Delphi Keyboard S

Note: This table assumes that you're using the default ⋯ ting, look at the Editor page of the Environment Optio⋯

Key	Purpose	Key	Purpose
Alt-0 (Zero)	Displays the Window list. You can use this option to select any of the Delphi windows. There are also direct key options included in this table.	Ctrl-Tab	Moves between pages of a window. For example, if you're in the editor, clicking on Ctrl-Tab will move you from unit to unit. Doing this in the Object Inspector will move you between the Events and Properties pages.
Alt-F4	Closes a dialog or form. You can use this in just about any situation—even to close Delphi itself.		
Alt-F10	Displays the context menu. Obviously this changes depending on what object you have selected.	Ctrl-U	Unindents a block of text.
Ctrl-E	Performs an incremental search. Using this key combination allows you to type one letter at a time within the editor. Delphi performs the search dynamically until you press Enter or the editor loses focus.	Ctrl-Z	Undoes the last editing action. The menu calls this action Undelete, but it actually does more.
		F1	This key displays a help screen, but it acts differently depending on what you have selected at the time. If you select a component on the form, it displays help for that component. If you select a component property or event, you'll see help on that property or event.
Ctrl-Enter	Displays a dialog associated with a property in the Object Inspector. Any time you see an ellipsis, you can display the editor associated with that property using this key combination. It also works in a few other places within Delphi.		
		F3	Use this key to perform the last search again without displaying the Find dialog.
Ctrl-F	This key displays the Find dialog.	F4	This key will run the source code to the current cursor position in the editor during a debugging session.
Ctrl-F2	Resets the program during a debugging session.	F5	Adds a breakpoint at the current cursor position.
Ctrl-F5	Displays the Add Watch dialog.		
Ctrl-F7	Evaluates or modifies a variable during a debugging session. Even though you can display this dialog if the program isn't running, you can't do anything with it.	F7	Traces into the current line of source code during debugging.
		F8	Steps over the current line of source code during debugging.
		F9	Runs the application. If the application needs to be compiled, Delphi will perform that action first.
Ctrl-F9	Compiles the source code.		
Ctrl-F12	Displays a list of units.	F10	Selects the main menu.
Ctrl-I	Indents a block of text. You can change the amount of indent on the Editor page of the Environment Options dialog. I normally set my indent to match the tab spacing I'm using.	F11	Displays the Object Inspector or selects it if you already have it open.
		F12	Toggles between the unit and the form.
		Shift-Ctrl-Z	Redoes the last editing action.
Ctrl-R	This key displays the Replace dialog.	Shift-F12	Displays a list of forms.
Ctrl-S	Saves the current file. This key combination doesn't save all the files.	Tab	Unless you're in the editor, this key moves you between items on the current page. Within the editor it inserts a tab into the source code.

Windows 95 Keyboard Shortcuts

Key	Purpose
Ctrl-Esc	Opens the Start menu on the Taskbar. You can use the arrow keys to select an application. Pressing Enter starts the application you selected.
Alt-F4	Ends the current application. Use this key to end Windows while at the Desktop.
Alt-Shift-Tab	Switches to the previous window.
Alt-Tab	Switches to the next window.
Esc	Cancels the last action in most cases. You can't back out of some actions, however-er.
F1	Displays online help. This help is general in nature, but it's application-specific.
F2	Pressing this while an icon is highlighted allows you to change the object name.
F3	Use this key to display the Find dialog while at the Desktop, Taskbar, or Start menu. You can also use it within some applications if they don't use the F3 key for some other purpose.
Left Alt-Left Shift-Num Lock	Turns on the MouseKeys feature of the Accessibility Options dialog. You can use this as a method for creating an alternate keyboard-driven mouse. The four arrow keys will allow you to move the mouse cursor as needed.
Left Alt-Left Shift-Print Screen	Turns on the high contrast feature of the Accessibility Options dialog.
Num Lock	Holding this key down for five seconds turns on the ToggleKeys feature of the Accessibility Options dialog
Right Shift	Holding this key down for eight seconds turns on the FilterKeys feature of the Accessibility Options dialog.
Shift 5 Times	Turns on the StickyKeys feature of the Accessibility Options dialog.
Shift-F1	Displays context-sensitive help when an application supports. Neither Delphi or Windows 95 seem to support this option. (Delphi's help is always context-sensitive.)
Shift-F10	Displays context menu for the currently selected object. This only applies to applications that provide a context menu. Most 32-bit applications provide a context menu.
Tab	Use this key while at Desktop to toggle between Desktop, Start menu, and Taskbar.

Form Design Keys and Mouse Movements

Key	Purpose
Alt-Drag	Performs a columnar block select.
Ctrl-Arrow	Moves a component one pixel at a time while on a form. Obviously you have to select the component before you can do this.
Ctrl-Drag	Allows you to select more than one component within a group box using the mouse.
Ctrl-Shift-Arrow	Moves a component one grid at a time while on a form.
Shift-Arrow	Sizes a component one pixel at a time.
Shift-Left Click	Selects one object at a time on a form.

Tip: You can copy a component to the clipboard. Paste it to a text processor and you'll see the code required to create the component. Paste it onto a form and you'll see a graphic representation of the component.

Handy Editor Tidbits

Any text after the last End statement in the source code is ignored by the compiler. You can use this feature to add notes that affect the application as a whole or to store routines that you plan to use later.

Delphi will automatically remove any procedures that you create accidentally by clicking on a component event in the Object Inspector. The only requirement is that nothing appear between the Begin and End statements.

Use the Color page of the Environment Options dialog to change the colors for various editor elements like symbols. You can access this dialog by selecting the Properties option in the editor's context menu.

Most of the Wordstar keystrokes work fine within the editor as long as you use the default keymapping.

The View | New Edit Window command allows you to create more than one edit window. This comes in handy if you need to track more than one section of the same source file or more than one source file at once. I also use it when I want to copy functions from one source file to another.

Peter Norton's

Guide to

Delphi® 2

John Paul Mueller

SAMS
PUBLISHING 201 West 103rd Street
Indianapolis, Indiana 46290

Copyright © 1996 by Peter Norton

PREMIER EDITION

International Standard Book Number: 1-672-30898-3

Library of Congress Catalog Card Number: 95-72346

99 98 97 96   4   3   2   1

Interpretation of the printing code: The rightmost double-digit number is the year of the book's printing; the rightmost single-digit, the number of the book's printing. For example, a printing code of 96-1 shows that the first printing of the book occurred in 1996.

Composed in Goudy and MCPdigital by Macmillan Computer Publishing

Printed in the United States of America

Trademarks

Publisher	Richard K. Swadley
Acquisitions Manager	Greg Wiegand
Development Manager	Dean Miller
Managing Editor	Cindy Morrow
Marketing Manager	Kristina Perry

Acquisitions Editor
Christopher Denny

Development Editor
L. Angelique Brittingham

Software Development Specialist
Steve Straiger

Production Editor
Mitzi Foster Gianakos

Technical Reviewer
Rich Jones

Editorial Coordinator
Bill Whitmer

Technical Edit Coordinator
Lynette Quinn

Resource Coordinator
Deborah Frisby

Formatter
Frank Sinclair

Editorial Assistants
Carol Ackerman
Andi Richter
Rhonda Tinch-Mize

Cover Designer
Tim Amrhein

Book Designer
Alyssa Yesh

Copy Writer
Peter Fuller

Production Team Supervisor
Brad Chinn

Production
Mary Ann Abramson, Stephen Adams, Carol Bowers, Charlotte Clapp, Jason Hand, Sonja Hart, Mike Henry, Ayanna Lacey, Clint Lahnen, Steph Mineart, Casey Price, Laura Robbins, Andrew Stone, Colleen Williams, Jeff Yesh

Overview

Contents

Dedication

This book is dedicated to my good friends Jack and Wally—fellow writers who really understand me.

Acknowledgments

Thanks to my wife Rebecca, for working with me to get this book completed. I really don't know what I would have done without her help in researching and compiling some of the information that appears in this book. She also did a fine job of proofreading my rough draft.

Rich Jones did an excellent job in technically editing the book.

I would like to thank Scott Clark for his help and direction. His input was instrumental in helping this book achieve the depth of information required.

Matt Wagner, my agent, deserves credit for helping me get the contract in the first place and taking care of all the details that most authors really don't think about.

Michael Li of InfoCan Management gets a special thank you for some of the technical details he provided me with. Likewise, the staff at Borland helped me through some rather sticky areas as I developed the code for this book.

Finally, I would like to thank Chris Denny and Angelique Brittingham of Sams for their assistance in bringing this book to print.

About the Author

John Mueller is a freelance author and technical editor. He has writing in his blood, having produced 28 books and almost 200 articles to date. The topics range from networking to artificial intelligence and from database management to heads-down programming. Some of his current books include a Delphi programmer's guide and a Windows NT advanced user tutorial. His technical editing skills have helped more than 22 authors refine the content of their manuscripts. In addition to book projects, John has provided technical editing services to both *Data Based Advisor* and *Coast Compute* magazines.

When John isn't working at the computer, you can find him in his workshop. He's an avid woodworker and candle maker. On any given afternoon, you can find him working at a lathe or putting the finishing touches on a bookcase. One of his favorite projects is making candle sticks and the candles to go with them. You can reach John on CompuServe at 71570,641.

Introduction

Introduction

Delphi—it sounds like something I should be consulting, rather than a programming environment based on Pascal. Those of us who grew up programming in DOS understand just how big a leap Delphi represents for the programmer in terms of programming speed and accuracy. When I first started writing code, we did just that—we had to write every line.

Fortunately, the tools available to programmers didn't remain static for very long. One of the first new tools was the code generator or automated coding environment. Code generators were a welcome change to the programming environment. At least I didn't have to write the same old "boiler plate" code over and over again, but it still fell to the programmer to write the vast majority of the specialty code that every application contains.

Today's RAD (rapid application development) environments—like the one provided by Delphi and Visual Basic—are so far removed from the days of DOS that it sometimes feels like I'm not programming at all. I see RAD as a natural extension of code generators. In essence, you define what you want to see and the programming environment creates the code to do it. Delphi takes care of so many programming tasks for you, that you may indeed feel as if you're consulting it, then adding a little input of your own, than creating an application.

Of course, all of the bells and whistles that allow you to prototype an application quickly break down when it comes time to actually make the application do something. Delphi provides all the tools you need to automatically generate the part of the application the user sees—the part that used to take so long to code by hand. You still have to provide the logic for making the user interface do productive work. That's where real programming skills still come into play and why you need this book. I'll take you on that next step, the one beyond the pretty interface. We'll explore all the things you'll need to do after you prototype an application (of course we'll visit the prototyping stage briefly as well).

What's in This Book

Now that I've piqued your curiosity a bit, let's look at what this book has to offer. I'm going to look at Delphi from the intermediate to advanced programmer level. I'm not talking about the Delphi programmer here, but any programmer. That's why I included the first four chapters of the book. They're designed to acquaint someone who knows how to program with the intricacies of using Delphi before we plunge into the deeper waters of advanced programming techniques. Even an experienced Delphi programmer will want to look at Chapter 1 "Introducing Delphi," because I provide an update of what's new and interesting in the 32-bit product.

So now that you have some idea of who is supposed to read this book, let's take a look at what it will cover. Here's an overview of the book that tells the four areas where you can expect to see me spend the bulk of my time.

1. Understand OLE Programming—This book covers all the details using words that the average reader can understand. Anyone who has spent time trying to figure out the OLE 2 specification knows that it's difficult at best to understand. Chapter 10, "Using Delphi with OLE," takes the pain out of learning OLE 2—a requirement for any application having the Windows 95 logo.

2. Take the Mystery Out of the Windows API—I've provided an overview of the Windows API in Chapter 5, "Accessing the Windows API," then broken it into four easily understood pieces in the following chapters. A lot of books tell you about the Windows API; some even show an example or two of how to use it. *Peter Norton's Guide to Delphi 2* provides major coverage of this very necessary area of programming.

3. Learn Database Management System (DBMS) Programming—It may look like I've only provided a single (albeit long) chapter for DBMS programming (Chapter 12, "Database Management Under Delphi"). However, there's more to DBMS programming than creating the application. You have to consider LAN security (Chapter 13, "Delphi on a LAN"), OLE links (Chapter 10), reports (Chapter 8, "Printer Magic"), and on-screen graphic representations of the data (Chapter 7, "The Windows GDI").

4. Create Delphi Extensions—If there's anything that I've learned over the years, it's that no programming product is an island. Sure, you can force a hammer to act as a screwdriver, but who'd want to if the screwdriver is available? That's what the fourth section of this book is going to do for you. I'm going to show you how to create extensions for Delphi with other languages. In other words, you'll leave with the knowledge that Delphi is a hammer, not a screwdriver. The extensions I'll show you how to create will act as the screwdriver.

Of course, this is just an overview. You'll find that I packed this book with all kinds of useful tips and hints about using Delphi to its fullest.

What You'll Need

You don't need anything special to use the majority of this book. If you already have a copy of Windows 95 and the 32-bit version of Delphi installed, you meet the software requirements. Of course, your hardware will have to support at least the minimum requirements of both Delphi and Windows 95 before you can use them. In essence, if you can run Delphi, you can use this book.

There are a few things that you'll probably find useful, but you don't absolutely have to have them to use this book. I'm not going to provide you with complete Windows API documentation in this book, so it would probably help if you had a good source of information for using the API. Unfortunately, the Windows API documentation supplied with Delphi tells you only about the tip, not the whole iceberg. (Then again, it's no worse than the Microsoft supplied documentation.)

A C/C++ compiler capable of creating Windows DLLs, VBXs, and OCXs is also a requirement for using the fourth section of this book. I plan to use Microsoft Visual C++ as my compiler. However, I plan to test all the examples with Borland's C/C++ product as well.

Conventions Used in This Book

What I'm talking about here are usage conventions. We'll cover programming conventions a little later on when I describe Hungarian notation and how to use it. I've used the following conventions in this book:

File | Open	Menus and the selections on them appear with a vertical bar. "File | Open" means "Access the File menu and choose Open."
`monospace`	It's important to differentiate the text that you'll use in a macro or type at the command line from the text that explains it. I've used monospace type to make this differentiation. Every time you see monospace text, you'll know that the information you see will appear in a macro, within a system file like CONFIG.SYS or AUTOEXEC.BAT, or as something you'll type at the command line. You'll even see the switches used with Windows commands in this text.
`italic monospace`	There are times you'll need to supply a value for a Windows or DOS command. For example, when you use the DIR command, you may need to supply a filename. It's convenient to use a variable name—essentially a placeholder—to describe what kind of value you need to supply. The same holds true for any other kind of entry—from macro commands to dialog box fields. Every time you see italic monospace text, you know that the name is a placeholder that you'll need to replace with a value. The placeholder simply tells you what kind of value you need to provide.
`<Filename>`	A variable name between angle brackets is a value that you need to replace with something else. The variable name I use usually provides a clue as to what kind of information you need to supply. In this case, I'm asking for a filename. Never type the angle brackets when you type the value.
`[<Filename>]`	When you see square brackets around a value, switch, or command, it means that this is an optional component. You don't have to include it as part of the command line or dialog field unless you want the additional functionality that the value, switch, or command provides.
italic	I use italic wherever the actual value of something is unknown. I also use italic where more than one value might be correct. For example, you might see FILE*xxxx* in text. This means that the value could be anywhere between FILE0000 and FILE9999.

Icons

This book contains many icons that help you identify certain types of information. The following paragraphs describe the purpose of each icon.

Note: Notes tell you about interesting facts that don't necessarily affect your ability to use the other information in the book. I use note boxes to give you bits of information that I've picked up while using Delphi, Windows NT, or Windows 95.

Tip: Everyone likes tips, because they tell you new ways of doing things that you might not have thought about before. Tip boxes also provide an alternative way of doing something that you might like better than the first approach I provided.

Warning: This means watch out! Warnings almost always tell you about some kind of system or data damage that will occur if you perform a certain action (or fail to perform others). Make sure you understand a warning thoroughly before you follow any instructions that come after it.

Peter's Principle: I usually include a Peter's Principle to tell you how to manage your Delphi or Windows environment more efficiently. Boxes with this icon might also include ideas on where to find additional information or even telephone numbers that you can call. You'll also find the names of shareware and freeware utility programs here.

Looking Ahead: It's always good to know what you'll find along the road. Whenever you see a Looking Ahead box, I'm providing a road sign that tells you where we're headed. That way, you can follow the path of a particular subject as I provide more detailed information throughout the book.

Knowing how something works inside is important to some people, but not so important to others. (It should always be a priority to any programmer who intends to directly access some part of the Windows API.) Whenever you see the architecture icon you know that I'm going to spend some time talking about the internal workings of Windows 95 or Windows NT. Knowing how Windows performs its job can help you determine why things don't work as they should.

Whenever you change something as important as your operating system or programming environment, there will be problems with older devices and applications that were designed for the older version. The Compatibility icon clues you in to tips, techniques, and notes that will help you get over the compatibility hurdle.

DOS is still with us and will continue to be for the foreseeable future. Microsoft at least provides better support for DOS applications under Windows 95. Whenever you see the DOS icon, I provide you with a tip, technique, or note about a way to make DOS applications and Windows coexist.

Even home users need to worry about networking these days. It's no surprise, then, that this book provides a wealth of networking tips and techniques that everyone can use. Expect to find one of these tidbits of knowledge wherever you see the Networking icon.

I use the Performance icon to designate a performance-related tip. There are many throughout this book, and they cover a variety of optimization techniques. You'll need to read them carefully and decide which ones suit your needs. Not every performance tip is for everyone. Most of them require a trade-off of some kind, which I'll mention.

Square pegs that had to fit in round holes: That's what some products were in the past. Recent standards efforts have helped reduce the number of square pegs on the market. I think it's important to know what those standards are so that you can make the best buying decisions possible. Getting a square peg at a discount rate isn't such a good deal when you need to spend hours making it round. Every time you see the Standards icon you'll know that I'm talking about some standard that defines a product that will fit into that round hole with relative ease.

Technical details can really help you localize a problem or decide precisely what you need to get a job done. They can also help improve your overall knowledge level about a product. Sometimes they're just fun to learn. However, there are times when you just need an overview of how something works; getting the details just gets in the way. I use the Technical Note icon to tell you when some piece of information is a detail. You can bypass this information if you only need an overview of a Delphi or Windows process or feature for the moment. These icons also provide you with clues of where you can look for additional information later.

Finding problems is one of the things that all of us do from time to time. Programmers probably spend more time than just about anyone else in this activity. It doesn't matter if the problem is hardware or software related if it's keeping you from getting your work done or that project finished. Every time you see the Troubleshooting icon you know that I'm providing you with a tool you'll need to find a problem.

It's helpful to compare the benefits of using one operating system over another. Every time I provide some insight into a comparison of Windows NT versus Windows 95, I use the Windows NT icon.

You should always know when a new feature in a product will either conflict with a feature in the old one, or if it simply wasn't available. Delphi 2 adds a lot of functionality that Delphi 1.0 didn't have. In fact, we devote the better part of Chapter 1 to this very topic. There are other areas where the 16-bit version of Delphi and the new 32-bit version conflict. Whenever you see this icon, it's telling you that you need to be aware of some new feature or a conversion issue.

An Overview of Hungarian Notation

Secret codes are the stuff of spy movies and a variety of other endeavors. When you first see Hungarian notation, you may view it as just another secret code. It contains all the elements of a secret code including an arcane series of letters that you have to decode and an almost indecipherable result when you do. However, it won't take long for you to realize that it's other programmers' code that's secret, not the Hungarian notation used in this book.

Hungarian notation can save you a lot of time and effort. Anyone who has spent enough time programming realizes the value of good documentation when you try to understand what you did in a previous coding session or interpret someone else's code. That's part of what Hungarian notation will do for you, document your code.

An understanding of Hungarian notation will also help you receive more information from the examples in this book and from the Delphi manuals in general. (Just about every Windows programming language vendor uses some form of Hungarian notation in their manuals.) In addition, these same concepts are equally applicable to Delphi, C, and Visual Basic code. The codes remain similar across a variety of programming languages, even when the language itself doesn't.

Don't think for a moment that this notation has remained static either. Many of the ideas presented in the original form of Hungarian notation have been discussed by developers at conferences and on bulletin board systems (BBSs). You'd be surprised at just how many forms of Hungarian notation have evolved since its inception.

So what precisely is Hungarian notation? It's a way of telling other people what you intend to do with a variable. Knowing what a variable is supposed to do can often help explain the code itself. For example, if I tell you that a particular variable contains a handle to a window, then you know a lot more about it than the fact that it is simply a variable. You can interpret the code surrounding that variable with the understanding that it's supposed to do something with a window.

The first stage of development for this variable naming system was started by Charles Simonyi of Microsoft Corporation. He called his system Hungarian notation, so that's the name we'll use here. There are many places that you can obtain a copy of his work, including BBSs and some of the Microsoft programming forums on CompuServe. His work was further enhanced by other developers. For example, Xbase programmers use their own special version of Hungarian notation. It takes the different types of variables that Xbase provides into account. An enhanced Xbase version of Hungarian notation was published by Robert A. Difalco of Fresh Technologies. You can find his work on a few DBMS specific BBSs, as well as the Computer Associates Clipper forum on CompuServe.

The basis for the ideas presented in this section are found in one of the two previously mentioned documents in one form or another. The purpose in publishing them here is to make you aware of the exact nature of the conventions I use and how to use them to their best advantage in your own code. There are four reasons why you should use these naming conventions in your programs.

1. Mnemonic Value—This allows you to remember the name of a variable more easily, an important consideration for team projects.

2. Suggestive Value—You may not be the only one modifying your code. If you're working on a team project, others in the team will most likely at least look at the code you have written. Using these conventions will help others understand what you mean when using a specific convention.

3. Consistency—A programmer's ability is often viewed as not only how efficiently they program, or how well the programs they create function, but how easily another programmer can read their code. Using these conventions will help you maintain uniform code from one project to another. Other programmers will be able to anticipate the value or function of a section of code simply by the conventions you use.

4. Speed of Decision—In the business world, the speed at which you can create and modify code will often determine how successful a particular venture will be. Using consistent code will reduce the time you spend trying to decide what someone meant when creating a variable or function. This reduction in decision time will increase the amount of time you have available for productive work.

Now that I've told you why you should use Hungarian notation, let's look at how I plan to implement it in this book. I'll use the following rules when naming variables. You'll also see me use them when naming database fields or other value related constructs. Some functions and procedures will use them as well, but only if Hungarian notation will make the meaning of the function or procedure clearer.

1. Always prefix a variable with one or more lowercase letters indicating its type. In most cases this is the first letter of the variable type, so it's easy to remember what letter to use. The following examples show the most common prefixes for Delphi and C. (There are literally hundreds of combinations used in Windows that don't appear here.) I also included a few database specific identifiers.

a	Array
c	Character
d	Date
dbl	Double
dc	Device Context
dw	Double Word
f	Flag, Boolean, or Logical
h	Handle
I	Integer

inst	Instance
l	Long
li	Long Integer
lp	Long Pointer
msg	Message
n	Numeric
o	Object
pal	Palette
psz	Pointer to a Zero Terminated String
ptr	Pointer (or P when used with other variables like psz)
r	Real
rc	Rectangle
rgb	Red, Green, Blue (color variable)
rsrc	Resource
sgl	Single
si	Short Integer
sz	Zero Terminated String
u	Unsigned
ui	Unsigned Integer or Byte
w	Word
wnd	Window

2. Some variables represent the state of an object like a database, a field, or a control. They might even store the state of another variable. Telling other programmers that a variable monitors the current state of an object can help them see its significance within the program. You can identify state variables using one of the following three character qualifiers:

New	a New state
Sav	a Saved state
Tem	a Temporary state

3. A standard qualifier can help someone see the purpose of a variable almost instantly. This isn't the type of information that the variable contains, but how it reacts with other variables. For example, using the Clr qualifier tells the viewer that this variable is used in some way with color. You can even combine the qualifiers to amplify their effect and describe how the variable is used. For example cClrCrs is a character variable that determines the color of the cursor on the display. Using one to three of these qualifiers is usually sufficient to describe the purpose of a variable. The following standard qualifiers are examples of the more common types:

Ar	Array
Attr	Attribute
B	Bottom
Clr	Color

Col	Column
Crs	Cursor
Dbf	Database File
F	First
File	File
Fld	Field
L	Last/Left
Msg	Message
Name	Name
Ntx	Index File
R	Right
Rec	Record Number
Ret	Return Value
Scr	Screen
Str	String
T	Top
X	Row
Y	Column

4. Once you clearly define the variable's contents and purpose, you can further define it with some descriptive text. For example, you might have a long pointer to a string containing an employee's name that looks like this lpszEmpName. The first two letters tell you that this is a long pointer. The second two letters tells you that this is a zero (or null) terminated string. The rest of the letters tell you that this is an employee name. (Notice that I used the standard qualifier, Name, for this example.) Seeing a variable name like this in a piece of code tells you what to expect from it at a glance.

5. There are times when you won't be able to satisfy every need in a particular module using a single variable. In those cases you might want to create more than one of that variable type and simply number them. You could also designate its function using some type of number indicator like those shown below:

1,2,3	State pointer references as in cSavClr1, cSavClr2, etc.
Max	Strict upper limit as in nFldMax, maximum number of Fields.
Min	Strict lower limit as in nRecMin, minimum number of Records.
Ord	An ordinal number of some type.

I

Delphi Nuts
and Bolts

1

Introducing Delphi

Delphi—it's the product that saved Borland from a sudden and terrible death as a company. However, it's a lot more than that; it's a Pascal derivative for the '90s. The RAD (rapid application development) environment that Delphi provides has captured the imagination of everyone who uses it. Even I'm impressed with just how fast I can develop at least a simple application in Delphi when compared to other languages like C or even Visual Basic.

So, what makes Delphi different? Pascal has long been known as a training language—something that colleges used to show new programmers how to create applications. Its highly structured format is the stuff that defines the difference between a good programmer, and one that produces miles of spaghetti code.

Delphi puts all this structure to good use. I've tried to read the code produced by code generators before—believe me, it's not a pretty sight. When code generator code works, it works well. When it breaks, no one can figure out what it was supposed to be doing in the first place. You certainly can't say the same thing about the code that Delphi produces—it's clean and simple. The reason is simple: Every piece of code fits into its own easily digested structure.

We'll take a quick look at Delphi in this chapter. I'm not going to tell you everything about it—that would take the fun of discovery out of learning Delphi for you. (It would also steal the thunder from a lot of areas in the rest of the book.) What we will do is get a feel for where Pascal is today, then look at what the new version of Delphi has to offer. I'll also spend some time looking at how Delphi compares to other languages—what you can expect and what you shouldn't even attempt.

An Overview of Pascal's History

Pascal is the brain child of Nicklaus Wirth—a programmer who needed a language he could use to teach other people to write something other than spaghetti code. He created what's now known as standard Pascal; a somewhat limited language designed to create small applications, in the year between 1970 and 1971. He was working at the ETH Technical Institute of Zurich after returning from teaching at Stanford University.

Pascal is a derivative of PL/1 (Programming Language 1) and ALGOL (ALGOrithmic Language). Pascal got its name from Blaise Pascal—a French mathematician who, in 1690, at the age of 18, created the first mechanical calculating machine. One of the major features of the first version of Pascal was that the compiler needed to use it required very little memory. When microcomputers started appearing on the scene in the late 1970s many educational institutions chose Pascal over assembler for teaching people how to program on these new machines.

Something happened along the way and Pascal didn't stay in the classroom as originally expected. The next version of Pascal (UCSD Pascal) was a bit more robust. It allowed the programmer to create full-fledged applications instead of the small utilities that Wirth originally designed Pascal to create. There were a lot of problems with UCSD Pascal though and those problems kept Pascal in the background. One of the biggest issues was the way that Pascal handled input and output. You had to write a lot of code just to access the display. Sure, that code was very readable, but it took too long to write. Another problem was that UCSD Pascal used a token system for storing the compiled application—this type of system slowed application performance significantly at a time when programmers jealously guarded every processor cycle.

When Borland introduced Turbo Pascal in 1984, the programming community really took notice. Here was a version of Pascal that was easy to use, provided a native code compiler, and made it easy to access the common peripherals like the keyboard and display. It was also very fast—at least for that day and age—to develop an application using Turbo Pascal. Borland made a big deal out of the fact that Turbo Pascal was one of the fastest compilers around for good reason: Every programmer was looking for any productivity enhancement he or she could find.

Borland continued to update and expand Turbo Pascal. When they released their Windows version of Pascal, it had very little to do with the Pascal originally created by Wirth. Turbo Pascal now includes object oriented programming (OOP) features along with a wealth of functionality that its creator probably dreamed about, but not much more. Suffice it to say that the Pascal of today is far removed from its ancestor—I feel that the vast changes in the language, more than any other element, probably account for Borland's new name for Turbo Pascal—Delphi.

What Is Delphi?

If you want to look at the short definition, Delphi is a RAD (rapid application development) version of Turbo Pascal for Windows. (Borland uses the term ObjectPascal to refer to the language now.) It provides an enhanced interface and many automated features that make it easier for you to develop an application. Figure 1.1 shows a typical Delphi display. I won't go into all the features right now—we'll do that in Chapters 2 through 4, but I did want to give you a quick tour and let you know what to expect. (The database components get covered in the database section of the book—Chapter 12, "Database Management Under Delphi.")

The combination of a speed bar and the various programming aids like the object inspector is what makes Delphi different. The speed bar is split into two sections. The left half contains the usual buttons that you might find in any application. For example, there's a set of buttons for opening individual files or projects. You can also use a speed button to add or delete units from your project. The run button allows you to compile, link, and run your application from within the IDE (integrated development environment) in one step.

On the right side of the speed bar you'll see several tabs. Each tabbed page contains one or more components. Essentially a component is a piece of predefined application code. For example, when you place a TButton component (the hint will show Button; Delphi adds a "T" in front of all components and other objects you'll use) on a form, it already knows how to do a few things like display itself and what to do when users press it. (This is the object oriented part of the component—we'll talk more about this later.) I'll show you every component that Delphi has to offer somewhere within the pages of this book. I think you'll be impressed with the number of things that you can do without adding a single line of code. In fact, I'll show you how to create a very simple database application in Chapter 12 that doesn't use a single line of hand written code. (Delphi does add some code to the application—but does that really matter much if you didn't have to code it?)

Figure 1.1.

Delphi provides an enhanced environment designed to make development fast and easy.

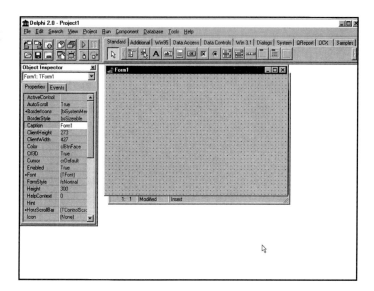

The Object Inspector—one of the design tools that you'll use—appears on the left side of the display directly below the speed bar. There are two tabbed pages in this window. The first page allows you to change the properties of any components that you place on a form or of the form itself. The second page allows you to assign specific procedures to events associated with a component. We'll spend a lot of time working with all of these items—so don't worry if it seems like I'm covering this material a bit fast right now.

To the right of the Object Inspector is a blank form. Delphi always displays a blank form for you when you start a new application. As with products like Visual Basic, you begin an application by putting the components you'll need onto the form, then using the Object Inspector to change their properties and add code to respond to specific events. For the most part you'll find that Delphi does a lot of the setup for you—all you need to do is worry about the actual mechanics and business logic of your application. For example, when you add a new TButton component to the display, all you really need to do is tell Delphi what to do when the user clicks on it.

Obviously this is an extremely brief look at Delphi. The whole intent was to show you what Delphi is. Simply telling you that it's a RAD development environment really doesn't say much. Knowing what this term really means is far more important. I've introduced you to some basic ideas behind a RAD environment in this section, but we've only touched on the very tip of the iceberg.

What Will Delphi Do for You?

The first question I asked myself when I looked at Delphi for the first time was why I would even need to use it. I started out using assembler in DOS. I played with Pascal for a while, but gave it up in favor of C somewhere along the way. In sum, I've probably played with ten or more different languages at one point or another in my career. The one thing that I've always observed is that every language is a tool. Each one has its strong and weak points. By the time I got to Windows programming, I had developed the skills required to use every tool in my toolbox—I really didn't need a new language (or so I thought).

So, what made me change my mind about Delphi? Someone told me that you could create a program without using much code with Delphi, then he proceeded to show me how. I think I counted 15 or 20 lines, not many when compared to some of the applications I've produced in the past. What did the application do? It allowed me to view a variety of files formats—both graphic and text— using a single application. I couldn't edit any of the files, but simply being able to view them with just a few lines of code was pretty impressive as far as I was concerned.

There are other programming languages on the market that could make a similar claim; Visual Basic certainly comes to mind. Obviously the ease of coding issue is important, but not enough for me to change my mind about using another language product. Delphi provides other features as well.

Consider the components that I described in the previous section. I find that they're an indispensable part of my programming environment because they do more than a VBX (Visual Basic eXtension) does. A VBX is a static piece of code—you can't really do anything more with it than its creator envisioned. If I don't like a Delphi component, I can inherit it; then change it to suit my needs. Try that with some of the other products out there.

The range of applications that Delphi is designed to create right out of the box was the feature that finally swayed me. I can create DLLs that are fast and very code efficient with my C compiler. The DBMS products I use certainly provide a lot in the way of data access tools. I really wouldn't want to give them up. However, Delphi falls in that middle range. Sure, I wouldn't want to write a real time inventory control system with it—that's what those DBMS products are for. But the idea that I can write anything from a small utility to a medium-sized DBMS application with one product is quite appealing to me and it should be to you as well.

Looking Ahead: If the features that I've described so far really don't help you make a decision, take a look at the new features section that follows this one. I think that you'll find that Delphi 2.0 adds quite a bit to the programming environment and still manages to improve things like execution speed. I was equally impressed to find that all of these new features didn't add to the size of my applications—if anything, my executable files are actually smaller than before.

New Features for this Version

This is the section where the veteran Delphi users will probably join in. Delphi 2.0 provides a lot of features that will make life a lot easier for those of you who used the 1.0 version. What I've done in the following paragraphs is provide a short synopsis of each new feature that Delphi 2.0 provides. I've tried to group the features according to type as well to make it easier to find the one you're looking for since the list of new features is so long.

Performance

Delphi 2.0 adds quite a bit when it comes to performance. Of course, everyone defines performance in different ways; so let me tell you what I mean by this term. There are actually three levels of performance that Delphi 2.0 enhances: programmer development, executable code speed, and compile times.

The following section will help you better understand how Delphi meets these three performance goals. I'm not saying that it's perfect, but it does improve on the performance provided by its predecessor and that's always good in my book. Obviously, hand-written C or assembly code is still going to be faster than Delphi, but you have to weigh the cost of developer time against the executable program speed you would gain. Likewise, some of these performance gains come at the cost of productivity. I wouldn't even dream of developing a large-scale database application with Delphi, but it does provide more than sufficient features to make it a good selection for many small- to medium-sized data applications.

The bottom line on performance is what you can reasonably expect from a product and still get the end result you need. Delphi 2.0 comes closer to that happy medium for everything from a small utility program to a full-fledged accounting system. The thing that you need to consider is how you spell performance.

Optimizing 32-Bit Compiler

Anyone who has spent much time reading the trade presses lately knows that corporate America is moving toward a 32-bit environment—probably not as fast as the home market—but they are making the move. Obviously you have to have a 32-bit compiler to create a 32-bit application—Delphi is that 32-bit compiler.

There's one big way in which the compiler you get with Delphi differs from a lot of other products on the market. It produces native code. So, how does this help you? Many of the products you'll use produce a tokenized application when you compile. In other words, the code you type is changed into tokens—not native 80x86 instructions. During run time your application has to actually interpret the tokens before it can execute them. There are two major benefits to native code compiling: smaller application size and faster execution.

One of the benefits of a native code compiler that you might not think about immediately is the difficulty in moving an application you create from place to place. With Visual Basic I always had to worry about which DLLs I needed to include with the product. Except for DBMS applications, you'll normally distribute just one file when using Delphi—the executable. Native code compilation normally means fewer if any supplementary files like DLLs.

The one problem that I have with this new feature is that the speed at which businesses are making the move. Delphi 2.0 doesn't provide any kind of 16-bit functionality—Borland will tell you to use the 1.0 product to write a 16-bit application. So, what you're going to end up with for the short term is two compilers on your machine. Hopefully Borland will combine the two compilers sometime in the future.

Full Windows 95 and Windows NT Support

This new version of Delphi will allow you to develop applications for either Windows 95 or Windows NT. In fact, you'll get full API support as part of the product. I like the way that Borland implemented the API support. They provided transition calls for most of the new API calls that both Windows 95 and Windows NT use. I'll get more into this topic when we reach Chapter 5, "Accessing the Windows API." Suffice it to say right now that most of the applications you wrote in Delphi 1.0 should move to 2.0 with very few coding changes.

There are a few minor problems with the support that Delphi provides. For one thing, instead of providing you with a Win32 API help file that contains Pascal examples, you get a rewarmed version for the Microsoft documentation—which uses all C code. If you find that you need to access the Win32 API—and most of you will at one time or another—you'll also need to learn a bit of C to get the job done.

Tip: The Delphi Win32 documentation does provide one interesting feature. Click on the Overview entry on each page of the Win32 API help file and you'll see which operating system the API call will work with. Windows 95 only supports a subset of the Win32 calls, so having this feature is extremely important. (Especially hard hit are the security API features—we'll discuss these problems in Chapter 13, "Delphi on a LAN.")

32-Bit Data Types

I was happy to see a variety of changes to Delphi's handling of various data types. For example, you no longer have a 255-character limit to worry about with strings. The new strings can actually contain more data than the Windows environment can handle. (The current size limit for a string under Windows 95 is about 1 GB and under Windows NT is about 2 GB—Delphi strings can be a theoretical 2 GB in size.) You'll find that arrays, records, and other data structures benefit from the new data size as well.

There are some areas where this feature will turn into a gotcha. For example, integers come in more sizes now. You'll have to specify which integer type you really want to use in some situations. The integer type is now 32-bits long—a very welcome enhancement for those of us with large numbers to manipulate.

Some 32-bit data type conversions are automatic. For example, all handles are now 32 bits. Thankfully, your code will continue to run just as it did under Delphi 1.0 because Delphi 2.0 takes care of the necessary conversions for you. (This assumes that you've used the Delphi supplied data types like THandle to define variables in your application.)

Delphi also provides some new 32-bit data types. Most of these data types are string specific. However, two new data types include: wide characters and variants. Wide characters are double byte Unicode character types for internationalization. Variants provide the ability to change the type of a variable at runtime for more flexible database and OLE automation.

One of the best features of 32-bit data types is the one that doesn't need any discussion. All 32-bit data types benefit from Windows flat address space. That means you no longer have 64 KB segments to worry about. In addition, all data is near; Delphi no longer wastes time managing far data segments.

New Math Unit

All of us write code that is less than optimal at times. In fact, there are times when I'll give up a bit of performance to write code that's clear rather than completely optimized. Math routines are often the hardest to reduce to the least common denominator. If you write an optimized piece of code to perform the computation, you could end up with an equation no one will ever be able to figure out—yourself included.

The new math unit included in this version takes all your equations and optimizes them. The result? You can write equations that make sense—they're presented in a way that most of us can figure out. Delphi compiles them in a way that optimizes application performance. You can now get the best of both worlds when it comes to complex programming situations.

You'll also find that the new math unit uses loop induction variables to reduce the amount of code executed in a loop. What this basically means is that Delphi increments a register for each iteration of a loop rather than recalculate the expression. This can produce a large increase in application execution speed in some cases. You'll also find that Delphi uses registers more efficiently in a lot of other places as well—reducing the need to move things in and out of memory.

OBJ File Support

Delphi 2.0 makes it even easier for you to use modules written in other languages. The native code compiler allows you to use (and create) DLLs, OCXs, automation servers, and OBJ files with equal ease. Obviously this feature provides a much stronger level of integration with Borland's C++ compiler, but I see it as a means for accessing other applications that generate OBJ or DLL files as well. (I'm talking about 32-bit development environments here—you'd need to write a thunking layer using Microsoft's thunking compiler to access anything written using a 16-bit development environment.)

TOleContainer Component

Version 1.0 of Delphi provided a simple TOleContainer component that provided basic OLE capabilities. Delphi 2.0 provides an updated TOleContainer component that provides full OLE 2.0 functionality. One advantage to this version, besides the OLE specific features, is its 32-bit roots. You'll find that your applications run faster when using this new component. The only thing I wish is that Borland had also provided additional components to make creating an OLE automation server easier to write; but at least the updated container component is a step in the right direction.

OLE Controls (OCXs)

The new version of Delphi provides full support for OCXs (OLE custom controls). This makes working with other applications a lot easier. As with VBXs (and just about everything else in Delphi for that matter) you can incorporate OCXs into any components that you create. There are the usual royalty and other considerations that you need to think about before you can send a component containing an OCX to someone else.

Note: Delphi 2.0 does support OCXs. It doesn't support VBXs. Borland's reason for this is that Microsoft doesn't support VBXs as part of Windows NT or Windows 95. The problem for the developer is that your investment in VBXs is gone unless one of two things happen: the VBX developer provides an updated OCX version of the VBX control or you use Microsoft's Thunking compiler to create your own C wrapper for the VBX controls. Obviously, even with a means for accessing the control, you'll lose the benefits of using 32-bit code when calling an older 16-bit VBX from Delphi.

Support for OLE Automation

If you really hate DDE (dynamic data exchange), you'll like OLE automation. What's the main reason that most people hate DDE? It's the lack of a standardized language that affects most programmers—you literally have to learn several different macro programming languages—one for each application you want to use. An OLE automation server doesn't require this investment in time; all applications that provide this service use one standard macro language.

OLE Automation Server Capabilities

Not only does Delphi 2.0 act as an OLE client (both a standard client and an automation client), but you can use it as an OLE automation server. You could create an OLE server using Delphi 1.0, but there was a lot of programming involved in doing so. This version of Delphi provides you with a complete set of instructions and all the tools you'll need to get the job done.

Looking Ahead: I'll provide a full discussion of both DDE and OLE in Chapter 10, "Using Delphi with OLE." We'll go through the various OLE server and client features that Delphi provides. I'll even show you how to create an automation server of your own. We'll also spend some time looking at a venerable standby—DDE.

Programmer Productivity Enhancers and Ease of Use Features

Delphi 2.0 now does more than ever before when it comes to making life easier for the programmer. I spoke in a previous section of the RAD environment that Delphi provides. This new version provides even more features that make RAD a reality.

Making tools more accessible was also one of the goals of the Delphi development team. I think that you'll find that most of the new features have some connection to that idea—making Delphi's features easy to access. Easy access almost always results in improved programmer efficiency.

The following paragraphs look at all the productivity-related features that Delphi 2.0 provides. Just how much they affect you is a matter of programming style and what types of applications you create. There are a few places where you'll just have to try a new feature out and see if it works for you. I found more than a few places where I thought a new feature was sort of so-so and found out later that it helped a lot more than I originally anticipated.

Multi-Error, Multi-Warning Compiler

I think some programmers must have screamed long and hard to get this particular feature. The frustration level of Delphi 1.0 was pretty high when it came to finding errors. Delphi 2.0 remedies this situation by pointing out all your errors—at least the ones it can find—up front. Figure 1.2 shows a typical error display. All you need to do to find an error is double-click on it and Delphi takes you right to it. (In fact, it highlights the flawed line of code with a red line and places the cursor next to the problem in most cases.)

Figure 1.2.
Delphi displays all the errors it can find in one pass of the compiler now.

You'll still find some situations where Delphi just won't find the right line of code right away. For example, if you forget to put a semicolon at the end of a line, the compiler still highlights the next line of code, but this isn't that big of a problem. Overall, you'll find Delphi is a lot faster to use because you can find all your errors in one compiler pass.

Improved Compiler Diagnostics and Error Messages

Don't you hate it when a compiler tells you that there is something wrong with your code, but the error message it provides is so cryptic that it could be anything? I've spent more than a few hours looking for one problem in my code, only to find out that the real problem had little or nothing to do with what the compiler told me was wrong. Even worse is a situation where the compiler simply accepts a bad piece of code without providing any form of warning at all. I've even lost data because of this particular short sightedness on the part of the compiler vendor.

I'm not going to go out on a limb and tell you that every error message that the Delphi compiler provides is complete and easy to understand, but I'll go so far as to say that the vast majority of them are. During my beta test time with this product I'd see the occasional "strange" message. As the product neared completion I noticed less and less of them. Part of the reason is my increased experience level in using the product, but the messages had a lot to do with it as well. Suffice it to say that you'll be able to actually believe the vast majority of the error messages you get now.

Smart-Caching Linker

Don't you hate it when the IDE insists on recompiling and linking everything in a project when you've changed a single line in the application? I've actually had time to get coffee and hold a somewhat serious conversation with another colleague during some compiles. I had to actually stop using the IDE of some early C products for this reason and resort to using the command line version of the compiler instead.

Delphi 2.0 gets around this problem with a new linking technology—or perhaps it's a smart implementation of something some of us have used all along. Borland calls it a smart-caching linker—I call it incremental linking (or at least some form of it).

No matter what you call this technology, what it does in the way of programmer productivity is pretty obvious. I can change a single line of code and get an almost instantaneous result under Delphi 2.0. Just hit the run button and your application—at least for the most part—will start running if you make small changes to fix a problem here or there.

Image Editor

I really like the Image Editor provided with Delphi 2.0. All it does is allow you to modify the contents of an RES file, but it's a lot nicer than having to use a third-party tool to accomplish the same thing. You can also use it to modify ICO, BMP, CUR, and DCR files. Figure 1.3 shows the Image Editor.

Figure 1.3.

Image Editor provides a fast and efficient method for modifying the graphics elements in your application.

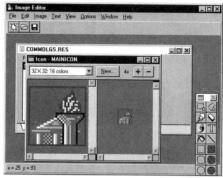

Looking Ahead: I'll cover the Image Editor in more detail in Chapter 4, "Adding Some Bells and Whistles." It's a good tool for giving your application that finished feeling once you get the basic code in place. For example, a change in cursor shape can give the user a much needed visual cue that your application is expecting him to do something or that it's performing some task in the background.

WinSight32

This is a new debugging tool for Delphi 2.0. It provides a wealth of information about the way that your application works with Windows. For example, it includes Spy—a method of viewing your application's conversations with Windows. You'll find that WinSight32 provides much of the functionality that you used to find in a variety of separate tools. Figure 1.4 shows a typical WinSight32 display.

Figure 1.4.

WinSight32 provides a variety of external debugging tools that you can use to find a variety of problems with your Delphi applications.

Some of the additional features of WinSight32 allow you to find and trace the activity of a particular process. You can use it much like you would the search capability of a standard application like a word process. The only difference is that you're tracing the activity of applications and using the search capability to find a specific application thread.

WinSight32 provides three kinds of information: window, class, and message. You can choose to view any of the three—the standard view shows the window and message information. In most cases you'll find that's what you use WinSight32 to obtain. Normally WinSight32 shows the active application with a blinking icon. It also tells you what kind of window, class, or message you're viewing. There is a lot of information hidden in each line of text—most of which we'll cover throughout the book as I pursue various topics. For example, if you look at the message window, you'll find that it tells you where a message is headed and what kind of message it is. These are items that you provide as part of the API function call that I'll talk about.

Visual Form Inheritance

tenets →

One of the tenants of OOP is that you're supposed to be able to reuse the vast majority of your code. Do any of the products out there today meet this goal? No! However, Delphi comes a lot closer.

Visual form inheritance is one of the reasons that Delphi comes to this ideal OOP condition. I have several new forms sitting in my gallery now—they're actually full-fledged applications—that I reuse all the time. One of them is the About Box I created for Delphi 1.0. It's probably the one example where I don't have to do anything at all with an inherited form. All I do is change the caption of one of the labels during run time to make this form work.

However, inheritance means a lot more than that. Whenever I make a change in an inherited form, it gets reflected in every other application that uses the form the next time I recompile. I also sub-class forms on a regular basis now. You can use this technique to create forms that are almost complete as a template. Inheriting the form allows you to create a basic application in a lot less time. Subclassing allows you to add the finishing touches to the form in a matter of hours instead of days.

Enhanced Gallery

Not only are forms in the gallery enhanced through inheritance, but you'll see more of them. Delphi 1.0 provided what I would term a full supply of standard forms and dialogs. In most cases you could use them as a starting point, but they didn't address some of the specialty needs of most developers.

Delphi 2.0 provides a wealth of new form and dialog types—even in some of the specialty areas like database management. You can store data modules (a new feature) for future products and use them just like you would any other form. What does this mean as far as productivity is concerned? Once you define a set of data sources you don't have to define them again if you store them in the gallery as a data module.

There are other new "form" types as well. For example, 32-bit applications support threads. You'll find a thread object in the gallery. All you need to do to create a thread of application is grab it from the New page of the New Items dialog. This same page contains the basic data module that I'll describe in Chapter 12 and new application types like DLLs. You'll even find an OLE automation object here.

TCollection Class for Component Writers

Anyone who has created components for Delphi will really like this new object. It provides the means of creating a container for the various objects that you create. For example, think of an expansion to one of the grid components that uses a special column object. You could create a collection of these objects using the TCollection class. Essentially, the TCollection object you create is an array of TCollectionItems. You access each item within the collection just as you would items in an array.

Form Linking with Smart Module Management

Anyone who has used Delphi for very long knows that it uses units so that you can compile each code module separately. However, some programmers found that manually updating the USES statement in a unit was tedious at best. Delphi 2.0 provides a new File Uses command that you can use to link forms into your application.

If this weren't enough, the IDE is more intelligent now and recognizes when it needs to update a USES statement. For example, if you reference Form2 (Unit2) inside of Form1 (Unit1), Delphi will prompt you to add Unit2 to your USES list when you recompile.

Delphi also includes a feature called automatic form. It allows you to create links across different modules. Even though Delphi has always allowed you to access the public objects, properties, and code in different forms using code, you couldn't access them in the design environment. All this has changed with Delphi 2.0. You can now link these components at design time across forms without having to write code. This makes it easier to create reusable modules that encapsulate data access and business rules separate from the user interface components.

Support for Windows 95 UI Controls

One of the big news items for Delphi 2.0 is the addition of Windows 95–specific components to the Visual Component Library (VCL). You'll find all the new Windows 95 components here, including tree views, track bars, sliders, progress bars, toolbars, rich text edit, list views, image list headers, and status bar controls. (One of my favorites is the rich text edit component—we'll take a look at it in Chapter 6, "Common Dialogs," when I show you how to use the common dialogs.) Not only that, but most of the existing components are updated to take advantage of the newer Windows 95 interface. For example, all the common dialogs look the same as the dialogs that most Windows 95–specific applications use (obviously, older versions of Windows NT can't provide this interface).

32-Bit Windows API Help System

You'd find all the new 32-bit features that Delphi provides a little difficult to use without the appropriate documentation. Likewise, there are still situations where you need to go to the Windows API to get some tasks done. Obviously you need a help system that includes the 32-bit calls that

Windows provides. For the most part you'll find that the Delphi-supplied help file is just the Microsoft documentation in disguise. However, it does include one especially nice feature—the overview section. Just click on this area of each entry in the help file to see which operating systems support a specific API call.

Improved IDE

Borland uses all the new components it developed to create a surprisingly versatile integrated development environment (IDE) in this version. You'll find that all the tools use the Windows 95 interface, making it easier to get from one place to another on the system.

If you're like me, you normally have a lot of program files for any project by the time you get done. Have you ever had to spend a half an hour looking for the right file because DOS limits you to an 8-character filename? Delphi 2.0 uses long filenames—you can provide a fairly long filename for each unit in your project. Obviously some of you are going to go crazy with this feature. Just remember that you'll have to use those unit names in your code—descriptive names are good, long ones that ramble for what seems like an eternity will be difficult to type.

Delphi Developer and Delphi Client Server Suite Productivity Enhancers

Borland is going to market more than one version of Delphi. The developer and client server suite versions of Delphi will contain some productivity tools that you won't find in other releases. Suffice it to say that if you need these features, you'll have to get one of these enhanced versions. The following paragraphs outline these additions and tell how they affect you.

Object Repository Support

Repository—I have to wonder who came up with that term. All this term means is that someone is using database technology to make life easier for the programmer. Delphi uses the repository for storing and reusing data models, business rules, objects, and forms. What this means to you as a programmer is that you'll spend less time coding and more time designing applications.

Not only does the repository encourage code reuse, it also reduces debugging time—something that I'm sure all of us like to avoid whenever possible. (Debugging often falls into the same category as paperwork for developers—a necessary evil akin to eating lemons without sugar.)

Unfortunately, application debugging is a necessary evil. In the past I used DLLs and other library formats to reuse the debugged code I created. Reusing code this way requires a conscious effort on the part of the developer. I think that you'll find that the repository is a lot more automatic.

Full-Featured Deployment/Installation Tool

Whether you design applications for a single company or you're a consultant who works for a lot of different companies, the need to distribute the applications you write is the same. You have to write some kind of utility to make the application easy to install (unless you have job security in mind—installing your application on a 1,000-node network would take quite some time). Normally writing such a utility is a bit time consuming, but it isn't too difficult.

Microsoft recently upped the ante on install utilities. Windows 95 (and soon Windows NT) require a method for uninstalling an application without resorting to a lot of hand editing of files. Trying to write such a utility from scratch every time you need to distribute an application is something most of us would rather not do. Just think of all those files that you have to remove from the SYSTEM folder without breaking anything on the user's machine and you'll see the same nightmare scenario that I do.

Enter InstallShield Express Lite. It's not what I would call the most complete install maker that I've ever seen, but it does take care of all of Windows 95 requirements. I found it extremely easy to use as well. All you really need to do is point and shoot. If you do find that the limitations of this product are getting in the way, you can always upgrade to the full-fledged product. Having a program that creates the installation utility you need to distribute applications is a dream come true for most of us.

Extended Open Tools API

When was the last time you wished you could use a favorite editor or other tool in place of the one provided with the IDE? Delphi 2.0 lets you add custom development tools directly into the Delphi environment using the extended Open Tools API. This feature allows you to link your favorite editor or other tool into the Delphi environment. You can even use the API to automate repetitive tasks by creating your own experts.

Database

One thing that has always intrigued me about Delphi is its ability to work in several environments. Take database programming for example. Most general purpose languages require a lot of extra code to do anything—one of the major reasons that I resorted to using DBMS specific language products in the first place. The flexibility of using a general purpose language just didn't pay off in this case; the features of a DBMS specific language allowed me to develop the application faster every time despite the limitations I encountered.

Delphi 2.0 increases its lead on other general purpose languages in this release. Sure, I still wouldn't use it in a situation that required heavy database processing; that's still the realm of the DBMS-specific languages. However, I can use Delphi in more situations now than ever before.

If you need the flexibility of a general purpose language, but still have to interact with a database, then Delphi is probably the way to go. You'll have to really work hard to overtax the capabilities that this product provides—at least when working with a moderately sized application.

> **Looking Ahead:** I'll explore the whole issue of database management in Chapter 12. However, that's not the only place you'll find some hints and tips you can use. Look at Chapter 13 for some tips on adding security to your application. I also show you some of the finer points of printing and using ReportSmith in Chapter 8, "Printer Magic." Finally, if you need to add OLE to your DBMS application, look at Chapter 10 for assistance.

32-Bit Borland Database Engine (BDE)

I was both happy and sad when I saw this feature. I think you'll find that the BDE looks about the same as it did in the 1.0 version. That was the unimpressive part. However, when I started working with the BDE, I realized that all the new features were under the hood. The most impressive feature—at least as far as I'm concerned—is the vast speed improvement that this version offers. Of course, you'll need to take it out on a test drive yourself to see the difference.

Database Form Expert

You may never start an application from scratch again once you try the new Database Form Expert. This particular feature enables you to get a database application going at a speed that you'll find amazing. In about five minutes—or maybe even less—you can get the basics together for a single or master/detail application. I expected to find tools like this in Access, but was surprised when I found a similar tool in Delphi.

Improved Database Desktop

Database Desktop has also improved in this version. You'll find it easier to configure because Borland added tabbed properties and preferences dialog boxes. The level of SQL support is also improved— you can query SQL tables directly now. I like the fact that I can customize the toolbars as well. You'll find a few other features in Database Desktop, but these are the major ones to look for.

Database Explorer

Explorer was a big change for me in Windows 95. Because of Explorer, I no longer resort to the DOS prompt every five minutes. I find that I can get work done faster if I explore my system using this new Windows 95 utility. Database Explorer promises to do about the same thing for Delphi.

There are two main features that you need to look at with this particular utility. First, you can look at the structure of the entire database. I'm not just talking about the tables; I'm talking about everything that the database contains. It doesn't matter what the source is—Database Explorer can access it (at least if Delphi provides the appropriate connectivity). In fact, we'll look at three different sources in Chapter 12 when I provide you with all the details of using this utility. Database Explorer is the perfect tool for figuring out exactly how to put your database application together; think of it as you would an outliner in a word processor.

The second feature is the data dictionary. You can get a real performance boost from starting your application using the Database Form Expert, but this feature is the one that will help you maintain the application later on. I was able to use the data dictionary for a variety of purposes including edit masks and creating a variety of business logic rules. This powerful tool will take a little time to learn, but you'll find it well worth the effort.

Database Component Enhancements

There are so many different component changes that I probably won't mention them all here. The first thing you'll notice are the enhancements to the TDBGrid component. The new version offers codeless support for quick searching and automatic lookup fields. You can also create multiple custom views to the same data using the TDBGrid column editors.

The TField component now offers support for lookup fields. What does this mean to you as a developer? Now you can tell Delphi to look up the value needed for a particular data entry field using a lookup table. I'll provide a lot more details on this particular feature in Chapter 12—we'll use it to define a lookup field for the categories used in at least one of the examples.

The TRecordGrid component allows you to use multi-record objects (MRO). Think of this particular component as the means to provide thumbnail sketches of a record. You'll see so many rows by so many columns of records on the display—in this respect it works much like a browser. However, the similarities end there because you'll see multiple custom forms instead of the spreadsheet-like rows and columns that many of us associate with a browse display.

Enhanced Integration with ReportSmith 3.0

ReportSmith used to require a lot of extra effort on the part of the Delphi developer. Even getting a report going was a major effort. I don't think that Borland will ever solve all the problems with their report generator, but they have solved one. Delphi 2.0 provides a new TReport component. All you do is stick it on a form. This particular component allows you to start a ReportSmith report with a simple command. I'll show you just how easy it is to use in Chapter 8.

Quick Report Components

Don't like the way that ReportSmith forces you to use a BASIC-like language for macros? Try the new Quick Report components. There are a lot of places where I found these new components just as useful as ReportSmith without all the hassle.

I won't get into a long winded discourse of all the virtues of these components here. However, think about this particular aspect of using Quick Reports—you don't have any external DLLs or run-time support to distribute. ReportSmith still requires all this baggage. The bottom line is that for small reports you'll want the ease of Quick Reports; ReportSmith is the heavy artillery that you'll use for those complex monster reports that take all night to print.

Data-Aware Controls

Delphi 2.0 provides a full set of data aware controls. Instead making the user guess what type of input you want, these components actually help the user enter the right kind of data. Any component on a form that helps the user, helps you as well.

Client-Server Development

Delphi places a special emphasis on client-server development. This is a relatively new area of DBMS programming where large companies need to downsize those huge databases lurking on mainframe computers. The following paragraphs describe some of the client-server enhancements that you'll find in Delphi 2.0.

32-Bit Local InterBase Server

Delphi 1.0 came with a single user license version of the Interbase server. It's a nice feature that helps a consultant create a great looking application in the shortest amount of time. The local Interbase server also allows you to move your sample data and upscale it to the full scale version of the product.

The 32-bit part of the Delphi 2.0 enhancement brings all the features that you might expect. You'll gain access to 32-bit data types and the stability of the 32-bit environment. However, that's not the big news.

The big news for Delphi 2.0 is the two user Windows NT server license that you'll get. The old single user product had a big problem. How could you test multi-user access of your database application if you didn't have a multi-user license for the server? This version of Delphi fixes that problem.

SQL Monitor

SQL Monitor helps you test, debug, and performance tune your database applications. One of its nicer features is the ability to trace calls between the client and server. SQL Monitor reports the amount of time spent on a single operation—helping you to find areas that you might need to optimize.

SQL Explorer

In the previous section we talked a little about the new Database Explorer utility provided with Delphi. SQL Explorer allows you to browse and modify server-specific meta data like stored procedures, triggers, and index descriptions. You'll also find SQL Explorer handy for modifying server specific information. Delphi provides connections for Oracle, Sybase, Microsoft SQL Server, and Informix.

Visual Query Builder

Visual Query Builder is a powerful SQL tool that helps you select the information you need from an SQL table. This is a graphical tool that automatically generates bug-free ANSI SQL-92 commands based on the criteria you specify. Obviously, even if the code is bug free, you'll still need to supply the right criteria to get the proper results.

32-Bit SQL Links Drivers

You'll love the new set of drivers provided with Delphi 2.0. They include 32-bit connections for Oracle, Interbase, Sybase, Microsoft SQL, and Informix. You'll also get new 16-bit drivers for Sybase System 10 and DB2. The best news is that you get an unlimited deployment license for all drivers, which means that you don't have to worry about licensing fees.

Delayed Update on Non-Live Result Sets

Delayed (cached) updates help improve server response time by reducing the amount of network traffic between a client and a server. What this feature does is wrap the transactions into batches. The multiple communications behave as a single transaction—reducing server contention and improving application performance.

Delphi Strengths and Weaknesses

Delphi is a great tool for most of the types of applications that you'll need to create. It's certainly the right tool for the user interface section of any application—the prototyping tools it provides are on par with those provided by Visual Basic and other RAD environments. Add in the team development tools and all the new components that this version of Delphi provides and I think you'll agree that it's certainly up to the tasks required of it in the Windows 32-bit environment.

I'll still probably use C from time to time, especially when I need to develop some low level or time critical code. I find that C still gives me better control over these application elements. It's also a bit faster, but Delphi certainly gives C a run for its money. Even Borland recognizes Delphi's limitations in this area. They purposely added features to this version to make it easier for you to interface Delphi with C as needed to get the job done. I applaud that attitude in a day when some vendors try to convince you that their product will do everything from brush your teeth to paint your house—they sort of remind me of the snake oil salesmen of old.

You'll probably want to keep your dedicated DBMS product around if you develop huge systems. In its favor, Delphi provides more connectivity features than any other general purpose language I've ever used. The codeless example I'll show you Chapter 12 certainly proves that Delphi can get the job done with a minimum of fuss. Still, when it comes time to start working with a large system, you'll find yourself getting mired in detail. Delphi just can't provide the level of tools that some of the complex DBMS tools provide. The very flexibility that makes it such a great general purpose tool keeps it from providing the things that a DBMS developer needs to create a huge system.

The following paragraphs take you on a tour of some of Delphi's strengths and weaknesses when compared to other languages. The purpose of this section is to help you understand where Delphi fits in the programmer's toolbox. As I mentioned earlier in this chapter, I don't believe in the one size fits all programming tool and neither should you.

Compared to C/C++

I think that C is always going to be king of the hill when it comes to working with low level features of the operating system. It provides a significantly better set of bit handling routines than Delphi does. I also find that I can access the hardware—when I need to—a bit faster using C. (Obviously this need is quickly going away—soon only an operating system or device driver programmer will ever need to worry about the hardware.) Then again, I thought that assembler would stick around as an adjunct to C, but it really hasn't. C simply included in-line assembler as part of its feature set—something that I still use on an occasional basis. Who knows, we may find that Delphi will incorporate in-line C sometime in the future.

Even though C may do the low level stuff better, Delphi does provide a faster programming environment. Unlike other RAD languages, Delphi provides a native code compiler. I want to emphasize this point because it's extremely important in regard to application execution speed and code size. Sure, machines today are getting faster and you can buy a huge hard drive for pennies. That's not the issue. The issue is that there are limitations to what you can expect from the hardware available today. Wouldn't it be better if all those processing cycles were doing something useful?

Compared to Visual Basic

Using Visual Basic taught me that RAD environments are great for getting a project started. Using one also eases the number of times you have to rewrite code to meet user expectations. With a little time and customer patience, I could usually design the entire user interface for an application in a few hours with the customer sitting by my side. I can honestly say that I can count on one hand the number of times I had to rework an interface that I created with Visual Basic.

The problem that I found with Visual Basic is that I quickly reached its limits. For example, anyone who has had to try and write a database application with Visual Basic will quickly tire of writing 10 lines of code for every one line in a specialty product. I finally ended up shelving Visual Basic in favor of some specialty programming languages that frankly didn't offer me much in the way of fast development.

Delphi is what Visual Basic should have been. It offers all of the promise of the RAD environment with few of the problems. I think you'll find that Visual Basic offers a few bells and whistles that Delphi doesn't in the form of direct third-party support. However, I'll exchange that support any day for faster development speed and fewer limitations.

Compared to CA-Visual Objects

Talk about a snarled IDE—CA-Visual Objects has it. I probably spent the better part of two days trying to figure everything out—that's really unusual for me. I'm not the only one who's complained about the steep learning curve of this product. In fact, the learning curve is so steep that I doubt many developers will try CA-Visual Objects out. That's really a shame because this is an extremely powerful product.

Once I got past the learning curve I found that developing a complex application using CA-Visual Objects is much faster than just about anything else I've used. Not only that, but using DLLs with this product is actually easier than using them with Delphi—if you can believe anything could be easier.

The fact still remains, if you want an easy-to-use product, CA-Visual Objects isn't the one to look at. If you need the power to develop really large DBMS application in a short amount of time, this is the way to go. The bottom line is that I'm probably going to stick with Delphi from now on for the vast majority of my DBMS applications and leave CA-Visual Objects for those monster jobs that I occasionally get.

32-Bit Versus 16-Bit

I'm not going to spend a lot of time telling you about all the differences between the 32-bit and the 16-bit versions of Delphi. I've already done that to some extent and I'll certainly add to the information you found in this chapter in future chapters. However, I'd be remiss in my duty to you if I didn't at least provide an overview of what you should expect to find in Delphi 2.0.

- Native Code Compiler—I can't stress this feature enough. If you want the power of Delphi with the speed of C, then you'll be very happy with this new version of the product.

- Flat Address Space—So what's this all about? A flat address space translates into even more speed. Every call is a near call. Every data segment is near as well. No longer will your code spend oodles of time working with Intel's segmentation scheme.

- 32-Bit Environment—The 32-bit environment offers all kinds of advantages to application programmers. Everything from better protection of your code to preemptive multitasking to speed enhancements like threads. I'm sure that you've seen all of these features of 32-bit applications acknowledged in any number of trade magazines. (If not, you'll certainly read about them in this book.)

- New Components—Delphi 2.0 provides a lot of new tools, some of them specific to Windows 95, others that are part of the 32-bit environment, and still others that the 1.0 version could have included, but didn't. I told you about all of these new features in the previous sections, so I won't cover them again here.

- Better Tools—From WinSight32 to the new Image Editor utility, you'll find that you're better equipped to produce great applications with Delphi 2.0. I'm going to cover the new utilities throughout the book. For example, we'll spend a lot of time talking about the new database tools in Chapter 12. I devoted an entire section to the Database Explorer and another to the BDE Configuration Utility.

Summary

This chapter has shown you some of the basic features of Delphi. We've talked about some of the reasons that I like to use it, what makes it a special tool that's worthwhile using. I've also provided some insights into how Delphi differs from its competition.

Don't get the idea that Delphi is the one and only tool that you'll ever need to get the job done—every programmer needs a fully outfitted toolbox of languages as far as I'm concerned. In fact, I'll demonstrate how you can mix languages together in the last section of this book. Using Delphi for its intended purpose is great, but hopefully this chapter has shown you that Delphi should be just one of many tools that you need to provide yourself with the very best programming environment possible.

Obviously all this introductory material doesn't do much for the veteran Delphi user. You already know why it's such a great development environment. However, this chapter also looked at all the new features that Delphi 2.0 has to offer. I haven't fully explored all of these new features, but you can be sure we'll do so throughout the rest of the book.

2

The Delphi
IDE

The Delphi IDE is designed to make programming as easy as possible—at least during the design phase of the project. All you really need to do is decide what your displays should look like, then drop the appropriate components in place to implement it. You can move the components around as needed and even add or delete components as needed. All of this functionality makes Delphi seem like a screen painter more than anything else when you start to use it.

Appearances can be deceiving—as you'll quickly find out. Once you have a form laid out, you can start modifying the properties of the various components that you placed on-screen. Properties include everything from the colors used to display the component to the caption used on a button. Properties can also affect component behaviors or the level of functionality they provide.

All of this is a prelude to coding. If you compiled and ran an application at this point, what you would see is a fully functional form. You could press the buttons and type information into any edit controls you provided. The memo components would act as full text editors. Everything would work to an extent—but they wouldn't really accomplish anything.

Up to this point you could have had the client at your side. The two of you could have worked on the appearance of the forms together. I view this as a very positive point in a RAD environment. Allowing the client to see the finished product—at least the only finished product that he's concerned with—is a big step in reducing the amount of reworking you'll have to do. The internal part of the program is the part you should, and will, concentrate on when writing an application.

This is the point where you'd start adding code to make buttons and menu entries do something. You'd take the shell that Delphi provided and change it into the finished application you or your client envisioned when you started the whole process. In other words, Delphi can provide a shell; you have to provide the works that make the shell worthwhile to use.

So, what's all this leading up to? This chapter is all about the IDE (integrated development environment) provided by Delphi. It's the part of the program that you'll use to create an application shell. You'll stay in the IDE to write the code that goes with the shell, but at that point any text editor would do an equally good job—well, with certain exceptions that I'll tell you about later. Suffice it to say that learning to use the IDE well will reduce the design time for the shell of your application and give you more time to work on the part that counts.

An Overview of the Delphi Speed Bar

Figure 2.1 shows a typical Delphi display. Right below the menu you'll find the speed bar. Believe it or not, this is where you'll spend the majority of your time during the user interface design phase of your application. Think of the Delphi IDE as a graphics program at this point and the components on the speed bar as the drawing tools that you'll use. It's a valuable analogy—one that will make the whole process of using Delphi easier.

Figure 2.1.
*The speed bar appears right
below Delphi's menu.*

There are actually two sections to the speed bar. The section on the right contains the speed buttons you'll use to perform tasks like saving the project or running it. The section on the right contains a full complement of components—it's called the visual component library or VCL for short.

Tip: Just about every Delphi object has a context menu you can display by right-clicking on it. The context menu normally contains an entry to get help. Other entries are object-specific. For example, if you right-click on a component, you'll see some options to align the component on the form. One of the options on the Object Inspector context menu allows you to hide it when no longer needed. Try right-clicking on the various elements of the Delphi environment to see what options the context menu contains.

Another form of Delphi help are hints. Just move your mouse pointer over a particular component or other object and you'll see a short description of it. You can add hints to your application too; I'll show you how later in the book.

Let's take a look at the speed buttons on the left side of the speed bar first. They're the ones you'll use to work with the project itself. There are three groups of buttons. The first group allows you to save your project or open a new one. The second group works with units and forms. The third group is what you'll use to compile and debug your application. The following list provides a quick rundown on each speed button on the list.

- Open Project—You'll use this button to open an existing project. Delphi displays all the DPR and PAS files in the current directory. Just like any file open display, you can maneuver to a new directory if needed. Figure 2.2 shows a typical File Open dialog used with Delphi. (The caption may change, but the functionality remains the same.)

Figure 2.2.
*A typical File Open dialog
used with Delphi.*

Tip: You can use the File | Reopen command to reopen a file or project that you recently worked on. Delphi will save up to eight files on the list: four DPR and four PAS.

- Open File—Use this speed button to open a standard file, one that isn't normally associated with the project. Delphi provides some standard file filters like PAS and DPR. It also includes a DFM filter. If your file type doesn't appear on the list, you can always select the All Files filter. Obviously the files you open are limited to the types that Delphi can read directly.

- Save All—This speed button saves all the files in your project, including the project file. You can also save all the files in a project by pressing Ctrl-S.

Tip: Delphi automatically saves all your files after it compiles the project as a default. This prevents you from losing any changes if your program should crash while you test it.

- Save File—You can use this option to save the currently selected file in the editor. The various files appear as pages on the editor screen (I'll show you how this looks a bit later). All you need to do is select the page you want to save, then press this speed button.

- Add File to Project—This speed button opens a dialog similar to the File Open dialog. It allows you to add another file to the current project. However, this speed button doesn't add any links between the various forms that you load.

Tip: You can use the File | Use Unit command to create any links you need between units. Simply select the unit that needs to use another unit, then select this option from the File menu. Delphi will ask which unit you want to use.

- Remove File from Project—Exercise caution when you use this speed button. It allows you to remove units that you no longer need to use with the project. (The file still exists on disk, but Delphi won't include it within the application.) Figure 2.3 shows a typical Remove From Project dialog. Notice that there are two columns. The left column contains the name of the unit. The right column contains the name of the associated form (if any).

- Select Unit from List—You don't have to display all the units that your project contains. The only unit that you have to display is the one that you're currently working on. Delphi automatically reads any non-displayed units from disk when it compiles. The View Unit dialog looks similar to the one in Figure 2.4.

Figure 2.3.
The Remove From Project dialog allows you to remove unneeded forms and units from the current project.

Figure 2.4.
The View Unit dialog allows you to select a unit from the current project to either view or edit.

Tip: Every form and unit that you display on-screen consumes Windows memory. This leaves less memory for the compiler and your sample application. If you run into memory problems when using Delphi, try closing all unneeded forms and units. This will free some memory for Delphi to use in running your application or compiling the code.

- Select Form from List—This speed button works much like the Select Unit from List button. The only difference is that it displays a list of units. The dialog looks similar to the one in Figure 2.4.
- Toggle Form/Unit—I actually found this button kind of useful even though I didn't think I would when I first started using Delphi. What it does is allow you to toggle between the unit that you're editing and the form that you're viewing. It comes in pretty handy when you have a lot of forms in the current project. You can select a unit from within the editor, then press this button to see which form the unit is associated with.
- New Form—One of the things that you'll do most often during the design phase of your application is create new forms. This button allows you to do just that without resorting to using the File | New command.

Tip: Don't automatically head for the New Form speed button just because it's handy. You'll find that you're missing a lot of what Delphi has to offer if you do. This new version contains a wealth of predefined forms and dialogs that are just too good to pass up. At least try using the File | New command long enough to become familiar with the various dialogs and forms that Delphi provides. That way, if you do run across a situation where one of these predefined forms would help, you'll know that they're available.

- Run—This speed button does more than you might think at first. Not only will it run your application, but it'll start the compilation process as well. Pressing the Run speed button tells Delphi to do whatever it takes to run your application.

- Pause—Once your application is running, you can use this speed button to pause it. Pausing your application puts you in debug mode where you can trace the various steps your application takes to perform the work you've asked it to do. An automatic way to pause your application is to set a breakpoint. A breakpoint tells your application to pause when it reaches a certain point in the execution sequence. I'll show you how to set breakpoints a little later.

- Trace Into—This speed button is used in debug mode only. It allows you to trace into a procedure. For example, say your code calls a function that you created. This button will take you to that function so that you can trace through the steps that it takes. Use the Step Over speed button if you want to stay in the current procedure or function.

- Step Over—Use this speed button to step over a function or procedure call. Delphi still executes the contents of that function or procedure, but you don't have to sit there and watch it do so. Use the Trace Into speed button if you actually want to see the contents of a function or procedure call execute. Obviously, you'll need a copy of the source code to do this.

Well, that's all the speed buttons on the left side of the display. As you can see, even though there aren't many of them, you can perform the vast majority of your design tasks without using the menu. About the only thing I would have preferred is the ability to choose something other than a standard form. It makes sense to display a list of the available forms since Delphi provides so many. This is actually a small complaint, but hopefully Borland will change this feature in a future release.

Now let's look at the VCL on the right side of the speed bar. Notice that this section contains tabbed pages. Figure 2.1 shows the default settings—you can add as many tabs as you deem necessary. This figure also shows the standard components. Delphi provides you with the means to add as many new components as you like. The following list will tell you about the default VCL tabs and some of the components they contain. We'll get into the components in detail as the book progresses.

Looking Ahead: Creating components is one way to make code reuse under Delphi a snap. Using a component is easy: all you have to do is click on it, then place it on a form wherever you want it to appear. The topic of components is so important that third party developers are flocking to create them. I recently saw a 55-page catalog containing nothing but Delphi components. We'll take a look at how you can create your own components in Chapter 17, "Building a Delphi VBX."

> **Tip:** Getting help on learning to use a component is easy. Just drop the component on a form, select it, then press F1. Delphi will provide context-sensitive help for that component.

- Standard—This tab contains all the standard components that you'll use with Delphi. It contains the basics like labels, menus, edits, and pushbuttons. You'll also find radio groups and panels in this section. Each of these components provides a basic function that most applications require. The components on this tab appear in Figure 2.1.

- Additional—Most of these components are graphic in nature. I really like the BitBtn component, it allows you to display an icon instead of (or with) a caption on a pushbutton. This tab also contains some of the basic graphic components like images and shapes. By the way, this is the tab that contains the speed buttons you'll need to create a speed bar for your application. Figure 2.5 shows the components on this tab.

Figure 2.5.

The Additional tab of the VCL contains most of the standard graphic components.

- Win95—Windows 95 offers a lot in the way of added functionality. Delphi 2.0 added this tab to the VCL so that you could access some of these features (some features, like the common dialogs, are automatic—you don't have to do anything special to see them). The components for this speed bar appear in Figure 2.6. I was surprised to find that I could figure out the functionality of most of the components simply by looking at Explorer. For example, the Tree List component acts just like the left pane of the Explorer display. You'll find some rather interesting components here as well. For example, the Image List component is essentially an array of images. You can add or delete images from here as needed. The end result is that creating an image editor should be a lot easier from this point on.

Figure 2.6.

The Win95 tab of the VCL contains all of the new interface components that the Windows 95 environment provides.

- Dialogs—Every version of Windows currently on the market makes the programmer's life just a bit easier by providing common dialogs. I spend an entire chapter (see Chapter 6, "Common Dialogs") looking at these components. Figure 2.7 shows the types of dialogs you can create using the components on this tab. They include the expected File Open and Save As dialogs, along with Font, Color, and Print dialogs. In essence, these dialogs allow you to incorporate into your application the same dialogs that every Windows application uses.

Figure 2.7.

Use the components on the Dialogs tab to add Windows common dialogs to your application.

- System—This tab contains some of the more interesting components that Delphi provides as a default. For example, this is the tab that you'll use to add timers to your application. It also contains a media player and the DDE components. You'll find that I describe the components here throughout the book. I make a special mention of the DDE components in Chapter 10, "Using Delphi with OLE," and the media player in Chapter 11, "Delphi and Multimedia Programming." Figure 2.8 shows all the components on the System tab.

Figure 2.8.

You'll find some of the more unusual components that Delphi offers on the System tab.

- Data Access—This is where you'll find the components that allow you access to your data. One of Delphi's specialties is the ability to grab data from just about anywhere, so you'll want to spend some time working with the components on this tab. Figure 2.9 shows what they look like. As you can see, you'll find data source, database, table, query, and other data-access components on this tab. I'll describe these components in more detail in Chapter 12, "Database Management Under Delphi."

Figure 2.9.

Gaining access to your data using the components on the Data Access tab is the first step to displaying it in your application.

- Data Controls—It doesn't matter how well you can access your data if you can't see it. Delphi provides a broad range of components that are specially designed to work with database data as shown in Figure 2.10. Notice that most of these components are extensions of the components on the Standard tab. The only real difference is that they have a database twist. (See Chapter 12 for more details.)

Figure 2.10.
The Data Controls tab contains all the components needed to display your database data.

- Win 3.1—Some of you are going to want to use the older Windows 3.x components in some circumstances. Say you need to add some additional functionality to an application you ported from the 16-bit environment and want to maintain the same appearance throughout the application. That's the purpose of the Win 3.1 tab shown in Figure 2.11. Notice that all your old favorites, including the tabbed notebook and the outline component, are here. This tab also includes two of the older database-related components: TDBLookupList and TDBLookupCombo.

Figure 2.11.
You'll find your old favorites from the 16-bit Delphi environment on the Win 3.1 tab.

- OCX—This is a new tab for Delphi 2.0. It contains sample OCX components and it's probably where you should install any new OCXs you buy (unless there are so many in the new package that it really needs its own tab). Figure 2.12 shows the default set of OCX components that you get with Delphi. Some of the more interesting offerings include a spelling checker, a graphing application, and a mini spreadsheet.

Figure 2.12.
Delphi 2.0 provides OCX support—this is where you tap into that support from a component level.

- Samples—Borland also provides you with some sample components that you can tear apart to learn how to build your own. They appear on the tab shown in Figure 2.13. I find that the gauge and the spin edit components are the ones I use the most. The calendar component also comes in handy from time to time. Of course, the main reason to look at these components is to learn how to build your own. (See Chapter 17 for more details.)

Figure 2.13.
The Samples tab provides some handy components, but its main purpose is to teach you how to create your own components.

- QReport—This was an unexpected, but very nice surprise when I worked with the beta product. Figure 2.14 shows the QReport component tab. It provides the means to send the information in a database to your printer. Theoretically, you might be able to use the components on this tab to provide output for general application needs as well. I'll show you the database end of these components in Chapter 12.

Figure 2.14.

QReport provides an alternative to using ReportSmith; the components act much like their display counterparts on the Data Controls tab.

Using the Object Inspector

Placing a component on a form doesn't necessarily configure it to your needs. It certainly doesn't add any of the code required to make the component do anything. The job of the Object Inspector is to allow you to configure the various objects in your application. In most cases these objects are going to be components that you grab from the VCL or forms from the New Items dialog.

So, how do you use the Object Inspector? It consists of two pages of data. The first page appears in Figure 2.15. It contains all the properties for a particular object. You'll find all of the things you expect here, including the height, width, and color of the object. Just about every component also includes special properties. For example, when you select a rich edit component, you'll see a property called Lines. It allows you to add any predefined text that you need to the component.

Figure 2.15.

The Object Inspector allows you to view and edit the properties associated with an object.

Tip: If you select multiple components on a form, you can view and edit their common properties in the Object Inspector. If the selected components don't have any common properties, the Object Inspector will show a blank page. This is one method for making changes to a lot of components at once. For example, you could use this technique to change the font size for some pushbuttons on the form to show default or standard actions that you want the user to perform.

You change the contents of a property by selecting it, then typing in a value in most cases. Some properties provide a combo box that you can use to select from a list of values. For example, you can choose from a list of border styles when configuring a form. Other property values will display an ellipsis next to the entry blank. This tells you that there is a dialog associated with this particular property. You'll use the dialog to change the value of the property (which probably won't appear in the blank once you edit it). The Lines property of a TMemo component falls into this category.

Tip: There is a keyboard method for selecting properties that you want to change. Press F11 to select the Object Inspector, then press Tab to select the left column of the Properties tab. Now all you need to do is type the first few letters of the property you want to change. Press Tab again to select the right column so that you can change the property's value. Use the Ctrl-Tab keyboard shortcut to switch between the Properties and the Events pages of the Object Inspector. This same technique works with other tabbed Delphi dialogs.

Tip: You can go right to the help for a particular property by selecting the property in the Object Inspector and pressing F1. If you need to get help on the component as a whole, make sure you select the component on the form and press F1.

The second page of the Object Inspector allows you to assign functions to events associated with an object. Figure 2.16 shows a typical example. The most common object event is click. When the user clicks on the object they normally expect something to happen. This is especially true for objects like pushbuttons.

Tip: Double-clicking on a component always assigns a procedure to its default event (the click event in most cases). Delphi will automatically create a procedure shell and place your cursor in the right place within the code editor. The name of the procedure is a combination of the object name and the event that you're defining. If you need to assign something other than the default procedure name to the default event, you'll need to select the Events page by hand to do it.

Figure 2.16.

You use the Events page of the Object Inspector to assign functions or procedures to specific object events.

Unlike the Properties page, Delphi always provides a combo box for each event on the Events page. This combo box contains a list of the procedures and functions you've already defined—allowing you to reuse code in some circumstances where the procedure is the same, but the object it acts on changes. (See Listing 11.7 in Chapter 11 for details on how to use this technique.)

Configuring Your Environment

You'll find that Delphi has a lot to offer when it comes to configuration options. In most cases the programmers at Borland made pretty good guesses as to what a programmer would want—probably because they used Delphi to write Delphi—but there are times where you may want something different.

The following paragraphs will take you through the various configuration options that Delphi provides. Use the Tools | Options command to display the Environment Options dialog used throughout this section. I'll also make some suggestions on which options you'll want to change and why.

Preferences

The Preferences page (see Figure 2.17) allows you to change the way that Delphi configures the IDE. Most generally you'll configure the options on this page once when you start using Delphi, then promptly forget that it exists. The following paragraphs provide an overview of each option.

- Desktop Contents—There are two radio buttons in this group. If you select the Desktop Only option, Delphi saves just the desktop configuration when you exit. This includes directory information, open editor files, and open windows. The second option adds the browser symbol information from the last successful compile.

- Autosave Options—You'll find two check boxes here. Delphi only checks the first one by default. I usually add the Desktop option as well. The reason is simple. If you don't add Save the Desktop configuration, you'll waste time rearranging things every time you open a file.

- Form Designer—There are actually two areas in this group. The first area controls the way that Delphi places and displays components. It automatically selects the first two options that display a position grid on all forms and snaps any components you place on the form to the grid. The third option displays a caption for each component, telling you what it is. I found that this was a handy feature when I first started using Delphi, but turned it off later because the captions tend to make the form look cluttered. The second area allows you to change the size of the grid. I kept this as the default value. Some people like to use a smaller grid, but that really makes it difficult to see the dots and use them accurately.

Figure 2.17.

The Preferences page of the Environment Options dialog allows you to change the IDE configuration.

Note: As of this writing, Delphi automatically displays the captions of any Data Access or other non-visual components that you place in a Data Module.

Tip: If you find that the grid increment is too coarse to position a particular component, then you can always bypass the Snap to grid option. Simply select the component, then use Ctrl-Arrow to move the component around on the screen. This allows you to micro-adjust the position of a component without defeating the purpose of the grid.

- Debugging—There are five different debugging options in this group. The first check box tells Delphi to use its integrated debugger. You'll normally keep this option checked unless you intend to use an external debugger. The second option tells Delphi to stop at the first unit with debug information. I normally keep this unchecked since I use breakpoints to stop the application as needed. The Hide Designer on Run option allows you to hide things like the Object Inspector when you run the application. I normally keep this checked so that I can use the space to display my Watch List dialog. The Break on Exception is a handy option in most cases. It tells you when your application does something that would normally cause a GPF in Windows (or some other error). It gets to be annoying though if you want to test for exceptions in an application. For example, in Chapter 11 I use the Try…Except construct to test for a non-existent file. I turned this option off when writing that example since it actually got in the way of getting the program to run. The final option in this group minimizes Delphi when you run your application. I normally keep it off so that I can easily access the Step Over and Trace Into speed buttons. It's a convenient option if you're trying to show a client how their application will actually look once you get it finished—the Delphi display tends to be distracting.

- Compiling—Delphi doesn't check this option by default and I've never understood why. It's essential to view the compiler's progress when writing an application. Some large applications could take a while to compile and this indicator at least shows you that Delphi is on the job.

Library

You'll use the Library page to control how Delphi interacts with libraries. In this case I'm talking about the units that Borland supplied with Delphi, such as the WINDOWS.PAS library. Figure 2.18 shows the groups on this page. The following paragraphs provide an overview of each group.

Figure 2.18.

Use the options on the Library page of the Environment Options dialog to change the way that Delphi works with library files.

- Map File—This is actually a general-purpose option. It tells the linker to create a map file—much like the map files you may have used in the DOS environment. The first option, the default, tells the linker not to provide a map file. The second option provides a map file containing the following entries: segment list, program start address, and any warning or error messages produced during the link. If you select the second option, Delphi adds a sorted list of public symbols to the previous list of entry. The third option provides a detailed report that also includes a detailed segment map. For most programming scenarios you'll want to keep this option set to Off.

- Messages—Delphi doesn't want to hound you with excess information, but at the same time it wants to provide as much as you need. The first option tells Delphi whether you want to see warning messages—essentially problems with your code that really don't rate as errors. The second option tells Delphi that you want to see messages that provide hints on improving program efficiency. I usually keep both options off, but you may want to turn them on while you learn to use Delphi.

- Options—There are two entries in this group. Use the first option if you want to add debug information to your library code. I find this feature handy if I want to see how Borland got a particular feature to work. It also comes in handy if I suspect there's a bug in the library code somewhere. The Save Library Code option allows you to save changes made to the library files. Normally Delphi doesn't save these changes to keep you from inadvertently introducing errors into them.

- Path—This option allows you to specify the path to your library files. Delphi normally sets it for you when you install it.

- Aliases—You probably won't need to change this option. It tells Delphi to use a library file in place of one listed in the USES section of your program. The only time you'll need to change this setting is when you port your applications from the 16-bit to the 32-bit environment. Notice that Borland automatically includes a reference to the new WINDOWS.PAS unit.

Editor

Code editors are one of the most personal elements that any programmer uses. I won't even pretend to tell you how to configure your editor for optimal use (although I'll offer some insights into the way I configure mine). Figure 2.19 shows the Editor page of the Environment Options dialog. As you can see, there are a ton of different options that you can use (in fact, they spill over into the next two pages). The following paragraphs provide a brief overview of each option.

Tip: You can display the three pages of the Environment Options dialog associated with the editor by right-clicking on the editor, then selecting Properties from the context menu. The same feature works with the speed bar and the VCL. Selecting properties from the context menu—when it appears—always displays the appropriate configuration dialog.

- Editor Speed Setting—Delphi provides four different speed settings that you can use. Essentially this allows you to set Delphi's editor to mimic another editor. Editor options include default keymapping, IDE classic (the Delphi 1.0 editor setup), Epsilon emulation, and BRIEF emulation.

- Editor Options—You can also configure individual editor options. This is the method I used since I like to use something a bit closer to some of the DOS editors that I've used in the past. About the only option that I really had to change was the tab settings. I usually have to move my code from my editor to a document—for example, in writing this book or as part of a final program documentation process. I set the Smart Tab option off and the Use Tab Character option on to make it easier to move my code from one environment to another.

- Block Indent—Indenting and unindenting your code is easy in the Delphi editor. Just select a block of code, then press Ctrl-Shift-I to indent and Ctrl-Shift-U to unindent. This setting controls how many characters the block moves for each indent. I usually set it for my default tab interval.

- Undo Limit—Each level of undo that you allow consumes some memory in the Windows environment. The actual amount of memory depends on the keystrokes that Delphi has to store. Since memory is a limited quantity on most machines, you might need to decrease the undo levels to free some up after a long editing session (Delphi automatically resets the undo feature after each code save). The only time I'd change this setting is if you were on a memory-starved system.

- Tab Stops—Delphi doesn't really provide many tab stops in the default configuration, so I added my own. I use a tab spacing of five characters to make it easy to see where one block ends and another begins. Obviously the interval you use is a matter of personal taste.

- Syntax Extensions—This next option is deceptively simple. I told you previously about the File Open button and the fact that it includes filters. You use this option to change the filter list. For example, I added *.TXT as one of the entries, which allows me to view README and other text files without leaving the editor or having to sift through too many entries to find them. There is one word of caution here. Make sure that you select registered file types for this entry—unregistered file types seem to cause problems.

Figure 2.19.

The Editor page allows you to change how your editor works within Delphi.

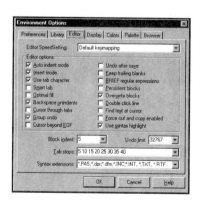

Display

The previous section told you about the options available for modifying the editor. For the most part, that page dealt with keystrokes and dialogs. This page deals with the way that the editor displays things on-screen. Figure 2.20 shows how this page looks. Notice that there are additional display-related emulation options on this page that allow you to make Delphi's editor look like some of the third-party products on the market.

Figure 2.20.
Use the Display page to change how code appears within the editor.

- Display and File Options—This group allows you to change the way that Delphi interacts with the file. The one compatibility option in this section is BRIEF Cursor Shapes, which changes the I-beam cursor shape to those used by BRIEF. The Create Backup File option is the one responsible for all those *.~* files in your source code directory. The Preserve Line Ends option tells Delphi to use hard carriage returns and to ignore the right margin. The final option, Zoom to Full Screen, tells Delphi to use the entire display for editing. I normally keep this turned off since I like having access to the speed bar during an editing session.

- Keystroke Mapping—The only purpose for this option is to determine what keystrokes to use in the editor. It allows you to change the control-key combinations to those used by your favorite editor.

- Right Margin—Most programmers aren't going to care about this option too much unless they regularly print out their code. It defines the right margin. I find that this option does come in handy because I can use it to determine when a line of code is too long to fit in my word-processed document. I always keep the Visible Right Margin option checked so that I can break long lines by hand.

- Editor Font—This is another option that's strictly up to the taste of the programmer. Delphi will allow you to use any monospaced font on your machine. All you need to do is select the font you want to use from the list, then select a font size. The box below this selection shows a sample of the font you selected.

Colors

Color serves far more than aesthetic appeal under Delphi—it helps you see the location of key words and other program features. The Colors page of the Environment Options dialog in Figure 2.21 allows you to define the colors that Delphi uses to highlight various elements.

Figure 2.21.
Color is important in Delphi because it allows you to highlight various program elements.

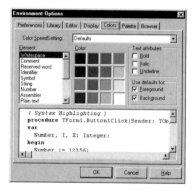

To change the color used for a particular element, just select the element you want to change from the list. Decide whether you want to use the default foreground and background colors by either checking or unchecking the appropriate check boxes. You can also decide to use bold, italic, or underlined fonts for emphasis. A left click on the color blocks determines the foreground color—a right click, the background color. The scroll box below the color settings shows what your changes will look like in the editor.

Palette

The Palette page of the Environment Options dialog is where you change the components that appear in the various pages of the VCL. I'm not going to cover this topic here—look in Chapter 17 for full details about creating and installing your own components in Delphi.

Browser

The final page in the Environment Options dialog, shown in Figure 2.22, contains the Object Browser options. Delphi allows you to browse the various objects in your application using the Object Browser (we'll get into Object Browser usage techniques in Chapter 4, "Adding Some Bells and Whistles"). The following paragraphs provide an overview of the various Browser page options.

Figure 2.22.
Delphi 2.0 offers an Object Browser—you use this page of the Environment Options dialog to configure it.

- Symbol Filters—These check boxes allow you to define what type of information you want to see in the Object Browser. Fortunately, you can also define which items actually get displayed from within the Browser itself, so I usually keep all the check boxes selected. This gives me a lot more control over what I see when I use the Object Browser.

- Initial View—You need to decide what you want to see first. I normally use the Object Browser because I need to know about a particular object. However, you may just want to browse through all objects in a unit—this option allows you to do that.

- Display—There are two options in this group. The first option, Qualified Symbols, tells Delphi to display the qualified identifier for a symbol. Normally only the symbol name is displayed.

- Object Tree—You have to be browsing an object to use this option. It tells Delphi which branches of the object tree to collapse.

Adding New Tools

You'll find that there are tools you use on a regular basis with Delphi. Wouldn't it be nice if you could simply launch them from a menu rather than resort to using the Start menu or Program Manager? That's what this section is all about. I'll show you how to add new entries to the Tools menu. Each of these entries will allow you to launch a utility program—any utility program. The following procedure shows you some of the ins and outs of adding your own programs to the Delphi Tools menu. (I'm assuming that you're already in Delphi at the start of this procedure.)

1. Use the Tools | Tools command to display the Tool Options dialog shown in Figure 2.23. This dialog displays a list of currently installed tools—not the actual tool executable filename, but the menu name that you assigned to it.

Figure 2.23.
The Tool Options dialog displays a list of tools that you can currently access from within Delphi.

Note: Your list of tools may vary from those shown in the figure, depending on what installation method you used. In most cases Delphi will automatically place all the tools you selected during the initial installation process on the Tools menu. Any tools you install after that probably won't appear—you'll have to add them manually.

2. Highlight an existing tool entry if you want to edit or delete it. Click on the Add, Edit, or Delete pushbuttons. If you select Delete, Delphi will remove the tool from the menu and you can exit the dialog (and this procedure). If you selected Add or Edit, Delphi will display the Tool Properties dialog shown in Figure 2.24.

Figure 2.24.
The Tool Properties dialog allows you to define a tool name and where to find it. You can also add optional parameters.

3. Decide on a new name for your tool and type it into the Title field. Press Tab. This is the name that Delphi displays on the Tools menu, so make sure you use something descriptive. In this case I decided to add the Image Editor to my Tools menu, so I typed its name in the Title field.

4. Type the name of your program in the Program field. Make sure you add any appropriate path information. As an alternative, you can press the Browse button. This will display a File Open dialog that you can use to find the program. Press Tab to move to the next field.

5. Type in the working directory for your tool. In most cases this is the same directory as the tool itself. However, you may want to make the working directory the same as your source code directory.

Tip: You can use the Browse button to enter the name of both your source code directory and the name of the tool by entering the fields in reverse. In other words, click on Browse and select a file in your source code directory first. This will change the Working Directory field to match your source code directory field. Use the Browse button a second time to select the tool you want to use. This second use will only change the contents of the Program field.

6. The final step is to add any command-line parameters that you need to start the tool. You can enter these by hand or use the macros that Delphi defines automatically. Figure 2.25 shows a list of macros. The most common macro is going to be $Name, which provides a filename as part of the opening parameters. If you do decide to use a macro, highlight the macro name and press the Insert pushbutton.

Figure 2.25.

Delphi provides a variety of macros you can use to provide information to the tool you want to use.

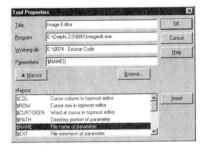

7. Click on OK to close the Tool Properties dialog. Click on Close to make the change to the Tools menu permanent.

As you can see, adding tools to your Delphi Tools menu isn't difficult and can make it a lot easier to access the utilities you need to write your application. I didn't mention it in the procedure, but you can use the arrow pushbuttons in the Tool Options dialog to move the tools around on the menu. That way you can place your favorite tools first on the list or arrange your tools in alphabetical order.

Summary

This chapter has provided you with an overview of the Delphi IDE. It's important to know how to use the tool you're going to use for programming—a fact lost on many of us when we rip open the package and install a new compiler without much thought of looking through the manuals.

I've also provided you with a wealth of usage tips that should make your time using the Delphi IDE a lot easier. A lot of these tips are in the documentation, but they're hidden away. The method I provided for changing the properties of multiple components at one time falls into this category. Some of them aren't even described in the documentation, for whatever reason. You won't find some of the keyboard tips that I provided anywhere in the documentation.

If you're a keyboard user and hate to spend too much time using the mouse, pay particular attention to all the keyboarding tips that I provided in this chapter. They'll make it easier for you to stick with the keyboard. In fact, I don't think that there is any area in Delphi where you absolutely have to use the mouse if you don't want to.

3

Building a Basic Program

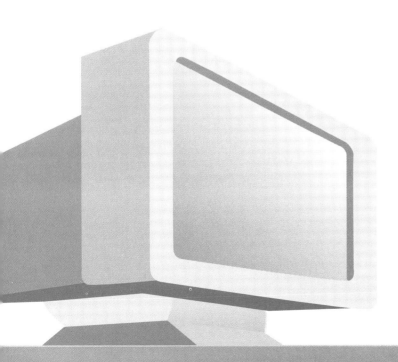

I had mentioned in Chapters 1 and 2 that one of the reasons Delphi is so popular is because it provides RAD programming environment. We all know that popular phrase, "Talk is cheap." It really is. Unless you see that a product performs, how do you know that what you're hearing isn't all hype? That's the purpose of this chapter. I want to introduce you to the physical part of Delphi's RAD capability—the part that really counts.

Creating a basic application—the starting point that you'll use for all of your applications—is one of the first things you'll need to learn when using Delphi. The first thing you need to understand is that RAD is a mind set as much as a technology. Just as OOP requires a different way of working and thinking, using a RAD environment to its full potential requires a change in the way you do things as well. The RAD environment requires an adjustment in the way that you think about an application; from the very first component you drop on the form to the last piece of code you attach to a pushbutton.

One of the basic things I always look at before I begin a new application is whether I have any "off-the-shelf" parts that I can use to start it. That's probably not a familiar idea to a programmer —you usually associate the phrase "off-the-shelf" with hardware of some kind. Delphi uses the idea of templates and components extensively to promote code reuse. These are nice new marketing terms, but I'll always think of them in terms of off-the-shelf parts. When you think about it, isn't this what components and templates really come down to being? (Realistically there are differences between the two that I'll get into in a little while.)

Using off-the-shelf parts saves you a lot of time and the client a lot of money. You both win when you use components and templates. OK, so you already do that with your current programming language—you reuse code to make creating new applications faster and less error prone. How is Delphi going to help? It's the way that Delphi helps you reuse code that makes a difference. You're not just reusing the code, but everything else in your application as well. A component is more than the code attached to it, as is a template. That's where the RAD perspective comes in.

The following sections will help you understand how to use Delphi with your new RAD hat in place. I'll show you how to create a basic application. However, in showing you this process I'll also get you acquainted with the RAD approach to writing an application. You'll find out that it's a lot more than just code reuse; it really does come down to using "off-the-shelf" parts to create the shell of an application. Think of yourself as a drag racer designer. Sure, you'll start with off-the-shelf parts to start the racer; but you'll make it worth running a race with the modifications you add.

Looking Ahead: We'll take a look at the templates portion of Delphi in the next section of this chapter. Look at the section entitled "An Overview of the Delphi Speed Bar" in Chapter 2, "The Delphi IDE," for an overview of the components that Delphi provides. I'll show you how to use both templates and components later in this chapter.

Using the Gallery

Templates—the forms and other applications shells you'll use to start an application—appear in the Gallery. You use the File | New command to display the New Items dialog shown in Figure 3.1. This is the Gallery. As you can see, it includes several predefined tabs. The following paragraphs provide an overview of the various tabs—we'll spend some time looking at specific tabs in detail a bit later.

Figure 3.1.

The New Items dialog displays a list of the templates that Delphi provides.

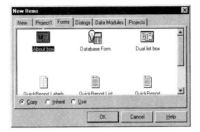

Note: You're going to see another term used for the Gallery in Delphi 2.0—depending on which version of the product you bought. The Object Repository is an advanced form of the Gallery. As far as I'm concerned, they're the same thing. To avoid confusing the issue any further, I'm going to use the term Gallery throughout the book to refer to the listing of templates that Delphi provides.

Tip: You don't have to use the New Items dialog to use some of the more common templates. The File menu contains several of them as standard entries. For example, you can use the File | New Form command to create a new standard form. The File | New Data Module command allows you to create a new data module—a type of form used to group non-visual components in one place. (Chapter 12, "Database Management Under Delphi," tells how to use a data module to make DBMS programming easier—you can use these same techniques with other non-visual components like timers.)

- New—This is the main tab. It contains a list of common form types along with some of the more unusual templates that Delphi provides. For example, you'll find the new TThread template here. Likewise, the Automation template allows you to create an OLE automation client or server. This tab also contains some application types. For example, you'll select the DLL template if you want to create a DLL instead of an application with Delphi.

- Project1—The exact name of this particular tab will change depending on what you call your project. What it contains is a complete list of all the templates in your application.

So, what good is this? What if you have a form in your application that looks similar to another form you need, but not quite? You could inherit that form and make any needed changes—reducing the amount of coding you'd need to do.

- Forms—Delphi provides more than just a standard form. It provides several default forms and you can add your own forms here as well. You'll probably want to take a look at the About Box template on this page—it provides everything that the typical developer will need. All you need to do is customize it with your company name and any other pertinent statistics. I find that the Dual List Box template is indispensable whenever I need the user to select one or more items from a list of items. This comes in very handy when creating configuration forms in database report programs. The Tabbed Pages form comes in handy for other types of configuration displays. In fact, I show you how to use this one in Chapter 7, "The Windows GDI" (just look at the Drawing Tool Configuration form in that chapter).

Tip: You can also access the Database Form template using the Database | Database Form Expert command. This is what happens when you select the Database Form entry on the Forms tab of the New Items dialog.

- Dialogs—I probably use this tab more than any of the others because it contains so many helpful templates. There are four different types of standard dialog on this page—two of them with Help buttons. I use the standard dialog quite a bit throughout the book, so you'll see plenty of chances to use it. The fifth dialog is a special password screen; I'll show you how to use it in Chapter 12. Suffice it to say that this dialog comes in very handy with database applications. However, you'll also need it to create certain types of network applications. (Look in Chapter 13, "Delphi on a LAN," for a description of how to use Delphi on the network.)

- Data Modules—I covered generic data modules in the New tab description. This tab contains specific data modules. Any time you create a data module, Delphi saves it for future use. That way you only have to define your data modules once, not every time you need to access the data. I find that this particular feature is extremely helpful for defining banks of other non-visual components as well.

Tip: You can save time and effort when creating applications that use common dialogs by defining a common dialog data module. Of course, this does consume a little more memory, especially if you don't use all the dialogs in every application. The trade-off is reduced programming time. You'll also find that using a data module reduces overall program memory requirements if more than one form uses the common dialogs.

- Projects—There are two kinds of projects that Delphi defines for you: an SDI application and a MDI application. I actually find that these are the least useful templates that Delphi provides because the applications are too generic to provide me with any useful benefit.

Suffice it to say that you'll probably want to add your own project templates here if you create a common application type. For example, I have a mailing list manager project defined here since I create more than a few of them. I also have a utility program template defined—it contains a single form and some basic menu options predefined along with some common dialogs like the File Open and Save As dialog entries. You can see an example of this project in Chapter 6, "Common Dialogs," where I tell you about the common dialogs. (The project in this chapter is actually a lot more complex than my project template, but looking through this chapter should give you some ideas.)

Now that I've introduced you to the Gallery, let's spend some time looking at how you can use it. The following sections tell you how to use and maintain the Gallery. This includes adding new templates to the Gallery, an important task if you want to create a customized array of "off-the-shelf" parts you can use to write applications faster.

Using Templates in Your Project

Getting a template from the Gallery to your project is easy. We've already looked at the first part of the process—using the File | New command to open the New Items dialog. Once you get the dialog open, you need to select the tab containing the template you want to use.

However, after you've worked with Delphi for a while, you might have more than a few templates to look through. Delphi provides an answer to this problem as well. If you right-click on any page in the Gallery, you'll see a context menu like the one shown in Figure 3.2.

Figure 3.2.

Like everything else in Delphi, the Gallery provides a context menu that allows you to change its appearance.

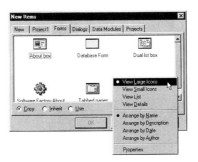

There are three groups of options in the context menu. The first group changes the way that Delphi displays the template list. All four of these items work much like their counterparts in Explorer. By default, you'll see a large icon display. The small icon display shown in Figure 3.3 comes in handy if you want to look at a lot of different templates at once. However, I find that it's a bit hard on the eyes to try to read descriptions this way. The List view shown in Figure 3.4 displays the templates in a list format. It doesn't look much different from the small icon display. The Details view shown in Figure 3.5 is the one that you'll use most often when searching for specific templates. It tells you the template name, a description, the date that the template was last modified, and the template's author.

> **Tip:** If you see a Details view template that contains N/A in the Modified field and a blank in the Author field, you know that it's a standard Delphi template. I always use standard templates as a starting point for new templates. (There are situations where I'll inherit an existing custom template, but doing this invites mystery errors in any applications that depend on the template.) Never modify the default Delphi templates—that way you'll always have a "baseline" template to use to create custom templates.

Figure 3.3.
The Small Icon view comes in handy when you need to see a lot of templates.

Figure 3.4.
The List view looks much like the Small Icon view—the only difference is the icon layout.

Figure 3.5.
You'll use the Detail view a lot if you have many templates on a specific page since it allows you to find a specific template quickly.

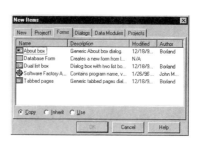

The next four options on the context menu allow you to change the presentation you'll see. At first this won't make much of a difference to you since all the templates you'll have are created by Borland. As time passes, you'll probably collect a lot of your own personal templates and perhaps a few from other people, so arranging them by author will become more important. Arranging your templates by date will allow you to see all your new templates first. You'll want to use author order to group all the templates that you've created. This allows you to find your personal templates quickly. The standard name order is probably the one that you'll use most. Sometimes you'll need to arrange the description order. Obviously, the uses for this particular option are quite limited unless you exercise a lot of care when writing the descriptions for your template. Of course, no matter how careful you are, the template descriptions written by other people won't be affected.

> **Tip:** You can click on the column headings in Detail view to arrange the templates using that criteria. For example, clicking the author column heading will arrange the templates in author order.

Let's complete the selection process. You should have noticed three radio buttons as you looked through the various pages in the New Items dialog. They define how you'll access the template. If you select Copy, then Delphi will place a copy of the template in your current project. This is the option that you'll use most often with "one time" projects—the projects that you don't intend to update a lot or use with a lot of different clients. The second option, Inherit, allows you to inherit the template. Any changes that you make to the template in the future will be reflected in an application that inherits the template. The advantages are obvious: Refinements in the template will ripple throughout all your projects making some changes automatic. I'd forget that the third option exists, for the most part. The Use option tells Delphi that you want to use the template itself in your application. Any changes you make will affect the template itself along with any applications that use inherited forms of the template. I'd never use this with one of Delphi's default forms; and with great care with any forms that I'd created myself. Suffice it to say, thinking ahead will prevent damage to your existing templates.

Once you decide which template you want to use and how you want to access it, click on OK to add it to your current application. What you'll see is a new form (or other template) added to your project in most cases. In other cases an expert will appear to guide you through the process of actually creating the new template. For example, the Database Form template works this way.

Adding a New Template

I previously mentioned adding new templates to those provided by Borland for Delphi. For example, I inherited the standard About Box form, then modified it for my own needs and saved it as a template. That way I don't have to create the About Box from scratch each time; it's already formatted the way I need it.

Since an About Box is one of the forms that everyone will need somewhere along the way, let's look at how you can modify the version supplied with Delphi. The following procedure takes you through the process of creating a new About Box template. Along the way you'll learn the general technique for creating any type of standard template. I'm assuming that you already have Delphi running.

1. Use the File | New command to open the New Items dialog shown in Figure 3.1. This is where you'll select the basic template to modify.

2. Select the About Box (or other standard Delphi template). You could also select one of your current custom templates if desired (we've already discussed the disadvantages of taking this approach).

3. Choose an access method. If you're using a standard Delphi template you'll probably want to inherit it unless you don't want to automatically incorporate any future changes Borland might make to the template. If you're using a custom template, you'll probably want to copy it. That way any changes you make to the custom template won't ripple through the new template you're creating.

4. Click on OK. You'll see a new copy of the About Box (or other template) appear.

5. Modify the About Box as needed. In my case I changed the logo and defined the OK button procedure to close the form. I also added a standard copyright statement. Notice that I didn't change the program name or version—those items get changed by the application when I use the template. My modified version of the About Box appears in Figure 3.6.

Figure 3.6.
The modified About Box template contains some personalized features like a standard icon and copyright statement.

6. Once you finish modifying the new About Box, try compiling it to make sure it works as expected. This means you'll have to save the source in one of your source directories. I always set aside a template-specific source code directory for this purpose. Now it's time to save your form as a template.

7. Right-click on the About Box. You'll see a context menu like the one shown in Figure 3.7. Notice that one of the options on this context menu allows you to save your template to the repository.

Figure 3.7.
The context menu for your new template contains an Add To Repository option.

8. Select the Add To Repository option. You'll see the Add To Repository dialog box shown in Figure 3.8. This is where you'll define all the fields that we saw in the Detail view of the New Items dialog shown in Figure 3.5.

Figure 3.8.
The Add To Repository dialog allows you to define the particulars of your new template.

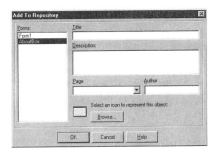

9. Type the name of the author and a title for your template in the appropriate fields as a minimum. You can also add a description to make it easier to figure out the purpose for your template later. Changing the icon will allow you to customize the appearance of the template within the New Items dialog. Finally, you'll want to select a specific page for your template within the New Items dialog.

Tip: Using a standard icon for your customized templates has the advantage of making them easy to see when you go into the New Items dialog. On the other hand, using specific icons for various template types makes it easier for you to categorize the template. For example, you could use one icon for standard templates and another for custom templates.

10. Click on OK to save the new template. Delphi will save the new template for you.

Creating templates is easy under Delphi and it's one of the things you'll need to do to start using the "off-the-shelf" approach to writing applications. With a few keystrokes we just created an About Box that you won't need to change. You could simply add the program name and version from within the calling application. The form does everything else that you need it to do. In essence, writing an About Box now consists of four steps: adding the form to your project and typing the three lines of code required to change the version, program name, and display the dialog itself. As you can see, that's an easy way to implement something you'd spend a few minutes creating for every application. (You might even create a standard application form with the required entries—making the process of adding an About Box totally automatic.)

Adding a Tab to the New Items Dialog

Delphi provides the tools you'll need to really organize the templates in your Gallery. I showed you how to add a new template to an existing page in the previous section. You don't have to do that—

you can create your own personal page for storing the templates you create. That's what we'll do in this section. I'll show you one method of adding a new page to the New Items dialog. (You'll see another method in the next section when I show you how to delete an old template.)

1. Use the File | New command to display the New Items dialog shown in Figure 3.1. This is the same dialog you used to use an existing template.

2. Right-click on the New Items dialog and you'll see the context menu shown in Figure 3.2.

3. Select the Properties option and you'll see the Object Repository dialog shown in Figure 3.9. There are two panes in this dialog. The left pane contains a list of pages; the right contains a list of templates on that page. You can actually do a few things with this dialog. For example, if you click on a page entry, you'll see a list of templates that the page contains in the right pane. If the page is empty, you can delete it. You can also use this dialog to rename the page. The arrows allow you to change the positions of the pages within the New Items dialog—just highlight the entry you want to move and use the arrow keys to move it. Our task in this procedure is to add a new page.

Figure 3.9.

The Object Repository dialog allows you to add new pages to the Gallery for storing customized templates.

Note: You can't work on templates using this dialog. I'll show you a procedure for removing old templates in the next section. The previous section provides a method for adding new templates. The only thing you can do in this dialog is work on the pages themselves.

4. Click the Add pushbutton and you'll see the Add Page dialog shown in Figure 3.10.

Figure 3.10.

The Add Page dialog allows you to add a new page to the Gallery.

5. Type the name of the new page, then click on OK. Make sure that you use a descriptive name. For example, I used Custom Database Forms for one of my pages. Obviously you

have to weigh the length of the name against the level of description you want. Using a long page name will increase the size of the tab used in the New Items dialog—hiding some of the pages you already have listed.

6. Click on OK to close the Object Repository dialog. You'll see a new page added to the New Items dialog.

Removing an Old Template

You're going to run into a situation where an old dialog or other template just isn't needed any more. Up until now, I've been showing you shortcut methods for using the Gallery. Now it's time to look at how you would access all the maintenance tools. The following procedure shows you how to remove a template from the Gallery. More important, it introduces you to the full fledged editor that you'll use to perform a variety of tasks. I'm assuming that you already have Delphi open. In this particular case, I'll remove the About dialog box that I added in the previous section. Obviously, you can use this procedure to remove any template.

1. Use the Tools | Repository command to open the Object Repository dialog shown in Figure 3.11.

Figure 3.11.
This is just another method of accessing the Object Repository dialog we saw in Figure 3.9.

2. Select the page that you want to remove a template from; then select the template that you want to remove from that page. I chose the Form Objects page, then the About Box I had previously created. Once you do this, Delphi will highlight several of the other pushbuttons shown on the dialog—including the Delete pushbutton. (You can also use the Edit Object pushbutton on this page to change information like the author and description of an existing template.)

3. Click on the Delete pushbutton. Delphi will display the dialog shown in Figure 3.12 that asks if you're sure that you want to delete the template.

4. Click on Yes to complete the process. You should see Delphi remove the template from the Object Repository dialog.

Figure 3.12.

*The Confirm dialog asks if
you're sure that you want to
remove the template.*

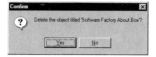

Changing Form Defaults

In the previous section I told you that you can't edit or delete Delphi's default templates. Yet, those are the templates used to create new applications and new forms. You access them directly using the File | New Application and the File | New Form commands. What if these default templates represent a lot of additional work for you—what if you want to use a custom form instead?

Delphi doesn't force you to use the default templates. You can change them using the two check boxes at the bottom of the Object Repository dialog shown in Figure 3.11. The first button—Main Form—changes the template used to create a new application. The second button—New Form—allows you to select the form that appears when you use the File | New Form command.

> **Tip:** You'll definitely want to change the default application and new form selections when working on group projects. Using this option makes it easier for everyone working on the project to use a consistent form style. It also means that applications will look more alike from project to project. Consistency will not only make project construction faster and more efficient, it'll reduce the learning curve for the people who use your applications.

Defining a Project

So far I've spent a lot of time in this chapter talking about the methods of creating off-the-shelf components. Now it's time to talk about a few housekeeping chores that you'll want to do to make this approach to programming a lot more efficient. After all, what good is it to create all these consistent components that you can just bolt together, if you can't keep track of where they are? Every hardware store that I've ever visited keeps an inventory of what they have on hand: so should you.

I didn't think about this particular problem at first because I had just a few templates to work with. However, as time went on, I started accumulating a whole list of off-the-shelf parts. I started spending more time working with the customer showing them what I had available, than what I could do to get the project done quickly. The same thing will happen to you after a while.

Why not borrow one of the techniques used by other types of businesses and create a catalog of your off-the-shelf parts? I maintain my catalog in a database. All it contains is a picture of the part, the template name, and a short description of what the template is for.

Now, what does this have to do with defining a project? Once you have a template catalog put together, you can use it to shop for project parts. In essence, you define a project by creating a list of stock parts that you can use to build the shell, then figuring out what customizations you'll need to add. If you use this approach to defining a project, you'll find that you have a lot more stock parts on hand that you probably thought you did.

It's during this design phase where I usually figure out the need for new templates. The trick is to design something that's specific enough to the project to make it useful, but generic enough that you can use it on future projects as well. For example, you'll notice that I defined an About Box that contained my stock logo and copyright statement. I left the application name and version blank since they'll change from project to project. That's the thing you need to consider as well—what will remain the same and what will change for every project you build.

Creating the Initial Window

There are three common application types that I create: database, editor, and utility. You'll see examples of all three kinds throughout the book. For example, Chapter 6 shows a typical editor. It contains a menu, main editing window, and a status bar. You'll find the utility type of application in several chapters starting with Chapter 5, "Accessing the Windows API," where I show you how to get the current task list and various other types of Windows status information. Chapter 12 contains the database examples for the book.

I think that you'll find that these three basic application types are the ones you'll create as well. The big thing you need to consider is that from a user's perspective, these three applications differ in their method of presentation. Presentation is a visual cue that tells the user what to expect from a particular application in regard to functionality. Consider the backup program provided with Windows 95—it's a utility program and the method of presentation tells you that. If you use Word for Windows, you'll see an editor display. The same holds true with CorelDRAW! (even though the editor display contains other elements, it still consists of a main window and associated menu of edit-related options). You'll find that products like Microsoft Access fall into the database category—the method of presentation fills you in right away.

There's a fourth category of application that we won't spend a lot of time with—spreadsheet. It isn't that this category is dead, but it provides the least potential for future applications. Delphi even provides all the spreadsheet interface items you'll need—including an OCX component. Needless to say, the number of times you'll actually have to write a spreadsheet is pretty limited.

The first step in designing an application, then, is to decide on what type presentation you want. Remember when I told you before about using an off-the-shelf approach to programming? Well, it begins with the application itself. Delphi provides two application experts, but I feel that they're too limited. What I've done is create my own set of three application experts—one for each type of application that I want to create.

So, how do you create your own application expert that works like the ones provided by Borland? It's surprisingly easy as long as you follow a few simple procedures. I'm going to take you through the steps to making your standard application into an expert similar in function to the SDI Application and MDI Application templates provided with Delphi. I'm assuming that you've already created an application, compiled and tested it, and that it's open in Delphi at the moment.

1. Place your application template in its own subdirectory in your TEMPLATE directory. The reason for this is simple: Delphi will copy the contents of this directory to a new project location whenever you select this new application. You'll notice that the SDIAPP and MDIAPP appear as subdirectories of the OBJREPOS directory—the place where Delphi stores all the forms and other templates found in the Gallery.

2. Use the Project | Add To Repository command to open the Add to Repository dialog shown in Figure 3.13. You can't create a new application template using the same method that we used to create a form template. Delphi makes a different set of entries in the Gallery for an application template than it does for other template types. (You can view the entries by looking in the DELPHI32.DRO file in the Delphi BIN directory—it contains the entries for all of the templates you make as well as those supplied by Borland.)

Figure 3.13.
The Add to Repository dialog allows you to create a new project (application) template.

3. Type in the Title, Description, and Author information. You can use something other than the default icon for the new project template by clicking on the Browse button and selecting one using the File Open dialog. Make sure you select a page to store the application template on; otherwise, it won't show up on the New Item dialog, even though you've added it to the Gallery.

4. Complete the new template entry by clicking on OK. You should see a new application template added to the Object Repository page that you specified in the Save Project Template dialog.

Tip: You can make an application template the standard application by clicking on it, then pressing the Default Project check box at the bottom of the Object Repository dialog.

Adding Components (Controls)

Now that I've shown you how to create all the standard elements, let's look at some customization details. Components represent the items that you'll add most often to an application beside menu entries. They allow you to define what type of data a user enters and the types of information your application will collect. You'll also use components as pushbuttons—not just the OK pushbutton that most of us use on a daily basis, but the media control and other specialty controls that Delphi provides.

There's a whole host of non-visual components as well. For example, you'll need to use timers from time to time. The only way you can tell that they're doing anything is to watch the clock and see what happens. Other non-visual components display common dialog boxes or control the user's access to data in outside sources of information. I could go on, but I think you get the point.

Adding components to a form is fairly easy. All you need to do is click on the component, then where you want it placed on the form. A faster method of getting components on the form is to simply double click on the component's icon on the VCL. Once placed on the form, you can move the component around as needed to get it placed just right.

I've already covered usage of the Object Inspector in Chapter 2. Once you have a component placed on the form, you'll use the Object Inspector to change its characteristics to suit your needs.

Arranging the Controls

Delphi provides a context menu for just about everything—components are no different. If you right-click on any component you'll see a context menu similar to the one shown in Figure 3.14. The following list provides a quick overview of the various menu options.

Figure 3.14.

The component context menu allows you to change the component's position with regard to the form and other components.

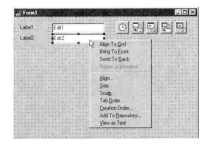

- Align To Grid—I talked about the various grid options in Chapter 2. This option allows you to align the component to the nearest grid setting. It uses the top left corner of the component as the positioning point.

- Bring To Front—When you use a bevel, panel, or other component that serves as a place to put other components, you might need to bring some of the smaller components to the front so that you can see them. This option brings whatever component you select to the front of the display area.

- Send To Back—This option sends the currently selected component to the bottom of a stack of components. In other words, the component is sent to the back of the display area. You can use this to keep components organized or to create special effects.

- Revert To Inherited—You'll only see this option active if you select an inherited component. It returns the current component's options to those used by the parent. I covered the differences between used, copied, and inherited components in the "Using Templates in Your Project" section of this chapter, so I won't go into that again. Suffice it to say that this represents one more advantage to using inherited components—you get a free super undo feature as part of the package.

- Align—You can align a component in one of two ways—against the form and against other components. I'll show you how to perform both types of alignment in just a bit.

- Size—Sometimes you'll want to change the size of your component using precise measurements without resorting to using the Object Inspector. This option does that and more. You can also use it to change the size of one or more components in a relative way. For example, you can use this option to make all the selected components the same size.

- Scale—Ever run out of room on a form before you run out of components to put there? How about the opposite situation—you need a form of a certain size, but the components used to fill it leave some blank spots? This option takes care of both problems by allowing you to scale your components to fit within the confines of a specific form space.

- Tab Order—There are times when I start creating a form and only later discover that I need to add one more edit component to it. The user would get confused if you made the new component the last one in the tab order list. This option allows you to change the tab order so that movement from one edit area to the next is smooth.

- Creation Order—Database management projects are very prone to error if you don't create the non-visual data access components in the right order. For example, you can't create a query before you have a data source to fill it. Think of the query as a glass that you want to fill with water—you can't fill it until you have the water (the data source). This option allows you to control the order in which Delphi creates the components during run time.

- Add To Repository—I've already covered this option. It's the one you use to add a component to the repository.

- View as Text—You'll find that this option comes in very handy at times. It allows you to view the visual form that you're creating as text—giving you very precise control over the placement, size, and other characteristics of the form and the components that it contains.

Now that you have a brief overview of all the context menu entries, let's take some time to look at specifics. The following paragraphs will show you how to use the various context menu entries to perform specific tasks.

Aligning Components

I usually get all the components I'm going to need on the form, then place them roughly where I need them. However, it's a lot faster to allow Delphi to complete the fine adjustment of component positions for me than to do it myself. For example, I might have a row of buttons at the bottom of a utility form or a dialog box. I'll place the first component precisely where I need it, then the others in a general location. I always make sure the last component is in its correct horizontal position.

To align the pushbuttons I simply select the first one in the group, then the rest in order. (I call the first component my anchor component since I'll use it to position the rest.) Make sure you always select the anchor component first. Once I have all the components selected, I right-click and select Align from the context menu. You'll see an Alignment dialog similar to the one in Figure 3.15.

Figure 3.15.
The Alignment dialog allows you to position one component in relation to the form or multiple components in relation to each other.

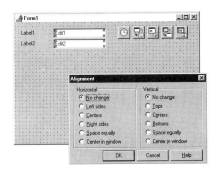

As you can see, there are a variety of positioning options on this dialog: a set for vertical and other for horizontal positioning. You can choose to position the components in relation to each other or the form itself. The option I like the best is spacing the components equally. Let's go back to my original example of pushbuttons at the bottom of a form. If I select the components in order, Delphi will take care of spacing them equally along the bottom. It'll also align all the components to the first one in the group. Using these two options in tandem gives me a professional looking display without a lot of hand positioning.

Sizing Components

Sometimes you'll have a pushbutton or other component that just isn't large enough to hold what you need it to. This happens to me all the time with pushbutton captions. You can select the pushbutton that requires change, right-click to display the context menu, and select the Size option. You'll see the Size dialog shown in Figure 3.16.

Figure 3.16.

The Size dialog allows you to change the size of a component in several ways.

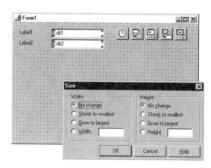

Notice that I can use either specific or relative measurements. In the case of a pushbutton that's too small to hold the caption I need to display, I'd use specific measurements to increase its size. Of course, that leaves me with another problem—the other pushbuttons don't match this one in size. All you need to do to fix this problem is select all the pushbuttons, then select the Grow to Largest option. In this case we're using a relative measurement.

Scaling Your Project

You're going to run into a situation where you can't fit all the components that you need on-screen using the standard component size. The form will be just a bit too small and you can't increase it for whatever reason. (Alternatively, you might find that the form is too big and you need to create larger components to fill it up.) One way to fix this situation is to change the size of the individual components—a relatively time-consuming way to do things.

There's another way to resolve the problem of too many components on too small a form—you can scale the components so they do fit within it. We're all familiar with what scaling does for a graphic image. You tell the graphics application to change the size of the various drawing elements by a certain percentage. All the drawing elements look the same as before; they're just smaller or larger. The idea here is to maintain the relationships between the various elements. Scaling under Delphi works the same way. All the work you put into creating a certain relationship between components is preserved; the only thing that changes is the component size.

Scaling components is a three-step process, just like the other operations I've told you about in this section. All you need to do is select the components you want to size, right-click to display the context menu, then choose the Scale option. You'll see a dialog like the one shown in Figure 3.17. All you need to do is type in a number in the range of 25 to 400. Numbers below 100 reduce the size of the components, while numbers greater than 100 increase their size.

Figure 3.17.
*Use the Scale dialog to either
increase or decrease the size
of the selected components by
a certain percentage.*

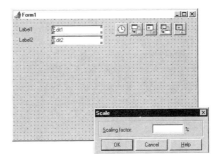

Changing the Creation Order

Non-visual components often provide vital services to the rest of the components on a form. For example, a timer can tell your application when it's time to perform a certain task. Database access components allow you to gain access to the data stored in tables.

Creating these components in a specific order might be important in some cases because the underlying application needs to have the component in place before it does something. For example, you'll need your data access components in place before you display the visual database elements if you use live data. Otherwise, Delphi will raise an exception when it tries to access a non-existent table. (Until the data access components are in place, there isn't any connection to the table—as far as Delphi is concerned, it doesn't exist.)

If you right-click on a form, you'll find a Creation Order option on the context menu. Selecting this option displays a dialog similar to the one shown in Figure 3.18. This is the dialog you'll use to change the creation order of non-visual components—it doesn't affect any visual components on the form. Components at the top of the list get created first. To change the order of a particular component, simply select it, then use the arrows to move the component higher or lower on the list.

Figure 3.18.
*The Creation Order dialog
lets you change the creation
order of non-visual
components.*

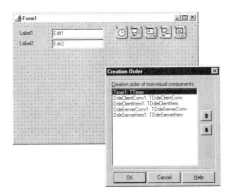

Viewing a Component as Text

A few of us still find it difficult to get precise results in a graphical design environment. Moving components around on a form just doesn't produce the results we had hoped for. Borland understands this and made provisions for another type of editing.

Right-clicking on a form and selecting the View as Text option removes the graphic display and replaces it with its text counterpart as shown in Figure 3.19. You'll find all the parameters that affect the visual representation of a component in a source code editor environment. All you need to do is read through the list of parameters and change them as needed.

Figure 3.19.
You can use the Text View of a form to make fine adjustments to various components and the form itself.

```
object Form1: TForm1
  Left = 252
  Top = 145
  Width = 435
  Height = 300
  Caption = 'Form1'
  Font.Color = clWindowText
  Font.Height = -11
  Font.Name = 'MS Sans Serif'
  Font.Style = []
  PixelsPerInch = 96
  TextHeight = 13
  object Label1: TLabel
    Left = 13
    Top = 16
    Width = 65
    Height = 17
    Caption = 'Label1'
  end
  object Label2: TLabel
    Left = 13
    Top = 40
    Width = 65
```

Moving between the text and graphic views is easy. All you need to do when you're done editing the text is right-click again. You'll see an option to View as Form on the context menu. Select it and you'll see the graphic representation of the form reappear.

Designing Menus

I'm not going to sit here and tell you about the basics of good menu design. The one piece of advice that I will offer is to look around at the applications you use. Which programs are fast and easy to use? You'll probably want to use that application as a source of ideas. I know that I've gone through the various menus of applications I like looking for ideas—you should do the same.

Delphi provides a lot more than you might think in regard to menus. I find that the off-the-shelf approach applies here as much as any other part of Delphi. Templates rule the creation of menus just like they do everything else in Delphi. The big difference is that there's a lot less room for individual achievement in this area. In other words, you'll find that the Delphi-supplied offerings will probably do for a start and that you'll eventually run out of new menu templates to add.

The following sections assume that you've gotten a form open (it doesn't matter what kind of form it is) and that there is a menu component on it. You'll want to open the Menu Designer. There are two ways to do this. Double-clicking on a menu component always opens the Menu Designer. You can also right-click on the component and select the Menu Designer option from the context menu. In either case, you'll see a blank menu like the one shown in Figure 3.20.

Figure 3.20.
The Menu Designer is where you'll add or remove options from a menu component.

Using an Existing Menu

I like to reduce my workload whenever possible by letting Delphi do as much of the work as possible for me. One way to do this is to use menu templates. Now, unless you paid careful attention to the context menus, this little feature might escape your notice. Right-click on the menu now and you'll see a context menu similar to the one shown in Figure 3.21.

Figure 3.21.
The Menu Designer context menu contains an option for using menu templates—a time-saving feature of Delphi.

Select the Insert From Template option. You'll see an Insert Template dialog like the one shown in Figure 3.22. Notice that Delphi provides a few of the more common menus as defaults. I've found that they're complete as is and I haven't had to edit them.

All you need to do to complete the action is select the menu template that you want to use and click on OK. You'll see the menu template added to your current menu. If you don't like what you see, press Delete and the menu will disappear as quickly as you added it.

Figure 3.22.
*The Insert Template dialog
allows you to add a menu
template to a menu
component.*

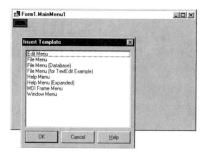

Creating a New Menu

Delphi doesn't provide every menu template that you'll ever need. For example, I like adding a View menu to some types of editor programs. I also use a custom File menu for most of my database applications. It doesn't matter why you need a new menu, the point is that you do. Why design that menu over and over again when you can design it once and save it for future use?

Once you design a new menu, Delphi enables the Save as Template option on the Menu Designer context menu. All you need to do is select it to display the Save Template dialog shown in Figure 3.23. Type in a name for the new menu and click on OK to save it.

Figure 3.23.
*The Save Template dialog
allows you to save custom
menu designs for future use.*

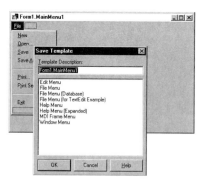

Tip: Use a consistent naming convention when you save your menu template. The existing entries should give you some ideas. I normally use the name of the initial menu entry followed by a comment in parentheses if necessary.

Summary

I haven't really shown you how to create an application in this chapter—I have an entire book of source code that shows you how to do that. What I've presented is one of the most important concepts that you can learn about using Delphi, an off-the-shelf part style of programming. I see this as one of the more important aspects of using any RAD environment. RAD—rapid application development—doesn't do much for you if you don't use the tools that it provides. That's what this chapter was all about. I've shown you how to create an inventory of off-the-shelf parts (objects in Delphi phraseology) —not just code, not just resources, but entire program pieces that you can bolt together then customize as needed.

We've looked at three basic forms of parts: forms, applications, and menus. There are other types of parts that you can create. For example, Delphi supports all the standard code reuse tools like DLLs and OBJ files. I'll show you how to use them later in the book. Likewise, you'll find that creating your own components is a must in many circumstances. We'll spend an entire chapter exploring that issue as well. However, this type of component creation requires some work on your part. The tools that I've presented in this chapter are things you can do without too much effort at all. The only thing you need to do is think about the possibility of saving the parts as you create them as part of your normal programming experience.

4

Adding
Some Bells
and Whistles

I spent most of the last chapter showing you how to use an off-the-shelf approach to programming. You'll find that using this approach will probably build a large part of the application for you. In fact, if you make sure that you always save the generic code used to activate the components on your forms, you'll probably save 60 to 70 percent of your coding effort in most cases.

However, there's still the other part of the application build—what I call bells and whistles. You need to fill out an application to give it the full functionality that the user needs. The dialog boxes and other features that make one application unique from the other just don't appear out of thin air.

This chapter is going to tell you how to get past a basic application, the part that you put together using off-the-shelf components, to the custom application that the user is looking for. Just like a race car mechanic doesn't stop at the stock car he puts together from spare parts, you can't stop building your application when you run out of pre-designed objects.

Deciding What To Add

Have you ever seen a program that contains dialog after dialog? I've actually seen some programs that use separate dialogs for everything from getting your name each time you save, to asking what you want to do about character formats. In some cases, it's probably better to combine several functions on one dialog than it is to keep all these separate dialogs hanging around. What about the program that contains seven layers of nested menu options that finally lead to something other than what you expected? Spreadsheet applications are especially prone to this problem for some reason. Both application defects are evidence of a design team that didn't really think ahead. While it's important to fill out an application's feature set, making the application difficult to use with too many gadgets just doesn't make sense.

The other problem I've been running into lately is programs that include too many modules. (The trade press has been hitting this subject pretty hard as well.) Think about applications like CorelDRAW! and Microsoft Word. They're both fine examples of the way to write a user friendly program—I find that they're both incredibly easy to use. However, my last copy of CorelDRAW! consumed three CDs. If that's not feature bloat, I don't know what is. While Word still fits on one CD, it contains more features than the average person will ever use. For example, what is a drawing program doing inside a word processor application? Obviously, somewhere along the way, some user requested this feature and the design team added it in without thinking about how many people would really use it. If you've run into this kind of application, you'll know what I'm talking about when I say that they're fat and bloated—almost to the point of being too expensive in terms of disk and processor utilization to use.

So, if these application examples tell you what you shouldn't do, then what is a good addition to an application? My short definition is this: If the user has to have a feature to reach a general application goal, then you need to add it. For example, a word processor has to have a spelling checker to really provide the level of functionality that the user needs. Producing error free text is one of the general goals of a word processor. Database management programs need extensive search capabilities. One of the general goals of a DBMS is to be able to find your data quickly and easily.

Another mandatory feature is inter-program communication. If the user needs a graphics application to draw pictures with, then wants to include those pictures in a word processed document, your word processor should provide the means to do so. In most cases this means adding OLE capabilities as a minimum. You might want to add OLE automation or DDE (or even both) as well. I'm all for giving the user all the tools they need to get the job done—I just don't like to see one application bloated to the point that I have to pay for every other user's needs as well. Inter-program communication is the way to allow users to build the set of tools they need to get their particular job done.

Looking Ahead: OLE is one of the hottest topics today—everything from the Internet to the latest version of Windows will use some version of it. Since this is such an important tool, I decided to devote an entire chapter to it. We'll look at all of the issues you'll face in adding DDE or OLE to your application in Chapter 10, "Using Delphi with OLE."

Message Boxes That Communicate

Message boxes are the things that application communications are made of. Whenever you have something to say to the person using your application, you'll use a message box of some sort to do it. Delphi provides three different ways to create message boxes—each one designed for a particular use. The following list describes each type in detail:

- ShowMessage()—I use this function to create general messages or troubleshooting messages to myself. All I need to provide is a message, so it's extremely fast to use as well. So, what constitutes a general message? You need to ask yourself a few questions to answer this one. How do you handle a situation where the user, Windows, or the application does something totally unexpected? Do you handle the situation with an error message? What if the event gets triggered by an error in one case, but is perfectly normal in another? This situation just doesn't happen often. However, there are cases where it does and that's the time you need to use a general message box instead of something more specific to avoid confusing the user. Let me give you an example. One application I used always displayed a save message box using an error icon. Some of the users of that application thought that it had experienced an error—even though it was only asking whether the user wanted to save the file or not. The same message box appeared when the application did experience an error one day. The user ended up corrupting his data because he had learned to disregard the message box. Obviously the programmer who wrote that application needed to detect the various save situations better, but the application does demonstrate a situation where a general message box would have been a little less confusing.

- MessageDlg()—This is the message box function that I use most often. It's a little more work to use, but I can customize it a lot more as well. You provide a message, an icon type, an array of one or more pushbuttons, and a help context. Using this message box type allows you to provide the user with a lot more input. The icon tells the user what kind of situation he is facing. The pushbuttons tell him what kind of actions he can take. If the situation is especially confusing, you can provide online help that'll describe the situation in detail.

Note: As of this writing, Windows doesn't always respond to the Delphi message box icons correctly. For example, you're supposed to hear a particular sound when an error message box appears and Windows doesn't provide this sound. Hopefully Borland will fix this problem by the time you read this, but you may want to watch for those situations anyway. What can you do about it? Make a separate call to the MCI (media control interface) subsystem before you call the dialog. I'll show you how to do this in Chapter 11, "Delphi and Multimedia Programming."

- Custom Form—There aren't too many situations where I'll use a custom form for a message box. However, there is one situation where I always use it. The About Box is a type of message box and it appears in every application. Why do I use a custom form in this case? Because a standard message box doesn't provide the space required to present all the information the user will need. That's the criteria you should use in other situations as well. If a message requires more space than a standard message box function call can provide, then take care of that need using a custom form. Obviously you'll want to limit the number of occasions where you use a custom form because they consume a lot more space than a function call does.

Now that you know about the three dialog box types, let's take a little time to see how they work. Figure 4.1 shows the main form for an application designed to display message boxes. You can fill out the various dialog boxes and create various messages boxes to see what they look like. Obviously, this little utility program isn't something you would actually use in a real application, but I do find it comes in handy for modeling purposes.

Figure 4.1.
*This form allows you to
select the criteria for creating
a message box.*

You'll also need to change the properties of some of the components on this form. In most cases I made the changes for aesthetic, not functional, reasons. Table 4.1 provides a complete list of the changes you'll need to make. (I didn't include captions since you can see those as part of the form in Figure 4.1.)

> **Note:** Table 4.1 shows the way in which I'll present complex component changes through-out the rest of the book. I'll give the name of the component in the Object column. The property column will contain the name of a property you need to change. The setting column will contain the actual setting you need to add to that property. I won't include such mundane things as sizing or position—those are elements that you'll normally want to decide on yourself and they don't affect the operating of the application.

Table 4.1. Message Box Display Utility Control Settings.

Object	Property	Setting
rgDialogType	ItemIndex	0
	Items.Strings	('Show Message' 'Message Dialog' 'Custom Message')
	OnClick	rgDialogTypeClick
rgIcon	Enabled	False
	ItemIndex	0
	Items.Strings	('Warning' 'Error' 'Information' 'Confirmation' 'Custom')
cbYes	Enabled	False
cbNo	Enabled	False
cbOK	Enabled	False
cbCancel	Enabled	False
cbHelp	Enabled	False
cbAbort	Enabled	False
cbRetry	Enabled	False
cbIgnore	Enabled	False
cbAll	Enabled	False
pbExit	OnClick	pbExitClick
pbTest	OnClick	pbTestClick

Once you get the form together, you'll need to add some code to make the program work. I'll explain the code later. For right now, type the code in Listing 4.1 into your application. (Some of the code is automatically generated by Delphi.) Make sure you add the proper declarations for the special procedures. Also add the declaration for our custom dialog box.

Listing 4.1. MBTest1.

```
unit MBTest1;

interface

uses
  Windows, Messages, SysUtils, Classes, Graphics, Controls, Forms, Dialogs,
  StdCtrls, ExtCtrls;

type
  TForm1 = class(TForm)
    rgDialogType: TRadioGroup;
    pbExit: TButton;
    Message: TEdit;
    Label1: TLabel;
    rgIcon: TRadioGroup;
    GroupBox1: TGroupBox;
    cbYes: TCheckBox;
    cbNo: TCheckBox;
    cbOK: TCheckBox;
    cbCancel: TCheckBox;
    cbHelp: TCheckBox;
    cbAbort: TCheckBox;
    cbRetry: TCheckBox;
    cbIgnore: TCheckBox;
    cbAll: TCheckBox;
    pbTest: TButton;
    procedure pbExitClick(Sender: TObject);
    procedure pbTestClick(Sender: TObject);
    procedure rgDialogTypeClick(Sender: TObject);
    function DispMessage: Integer;
    function MessageDialog: Integer;
    function CustomMessage: Integer;
    procedure DoCloseForm(Sender: TObject);
  private
    { Private declarations }
  public
    { Public declarations }
  end;

var
  Form1: TForm1;
  MsgDlg: TForm;          {Our custom dialog box.}

implementation

{$R *.DFM}
```

```
procedure TForm1.pbExitClick(Sender: TObject);
begin
    {End the application.}
    Application.Terminate;
end;

procedure TForm1.pbTestClick(Sender: TObject);
var
    iResult: Integer;    {User's button selection in message dialog.}
begin
    {Select the message display procedure.}
    Case rgDialogType.ItemIndex of
        0: iResult := DispMessage;
        1: iResult := MessageDialog;
        2: iResult := CustomMessage;
    end;

    {Display a message box showing the result.}
    case iResult of
        mrYes: ShowMessage('User pressed: Yes');
        mrNo: ShowMessage('User pressed: No');
        mrOK: ShowMessage('User pressed: OK');
        mrCancel: ShowMessage('User pressed: Cancel');
        mrNone: ShowMessage('User pressed: Nothing');
        mrAbort: ShowMessage('User pressed: Abort');
        mrRetry: ShowMessage('User pressed: Retry');
        mrIgnore: ShowMessage('User pressed: Ignore');
        mrAll: ShowMessage('User pressed: All');
    end;
end;

procedure TForm1.rgDialogTypeClick(Sender: TObject);
begin
    {Enable or disable buttons based on user input.}
    if (rgDialogType.ItemIndex = 0) or (rgDialogType.ItemIndex = 2) then
        begin
        rgIcon.Enabled := False;
         cbYes.Enabled := False;
         cbNo.Enabled := False;
         cbOK.Enabled := False;
         cbCancel.Enabled := False;
         cbHelp.Enabled := False;
         cbAbort.Enabled := False;
         cbRetry.Enabled := False;
         cbIgnore.Enabled := False;
         cbAll.Enabled := False;
        end
    else
        begin
        rgIcon.Enabled := True;
         cbYes.Enabled := True;
         cbNo.Enabled := True;
         cbOK.Enabled := True;
         cbCancel.Enabled := True;
         cbHelp.Enabled := True;
         cbAbort.Enabled := True;
         cbRetry.Enabled := True;
```

continues

Listing 4.1. continued

```delphi
            cbIgnore.Enabled := True;
            cbAll.Enabled := True;
         end;

end;

function TForm1.DispMessage: Integer;
begin
    {Display a standard show message dialog.}
    ShowMessage(Message.Text);
    Result := mrOK;
end;

function TForm1.MessageDialog: Integer;
var
    eIconType: TMsgDlgType;        {Icon selected in Icon Type radio group.}
    eButtons: TMsgDlgButtons;      {Buttons selected in the Button Types group.}
begin
    {Determine the icon type.}
    case rgIcon.ItemIndex of
        0: eIconType := mtWarning;
        1: eIconType := mtError;
        2: eIconType := mtInformation;
        3: eIconType := mtConfirmation;
        4: eIconType := mtCustom;
        end;

    {Determine which buttons to display.}
    eButtons := [];    {Clear the variable before we use it.}

    if cbYes.Checked then
        eButtons := eButtons + [mbYes];
    if cbNo.Checked then
        eButtons := eButtons + [mbNo];
    if cbOK.Checked then
        eButtons := eButtons + [mbOK];
    if cbCancel.Checked then
        eButtons := eButtons + [mbCancel];
    if cbHelp.Checked then
        eButtons := eButtons + [mbHelp];
    if cbAbort.Checked then
        eButtons := eButtons + [mbAbort];
    if cbRetry.Checked then
        eButtons := eButtons + [mbRetry];
    if cbIgnore.Checked then
        eButtons := eButtons + [mbIgnore];
    if cbAll.Checked then
        eButtons := eButtons + [mbAll];

    {Display a standard message dialog.}
    Result := MessageDlg(Message.Text, eIconType, eButtons, 0);
end;

function TForm1.CustomMessage: Integer;
var
    lMessage: TLabel;    {The message in our dialog.}
    pbOK: TButton;       {An OK pushbutton to close the dialog.}
```

```
begin
    {Create and configure the initial dialog.}
    MsgDlg := TForm.Create(Application);
    MsgDlg.Width := Message.Width + 20;
    MsgDlg.Height := 120;
    MsgDlg.BorderStyle := bsDialog;
    MsgDlg.Caption := 'Custom Message Dialog';

    {Create and configure the message.}
    lMessage := TLabel.Create(MsgDlg);
    lMessage.Width := Message.Width;
    lMessage.Left := 10;
    lMessage.Top := 10;
    lMessage.Caption := Message.Text;

    {Add the message to our dialog.}
    MsgDlg.InsertControl(lMessage);

    {Create and configure the pushbutton.}
    pbOK := TButton.Create(MsgDlg);
    pbOK.Caption := 'OK';
    pbOK.Top := 50;
    pbOK.Left := (MsgDlg.Width - pbOK.Width) div 2;
    pbOK.OnClick := DoCloseForm;

    {Add the pushbutton to our dialog.}
    MsgDlg.InsertControl(pbOK);

    {Display the completed dialog.}
    MsgDlg.ShowModal;

    {Send back the result.}
    Result := mrOK;

    {Free the memory used by the dialog.}
    MsgDlg.Free;

end;

procedure TForm1.DoCloseForm(Sender: TObject);
begin
    {Close our dialog box.}
    MsgDlg.Close;
end;

end.
```

You'll find that the code in this example demonstrates how easy or how difficult you can make things for yourself under Delphi. The ultimate in flexibility often requires the most extensive coding on your part. The bottom line is just how far you're willing to go to make the program work precisely the way you want it to. Obviously custom code has a few drawbacks as well. For one thing, it doesn't fit very well into the off-the-shelf programming strategy that Delphi promotes. Another problem is that you'll spend orders of magnitude more time in creating an application if you use custom code.

Let's take a look at the simplest method of creating a message box—the one shown in the DispMessage function. It doesn't take long to figure out that this single line of code provides the least flexibility, but I think it does an adequate job for the two or three seconds it took to write it. Delphi provides a lot of functions like this. You can write them in a matter of seconds—the problem is that you'll give up some flexibility in the exchange. Figure 4.2 shows the output from this function—not very impressive. You can't even display an icon or specific buttons with this particular function. Moreover, you can only provide one type of feedback for your application—the fact that the user pressed OK.

Figure 4.2.

The ShowMessage function is quick, but very limited in its functionality.

The second method takes quite a few more lines of code to implement, but the main line is the MessageDlg function. You have to supply a bit more information to use this function, but theoretically you could implement it in one line. However, that approach would remove one of the advantages of using this function—the ability to get more than one kind of input from the user. A more realistic coding size for this function is one line of code for the function itself, and a minimum of one line for each pushbutton you select. Obviously the actual amount of code you'll need to provide when using this function is based on the way you react to the user's input.

I've had to add a few additional lines of code to my example that you probably won't need in yours. One section of the code defines the icon that the message box displays based on your selection in the Icon Type radio group. Another code section builds a list of buttons based on the check boxes you select in the Button Types group. Figure 4.3 shows a representative sample of the output from this function. Note that the utility allows you to try a variety of buttons and icons so that you can better see how this function works.

Note: There is an extended version of the MessageDlg function named MessageDlgPos. Normally Delphi displays the message dialog in the middle of the screen. This version of the function also allows you to change the screen message dialog's screen position.

Figure 4.3.

The MessageDlg function requires a little more work on the programmer's part, but provides better input from the user.

Now we come to the most code intensive method of creating a message box. You can use a custom form in place of Delphi's built in functions to build your own dialog boxes whenever you need to. That's the main purpose of the CustomMessage function. There are certain advantages to this approach. I can dynamically create dialog boxes and then release the memory they use—a distinct advantage in memory starved applications. More important, you can use the technique I show you here to create any kind of form you might need. The only time the form would actually use memory is if the user opened it. I find this particular approach comes in handy for configuration or other types of forms that seldom get used. You'll need to decide between the speed of writing an application using off-the-shelf components and the memory usage reducing features of custom code.

Tip: Even though this example doesn't show it, using custom message boxes allows you to define some special features. For example, you could provide a custom set of icons for the message dialog to make it more application specific or user friendly. You can also take control of things like the form caption and the types of information that the message box displays.

One thing you should notice is that I actually declare the MsgDlg object outside of the function right after the Form1 declaration. The reason is simple: I wanted to attach code to the click event of my pushbutton. Doing things this way makes it easier for me to add an event procedure. There are other ways of getting the job done, and I'll explore them with you throughout the book.

A disadvantage of this method of creating a message box becomes apparent almost immediately. You should have noticed by now that I have to define each and every property of every part of the dialog unless I want to accept the default values. That's one of the prices you have to pay for flexibility—the loss of automatic definitions. I found one parameter assignment interesting. It appears as if you would assign a string to an event. Look at the pbOK.OnClick assignment. There aren't any quotes around DoCloseForm. When you want to assign an event to a component, you actually assign the event—not a representation of the event in string form.

Simply creating a pushbutton or a label isn't enough to get it on the message box when you display it. Notice how I used the InsertControl method to add the new components after I defined them. If you want to add a component to any kind of Delphi container, you need to use the InsertControl method to do it. By the way, this same method works with other kinds of components, such as group boxes and panels.

You'll probably be a little disappointed when you see the form produced by this function—it appears in Figure 4.4. Remember that the purpose for using this technique was to gain added flexibility. I could have made the message box look like the one in Figure 4.3, or anything else for that matter. Using this technique gives you the flexibility to do anything you want—within reason—but requires a lot of extra work on your part.

Figure 4.4.

The third method of creating a message box—a custom form—is a lot more flexible than any other method you might use.

There's one last section of code in this example. It appears in the pbTestClick procedure. There are actually two sections. The first section selects a message box display method based on your selection in the Message Box Type radio group. The second section acts on the return value from the function call. In this case I simply tell you which button the user pressed. Figure 4.5 shows the output from one function call.

Figure 4.5.

Testing for the return value from a message box call is one way to provide custom handling for specific user needs.

Dialogs for Quick Selections

Just about every edit or database class of application you'll ever write requires the use of dialogs. In some cases you'll also add dialog boxes to utility programs as well. So, what does a typical dialog box do? In my book there are two types: configuration and selection. A File Open dialog allows you to select a file from your hard drive, while an Options dialog allows you to configure the application. They both have their uses within Windows applications.

There are other distinctions within the Windows environment. Some dialogs appear within DLLs. For example, you'll probably use the File Open dialog that Windows provides instead of creating your own. Other dialogs are made from scratch—every configuration dialog will fall into this category. (Obviously there are several ways to create a dialog from scratch: you can start with a standard form and add components to it or even create it dynamically. We'll look at many methods of getting the job done throughout the book.)

Delphi also provides several pre-built dialogs that you can use. We went through the majority of this in Chapter 3, "Building a Basic Program," when I talked with you about the New Items dialog. Essentially you'll find the dialogs that Delphi provides on the Dialogs page of the New Items dialog as shown in Figure 4.6. The following paragraphs describe the three basic types of dialogs that you'll find here.

Figure 4.6.

Delphi provides three different types of dialogs as part of the default setup.

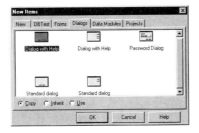

- Dialog with Help—There are two arrangements of this particular dialog. One has the buttons running vertically along the right edge of the dialog. The other has the buttons running along the bottom. The distinctive feature of this dialog is that it includes a Help pushbutton. I use it when I need to create a complex configuration or selection dialog.

- Standard Dialog—You'll find that this dialog type comes in handy when you need to create something simple. For example, you might want to have the user choose between two colors for the text of your application. I use this dialog when the configuration or selection options are limited—when I can make the user understand what I want by using labels. Obviously, the lack of a Help button makes programming faster and also reduces the memory requirement for using this dialog.

- Password Dialog—I'm going to tell you a lot more about this dialog in Chapter 12, "Database Management Under Delphi." Suffice it to say that this is the only special purpose dialog provided with Delphi. You'll find that the password field doesn't display the characters that a user types—it uses asterisks instead.

I include several of the forms on the Forms page shown in Figure 4.7 as dialogs. They allow you to select items or perform configuration tasks without a lot of added programming. The following list talks about each of the form dialogs.

Figure 4.7.

Several of the forms on the Forms page really qualify as dialogs since you wouldn't use them in any other capacity.

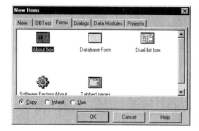

- About Box—We've already spent some time talking about this dialog box in Chapter 3. In fact, I showed you how to modify it for your own needs there. Even a utility program normally requires some type of About Box to tell others about copyright and version information.

- Dual List Box—This is the handiest dialog box in Delphi when you need to have the user select from a list of something. The whole range of choices appears on the left side; the choices that the user wants appear on the right side. I use this particular dialog for setup programs. You'll also find that it comes in handy for database management programs. For example, you might need to categorize something in several ways. You could put a list of descriptive words in the left pane and allow the user to move the ones that apply to the current entry to the right pane.

- Tabbed Pages—Remember what I said at the beginning of this chapter about some applications using too many dialog boxes? I look at this dialog as one cure for that problem. You can use it to put all the configuration information needed for the entire application into one dialog. The user merely goes from page to page as needed to change specific configuration options. Just about every major application I can think of uses this technique now.

Now that we've looked at the dialog boxes, let's take a look at an example of how to use one. Figure 4.8 shows the form we'll use. I wanted to show you what the various dialog boxes look like in action and how you can respond to user input. Obviously you wouldn't create something like this as a practical application, but it does come in handy for showing what features Delphi provides. The only component property I changed was to set the Memo1.Align property to alClient. The project also includes the six dialog types that I talked about in the previous paragraphs. I added some components to the Tabbed Page Dialog so that you could see how to interact with them. The only change I made here was to set the ItemIndex property of the radio group on page 2 to 0. This provides a default setting just in case the user doesn't select anything. Figures 4.9 through 4.11 show the various dialog box additions.

Figure 4.8.

This form allows you to select the various dialog box types and see what they look like.

Figure 4.9.

Page 1 of the Tabbed Notebook Dialog contains a check box.

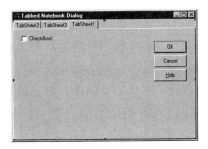

Figure 4.10.

There is a radio group on page 2 of the Tabbed Notebook Dialog.

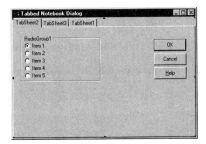

Figure 4.11.

On page 3 of the Tabbed Notebook Dialog, you'll find a list box.

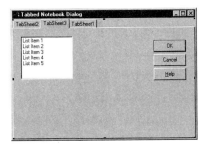

Once you have the form put together and a set of dialogs to test it with, you'll need to add some code. Listing 4.2 contains the code for this example. It's not very complex—the purpose of this example is to simply show how the dialogs look and how to access the data they contain. I also provide some clues on how to handle the dialogs once the user closes them.

Listing 4.2. DBTest1.

```
unit DBTest1;

interface

uses
  Windows, Messages, SysUtils, Classes, Graphics, Controls, Forms, Dialogs,
  Menus, StdCtrls;

type
  TForm1 = class(TForm)
    MainMenu1: TMainMenu;
    File1: TMenuItem;
    Exit1: TMenuItem;
    DialogForms1: TMenuItem;
    StandardDialogs1: TMenuItem;
    TabbedPages1: TMenuItem;
    AboutBox1: TMenuItem;
    DualList1: TMenuItem;
    StandardDialog1: TMenuItem;
    DialogwithHelp1: TMenuItem;
    PasswordDialog1: TMenuItem;
    Memo1: TMemo;
    procedure Exit1Click(Sender: TObject);
    procedure TabbedPages1Click(Sender: TObject);
    procedure AboutBox1Click(Sender: TObject);
    procedure DualList1Click(Sender: TObject);
    procedure StandardDialog1Click(Sender: TObject);
    procedure DialogwithHelp1Click(Sender: TObject);
    procedure PasswordDialog1Click(Sender: TObject);
  private
    { Private declarations }
  public
    { Public declarations }
  end;

var
  Form1: TForm1;

implementation

uses DBTest3, DBTest2, DBTest4, DBTest5, DBTest6, DBTest7;

{$R *.DFM}

procedure TForm1.Exit1Click(Sender: TObject);
begin
    {Exit the Application.}
    Application.Terminate;
end;

procedure TForm1.TabbedPages1Click(Sender: TObject);
begin
```

```
    {Display the dialog.}
    PagesDlg.ShowModal;

    {Clear the display area.}
    Memo1.Lines.Clear;

    {Use the dialog box.}
    with PagesDlg do
    begin

    {Display the status of page 1.}
    if CheckBox1.Checked then
        Memo1.Lines.Add('The user checked the box on page 1.')
    else
        Memo1.Lines.Add('The user didn''t check the box on page 1.');
    Memo1.Lines.Add('');

    {Display the status of page 2.}
    Memo1.Lines.Add('User selected ' + RadioGroup1.Items[RadioGroup1.ItemIndex] + ' on
page 2.');
    Memo1.Lines.Add('');

    {Display the status of page 3.}
    if ListBox1.ItemIndex >= 0 then
        Memo1.Lines.Add('User selected ' + ListBox1.Items[ListBox1.ItemIndex] + ' on page
3.')
    else
        Memo1.Lines.Add('The user didn''t select anything on page 3.');
    end; {with PagesDlg do}
end;

procedure TForm1.AboutBox1Click(Sender: TObject);
begin
    {Display the dialog.}
    AboutBox.ShowModal;

    {Clear Memo1 so the user will know there isn't any output.}
    Memo1.Lines.Clear;
end;

procedure TForm1.DualList1Click(Sender: TObject);
var
    iCount: Integer;    {Number of items in the left list.}
begin
    {Display the dialog.}
    DualListDlg.ShowModal;

    {Display the user's selections.}
    Memo1.Lines.Clear;

    Memo1.Lines.Add('User selected:');

    For iCount := 0 to DualListDlg.DstList.Items.Count - 1 do
        Memo1.Lines.Add(DualListDlg.DstList.Items[iCount]);
end;

procedure TForm1.StandardDialog1Click(Sender: TObject);
var
```

continues

Listing 4.2. continued

```
    fResult: Integer;    {Which button did the user press?}
begin
    {Display the dialog.}
    fResult := OKRightDlg.ShowModal;

    {Clear the display.}
    Memo1.Lines.Clear;

    {Determine which button the user pressed.}
    if fResult = mrOK then
        Memo1.Lines.Add('User pressed OK.')
    else
        Memo1.Lines.Add('User pressed Cancel.');
end;

procedure TForm1.DialogwithHelp1Click(Sender: TObject);
var
    fResult: Integer;    {Which button did the user press?}
begin
    {Display the dialog.}
    fResult := OKHelpBottomDlg.ShowModal;

    {Clear the display.}
    Memo1.Lines.Clear;

    {Determine which button the user pressed.}
    if fResult = mrOK then
        Memo1.Lines.Add('User pressed OK.')
    else
        Memo1.Lines.Add('User pressed Cancel.');
end;

procedure TForm1.PasswordDialog1Click(Sender: TObject);
const
    sPassword = 'SECRET';
var
    fResult: Integer;    {Did the user press Cancel?}
begin
    {initialize our result variable.}
    fResult := mrCancel;

    {Don't allow the user to cancel out of the password dialog.}
    while (fResult = mrCancel) or (PasswordDlg.Password.Text <> sPassword) do

        {Show the dialog.}
        fResult := PasswordDlg.ShowModal;

    {Clear the display.}
    Memo1.Lines.Clear;

    {Display a success message.}
    Memo1.Lines.Add('User entered correct password!');
end;

end.
```

Let's take a look at the code for this example. There are a few things that you need to do to access data on a dialog. One of the most important things is to add each of the dialogs to your Uses statement as shown in the listing. Notice that this Uses statement appears as part of the implementation part of the program—you need to place it here instead of with the library modules that you plan to use.

Tip: The File | Use Unit command provides a fast and easy method for adding references to the dialogs in your main application. Simply select each of the dialogs from the list presented and click on OK. Delphi will add the appropriate Uses statement to your code automatically.

Notice that the list box in our Tabbed Notebook Dialog only allows a single selection. This reduces the complexity of the list box code for that part of the example. Contrast this with the code I've provided for the Choices Dialog where the user can select anywhere from none to all of the available choices. Instead of a single line statement that displays the selected value, this routine uses a for loop to display all the items in the right hand list box.

I've played around with several different methods for implementing the Password Dialog. In this case I used a while loop to get the job done. The Password Dialog won't close until the user types the right password (SECRET in this case) and clicks on OK. Obviously you'd need something a bit more robust to provide real security. For one thing, you'd have to find out what the user's password is from an access database. I'll cover that topic in more detail in Chapter 13, "Delphi on a LAN," when we cover security on the network.

Client Windows to Display Special Data

Message boxes talk to the user and dialog boxes allow the user to enter information. However, you still need a way to give the user some kind of feedback. I'm talking about data manipulation here—the whole reason to use an application in the first place. The normal way to do this is the approach that I took in Figure 4.8. All I did was add a TMemo component to the main form and display any results there.

You're going to run into situations where this approach won't work very well. For example, your application might handle text for the most part, but for some reason you need to display graphics as well. I can think of a number of utility programs that fall into this category—normally they display statistics, but you might want to see something like system performance as a graph. DBMS applications often fall into this category as well. Normally you use custom forms and browses to add textual data to the database. However, in some situations you might want to see a graphic representation of that data in a separate window.

Giving the user feedback in the right way is what client windows are all about. A word processor can display text and graphics together because that's the way that the user will eventually print them out—a database manager can't say the same thing. A user of that type of application normally expects to see pure text (unless the database is designed to handle BLOBs, which are just another form of data input in this case). Placing a graph of last week's sales in a separate window makes sense in this situation.

I've already shown you several ways to create new forms. We've looked at creating them during design time as discrete units of your application. I've also shown you one method for creating a form dynamically. Suffice it to say that the method you choose depends a great deal on the memory constraints of your system, the complexity of the data and the form used to display it, and the number of times you actually plan to use the form. If you need to display a simple graph on an infrequent basis, then creating a client window dynamically is probably the best way to go.

Using Image Edit for Cursors, Icons, and Bitmaps

One of my favorite updates to Delphi 2.0 is the enhanced version of the Image Edit utility. It was the first thing that I added to my Tools menu. (We covered the procedure for doing this in Chapter 2, "The Delphi IDE." See the section entitled "Adding New Tools.") In this section I'm going to show you how to use this tool to add some special bells and whistles to your application—some of which you normally associate with higher end applications. I'm also going to show you some of the more mundane things like creating your own application icon and storing multiple icons in one file.

The first thing we'll need to do is look at the Image Editor itself. Figure 4.12 shows a typical example of how the Image Editor utility looks after you load a resource file. Notice that the resource file dialog uses a hierarchical display. There are three kinds of resources you can edit with the Image Editor: bitmaps, cursors, and icons. In some cases you'll also see a String resource tree in the window, but you can't edit it with the program. You can use the hierarchical display to add new resources to your application, then call on those resources to dress up a display.

Figure 4.12.
The Image Editor utility will help you add some special bells and whistles to your application.

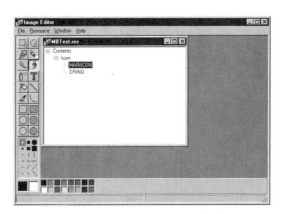

Let's look at the Icon branch first (the one shown in Figure 4.12). Every Delphi application contains a MAINICON icon. It's the one that you see when you look at the application's icon within Explorer. The default icon is the Delphi icon (the temple with a flaming torch in front of it).

> **Tip:** You can change the default icon by using the Project | Options command to display the Project Options dialog. The Application tab of this dialog contains an entry for the main program icon. Simply load a new icon from disk by clicking on the Load Icon button.

As with everything else in Delphi, you can display a context menu by right-clicking on the display. Figure 4.13 shows the context menu for the Image Editor. The New option allows you to create a new cursor, bitmap, or icon. Selecting the New option displays the submenu shown in the figure. Simply select the type of resource you want to create. If you select a bitmap, you'll see the Bitmap Properties dialog shown in Figure 4.14. Simply select the number of colors you want and the size of the bitmap. You'll see a similar dialog if you select an icon. Figure 4.15 shows the Icon Properties dialog. Notice that you're restricted to specific sizes for icons—bitmaps are more flexible in this regard. Cursors don't require any configuration. The Image Editor utility will create a new tree entry for each of the resources you select. Double-clicking on an entry displays the editor shown in Figure 4.16. Notice that it's just like any other paint program you've used in the past.

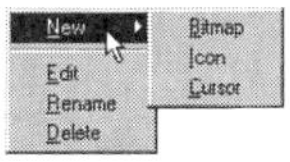

Figure 4.13.
The first step in creating a new resource is selecting the type you want.

Figure 4.14.
The Bitmap Properties dialog allows you to configure your new bitmap before you draw it.

Figure 4.15.
The Icon Properties dialog allows you to choose from a variety of icon sizes and color specifications.

There are a few special features that you'll need to know about when using this editor. To select a foreground color you left-click on the color palette. The background color is selected with a right-click. An important non-color for icons and cursors is the transparent color attribute. You select it by right- or left-clicking on that entry in the color area. It allows whatever you see below the icon or cursor to show through. In addition to color, you'll find that the Image Editor utility also provides a good selection of patterns and line widths. They appear on the left side of the display below the drawing tools—a simple click is all you need to select one. Obviously there are limitations to what you can use in the small area of an icon or cursor, but it's good to know that the features are there when you need them.

Figure 4.16.
You'll find that the Image Editor provides capabilities similar to most paint programs.

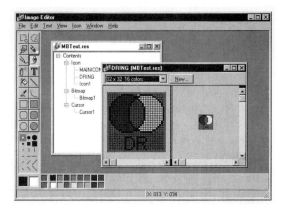

Looking Ahead: Figure 4.16 shows an icon that I created using the editor. You may want to try creating your own icon. I'll show you how to use an icon resource in the next section. This same procedure will work with every other resource you can add to an RES file—only the actual Windows API function call changes.

If you decide to change a resource's appearance later, just highlight it and select the Edit option from the context menu. Double-clicking on the entry will also allow you to edit it. You'll see an editing display similar to the one shown in Figure 4.16. Press the New pushbutton in the editor if you decide to start from scratch. You'll see a dialog telling you that the resource already exists. Simply press Yes when asked if you want to replace it.

The Image Editor utility automatically names the icons and other resources you create using the resource type followed by a number. For example, the first icon you would create is named Icon1. Even though this is an easy name to remember, it doesn't really say much about the functionality of the icon. Changing the name of a resource is easy; all you do is highlight the entry and select the Rename option of the context menu. You'll see an editing box similar to the one shown in Figure 4.17. This box works just like the one in Explorer. You'll need to refer to this name to use an icon or other resource within an application, so picking something descriptive is important.

Removing resources from an RES file is easy. All you need to do is highlight the resource and select the Delete option of the context menu. Just click on Yes when Image Editor asks if you want to delete the resource. Make sure you really want to delete the resource, since there isn't any undo feature for returning the resource once it's gone. The bottom line? Always delete resources with care.

Figure 4.17.

The editing box shown here allows you to change the name of an icon or other resource.

Special Image Edit Considerations for Resource Files

Now that you've gotten down the basics of using the Image Editor utility, you may wonder why you would go to all this trouble to add an icon to your application. There are several situations where RES files become more than a little important. The most common way to add an icon to a Delphi application is to add a TImage component, then specify an icon to fill it. However, what if there's a chance that you'll need to display more than one icon in that position? Our custom message box in Figure 4.4 might use any one of several icons depending on what type of message you want to display. You could use the Load From File method for the TImage component, but you can't always depend on the icon file being available on disk. Using an RES file places the icon in your EXE file. That way you always know that the icons or other resources you need to perform a particular task are available.

Once you see the importance of RES files, it's hard to figure out how you ever got by without them in certain situations. Of course, the problem now is to get the icon from your EXE file to your display. There's a long and error prone Windows API method to getting the job done, but we'll explore the much easier Delphi alternative in this chapter.

Remember how the custom message box example shown in Figure 4.4 lacked much pizzazz? I'm going to show you how to add a feature to it that you can't get in a standard message box. Listing 4.3 contains the modified source code for the custom message box function.

Listing 4.3. Custom message box function.

```
function TForm1.CustomMessage: Integer;
var
    lMessage: TLabel;      {The message in our dialog.}
    pbOK: TButton;          {An OK pushbutton to close the dialog.}
    DRing: TIcon;           {A new icon for our dialog.}
    Image1: TImage;       {An image to hold the icon.}
begin
    {Create and configure the initial dialog.}
    MsgDlg := TForm.Create(Application);
    MsgDlg.Width := Message.Width + 55;
    MsgDlg.Height := 120;
```

continues

Listing 4.3. continued

```
MsgDlg.BorderStyle := bsDialog;
MsgDlg.Caption := 'Custom Message Dialog';

{Create and configure the message.}
lMessage := TLabel.Create(MsgDlg);
lMessage.Width := Message.Width;
lMessage.Left := 45;
lMessage.Top := 10;
lMessage.Caption := Message.Text;

{Add the message to our dialog.}
MsgDlg.InsertControl(lMessage);

{Create and configure the pushbutton.}
pbOK := TButton.Create(MsgDlg);
pbOK.Caption := 'OK';
pbOK.Top := 50;
pbOK.Left := (MsgDlg.Width - pbOK.Width) div 2;
pbOK.OnClick := DoCloseForm;

{Add the pushbutton to our dialog.}
MsgDlg.InsertControl(pbOK);

{Create and configure the icon.}
DRing := TIcon.Create;
DRing.Handle := LoadIcon(hInstance, 'DRING');

{Create and configure the image.}
Image1 := TImage.Create(MsgDlg);
Image1.Left := 5;
Image1.Top := 5;
Image1.Height := DRing.Height;
Image1.Width := DRing.Width;
Image1.Canvas.Draw(0, 0, DRing);

{Add the image to our dialog.}
MsgDlg.InsertControl(Image1);

{Display the completed dialog.}
MsgDlg.ShowModal;

{Send back the result.}
Result := mrOK;

{Free the memory used by the dialog.}
MsgDlg.Free;

end;
```

In addition to changing some of the configuration values for the message box to make room for an icon, I also added a TIcon and a TImage variable to the function. Notice how I created the icon first, then the image. An image is a component—you can add it to a dialog. On the other hand, icons are drawn onto the canvas of components.

I still have to use a Windows API call to load the icon. The LoadIcon function returns a handle to an icon stored in an EXE file. (You'd use the LoadBitmap function to load a bitmap and the LoadCursor function to load a cursor.) All you have to do to access it is make the icon's handle equal to the handle returned by the function call. So how does our new dialog look? Figure 4.18 shows the new version of our custom message dialog. Notice that I used the custom icon that we created in the previous section to dress up the dialog.

Figure 4.18.
The new version of the custom message box looks a lot better than the previous one.

Tip: Windows 95 also provides a LoadImage function that allows you to load any image type using a single call. The advantage to using this call is that you can use a generic procedure for loading a variety of image types. It's also more flexible than the older calls. For example, you get to specify an image size. The disadvantage is that this new call requires a lot more information to use.

Windows also provides a group of default icons—the ones that you commonly see in the standard message boxes. This allows you to create standard and custom dialogs using one function. Table 4.2 lists the standard message box values. You don't enclose these values in quotes as we did with the custom icon.

Table 4.2. Standard Windows Icon Values.

Value	Icon Type
IDI_APPLICATION	This is the default application icon. It's the one listed as MAINICON in the RES file.
IDI_ASTERISK	The asterisk icon is commonly used in informative messages.
IDI_EXCLAMATION	Exclamation points are used in warning messages.
IDI_HAND	You'll see this hand-shaped icon used in serious warning messages. In most cases you'll want to reserve this icon for system use since it indicates some type of serious system failure.

continues

Table 4.2. continued

Value	Icon Type
IDI_QUESTION	The question mark icon is used in prompting messages. You'll use it if you want to ask the user a question such as whether they want to save a file before they exit the application.
IDI_WINLOGO	You can only use this icon with Windows 95. It displays the Windows 95 logo.

Executing Tasks in the Background Using TThread

Working in a 32-bit development environment has more than a few advantages. We'll spend quite a bit of time in this book looking at ways to do just that. The first thing that I'd like to show you is how to create a thread of execution.

What precisely is a thread? It's a way of putting some task in the background and pursuing your main application goal. For example, users are using a word processor and decide to print, they don't want their machines tied up while they wait for the print routine to finish. The main purpose of the word processor, at least from the users' perspective, is to accept their input. Putting the print routine in a thread so that it can execute in the background is a more efficient and user friendly way to handle this job.

We had previously talked about the thread object in the New Items dialog. This is where you'll start creating a thread. Simply select the thread object from the New Items dialog and you'll see the dialog shown in Figure 4.19. You have to give your thread a name so that Delphi can access it later.

Figure 4.19.
Creating a thread object is the first step in adding threads to your application.

Once you supply the requested thread name, Delphi will add a new unit to your application. Inside this unit is a new procedure called Execute. You'll place your main thread code here. You'll also see another procedure that's commented out. It provides an example of how to tell the user that the thread is working. In this case Borland is suggesting that you could update your main application form's caption to reflect the change. I prefer to provide something a bit more active than that in a status bar. In the case of a print routine you could show the current page being printed or some other type of status information that tells the user that the thread is working. (Make sure you observe Borland's recommendation that you not allow a thread to write to VCL components directly, but use a synchronization method instead. What this means is that all VCL operations are performed by the main thread—all child threads must request those services as part of a synchronization call to the main thread.)

Working with threads is different than working with other types of Delphi components or objects. For example, in most cases you need to do something with a component once you create it. Threads are either active or suspended when you create them. You tell Delphi in which state to start the thread as part of the Create method. Unlike other objects, the application always owns a thread, so you don't need to supply this parameter. Of course, all this assumes that you use the standard methods—you can always override any of these methods for a thread to allow it to accept other parameters. Obviously this is a greater possibility when creating a thread, since you'll need to tell it how to interact with the main thread. Listing 4.4 shows an example of how you would create a thread. In this case I created a thread to print the contents of a rich text edit field, so I used the standard constructor.

Listing 4.4. Creating a thread.

```
procedure TForm1.pbTestClick(Sender: TObject);
var
    NewThread: PrintIt;    {New thread of execution.}
begin
    {Create the thread.}
    NewThread := PrintIt.Create(False);
end;
```

There are two other methods that you'll usually use with threads. One is the Suspend method. You might need to suspend a thread to meet user processing needs or to synchronize two threads of operation. A user may simply request that you suspend a thread to allow him to perform another task. For example, it's not all that unusual that a print routine would get suspended if the user needed to do something else with the machine for a minute or two. Error correction is another situation where a thread might become suspended. What happens if a printer runs out of paper? Suspending the thread would allow the user to add more paper, then resume the printout. If you can suspend a thread of execution, it only makes sense that you can resume it. That's the other commonly used method.

You always have to terminate a thread using the Terminate method when it gets done doing its work. (Delphi also provides a Destroy method, but I avoid using it for any component or object.) Otherwise the thread will continue to run in the background and Delphi won't deallocate the memory it uses after the main thread terminates. You might see other strange effects under Windows 95 as well, since it doesn't protect memory as well as Windows NT does. However, even though it would seem that you would do this from outside of the thread within the main thread, the opposite is true. Always add the Terminate method as the last step of a thread.

Note: As of this writing, the identifier used by a thread doesn't get deallocated until the application exits. This means that even though the thread is no longer in use, the reference to it still exists. You'll still see the thread in the Thread Status window as you debug the application.

Threads also have priorities. A priority tells the system how much time to devote to a particular thread. So, a high priority thread would provide the best execution speed, while a low priority thread would produce the least effect on overall system throughput. There are two TThread methods that deal with priorities: SetPriority and GetPriority. Delphi defines seven constants you can use to adjust or monitor a thread's priority. They range from THREAD_PRIORITY_IDLE (the lowest priority) to THREAD_PRIORITY_TIME_CRITICAL (the highest priority).

Summary

The overall intent of this chapter was to help you understand the various types of bells and whistles you can add to a program. There are a lot of ways to get information from the user or to provide them with the information needed to use your application. However, to truly communicate with the user, you need to learn what type of dialogs to use and when to use them.

We also spent some time looking at various types of dialog boxes that Delphi provides and a few that you can create on your own. Message boxes always communicate some type of message. In some cases they also ask the user what to do about a particular situation. Dialog boxes are mainly configuration and data information gathering devices. In this case, you're asking the user for some type of input. Remembering which types of dialog to use in specific situations can help make your application easier to use.

This chapter also talked about the new Image Editor utility. Adding icons and other resources to your application is essential to making it fun to use. You can't always depend on a specific resource being available on disk—it's better to incorporate it into your EXE file so you can simply grab it when needed.

Finally, we looked at one of the advantages of using a 32-bit programming environment. The TThread component may take a little getting used to, but I think you'll find that it's essential to making a program user friendly and fast to use.

II

Delphi and the Windows Environment

5

Accessing the Windows API

One of the first things you need to know to expand Delphi's programming horizons is how to access the Windows API (application programming interface). The Windows API is vast, it provides access to all of the features that Windows provides, yet many programmers still find it limited. Even with these limitations, there are times when you need to gain access to a particular Windows feature, but Delphi doesn't provide access to it for you. (It's certain that Delphi provides access to the vast majority of the Windows API through the VCL, but I'll show you quite a few features it doesn't even touch in the next several chapters.)

So, what kinds of things can you do with the API that you can't do directly with Delphi? Some of the answers are fairly obvious. For example, you might need to provide some low level network functionality that Delphi doesn't support directly. Using the NetWare bindery or NDS (NetWare Directory Services) features directly would fall into this category. An OLE server will also require you to access the Windows API to perform some types of work. Think about all the hidden DDE functions that the Windows API supports that you can't find in Delphi.

Some of the other forms of API access are a little more subtle though, and it might be easy to miss them. What types of common dialog support does Delphi provide? You might be surprised to find that the Windows API functions are a lot more flexible. So you have a choice. You can either use the Delphi provided functionality and decrease your programming time or you can use the Windows API and increase program flexibility.

> **Tip:** Insulating yourself from operating system and programming environment changes is always a good idea. You should avoid using the Windows API if Delphi provides a function to do the work you need it to do. Using the built-in functions whenever possible puts the burden of upgrading application functionality on the vendor instead of yourself. When it comes time to update your program to make use of a new operating system feature, you might be able to implement it by recompiling the application. The vendor may provide an automated tool to allow you to make use of a new programming environment feature, but you can be certain that the tool will only work with what most vendors call standard code. Standard code never includes direct API calls. Using the built-in features also allows you to make better use of all the automated tools that a particular programming environment provides.

Obviously I can't enumerate every instance where you would want to use the Windows API instead of Delphi functions here. Suffice it to say that there are two categories of Windows API access for the Delphi programmer: necessity and convenience. You'll always have to use the Windows API when Delphi doesn't support a particular Windows feature, making the API call a necessity. Convenience is another word for flexibility in this case. The Windows API provides greater flexibility than the Delphi functions do in some situations. However, in this case you have a choice of whether to use the Windows API or not.

What Is the Windows API?

The Windows API is somewhat difficult to categorize; it means different things to different people. Talking to a room full of programmers will probably yield a room full of different answers on exactly what the Windows API contains. Some programmers will tell you that it's a list of all the functions in the Windows API help file (a very limited view), while others will tell you that it's a combination of all the DLLs and other executables in your SYSTEM directory. There's no dictionary definition of what the Windows API contains and what it excludes, so most programmers come up with their own definition.

I always look at the scope of the Windows API as the entry points to all the functions contained in the various DLLs, VxDs, VBXs, OCXs, and other Windows executables on a particular machine. For example, the Windows API includes all the exported functions you find when looking at the USER32.DLL. If you use the Windows 95 Quick View utility to look at USER32.DLL, you would see something like Figure 5.1. The Export Table section will tell you which functions the DLL makes available for a programmer to use. If you look up the AdjustWindowRect entry in your Windows API help file, you'll see something like the entry in Figure 5.2. However, this DLL contains more functions than you'll find in any help file. For example, try to find some information on the ActivateKeyboardLayout function. Even though this function is part of the API, it doesn't appear in your Delphi documentation. You'd probably find this information in the Microsoft documentation, as part of a white paper on their Internet or CompuServe forums, or in a "hidden" functions book. The point is that you'll want to spend some time digging around in the actual DLLs before you assume that Windows is missing some bit of functionality that you need—the functionality may simply be hidden.

> **Tip:** You can access the Windows Quick View utility by right-clicking on a file and selecting the Quick View option from the context menu. If you don't see a Quick View entry, that means Quick View probably doesn't support that particular file extension. You can still use Quick View to look at most executable file formats by making a copy of the file, then changing its extension to DLL. Make sure you do this on a copy of the file and then erase the copy when you're finished looking.

Figure 5.1.

Looking at the Export Table entries for a DLL using the Windows 95 Quick View utility can tell you a lot about the services that it offers.

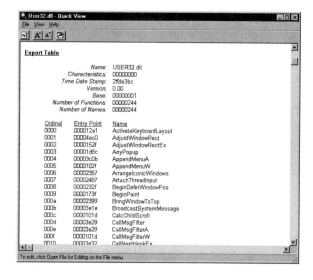

Figure 5.2.

The Windows API help file supplied with Delphi 2 will tell you about many of the entries in USER32.DLL.

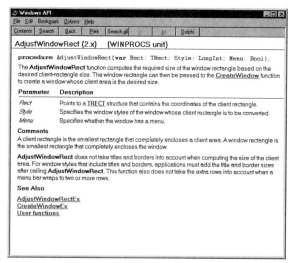

Tip: While every DLL will contain one or more functions in the Export Table section, you should also look at the other sections in the file to gain a better understanding of how it interacts with the rest of the Windows API. The Import Table section will tell you what resources—in the form of functions found in other DLLs—this DLL needs to work. Mapping out a hierarchy of needed DLLs can make it easier to see how your application fits into the Windows environment. In fact, this map can be a valuable troubleshooting aid when a user is having problems and all you have is a mysterious error message that indicates there is a file missing. All you need to do is look at your DLL map and make sure those files are present in the SYSTEM directory.

However, the Windows API is more than just a collection of Export Table entries. What you can consider is that the Windows API also varies on an application basis. Some applications may have access to more of the API than others do. The reason is simple. Because the Windows API is made up of modules, you can add to it by simply adding a new DLL or other executable file. The pen functions are one example of this extended functionality; multimedia is another example. If a particular machine lacks a sound board, you can bet that you won't have access to those multimedia features. The installed base of software also affects the extended base of Windows API function. For example, if one machine has a particular application—say a spreadsheet—installed, you can bet there will be features added to the Windows API. (At the very least you might find that there's an added layer of processing.)

Of course, if you simply look at the API this way, its configuration would change from machine to machine based on what features and application programs the user installed. A programmer has to come up with a definitive set of API calls that he can use while writing an application. This is the Windows API that the application needs to work properly on every machine where it's installed and the only API that makes a bit of difference to you as the programmer. To do this, I came up with three levels of API calls that I feel I can safely use.

The upper level contains the functions that I would always expect a machine to have available. You need this layer of functions to start your application and check for the presence of any other functions you may need. I limit my strict definition of the Windows API to those executables that make up the central portion of Windows—those DLLs and other executable files that the user has to install to gain the minimum level of Windows functionality. You can always depend on the existence of these Windows API functions because the user has to install them to make Windows work. Of all the DLLs and other executables on your machine, you have to have the USER, GDI, and KERNAL functions to make Windows work. (I'll tell you more about these functions as time goes on, but you can use the Quick View utility to check these DLLs out any time you want to verify the absolute presence of a specific function.)

Looking Ahead: We're only getting started with the Windows API in this chapter. Look through Chapters 6 through 9 for more information about the architectural part of the Windows API. Chapter 10, "Using Delphi with OLE," will enlighten you about the intricacies of OLE programming, including a look at some of the registry elements you may not have heard about before. Chapter 11, "Delphi and Multimedia Programming," talks about multimedia programming, including some additional considerations for using the Windows API.

Once you get past this minimal level of functionality, you start looking at what I call a Windows API extension. These are the functions that appear in DLLs and other executables that a user could install as part of Windows (as contrasted with a DLL installed as part of an application). For example, you don't have to install a backup program, so the DLLs that make it up might not be present. In addition, you may find that the DLLs for some devices—especially multimedia devices—differ in their capabilities from installation to installation, so you have to consider which functions are essential and which are only nice to have. (Using an advanced feature means that you'll have to test for that capability before you use it.) For example, an older 8-bit sound board won't provide the same number of capabilities as a newer 32-bit board. Even if there's a limited capability, you can always count on a few basic functions (the API documentation usually tells you the minimal functionality that you can expect). Of course, the best news is that since these DLLs are provided as part of Windows; you can make their installation a requirement for using your application. In other words, you can depend on the existence of these functions if a user actually installs a Windows feature. If the user hasn't installed the feature, you can ask them to do so and still maintain strict Windows compatibility.

The final level of API functions is the application API. This is the set of DLLs and other executables that a user would probably install as part of another application. Say for instance that you want to create an add-on product for Lotus 1-2-3. You could rightfully make installing Lotus 1-2-3 a requirement for using your application. If you had access to the functions within the Lotus 1-2-3 supplied DLLs, then you could use them in place of developing your own low level functions.

Of course, this is an oversimplification of all the issues you'll face when deciding what DLLs and other files make up your version of the Windows API. In fact, you'll find the various modules I've just described talked about as this API or that. The fact of the matter is that all of them affect your access to Windows functionality. In my book that makes them all part of your Windows API. It doesn't really matter whose tool kit originally contained the DLL, you need it today to get an application working.

A Quick Overview of the API Components

Any discussion of the Windows API will necessarily include a look at the architecture itself. I've provided a generalized architectural view in the following paragraphs. It has a very definite Windows 95 slant, but most of the features I describe are also available in Windows NT. We'll take a more in-depth look at specifics in Chapters 6 through 9.

Rings of Protection

Before I begin a discussion of individual Windows architectural components, I'd like to direct your attention to the "rings" of protection that the 80386 (and above) processor provides. There are four security rings within the Intel protection scheme, but most operating systems use only two (or sometimes three) of them. The inner security ring is ring 0. This is where you'll find the operating system proper. The outermost ring is 3. That's where the applications reside. Sometimes an operating system gives device drivers better access to some operating system features than an application gets by running them at ring 1 or 2. Windows doesn't make any concessions; device drivers run at ring 0 or 3, depending on their purpose.

Windows uses these protection rings to make certain that only operating system components can access the inner workings of Windows, and that an application can't change settings that might cause the entire system to crash. For example, Windows reserves the right to allocate memory from the global pool; therefore, the capabilities needed to perform this task rest at ring 0. On the other hand, applications need to access memory assigned to them. That's why Windows assigns local memory a protection value of 3.

Think of each ring as a security perimeter. Before you can enter that perimeter, you have to know the secret password. Windows gives the password only to applications that it knows it can trust; everyone else has to stay out. Whenever an application does try to circumvent security, the processor raises an exception. Think of an exception as a security alarm. The exception sends the Windows police (better known as an exception handler) after the offending application. After its arrest and trial, Windows calmly terminates the offending application. Of course, it notifies the user before performing this task, but the user usually doesn't have much of a choice in the matter.

Figures 5.3 and 5.4 give you a pretty good idea of exactly whom Windows trusts. Applications and device drivers running at ring 3 have very few capabilities outside their own resources. In fact, Windows even curtails these capabilities somewhat. Some of the activities that a DOS application could get by with, such as directly manipulating video memory, aren't allowed here. The reason is simple: Video memory is a shared resource. Whenever another application would need to share something, you can be certain that your application wouldn't be able to access it directly.

Now, on to the various components that actually make up Windows. The following sections break the Windows components into main areas. Each of these general groups contains descriptions of the individual components and what tasks they perform. Remember that this is only a general discussion. Windows is much more complex than it might first appear. The deeper you get as a programmer, the more you'll see the actual complexity of this operating system.

Architecture

Several elements make up the Windows architecture. Figure 5.3 shows an overview of the Windows 95 architecture, while Figure 5.4 shows the same thing for Windows NT. Each element takes care of one part of the Windows environment. For example, the Windows API (Application Programming Interface) layer lets applications communicate with Windows internals such as the file management system. Even though these elements are separate modules from a conceptual point of view, you'll find that they work together in unison. In reality, it's difficult at best to separate the various architectural elements from a practical point of view. (For example, you can't separate the API layer from the components it interacts with in a real sense, but I do so in this section to make the purpose of each element a bit clearer.) I describe each of these main components in detail in the following sections.

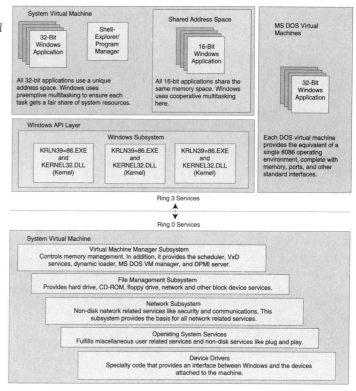

Figure 5.3.
Windows 95 contains several major elements. Each element provides a different service to the user and other applications running under Windows.

System Virtual Machine

The System Virtual Machine (VM) component of Windows 95 contains three main elements: 32-bit Windows applications, the shell, and 16-bit Windows applications. Essentially, the System VM component provides most of the Windows 95 user-specific functionality. Without it, you couldn't run any applications. Notice that I don't include DOS applications here. This is because Windows uses an entirely different set of capabilities to run DOS applications. It even runs them in a different processor mode.

Windows NT includes all the capabilities of Windows 95 and adds two more: OS/2 and POSIX support. Notice that there's a client side to this support in the System Virtual Machine area of the diagram and a server side in the Windows API Layer part of the drawing. Windows NT uses a client and server approach to managing applications so that it can quickly adapt to applications designed for other operating systems by using this technique. We really won't discuss this added support much in this book, but you should at least be aware that it exists. Windows NT also provides a higher level of protection for 16-bit Windows applications—that's why I moved them to the DOS Virtual Machine area of the diagram.

Figure 5.4.

Windows NT contains many of the same features as Windows 95, but it adds security, multiplatform/multiprocessing support, and more 32-bit processing elements.

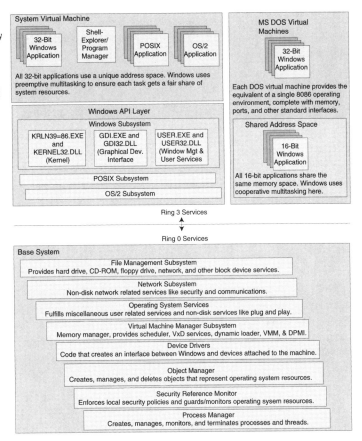

Warning: It may appear that you could run applications designed for different operating systems together under Windows NT and share their data. While Windows NT will run more than one operating system's applications, it won't share data between them. For example, a POSIX application creates file handles differently than a Windows 32-bit application does. The POSIX file handle would be meaningless to the Windows NT application. The same idea holds true for any other type of data that an application may generate. In short, it's never a good idea to pass data from one application to another unless you use some documented method to do so.

Theoretically, the System VM also provides support for the various Windows API layer components. However, since these components provide a different sort of service, I chose to discuss them in a separate area. (Needless to say, the distinction between the client or System VM and server or

Windows API layer parts of Windows NT architecture are a lot clearer than under Windows 95.)
Even though applications use the API and users interact with applications, you really don't think
about the API until it comes time to write an application. Therefore, I always think of the API as a
programmer-specific service rather than something that the user really needs to worry about. The
following list describes the System VM components in detail:

- 32-bit Windows applications: This entry means something slightly different for Windows
  95 and Windows NT. Windows NT can use a wide variety of fully functional 32-bit
  applications, some of which will not run under Windows 95. For Windows 95, these are
  the new Win32-specific applications that use a subset of the Windows NT API. In fact,
  many Windows NT applications, such as Word for Windows NT, will run just fine under
  Windows 95. A 32-bit application usually provides better multitasking capabilities than its
  16-bit counterpart. In addition, many 32-bit applications support new Windows features
  such as long filenames, while most 16-bit applications do not. 32-bit applications provide
  two additional features. The more important one is the use of preemptive versus coopera-
  tive multitasking. This makes your work flow more smoothly and forces the system to wait
  for you as necessary, rather than the other way around. The second one is the use of a flat
  memory address space. This feature really makes a difference in how much memory an
  application gets and how well it uses it. In addition, an application that uses a flat address
  space should run slightly faster since it no longer has to spend time working with Intel's
  memory segmentation scheme.

- The shell: Two shells are supplied with Windows 95 (the new version of Windows NT will
  also support both shells—the current version only supports Program Manager), and you
  can choose either. The newer shell, Explorer, provides full 32-bit capabilities. It also sports
  the new interface shown in Figure 5.5. Explorer combines all the features you used to find
  in Program Manager, Print Manager, and File Manager. You can also use the older Program
  Manager interface with Windows 95 (see Figure 5.6). It doesn't provide all the bells and
  whistles that Explorer does, but it will certainly ease the transition for some users who
  learned the Program Manager interface. Switching between shells is easy. All you need to
  do is change the Shell= entry in the [Boot] section of SYSTEM.INI. Of course, Windows
  95 also lets you choose which shell you want to use when you install it.

- 16-bit Windows applications: All your older applications—the ones you own right now—
  are 16-bit applications unless you bought them for use with Windows NT. Windows 95
  runs all these applications in one shared address space. Essentially, Windows 95 organizes
  all these 16-bit applications into one area and treats them as if they were one task. You
  really won't notice any performance hit as a result, but it does make it easier for Windows
  95 to recover from application errors. With it, Windows 95 can mix 16-bit and 32-bit
  applications on one system.

Figure 5.5.
Windows 95 sports a new interface that should make life a lot easier for the novice user.

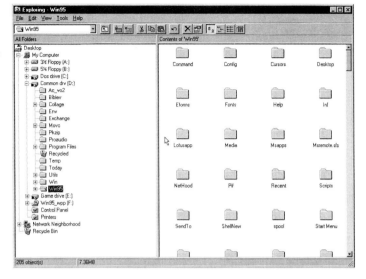

Figure 5.6.
Windows versions 3.0 and above offer one of the things that users need to use a computer efficiently: a graphical user interface (GUI).

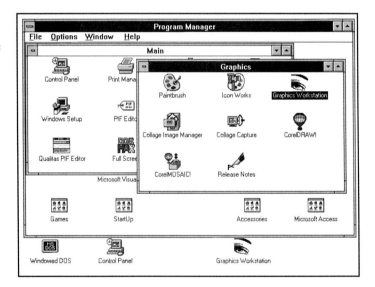

- POSIX Application: I've never seen anyone use this particular feature, so I can't tell you how well it works. This is a government specified form of UNIX that's supposed to be portable across a variety of platforms. It appeared in 1988 as IEEE Standard 1003.1-1988. Suffice it to say that you probably won't need to interact with this interface element unless your system is running a POSIX application. It's interesting to note that the current POSIX interface only supports character mode applications.

- OS/2 Application: The OS/2 support under Windows NT is somewhat disappointing. The only things you can run with the current version of Windows NT are the character mode programs used with OS/2 version 1.0. You can't run any of the Program Manager capable programs. Hopefully this will change in the future.

The Windows API Layer

Two Windows APIs are included with Windows 95. The first API is exactly like the old one supplied with Windows 3.1. It provides all the 16-bit services that the old Windows had to provide for applications. An older 16-bit application will use this API when it runs. The other API is the new Win32 API used by Windows NT. It provides a subset of the features that all 32-bit applications running under Windows NT can access. The 32-bit API provides about the same feature set as the 16-bit API, but it's more robust.

To support multiple operating systems, Windows NT also has to provide multiple API levels. Microsoft calls these API layers servers. The client for a particular operating system calls the API layers. These layers translate system requests like opening a file or printing a document into something that Windows NT can understand. From a programmer's point of view the Windows NT 32-bit API looks just the same as the one you'll find in Windows 95 (even though it does provide a wider range of calls). It's the actual operating system implementation that differs. Windows 95 provides a single API. Windows NT provides multiple API servers. I won't talk about the OS/2 or POSIX API in this book since you can't access them from your Windows 32-bit application.

Let's take a closer look at the 32-bit Windows API, the one we'll be interested in throughout the book. Of course, the biggest benefit that you'll hear most programmers talk about is the flat memory address space. Every application running under Windows has had to spend time working with Intel's segmented address scheme—until now. A 32-bit application doesn't need to worry about segmentation anymore. Every call is a near call; every call is in a single segment.

Notice that our diagram shows six system files for both Windows 95 and Windows NT. They're broken up into three operating system areas. Each area contains two files: one 16-bit and the other 32-bit. This is the upper level of API support that I mentioned previously. No matter which API you use, your application will address these three basic components. The 16-bit versions of these files are GDI.EXE, USER.EXE, and KRNL386.EXE. The 32-bit versions of these files are GDI32.DLL, USER32.DLL, and KERNEL32.DLL. The following list describes these three components in detail:

- Windows kernel (KRNL386.EXE or KERNEL32.DLL): This part of Windows 95 provides support for the lower-level functions that an application needs to run. For example, every time your application needs memory, it runs to the Windows kernel to get it. This component doesn't deal with either the interface or devices; it interacts only with Windows itself.

- Graphical device interface (GDI.EXE or GDI32.DLL): Every time an application writes to the screen, it uses a GDI service. This Windows component takes care of fonts, printer services, the display, color management, and every other artistic aspect of Windows that users can see as they use your application.

- User (USER.EXE or USER32.DLL): Windows is all about just that—windows. It needs a manager to keep track of all the windows that applications create to display various types of information. However, User only begins there. Every time your application displays an icon or pushbutton, it's using some type of User component function. It's easier to think of the User component of the Windows API as a work manager; it helps you organize things and keep them straight.

There's actually one more piece to the Windows API, but it's a small piece that your application will never use. Both Windows NT and Windows 95 still start out as 16-bit applications in order to implement plug and play. The plug and play BIOS contains separate sections for real mode and 16-bit protected-mode calls. If Windows started out in 32-bit mode, it couldn't call the plug and play BIOS to set up all your devices without a lot of overhead (see the discussion of thunking in the next section to understand why). All device configuration has to occur before Windows actually starts the GUI.

However, 16-bit mode operations end very soon after you start Windows 95. The user shell is a 32-bit application. As soon as the 16-bit kernel sees the call for the shell, it loads an application called VWIN32.386. This little program loads the three 32-bit DLLs that form the Win32 API. Once it completes this task, VWIN32.386 returns control to the 16-bit kernel, which in turn calls the 32-bit kernel. Windows runs in 32-bit mode from that point on.

The Base System

The Base System component of Windows 95 and Windows NT contains all the operating-system-specific services. This is the Windows core, the part that has to be operating in order for Windows to perform its work. Notice that Figure 5.4 contains several elements that Figure 5.3 doesn't. Windows NT is far more robust than Windows 95 and needs additional components to get the job done. The following paragraphs describe each part of the Base System in detail.

- File Management Subsystem: This part of the Base System provides an interface to all the block devices connected to your machine. It doesn't matter how the connection is made— physically or through a network. All that matters is that your machine can access the device. The big thing to remember about the File Management Subsystem is that Windows 95 no longer relies on DOS to manage files. Of course, Windows NT never relied on DOS in the first place.

- Network Subsystem: Windows for Workgroups was the first version of Windows to address the networking needs of the workgroup. It even incorporated networking as part of the operating system rather than as a third-party add-on product. Windows 95 extends this capability. Not only can you run a Microsoft peer-to-peer network, but Windows 95 provides protected-mode hooks for most major LAN products as well. In fact, you can keep more than one network active at a time. The modular nature of the Network Subsystem enables other vendors to add to Windows 95-inherent capabilities through the use of VxDs (virtual anything drivers). Windows NT provides an even more complex networking scheme. For example, it includes much stronger network security and the resources required to implement domains.

- Operating System Services: This is the part of the operating system that deals with features such as plug and play. It also fulfills miscellaneous user and operating system requests. For example, every time the user asks Windows for the time of day, he is requesting a service from this Windows component.

- Virtual Machine Manager: Ever wonder where the exact center of Windows is? This is it; this is the component that holds everything else together. The Virtual Machine Manager takes care of task scheduling, and it starts and stops every application on the system (including any DOS applications that you might run). This operating system component manages virtual memory on your machine as well. Of course, your application uses the Windows API to make the request instead of talking with this part of the system directly. Since the Virtual Machine Manager handles all memory allocations, it also has to act as a DPMI (DOS Protected Mode Interface) server for DOS applications that run in protected mode. When a DOS application makes a memory request, it's actually calling routines in this component of Windows. As with Windows applications, DOS applications can't directly access this component of Windows. The DOS application uses a DOS extender API to make its call. Finally, the Virtual Machine Manager is responsible for intertask communication. All this means is that all DDE and OLE requests filter through this section of the operating system.

- Device Drivers: Windows would never know what to do with your system if it weren't for the lowly device driver. This bit of specialty code acts as an interpreter. It takes Windows requests and provides them to the device in a format it can understand. Windows 95 supports two forms of device drivers. The first type is the real-mode device driver that you used with Windows 3.1. The problem with using this type of driver is that Windows has to keep switching between real and protected mode to use it. Windows 95 also provides the VxD, or virtual device driver, which lets Windows talk to the devices on your system without switching to real mode. There are three reasons to use VxDs over standard real-mode device drivers: Your system remains more stable, runs faster, and recovers from errors better. Obviously, Windows NT only provides support for the virtual 32-bit driver. There's no real mode driver support in this environment.

- Object Manager: This component of Windows NT creates, manages, and deletes objects. Most of these objects represent abstract operating system resources like memory. The Windows NT environment is a lot more complex and it uses more modular components than Windows 95 so it needs this extra base system component. Every time you need to create a new system object like an icon or dialog box, you call the Object Manager.

- Security Reference Monitor: Windows NT provides a very major feature that you'll never find in Windows 95—Class C2 level security that restricts access to computer resources on a need to know basis. Implementing this level of security requires a lot of work on the part of the operating system in general and this module in particular. You'll find all the qualifications for C2 level security in DOD manual 5200.28-STD. The security levels range from Class D (least secure) to Class A (most secure). In essence, this added level of security allows government agencies to use Windows NT in a secure environment. It probably won't affect you much as a Delphi programmer unless you write applications for the government. There have been rumors that a future version of Windows NT may even support higher security levels than this. Part of the Security Reference Monitor's job is to monitor system resources. This prevents one process or thread from grabbing all the system resources like memory. The bottom line is that the module prevents the operating system from losing control for too long. An application is forced to work with the operating system in such a way that every process and thread gets a fair share of the computing resources. Finally, the Security Reference Monitor provides statistical data that a network administrator can use to monitor system performance.

- Process Manager: Windows NT also supports a wider range of processing options than Windows 95 does. Multiprocessing environments require the use of heavier duty process management techniques. The Process Manager creates, manages, and terminates both processes (applications) and threads (streams of execution within an application). It also allows the operating system to suspend and resume processes and threads as needed to keep the overall system stable. Like the Security Reference Monitor, the Process Manager provides statistical data that a network administrator can use to monitor system performance.

DOS Virtual Machine

I've separated the DOS Virtual Machine component of Windows from the other components for several reasons. DOS applications have formed the basis for using the PC for a long time. In fact, for many years, nothing else was available. Yet most of these applications were written at a time when the standard PC ran one application and one application only. That one application had total control of the entire machine.

Windows 95 deals with DOS applications differently than it deals with the Windows-specific applications on your machine. Each DOS application runs on what Intel terms a *virtual machine*. Essentially, the processor fools the application into thinking that it is the only application running on your machine at the moment. Each virtual machine has its own memory space and access to devices on the system. The amazing thing is that you can have many virtual machines running on your one physical machine at a time. We'll take a more detailed look at the DOS Virtual Machine later. Suffice it to say that Windows 95 has to literally perform backflips to make this whole concept work properly, especially when you consider Windows-hostile applications such as games.

Windows NT takes a slightly different approach to the whole virtual machine picture. It creates a DOS Virtual Machine, then executes a copy of 16-bit Windows on it to run your 16-bit applications. All of your 16-bit Windows applications run in precisely the same environment they did before. The big difference is that they are completely encapsulated and separated from every other application type running on your machine. Of course, all the 16-bit applications share one address space, just like they did under Windows 3.x. DOS applications all run under separate DOS Virtual Machines, just like they do under Windows 95. Again, the big difference would be in the way that these virtual machines are handled. Windows NT provides a much higher level of encapsulation than Windows 95 does.

The Plug and Play BIOS

The first question you're all going to ask is why we should even worry about plug and play (PNP) in a book on programming. Before now, you as a programmer could always count on a specific set of devices remaining in place during any given session. For that matter, you could probably count on those devices being present from session to session for the most part. That isn't true any longer. The use of notebook computers and PCMCIA components means that you can't count on a piece of hardware being present from one moment to the next any longer. It means that your application has to fail gracefully when it expects to find a piece of hardware that the user just unplugged. Fortunately for you, Windows does provide a wealth of API functions for dealing with this situation. Now you know why we need to worry about PNP, but just what is it?

PNP was big news for Windows 95. Windows NT will also implement this feature completely in the next version (it already does to a certain extent). The first misconception that I want to clear up is that this is some new piece of "magic" that Microsoft pulled from its bag of tricks. PNP isn't magic, nor is it even all that new. The only thing that Windows does differently is actually use the capabilities provided by PNP hardware.

Let's go back a bit. The very first MCA (microchannel architecture) machine produced by IBM contained everything needed by PNP except one thing—an operating system. The same can be said of many EISA machines.

The problem wasn't simply a matter of adding some capabilities to an operating system. You have to build this feature into every aspect of the operating system; it can't be added on. In addition, you need routines that will handle problems between the various pieces of hardware vying for a particular port address or interrupt. Finally, the BIOS itself has to provide a standardized interface, and these earlier offerings were anything but standard.

PNP is actually the work of three system components: hardware, BIOS, and operating system. The BIOS queries all the system components during startup. It activates essential system components such as the disk drive and display adapter. Everything else waits on the sidelines until the operating system boots. During the boot process, the operating system finishes the task of assigning interrupts and port addresses to every system component. It also asks the BIOS to provide a list of previous assignments so that it won't use them again.

The EISA and MCA BIOS weren't prepared for this kind of interaction with the operating system. Enter the PNP BIOS. This isn't the work of Microsoft, but of Compaq Computer Corporation, Phoenix Technologies Ltd., and Intel Corporation.

In addition to cooperating with the operating system, the PNP BIOS provides something very important that the EISA and MCA BIOS don't—protected-mode routines. The current BIOS specification only requires vendors to provide 16-bit protected-mode routines. That's why Windows still starts in 16-bit mode instead of 32-bit mode. In addition, that's one of the reasons why a real-mode DOS stub (a functional subset of the DOS that you are familiar with) is part of the picture when using Windows 95. (The version of real-mode DOS provided with Windows 95 also executes the AUTOEXEC.BAT and CONFIG.SYS.) You can't use the protected-mode routines without first gathering the information that the BIOS needs in real mode. The real mode DOS stub performs this function for the BIOS. Since Windows NT doesn't support real mode drivers, it uses a special protected mode loader to check the PNP status. There's no DOS in Windows NT (at least not during startup).

Note: A few people out there will try to convince you that their systems are fully PNP-compatible. If you look inside, you'll see shiny new components, all of which are indeed PNP-compatible. But, unbeknownst to you, something is missing. A lot of folks find out too late that their system lacks a PNP BIOS. So how can you avoid the same fate?

Intel, inspired by the PNP BIOS problems, created a test utility to check your PNP BIOS. You can download a copy of this BIOS test program from the plug and play forum (GO PLUGPLAY) on CompuServe. Look in Library 6 for BIOTST.ZIP. You might want to check out BIO10A.DOC (BIO1A.ZIP) while you're at it. This specification talks about the capabilities of the plug and play BIOS. It also provides some information about the peripheral board setup.

When looking at a PNP-compatible system, you should see a lot more than just three different entities cooperating to provide automatic system configuration. PNP wouldn't be worth all the hubbub if that's all it provided. The following paragraphs provide a list of additional features that you get as part of a PNP system.

- Identify installed devices: Windows automatically detects all of the plug and play components attached to your system. This means that you need to provide a minimum of information during installation and nothing at all during subsequent reboots. Contrast this with the almost continuous flow of information needed under Windows 3.x.

- Determine device resource needs: Every device on your computer needs resources in the form of processor cycles, input/output ports, DMA channels, memory, and interrupts. Windows works with the BIOS and peripheral devices to meet these needs without any intervention.

- Automatic system configuration updates and resource conflict detection: All of this communication between peripheral devices, the BIOS, and the operating system allows Windows to create a system configuration without any user intervention. The Device Manager configuration blocks are grayed out because the user doesn't need to supply this information anymore. The enhanced level of communication also allows Windows to poll the peripherals for alternative port and interrupt settings when a conflict with another device occurs.

- Device driver loading and unloading: CONFIG.SYS and AUTOEXEC.BAT used to contain line after line of device driver and TSR statements. This is because the system had to bring these devices online before it loaded the command processor and Windows 3.x. Windows 95 can actually maintain or even enhance the performance of a plug-and-play–compatible system without using an AUTOEXEC.BAT or CONFIG.SYS (Windows NT never needed them). Plug and play compatibility allows Windows to load and unload any device drivers that your system needs dynamically.

- Configuration change notification: Plug and play might make system configuration changes automatic, but that doesn't mean that Windows 95 leaves you in the dark. Every time the system configuration changes, Windows notifies you by displaying a dialog box on-screen. Essentially, this dialog box tells you what changed. This capability provides an additional side benefit. Windows also notifies you whenever your equipment experiences some kind of failure. When a piece of equipment fails, Windows notices that it is no longer online. Plug and play requires three-way communication, and a defective device usually fails to communicate. Instead of your finding out that you no longer have access to a drive or other device when you need it most, Windows notifies you of the change immediately after it takes place.

Getting 16-Bit and 32-Bit Applications to Work Together

Windows 95 and Windows NT both run a combination of 16-bit and 32-bit applications. All those older applications and device drivers you use now have to work within the same environment as the new 32-bit drivers and applications that Windows provides. You already know how Windows takes care of separating the two by using different memory schemes. The 16-bit applications work within their own virtual machine area. It would be nice if things ended there, but they can't.

There are times when 16-bit and 32-bit applications have to talk to each other. This doesn't just apply to programs the user uses to perform work, but to device drivers and other types of Windows applications as well. Most Windows applications use a memory structure called the *stack* to transfer information from one application to another. Think of the stack as a database of variables. Each record in this database is a fixed length so that every application knows how to grab information from it. Here's where the problems start. The stack for 32-bit applications is 32 bits wide. That makes sense. It makes equal sense that the stack for 16-bit applications should be 16 bits wide. See the problem?

Of course, the problems are only beginning. What happens when you need to send a 32-bit value from a 16-bit application to a 32-bit application? The 32-bit application will expect to see the whole value in the EAX register. On the other hand, the 16-bit application expects to see the value in a combination of the DX and AX registers. This same problem translates to pointers as well. A 32-bit application, for example, will use the SS:ESP register pair to point to the stack.

But wait, there's more! Remember that 16-bit applications use a segmented address space. An address consists of a selector and an offset. A 16-bit application combines these two pieces to form a complete address. On the other hand, 32-bit applications use a flat address space. They wouldn't know what to do with a selector if you gave them one. All they want is the actual address within the total realm of available memory. So how do you send the address of a string from a 16-bit to a 32-bit application?

By now you're probably wondering how Windows keeps 16-bit and 32-bit applications working together. After all, there are a number of inconsistencies and incompatibilities to deal with. The stack is only the tip of the incompatibility iceberg. It's easy to envision a method of converting 16-bit data to a 32-bit format. All you really need to do is pad the front end of the variable with zeros. But how does a 32-bit application send data to a 16-bit application? If the 32-bit application just dumps a wide variable onto the stack, the 16-bit application will never know what do to with the information it receives. Clearly the data needs to go through some type of conversion. Windows uses something called the *thunk layer* to allow 16-bit and 32-bit applications to communicate. Figure 5.7 shows the interaction of 16-bit and 32-bit applications through the thunk layer.

As you can see, the three components of the API layer also provide translation services in addition to the other services they perform. Each API component translates the data and addresses within its area of expertise. For example, the two GDI components translate all graphics data between 16-bit and 32-bit applications.

Most thunking is pretty straightforward. For example, Windows simply moves register data to the appropriate register. The thunk layer builds a new stack to meet the needs of the application receiving it. Address translation takes a little more work. In addition, address translation is very expensive timewise. Every time Windows has to translate an address, it must perform several selector loads. The processor has to verify every selector load, so these translations can get cumbersome.

Figure 5.7.

The thunk layer makes it possible for 16-bit and 32-bit applications to coexist peacefully under Windows.

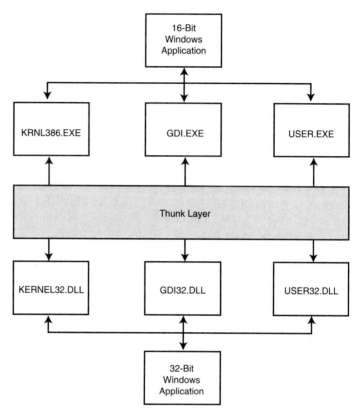

Fortunately, you as an application programmer won't have to worry too much about the actual thunk process as long as you use all 32-bit code or you rely on Delphi's built-in features. What you do need to worry about is making certain that the process actually takes place when calling a piece of code that needs it. For example, if you write your own DLL and it calls a piece of 16-bit code, then you'll need to make sure that the proper changes get made. If you use straight API calls, there is usually a 32-bit version of the call even if Windows relies on 16-bit code to implement the call. Windows 95 is just packed with routines of this type since it still contains a lot of 16-bit code. Your 32-bit application will take a performance hit every time that you use an API call that requires a thunk in this environment. Windows NT doesn't have this problem since it's mostly 32-bit code.

Windows and DLLs

Under DOS, an application must contain every component it needs in order to execute. The programmer links in library support for graphics, low-level utilities, and a variety of other needs. Of course, this whole scenario is based on the fact that the application is the only thing running under DOS.

Windows is a different kind of environment. There's always more than one task running under Windows. Somewhere along the way, someone figured out that if you have multiple applications running, there might be some duplicate code out there as well. For example, the display routines used by one application are probably the same as the display routines used by another application at some particular level. The same person probably figured out that you could reduce the overall memory requirements of a system if you allowed all the applications to share these redundant pieces of code instead of loading them from scratch for each application.

The DLL (dynamic link library) is the culmination of just such an idea. There are two forms of linking under Windows (or OS/2 or UNIX, for that matter). The first link combines all the object modules required to create a unique application. That link cycle happens right after the programmer finishes compiling the code. The second link cycle happens when the user goes to load the application. This is where the DLL comes in.

Every Windows application has unresolved references to functions. Microsoft calls them import library calls. What these calls do is load a DLL containing the code required to satisfy that function call. If the DLL happens to be in memory when Windows calls it, Windows increments the DLL's usage level to indicate that more than one application is using the DLL. When an application stops using a DLL, Windows decrements its usage level. When the DLL's usage count goes to 0, Windows can unload it from memory. In effect, using DLLs can save quite a bit of memory when you're loading multiple applications.

So what does this have to do with the API? The Windows API starts with three files, as just described. However, these three files call other files—DLLs, to be exact. Rather than create three huge files, Microsoft chose to reduce the size of the Windows kernel by using DLLs.

This capability also makes Windows more flexible. Consider printer support. All you need to do to add printer support for a new printer is copy some files to disk. At least one of those files will be a DLL. Every printer DLL contains the same entry points (function names), so Windows doesn't need to learn anything new to support the printer. The only thing it has to do is install a new DLL. Your application performs the same task when you tell it to print. It looks at the DLLs currently installed for the system. The application doesn't have to care whether the printer is a dot matrix or a laser. All it needs to know how to do is tell the printer to print; the DLL takes care of the rest.

Direct API Access

Now that you know about the Windows API and have at least an overall understanding of the architectural details behind it, let's take a look at what you need to do to use the Windows API in an application. The first thing you need to know is that Delphi helps you out quite a bit by providing several preprogrammed units. For example, what if you want to access the common dialogs? Delphi helps you out by providing the COMDLG unit. Using the Delphi-specific Windows API help will tell you which unit to use when accessing a specific part of the API.

Of course, there's more to accessing the Windows API than just loading a preprogrammed unit and calling one or more functions in it. Remember that Windows is a user-oriented operating system. The user can move from place to place on the Desktop without much regard for which applications are currently running. One moment your application could have the focus, another it might be in the background.

Before we get mired in too many details, let's take a look at some practical examples of accessing the Windows API. Of course, these applications won't show you every aspect of using the API, but they will help you get your feet wet. The following sections look at several common API access situations like determining the system status by looking at the Windows flags.

Looking at the Windows Flags

Windows doesn't keep the status of anything a secret—at least of anything that you really need to know about as a programmer. One of my favorite things to check during the days of the 80386 was whether a machine had a math coprocessor. Using the math coprocessor to speed the execution of real number math was one of the things I did to give my applications that snappy feel that people expect. Today you'll find that a wide variety of programming environments use the math coprocessor by default if you specify certain libraries. Of course, C has always provided this capability through the use of various math coprocessor specific and emulation libraries.

Note: I'm covering both the 16-bit and 32-bit versions of the Windows API in this section. There are several reasons for this and you really need to think about them as you read. The main reason I'm doing this is to show you that the two APIs do provide similar functionality, but that the 32-bit API's support is a lot more versatile and updated to meet the needs of today's programmer. I also want to encourage you to take a look at both APIs. In more than a few cases the 32-bit version of a call provides a mere extension of the flexibility of the 16-bit call. Most of the calls use the same name with an "EX" extension. I find that these little "additions" can make it difficult to find something in the help file. If you can't find a function because Microsoft superseded it with a new one, then try adding an EX extension to the old call name. In this particular case, the function names are totally different. However, Microsoft is pretty good about documenting these name differences in their help file. It only takes a few seconds to look up a missing function call that could cost you hours in programming time otherwise.

There are a lot of different flags in Windows and you need to use a variety of API calls to get their status, but we'll concentrate on the GetWinFlags function for now. This is the 16-bit function call that anyone using Delphi 1.0 will need to use. The GetWinFlags function can tell you a few things about the hardware your program is running on. The following list tells you the types of information you will find.

- Math Coprocessor Present—This function won't tell you what kind of math coprocessor the machine has, but it will tell you whether or not one is present. Obviously, the 80387 math coprocessor provides many transcendental functions that the 80287 and below don't provide. I especially like the way it handles trigonometric functions. Unfortunately, the math library provided with Windows makes these functions inaccessible to the programmer. You'd have to write your own math library if you actually wanted to differentiate between an 80287 and an 80387. Suffice it to say that I hope Microsoft fixes this problem sometime in the near future.

- Processor Type—You can check for a specific processor type on the host machine. Windows differentiates between the 80286, 80386, and the 80486 in its present state. Knowing this information could help someone writing a real time program customized application speed to the capabilities of the machine.

- Windows Operating Mode—This is becoming less of an issue as new versions of Windows come out. It certainly isn't an issue at all with Windows NT or Windows 95. However, you can still use this particular flag to determine whether you are in enhanced or standard mode.

- Paged Memory—Most machines use paged memory these days, so this flag won't provide too much useful information either. A machine that uses paged memory usually provides better memory handing capabilities than a machine that doesn't. Obviously this is another flag that could help you adjust the speed of a real time application to meet the capabilities of the installed hardware.

- Protected Mode—You'll notice that I didn't even check the status of this flag in the example that follows. Every version of Windows since 3.1 sets this flag automatically, so it doesn't really pay to check its status. Besides, do you really question whether the host machine is operating in protected mode? Hopefully Microsoft will remove this flag and replace it with something we can use sometime in the future. I really doubt that too many people have old applications that need to know whether they are in protected mode or not.

So, what will you 32-bit users need? Microsoft chose not to support the GetWinFlags function when it created the 32-bit Windows API. They provide a new function call GetSystemInfo. This new function adds support that you'll really need in the 32-bit environment like the number of processors that a machine supports. It's unfortunate that the new call doesn't support some of the old features, but then how many 80386 machines are still out there? You'll also see another difference in this function. It uses a structure instead of a variable to return the system information. This makes the GetSystemInfo function a lot more flexible than its 16-bit counterpart. Microsoft can expand a structure if need be to handle new computing situations or add new values to existing entries as new hardware appears on the market. The following list tells you all about the entries in the system information structure.

- OEM ID/Processor Architecuture—This entry defines who made the processor or its architecture type. The current call supports Intel, MIPS, Alpha, and Power PC machines.

- Page Size—It's always helpful to know just how big a page the operating system is using. The page size determines how big a chunk of memory that the processor moves at a time. The processor manages memory in pages, not by the byte since this would consume too many processing cycles.

- Minimum/Maximum Application Address—These two entries tell you the minimum and maximum memory address that an application or DLL can access. It doesn't necessarily reflect the amount of memory in the machine, but it does reflect the amount of usable memory. Of course, your application won't get to use all of it, there are other applications that need memory too.

- Active Processor Mask—Multiple processors have become a fact of life in today's computing environment. That means you have one more item to think about from a theoretical perspective. A machine with more processors can provide a better level of processing—you can stick more things in the background without bogging the processor down. However, there is no guarantee that every processor in the machine is even working, much less available for your use. This entry tells you which processors are active. It's a 32-bit word—one bit for each processor that Windows NT can support. To find out which processors are active, just look for a 1 in its bit position starting with 0.

- Number of Processors—There are times where you just need to know the number of processors a machine contains. For example, you might want to tell the user how many processors their machine has from within a Help About dialog box or within a maintenance screen. That's what this particular entry will tell you, the actual number of processors in the machine. It won't tell you how many of those processors are actually active though; look at the previous entry for that information.

- Processor Type—This entry provides you with better information about your processor than the Processor Architecture entry did. It returns an actual processor number like 386 for an 80386 machine. You'll find values here for the Intel, MIPS, and Alpha machines—use the Processor Level entry if you have a Power PC.

- Allocation Granularity—While the Page Size entry tells you how the processor moves memory, this entry tells you how it allocates it. The Page Size entry is always less than or equal to this entry. The standard allocation size for Intel processors is 64 KB, the size of a segment. Other processors will have a different allocation size.

- Processor Level—As far as an Intel processor is concerned, this entry won't matter much. It returns the same 80386 or above entry that the Processor Type entry did. Other processor vendors actually provide a processor level value though. For example, the Power PC currently provides six levels including: 601, 603, 604, 603+, 604+, and 620.

- Processor Revision—This is an important entry if you're looking for specific problems associated with a processor. For example, you can use this entry to determine the step level and stepping of an Intel processor. One way you can do this is part of an installation process. Windows 95 uses it to detect the B step 80386 processor. That particular processor won't work with Windows 95. You'll have to refer to vendor documentation to find out the specifics of each processor step and stepping level.

It's time to write our first API function. In this case we're going to do one of my favorite activities, check the hardware status of the machine using the GetSystemInfo function. I created the simple form shown in Figure 5.8. All you really need is some type of display area and a Test button. I used a memo control for my display area, but you could just as easily use something like a group of single line edits to accomplish the same purpose.

Figure 5.8.
This simple form will allow you to build a simple test routine for the Windows Flag function calls.

Note: If you're using Delphi 1.0, you must add the WinProcs and WinFlags units to your application before it will work. Simply use the Add File to Project button on the Project speedbar. Delphi will automatically add the files to the Uses statement for you. These two units provide all the calls required for the Delphi supported Windows API routines. The Delphi help file will usually tell you about the WinProcs unit, but fails to mention the WinFlags unit. Adding them both to your program usually results in fewer problems along the way. It also allows you to quickly check the contents of the units as needed during programming. Delphi 2.0 replaces these two units with a single Windows unit. Fortunately, the new version of Delphi can still work with the two unit call—it performs an automatic conversion for you as part of the library setup.

Obviously the "program" can't do anything yet since we haven't attached any code to the Test button. Just double click on the Test button and add this code to your test unit. We'll use the code in Listing 5.1 to test the status of the various hardware components on the host machine. Notice that the function's output appears in the memo control area.

Listing 5.1. Code to test hardware status.

```
procedure TForm1.Button1Click(Sender: TObject);
const
    {Processor families.}
    PROCESSOR_ARCHITECTURE_INTEL = 0;
    PROCESSOR_ARCHITECTURE_MIPS = 1;
    PROCESSOR_ARCHITECTURE_ALPHA = 2;
```

continues

Listing 5.1. continued

```
        PROCESSOR_ARCHITECTURE_PPC = 3;
        PROCESSOR_ARCHITECTURE_UNKNOWN = $FFFF;

        {Processor types.}
        PROCESSOR_INTEL_386 = 386;
        PROCESSOR_INTEL_486 = 486;
        PROCESSOR_INTEL_PENTIUM = 586;
        PROCESSOR_MIPS_R4000 = 4000;
        PROCESSOR_ALPHA_21064 = 21064;

var
    SystemInfo: TSystemInfo;                 {Status variable}
begin

    {Clear the current comment from the memo control.}
    Memo1.Lines.Clear;

    {Get the current Windows Flags.}
    GetSystemInfo(SystemInfo);

    {Display the information.}
    with SystemInfo do
    begin

    {Display the current processor family.}
    case wProcessorArchitecture of
        PROCESSOR_ARCHITECTURE_INTEL: Memo1.Lines.Add('Intel Processor Found');
        PROCESSOR_ARCHITECTURE_MIPS: Memo1.Lines.Add('MIPS Processor Found');
        PROCESSOR_ARCHITECTURE_ALPHA: Memo1.Lines.Add('Alpha Processor Found');
        PROCESSOR_ARCHITECTURE_PPC: Memo1.Lines.Add('Power PC Processor Found');
    end;

    {Display the number of processors.}
    Memo1.Lines.Add('Number of Processors: ' + IntToStr(dwNumberOfProcessors));

    {Display the processor type.}
    case dwProcessorType of
        PROCESSOR_INTEL_386: Memo1.Lines.Add('Processor Type Is: 80386');
        PROCESSOR_INTEL_486: Memo1.Lines.Add('Processor Type Is: 80486');
        PROCESSOR_INTEL_PENTIUM: Memo1.Lines.Add('Processor Type Is: Pentium');
        PROCESSOR_MIPS_R4000: Memo1.Lines.Add('Processor Type Is: R4000');
        PROCESSOR_ALPHA_21064: Memo1.Lines.Add('Processor Type Is: 21064');
    end;

    {Display Memory Statistics.}
    Memo1.Lines.Add('');
    Memo1.Lines.Add('Memory Statistics');

    {Display the memory page size and allocation granularity.}
    Memo1.Lines.Add('Current Page Size is: ' + IntToStr(dwPageSize));
    Memo1.Lines.Add('Allocation Granularity is: ' + IntToStr(dwAllocationGranularity));

    end; {with SystemInfo do}

end;
end.
```

Now all you need to do is run the application. You should get output similar to that shown in Figure 5.9. Notice that my machine has a single 80486 processor. The operating system allocates memory in 64 KB chunks and moves it around in 4 KB pages. Obviously this isn't all the information you could obtain from the GetSystemInfo function, but it does give you a good idea of what's possible.

Figure 5.9.

Most machines now come equipped with an 80486 or above processor, but determining the number and type of processors can help you tailor your application for a specific machine type.

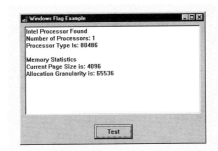

Manipulating the Serial Port

Communicating with other people has become less of a luxury and more of a requirement. Not only do we have local BBSs, online services, and custom applications like pcAnywhere to deal with, but there's the Internet to consider as well. Corporate America, and to a lesser extent everyone else, can't get by without some form of computer communication. In fact, I checked my machine this morning and was startled to find five communication programs and at least two other programs with their own built-in communication capabilities.

Suffice it to say that there is a good chance you will spend some time working with some type of communications in your application. As we all know, communication requires some type of inter-action with the serial port. Now, the last thing I want to think is that there is any lack of existing software on the market to take care of your communication needs. One look at Appendix A, "A Guide to VBXs and OCXs," will tell you that more than a few people are interested in communications. In fact, after a few hours of trying to work with the serial port using Delphi's built-in capabilities and the Windows API, I'm sure you'll agree with me that those third party libraries look good.

However, there are times when you will need to do some type of very quick check and not much more. It helps to know the location of a modem, for example, and that only takes a few seconds to check. It hardly pays for you to import an entire library of functions if your only purpose is to check for the modem attached to COM1. It's also handy to know if there's some kind of a problem with the serial port. For example, I had one application that left the port open. Leaving the port open effectively locks everyone else out. With that in mind, let's take a look at how you would interact with the serial port under Windows. We'll use the same form as shown in Figure 5.8, a simple memo control and Test button, to perform this task. I did lengthen my form and memo control to make it easier to see all the port data at a glance.

The code in this example polls the COM1 serial port to see if we can access it. You'll notice that we have to use a device control block (DCB) to retrieve the data. Windows uses a plethora of structures to pass data from one location to another. Doing so saves on stack space and makes it possible for Windows to communicate with a program even if large quantities of data are required. Our example shows all the kinds of data you can expect to find in the port DCB. The same DCB is used for serial and parallel ports, but parallel ports disregard a lot of the entries. Once our example interprets the results of the query, it displays the results in the memo control. Listing 5.2 contains the code you'll use to make the Test button get the job done.

Listing 5.2. Code for the Test button.

```
procedure TForm1.Button1Click(Sender: TObject);
const
        {Serial port flag values.}
    DCB_BINARY = $0001;
    DCB_PARITY = $0002;
    DCB_OUTXCTSFLOW = $0004;
    DCB_OUTXDSRFLOW = $0008;
    DCB_DTRENABLE = $0010;
    DCB_DTRFLOW = $0020;
    DCB_DSRSENSE = $0040;
    DCB_TXCONTONXOFF = $0080;
    DCB_OUTX = $0100;
    DCB_INX = $0200;
    DCB_PECHAR = $0400;
    DCB_NULL = $0800;
    DCB_RTSENABLE = $1000;
    DCB_RTSFLOW = $2000;
    DCB_RTSTOGGLE = $3000;
    DCB_ABORT = $4000;

    {Tab character.}
    CHR_TAB = chr(9);
var
    lpszCommName: PChar;              {Serial Port Name}
    hCommPort: THandle;              {Port handle.}
    iAccess: Integer;              {Type of access needed.}
    dwCreation: DWORD;              {Creation flags.}
    lResult: BOOL;              {Boolean return code from functions.}
    DeviceControlBlock: TDCB;              {Serial Port Control Stucture}
    sCommBuffer: String;              {Communications buffer.}
    sNumConv: String;              {Conversion string.}
begin

    {Define the parameters for the first port, then open it.}
    lpszCommName := 'COM1';
    iAccess := GENERIC_READ or GENERIC_WRITE;
    dwCreation := OPEN_EXISTING;
    hCommPort := CreateFile(lpszCommName, iAccess, 0, NIL, dwCreation, 0, 0);

    {Check to see if we opened it sucessfully.}
    if hCommPort >= 0 then
      begin
      Memo1.Lines.Add('The port is open.');
```

```
{Get the Port Status.}
lResult := GetCommState(hCommPort, DeviceControlBlock);

{Were we successful in querying the port?}
if lResult then
   begin
   Memo1.Lines.Add('Successfully queried serial port.');

   {Display the current baud rate.}
   case DeviceControlBlock.Baudrate of
        CBR_110: Memo1.Lines.Add('Baud rate: 110');
        CBR_300: Memo1.Lines.Add('Baud rate: 300');
        CBR_600: Memo1.Lines.Add('Baud rate: 600');
        CBR_1200: Memo1.Lines.Add('Baud rate: 1200');
        CBR_2400: Memo1.Lines.Add('Baud rate: 2400');
        CBR_4800: Memo1.Lines.Add('Baud rate: 4800');
        CBR_9600: Memo1.Lines.Add('Baud rate: 9600');
        CBR_14400: Memo1.Lines.Add('Baud rate: 14400');
        CBR_19200: Memo1.Lines.Add('Baud rate: 19200');
        CBR_38400: Memo1.Lines.Add('Baud rate: 38400');
        CBR_56000: Memo1.Lines.Add('Baud rate: 56000');
        CBR_128000: Memo1.Lines.Add('Baud rate: 128000');
        CBR_256000: Memo1.Lines.Add('Baud rate: 256000');
   else
        {If Windows didn't use a define, then it provided a number.}
        Str(DeviceControlBlock.Baudrate, sCommBuffer);
        Memo1.Lines.Add('Baud rate: ' + sCommBuffer);
   end;

   {Display the byte size.}
   Str(DeviceControlBlock.ByteSize, sCommBuffer);
   Memo1.Lines.Add('Byte size: ' + sCommBuffer);

   {Display the parity setting.}
   case DeviceControlBlock.Parity of
        EVENPARITY: Memo1.Lines.Add('Parity: EVEN');
        MARKPARITY: Memo1.Lines.Add('Parity: MARK');
        NOPARITY: Memo1.Lines.Add('Parity: NO');
        ODDPARITY: Memo1.Lines.Add('Parity: ODD');
   end;

   {Display the number of stop bits.}
   case DeviceControlBlock.StopBits of
        ONESTOPBIT: Memo1.Lines.Add('Stop Bits: 1');
        ONE5STOPBITS: Memo1.Lines.Add('Stop Bits: 1.5');
        TWOSTOPBITS: Memo1.Lines.Add('Stop Bits: 2');
   end;

   {Check the mode flag status.}
   if (DeviceControlBlock.Flags and DCB_BINARY) = DCB_BINARY then
      Memo1.Lines.Add('Mode: Binary')
   else
        Memo1.Lines.Add('Mode: Character');

   {Check the signal flag status.}
   Memo1.Lines.Add(' ');
   Memo1.Lines.Add('Signal Flags:');
```

continues

Listing 5.2. continued

```
   if (DeviceControlBlock.Flags and DCB_RTSENABLE) = DCB_RTSENABLE then
      sCommBuffer := 'RTS: Enabled'
   else
       sCommBuffer := 'RTS: Disabled';

   if (DeviceControlBlock.Flags and DCB_PARITY) = DCB_PARITY then
      sCommBuffer := sCommBuffer + CHR_TAB + 'CTS: Enabled'
   else
       sCommBuffer := sCommBuffer + CHR_TAB + 'CTS: Disabled';

   if (DeviceControlBlock.Flags and DCB_DTRENABLE) = DCB_DTRENABLE then
      sCommBuffer := sCommBuffer + CHR_TAB + 'DTR: Enabled'
   else
       sCommBuffer := sCommBuffer + CHR_TAB + 'DTR: Disabled';
   Memo1.Lines.Add(sCommBuffer);

   {Check the flow flag status.}
   Memo1.Lines.Add(' ');
   Memo1.Lines.Add('Flow Control:');
   if (DeviceControlBlock.Flags and DCB_RTSFLOW) = DCB_RTSFLOW then
      sCommBuffer := 'RTS: Enabled'
   else
       sCommBuffer := 'RTS: Disabled';

   if (DeviceControlBlock.Flags and DCB_OUTXCTSFLOW) = DCB_OUTXCTSFLOW then
      sCommBuffer := sCommBuffer + CHR_TAB + 'CTS: Enabled'
   else
       sCommBuffer := sCommBuffer + CHR_TAB + 'CTS: Disabled';

   if (DeviceControlBlock.Flags and DCB_DTRFLOW) = DCB_DTRFLOW then
      sCommBuffer := sCommBuffer + CHR_TAB + 'DTR: Enabled'
   else
       sCommBuffer := sCommBuffer + CHR_TAB + 'DTR: Disabled';

   if (DeviceControlBlock.Flags and DCB_OUTXDSRFLOW) = DCB_OUTXDSRFLOW then
      sCommBuffer := sCommBuffer + CHR_TAB + 'DSR: Enabled'
   else
       sCommBuffer := sCommBuffer + CHR_TAB + 'DSR: Disabled';
   Memo1.Lines.Add(sCommBuffer);

   if (DeviceControlBlock.Flags and DCB_OUTX) = DCB_OUTX then
      sCommBuffer := 'XON/XOFF Xmit: Enabled'
   else
       sCommBuffer := 'XON/XOFF Xmit: Disabled';

   if (DeviceControlBlock.Flags and DCB_INX) = DCB_INX then
      sCommBuffer := sCommBuffer + CHR_TAB + 'XON/XOFF Receive: Enabled'
   else
       sCommBuffer := sCommBuffer + CHR_TAB + 'XON/XOFF Receive: Disabled';
   Memo1.Lines.Add(sCommBuffer);

   Memo1.Lines.Add(' ');
   Memo1.Lines.Add('Replacement Character Status:');
   if (DeviceControlBlock.Flags and DCB_PECHAR) = DCB_PECHAR then
      Memo1.Lines.Add('Parity Error Replacement: Enabled')
   else
       Memo1.Lines.Add('Parity Error Replacement: Disabled');
```

```
          if (DeviceControlBlock.Flags and DCB_NULL) = DCB_NULL then
             Memo1.Lines.Add('Null Character Discard: Enabled')
          else
              Memo1.Lines.Add('Null Character Discard: Disabled');

          {if (DeviceControlBlock.Flags and DCB_CHEVT) = DCB_CHEVT then
             Memo1.Lines.Add('Event Character Flagging: Enabled')
          else
              Memo1.Lines.Add('Event Character Flagging: Disabled'); }

          {Display the various replacement characters.}
          Memo1.Lines.Add(' ');
          Memo1.Lines.Add('Replacement Characters:');
          Str(Ord(DeviceControlBlock.XOnChar), sNumConv);
          sCommBuffer := 'XON: ' + sNumConv;
          Str(Ord(DeviceControlBlock.XOffChar), sNumConv);
          sCommBuffer := sCommBuffer + CHR_TAB + 'XOFF: ' + sNumConv;
          Str(Ord(DeviceControlBlock.ErrorChar), sNumConv);
          sCommBuffer := sCommBuffer + CHR_TAB + 'Parity: ' + sNumConv;
          Str(Ord(DeviceControlBlock.EofChar), sNumConv);
          sCommBuffer := sCommBuffer + CHR_TAB + 'EOF: ' + sNumConv;
          Str(Ord(DeviceControlBlock.EvtChar), sNumConv);
          sCommBuffer := sCommBuffer + CHR_TAB + 'Event: ' + sNumConv;
          Memo1.Lines.Add(sCommBuffer);

          end
      else
          {If we didn't get the port status, display an error message.}
          Memo1.Lines.Add('Failed to get port status.');

      {Close the communications port.}
      CloseHandle(hCommPort);
      end
   else
       begin

       {If we weren't able to open the port, find out why.}
       case hCommPort of
           IE_BADID: Memo1.Lines.Add('Invalid device identifier.');
           IE_BAUDRATE: Memo1.Lines.Add('Baud rate not supported.');
           IE_BYTESIZE: Memo1.Lines.Add('Invalid byte size.');
           IE_DEFAULT: Memo1.Lines.Add('Invalid default parameters.');
           IE_HARDWARE: Memo1.Lines.Add('Device is locked.');
           IE_MEMORY: Memo1.Lines.Add('Invalid queue size.');
           IE_NOPEN: Memo1.Lines.Add('The device is not open.');
           IE_OPEN: Memo1.Lines.Add('The device is already open.');
       else
           Memo1.Lines.Add('Unidentifiable Error.');
       end;
   end;

end;
end.
```

Now that we've gotten the program built, let's go ahead and test it. If you run this application you'll see some output similar to that shown in Figure 5.10. Notice that the program displays all the status information for the COM1 serial port.

Figure 5.10.

There are a lot of reasons to poll the serial ports on your system, not the least of which is to look for a modem.

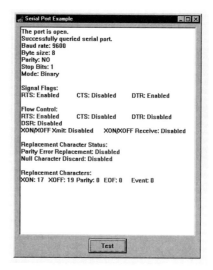

Checking the Status of Windows Objects

Once you get past the standard flags and some of the hardware, you're left with looking at Windows itself. Everywhere you look, you'll see a lot of talk about Windows objects. In fact, the term object seems to apply to just about everything you can see and a few things you can't. For example, every application running under Windows could be considered an object. Certainly all the dialogs, bitmaps, controls, fields, and every other part that makes up the application is an object of some sort.

Keeping track of all these objects could get quite confusing if the Windows API didn't provide so many functions to help you out. The problem isn't a lack of functions, but one of functions appearing everywhere. For example, if you want to find out which tasks are currently running on the machine, then you'd have to look under the Windows functions. On the other hand, methods for keeping track of your bitmaps appear with the GDI functions. It won't take you too long to figure out that you'll really need to look to find the management functions you need. The key, of course, is to look where you would expect to find the functions to manage that type of an object.

Tip: Just about every object query function that Windows has to offer begins with the word "get." Using the advanced search capabilities offered by Windows 95 (and hopefully the next version of Windows NT) should allow you to create a list of all the available query functions. Maintaining a list of these functions could greatly reduce the amount of time you spend scanning the help files looking for the function you need.

The code in the example for this section shows you how to find out which tasks are currently running. This is an important piece of information if you want to keep a user from starting multiple copies of your application. You can also use it to find out if an application you need to interact with for OLE or DDE purposes is active. Finally, this technique comes in handy when you need to check for the presence of an application server. Some graphics applications use a graphics server to process drawing information and present a copy of it on screen or a printer. We'll use the initial dialog shown in Figure 5.8 to create this example. Listing 5.3 contains all the code you need to make the example work.

Listing 5.3. Making the example work.

```
unit Tasklst;

interface

uses
  SysUtils, Windows, Messages, Classes, Graphics, Controls,
  Forms, Dialogs, StdCtrls;

type
  TForm1 = class(TForm)
    Memo1: TMemo;
    Button1: TButton;
    procedure Button1Click(Sender: TObject);
  private
    { Private declarations }
  public
    { Public declarations }
  end;

{Declare our callback function.}
function DoEnumWindow(hwnd: THandle; lIntParam: LPARAM):BOOL stdcall;

var
  Form1: TForm1;

implementation

{$R *.DFM}

procedure TForm1.Button1Click(Sender: TObject);
var
      lpCallback: TFNWndEnumProc;      {Pointer to our callback function.}
begin
      {Clear the display area.}
    Memo1.Lines.Clear;

      {Get the address of our callback function.}
      lpCallback := @DoEnumWindow;

    {Start the enumeration process.}
      EnumWindows(lpCallback, 0);
end;

function DoEnumWindow(hwnd: THandle; lIntParam: LPARAM):BOOL;
var
    sWindowName: String;       {Window name.}
```

continues

Listing 5.3. continued

```
begin
      {Set the length of our display string.}
      SetLength(sWindowName, 255);

   {Make sure we  have a window handle.}
      if IsWindow(hwnd) then
      begin

        {Get the name of the window and display it.}
        GetWindowText(hwnd, PCHAR(sWindowName), 255);
        Form1.Memo1.Lines.Add(sWindowName);
        end;

   {Return True so that we'll get the next window handle.}
      Result := True;
end;

end.
```

Now that we've gotten the program built, let's go ahead and test it. If you run this application you'll see some output similar to that shown in Figure 5.11. All this program does is display a list of the current tasks running.

Figure 5.11.

Learning which tasks are running could help you determine whether you need to start an application or not before making a DDE call.

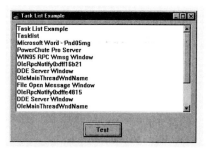

This example uses a couple of advanced techniques that we'll build on as the book progresses. The first thing you should notice is that the code attached to our Test button is rather short. All it does is clear the display, get the address of a callback function (I'll explain this term in a few seconds), and then call the EnumWindows function. This function allows you to list all of the top level windows—it doesn't concern itself with child windows. You could get a list of child windows as well using the EnumChildWindows call.

Now, what's a callback function? Under DOS, you had to create a loop function and get a list of items one item at a time. The directory list functions work this way. Windows 3.x worked this way to a certain extent as well. If you wanted to find out what tasks were active on your machine you would call TaskFirst, then TaskNext within a loop. I even know of a few Windows 95 functions that work this way—GetWindow is one of them. However, there's a better way. When you call the EnumWindows you're telling Windows to handle the looping part of the equation for you. This promotes the very best kind of multitasking and reduces the need for you to write a lot of extra code to handle the overhead portion of a task. The EnumWindows function accepts the address of a function in your application. Windows sends this function the handle for each top level window one at a time. This is why the second function is called a callback function.

DoEnumWindow is an example of a very simple callback function. All it does is accept the handle that Windows passes it, checks to make sure that it really is a window, then displays the information about that window—the title in this case. Notice that I have the function return True. That's a signal to Windows that you want it to send more information. If you want to stop processing information, you pass False.

There is one other bit of information you need to look at. Notice our function declaration uses stdcall. Pascal and Windows use different calling techniques—I'll get into more detail about this in later chapters. For right now, what you need to remember is that stdcall allows Windows to interact with functions in your application. A callback function always needs to add stdcall to its declaration so that it will be able to talk with Windows.

Looking Ahead: Our discussion of Windows objects certainly doesn't end here. Chapter 6, "Common Dialogs," will enlighten you about the various common dialogs that Windows has to offer. You'll also spend some time learning about bitmap and other graphic objects in Chapter 7, "The Windows GDI."

Other Types of Direct API Access

We've only just begun to look at the variety of things you can do with the Windows API. There are literally hundreds of API calls you can make to adjust a display or send output to a printer. You can build an OLE server or perform a variety of other tasks using API calls. I use a lot of the Version functions when writing an installation program. For example, you'll find two rather useful functions: GetSystemDir and GetWindowsDir there. These two functions tell you the location of the user's Windows directory and the System directory—a requirement for installation programs that work properly. There are even calls that allow you to reconfigure the system to meet the needs of your application. For example, Windows 95 allows you to change the display resolution on the fly (provided you have the right kind of display adapter). Some game programs use this feature to reconfigure the display to a specific resolution.

Of course, all the programs we've looked at so far have had one thing in common. They all took a look at some piece of information that the Windows API had to offer, then returned a result. What if you need to do something more complicated than that? Getting information is one way to get work accomplished, but there are many other ways to use the API to your advantage. Chapters 6 through 9 will show you a variety of techniques for accessing every part of the Windows API in one way or another.

Before we can move ahead though, you need to learn some additional programming techniques. The following sections will start to show you some of the advanced techniques you'll need to know to really use the Windows API to its fullest. You'll need to learn about the Windows message queue and the way that it calls an application back with a bit of information or some type of task. You'll also learn about a very important Delphi limitation and how to get around it.

Getting a Handle on Windows Resources

More than a few Windows functions will ask you to provide a handle of some sort. These functions need the handle to access whatever it is that you want them to work with. Every Windows object—windows, dialog boxes, even controls—have a handle. Think of a handle as the street address on your house; it's the method that Windows uses to identify a particular object.

The only problem for the Delphi programmer is that you normally don't have to deal with handles. Delphi takes care of all these details for you when you create dialog boxes and the like. It's all part of the RAD (rapid application development) environment that products like Delphi provide.

So, how do you figure out what the handle is for something in your application? The answer is easier that you might think. All you need to do is use the word "handle" to get the handle for any object in Delphi. For example, if you have a control named Memo1 on a form, then you would use something like hMemo1 := Memo1.handle to get the handle for that particular object.

Of course, now you can run into another problem. It's never safe when programming in Windows to assume that the handle you got a few minutes ago is valid right now. The user could have closed the window or other object and invalidated its handle. Always get the handle you need for an API call immediately before you make the call. Get the handle again each time you need to make the API call. Unlike DOS file handles, you always have to verify the handles you use under Windows.

Starting a Conversation with Windows

Starting a conversation with someone or something always involves some form of information exchange. It's the exchange of knowledge that makes a conversation worthwhile. Programmers have been sending messages to the operating system in a variety of ways throughout the years. Witness the DOS interrupt system. You told DOS what you wanted to do and it provided some kind of response. There was an exchange of information, albeit in a nearly incomprehensible format.

Windows couldn't use a static system of exchanging information with an application. For one thing, these older systems just wouldn't allow for more than one message at a time. This won't work under Windows because the user could be running any number of applications—all of which could be requesting some type of service. The message system is the Windows way of communicating. You send

Windows a message when you need to get something done. Likewise, Windows will send your application a message when system conditions change and you have to do something about it.

I like to think of the Windows message system as similar to the message system provided by an online network. You leave a message for someone, they answer back, and you start a conversation in which neither party is talking directly to each other. Each party simply attaches a new message to the response made by the other party. The messages form what most people call a thread. The Windows message queue works in about the same way. You send a message, and your application has to wait for a response. Needless to say, you have to speak the same language that Windows does to get anything out of the messages it sends or even know how to ask intelligent questions. The following paragraphs will tell you how to speak Windows' language. They'll give you a basic understanding of the Windows message queue that we'll refine as the book progresses.

Understanding the Message Queue

Messages aren't at all like the interrupts that DOS used. Sure, you are trying to accomplish sort of the same thing by gaining the operating system's attention, but the whole process stops there. A DOS application could send out one message at a time and then had to wait until DOS had a chance to answer. Windows works in a completely different way. Your application can perform other processing while it waits for an answer. We're not talking DOS here where an application would poll the keyboard, waiting for a response. For that matter, you can send more than one message to Windows while you wait for the response to the first one. Windows will handle each message in turn until it runs out of messages to process.

Messages aren't limited to the operating system. You can send messages to other applications or even to yourself. We'll see how that's important in just a bit. Just remember for the moment that messages in Windows work like the messages you send over e-mail or through an online service.

There are a variety of messages you can send. For example, you can send Windows a WM_PAINT message. It essentially tells Windows that you need to repaint some portion of the screen. You could use this message to tell yourself to repaint your main window. Yes, it sounds like you're talking to yourself, and in a way you are, but that's how things work.

Now, what happens if someone sticks a window on top of yours? Part of your window will get overwritten by that other application. So, what happens when the user removes the window? Windows will send you a WM_PAINT message of course. It's the same message, but different sources are sending it to your application. It doesn't matter why you need to repaint the window; the fact is that it needs to be repainted.

The combination of the message queue and a message handling loop in your application allows you to create an application that uses one standard technique to handle a variety of situations. The message handling loop gets called each time Windows has a message for you to process. The loop passes control of the message from to the routine designed to handle it.

There is one more piece to this puzzle. The Windows API actually groups some messages and functions together. For example, when an application calls the CreateWindow function, it's actually asking Windows to generate a WM_CREATE message. Of course, there's more involved than a simple message. The function call includes a number of parameters including the window name, its size and position, the menu associated with it, and a few other parameters that affect the window's appearance and characteristics.

Normally Delphi takes care of the message queue and the message handling loop for you. However, if you start working with the Windows API directly, you may find that you have to handle the message queue yourself—the standard Delphi routines won't know how to handle your application's special needs. The following paragraphs are going to explore the Windows message queue and help you see how to handle it within a Delphi application.

Window Management Messages

You're going to find that you spend the majority of your time taking care of the GUI aspects of your application, despite all the RAD tools that Delphi provides. The reason is simple: the GUI interacts with the user, the whole reason for writing an application in the first place.

This fact wasn't lost on Microsoft when they designed Windows. There are more window management messages than you probably care to know about. (A recent count in several of my API guides showed that there are between 140 and 150 of these messages floating around.) Each one is designed to help you, as the programmer, get some important task done or take care of some important user need. As I mentioned before though, Delphi takes care of the greater part of these messages for you so you don't need to worry about them.

The time that you do need to start worrying about these messages is when you start directly interacting with the Windows API. Delphi may not know how to handle a particular message if you've set up a specific set of parameters in a window. For the most part, it knows how to repaint and resize the window and not much else. (Although you can add other capabilities using controls and other built-in Delphi features.)

So, how can you tell a window management message from any other message that Windows generates? Every window message begins with the letters WM. Anytime you see a message that begins with WM, you know that it provides some type of window management message. Of course, the actual topics for these messages vary a great deal. For example, you'll find several messages for scrolling the contents of a window—not too unexpected. Some of the more exotic messages deal with DDE like WM_DDE_EXECUTE, MDI (multiple document interface) like WM_MDICREATE, and the clipboard like WM_SIZECLIPBOARD. There are also messages to end the window and thereby end the application.

Using the PostMessage() and PostThreadMessage() Functions

There are more than a few message related functions in Windows. The two that I use the most often for sending messages are PostMessage() and PostThreadMessage(). (I usually use the GetMessage() and PeekMessage() functions to retrieve messages.) The PostMessage() function will work with any window. The PostThreadMessage() is the one designed for sending messages to your application. For that matter, you can use it to post messages to any task. You can't use it for other window types.

Now that we've gotten an idea of what messages are and how Windows uses them, let's look at an example of a program that sends a series of messages out to change its appearance. In this case, we'll put some data in a window and scroll it around using some arrow keys. (Of course, you could accomplish the same thing by adding scroll bars to the window, but this particular example does a good job of showing how to use various messages to your advantage.) Once you get the basic idea of how to use messages down, you'll find all kinds of uses for them in your application.

The first thing you'll need to do is create a form with a memo control and four pushbuttons as shown in Figure 5.12. Notice that we used some arrows in this case. I used the BitBtn control in place of the regular pushbutton. You'll find the bitmaps for the arrows in the IMAGES\BUTTONS directory.

Figure 5.12.
The message example includes four pushbuttons and a memo field. The pushbuttons control the way that the memo field reacts.

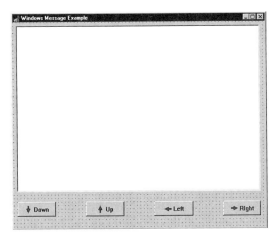

Once you create the form, add the button click code shown in Listing 5.4 to each of the four pushbuttons. It's important to add the right message to each pushbutton. The message you choose affects how the button controls the contents of the memo control. Check little things like the scroll direction message you send to the message handling routine.

Listing 5.4. Adding the button click code.

```pascal
unit Winmsg;

interface

uses
  SysUtils, WinTypes, WinProcs, Messages, Classes, Graphics, Controls,
  Forms, Dialogs, StdCtrls, Buttons;

type
  TForm1 = class(TForm)
    Memo1: TMemo;
    BitBtn1: TBitBtn;
    BitBtn2: TBitBtn;
    BitBtn3: TBitBtn;
    BitBtn4: TBitBtn;
    procedure BitBtn1Click(Sender: TObject);
    procedure BitBtn2Click(Sender: TObject);
    procedure BitBtn3Click(Sender: TObject);
    procedure BitBtn4Click(Sender: TObject);
  private

    {Always add the message handling procedures to the private area.}
    procedure WMVScroll(var Msg: TWMVScroll); message WM_VSCROLL;
    procedure WMHScroll(var Msg: TWMHScroll); message WM_HSCROLL;
  public
    { Public declarations }
  end;

var
  Form1: TForm1;

implementation

{$R *.DFM}

procedure TForm1.BitBtn1Click(Sender: TObject);
var
   hTask: THandle;                   {Handle of the Current Task}
   hMemo: HWND;                      {Handle of the Memo Control}
   lParam: Longint;                  {32-bit Message Parameter}
   fResult: BOOL;                    {Result of move.}
begin
    {Initialize our varibles.}
    hTask := Form1.Handle;           {Get the current task handle.}
    hMemo := Memo1.handle;           {Get the memo control handle.}
    lParam := hMemo;                 {Place it in the low word of lParam.}
    lParam := lParam * $10000;       {Move it to the high word of lParam.}

    {Send a message to the control via the task.}
    fResult := PostMessage(hTask, WM_VSCROLL, SB_LINEUP, lParam);
end;

procedure TForm1.BitBtn2Click(Sender: TObject);
var
   hTask: THandle;                   {Handle of the Current Task}
   hMemo: HWND;                      {Handle of the Memo Control}
   lParam: Longint;                  {32-bit Message Parameter}
   fResult: BOOL;                    {Result of move.}
```

```
begin
    {Initialize our varibles.}
    hTask := Form1.Handle;            {Get the current task handle.}
    hMemo := Memo1.handle;           {Get the memo control handle.}
    lParam := hMemo;                 {Place it in the low word of lParam.}
    lParam := lParam * $10000;       {Move it to the high word of lParam.}

    {Send a message to the control via the task.}
    fResult := PostMessage(hTask, WM_VSCROLL, SB_LINEDOWN, lParam);

end;

procedure TForm1.BitBtn3Click(Sender: TObject);
var
    hTask: THandle;                  {Handle of the Current Task}
    hMemo: HWND;                     {Handle of the Memo Control}
    lParam: Longint;                 {32-bit Message Parameter}
    fResult: BOOL;                   {Result of move.}
begin
    {Initialize our varibles.}
    hTask := Form1.handle;           {Get the current task handle.}
    hMemo := Memo1.handle;           {Get the memo control handle.}
    lParam := hMemo;                 {Place it in the low word of lParam.}
    lParam := lParam * $10000;       {Move it to the high word of lParam.}

    {Send a message to the control via the task.}
    fResult := PostMessage(hTask, WM_HSCROLL, SB_LINEDOWN, lParam);

end;

procedure TForm1.BitBtn4Click(Sender: TObject);
var
    hTask: THandle;                  {Handle of the Current Task}
    hMemo: HWND;                     {Handle of the Memo Control}
    lParam: Longint;                 {32-bit Message Parameter}
    fResult: BOOL;                   {Result of move.}
begin
    {Initialize our varibles.}
    hTask := Form1.handle;           {Get the current task handle.}
    hMemo := Memo1.handle;           {Get the memo control handle.}
    lParam := hMemo;                 {Place it in the low word of lParam.}
    lParam := lParam * $10000;       {Move it to the high word of lParam.}

    {Send a message to the control via the task.}
    fResult := PostMessage(hTask, WM_HSCROLL, SB_LINEUP, lParam);

end;

procedure TForm1.WMVScroll (var Msg: TWMVScroll);
begin

    {Determine which direction we should scroll, then do it.}
    case Msg.ScrollCode of
        SB_LINEUP: Memo1.ScrollBy(0, 12);
        SB_LINEDOWN: Memo1.ScrollBy(0, -12);
        end;
```

continues

Listing 5.4. **continued**

```
        {Make sure to pass the message along to the ancestor's object handler.}
        inherited;
end;

procedure TForm1.WMHScroll (var Msg: TWMHScroll);
begin

        {Determine which direction we should scroll, then do it.}
        case Msg.ScrollCode of
            SB_LINEUP: Memo1.ScrollBy(12, 0);
            SB_LINEDOWN: Memo1.ScrollBy(-12, 0);
            end;

        {Make sure to pass the message along to the ancestor's object handler.}
        inherited;
end;

end.
```

There are several other important features in this program. First of all, notice the two new entries in the unit's private area. You have to tell the unit that it's supposed to process some additional messages and this is the way that you do it. Essentially, the declaration contains a prototype of your message handling function, followed by the key word message and the type of message you want to handle.

The other section you should notice is the addition of two procedures near the end of the unit. These procedures perform the actual message processing. Delphi provides you with simplified record structures you can use in place of Windows normal message structures. I strongly suggest you use them because manipulating the data in the standard structures can get to be very time consuming. Notice that I only selected to process the SB_LINEUP and SB_LINEDOWN messages for each scroll type. Normally you would provide some type of handler for all the types of scrolling that the WM_VSCROLL and WM_HSCROLL messages can handle.

Now that we've gotten the program built, let's go ahead and test it. You'll need to type some text in the memo field; it doesn't really matter what text you type. Once you add some text, you'll see some output similar to that shown in Figure 5.13. You can use the four arrow keys to move the text around as desired.

Other Types of Windows Messages

There are a whole range of other Windows message types. We've already seen some of them in this chapter. Others will appear throughout the rest of the book. Some of the messages are pretty easy to figure out just by the prefix that Windows assigns to them; others will require a little reading on your part.

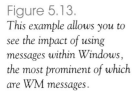

Figure 5.13.
This example allows you to see the impact of using messages within Windows, the most prominent of which are WM messages.

The following list shows some of the more common prefixes. This will help you get a quick start on the messages that you'll use within the Windows environment. All you need to do is look the needed prefix up in the help file to see what types of messages it supports.

- BM—Bitmaps
- CB—Combo box
- DM—Default message (used with standard pushbuttons like OK)
- EM—Edit controls (both multi-line and single line controls)
- LB—List box
- SB—Scroll bars
- STM—Normally associated with icon resources

Beside these message types, you'll run across a variety of other predefined values that work with messages, but don't necessary act as messages. For example, the BN prefix is used for a bitmap notification. You'll find a WN prefix as well. It's used as a window notification. See the pattern forming here? Once you have these basic message types, there are a variety of other prefixes that directly relate to them, deciphering their meaning is usually easy.

Replacing the Application Window

Remember that Delphi limitation that I mentioned previously? There are times where you have to replace the application window routine to make an application work. This is especially true if you are using your own external DLLs or directly accessing some parts of the Windows API.

Let's look at the Windows API aspect first. There are some API calls that require you to provide a callback routine. Since the standard Delphi application window won't know what to do when

Windows calls it back, you have to create a new one that does. The callback routine processes messages that Windows sends to it. For example, if you wanted to create a list of all the applications currently running on the system, you'd have to create a callback routine to handle the messages that Windows would send it. Each callback would contain the name of one active application.

You may find that you need to create complex DLLs that can't process everything you ask of it in one time slice. In that case you'll have to implement some kind of callback strategy to give other applications a chance to execute. Your DLL will process one piece of the puzzle at a time. Each time it completes a piece, it will call the Delphi application back and deliver it. That's how a callback system works: it allows the server routine to call the client back as it accomplishes the requested task.

Normally callback routines are limited to information processing of some sort. Your application has asked a DLL to provide it with some type of information, such as a list of all the active applications running under Windows.

Understanding the Application Window

Delphi does provide the application windows that it creates with adequate callback processing in most cases. You'll find that the message example in this chapter will allow you to intercept the vast majority of the callback messages that Windows might send to your application. The application class even provides an OnMessage event that you can monitor for incoming messages.

A problem arises when a DLL or other external source uses something other than the PostMessage() or PostThreadMessage() functions to send your application a message. The Delphi supplied application window's OnMessage event won't alert you to the presence of a message sent using the SendMessage() function. That's the message that many DLLs use when they need to alert your application to an error condition of some sort.

So, why would a DLL try to make life difficult for you and your application by using one function for standard messages and another for error messages? The PostMessage() and PostThreadMessage() functions return only a logical response—true if Windows was able to deliver the message to a message queue, false otherwise. That response doesn't tell the DLL very much, but it works in most cases. The SendMessage() function returns a specific value to the DLL. It doesn't just dump the message in the message queue and exit; it waits until the application has a chance to process the message and return some kind of a result. See the difference? The DLL can use the return value to figure out a course of action for repairing some kind of error condition. Obviously, there are a lot of other situations where the SendMessage() function is a lot more useful than the PostMessage() or PostThreadMessage() functions. You may even want to use it in your own DLLs.

Here's an example of an error that a DLL could repair if it had some application input. Say the user tries to look at the A drive, but there isn't any disk there. Your application could simply take a nose dive, or it could display a helpful dialog telling the user that that drive is empty and then tell the

DLL to redirect the current drive to the previous drive. That kind of processing is a lot more helpful to the user and prevents the kind of instability that users have cited Windows for in the past.

By now you're asking why Borland didn't simply add this additional feature to Delphi in the first place. Why should you have to replace the application window? The answer is speed. Most applications don't require the additional processing that I just talked about because Windows or Delphi takes care of that processing for you. The only time you really need it is when you're using a custom DLL or you need to do something special with the Windows API.

Subclassing the Delphi Window

Now that you have some idea of why you would want to replace the application window with something that'll respond to a function like SendMessage(), let's take a look at implementation. What we need to do here is subclass the current application window—after all, it already does just about everything we need it to. All we really want to do is add some extra message processing capabilities.

We'll use the same form shown in Figure 5.8 that we have for most of the examples in this chapter. Once you have the form created, add the code in Listing 5.5. Simply add the Button1Click() procedure code to the test button. You'll also need to change the project code shown in Listing 5.6. The NewAWnd unit receives a standard window handler procedure called UserMessageHandler. You'll also need to add the NewAppWindow() function and MakeNewAppWindow() procedure code to the new MakeAWnd unit. Finally, you'll need to modify the NEWAPWND.DPR file as shown at the beginning of the listing. Notice that we have to add two entries: one for the new window handler and another for the standard window handler.

Listing 5.5. **Code to add.**

```
unit Newawnd;

interface

uses
  SysUtils, Windows, Messages, Classes, Graphics, Controls,
  Forms, Dialogs, StdCtrls;

type
  TForm1 = class(TForm)
    Memo1: TMemo;
    Button1: TButton;
    procedure Button1Click(Sender: TObject);
  private
    { Private declarations }
  public
    procedure UserMessageHandler(var Msg: TMsg; var fHandled: Boolean);
  end;

var
  Form1: TForm1;
```

continues

Listing 5.5. continued

```
implementation

{$R *.DFM}

procedure TForm1.Button1Click(Sender: TObject);
type
    ResultString = String[10];        {Return value string length}
var
   liResult: Longint;                 {Return value.}
   sResult: ResultString;             {Return value in string form}
begin
    {Send a message instead of posting it this time.}
    Memo1.Lines.Add('Testing the SendMessage function.');
    liResult := SendMessage(Application.handle, WM_USER, 0, 0);
    Str(liResult, sResult);
    Memo1.Lines.Add('The return value for SendMessage was: ' + sResult);

    {Now try a PostMessage function call.}
    Memo1.Lines.Add(' ');
    Memo1.Lines.Add('Testing the PostMessage function.');
    PostMessage(Application.handle, WM_USER, 0, 0);
end;

procedure TForm1.UserMessageHandler(var Msg: TMsg; var fHandled: Boolean);
begin
    {This procedure only works if we use a PostMessage function.}
    if Msg.Message = WM_USER then
        Memo1.Lines.Add('Received by the UserMessageHandler procedure.');
end;

end.
```

Listing 5.6. Project code.

```
program Newapwnd;

uses
  Forms,
  Newawnd in 'NEWAWND.PAS' {Form1},
  WinProcs in '\DELPHI\LIB\WINPROCS.PAS',
  WinTypes in '\DELPHI\LIB\WINTYPES.PAS',
  Makeawnd in 'MAKEAWND.PAS';

exports
        {Export our new window function to Windows.}
        NewAppWindow;

{$R *.RES}

begin
  MakeNewAppWindow;           {Register our new application window procedure}
  Application.CreateForm(TForm1, Form1);
  Application.OnMessage := Form1.UserMessageHandler; {Standard handler entry}
  Application.Run;
end.
```

The two new procedures in our example work hand-in-hand to subclass the default Delphi application window procedure. The MakeNewAppWindow() procedure is the one that does the actual work of subclassing the window. The NewAppWindow() function performs the additional processing work.

Notice the way that we defined the NewAppWindow() function. Every application window function has to have four parameters—the same four parameters that every message has: a handle to the window, the message type, one parameter of a word length, and one parameter of a long integer length. You'll also see that we added the "export" key word to this function. Adding export to the function allows other application and Windows to see your application window function, a requirement if you want to receive any messages.

Now that we have all the required code in place, let's take a look at the result. You should see a display similar to the one in Figure 5.14 when you run this application. Notice that the SendMessage() function works only with our new application window handler. The PostMessage() function works with both. The SendMessage() function also returns a result; the PostMessage() function doesn't.

Figure 5.14.
The New Application Window example shows the added flexibility of using a custom application window routine.

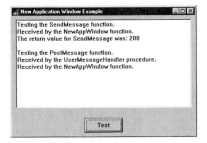

> **Tip:** From a speed perspective, using PostMessage() is faster. You can send a message somewhere and the function returns immediately. SendMessage() is slower because it has to wait for a result from the called application. However, it has the advantage of providing more information on return, allowing you to react to potential error conditions.

Hooking What You Need

Imagine you're sitting beside a stream, fishing rod in hand. You cast your hook into the water and reel in a big fish—the result of a great day of fishing. Windows has a stream too. It contains messages and you grab them out of the stream using a hook function. Of course, this form of fishing lacks the arbitrary nature of fishing beside a stream. Your hook function will grab only specific messages, those that you ask Windows to send your way.

Creating a Hook

There are several steps in creating a hook. The first thing you need to decide is which messages you want to receive. Windows will send you all of the messages of a particular type. Table 5.1 shows the message types that Windows provides.

Table 5.1. Windows Hook Types.

Type	Purpose
WH_CALLWNDPROC	Installs a window filter. Use this particular filter with caution since it affects system performance.
WH_CBT	Installs a computer-based training (CBT) filter.
WH_DEBUG	Installs a debugging filter.
WH_GETMESSAGE	Installs a message filter (on debugging versions only). Use this particular filter with caution since it affects system performance.
WH_HARDWARE	Installs a nonstandard hardware-message filter.
WH_JOURNALPLAYBACK	Installs a journaling playback filter.
WH_JOURNALRECORD	Installs a journaling record filter.
WH_KEYBOARD	Installs a keyboard filter.
WH_MOUSE	Installs a mouse-message filter.
WH_MSGFILTER	Installs a message filter.
WH_SYSMSGFILTER	Installs a system wide message filter.
WH_CALLWNDPROCRET	Installs a window filter. Unlike WH_CALLWNDPROC, this hook passes a return value from the window procedure that processed the message, as well as the message parameters associated with the message.

Hook functions are chained together, much like device drivers are in the DOS environment. You have to provide room in your hook function for the address of the next hook function in the chain. When you decide to unhook your function from the chain later, you have to pass this address back to Windows. Each hook in the chain gets a chance to look at the messages that Windows receives, and it then passes them on to the next hook in the chain.

Obviously, using a hook affects all the messages on the machine, so you have to build a filter function to use with the hook. The filter function removes the messages that you need from the stream and sends the rest on to the next hook in the chain. A filter function works just as you think it would. It looks for specific information in the message, decides whether this messages fulfills the criteria you selected, and then passes the message on or keeps it.

Creating a filter function takes a little time. The first thing you should decide is whether your filter is a system wide or an application specific filter. A system wide filter must reside in a DLL. Windows allows you to place an application specific filter in a DLL or within the application itself. You should always follow this four step process when adding a filter to the system to make sure that it gets registered properly. The alternative is a frozen machine when your filter disrupts the hook chain for a particular type of message.

1. Export the function in its module definition (DEF) file. We'll take a look at the exact process for doing this in Chapter 15, "Creating Your Own DLLs Using Delphi," when we create a SendKeys() function (it's actually pretty easy). So what is an exported function? Remember the functions we saw listed in Figure 5.1? Every entry in the Export Table is an exported function. Windows (and other applications) can only call exported functions. Exporting a function makes it public, so that other Windows processes can call it to perform specific kinds of work.

2. Get the function's address using the GetProcAddress function if it's in a DLL or the MakeProcInstance function if it's in an application. You won't need MakeProcInstance in 32-bit applications since you can call Win32 functions directly. You'll need a module handle (it's location in memory) and the function name (exactly as it appears in the Export Table entry) to use the GetProcAddress function. Using MakeProcInstance is a little different. You need to supply the procedure's address and an instance handle (the identifier for this particular instance of the program in memory).

3. Call the SetWindowsHookEx function. You'll need to supply the type of filter you want to register and the address you obtained using either GetProcAddress or MakeProcInstance.

4. Store the handle you get back from the SetWindowsHookEx function. This is the handle of the previous hook in the chain. You'll need to call it with any messages you don't want to process. Windows will also need this information when you want to unhook your filter from the hook chain.

Understanding the SendKeys() Function

Hooks have a lot of practical applications in Delphi, not the least of which is to get around some of the limitations of this product. Anyone who has programmed in Visual Basic or just about any Microsoft application product like Word Basic for that matter knows about the SendKeys() function. It allows you to send keystrokes to another application, just as if they were typed at the keyboard. Some programmers use this function to execute macros in another application without resorting to DDE.

For whatever reason, Borland decided not to provide a SendKeys() function as part of Delphi. (Interestingly enough, Paradox for Windows does provide this functionality.) Perhaps they felt it was outdated with all the advances in OLE over the years. Obviously, SendKeys() is still a useful function for those quick macro programming jobs.

A hook function can help you build SendKeys() function into your Delphi application. This allows other programs, like Paradox or Word for Windows, to send keystrokes to your application. To implement a SendKeys() function in your application, you would need to create a journal playback hook using the WH_JOURNALPLAYBACK type.

Looking Ahead: I'll show you how to create your own SendKeys() function in Chapter 15. A Delphi application requires you to create a DLL to implement a hook of this type. Fortunately, you don't have to resort to C to do it.

Summary

This chapter has covered a lot of territory. First, we looked at what the Windows API is and what it means to you as an application programmer. It's important to define the terms we use since so many people misuse them. Second, we looked at all the architectural considerations behind the Windows API. You need to understand the Windows architecture before you try to access it using an API call; otherwise, you're like the person who got lost in a cave without a candle. There isn't any way that you'll figure out where to go or what to do. Finally, we looked at the implementation details of actually creating a small application that calls on the Windows API. Practical experience never hurts when it comes to something as complex as accessing the Windows API.

6

Common
Dialogs

Anyone who uses Windows for very long can't help but notice that just about every dialog they'll see has a common format. An Open dialog in one application looks much the same as one under another. The reason is simple: Microsoft provides these dialogs (at least the code that determines how they look) as part of Windows. There are two common looks in Windows 95—the old Program Manager look and that provided by the newer Explorer interface. The code for the 16-bit Program Manager version appears in the COMMDLG.DLL in your SYSTEM directory. You can see the entries for this DLL in Figure 6.1. The 32-bit code for the Explorer version of the common dialogs appears in the COMDLG32.DLL in the SYSTEM directory (see Figure 6.2).

Figure 6.1.

The 16-bit common dialog code appears in COMMDLG.DLL.

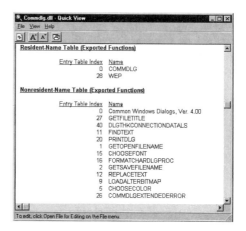

Figure 6.2.

The 32-bit Explorer style common dialogs appear in COMDLG32.DLL and reflect the differences found in that interface.

It's important to remember why the "common" in common dialogs is so important. Instead of writing the same code over and over again, Windows encourages code reuse by providing some objects—like dialogs—as part of the overall Windows API. You'll find a lot of other objects in Windows share this characteristic as well. For example, take a look at the COMMCTRL.DLL and COMCTL32.DLL files in the SYSTEM directory. You'll find a lot of the controls you might think are part of a programming environment there.

There's something else that's special about these DLLs. All 16-bit DLLs provide at least one of two exported entry points: WEP (Windows Entry Point) and LibMain. Most 32-bit DLLs use a DLLEntryPoint entry point in place of these two entries. When you look at COMDLG32.DLL, you see one of the exceptions to this rule. It has a WEP entry to maintain compatibility with previous versions of Windows.

> **Tip:** If you notice that a lot of applications seem to use common controls or provide similar features, it's a safe bet that there's a Windows DLL that provides that feature somewhere in your SYSTEM directory. Knowing what your SYSTEM directory contains can help when you notice a deficiency in the way that Delphi handles a particular task. You can always use the Windows API to access the features in that DLL instead of relying on Delphi's built-in feature set.

Common Dialog Box Overview

Now that we have a good idea of why they're called common dialogs, let's take a look at what those dialogs will allow us to do. There are eight different common dialogs provided in Windows, Windows 95, and Windows NT: Color, Find, Font, Open, Print, Print Setup, Replace, and Save As. The differences you see between a common dialog used in one application and one used in another application are largely a matter of flags. Microsoft provided enough flags for the common dialogs that you can choose whether a feature appears or not.

To get an idea of just how many flags there are, take a look at the Object Inspector Options entry for any of the common dialogs. For example, the Replace dialog provides no less than 13 flags. They control such things as whether the Up/Down radio buttons are enabled. You can even choose whether you want to enable them, disable them, or hide them completely from view. There's one common dialog that doesn't accept any flags. Windows takes care of processing the Print Setup dialog itself, so it reserves the right to configure this dialog as it sees fit.

Note: You can usually identify common dialogs and common control flags in Delphi code because they start with an "fd" (flag definition) or "fr" (flag response) prefix. Printer dialogs usually use "po" (print option) and "pr" (print response) prefixes.

Common dialogs share a few other things in common as well. Most of them display the dialog, but rely on the application to respond to any user input. (The only exception to this rule is the Print Setup dialog, which Windows takes care of completely.) Delphi handles this by wrapping the common dialog code in a class definition. Every common dialog displays itself when you use the Execute method (which we'll see later in this chapter in the example code). The class always returns a Boolean value. If the user presses OK or indicates a selection in some other way (like double-clicking on a filename), then the object always returns true. Getting a true response means that you'll need to look at the object's properties to determine how to react to the user action. This common interface greatly reduces the learning curve for using the common dialogs.

Because of the differences between the 16-bit and 32-bit versions of the common dialogs (they don't even use the same API calls), this chapter will mainly deal with the common dialogs as Delphi presents them. You should be able to use the example code in either Delphi version with a few minor changes. The code, as presented, runs in the 32-bit environment. You'll need to replace the TRichEdit control with a standard Tmemo control if you decide to run this program in the 16-bit environment. Unfortunately, this means you'll also lose the ability to handle rich text format (RTF) files without adding some code to handle them. The 16-bit version of Delphi doesn't support the TStatusBar class either. Since it really doesn't do much for the purposes of this example, you can safely ignore it.

Using Common Versus Custom Dialogs

By now you may be asking yourself why anyone would use a custom rather than a common dialog. Delphi provides a wealth of controls that you can use to build your own dialogs, and I've seen more than a few programmers use them. There are two good reasons to use custom dialogs (and many people cite even more).

A custom dialog allows you to remove certain common dialog features from user view. For example, if you used a common dialog on a Novell network, the user could end up changing their drive mappings. Selecting a mapped drive and then changing directories effectively changes the mapping to the new location. A programmer could use custom dialogs to prevent the user from shooting himself in the foot by changing the drive mappings.

Another good reason is security. Some programmers may want to hide the details of where data's stored, yet allow the user access to all the files they have rights to. The way to do this is to use a custom dialog in place of the common dialogs. Presenting the user with a specific list of files is certainly one way to reduce security problems while making the program easier to use.

Custom dialogs have a lot of drawbacks and you probably shouldn't use them unless you absolutely have to. The biggest drawback is that you have to code them by hand. Windows promotes code reuse. When you decide to code your own dialogs, you are effectively ignoring that advantage to gain some specific end goal. Whether that end goal is security or ease of use, you have to decide if it's worth the time to do it. Obviously, you'll still have to write the logic part of a common control—the business end that does something with the user's input, but at least you don't have to write the code for the dialog itself.

The time writing the code to display the dialog is only the down payment in time that you'll spend maintaining custom dialogs. Think about the transition between the 16-bit and 32-bit versions of Delphi for a moment. If you used common dialogs in your code, then you'll automatically reap the benefits of long filenames and other Windows 95 features with a simple recompilation of your code. Using custom dialogs means that you'll have to rewrite them from scratch before you'll see any Windows 95 benefits.

You could accidentally make your application harder, not easier, to use with custom dialogs as well. Let's face it, most users get into ruts quite easily. Change their environment, even a little bit, and they have to think about what they're doing with the application rather than the work they're trying to get done. The end result is user dissatisfaction. Always think twice before you change a user's environment. Even if the dialog is easier to use, it'll be harder because it's not what the user is accustomed to using.

Accessing the Common Dialogs

Delphi almost makes the job of accessing the common dialogs too easy if all you want is the "standard" look. All you have to do is add an appropriate menu and toolbar entry to your application, drop a control from the Dialog tab of the Control Palette, and add a bit of code to tie everything together. However, as soon as you want to depart from the standard look, the job of making the common dialogs work properly using the Delphi controls gets a little more difficult. In most cases you can make the required changes using flags. This is the best choice if you need to maintain compatibility between the 16-bit and 32-bit versions of your Delphi code. If compatibility isn't an issue, you can always resort to using custom dialog boxes or directly calling the API functions yourself.

Peter's Principle: When you start working with a lot of procedures and functions in one unit, it becomes difficult to find one particular procedure out of the list. One of the ways that I impose a little order on my applications is to place the procedures in a specific order.

There are a variety of ways of ordering your procedures and functions. Some programmers use a strict alphabetical ordering. All the A functions appear first, followed by the Bs, and so forth. That's fine in some situations, but I find it a bit time-consuming to move everything around.

The way that I order my procedures is by functional area first, then in sequence of use within those groupings. For example, I place all my menu functions first. Then those for speedbar buttons, followed by functions that the other functions need to work. All of my menu functions appear in menu order. So, for example, the function associated with the File | New menu command would appear first in the source code. The File | Exit function would appear last in the File menu group, but before any of the Edit menu functions. You get the idea.

Using this method of ordering functions works well for me because that's the order in which I code them. I simply build the interface, then the menu, then the speedbar, and so on until I have all the user interface elements in place. Once I get that done, it's time to add some code to each user interface object. What better way than to start at the beginning and work your way down. I start with the File | New menu entry and work my way from there. Programming this way makes it a snap to keep my functions in order with very little wasted time or effort. Of course, the benefit of all this added work is being able to quickly find the source you need to modify later on.

Our example program uses a text editor as a basis for showing you how to use the common dialogs. Figure 6.3 shows how to design your application interface. There are several special features in this example. The first is the use of a TRichEdit component in place of the more familiar Memo component. Using a TRichEdit component allows us to support both text and RTF files without much additional programming. In fact, all we'll really have to do is change one of the RichEdit1 object properties (PlainText) to get the job done. Notice also the status bar at the bottom of the display. We won't do much with it right now, but it'll come in handy in later chapters as we tackle more difficult topics from a user perspective. The toolbar background is a standard panel. I simply added the appropriate SpeedButton components to the panel after I got it in place. Notice also that there are eight dialog components in the RichEdit1 area of the form. These common dialog controls come from the dialogs page of the component library. All you need to do is place them somewhere on the form for right now. I found that placing them in the RichEdit1 object was the easiest way to keep track of their position (the controls disappear when you run the application).

Figure 6.3.

The sample application in this chapter uses a text editor as a starting point.

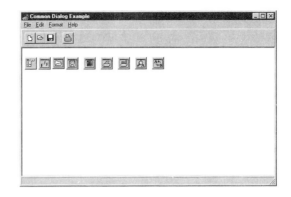

Once you get your form designed, you'll need to make some changes to the object properties to get it to look like mine. Table 6.1 provides the names of the objects, the properties, and the changes you need to make. Don't worry too much if your application doesn't look precisely like mine, it's the functionality of the program that matters, and we'll cover that in the following sections.

Table 6.1. Common Dialog Example Object Changes.

Object	Property	Setting
RichEdit1	Align	alClient
	ScrollBars	ssBoth
	WantTabs	True
Panel1	Align	alTop
StatusBar1	Align	alBottom
OpenDialog1	DefaultExt	RTF
	Filter	Rich Text Format | *.RTF | Text Files | *.TXT | All Files | *.*
	Options	[]
SaveDialog1	DefaultExt	RTF
	Filter	Rich Text Format | *.RTF | Text Files | *.TXT | All Files | *.*
	Options	[]
PrintDialog1	Options	[]
FindDialog1	Options	[frHideUpDown]
	OnFind	FindDialog1Find
ReplaceDialog1	Options	[frHideUpDown]
	OnFind	ReplaceDialog1Find
	OnReplace	ReplaceDialog1Replace

This program includes a menu. All you need to do to create it is drop a MainMenu control somewhere on the form. Double-click on the MainMenu to display a blank menu editor screen. I didn't do anything fancy here. All you need to do is right-click on the menu entry to display the context menu. Select Insert From Template to display the Insert Template dialog. I chose the four default menus for File, Edit, and Help. The Format menu contains two entries: Color and Font. Adding them in is fairly easy (we covered this whole process in Chapter 3, "Building a Basic Program").

I had to add some code for some of the default functions. Listing 6.1 contains the code required to implement the File | New and File | Exit menu options. It also contains all the entries you should have at the beginning of your application. You'll find that Delphi makes most of these entries for you. I included this listing just in case it misses an entry or two. You'll definitely need to add two entries. The first is in the Uses section. Make sure you add the Printers entry or Delphi will raise an error every time you want to print something. You'll also need to add the EditWindowSave procedure to the Public area once we get to the Save As section of the chapter. Finally, you'll probably want to check to make sure that Delphi adds the FindDialog1Find, ReplaceDialog1Find, and ReplaceDialog1Replace entries to the Type section.

Listing 6.1. Code to implement File | New and File | Exit menu options.

```
unit CmnDlgs;

interface

uses
  SysUtils, Windows, Messages, Classes, Graphics, Controls, Forms, Dialogs,
  StdCtrls, ComCtrls, Menus, Buttons, ExtCtrls, Printers;

type
  TForm1 = class(TForm)
    RichEdit1: TRichEdit;
    MainMenu1: TMainMenu;
    File1: TMenuItem;
    Exit1: TMenuItem;
    N1: TMenuItem;
    PrintSetup1: TMenuItem;
    Print1: TMenuItem;
    N2: TMenuItem;
    SaveAs1: TMenuItem;
    Save1: TMenuItem;
    Open1: TMenuItem;
    New1: TMenuItem;
    Edit1: TMenuItem;
    Object1: TMenuItem;
    Links1: TMenuItem;
    N3: TMenuItem;
    GoTo1: TMenuItem;
    Replace1: TMenuItem;
    Find1: TMenuItem;
    N4: TMenuItem;
    PasteSpecial1: TMenuItem;
    Paste1: TMenuItem;
```

```
    Copy1: TMenuItem;
    Cut1: TMenuItem;
    N5: TMenuItem;
    Repeatcommand1: TMenuItem;
    Undo1: TMenuItem;
    Help1: TMenuItem;
    About1: TMenuItem;
    HowtoUseHelp1: TMenuItem;
    SearchforHelpOn1: TMenuItem;
    Contents1: TMenuItem;
    OpenDialog1: TOpenDialog;
    Format1: TMenuItem;
    Color1: TMenuItem;
    Font1: TMenuItem;
    FontDialog1: TFontDialog;
    SaveDialog1: TSaveDialog;
    StatusBar1: TStatusBar;
    Panel1: TPanel;
    SpeedButton2: TSpeedButton;
    SpeedButton3: TSpeedButton;
    SpeedButton1: TSpeedButton;
    ColorDialog1: TColorDialog;
    PrintDialog1: TPrintDialog;
    PrinterSetupDialog1: TPrinterSetupDialog;
    FindDialog1: TFindDialog;
    ReplaceDialog1: TReplaceDialog;
    SpeedButton4: TSpeedButton;
    procedure Exit1Click(Sender: TObject);
    procedure Open1Click(Sender: TObject);
    procedure Font1Click(Sender: TObject);
    procedure Save1Click(Sender: TObject);
    procedure SpeedButton2Click(Sender: TObject);
    procedure Color1Click(Sender: TObject);
    procedure SaveAs1Click(Sender: TObject);
    procedure SpeedButton3Click(Sender: TObject);
    procedure New1Click(Sender: TObject);
    procedure SpeedButton1Click(Sender: TObject);
    procedure Print1Click(Sender: TObject);
    procedure PrintSetup1Click(Sender: TObject);
    procedure SpeedButton4Click(Sender: TObject);
    procedure Find1Click(Sender: TObject);
    procedure FindDialog1Find(Sender: TObject);
    procedure Replace1Click(Sender: TObject);
    procedure ReplaceDialog1Replace(Sender: TObject);
    procedure ReplaceDialog1Find(Sender: TObject);
  private
    { Private declarations }
  public
    procedure EditWindowSave;
  end;

var
  Form1: TForm1;

implementation

{$R *.DFM}
```

continues

Listing 6.1. continued

```
procedure TForm1.New1Click(Sender: TObject);
var
    wResult: Word;     {Result of Save File query.}
begin

    {See if the file has changed before we erase the window contents.}
    if RichEdit1.Modified then
        begin

            {If the file has changed, display a warning message.}
            wResult := MessageDlg('Save changes to file?', mtWarning, [mbYes, mbNo,
mbCancel], 0);

                {Act on the user's response.}
                case wResult of
                    mrYes: EditWindowSave;
                    mrCancel: Exit;
                end;
            end;

    {If everything is ok to proceed, then clear the display.}
    RichEdit1.Lines.Clear;
    RichEdit1.PlainText := False;
    SaveDialog1.Filename := '';
    OpenDialog1.Filename := '';
    RichEdit1.Modified := False;
end;

procedure TForm1.Exit1Click(Sender: TObject);
begin
    Halt;     {Exit the program}
end;

end.
```

Looking Ahead: Obviously we won't use all the menu entries in this chapter. I'll show you how to implement the OLE entries in Chapter 10, "Using Delphi with OLE." This includes the cut, copy, and paste entries. Chapter 14, "Packaging Your Application," will not only show you how to create a help file, it'll show you how to tie that help file into the rest of your application. We'll define the Help menu commands in that chapter.

Now that we've spent some time getting the initial form together, we can start programming the rest of the menu entries. I've placed the code for the various menu commands in alphabetic order in the following sections. You can add the code to the application in any order you like. Each module is self-contained—one menu command doesn't rely on the code used for any other command.

There's one more thing you need to think about. I placed some SpeedButton controls on the toolbar to make things faster and easier for the user. All I did then was double-click on the control to display its procedure, and then copy the code that I used for the corresponding menu item. You'll find that creating all the menu items first and debugging them makes adding the toolbar buttons a breeze for you and the user alike.

Color

The Color dialog in this example is just like the one you've seen in any number of applications. It appears in Figure 6.4. Of course, simply displaying the dialog does nothing for our application. You have to interpret the user selections, and then apply those selections to the text attributes. Fortunately, the TRichEdit control contains a Color parameter. All you need to do is apply the contents of the TColorDialog Color property to the selected text within the control.

Figure 6.4.
Use the ColorDialog1.Execute command to display the Color dialog object.

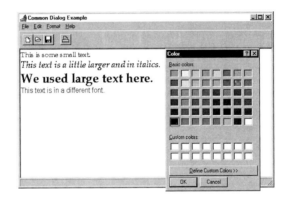

RTF files use an interesting technique to keep track of the colors that the user wants within the file. There are two entries. The first entry defines the available color selections as shown below:

```
{\colortbl\red0\green0\blue0;\red255\green0\blue0;\red0\green128\blue0;\red0\green0\blue255;}
```

Notice that each entry is separated by a semicolon. The default color, black in this case, is always defined as the first entry. A color table entry contains one value each for red, green, and blue.

Once you have a color table, accessing it is easy. An RTF file will contain numerous entries that look like this:

```
\plain\f4\fs24\cf3
```

The important part of this entry is \cf3 (we'll discuss the other entries later). The \cf command tells an RTF capable editor which color to use from the color table when displaying a particular section of text. The color remains for all text until the editor runs across another \cf entry. In this case, we're looking at the fourth entry (since the table begins at a 0 offset) or the color blue.

The Color dialog provides a minimum of configuration flags. Table 6.2 provides a complete listing of the flags and tells you how to use them.

Table 6.2. Color Dialog Flags.

Flag	Description
cdFullOpen	The dialog will display the custom coloring options when it opens.
cdPreventFullOpen	Windows will disable the Create Custom Colors button in the Color dialog box so the user cannot create their own custom colors.
cdShowHelp	This flag adds a Help button to the Color dialog box.
cdSolidColor	Selecting this option forces the dialog to display only solid colors— even if there are predefined dithered colors that the dialog could display.
cdAnyColor	This flag doesn't appear operational in the current version of Delphi. It should allow the user to select any color, not just predefined colors, from the Color dialog. Delphi normally keeps this option enabled whether you select this option or not.

Now that you have a better idea of how the Color dialog works and acts from a user perspective, let's look at some Delphi code to implement it. Listing 6.2 contains the code required to use a standard Color dialog box within Delphi to change the color of text typed into our editor. The techniques you'll use for other types of objects will vary slightly; you may need to change your strategy for figuring out which objects are selected or the method used to change their color.

Listing 6.2. Code required to use standard Color dialog box.

```
procedure TForm1.Color1Click(Sender: TObject);
begin
    {Assign the current color to our dialog.}
    ColorDialog1.Color := RichEdit1.SelAttributes.Color;

    {If the user selects OK or double clicks on a color.}
    if ColorDialog1.Execute then

        {If the user has selected some specific text.}
        if RichEdit1.SelLength > 0 then

            {Set the selected text color.}
            RichEdit1.SelAttributes.Color := ColorDialog1.Color
        else

            {Change the default text color.}
            RichEdit1.DefAttributes.Color := ColorDialog1.Color;

    {Return focus to our editing window.}
    RichEdit1.SetFocus;

end;
```

Overall, the dialog implementation in this example is very straightforward and easy to understand. However, there is one subtle point that you need to consider. Contrast the text selection method used in this example with the method used later on for fonts. The Fonts dialog affects more than one text attribute so you have to treat it differently than the Color dialog, which only affects one text attribute. Differences between dialogs like this are important to remember; you need to think about how the dialog will affect your application. If you don't, what might appear as a straightforward implementation can quickly turn into a nightmare.

Find

The Find and Replace dialogs are the most complex to implement in your application. Both of them require more than one routine to perform any useful work. Figure 6.5 shows the Find dialog implementation for our program. You display the Find dialog using the FindDialog1.Execute command, just as you do with any other common dialog. It's the OnFind event definition that makes the difference in this case. Every time the user presses the Find pushbutton in the dialog, Windows will call the OnFind event. We implement that code in the FindDialog1Find procedure in this example.

Figure 6.5.
Creating a Find dialog for your application requires a lot more code than any other dialog except the Replace dialog.

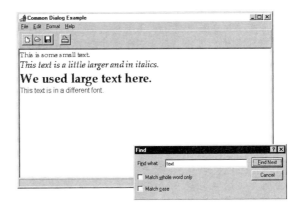

The Find dialog is also one of the more complex common dialogs to customize. You have a choice of 13 different flags to choose from when deciding what to include. Some of the flags appear to duplicate functions. For example, there's one flag for disabling the Up and Down radio buttons and another flag for hiding them. The difference is in what the user sees. You would probably disable the buttons if the user were already at the top or bottom of a document, then enable them once the user got past this point. The hiding option comes in handy if you always want the user to search in the same direction (as is the case for our example). Table 6.3 shows the various Find dialog flags and explains their uses.

Table 6.3. Find Dialog Flags.

Flag	Description
frDisableMatchCase	Use this flag to disable the Match Case check box and prevent users from checking it. Remember to use the UpperCase function (as shown in the example code) to perform a case-insensitive search.
frDisableUpDown	This is the flag that disables the Up and Down radio buttons. The user can still see them, but they can't select them. Delphi defaults to searching down. You can still change the direction selection that the dialog returns using the frDown flag.
frDisableWholeWord	Use this flag to disable the Match Whole Word Only check box and prevent users from checking it. I usually add a space to either side of the search word if the user does check this box. Using a space on both sides ensures that you find only whole words. A little extra code would deselect the spaces once you found the appropriate entry in the text.
frDown	Setting this flag to true tells your application to search in a downward direction if you have that option enabled. There isn't any magic here. If you keep the frDown flag active, the only thing it'll tell you is what direction to search, not the way to accomplish that task.
frFindNext	This flag is kind of useless in most cases. It gets set when the user chooses the Find Next button. When frFindNext is True, your application should search for the string in the FindText property. Of course, if you implement a two function approach like the one shown in the example, you won't even need this flag.
frHideMatchCase	This flag will hide the Match Case check box. It isn't visible in the dialog box so the user can't select it.
frHideWholeWord	This flag will hide the Match Whole Word Only check box. It isn't visible in the dialog box so the user can't select it.
frHideUpDown	This flag will hide the Direction Up and Down radio buttons. They aren't visible in the dialog box so the user can't select them. If you query the dialog box about direction, it will return the default setting—the one selected with the frDown flag.
frMatchCase	Use this flag to determine whether the user has checked the Match Case check box. A return value of true means that it's selected. You can also use this flag to automatically check the check box at runtime.
frReplace	Available, but not functional in this dialog.

Flag	Description
frReplaceAll	Available, but not functional in this dialog.
frShowHelp	Windows doesn't force you to provide help to the user. This flag, which defaults to false, displays a Help pushbutton when you set it to true. You'll need to set the HelpContext property to provide any meaningful level of help. We'll take a better look at the methods for implementing help in Chapter 14.
frWholeWord	Use this flag to determine whether the user has checked the Match Whole Word Only check box. A return value of true means that it's selected. You can also use this flag to automatically check the check box at runtime.

There are two different procedures required to implement the Find dialog in our example. The first procedure simply displays the dialog using the FindDialog1.Execute method. Windows will execute all the instructions in this procedure before it displays the dialog and allows the user to interact with it. You won't return to the procedure at all once the dialog is displayed. The bottom line is don't bother to put anything other than the Execute method in here unless you need to perform some type of setup before you display the Find dialog.

The second procedure is a lot more complex. It gets called every time the user presses the Find Next pushbutton. Part of the routine performs some setup. You'll need to ensure that the variables are set correctly before you start the search process. In many cases this means compensating for the current cursor position if the user is anywhere but the beginning or end of the file. Listing 6.3 shows both of the Find dialog procedures.

Listing 6.3. Find dialog procedures.

```
procedure TForm1.Find1Click(Sender: TObject);
begin
    {All we need to do here is display the dialog; the
     FindDialog1Find procedure does the rest of the work.}
    FindDialog1.Execute;
end;

procedure TForm1.FindDialog1Find(Sender: TObject);
var
    sFindText: String;        {Search String}
    iLineNumber: Integer;     {Search Line Counter}
    iCurrentLine: Integer;    {Search Start Position}
    iFoundPosit: Integer;     {String position within line.}
    iLength: Integer;         {SelStart Position}
    fWordWrap: Boolean;       {Current WordWrap Status}
begin

    {Initialize our variables.}
```

continues

Listing 6.3. continued

```
sFindText := FindDialog1.FindText;
iCurrentLine := 0;
iLength := 0;
fWordWrap := RichEdit1.WordWrap;

{Change the search variable as needed if whole words were selected.}
if FindDialog1.Options*[frWholeWord] = [frWholeWord] then
    sFindText := ' ' + sFindText + ' ';

{Change the search variable to reflect case sensitivity.}
if FindDialog1.Options*[frMatchCase] <> [frMatchCase] then
    sFindText := UpperCase(sFindText);

{Turn off word wrap so it won't interfere with the search.}
RichEdit1.WordWrap := False;

{If this is the second or subsequent find, then locate the starting line.}
while iLength < RichEdit1.SelStart do
    begin
     {The length of a line is equal to the text it contains and the end
      of line characters.}
    iLength := iLength + Length(RichEdit1.Lines[iCurrentLine]) + 2;
    iCurrentLine := iCurrentLine + 1;
    end;

{Continue looking from the current position to the end of the edit window.}
for iLineNumber := iCurrentLine to RichEdit1.Lines.Count do
    begin

    {A return value of 0 tells us that the text doesn't appear in
     this line.  We use the UpperCase function to convert all text to
     upper case unless the user requested a case sensitive search.}
    if FindDialog1.Options*[frMatchCase] = [frMatchCase] then
        iFoundPosit := Pos(sFindText, RichEdit1.Lines[iLineNumber])
    else
        iFoundPosit := Pos(sFindText, UpperCase(RichEdit1.Lines[iLineNumber]));

    {If we found the search text, then let's highlight it.}
    if iFoundPosit > 0 then
        begin

        {Give the edit window focus.}
        RichEdit1.SetFocus;

        {Change the selected text starting position.}
        RichEdit1.SelStart := iLength + iFoundPosit - 1;

        {Set the length equal to our search string.}
        RichEdit1.SelLength := Length(sFindText);

        {Return word wrap to its previous state.}
        {RichEdit1.WordWrap := fWordWrap;}

        {Exit this procedure and return to the program.}
```

```
        exit;
      end;

    {Add the length of the current line to our length variable if we
     haven't found the search text.}
    iLength := iLength + Length(RichEdit1.Lines[iLineNumber]) + 2;
    end;

  {if we reached the end of the file, then display a message.}
  MessageDlg('Reached the end of the file.', mtInformation, [mbOK], 0);
end;
```

There are a few interesting components to the search routine. First, notice that we exit from the procedure using the Exit command once we find what we need. You have to do three things before you can exit the search routine. First, you need to give the Edit window focus, or the user won't be able to see the text you've highlighted (to show that you found the next occurrence of the specified text). Second, you need to set a starting position. Both the TMemo and TRichEdit controls set the first position in the file as 0, so you need to compensate for this by subtracting 1 from the final search position. The SelStart parameter contains the starting position (the beginning of the search work in the edit window). Third, you need to set the length of the selection area, the area that'll appear highlighted in the Edit window.

Another interesting feature of this routine is the MessageDlg call at the very end. You need to provide the user with some type of input when he reaches the end of the file. There isn't any text to highlight, so there really isn't any reason to turn control over to the Edit window. Without this input the user might assume any number of things about your application (he may even assume that it's frozen). It's only one line of code, but a very important line from the user's perspective.

You'll want to pay particular attention to the way that I implemented the various user selections for this dialog. There are a number of important search parameters that you'll want to include with any application, including the ability to perform both case-sensitive and case-insensitive searches. I chose not to implement the up and down radio buttons in the example to keep the search routine simple. Adding that feature would simply be a matter of counting down instead of up from a specific position in the edit window.

Fonts

Fonts are an essential part of any application. In fact, I can't think of a single application on my machine that lacks some form of font control—even though more than a few of them lack any form of color controls. Our example (shown in Figure 6.6) supports fonts in RTF files in about the same way as it supports color. RTF files use two entries for fonts, just like they did for color. There are some subtle differences though, and you need to be aware of them.

Figure 6.6.
*The Font dialog can provide
as few or many options as
you think the user needs.*

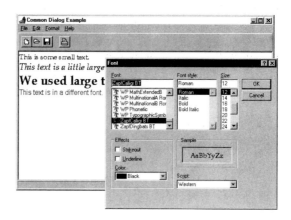

The font table entry contains one font description for each font that you use in the file. The description includes the font number, style, and name as shown below:

```
{\fonttbl{\f0\fnil MS Sans Serif;}{\f1\fnil\fcharset2 Symbol;}{\f2\fswiss\fprq2
System;}{\f3\fnil ZapfCalligr BT;}{\f4\fnil Arial;}}
```

You'll notice that there really isn't enough information to define a font style for anything in this description. Unlike the self-contained color table entries, the font table is only a starting point. The rest of the definition appears with the text itself as shown below:

```
\plain\f3\fs32\cf0\i
```

This description starts by telling you that the text uses font number 3 or ZapfCalligrBT in this case. The \fs parameter tells you the font size in points. We're looking at a 32-point font in this example. The final entry on the line is a \i. This tells you that the font is italicized. RTF files use \b for bold or a combination of \b\i for bold italic fonts. You'll also see \ul for underline and \strike for strikethrough here.

Unlike the Color dialog, the Font dialog provides a wealth of configuration flags. In fact, it provides even more flags than the Find or Replace dialogs. Notice especially the Windows 95 specific fdApply flag provided with the 32-bit version of Delphi. Table 6.4 provides a complete listing of the flags and tells you how to use them.

Table 6.4. Font Dialog Flags.

Flag	Description
fdAnsiOnly	This flag only allows the user to select fonts that use the Windows character set when set to true. In other words, the Font combo box won't display any of the symbol fonts installed on the machine.

Flag	Description
fdEffects	You can add some pizzazz to your Font dialog by setting this flag to true. It displays both the Effects check boxes and the Color list box in the Font dialog box. The user uses the Effects check boxes to specify strikeout or underlined text. The Color list box allows the user to select a color for the selected font.
fdFixedPitchOnly	Use this flag if you only want to display monospaced (non-proportional) fonts in the Font combo box. This comes in handy for terminal applications where you want to simulate something like a DOS environment.
fdForceFontExist	Windows usually tries to find the closest matching font if the user types in the name of a non-existent font. This flag tells Windows to display an error dialog instead of accepting the font selection. (Yes, there are a few automated flags in the list—you don't have to supply any code to make this one work.)
fdLimitSize	Setting this flag to true enables the MinFontSize and MaxFontSize properties. These properties will limit the number of fonts available in the Font combo box to those that provide font sizes between the specified point size limits.
fdNoFaceSel	Use this flag if you don't want to automatically select a font name in the Font combo box when the dialog opens.
fdNoOEMFonts	Use this flag if you only want to display raster (non-vector) fonts in the Font combo box.
fdScalableOnly	Use this flag if you only want to display scalable fonts in the Font combo box.
FdNoSimulations	Use this flag if you only want to display fonts that aren't GDI simulations in the Font combo box.
fdNoSizeSel	Use this flag if you don't want to automatically select a font size in the Size combo box when the dialog opens.
fdNoStyleSel	Use this flag if you don't want to automatically select a font style in the Style combo box when the dialog opens.
fdNoVectorFonts	Same as fdNoOEMFonts.
fdShowHelp	Windows doesn't force you to provide help to the user. This flag, which defaults to false, displays a Help pushbutton when you set it to true. You'll need to set the HelpContext property to provide any meaningful level of help. We'll take a better look at the methods for implementing help in Chapter 14.

continues

Table 6.4. continued

Flag	Description
fdTrueTypeOnly	Use this flag if you only want to display TrueType fonts in the Font combo box.
fdWysiwyg	Use this flag if you only want to display fonts that are available to both the printer and the screen in the Font combo box.
fdApply	Windows 95 provides a new feature in most of its dialog boxes. Instead of having to press OK and exit the dialog to see the effect of the changes you request, you can click on the Apply pushbutton. This flag enables the Apply pushbutton in the dialog. You need to supply a procedure name in the OnApply event if you choose this option.

Now that you have a better idea of how Font dialog works and acts from a user perspective, let's look at some Delphi code to implement it. Listing 6.4 contains the code required to use a standard Font dialog box within Delphi to change the attributes of text typed into our editor. Notice that these attributes affect a variety of things including the font name, size, and attribute. However, there are other attributes like underline that are implemented as part of the editor screen routines, not the font itself.

Listing 6.4. **Code to use standard Font dialog box.**

```
procedure TForm1.Font1Click(Sender: TObject);
begin

    {Assign the current font attributes to our dialog.}
    FontDialog1.Font.Assign(RichEdit1.SelAttributes);

    {If the user selects OK or double clicks on a color.}
    if FontDialog1.Execute then

        {If the user has selected some specific text.}
        if RichEdit1.SelLength > 0 then

            {Set the selected text font attributes.}
            RichEdit1.SelAttributes.Assign(FontDialog1.Font)
        else

            {Set the default text font attributes.}
            RichEdit1.DefAttributes.Assign(FontDialog1.Font);

    {Return focus to our editing window.}
    RichEdit1.SetFocus;
end;
```

As you can see, implementing the font routines is fairly straightforward. I've already discussed the differences between this routine and the one used to implement a Color dialog in the color section of the chapter, so I won't talk about it again here. One important method used in this procedure that doesn't appear in most of the other procedures in this chapter is the Assign method. You can normally assign the attribute in one object to another object as long as they're compatible.

Open

Every application has to have an Open dialog (unless it's a custom application that only uses one set of files under strict program control). The Open dialog for our example appears in Figure 6.7. The first thing you'll notice is that the Windows 95 version provides the ability to create new folders from within either the Open or Save dialogs. You can also rename files (the programmer doesn't have to add a single line of code to implement this capability). The new tree structure and long filename support make this dialog a lot easier to use as well.

Figure 6.7.
The Windows 95 version of the Open dialog provides a lot more functionality than its predecessor did.

Like every other dialog that we've discussed so far, you control the appearance of the Open dialog using a selection of flags—a whopping count of 18 in this case. There is one Windows 95–specific parameter and three that refer to both Windows 95 and Windows NT: ofNoLongNames, ofNoNetworkButton, ofOldStyleDialog, and ofNoDereferenceLinks. Table 6.5 describes them all for you.

Table 6.5. Open Dialog Flags.

Flag	Description
ofAllowMultiSelect	Set this flag to true if you want to allow the user to select more than one filename in the dialog.
ofCreatePrompt	This flag will allow the user to create a new file from the Open dialog. Windows will display a dialog asking the user if he wants to create a new file when he enters a non-existent filename if you set this flag to true. Since Windows creates the new file for you, your application will still react as if it had opened an existing file.

continues

Table 6.5. continued

Flag	Description
ofExtensionDifferent	Delphi sets this option when the filename returned from the dialog box has an extension that differs from the default file extension (the DefaultExt property). Obviously, this flag allows you to detect when your application needs to treat a file differently. For example, in our example, we treat text files differently than RTF files.
ofFileMustExist	Use this flag if you want Windows to tell the user when he has entered a non-existent filename. What the user will see is a dialog saying the file doesn't exist and he should check his path and filename. The advantage to using this flag is that your application will always receive the name of an existing filename when the user clicks on OK.
ofHideReadOnly	Use this flag to hide the Read Only check box.
ofNoChangeDir	This option doesn't prevent the user from changing the directory or drive shown in the Open dialog. It does, however, return the current directory to the one shown when the dialog opened when the user closes the dialog. This comes in handy if you need to look for files in the application directory and don't want to keep checking for the right directory in your application code.
ofNoReadOnlyReturn	Use this flag to tell Windows to display a dialog every time the user selects a read-only file.
ofNoTestFileCreate	Available, but not functional in this dialog.
ofNoValidate	Use this flag if you want to disable filename validation. Normally, Windows displays a dialog if the user enters invalid characters for a filename.
ofOverwritePrompt	Available, but not functional in this dialog.
ofReadOnly	This flag tells you that the user checked the Read Only check box when true.
ofPathMustExist	Use this flag if you want Windows to tell the user when he has entered a non-existent path. What the user will see is a dialog saying the path doesn't exist. The advantage to using this flag is that your application will always receive the name of an existing path when the user clicks on OK.
ofShareAware	Windows normally tries to protect the user from opening a file that someone else has already opened. Setting this flag to true disables sharing violation protection. Of course, disabling the protection will allow two users to overwrite each other's data unless your application provides some type of sharing protection.

Flag	Description
ofShowHelp	Windows doesn't force you to provide help to the user. This flag, which defaults to false, displays a Help pushbutton when you set it to true. You'll need to set the HelpContext property to provide any meaningful level of help. We'll take a better look at the methods for implementing help in Chapter 14.
ofNoLongNames	This flag allows you to disable long filename support to use the standard DOS 8,3 filenames. The only time you would need this flag is if you needed an application to work with both Windows 3.x and Windows 95 systems.
ofNoNetworkButton	You can use this flag to hide the Network button on old style dialogs. Obviously it doesn't have any meaning for the newer Explorer dialogs that make every network drive automatically available.
OfOldStyleDialog	Use this flag if you want to use an old style Open dialog. You may find it easier than trying to support two types of application interface.
ofNoDereferenceLinks	This flag disables dereference link support.

Now that we've gotten the particulars of the Open dialog down, let's look at some sample code. Listing 6.5 provides everything that you need to implement an Open dialog. Notice that it includes necessary features like the ability to detect the file type. It also saves the filename to our Save dialog, a necessary step if you want your application to provide the user with a default filename. Using this setup also enables the user to save a file without going through the Save As dialog first.

Listing 6.5. **Implementing an Open dialog.**

```
procedure TForm1.Open1Click(Sender: TObject);
var
    sFilename: TFilename;          {User file selection}
begin

    {If the user clicks on OK or double clicks on a filename.}
    if OpenDialog1.Execute then

        {Assign the filename to a string.}
        begin
            sFilename := OpenDialog1.Filename;

            {Determine the file type and set the editor as appropriate.}
            if Pos('.RTF', UpperCase(sFilename)) > 0 then
                RichEdit1.PlainText := False
            else
                RichEdit1.PlainText := True;

            {Open the File.}
            RichEdit1.Lines.LoadFromFile(sFilename);
```

continues

Listing 6.5. continued

```
            {Save the filename to our Save As dialog.}
            SaveDialog1.Filename := sFilename;
    end;

    {Return focus to our editing window.}
    RichEdit1.SetFocus;
end;
```

Tip: Just to show you that there are always several ways of accomplishing the same task in Delphi, find the line of code that looks like this:

```
if Pos('.RTF', UpperCase(sFilename)) > 0 then
```

This is one way to look for a file extension. Another way is to use this statement in its place:

```
if ExtractFileExt(sFilename) = 'RTF' then
```

Is either method better? Probably not. However, the ExtractFileExt method is more flexible. It's the method that you'll see me use in several other pieces of code in the book. I think it's important to know the various ways to get something done—you never know when your favorite way won't work in a given situation and you'll have to resort to an alternative.

Print

Once you get past data entry and manipulation, you have reports of various kinds to contend with. I have a few database applications where I spent two or three times the hours programming the report section of the application than I did everything else combined. A good report can help the user derive the very most out of the application you design. After all, what good is the data you put in if you can't get it back out again? Most of us are familiar with the Print dialog shown in Figure 6.8. However, I was surprised when I found out how easy it is to implement a simple routine for handling this dialog in Delphi.

Figure 6.8.

Delphi provides many tools that make it easy to design and implement print routines in your application.

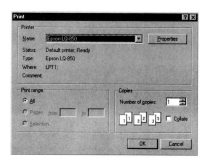

Looking Ahead: We'll only look at the very tip of the printing iceberg in this chapter. Printing is such an important topic that I decided to devote an entire chapter to it. Look in Chapter 8, "Printer Magic," for more information on how to print in Delphi.

The Print dialog only provides six configuration flags as shown in Table 6.6. Unlike the other dialogs in this chapter, there are few things that you can really control in the Print dialog. About the only area of real support is the ability to select how much of the document to print. This means that your application has to provide a lot of strong support internally for a standard print situation. It also means that this is one of the few dialogs that you'll probably skip in favor of custom dialogs for many applications. Database applications usually require very specific reports, something not supported by the Windows common dialogs.

Table 6.6. **Print Dialog Flags.**

Flag	Description
poHelp	Windows doesn't force you to provide help to the user. This flag, which defaults to false, displays a Help pushbutton when you set it to true. You'll need to set the HelpContext property to provide any meaningful level of help. We'll take a better look at the methods for implementing help in Chapter 14.
poPageNums	Set this flag to true if you want to enable the Pages radio button. This allows the user to select a range of pages to print. (Obviously, this also means that your application must provide a pagination routine.)
poPrintToFile	Set this flag to true if you want to allow the user to print to a file instead of the printer. This option is very handy if you have users that use portable machines. They can work off-site, then print any reports they create when they return to work.
poSelection	You'll need to set this flag carefully. The first step is to make sure that the user has selected a range of text. Once you do that, you can enable the flag to allow them to print just the selected text.
poWarning	This is another flag that you'll find useful for applications that have to react to the needs of portable users. It tells Windows to display a message if the user tries to print and there is no printer attached to the machine.
poDisablePrintToFile	Setting this flag to true enables the Print to File check box. The poPrintToFile flag only displays the check box and associated prompt. This flag allows the user to actually select the option.

Now that we have some idea of how to use the Print dialog, let's look at some very basic code for using it. The purpose of this example isn't to show you the most complex print routine in the world, it's there to show you the very minimum you can provide to enable a user to print. This routine will send an entire document to the printer; it doesn't do anything else. We'll take a look at all the bells and whistles you can add to a print routine in Chapter 8.

Listing 6.6. Print routine.

```
procedure TForm1.Print1Click(Sender: TObject);
begin

    {if the user selected a print option, then act on it.}
    if PrintDialog1.Execute then

            {Print everything.}
            RichEdit1.Print('Common Dialog Example');
end;
```

Print Setup

The Print Setup dialog (shown in Figure 6.9) is the only "fire and forget" common dialog that Windows provides. The only thing you need to do to use it is execute it as shown in Listing 6.7. There are no flags or other configuration options provided with this dialog, so you don't even have to worry about responding to any user input.

Figure 6.9.

Windows handles every aspect of the Print Setup dialog; all you need to do is display it.

Listing 6.7. Execute the Print Setup dialog.

```
procedure TForm1.PrintSetup1Click(Sender: TObject);
begin
    {All we need to do is display the dialog; Windows takes care of the rest.}
    PrinterSetupDialog1.Execute;
end;
```

Replace

Like the Find dialog, implementing the Replace dialog shown in Figure 6.10 is a complex issue. Fortunately, you can use most of the code that you created for your Find dialog with just a few tweaks here and there to change object names. (I tried to come up with a generic routine for this chapter, but Delphi wouldn't provide that capability at the time of this writing—you may be able to implement the find part of a Replace dialog using the same routine that your Find dialog uses.)

Figure 6.10.
The Replace dialog provides a lot of configuration options and requires a lot of work on the programmer's part to implement properly.

You might be tempted to think that the Replace dialog has precisely the same configuration options as the Find dialog—and for the most part it does—but there are differences. Table 6.7 provides a complete listing of the Replace dialog flags and their meanings.

Table 6.7. Replace Dialog Flags.

Flag	Description
frDisableMatchCase	Use this flag to disable the Match Case check box and prevent users from checking it. Remember to use the UpperCase function (as shown in the example code) to perform a case-insensitive search.
frDisableUpDown	This is the flag that disables the Up and Down radio buttons. The user can still see them, but they can't select them. Delphi defaults to searching down. You can still change the direction selection that the dialog returns using the frDown flag.
frDisableWholeWord	Use this flag to disable the Match Whole Word Only check box and prevent users from checking it. I usually add a space to either side of the search word if the user does check this box. Using a space on both sides ensures that you find only whole words. A little extra code would deselect the spaces once you found the appropriate entry in the text.
frDown	Setting this flag to true tells your application to search in a downward direction if you have that option enabled. There isn't any magic here. If you keep the frDown flag active, the only thing it will tell you is what direction to search, not the way to accomplish that task.

continues

Table 6.7. continued

Flag	Description
frFindNext	This flag is kind of useless in most cases. It gets set when the user chooses the Find Next button. When frFindNext is True, your application should search for the string in the FindText property. Of course, if you implement a two-function approach like the one shown in the example, you won't even need this flag.
frHideMatchCase	This flag will hide the Match Case check box. It isn't visible in the dialog box, so the user can't select it.
frHideWholeWord	This flag will hide the Match Whole Word Only check box. It isn't visible in the dialog box, so the user can't select it.
frHideUpDown	This flag will hide the Direction Up and Down radio buttons. They aren't visible in the dialog box, so the user can't select them. If you query the dialog box about direction, it'll return the default setting— the one selected with the frDown flag.
frMatchCase	Use this flag to determine whether the user has checked the Match Case check box. A return value of true means that it's selected. You can also use this flag to automatically check the check box at runtime.
frReplace	A Replace dialog, unlike the Find dialog, contains more than one button. The only way that you can determine which button the user pressed is if the system tells you. This flag is set to true if the user presses the Replace pushbutton.
frReplaceAll	A Replace dialog, unlike the Find dialog, contains more than one button. The only way that you can determine which button the user pressed is if the system tells you. This flag is set to true if the user presses the Replace All pushbutton.
frShowHelp	Windows doesn't force you to provide help to the user. This flag, which defaults to false, displays a Help pushbutton when you set it to true. You'll need to set the HelpContext property to provide any meaningful level of help. We'll take a better look at the methods for implementing help in Chapter 14.
frWholeWord	Use this flag to determine whether the user has checked the Match Whole Word Only check box. A return value of true means that it's selected. You can also use this flag to automatically check the check box at runtime.

So, what's different about a Replace dialog? For one thing, you have to do something with the text you select. There are basic problems that a Replace dialog is trying to solve. First, you have to find the text that you want to replace. We already covered that issue in the Find dialog section of the chapter.

Once you find the text, you have to modify it. That part of the process is actually pretty easy. Listing 6.8 shows you everything you need to implement a basic Replace dialog with the same limitation (unidirectional search) that our Find dialog had. The difference is the inclusion of a third routine (ReplaceDialog1Replace).

Listing 6.8. **Implementing a basic Replace dialog.**

```
procedure TForm1.Replace1Click(Sender: TObject);
begin
    {All we need to do here is display the dialog. The
     FindDialog1Find procedure does the rest of the work.}
    ReplaceDialog1.Execute;
end;

procedure TForm1.ReplaceDialog1Find(Sender: TObject);
var
    sFindText: String;          {Search String}
    iLineNumber: Integer;       {Search Line Counter}
    iCurrentLine: Integer;      {Search Start Position}
    iFoundPosit: Integer;       {String position within line.}
    iLength: Integer;           {SelStart Position}
    fWordWrap: Boolean;           {Current WordWrap Status}
begin

    {Initialize our variables.}
    sFindText := ReplaceDialog1.FindText;
    iCurrentLine := 0;
       iLength := 0;
    fWordWrap := RichEdit1.WordWrap;

    {Change the search variable as needed if whole words were selected.}
    if ReplaceDialog1.Options*[frWholeWord] = [frWholeWord] then
        sFindText := ' ' + sFindText + ' ';

    {Change the search variable to reflect case sensitivity.}
    if ReplaceDialog1.Options*[frMatchCase] <> [frMatchCase] then
        sFindText := UpperCase(sFindText);

    {Turn off word wrap so it won't interfere with the search.}
    RichEdit1.WordWrap := False;

    {If this is the second or subsequent find, then locate the starting line.}
    while iLength < RichEdit1.SelStart do
        begin
         {The length of a line is equal to the text it contains and the end
          of line characters.}
         iLength := iLength + Length(RichEdit1.Lines[iCurrentLine]) + 2;
         iCurrentLine := iCurrentLine + 1;
         end;
```

continues

Listing 6.8. continued

```
    {Continue looking from the current position to the end of the edit window.}
    for iLineNumber := iCurrentLine to RichEdit1.Lines.Count do
        begin

            {A return value of 0 tells us that the text doesn't appear in
             this line.  We use the UpperCase function to convert all text to
             upper case unless the user requested a case sensitive search.}
            if ReplaceDialog1.Options*[frMatchCase] = [frMatchCase] then
                iFoundPosit := Pos(sFindText, RichEdit1.Lines[iLineNumber])
            else
                iFoundPosit := Pos(sFindText, UpperCase(RichEdit1.Lines[iLineNumber]));

            {If we found the search text, then let's highlight it.}
            if iFoundPosit > 0 then
                begin

                    {Give the edit window focus.}
                    RichEdit1.SetFocus;

                    {Change the selected text starting position.}
                    RichEdit1.SelStart := iLength + iFoundPosit - 1;

                    {Set the length equal to our search string.}
                    RichEdit1.SelLength := Length(sFindText);

                    {Return word wrap to its previous state.}
                    RichEdit1.WordWrap := fWordWrap;

                    {Exit this procedure and return to the program.}
                    exit;
                end;

            {Add the length of the current line to our length variable if we
             haven't found the search text.}
            iLength := iLength + Length(RichEdit1.Lines[iLineNumber]) + 2;
        end;

    {If we reached the end of the file, then display a message.}
    MessageDlg('Reached the end of the file.', mtInformation, [mbOK], 0);
end;

procedure TForm1.ReplaceDialog1Replace(Sender: TObject);
begin

    {We need to make sure that the current text is what we want
     to replace.}
    if (RichEdit1.SelLength = 0) or (RichEdit1.SelText <> ReplaceDialog1.FindText) then
        ReplaceDialog1Find(Sender);

    {If we still haven't found something to replace, exit the routine.}
    if RichEdit1.SelLength = 0 then
        Exit;

    {Once we find something to replace, then replace it.}
    RichEdit1.SelText := ReplaceDialog1.ReplaceText;
```

```
    {Look for the next piece of text to replace.}
    ReplaceDialog1Find(Sender);
end;
```

Let's spend a little time talking about the ReplaceDialog1Replace routine in this example. You have to take three steps before you can replace text in an Edit dialog.

1. Check to make sure some text is highlighted. If the user hasn't highlighted some text and they haven't looked for it either, then you'll need to look for the text he wants to replace.

2. If there is text highlighted, then make sure it's the right text. It wouldn't serve the user's needs if you simply replaced any highlighted text with the replace value.

3. Replace the text, then look for the next value. Just like the Find dialog, the user won't know when he's reached the end of the file unless you tell him. Always check for the end of the file by checking for the next piece of text to replace.

Save As

We've come to the final dialog in our discussion. The Save As dialog, show in Figure 6.11, allows you to save a file to disk. However, it actually gets used in more places than any other dialog and in different ways. Every application I can think of uses the Save As dialog for at least three different menu commands: File | Save, File | Save As, and File | New. That's right, before you can create a new file, you really should ask the user if he wants to save the existing one. If your application only supports one file at a time, you should probably add a Save As dialog routine to the File | Open menu option as well.

Figure 6.11.

The Save As dialog gets used in more places than any other dialog.

Many of the Save As dialog options are the same as the Open dialog. However, there are some minor differences between them. For example, the Save As dialog actually does something with the ofNoTestFileCreate and ofOverwritePrompt flags. Table 6.8 describes each of the Save As dialog flags in detail.

Table 6.8. Save As Dialog Flags.

Flag	Description
ofAllowMultiSelect	Set this flag to true if you want to allow the user to select more than one filename in the dialog.
ofCreatePrompt	This flag will allow the user to create a new file from the Open dialog. Windows will display a dialog asking the user if he wants to create a new file when he enters a non-existent filename if you set this flag to true. Since Windows creates the new file for you, your application will still react as if it had opened an existing file.
ofExtensionDifferent	Delphi sets this option when the filename returned from the dialog box has an extension that differs from the default file extension (the DefaultExt property). Obviously, this flag allows you to detect when your application needs to treat a file differently. For example, in our example, we treat text files differently than RTF files.
ofFileMustExist	Use this flag if you want Windows to tell the user when he has entered a non-existent filename. What the user will see is a dialog saying the file doesn't exist and that he should check his path and filename. The advantage to using this flag is that your application will always receive the name of an existing filename when the user clicks on OK.
ofHideReadOnly	Use this flag to hide the Read Only check box.
ofNoChangeDir	This option doesn't prevent the user from changing the directory or drive shown in the Open dialog. It does, however, return the current directory to the one shown when the dialog opened when the user closes the dialog. This comes in handy if you need to look for files in the application directory and don't want to keep checking for the right directory in your application code.
ofNoReadOnlyReturn	Use this flag to tell Windows to display a dialog every time the user selects a read-only file.
ofNoTestFileCreate	There are times where you want to create files in a network directory where the user has create, but not modify, rights. For example, you may want the user to fill out a company survey where he doesn't have an option to change the survey contents once it's completed. Use this flag if you want to take full control of file operations. Your application won't check for write protection, a full disk, an open drive door, or network protection when saving the file because doing so creates a test file.

Flag	Description
ofNoValidate	Use this flag if you want to disable filename validation. Normally, Windows displays a dialog if the user enters invalid characters for a filename.
ofOverwritePrompt	Normally Windows doesn't care if the user decides to overwrite an existing file. You can set this flag to display a dialog telling the user when he is about to overwrite an existing file. The dialog gives him a choice of overwriting it or saving to a different filename.
fReadOnly	This flag tells you that the user checked the Read Only check box when true.
ofPathMustExist	Use this flag if you want Windows to tell the user when he has entered a non-existent path. What the user will see is a dialog saying the path doesn't exist. The advantage to using this flag is that your application will always receive the name of an existing path when the user clicks on OK.
ofShareAware	Windows normally tries to protect the user from opening a file that someone else has already opened. Setting this flag to true disables sharing violation protection. Of course, disabling the protection will allow two users to overwrite each other's data unless your application provides some type of sharing protection.
ofShowHelp	Windows doesn't force you to provide help to the user. This flag, which defaults to false, displays a Help pushbutton when you set it to true. You'll need to set the HelpContext property to provide any meaningful level of help. We'll take a better look at the methods for implementing help in Chapter 14.
ofNoLongNames	This flag allows you to disable long filename support to use the standard DOS 8.3 filenames. The only time you would need this flag is if you needed an application to work with both Windows 3.x and Windows 95 systems.
ofNoNetworkButton	You can use this flag to hide the Network button on old style dialogs. Obviously, it doesn't have any meaning for the newer Explorer dialogs, which make every network drive automatically available.
OfOldStyleDialog	Use this flag if you want to use an old style Open dialog. You may find it easier than trying to support two types of application interface.
ofNoDereferenceLinks	This flag disables dereference link support.

The code in Listing 6.9 shows you how to implement both a File | Save and a File | Save As menu command. Not surprisingly the File | Save As command is the simpler of the two since you can assume a little more when writing it.

Listing 6.9. Implementing a File | Save and File | Save As command.

```
procedure TForm1.SaveAs1Click(Sender: TObject);
var
        sFilename: TFilename;    {User file selection}
begin

    {If the user clicks on OK or double clicks on a filename.}
    if SaveDialog1.Execute then

        {Get the user selection.}
        begin
            sFilename := SaveDialog1.Filename;

        {Determine the file type and set the editor as appropriate.}
        if Pos('.RTF', UpperCase(sFilename)) > 0 then
            RichEdit1.PlainText := False
        else
            RichEdit1.PlainText := True;

        {Save the file.}
        RichEdit1.Lines.SaveToFile(sFilename);
        end;
end;

procedure TForm1.Save1Click(Sender: TObject);
begin
    {Save the edit window contents.}
    EditWindowSave;
end;

procedure TForm1.EditWindowSave;
var
    sFilename: TFilename;    {User file selection}
begin
    {Check to see if the user has saved this file before.}
    if Length(SaveDialog1.Filename) > 0 then

        {Save the file without displaying a dialog.}
         RichEdit1.Lines.SaveToFile(SaveDialog1.Filename)
    else
        {If the user clicks on OK or double clicks on a filename.}
        if SaveDialog1.Execute then

            {Get the user selection.}
                begin
                    sFilename := SaveDialog1.Filename;

                {Determine the file type and set the editor as appropriate.}
                if Pos('RTF', UpperCase(sFilename)) > 0 then
                        RichEdit1.PlainText := False
                else
                    RichEdit1.PlainText := True;

                {Save the file.}
                RichEdit1.Lines.SaveToFile(sFilename);
            end;
end;
```

As you can see from the code, the File | Save As command is a subset of the File | Save command; so let's take a look at it. Looking at the File | Save command, you'll see that it simply calls the EditWindowSave procedure. I did this so that I could use one save routine in a variety of places. The first thing that the EditWindowSave procedure checks is whether we've saved the file before. If so, the routine simply saves the contents of the edit window to the same file. That's why we can't use this routine for the File | Save As command that always displays the Save As dialog. If the user hasn't saved the file before, we have to display the Save As dialog. This dialog provides two different file types—text and RTF (plus an all consuming *.* wildcard type). Saving the file isn't difficult; all we do is copy the edit window's contents to it. The trick is to save the file in the right format. Notice that we change the edit window PlainText property to match the kind of file we want to create. This is an important part of the save process. Setting the PlainText property true removes the RTF formatting codes from the file, enabling us to view it with a text editor.

Summary

This chapter began by helping you understand what a common dialog is and where the code for common dialogs appears in the Windows SYSTEM directory. Knowing this information can help you find useful bits of code in other Windows-supplied DLLs.

We also explored why common dialogs are so important. Code reuse is a major reason to use Windows. Allowing the operating system to take care of some of the details—like dialogs—for you can greatly reduce the time required to code an application. More important than that is the time you'll save in updates and application debugging later.

Finally, we took a look at the eight common dialogs that Windows provides: Color, Find, Font, Open, Print, Print Setup, Replace, and Save As. You can configure each of the dialogs, except the Print Setup dialog, as needed by your application. We looked at the various configuration issues as well as how you would implement a common dialog within Delphi.

7

The Windows GDI

The Graphic Device Interface (GDI) is one of the most complex areas of Windows for the programmer to tackle. Some people view the GDI as a means to display pretty pictures on screen, but they're wrong. It's not just a matter of understanding how Windows interacts with the display adapter or printer; there are a lot of other considerations as well. For example, when you draw a circle on the display, will it look round? That all depends on the display's aspect ratio. What about the jagged lines that we all had to get used to under DOS? Are they acceptable in Windows as well? You'll find that they aren't, so your application may need to perform some type of anti-aliasing. How will the circle you display on screen look when you print it? Most of us realize that in the past WYSIWYG (what you see is what you get) was a pipe dream. Today this may not be the case with the proper programming skills.

There are other issues beyond simple graphics that you need to consider as well. Multitasking environments tend to create a wealth of problems for the application programmer. For example, how will Windows interact with your application if it continues to draw a graph or chart in the background? I've seen some strange things happen when an application continues to assume that it's in the foreground when it's not. The least that you can expect to see is some type of display corruption. What about the use of palette? Your application can control how things appear while it's in the foreground, but it can't while in the background. This isn't that big of a problem if the user is concentrating on something else, but they might be surprised to see the nice green in their chart turn blue when the foreground application changes the palette. All of these considerations—and more—are also part of the GDI.

Lest you think that the Windows GDI is going to be too difficult to understand, consider some of the tools at your disposal. For one thing, Delphi provides you with more than a few capabilities when it comes to the GDI. The 16-bit version provided some tools, the newer 32-bit version provides even more (we covered these new features in Chapter 1, "Introducing Delphi"). Delphi also takes care of some of the management questions for you. For example, we saw in Chapter 5, "Accessing the Windows API," that it takes care of the WM_PAINT message for you, which is responsible for updating things like the display palette and the image itself when the user brings your application to the foreground. The new capabilities found in Windows 95 also help a great deal (we'll talk about these features in the architectural section of the chapter). Add to that the proliferation of graphics libraries like Graphics Server from Pinnacle Publishing and end user products like Microsoft's Plus Pack and you have an environment that's much improved from a programmer perspective. (Graphics Server helps you create graphs and charts with a minimum of effort, while the Plus Pack contains software that performs some anti-aliasing for all applications.)

An Architectural Overview of the GDI

Video is the most noticeable architectural component of Windows. It's the underlying combination of hardware and software that allows you to see the graphics, dialog boxes, icons, and other elements that make Windows worth using. Under DOS, text and graphics were separate elements and used different video adapter display modes for the most part. Windows displays everything in graphics mode, so it would seem that the problem would be simpler, not more complex. The truth is a lot different than most people expect. That dialog box is an object, not simply a picture. An object has properties and it maintains its separate identity. When Windows draws a dialog box, it isn't drawing a picture, but the representation of a screen object. The same holds true for all the other graphics you see on screen. The GDI is ultimately responsible for managing all of these graphic components. It does so using a variety of structures and other programming devices that we'll study in the next section.

Let's begin with a look at the GDI architecture. There are three elements that I consider crucial to an understanding of the GDI architecture. You need to consider inter-component communications (a statement of video display problems and interfaces), current standards used to create the GDI (methods used to define solutions to various display problems and a description of the interfaces), and the GDI itself (the implementation of the standards). We'll look at each of these three areas in the following sections. You should have a good understanding of what the GDI does by the time we're through.

Note: I've included two different GDI architecture sections—one for Windows 95 and another for Windows NT. The Windows 95 section is complete in every detail. The Windows NT section builds on the information in the Windows 95 section to help you understand the differences between the two operating systems.

Communication Is Key

Inter-component communication is key to making the Windows GDI work properly. The problem isn't simply one of displaying a picture on-screen; that would be easy to manage. The problem is one of communication between the various elements that create and manage the picture in the first place. You need to remember that the GDI has a lot more to worry about than your application—or even all the Windows applications running on a machine for that matter. The GDI has to manage every application that Windows is running, no matter in what environment the application is running. That includes both DOS and Windows applications for Windows 95. Windows NT has even more to manage because it also provides OS/2 and POSIX operating environments. The following list illustrates some of Windows communication problems:

- Application level: Three different kinds of applications use Windows 95. Windows NT, as previously stated, provides a minimum of five different application levels. DOS applications normally think they are alone in the world, so they violate just about every imaginable rule for displaying information. In fact, this lack of control prevents some DOS applications from running under Windows NT. Game programs are the worst in this area;

you can count on them to change the display adapter registers in unusual ways and write directly to video memory with nary a thought that anyone else might be using the system. Although 16-bit Windows applications are a bit more conscientious than their DOS counterparts, they still use an older interface to draw to the display. (Even though Windows 95 and Windows NT manage 16-bit applications differently internally, you as a programmer won't see any differences worth noting.) Newer 32-bit Windows might offer the ultimate in available features right now, but they're often hampered by other applications running on the machine. Windows NT also has to manage OS/2 and POSIX applications. Fortunately, these programs tend to be better behaved than their DOS counterparts, so the amount of additional management needed is fairly minimal.

- Device driver: I own an older display adapter that drives me crazy when I use Word for Windows. It's not really a problem with the adapter; it's a problem with the drivers that support the adapter. If the display driver doesn't correctly interpret the commands issued by applications running under Windows, or if those applications use undocumented command features, there's a good chance of miscommunication. In the case of my faulty setup, the adapter misinterpreted some of the commands that Word and a few other applications used, resulting in an unreadable screen.

- Adapter: In the beginning, IBM set the tone and the baseline for all display adapters. Its leadership was responsible for the somewhat standard way in which the CGA and EGA display adapters worked. By the time VGA came around, IBM was starting to lose its leadership position. Then came SVGA (super VGA) and there was no IBM standard to follow. For a while there was a lack of any kind of standardization for the extended modes that vendors built into their display adapters. The result was total chaos. How do you build a set of standardized drivers for an operating system when there's no standard to follow? We'll look at how this problem finally was resolved a little later in this chapter.

- Monitor: There's less of a standardization problem with monitors, but it's still present. This problem manifests itself in setups where one monitor works fine but another doesn't. The problem is in the signals coming from the display adapter. With today's ergonomic concerns, like the 70 Hz refresh rate needed to reduce eyestrain, frequency ranges have expanded dramatically. Some monitors just can't handle the increased frequency requirements. Add to that some level of ambiguity on the part of vendors. I'll never get over the fine-print problem with several monitors I looked at. A monitor supposedly supports 1024 × 768 mode. When you look at the fine print, though, it becomes obvious that this support is good only in interlaced mode. This led to a problem with one monitor when I installed Windows NT. I got the upper half of the picture just fine, but the lower half disappeared. The problem was some combination of adapter, driver, and monitor. If the monitor had supported 1024 × 768 non-interlaced mode, there wouldn't have been a problem.

- Operating system requirements: Normally, the operating system itself is the least of your worries with the display. However, sometimes it can actually be the source of your problems. Take icons, for example. We all take them for granted because they generally work without any difficulty. But what happens if some file that the operating system needs is changed by an application or is corrupted somehow? On one machine, the system files had suffered some type of damage, and all the icons disappeared. No amount of work would bring them back, so I finally ended up reinstalling everything from scratch to get them back.

Now that you have a better idea of the communication problems that Windows suffers from, you might wonder why it works at all. We discussed the Windows system of messages in Chapter 5. It's this message (event) loop that allows every application running within Windows to communicate with each other and Windows itself. In addition, Windows doesn't allow an application to draw to the real display buffer (some programmers call this area of memory the video buffer). You actually draw to a virtual buffer. When you switch from one environment to another—say Windows to DOS—Windows takes away one virtual screen and replaces it with another. The combination of an event loop and constant redrawing enables Windows to keep your display up-to-date, even if small amounts of miscommunication do occur.

Graphics Standards

The second part of our GDI architecture triad is standards. Many different standards organizations help keep things running smoothly on your computer. Several competing standards affect how your modem works. One of these organizations, the CCITT, has become a major contributor as of late. Another organization, EIA, defines specifications for the various port connectors, serial and parallel, which attach your machine to the outside world and peripheral devices. The standards organization you want to keep your eye on for display adapters and monitors, though, is the Video Electronics Standards Association (VESA). This organization does a lot more than simply define the electronics behind a monitor or display adapter; it also defines the programming interface. For example, when IBM wouldn't publish the specifications for the 8514/A display adapter, VESA got together with several other companies and published one in IBM's stead. When someone creates a device driver for Windows, it's the VESA standards that they use when designing the hardware interface section of the code. Your application indirectly interacts with that driver through the GDI. When you ask Windows to tell you the capabilities of a particular device, it can do so because the display adapter and its driver use a standard interface that Windows can understand.

Tip: VESA can provide you with detailed specifications for a number of display adapter and monitor standards. You can usually get copies of these standards from online sources such as CompuServe. They also often appear in the manuals that come with your adapter or monitor. You can contact VESA directly using the following information:

Video Electronics Standards Association
2150 North First Street, Suite 440
San Jose, CA 95131-2029
Voice: (408) 435-0333
Fax: (408) 435-8225

I first ran into this organization in 1989, but they were probably around a while before that. IBM had dropped VGA in favor of its proprietary 8514/A display adapter. Without a leader in the field to dictate a standard, the entire display adapter arena fell into a state of disarray. At the time I first heard about VESA, they were working on a standard to fix the SVGA problem. Of course, the resolutions and number of colors were severely limited in comparison to what you can get today.

The main difficulty that the graphics community was facing was communication. Before this time, every display adapter used the same programming interface, in the form of a BIOS call, to change display settings and otherwise control the display adapter. All the old display methods worked, but vendors chose to differentiate their products by implementing the VGA "extended" modes differently. The resulting chaos made it impossible for any programmer to write an application that used SVGA modes without writing a different driver for each adapter.

VESA stepped in to make sense of all this chaos. The result of these initial efforts were several VESA standards and some additional software for each display adapter. That VESA driver that you load for some applications is actually a BIOS extension that allows display adapters to use a standardized SVGA interface. The extension translates VESA standard BIOS calls into something adapter-specific. As a result, an application can use one set of BIOS calls to configure and control the display adapter. Newer display adapters no longer require you to load a special driver; their BIOS chips come with VESA support installed. Table 7.1 shows many of the common standards that VESA has produced. There are also older standards that will shed some light on some issues that these newer standards don't cover. A representative at VESA will be more than happy to answer any questions you might have.

Table 7.1. VESA Standards for Display Adapters and Monitors.

Standard	Title	Purpose
VS911020	Super VGA protected-mode interface	This document provides information on a standardized method of accessing the BIOS routines from a protected-mode program.
VS911021	Video cursor interface	Use this standard to learn how to build an interface between a pointing device and the display adapter.

Standard	Title	Purpose
VS911022	Super VGA BIOS extension	This is the document you'll need in order to learn about VESA standard display modes for the SVGA.
VXE 1.0	XGA extensions standard	This document tells you about some of the standardization efforts under way for the XGA.
VS910810	Monitor timing standard for 1024 × 768 with 70 Hz refresh rate	This standard helps provide a consistent method of providing ergonomically correct displays. It allows a vendor to create a display adapter and monitor that will work together at the 70 Hz refresh rate, which greatly reduces eye strain.
VS900601	Standard 8514/A register bit fields	A programmer needs to know the details of how a register works. This standard provides that information.
VS890803	Standard VGA passthrough connector	There was a lot of confusion on how to get a high-resolution display adapter to work with a standard one. The passthrough connector seemed an ideal way to do it, but the connections for it weren't standardized. That's what this standard does: It defines the passthrough connector and allows you to use multiple adapters in one machine.
VS890804	Standard 8514/A registers	Before you can program a register, you need to know what to call it. This standard defines what registers an 8514/A contains. Remember that IBM didn't want to share this information with anyone.

Of course, this selection of standards is by no means complete. VESA works on a whole array of other standardization efforts, such as industrial guidelines for the manufacture of computer components. Its most famous nondisplay-related standard is probably the VL bus. This was such an important standard at one time that in 1993, Dell wanted to take VESA to court over the matter of who owned the standard.

The Windows 95 Graphics Architecture

Now that you have some idea of the problems that Microsoft (and any other vendor) faces when it comes to providing something for you to look at, it's time to discuss how they do it. Display adapters and monitors have both moved beyond the simpler requirements of the time when IBM was at the helm. In the interim, we've seen the emergence of even higher resolutions and a new adapter called the XGA. The SVGA is also improving on an almost daily basis. It used to be that 640 × 480 resolution and 256 colors were something to whistle about. Today an adapter is considered almost inadequate at 1024 × 768 resolution and 24-bit (16.7 million) colors. Windows 95 endeavors to handle this wide range of capabilities using the same centralized control mechanism that it uses for printing—a combination of the minidriver and DIB engine.

One of the main architectural components is the GDI. This is the part of the graphics architecture that you, as a programmer, will interact with. (Even if you don't interact with it directly, you can be certain that the Delphi supplied components, functions, and DLLs do.) The GDI has been tuned and retuned throughout the various incarnations of Windows. It's no surprise that Microsoft has spent so much time in this area, since many benchmark tests focus on graphics performance. In fact, from a user perspective, the thing they notice most is the way the graphics engine performs. Microsoft did some more tuning of the GDI for Windows 95, but I'd term this tuning more incremental than major. The following list provides details on some of the more significant changes.

- DIB engine: The new DIB engine is handcrafted assembly language. Not only is this area heavily used in rendering graphic images, but it's used for the printer as well. The GDI and DIB engine work together with the display device driver to produce the picture you'll eventually see on-screen. Unlike previous versions of Windows, though, Windows 95 doesn't force every graphics instruction to go through the DIB engine. If a display adapter provides a coprocessor that can handle the operation more efficiently, Windows uses it in place of the DIB engine.

- TrueType rasterizer: This is the component responsible for changing the font descriptions in your TTF files to a bitmap that Windows can display on-screen. Microsoft moved the data for this part of the GDI out of the 64 KB heap area to a 32-bit area. They also rewrote the rasterizer code in 32-bit format to improve overall performance.

- GDI component duplication: We talked about the use of a thunk to convert 16-bit data to 32-bit format in Chapter 5. Thunks cost time. This isn't a big deal in most cases, because a thunk can be a lot less expensive than a transition to real mode to handle a device need. However, some operations are performed so often that Microsoft decided to provide both a 16-bit and a 32-bit version in Windows 95. This allows for a small but noticeable speed improvement over Windows NT.

- Path support: A Windows application used to create complex objects using lots of standard objects such as squares, triangles, and circles. All these little calls could eat up a lot of processor time if the program needed to create something really complicated. Using paths allows a Windows 95 application to describe a complex shape in one function call. The GDI can then figure out the most efficient way to present it. The result is that the programmer spends less time describing the object, and the user sees a performance improvement.

- Metafile support: A metafile contains drawing commands that describe the drawing instead of actually providing a bitmap for it. Each command is called a *record*. The GDI processes records to reconstruct the image. The advantage of a metafile is that you can make it any size you want and adapt it to any device resolution. Windows 3.x didn't provide metafile support as part of the operating system even though some applications did provide this support. Windows 95 improves on this by providing partial metafile support as part of the API. It doesn't include the full range of metafile commands that Windows NT does, but it does provide some. The result is that you gain the advantages of using a metafile, but Windows 95 won't completely understand some Windows NT metafiles. Fortunately, if the GDI doesn't understand a particular command, it ignores it and goes on to the next one.

- Bézier curve drawing: A Bézier curve is drawn using a set of points. A curved freeform line connects the points. The idea isn't to necessarily touch all the points, but to draw a line that most nearly defines a shape that flows from point to point. Many advanced graphics applications such as CorelDRAW! support this feature right out of the box. Windows 95 adds this feature so that an application can describe a curve using points and allow the GDI to figure out how to draw it.

- Image color matching (ICM): It wasn't long ago that everyone used green screens and black-and-white printers. Today the cost of a color printer is dropping rapidly, and color displays are standard on every machine. There's a problem in trying to get the color on your screen to match the color on your printer, however. For one thing, the two devices use different methods to create colors. Another reason is that it's nearly impossible to create some colors on certain devices. The technical details of all this are keeping several standards groups talking right now, so it's impossible to say how the problem occurs or what to do about it. Still, the problem remains. With the emergence of color as a major new component of computing, Microsoft saw the need to provide color matching between devices. Although it's not a perfect solution, ICM is a good start for people who can't afford professional publishing equipment.

Improvements in the GDI aren't the only change in Windows 95. There are some pretty big architectural changes as well. Let's take a look at the overall architecture. I won't get into bits and bytes here, but I will tell you about the basic components required to display something on-screen. Figure 7.1 is an overview of the Windows 95 architecture. The following paragraphs tell you what task each of the components performs.

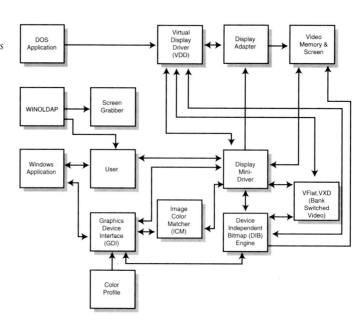

Figure 7.1.
An overview of the Windows 95 graphics architecture.

- WINOLDAP: This is a module that senses when a DOS application is about to take control of the display area. It notifies USER and the screen grabber so that they can preserve the graphics system status information. You'll find this module listed as WINOA386.MOD in your \SYSTEM directory.

- Screen grabber: I always think of this as a camera. In essence, that's what it is. The screen grabber takes a picture of the screen and preserves it for later. This allows Windows to restore the screen to its former appearance after you exit a DOS session. Any file with a .2GR or .3GR extension in your \SYSTEM directory is a screen grabber. You don't need the 2GR files for Windows 95, because it doesn't support standard mode. In addition, you need only one 3GR file—the one designed for your display adapter.

- User: We've already discussed the uses for this module extensively. This module tracks the state of all the display elements, such as icons and dialog boxes, in addition to drawing them. That's why it needs to be informed before a DOS session comes to the foreground—so that it can take a snapshot of the current state of these components. As I stated earlier, there are actually two User-related files on disk—a 16-bit and a 32-bit version.

- GDI: This is another module that we've spent a lot of time discussing. Like the User module, there are two physical files—one for 16-bit and another for 32-bit needs. The GDI module works with the display driver and the DIB engine to produce the graphic components of a Windows display.

- Display minidriver: With Windows 3.x, every video signal went through the Virtual Display Driver (VDD). The VDD would process the signal and send it to the display adapter. Windows 95 can use a combination of the display minidriver and the DIB engine for adapters that can support them. Using this driver combination results in a speed increase from 32-bit code. The name of this file varies, depending on the type of display you're using. On my system, it's named SUPERVGA.DRV. Unlike the VDD, which performs all video processing, the display minidriver takes care of only device-specific details. The DIB engine takes care of graphics rendering. A minidriver contains a lot less code than a full-fledged VDD, reducing the amount of code that a vendor must write.

- Device-independent bitmap (DIB) engine: The DIB engine takes the graphics instructions provided by the GDI and renders them into an image. Unlike printing, in which the DIB engine doesn't do the whole job, it actually draws the rendered image on the frame buffer. A *frame buffer* is a piece of system memory set aside to represent video memory. When the drawing on the buffer is complete, the entire buffer is sent to video memory at one time. Anything sent to video memory usually ends up on the display. This process is known as *virtualization*. The DIB engine itself is found in DIBENG.DLL. There's also a compatibility module for Windows 3.x applications called DISPDIB.DLL, which was the predecessor to the DIB engine. This second DLL allowed Windows 3.x to use a DIB for small objects instead of the entire display. You might also find several DIB*.DRV files in your \SYSTEM directory. Each one of these files provides some type of expanded display or memory management function for Windows 3.x DIBs. In almost all cases, these drivers are designed to work on individual objects rather than the entire display. The frame buffer management routines are found in FRAMEBUF.DRV.

- Color profile: This is a data file that contains the color capabilities for your output device. It doesn't matter whether the device is a printer or a display adapter; the type of information is the same. The purpose of a color profile is to provide the ICM with the information it needs to keep the display and other color devices in sync. That way, when you select dark red on the display, you get the same dark red on your printer. We talked about some of the problems with color matching earlier, so I won't go into them again here. You'll find all the color profile files in the COLOR folder in the SYSTEM folder. All these files have an .ICM extension. The Properties dialog associated with each one will give you many more technical details about the actual profile.

- Image color matcher (ICM): The whole process of matching the output of your printer to what you see on the display is complex—much too complex to really cover here. We discussed the problem of color matching earlier in this chapter. The ICM is the module that actually performs the work. It subtly changes the output of your printer and display so that they match. The GDI, display minidriver, and ICM work together to compare the current color set and translate it into something that will work on both devices. It's not a perfect solution, but it works for the most part. Let's just say that the results are very close, but not absolutely the same. Most of us wouldn't notice, but a professional artist might. Of course, this solution can't take into account the many details that a professional would, such as temperature, humidity, and other environmental aspects beyond Windows' control. The files that contain the ICM include ICM32.DLL and ICMUI.DLL; both appear in the SYSTEM folder.

- VFLATD.VXD: This module is only used for bank-switched video adapters. Its main purpose is to manage the video memory window that these devices provide. Banked-switched video memory works much like expanded memory—a large amount of memory is accessed through a movable window. The display adapter on your machine could contain a very large amount of memory. Unfortunately, there's only a 64 KB window set aside to access that memory. Depending on your adapter's configuration, Windows might not be able to get around this limitation. VFLATD.VXD can manage up to a 1 MB frame buffer. It reads this buffer into video memory as required in 64 KB chunks.

- Virtual display driver (VDD): Windows 3.x used this module as its sole source of communication with the display adapter. Windows 95 provides it for compatibility purposes and for DOS applications. In most cases, the name of this file contains some part of the name of the display adapter vendor. For example, the name of the VxD for my system is VIDEO7.VXD. You'll find it in the SYSTEM folder. This driver converts drawing commands into signals that the display adapter can use. It also manages the display adapter and performs a variety of other tasks related to the way that all the applications on your machine share the display adapter. In essence, it's a 16-bit version of the display minidriver and DIB engine combination.

- Display adapter: This is the physical piece of hardware in your machine.

- Video memory and screen: Video memory is where the electronic form of the image that you see on-screen is stored.

Keep in mind that this was a quick tour of the video subsystem. The actual inner workings of this part of Windows are a lot more complex than you might think. To give you a better idea of the way things work, think of Windows as having three video paths (it's more complex than that, but let's not get mired in too much detail at this point): one 16-bit DOS, one 16-bit Windows, and one 32-bit Windows. The path that Windows uses depends on what applications you're using, the type of adapter you have, and the video performance settings you select in the System Properties dialog. The 16-bit DOS path consists of the VDD, display adapter, and video memory. It also might include VFLATD.VXD if required. The 16-bit Windows path adds WINOLDAP, the screen grabber, User, and the GDI. The 32-bit path includes User, the GDI, the display minidriver, the DIB engine, and video memory. It also includes VFLATD.VXD if your display adapter uses bank-switched memory. Both Windows paths could include the ICM and the associated color profiles. It depends on your setup, the drivers that Microsoft eventually includes, and the capabilities of the devices you're using.

Windows NT Graphics Architecture

This section assumes that you've read through the Windows 95 architecture description I provided in the previous section. Windows NT provides many of the same elements that Windows 95 does. However, it has some additional considerations that Windows 95 doesn't, such as:

- Portability—Windows NT is meant to be portable. That means that Microsoft had to design it to run on a variety of platforms (or computers) with a minimum of changes. We'll see in a few moments how that affected their design strategy for the GDI in Windows NT.

- OS/2 and POSIX Support—You can't provide support for applications designed for another operating system without also supporting the graphics needs of those applications. Windows NT uses a client system to provide this support. There's a client for OS/2 and another for POSIX. This client architecture could conceivably allow Windows NT to support any number of operating systems. It represents a major difference between it and Windows 95.

- Multiprocessor Support—Any time you introduce more than one processor into the computing picture, you have to also add code to handle it. Graphics is the largest consumer of resources on your machine. Not only does it take large quantities of memory, but it needs a lot of processor cycles as well. Windows NT had to provide support for using more than one processor to complete graphics tasks to make multiprocessing a reality.

- Improved Reliability—Reliability is a major concern with Windows NT—much more so than with Windows 95. DOS applications that write directly to the video adapter and change its registers without much thought are a threat to that security. You'll find that Windows NT is a lot less tolerant of ill-behaved applications than Windows 95 is. Much of that intolerance is found in the GDI and other graphics elements.

There's an interesting bit of information to note about the Windows NT GDI: It's one of the few pieces that Microsoft wrote mostly with C++ (the rest of Windows NT uses a combination of C and C++). I think you'll also see more than a few differences between the Windows 95 GDI and the one used in Windows NT in Figure 7.2. I'm not going to reiterate everything I said in the previous section here. The following paragraphs do describe the differences between the Windows NT architecture and that found in Windows 95.

- WIN32 Subsystem: Remember that Windows NT uses a client and server approach to taking care of the needs of the various applications it supports. The way it does that is through the WIN32 subsystem—a buffer layer that translates foreign operating system calls into something that Windows NT can understand. Think about POSIX for a second. Filenames and other entities are case sensitive in that environment. Contrast this to the case insensitive nature of DOS. You'll also remember that OS/2 is a 32-bit operating system, even in character mode, which makes a big difference in the way its applications react. The actual number of differences between the various operating system applications are too vast to really discuss in detail here, and we really don't need to know them to program adequately in Delphi. On the other hand, it's always nice to know that something exists even if you don't need it.

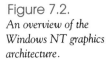

Figure 7.2.
An overview of the
Windows NT graphics
architecture.

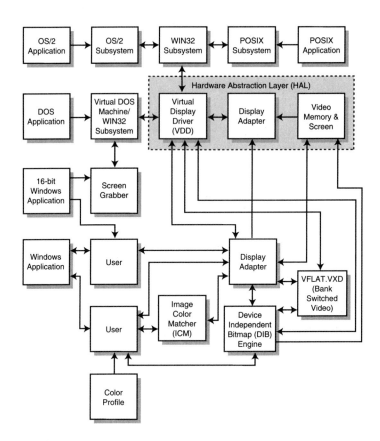

- Virtual DOS Machine (VDM): Windows NT places each DOS application in its own VDM. The reason is simple: To provide the higher level of system reliability that Windows NT users demand, Microsoft had to make sure that each application had its own environment, an environment that is completely separate from that used by any other application. It's also important to remember that 16-bit Windows applications share one VDM. You need to remember that Windows NT always starts a VDM, then runs a copy of 16-bit Windows in it to service the needs of 16-bit Windows applications. This effectively adds two layers to every interaction—one for the VDM and another for the WIN32 Subsystem. As with everything else, this additional layering is transparent to the programmer. You still use the same interfaces as before.

- OS/2 Application, OS/2 Subsystem, POSIX Application, and POSIX Subsystem: I included these four elements so that you would know that they're there, but I really don't plan to say much about them since you won't use them with Delphi. Suffice it to say that Windows NT provides support for OS/2 and POSIX.

- Hardware Abstraction Layer (HAL): This is another conceptual type of element in Windows NT. Microsoft wrote the drivers and other software elements in such a way that they could easily move Windows NT to other platforms. That's how they moved Windows NT to the MIPS and Alpha machines. The basic architecture of Windows NT is the same, but the low level drivers—the ones that directly interface with the hardware—are different. Figure 7.2 shows the elements for an Intel processor machine. You might see something slightly different when using an Alpha or MIPS machine. The important thing to remember is that as far as your application is concerned, it's still running on an Intel machine. The only time you'll run into trouble is if you bypass the Windows API and go directly to the hardware.

The short take on all this is that you won't notice much difference between the Windows NT GDI and that used under Windows 95 as a Delphi programmer. You can even use the API directly and not get too worried about anything. There are a few situations in which you might notice differences, though, if you decide to create your own DLLs. The big thing to remember is that Windows NT runs on more than one hardware platform. If you plan on creating an application to run under both Windows 95 and Windows NT, then you can't assume anything about the hardware that your application will run on. You have to use the API in a device independent manner and rely on it exclusively. That's going to be hard where the Windows API falls short on special device support. Then again, would you really run an application that requires a special device on another platform? The problem of directly accessing the hardware tends to take care of itself if you take the time to think your application through.

Creating a Device Context

The first thing that you'll need to learn about when using the GDI is the device context. I previously mentioned that all Windows applications (and DOS for that matter) use a virtual screen and printer instead of the real thing. Windows essentially issues everyone a blank piece of paper and a pencil. Your application records what it wants to display on screen or on the printer using its paper and pencil. Windows looks at what all the applications have drawn and makes the appropriate changes to the real display memory. The paper and pencil are a device context.

You'll need separate device contexts for anything you want to draw to the screen or the printer. A device context isn't simply memory, it's an object. It has properties just like all the Delphi objects that you create. You can change these properties to provide certain special effects for your application. The device context also provides a variety of management tools. For example, there are a number of function calls that you can use to ascertain the current status of the device context (or any object within the device context).

So, how does this affect you within Delphi? It doesn't if you're going to use Delphi's built-in features to access the display. Delphi takes care of the sheet of paper for you. On the other hand, if you decide to directly access the Windows API, you'll need to get a piece of paper from Windows and maintain it yourself. That's one of the tradeoffs of using the Windows API.

Now that you've gotten the idea of a device context down, you'll need to know something else about it. Windows doesn't actually allow you to do anything directly to the device context. You have to use function calls to manipulate its contents. When I think about the way Windows handles a device context, I often get the picture of someone manipulating an object in one of those clean rooms using mechanical arms. You can see everything in the room and interact with it, but you have to use the mechanical arms to do so.

So, how do you even know that you have access to a device context? You use a special function call to create one or you get the current device context from an existing window (we'll see how this is done in a few moments). If you provide Windows with the proper information, it returns a handle to the device context. This brings up one of the first compatibility issues between the 32-bit and 16-bit Windows environment. The handle you get when you create a device context for a Windows NT or 95 application is 32 bits long, just like everything else in these environments. The handle for a 16-bit Windows application is only 16 bits long. So, does this mean you have to change a lot of code if you're moving from the 16-bit environment to the 32-bit environment? No, if you used the right kind of variable type for your device context handle, you shouldn't experience any problem at all. Both 16-bit and 32-bit Windows use the HDC variable types for device context handles. The only thing you need to do is change your documentation to reflect the change in handle size and recompile. Your compiler will take care of the rest.

Our first example is what I call the hard way—I'll tell you why after we look at the example. Listing 7.1 shows the code you'll need to access the current device context. Figure 7.3 shows the form I used for this example. The only things I did were to add a menu containing a File | Exit and a Test command. I also changed the Form1 Color parameter to clWhite.

Figure 7.3.
This version of the Test form comes in handy for graphics because you don't have any buttons in the way and can draw directly on the form.

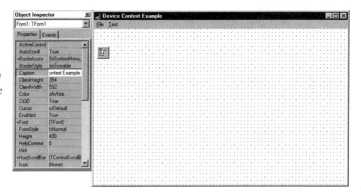

Listing 7.1. Creating a device context.

```
unit DC1;

interface

uses
```

```
   SysUtils, Windows, Messages, Classes, Graphics, Controls, Forms, Dialogs,
   Menus, StdCtrls;

type
  TForm1 = class(TForm)
    MainMenu1: TMainMenu;
    File1: TMenuItem;
    Exit1: TMenuItem;
    Test1: TMenuItem;
    procedure Exit1Click(Sender: TObject);
    procedure Test1Click(Sender: TObject);
  private
    { Private declarations }
  public
    { Public declarations }
  end;

var
  Form1: TForm1;

implementation

{$R *.DFM}

procedure TForm1.Exit1Click(Sender: TObject);
begin
    Halt;    {Exit the program}
end;

procedure TForm1.Test1Click(Sender: TObject);
var
    hdc: HDC;                  {Handle to a device context}
begin
    {Get the handle to the current device context.}
    hdc := GetDC(handle);

    {Use some functions to draw on the window.}
    MoveToEx(hdc, 100, 0, NIL);     {Move to a specific point}
    LineTo(hdc, 0, 100);          {Draw a line from that point to another point}
end;


end.
```

Notice that we use Delphi's predefined "handle" for the window handle. You could just as easily have used the GetActiveWindow API call. Using the predefined handle provides you with a little more flexibility. For example, you don't have to draw on the main form; you could just as easily add a TMemo control to the form and draw on it instead. Keeping the TMemo control the same size would reduce the number of resize problems you'd have using a standard form.

Overall, the code in this example should look fairly simple. There is one thing that you should notice about the MoveToEx function call. You won't find it in the Windows 3.x API. Microsoft tried to reduce the complexity of using the Windows API as much as possible—especially when it came to moving from the 16-bit to 32-bit environment. In some cases they couldn't make the 32-bit call precisely the same as its 16-bit counterpart. That's why the 32-bit version of MoveTo is MoveToEx (the Ex is extended). The 32-bit version takes a fourth parameter (a point structure that contains the previous location on return). We didn't need it for this example, so I simply passed a value of NIL to the function.

Once you type this code, you can run it. You should see a display similar to the one shown in Figure 7.4. It's not much to look at, but it'll get you started with device contexts.

Figure 7.4.

This simple device context example shows you the basics of working with them in Windows.

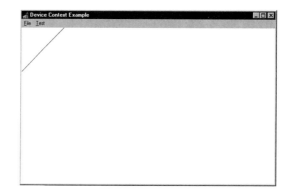

Remember that I told you the previous example is the hard way. So, what's the easy way? Delphi provides a predefined device context for you. It's called a canvas—think of an artist's canvas and you can't go wrong. Take a look at Listing 7.2. It shows the same device context example as before, but this time we use the predefined canvas instead of getting the device context ourselves.

Listing 7.2. An easier way to create a device context.

```
procedure TForm1.Test1Click(Sender: TObject);
begin
    {Use some functions to draw on the window.}
    Canvas.MoveTo(100, 0);    {Move to a specific point}
    Canvas.LineTo(0, 100);    {Draw a line from that point to another point}
end;
```

As you can see, this version of the Text1Click procedure is even simpler than the previous one. We've also used one less variable and made the code a bit easier to read. Notice that we can use exactly the same code in both the 16-bit and 32-bit versions of Delphi as well. The downside is that you probably won't get the same level of flexibility as you did using the API directly. For example, our new version of the function won't return the previous pointer position, something that the new MoveToEx call to the GDI will do for us. You may see this as a minor point, but it could become a major issue in some programming projects.

We have to take a look at a few more issues regarding device contexts under Windows. For one thing, there's more than one type of device context. Windows supports the four device context types shown in Table 7.2.

Table 7.2. Windows Device Context Types.

Context Type	Description
Display	This is the one that we've already looked at in this section. A display device context is usually attached to a window or some other area that you can draw on like a TMemo control. Drawing on a display device context always sends information to the screen. There are three types of display device context: class, common, and private. You would use the class type to support older applications. Always use a private display device context with 32-bit applications. Windows maintains a group of common device contexts. You can use one of them if your application doesn't do a lot of drawing. For example, you might want to use a common device context to quickly output a graph or chart. You can use the GetDC, GetDCEx, or BeginPaint functions to get a common device context. Obviously, you'll also want to give up the handle you receive quickly since Windows only has a limited number of these device contexts available. Private device contexts are actually owned by applications. You can draw on them as much as you like before giving them back to Windows. CAD and drawing applications will probably use this type of display device context.
Printer	Like the display device context, anything you send to the printer display context is printed immediately. Windows also uses the printer device context for alternate output devices like plotters. Obviously you have to have the right device drivers loaded before you can use a plotter or other alternate output device. (Strangely enough, none of the Windows documentation mentions where faxes are supposed to fit in—I've found that the vast majority of them use the serial port services and require a memory device context.)
Memory	Anything you can send to a device or a printer device context you can also send to memory. You create a memory device context using the CreateCompatibleDC function. I always look at a memory device context as print or display now, output later. You'll also use this device context type for things like bitmaps.
Information	Before you can really use a device, it's nice to know its capability. This isn't such a big deal when working with the display since Windows does such a great job of dealing with it. However, printers are another story. For example, if you have a color document to output to the printer, it would be nice to know if the printer supported color output. You might want to add a special dithering routine to support black-and-white printers. You create an information device context using the CreateIC function. Once you create the device context, you can object information about a specific object using the GetCurrentObject or GetObject functions.

A device context doesn't just sit around and wait for you to draw on it. You have to fill it with any number of graphic objects before you can really use it. Delphi takes care of some of this for you, but you may find reason to add some graphic objects of your own. For example, you might want to add an additional palette (group of colors) or a font. Windows recognizes seven different graphic objects—primitives that it uses to create every other object you can use within Windows. Table 7.3 contains a complete list of these objects. (We'll cover their use in the next few sections.)

Table 7.3. Windows Graphic Objects.

Object Type	Purpose and Attributes
Bitmap	A bitmap is a raster picture of some type. For example, BMP files fall into this category as do icons and PCX files. A bitmap object has the following attributes: size in bytes, dimensions in pixels, color format, and compression scheme. You'll find that bitmap objects also have a variety of other attributes based on their specific type. We'll cover the more common bitmap types in the following section.
Brush	Brushes are for applying color. You use a brush to apply paint on a wall. Windows uses brushes to paint the interior of other graphic objects like polygons and paths. There is a wide variety of brush types. You can even use a bitmap as a brush to create a patterned fill. Brushes have the following attributes: style, color, pattern, and origin.
Palette	An artist couldn't create much without an entire palette of colors. Windows allows you to define a wealth of colors, but some video adapters only allow you to display 256 at a time. That's why you might want to use more than one palette. You could ensure clear and solid colors on screen by using a different palette each time you need a different set of 256 colors. Palettes have the following attributes: colors and size (number of colors in the palette).
Font	Every bit of text you see in Windows is stored in a font. You couldn't write anything at all to screen without using one. Fonts have a lot of different attributes. However, the ones that you'll use most often include: Typeface name, width, height, weight, and character set.
Path	Think of one of those hedge mazes in Europe when you see this word and you'll find it easier to remember what this object type is. This doesn't refer to the path you use to access files; it refers to some type of drawn object like a polygon, arc, line, or circle. Windows has a lot of different path functions and they all have different attributes. We'll talk about this topic fully in the next section.

Object Type	Purpose and Attributes
Pen	You write with a pen. Windows writes with one as well; it uses a pen object to draw lines. Think of the different pens that a calligrapher uses and you'll have a better idea of what Windows means when it talks about a pen. Pen objects have the following attributes: Style (nib type), width (nib size), and color.
Region	A region is just that, the dimensions of some area within the device context. There are times that you'll want to tell Windows to work with one area of the canvas and not another. Region objects allow you to do just that. Needless to say, region objects have the following attributes: location and dimension.

Device contexts need one more thing to make them worth using. We already defined the container by specifying a device context type. I told you about the objects that we put into the container. Now it's time to look at the way that those objects will interact with each other. A graphic mode does just that, it tells Windows how you want the objects in your device context container to interact with each other. The way that they interact largely determines what kind of a screen effect you'll get when using specific types of functions. This is especially true when you fill an area using a brush and, to a lesser extent, when you draw something on screen. The graphic modes even tell Windows what to do when you cover one color with another. For example, will the two colors combine, or will the new color replace the old one? If you do choose to let the color combine, how will they combine? There are several different mixing methods that Windows supports. Unlike modes in the conventional sense (something that you select from a list of possible items), Windows uses all five modes listed below at the same time. Think of a mode as a way to defining one aspect of the way Windows handles graphics. Table 7.4 will give you a better idea of how the graphics modes work, but we'll cover them in detail in the next few sections.

Table 7.4. Windows Graphics Modes.

Mode	Description
Background	This defines how Windows mixes background colors. It tells whether Windows replaces one color with another or if it merges the two together to form a new color. You'll normally see this mode used with text and bitmap operations.
Drawing	You use this mode to tell Windows how to mix foreground colors together. You'll normally see this mode used in pen, brush, text, and bitmap operations.
Mapping	Windows allows you to define device contexts in a variety of ways. One of the things that you can decide to do is create world space—in essence, the biggest sheet of paper in the world since it's theoretically limited in size by

continues

Table 7.4. continued

Mode	Description
	the memory in your machine. Once you use this huge piece of paper, you have to decide how to show it on a physical device like a printer or a display. The mapping mode tells Windows how you want sizing issues solved.
Polygon-Fill	This mode defines how Windows fills the interior of polygons and other shapes. In essence, it decides what shape and size brush that Windows will use for painting.
Stretching	When you compress an image, you lose some of the detail that it contains. Windows needs to know how to mix colors together to maintain the quality of the image as much as possible. For example, when you scale a 1 point line down to the point where the user can no longer truly see it, how should Windows continue to represent the line? There are a variety of things you can do to give the user the feeling that the 1 point line is still there even though it isn't.

Using Graphics Drawing Primitives

Windows provides a number of graphics primitives that you can combine in various ways to create images. It's this list of graphics primitives that enables applications like CAD and high end drawing products to store only the numbers required to create a drawing, rather than the drawing itself. For example, you can choose to store the bitmap used to create an image (raster graphics), or the numbers used to compute it (vector graphics).

There are a number of advantages to both graphic formats. Obviously we don't have space here to discuss them all. However, you'll find, for the most part, that vector graphics offer advantages in scaleability and storage size. An equation can't lose resolution, nor can you distort it. However, raster graphics have a distinct advantage in display speed. An application needs to recalculate all the graphics primitives used to create a vector image; raster images are ready to display as stored. You'll also find that raster graphics are a great deal easier to program and that they have certain advantages when it comes time to perform detailed editing. You can't easily edit a vector image at the pixel level.

I'm going to show you four different Windows graphic primitives in the following example. Making the example flexible enough for you to try out the various coordinates that the primitives need as input required the addition of a few extra forms. Figures 7.5 through 7.7 show the forms you'll need to create for this example.

Figure 7.5.
The main form looks much like our previous example. It includes a simple menu that allows you to see the various primitives in action.

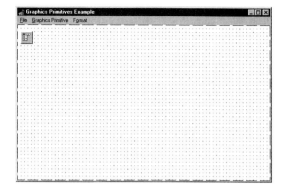

Figure 7.6.
We needed a coordinate entry dialog to make some of the primitives work. Some primitives also require the addition of a bounding box.

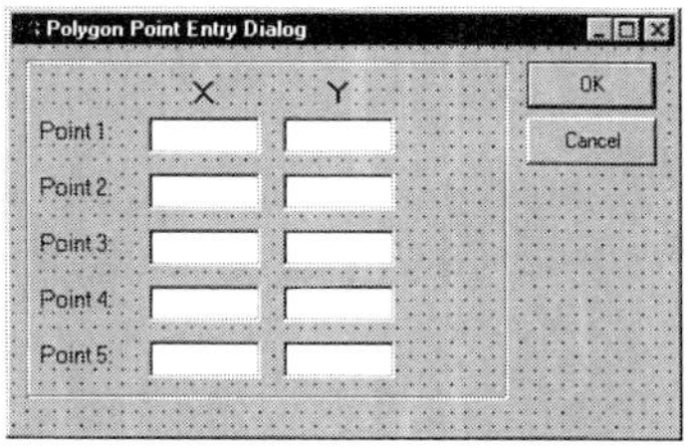

Figure 7.7.
This dialog works with primitives that provide non-uniform output like the Polygon method.

The main form, Form1, looks much the same as the one in the previous example. In this case I added a more complex menu. It contains a File | Exit command as before. The Graphics Primitives menu contains four commands: Arc, Ellipse, Polygon, and Rectangle. You can look at the Tcanvas documentation supplied with Delphi for a list of other primitives that Windows supports. A Format menu (which we'll flesh out later) contains a single entry for now—Stretch. You'll want to set the Form1.Color property to clWhite. I also added an Image control to this setup to make some features—like resize and repaint—a little more automatic. You'll need to set the Image1.Align property to alClient so it maintains its shape to match that of Form1.

I copied the two dialogs from the Standard Dialog Box gallery entry. Make sure you copy, not inherit, these forms. Using copies tends to be a little less error prone when you're experimenting with new techniques. I didn't include the code for these two dialogs in the source code listing below because Delphi automatically makes all the appropriate entries for you.

The Coordinate Point Entry dialog contains two sections. The upper section is where the user enters coordinates. These coordinates normally decide the upper left and lower right boundaries of the object you want to draw. I named the edit controls in this section: X1, Y1, X2, Y2. The first two coordinates define the upper left corner of the object. The last two coordinates define the lower right corner of the object. In the case of an arc, what you're really telling Windows is the starting and stopping points of the arc. The bottom section provides the coordinates for the arc bounding box. I named the edit controls in this section: BoundX1, BoundY1, BoundX2, and BoundY2. As with the other coordinates, the first set of coordinates defines the upper left corner, while the second set of coordinates defines the lower right corner of the bounding box. Only the arc requires a bounding box in this example. (You'll find other situations where you need a bounding box to fully define a graphic primitive of some type.) Both the rectangle and circle are enclosed figures, they only need the upper left and lower right points defined to describe them.

Some graphics primitives allow you to draw lines or make non-uniform shapes like stars and trapezoids. You couldn't easily describe a star using two sets of X and Y coordinates. What you really need to do is describe the starting and ending point of each line that the star uses. You can actually reduce this to one starting and several ending points if you assume that each new line starts where the previous line ended. That's precisely what the Polygon method does; it assumes that you only need to define one starting point. So, if you wanted to describe a five pointed figure, you would need six entries: One for the starting point and five for each ending point. Graphics primitives that draw non-uniform figures like this always use an array for passing the required list of coordinates.

The Polygon Point Entry dialog shows one way to handle multiple point entry. Since we assume a fixed number of entry points, I could use an array to hold the required parameters. The edit controls on this form are named PX1 through PX5 for the X coordinates and PY1 though PY5 for the Y coordinates. A grid control—used to create a spreadsheet type interface—would also work in this situation. You'd have to use a grid control if you wanted to allow the user to enter multiple points.

Tip: You could use a combination of a dialog box and a routine for monitoring user clicks on the Image1 control to create a polygon. Using the familiar click, then drag would work just fine for graphics primitives like circles and rectangles, but wouldn't work at all well for polygons. An arc would probably require a combination of two click drags—the first time you would prompt the user for a bounding box, the second the actual arc. Products like Corel Draw take care of this problem by having the user draw a circle as a starting point for the arc. The user then grabs handles on the circle perimeter to define the ends of the arc.

Now that you have an idea of what kind of graphics primitives we're going to see, look at Listing 7.3. This contains all the code you need to create the four graphics primitives demonstrated in this example. I added some extra code so that you could experiment with the coordinate system and see the effects of various entries. I also made sure that each primitive provided a default set of coordinates that you could select by clicking OK when one of the two dialogs appeared.

Listing 7.3. Using the graphics drawing primitives.

```
unit GrphPrm1;

interface

uses
  SysUtils, Windows, Messages, Classes, Graphics, Controls, Forms, Dialogs,
  Menus, ExtCtrls;

type
  TForm1 = class(TForm)
    MainMenu1: TMainMenu;
    File1: TMenuItem;
    Exit1: TMenuItem;
    GraphicsPrimitives1: TMenuItem;
    Arc1: TMenuItem;
    Ellipse1: TMenuItem;
    Rectangle1: TMenuItem;
    Polygon1: TMenuItem;
    Format1: TMenuItem;
    Stretch1: TMenuItem;
    Image1: TImage;
    procedure Exit1Click(Sender: TObject);
    procedure Arc1Click(Sender: TObject);
    procedure Ellipse1Click(Sender: TObject);
    procedure Polygon1Click(Sender: TObject);
    procedure Rectangle1Click(Sender: TObject);
    procedure Stretch1Click(Sender: TObject);
    procedure FormResize(Sender: TObject);
  private
      procedure EnableBoundingBox;
    procedure DisableBoundingBox;
    procedure NewBitmap;
  public
    { Public declarations }
  end;

var
  Form1: TForm1;

implementation

uses GrphPrm2, GrphPrm3;

{$R *.DFM}

procedure TForm1.Exit1Click(Sender: TObject);
begin
    Halt;    {Exit the program.}
end;

procedure TForm1.Arc1Click(Sender: TObject);
var
    X1, Y1, X2, Y2: Integer;    {Arc coordinates entered by user.}
    B1, B2, B3, B4: Integer;    {Bounding box coordinates.}
begin
```

continues

Listing 7.3. continued

```
    {Initialize our coordinate dialog box.}
    Coordinate.X1.Text := IntToStr(0);
    Coordinate.Y1.Text := IntToStr(0);
    Coordinate.X2.Text := IntToStr(0);
    Coordinate.Y2.Text := IntToStr(0);

    {Initialize the bounding box variables.}
    Coordinate.BoundX1.Text := IntToStr(0);
    Coordinate.BoundY1.Text := IntToStr(0);
    Coordinate.BoundX2.Text := IntToStr(Image1.Picture.Bitmap.Width);
    Coordinate.BoundY2.Text := IntToStr(Image1.Picture.Bitmap.Height);

    {Get the user's input for bounding box and coordinates.}
    if Coordinate.ShowModal = mrCancel then
        Exit;

    {Convert the user input to numbers.}
    X1 := StrToInt(Coordinate.X1.Text);
    Y1 := StrToInt(Coordinate.Y1.Text);
    X2 := StrToInt(Coordinate.X2.Text);
    Y2 := StrToInt(Coordinate.Y2.Text);
    B1 := StrToInt(Coordinate.BoundX1.Text);
    B2 := StrToInt(Coordinate.BoundY1.Text);
    B3 := StrToInt(Coordinate.BoundX2.Text);
    B4 := StrToInt(Coordinate.BoundY2.Text);

    {Display a rectangle to show the bounding area.}
    Image1.Canvas.Rectangle(B1, B2, B3, B4);

    {Display the arc.}
    Image1.Canvas.Arc(B1, B2, B3, B4, X1, Y1, X2, Y2);
end;

procedure TForm1.Ellipse1Click(Sender: TObject);
var
    X1, Y1, X2, Y2: Integer;    {Circle coordinates entered by user.}
begin
    {Initialize our coordinate dialog box.}
    Coordinate.X1.Text := IntToStr(0);
    Coordinate.Y1.Text := IntToStr(0);
    Coordinate.X2.Text := IntToStr(Image1.Picture.Bitmap.Width);
    Coordinate.Y2.Text := IntToStr(Image1.Picture.Bitmap.Height);

    {Disable the bounding box coordinates.}
    DisableBoundingBox;

    {Get the user's input for bounding box and coordinates.}
    if Coordinate.ShowModal = mrCancel then
        begin
        {If the user selected cancel, then enable the bounding box and exit.}
        EnableBoundingBox;
        Exit;
        end;

    {Convert the user input to numbers.}
    X1 := StrToInt(Coordinate.X1.Text);
    Y1 := StrToInt(Coordinate.Y1.Text);
```

```
    X2 := StrToInt(Coordinate.X2.Text);
    Y2 := StrToInt(Coordinate.Y2.Text);

    {Display the ellipse.}
    Image1.Canvas.Ellipse(X1, Y1, X2, Y2);

    {Enable the bounding box before we leave.}
    EnableBoundingBox;
end;

procedure TForm1.Polygon1Click(Sender: TObject);
var
    aPointList: array[1..5] of TPoint;     {Points to draw on screen.}
begin
    {Initialize the dialog box variables.}
    Polygon.PX1.Text := IntToStr(150);
    Polygon.PY1.Text := IntToStr(0);
    Polygon.PX2.Text := IntToStr(300);
    Polygon.PY2.Text := IntToStr(150);
    Polygon.PX3.Text := IntToStr(200);
    Polygon.PY3.Text := IntToStr(300);
    Polygon.PX4.Text := IntToStr(100);
    Polygon.PY4.Text := IntToStr(300);
    Polygon.PX5.Text := IntToStr(150);
    Polygon.PY5.Text := IntToStr(0);

    {Get the user's input.}
    if Polygon.ShowModal = mrCancel then
        Exit;

    {Convert the user input into an array.}
    aPointList[1].X := StrToInt(Polygon.PX1.Text);
    aPointList[1].Y := StrToInt(Polygon.PY1.Text);
    aPointList[2].X := StrToInt(Polygon.PX2.Text);
    aPointList[2].Y := StrToInt(Polygon.PY2.Text);
    aPointList[3].X := StrToInt(Polygon.PX3.Text);
    aPointList[3].Y := StrToInt(Polygon.PY3.Text);
    aPointList[4].X := StrToInt(Polygon.PX4.Text);
    aPointList[4].Y := StrToInt(Polygon.PY4.Text);
    aPointList[5].X := StrToInt(Polygon.PX5.Text);
    aPointList[5].Y := StrToInt(Polygon.PY5.Text);

    {Display the polygon on screen.}
    Image1.Canvas.Polygon(aPointList);
end;

procedure TForm1.Rectangle1Click(Sender: TObject);
var
    X1, Y1, X2, Y2: Integer;     {Rectangle coordinates entered by user.}
begin
    {Initialize our coordinate dialog box.}
    Coordinate.X1.Text := IntToStr(20);
    Coordinate.Y1.Text := IntToStr(20);
    Coordinate.X2.Text := IntToStr(Image1.Picture.Bitmap.Width - 20);
    Coordinate.Y2.Text := IntToStr(Image1.Picture.Bitmap.Height - 20);

    {Disable the bounding box coordinates.}
    DisableBoundingBox;
```

continues

Listing 7.3. continued

```
    {Get the user's input for bounding box and coordinates.}
    if Coordinate.ShowModal = mrCancel then
        begin
         {If the user selected cancel, then enable the bounding box and exit.}
         EnableBoundingBox;
        Exit;
         end;

    {Convert the user input to numbers.}
    X1 := StrToInt(Coordinate.X1.Text);
    Y1 := StrToInt(Coordinate.Y1.Text);
    X2 := StrToInt(Coordinate.X2.Text);
    Y2 := StrToInt(Coordinate.Y2.Text);

    {Display the rectangle.}
    Image1.Canvas.Rectangle(X1, Y1, X2, Y2);

    {Enable the bounding box before we leave.}
    EnableBoundingBox;
end;

procedure TForm1.Stretch1Click(Sender: TObject);
begin

    {Change the status of the Image1 Stretch property based on its
     current state.}
    if Image1.Stretch then
        begin
         Image1.Stretch := False;        {Change the stretch mode.}
         Image1.Refresh;               {Repaint the image.}
         Form1.Refresh;
         Stretch1.Checked := False;    {Change the menu check.}
         end
    else
        begin
         Image1.Stretch := True;
         Image1.Refresh;
         Form1.Refresh;
         Stretch1.Checked := True;
         end;
end;

procedure TForm1.DisableBoundingBox;
begin
    {Disable the bounding box coordinates.}
    Coordinate.BoundX1.Enabled := False;
    Coordinate.BoundY1.Enabled := False;
    Coordinate.BoundX2.Enabled := False;
    Coordinate.BoundY2.Enabled := False;
    Coordinate.BoundX1.Color := clBtnFace;
    Coordinate.BoundY1.Color := clBtnFace;
    Coordinate.BoundX2.Color := clBtnFace;
    Coordinate.BoundY2.Color := clBtnFace;
end;

procedure TForm1.EnableBoundingBox;
begin
```

```
      {Enable the bounding box coordinates.}
      Coordinate.BoundX1.Enabled := True;
      Coordinate.BoundY1.Enabled := True;
      Coordinate.BoundX2.Enabled := True;
      Coordinate.BoundY2.Enabled := True;
      Coordinate.BoundX1.Color := clWindow;
      Coordinate.BoundY1.Color := clWindow;
      Coordinate.BoundX2.Color := clWindow;
      Coordinate.BoundY2.Color := clWindow;
end;

procedure TForm1.NewBitmap;
var
    oNewBitmap: TBitmap;     {New Bitmap Object}
begin
    oNewBitmap := TBitmap.Create;            {Create the object.}
    oNewBitmap.Width := Image1.Width;        {Set its width.}
    oNewBitmap.Height := Image1.Height;    {Set its height.}
    Image1.Picture.Bitmap := oNewBitmap;    {Assign the blank bitmap to Image1.}
end;

procedure TForm1.FormResize(Sender: TObject);
begin
    {If Image1 is set to stretch the image, then we don't need to create a
     new bitmap.}
    if not Image1.Stretch then

        {Create a new bitmap to hold the drawing.}
        NewBitmap;
end;

end.
```

There are several features you should notice about this code. The first one is the fact that I use the current Image1.Picture.Bitmap height and width parameters instead of using the window parameters. There are two reasons for this. First, if you're working in stretch mode, then the window parameters are actually warped when compared to those of the bitmap. Remember that you're stretching the bitmap to fit the window. The bitmap stays the same size, only its appearance changes. Second, Delphi automatically clips any image you draw within an Image control to match the size of the Bitmap property. What this means is that even though the Image control itself has more drawing space, the bitmap doesn't. The bitmap size is static—you can't change it.

Once you get used to the idea of a static bitmap size, you'll see the reason for two of the other functions in this example. We need to monitor the Form1 Resize event. To do that we create the TForm1.FormResize function. Within this function you'll see a call to the second function—NewBitmap. If we resize the form, then we need to create a new bitmap for Image1 that matches its size. This allows you to use all of the drawing area that the Image1 control provides.

The Stretch1Click procedure allows us to change the Stretched property of Image1. All we do in this procedure is test the current state and reverse it. The maintenance tasks for this function include updating the checked status of the menu entry and redrawing the display. Notice that the redraw step consists of two parts, redrawing the image itself, then redrawing the form. What you'd see is fragments of the previous image if you changed the stretch mode without redrawing the display.

Now that we have everything needed to test these graphics primitives out, let's take a look at them. Figures 7.8 through 7.11 show what you should expect to see when you test the various options out. As I mentioned previously, you can use each one of these primitives to create a complex picture.

Figure 7.8.

The arc graphics primitive is useful for drawing pie charts or parts of circles (there is also a primitive for drawing pie wedges).

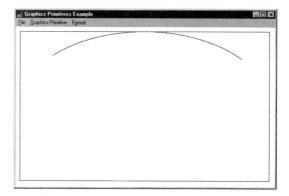

Figure 7.9.

The ellipse graphics primitive can draw either an ellipse or a circle. All you need to do is make sure the coordinates describe a square region if you need a circle.

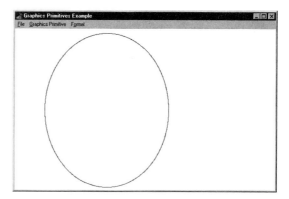

Figure 7.10.

The polygon graphics primitive can obviously accept more than five array entries. However, five is more than enough to show what this primitive can do.

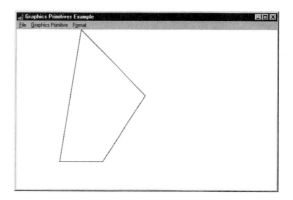

Figure 7.11.

Rectangles are the basis for a lot of drawing projects. You may even see them used to define other objects.

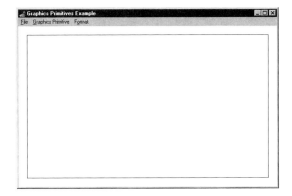

I've obviously made some decisions in this example that you might not want to make for your own programs. For example, what alternative do you have if you don't want to manage the bitmap size the way that I did? One option that you could use is the same option that programs like Paintbrush or MS Paint use—you can have the user define a specific image size, then use that image size throughout the drawing process. If the user wants to change the drawing size, then he'll need to copy the existing image into a new bitmap.

You may also find the Stretch mode that I incorporated into my program a little less than useful in some situations. For example, what if you want to provide the user with a true perspective of the drawing rather than forcing the drawing to fit in the space provided? You could use scroll bars to allow the user to scroll around the display. I also find the ScaleBy property very useful in these cases. Instead of stretching the drawing, you simply find the smaller of the two space constraints and scale the image by that amount.

Selecting Colors, Pens, and Brushes

Adding color and patterns to the graphics you create is simply taken for granted under Windows— that is, unless you're the programmer creating an application. Windows offers a somewhat confusing array of pen and brush options. Within those pen and brush option selections is a place for color.

We already started looking at the process of creating an image editor of sorts in the previous section. The example showed you how to create various shapes (graphics primitives) within an application. Now it's time to look at the effect of using various brushes and pens within an application. To start this particular example, I added two more entries to our Format menu in Form1 (see the previous section for details): Pen Parameters and Brush Parameters. The form itself is unchanged and I haven't added any new controls to it. You'll need to add the source code shown in Listing 7.4 to make these menu commands work. Make sure that you also add the GrphPrm4 unit to the Uses statement in the Implementation section of GrphPrm1. Delphi should automatically take care of any other entries for you.

Listing 7.4. Selecting colors, pens, and brushes.

```
procedure TForm1.PenParmeters1Click(Sender: TObject);
begin
    with DrawToolConfig do
        begin

        {Select the correct page in our configuration dialog.}
        PageControl1.ActivePage := PageControl1.Pages[0];

        {Display the dialog.}
        if ShowModal <> mrCancel then
            begin

            {If the user changes the pen width value, then change the
             actual width in our canvas area.}
            Form1.Image1.Canvas.Pen.Width := StrToInt(PenWidth.Text);

            {Change the pen style as needed.}
            case PenStyle.ItemIndex of
                0: Form1.Image1.Canvas.Pen.Style := psSolid;
                1: Form1.Image1.Canvas.Pen.Style := psDash;
                2: Form1.Image1.Canvas.Pen.Style := psDot;
                3: Form1.Image1.Canvas.Pen.Style := psDashDot;
                4: Form1.Image1.Canvas.Pen.Style := psDashDotDot;
                5: Form1.Image1.Canvas.Pen.Style := psClear;
                6: Form1.Image1.Canvas.Pen.Style := psInsideFrame;
                end;

            {Change the pen mode as needed.}
            case PenMode.ItemIndex of
                0: Form1.Image1.Canvas.Pen.Mode := pmBlack;
                1: Form1.Image1.Canvas.Pen.Mode := pmWhite;
                2: Form1.Image1.Canvas.Pen.Mode := pmNop;
                3: Form1.Image1.Canvas.Pen.Mode := pmNot;
                4: Form1.Image1.Canvas.Pen.Mode := pmCopy;
                5: Form1.Image1.Canvas.Pen.Mode := pmNotCopy;
                end;

            {Set the pen color to the value stored in the
             ColorDialog1 Tag Parameter.}
            Form1.Image1.Canvas.Pen.Color := ColorDialog1.Color;

        end; {if ShowModal <> mrCancel}
    end; {with DrawToolConfig do}
end;

procedure TForm1.BrushParameters1Click(Sender: TObject);
begin
    with DrawToolConfig do
        begin
        PageControl1.ActivePage := PageControl1.Pages[1];
        if ShowModal <> mrCancel then
            begin

            {Set the pen color to the value stored in the
             ColorDialog1 Tag Parameter.}
            Form1.Image1.Canvas.Brush.Color := ColorDialog2.Color;
```

```
        {Set the brush style.}
        case BrushStyle.ItemIndex of
             0: Form1.Image1.Canvas.Brush.Style := bsSolid;
             1: Form1.Image1.Canvas.Brush.Style := bsClear;
             2: Form1.Image1.Canvas.Brush.Style := bsBDiagonal;
             3: Form1.Image1.Canvas.Brush.Style := bsFDiagonal;
             4: Form1.Image1.Canvas.Brush.Style := bsCross;
             5: Form1.Image1.Canvas.Brush.Style := bsDiagCross;
             6: Form1.Image1.Canvas.Brush.Style := bsHorizontal;
             7: Form1.Image1.Canvas.Brush.Style := bsVertical;
             end;

        end; {if ShowModal <> mrCancel then}
     end; {with DrawToolConfig do}
end;
end.
```

The first thing you should notice is that these two routines call a paged form called DrawToolConfig. You'll find this form in the Form page of the Delphi gallery under Tabbed Pages. We need to select a page in this form. Unlike Delphi 16, we have to provide this form with an object, not a page index. We get this page index using the Pages property of PageControl1.

It won't take too long to figure out what the rest of the code does. There are a variety of case and assign statements that take the input from the tabbed pages form and reconfigure the pen or brush on our canvas. Except for the pen mode, I've included every possible value in the example so that you could fully test them out.

Figures 7.12 and 7.13 show the DrawToolConfig form. There are two pages in this form. Notice that I've included two Color Dialog controls in this case. One color dialog is for the pen color; the other is for the brush color. Using a tabbed form means that the user could move from one configuration area to the next. It also means that you'll need to provide separate dialogs for each color setting. That way you can act on the color settings after the user presses OK. If you tried to act on the new color settings immediately after the user selected them, then there wouldn't be any way for the user to back out of a selection and the Cancel button would be meaningless.

Figure 7.12.
The first page of our tabbed form allows the user to reconfigure the pen options.

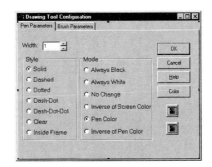

Figure 7.13.
The second page of the
tabbed form contains all the
options for the brush.

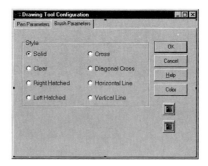

You'll need a little more information to complete the Pen Parameters TTabSheet control. I provided two methods for changing the pen width: the PenWidth edit control and a TUpDown control named UpDown1. You won't need any code to make the up/down control work with the edit control; all you need to do is enter the edit control's name in the Associate parameter of the TUpDown control. Pen Parameters also contains two radio button group controls named PenStyle and PenMode. You don't need to add any radio buttons to these controls—just add the strings shown in the figure to the Items property of each control. The Color button isn't part of the standard dialog either. All you need to do is add the button directly below the standard Help button. The button's code simply executes the ColorDialog1 dialog.

The Brush Parameters TTabSheet is even easier to put together than the Pen Parameters control was. All you need in this case is a radio button group control and a Color pushbutton. The method for configuring the two controls is the same as before. The only difference is that I named the radio group control BrushStyle. The Color pushbutton accesses the ColorDialog2 dialog for reasons that I'll describe later. The final touch to both TTabSheet controls is to add the requisite TColorDialog controls.

Let's take a look at the code to make this form perform some useful work. Listing 7.5 contains all the code required to make the tabbed form work. Two of the procedures in this unit—PenParmEnter and BrushParmEnter—keep the configuration dialog in sync with the Image1 control on Form1. The other two procedures simply execute the appropriate color dialog when the user wants to change the color setting for a pen or brush. Notice that we don't do anything with the color change in this unit—that's taken care of in GrphPrm1.

Listing 7.5. Creating a tabbed form.

```
unit GrphPrm4;

interface

uses Windows, SysUtils, Classes, Graphics, Forms, Controls, StdCtrls,
  Buttons, ComCtrls, ColorGrd, Dialogs, ExtCtrls;

type
```

```
  TDrawToolConfig = class(TForm)
    PageControl1: TPageControl;
    OKBtn: TButton;
    CancelBtn: TButton;
    HelpBtn: TButton;
    BrushParm: TTabSheet;
    PenParm: TTabSheet;
    Label1: TLabel;
    PenWidth: TEdit;
    UpDown1: TUpDown;
    PenColor: TButton;
    ColorDialog1: TColorDialog;
    PenMode: TRadioGroup;
    PenStyle: TRadioGroup;
    BrushColor: TButton;
    ColorDialog2: TColorDialog;
    BrushStyle: TRadioGroup;
    procedure PenParmEnter(Sender: TObject);
    procedure PenColorClick(Sender: TObject);
    procedure BrushColorClick(Sender: TObject);
    procedure BrushParmEnter(Sender: TObject);
  private
    { Private declarations }
  public
    { Public declarations }
  end;

var
  DrawToolConfig: TDrawToolConfig;

implementation

uses
GrphPrm1;

{$R *.DFM}

procedure TDrawToolConfig.PenParmEnter(Sender: TObject);
begin

    {Get the current pen width on entry to the dialog.}
    PenWidth.Text := IntToStr(Form1.Image1.Canvas.Pen.Width);

    {Select the appropriate pen style on entry.}
    case Form1.Image1.Canvas.Pen.Style of
        psSolid: PenStyle.ItemIndex := 0;
        psDash: PenStyle.ItemIndex := 1;
        psDot: PenStyle.ItemIndex := 2;
        psDashDot: PenStyle.ItemIndex := 3;
        psDashDotDot: PenStyle.ItemIndex := 4;
        psClear: PenStyle.ItemIndex := 5;
        psInsideFrame: PenStyle.ItemIndex := 6;
        end;

    {Select the appropriate pen mode on entry.}
    case Form1.Image1.Canvas.Pen.Mode of
        pmBlack: PenMode.ItemIndex := 0;
```

continues

Listing 7.5. **continued**

```
        pmWhite: PenMode.ItemIndex := 1;
        pmNop: PenMode.ItemIndex := 2;
        pmNot: PenMode.ItemIndex := 3;
        pmCopy: PenMode.ItemIndex := 4;
        pmNotCopy: PenMode.ItemIndex := 5;
        else PenMode.ItemIndex := 0;
        end;

    {Initialize the color dialog.}
    ColorDialog1.Color := Form1.Image1.Canvas.Pen.Color;
end;

procedure TDrawToolConfig.PenColorClick(Sender: TObject);
begin
    {Display a color dialog.}
    ColorDialog1.Execute
end;

procedure TDrawToolConfig.BrushParmEnter(Sender: TObject);
begin

    {Initialize the color dialog.}
    ColorDialog2.Color := Form1.Image1.Canvas.Brush.Color;

    {Get the brush style.}
    case Form1.Image1.Canvas.Brush.Style of
        bsSolid: BrushStyle.ItemIndex := 0;
        bsClear: BrushStyle.ItemIndex := 1;
        bsBDiagonal: BrushStyle.ItemIndex := 2;
        bsFDiagonal: BrushStyle.ItemIndex := 3;
        bsCross: BrushStyle.ItemIndex := 4;
        bsDiagCross: BrushStyle.ItemIndex := 5;
        bsHorizontal: BrushStyle.ItemIndex := 6;
        bsVertical: BrushStyle.ItemIndex := 7;
        end;
end;

procedure TDrawToolConfig.BrushColorClick(Sender: TObject);
begin
    {Display the color dialog.}
    ColorDialog2.Execute;
end;

end.
```

Most of this code will work as shown in Delphi 16. You'll need to replace the Windows 95–specific TPageControl with a TTabbedNotebook control. The easiest way to do this is to select a different dialog type when you create the new form. The business end of the code—the code that actually makes the program do something useful—should work equally well under both 16-bit and 32-bit versions of Delphi.

Now that we've gotten all the code together for our program, let's take a quick look at one example of what you can do with it. Figure 7.14 shows one example of what the example can do now. I chose a 4-pixel pen line and a cross hatched brush to display a full sized ellipse on screen. Obviously there are too many selections to show here, but the figure does give you an idea of what's possible. Take the time to try out the various options so that you can see how they interact. You might be surprised at how some of the pen mode settings affect the way that the brush looks on screen. On the other hand, none of the brush settings appear to affect the pen at all.

Figure 7.14.

Adding pen and brush configuration settings can greatly enhance the flexibility of your application.

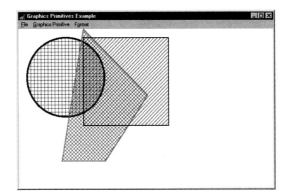

Displaying and Creating Metafiles

So far we've spent a lot of time looking at bitmaps—raster graphics. We initially started talking about both raster and vector graphics in this chapter. The WMF (Windows Metafile) format is a vector graphic. It has all the advantages and disadvantages of that particular medium. Essentially, a metafile describes how to build the graphic image; it doesn't actually contain a bitmap of that image. A program is responsible for reading the metafile, then building an image based on the instructions that it contains. As I previously mentioned, there are two benefits to this method: The ability to scale the image to any size without loss of resolution and the size of the resulting file (it takes less room in most cases to store the instructions to build a graphic image than to store the image itself).

One of the things that we haven't covered to date is the way that Delphi handles various file formats. When you place a TImage control on a form, you don't just get the control itself, but all of the objects that the TImage control contains. As far as Delphi is concerned, there are four different graphic file formats: Bitmap, icon, metafile, and custom. It can load and save the first three file formats without much help from the programmer—all you really need to do is load them and Delphi takes care of displaying them for you (as we'll see in the example for this section). The big thing that you need to remember as a programmer is that Delphi provides three different object types to store and manipulate the file formats that it supports. A TImage picture actually contains a TIcon, TBitmap and a TMetafile object. You need to place the graphic you want to display into the correct object or Delphi will display a runtime error.

Tip: All three of the image file types that Delphi supports are based on the TGraphic class. You could potentially derive new graphic file classes using the TGraphic class as a starting point. Obviously this would require low level knowledge of the precise file format that you wanted to support.

Warning: You can't read a graphic file into one area of a TImage control—say a metafile into the metafile object, and output it as a different file type like a bitmap. Delphi won't perform any kind of file translation for you. In fact, if you attempt to do this within an application (at least as of this writing) Delphi will raise an exception error, but only after it has overwritten both your original and the target file. You'll lose the data stored in the original file. Make absolutely certain that you always keep track of which graphics file format is contained in a TImage control. Always output the image to the same file type when you save it.

So, how do you build an application that can make maximum use of the capabilities that Delphi provides? Listing 7.6 shows one way of at least starting the job. You have to open the files and store them in the correct file before you can use them. This example shows you how to open the file, detect the file type, then save the file in its original format.

Listing 7.6. Displaying and creating metafiles.

```
unit WMF1;

interface

uses
  Windows, Messages, SysUtils, Classes, Graphics, Controls, Forms, Dialogs,
  OleCtrls, ChartFX, Menus, ExtCtrls, StdCtrls;

type
  TForm1 = class(TForm)
    MainMenu1: TMainMenu;
    File1: TMenuItem;
    Exit1: TMenuItem;
    N1: TMenuItem;
    PrintSetup1: TMenuItem;
    Print1: TMenuItem;
    N2: TMenuItem;
    SaveAs1: TMenuItem;
    Save1: TMenuItem;
    Open1: TMenuItem;
    New1: TMenuItem;
    OpenDialog1: TOpenDialog;
    SaveDialog1: TSaveDialog;
    Image1: TImage;
    procedure Exit1Click(Sender: TObject);
```

```
    procedure Open1Click(Sender: TObject);
    procedure SaveAs1Click(Sender: TObject);
    procedure Save1Click(Sender: TObject);
  private
    procedure ShowSaveDialog;
  public
    { Public declarations }
  end;

var
  Form1: TForm1;

implementation

{$R *.DFM}

procedure TForm1.Exit1Click(Sender: TObject);
begin
    Halt;    {Exit the program.}
end;

procedure TForm1.Open1Click(Sender: TObject);
begin
    {Open the dialog and see if the user selects a file.}
    if OpenDialog1.Execute then
        begin

          {Determine which type of file the user selected.}
          if Pos('WMF', UpperCase(OpenDialog1.Filename)) > 0 then
              begin

                {Load the image.}
                Image1.Picture.Metafile.LoadFromFile(OpenDialog1.Filename);

                 {Set the scrollbars so they track the image properly.}
                 Form1.VertScrollBar.Range := Image1.Picture.Metafile.Height;
                 Form1.HorzScrollBar.Range := Image1.Picture.Metafile.Width;

                 {Change the default extension in our Save dialog to match
                  the current file type.}
                 SaveDialog1.DefaultExt := 'WMF';
                 SaveDialog1.FilterIndex := 1;
                 end
            else if Pos('ICO', UpperCase(OpenDialog1.Filename)) > 0 then
               begin
                 Image1.Picture.Icon.LoadFromFile(OpenDialog1.Filename);
                  Form1.VertScrollBar.Range := Image1.Picture.Icon.Height;
                  Form1.HorzScrollBar.Range := Image1.Picture.Icon.Width;
                  SaveDialog1.DefaultExt := 'ICO';
                  SaveDialog1.FilterIndex := 3;
                  end
            else if Pos('BMP', UpperCase(OpenDialog1.Filename)) > 0 then
                begin
                  Image1.Picture.Bitmap.LoadFromFile(OpenDialog1.Filename);
                   Form1.VertScrollBar.Range := Image1.Picture.Bitmap.Height;
                   Form1.HorzScrollBar.Range := Image1.Picture.Bitmap.Width;
                   SaveDialog1.DefaultExt := 'BMP';
```

continues

Listing 7.6. continued

```
                    SaveDialog1.FilterIndex := 2;
                end
        else
                MessageDlg('File Format Not Supported', mtError, [mbOK], 0);

        {Store the current filename for future use.}
        SaveDialog1.Filename := OpenDialog1.Filename;
        end; {if OpenDialog1.Execute then}
end;

procedure TForm1.Save1Click(Sender: TObject);
begin
    {See if there is a file in use.}
    if Length(SaveDialog1.Filename) > 0 then
        begin

        {Select a file save technique suited to the needs of the file}
        case SaveDialog1.FilterIndex of
            1: Image1.Picture.Metafile.SaveToFile(SaveDialog1.Filename);
            2: Image1.Picture.Bitmap.SaveToFile(SaveDialog1.Filename);
            3: Image1.Picture.Icon.SaveToFile(SaveDialog1.Filename);
            end; {case SaveDialog1.FilterIndex of}
        end
    else

        {Display the Save As dialog.}
        ShowSaveDialog;
end;

procedure TForm1.SaveAs1Click(Sender: TObject);
begin
    {Display the Save As dialog.}
    ShowSaveDialog;
end;

procedure TForm1.ShowSaveDialog;
begin
    {See if the user selected a file.}
    if SaveDialog1.Execute then
        begin

            {Select a file save technique suited to the needs of the file}
            case SaveDialog1.FilterIndex of
                1: Image1.Picture.Metafile.SaveToFile(SaveDialog1.Filename);
                2: Image1.Picture.Bitmap.SaveToFile(SaveDialog1.Filename);
                3: Image1.Picture.Icon.SaveToFile(SaveDialog1.Filename);
                end; {case SaveDialog1.FilterIndex of}
        end; {if SaveDialog1.Execute then}
end;
end.
```

The form for this program appears in Figure 7.15. As with the other examples in this chapter, I changed the Form1 Color property to clWhite. I also added a main menu, a TImage control, and both an Open and a Save As dialog to the form. I changed the Image1 Align property to alClient. The main menu contains a single File command that I created using the standard File template.

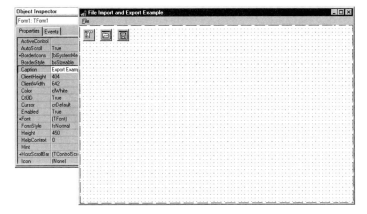

Figure 7.15.
Handling graphic image file services requires a dialog setup similar, but not the same, as that used for a text editor.

You should also see a few differences in the source code for this example from the source for a File | Open and File | Save command from Chapter 6, "Common Dialogs." Notice that I had to detect the file type and place the image in the correct area of the Image1 control. I saved this information in the SaveDialog1 dialog in two areas—the DefaultExt and the FileIndex properties. Using this technique greatly simplifies the amount of work required to save the file properly. In addition, you can always check the contents of these properties when it comes time to modify the drawing.

I found it interesting that you can use the same drawing tools for every graphic type in Delphi. The only difference is the TImage control object that you actually work with. All the graphic primitive techniques that I showed in the previous section of this book will work equally well with icons, bitmaps, and metafiles. Of course, you need to make sure that you're working with the right object. As far as icons are concerned, the only other limitation is that you're severely limited in the size of the icons you can create.

Once you get the example put together, you can use it to view any of the three file types that Delphi supports. There's one other nice feature to note. When I open the file, I use the graphic object's width and height controls to set the range for the form's scroll bars. If the form isn't large enough to hold the image, you'll see the scroll bars appear along the right and bottom sides of the form. This feature makes it a lot easier for the user to move around the image.

Summary

This chapter has provided you with a whirlwind tour of the Windows GDI. We began by looking at the Windows graphics architecture. I feel that it's important for a programmer to be at least aware of the structure that allows him to write an application in a certain way. You don't always have to know the bits and bytes of every part of the Windows API, that's what manuals are for; but knowing how things fit together can be a great aid in getting your application completed on time.

The next section looked at the most essential element of any discussion of the Windows GDI—the device context. Delphi talks about the device context as a canvas. That's probably an accurate enough description for most of the work you'll want to perform. It's definitely accurate enough for the kinds of things that the built-in Delphi functions allow you to perform. The important idea to remember is that a canvas can refer to more than just the main window of an application. For example, memo fields provide an excellent drawing board in most cases and you can keep a tight rein on their size without affecting the user's ability to resize the form as a whole.

After we got the mechanical portion of the GDI taken care of, we spent several sections taking a look at the various tools that Windows provides for drawing on the display. It's important to know which tools you have at your disposal and what type of input they require to get the job done.

8

Printer Magic

Printers always seem to bring out the worst qualities in any application. It's not too difficult to figure out why—every printer is an individual—making the job of writing a specific output routine difficult at best. At least, that was one of the more significant problems under DOS.

Windows has tamed the printer more than any other piece of equipment attached to your computer. As with the graphic interface, you use a device context to write to the printer under Windows. Essentially you have a blank sheet of paper to write on and Windows does some of the work needed to get it to the printer.

DOS programmers had to be experts on a variety of printers because they needed to know the escape code sequences to control the printer's actions. This is the part of the work that Windows takes over for you—no longer does the programmer have to worry about sending codes to control the printer. You'll use the same commands to send output to a laser printer that you use for your standard dot matrix. The Windows drivers take care of the details of implementing the commands you provide.

Another major problem in the past was detecting and resolving print errors. You can still choose to manage the printer, but doing nothing won't produce the catastrophic results they did in the past. Windows Print Manager does an adequate job of telling the user that there is a printer error. In fact, Windows 95 has greatly improved on this particular area. I used to take care of some kinds of printer errors myself because Print Manager was inadequate in some areas—especially when it came to print errors on a peer-to-peer network. I got the "Printer does not respond" error message for everything from a paper out problem to a major failure. The new version of Print Manager not only provides better error messages, it constantly rechecks the status of the printer so you don't have to worry about resetting anything once the error is fixed.

However, there are still a lot of issues that the programmer does need to worry about. Windows hasn't removed the need for ensuring that the data fits on a standard printed sheet. Fiddling around with the width of data fields is one issue that I expect programmers to have to deal with until the end of time. Font differences between what you see on-screen and what you'll get out of the printer don't help much. Even though the fonts all look standard on-screen, you'll find that some print drivers are more adept at reproducing them than others. I still haven't found a font that looks exactly the same on-screen and on the printed page. (Windows 95 does get a lot closer in this regard though and I expect that the next release will remove most, if not all, of the printer versus screen font issues.) Even if you do get everything to work just right, you'll still run into situations that defy logic— the text fits on all but one of the printers you need to service.

Peter's Principle: In addition to all their other failings, printers are unusually susceptible to problems in the computing environment. One of the things that I always do before I start on a programming project is check my hardware and drivers. I've run into more than one situation where an application I created worked just fine on all but one machine. Usually the culprit turns out to be a bad driver or perhaps an old BIOS chip. Checking the test platform before you start the programming effort is one way to make sure the bugs you see are actually bugs and not a problem with the environment.

You'll also find it essential to read through the vendor's README file or other documentation. Look at their BBS or other online service for updates on the latest bugs in a compiler. Apply any needed patches before beginning a programming project and you'll reduce the chance of inducing bugs that you can resolve by changing your code.

Obviously this is good advice for any part of the programming effort, but especially so for any printer specific tasks. Trying to get the type that the printer outputs on paper to look the same as what you see on-screen is difficult enough without introducing bugs that you can't fix. Take the time to check out your computing environment before you begin a project, then again before you start writing the printer routines.

There are speed issues to consider when writing generic printer code as well. A dot matrix printer produces output a lot faster if you use its internal fonts; the same could be said of other printer types but to a lesser degree. If you use one of Windows generic fonts, you can be certain that everyone who uses your application will have that font available—you can also be certain that none of the printers that you'll output data to will have that font. The end result is that it'll take a lot longer for someone to produce output from your application than they really need to.

This is just the tip of the iceberg. The method you use to output multiple copies could cause problems as well. Many applications provide an option to collate the output. Whether you include this feature or not is something you'll have to think about. Adding a feature like this will certainly increase the time it takes to produce an end application. What you need to determine is how many users will actually need such a feature.

Now that I've gotten your attention, let's take a look at the magic you'll need to get a printer to work with your application. We'll start by looking at the Windows architecture—just like we did for the GDI chapter—then I'll show you some practical programming examples. I'll look at both stand-alone print routines and those you can create using ReportSmith in this chapter.

An Architectural Overview of the Printer Subsystem

Any discussion of printer programming techniques has to start with an understanding of the Windows printer architecture. Knowing which components interface with each other when you print will often provide ideas on new techniques you can use for getting the job done faster and with fewer mistakes. The emphasis here is on fewer. Anyone who has spent an entire evening looking at the answer to a bug in their application will understand what I mean when I say that ignorance really isn't all that blissful when it comes to application development. Sometimes you really do need to know what the operating system is doing with the call you make to find a problem in your code.

However, you'll get more out of this section than a simple description of how to program the printer under Windows; you'll also gain a better understanding of printing from a user perspective. An understanding of how printing works at the user level will often help you discover new optimization techniques or track down an equipment failure with less difficulty. This kind of knowledge will also help you make your applications more user friendly and make it easier for you to communicate with the people who use your application once you get it installed.

Figure 8.1 provides you with an overview of the Windows 95 print architecture. You'll find the Windows NT version of the architecture (based on the new additions to version 3.51) in Figure 8.2. Both operating systems use about the same strategy, so I'll describe them together and add notes as appropriate. In most cases you'll find that Windows NT adds one or more additional layers to the picture to take care of various needs like platform independence. Most important of these additional layers, of course, is the hardware abstraction layer—see the figure and the accompanying description for more details.

Figure 8.1.
Windows 95 uses an improved print architecture that depends on minidriver support.

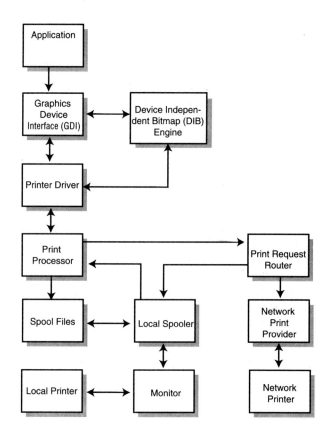

Figure 8.2.

Windows NT uses about the same print architecture as Windows 95, but adds additional layers to enforce device and platform independence.

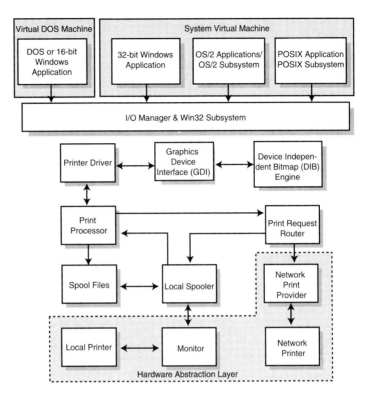

- Application: Windows 95 looks at a single application type for the most part when it comes to printing. In fact, as far as a programmer is concerned, you won't see any differences (except in the actual programming techniques used to access the printers—which goes without saying). Windows NT is another story. Remember that it supports various applications through servers. A 32-bit application receives a different level of support than a 16-bit or DOS application does. A POSIX application—which requires special support for case-sensitive names and asynchronous handling of certain system requests—receives different support than an OS/2 application. The fact that each virtual DOS machine is a separate entity also changes the equation a little. Fortunately, Delphi and the Windows API mask most of these considerations from the programmer.

- Virtual DOS Machine (VDM): Windows NT places each DOS application in its own VDM. The reason is simple: To provide the higher level of system reliability that Windows NT users demand, Microsoft had to make sure that each application had its own environment, an environment that's completely separate from that used by every other application. It's also important to remember that 16-bit Windows applications share one VDM. You need to remember that Windows NT always starts a VDM, then runs a copy of 16-bit Windows in it to service the needs of 16-bit Windows applications. This effectively adds two layers to every interaction—one for the VDM and another for the WIN32 Subsystem.

As with everything else, this additional layering is transparent to the programmer. You still use the same interfaces as before.

- OS/2 Application, OS/2 Subsystem, POSIX Application, and POSIX Subsystem: I included these four elements so that you would know that they're there, but I really don't plan to say much about them since you won't use them with Delphi. Suffice it to say that Windows NT provides support for OS/2 and POSIX.

- WIN32 Subsystem: Remember that Windows NT uses a client and server approach to taking care of the needs of the various applications it supports. The way it does that is through the WIN32 subsystem—a buffer layer that translates foreign operating system calls into something that Windows NT can understand. Think about POSIX for a second. Filenames and other entities are case-sensitive in that environment. Contrast this to the case-insensitive nature of DOS. You'll also remember that OS/2 is a 32-bit operating system, even in character mode, which makes a big difference in the way its applications react. The actual number of differences between the various operating system applications are too vast to really discuss in detail here, and we really don't need to know them to program adequately in Delphi. On the other hand, it's always nice to know that something exists even if you don't need it.

- I/O Manager: Windows NT uses a slightly different interface for managing input and output than Windows 95 does. One of the big differences is that Windows NT needs an I/O Manager to get the job done. The I/O manager accepts requests from applications and delivers them to the various device subsystems in the form of packets—input/output request packets (IRPs). The I/O Manager doesn't actually do any of the work; its job is to ensure that any application or operating system requests get passed to the right subsystem. The subsystem takes the IRP that the I/O Manager generates and interprets it. The end result is much the same as we have under Windows 95. So, why should we even bother with this added layer of processing? Because Windows NT is designed to act as a server, it's reasonable to think that it will experience a higher level of I/O than Windows 95. It needs the added layer to effectively manage all the I/O requests and provide feedback to the network administrator. Another reason is the number of platforms that Windows NT works with; you need this extra layer of processing to make sure that a request for printing services from a RISC machine like an Alpha gets sent to a print driver that understands the Alpha's language. Just like any other manager, the I/O Manager waits until the device driver reports that it has completed its assigned task. Once the I/O Manager receives this confirmation, it destroys the IRP. Device drivers can also pass requests for services to the I/O Manager. For example, the printer driver may need the services of a network driver to pass requests on to another machine. The I/O Manager also calls on the Object Manager (not shown in our diagram). Every resource—file, pipe, device, or memory allocation—under Windows NT is an object. Every object has a unique name. Since some operating systems like POSIX use case-sensitive names, and others like DOS use case-insensitive names, Windows NT has to have a way of handling both situations. The use of objects for every component answers this need.

- Graphics device interface (GDI): We've talked about this particular element of the printing picture in the past. The GDI is the API that an application uses to talk to the printer. An application doesn't directly access a printer like DOS did. It uses the Windows services. This allows for centralized scheduling and control of print jobs, a necessary requirement of a multitasking environment.

- Device-independent bitmap (DIB) engine: The DIB engine is normally associated with the display adapter. It works with the GDI to produce the bitmap you see on-screen. For example, when Windows displays wallpaper on the Desktop, it's the DIB engine that actually produces the bitmap under the instruction of the GDI. We talked about this topic in Chapter 7. As far as a printer is concerned, the DIB engine provides a convenient method of manipulating graphics. For example, if you choose to print a file in graphics mode instead of text mode, the DIB engine helps prepare the print job for you.

- Printer driver: This is the third piece of the print page preparation. It interfaces with both the GDI and the DIB engine to produce printer-specific output in the form of journal records. Think of a journal record as the disassembled pieces of a puzzle. All the pieces will eventually be put together; but for right now, each record is just a piece of that puzzle. Just like with puzzle pieces, you can look at them individually and recognize what they will eventually become. We'll spend a little more time talking about journal records later in this chapter. For right now, it's only important to know that they exist and that each record is one piece of the print job.

Note: Since Windows NT supports both RISC and Intel platforms (and perhaps even more in the future), you could end up with more than one version of each print driver on a printer server. Windows NT allows the network administrator to place the print drivers on the host machine or the workstation. Many will place the drivers on the host machine to make updates easier to perform. Make certain you reference the correct driver file if you plan to access the print driver directly.

- Print processor: The print processor accepts the printer-ready data from the printer driver. Its only function at this point is to despool the data to the print request router. In other words, it sends the journal records out single file in an orderly manner. Later, the print processor takes care of spooling the data to the local hard drive (spool files) if this is a local print job. This means that it takes all the puzzle pieces (journal records) and connects them into a single document.

- Print request router: This component routes the formatted data to the appropriate location. It determines whether the job is for a local or remote printer. If it's for a remote printer, the print request router sends the data to the network print provider. Otherwise, it sends the data to the local spooler.

- Network print provider: The network print provider is network-specific. It's the interface between your machine and the beginning of the network data stream. Its job is to accept the journal records, connect them into a single document, convert the document into a network-specific format (if required), and transmit the converted data to the next component in the network data stream. If all goes according to plan, this data will eventually find its way to a network printer.

- Local spooler: The first job of this particular component is to hand off print jobs to the print processor. The print processor converts the journal records it receives into a document. The local spooler reads the data files that the print processor stores on disk and sends them to the monitor. It also accepts messages from the monitor regarding the status of the printer. We'll discuss the types of information it receives when we discuss the monitor.

- Spool files: These are the physical files that the print processor stores in the Spool folder under the main Windows folder. Each printer type has its own storage location in this folder.

- Monitor: The monitor handles all communication with the printer. It accepts data from the spooler and transmits it to the printer. The monitor is also responsible for providing the spooler with plug and play information about the printer. Finally, the monitor provides the spooler with printer error information. Instead of giving you a "printer not ready" message, printers that support a bidirectional port can supply an "out of paper" or "toner low" message.

- Hardware Abstraction Layer (HAL): This is another conceptual type of element in Windows NT. Microsoft wrote the drivers and other software elements in such a way that they could easily move Windows NT to other platforms. That's how they moved Windows NT to the MIPS and Alpha machines. The basic architecture of Windows NT is the same, but the low-level drivers—the ones that directly interface with the hardware—are different. This drawing shows the elements for an Intel processor machine. You might see something slightly different when using an Alpha or MIPS machine. The important thing to remember is that as far as your application is concerned, it's still running on an Intel machine. The only time you'll run into trouble is if you bypass the Windows API and go directly to the hardware.

This might look like a lot of work just to get your document from an application to the printer that's connected to your machine. You're right. If that's all the tasks that Windows 95 and Windows NT could handle, this architecture would be very inflated indeed. However, there's much more here than meets the eye. Using this kind of interface provides the user with a lot more freedom in regard to printer usage. It ensures that everyone gets equal access to the printer. Programmers benefit as well because it's easier to write print drivers. The DIB engine improves the quality of your output. I could go on, but I think the point is made. The printing architecture might be complex, but it makes printing easier from a user perspective.

Windows NT has to do a lot more than just support the architecture that I've shown here. The diagram in Figure 8.2 is a very simplistic version of what actually has to go on. Here are some additional things to consider—especially if you plan to write a printer DLL or interact with the printing subsystem in some other way.

- Platform Independence—I've talked about this topic more than a few times in regard to Windows NT. The printing subsystem is one area where you have to be especially careful in regard to platform independence. Windows NT can support printing for workstations that use other processors on your machine. That's right, someone with an Alpha or a MIPS machine could send data through their print driver, over the network connection, to your machine. If you write some type of printer add-on that doesn't take that fact into account, you could end up spending some sleepless nights trying to get those network connections working again.

- Version Control—We're entering a time when there are going to be multiple versions of Windows NT to deal with. That's not so bad, but there are other issues to deal with. The trade presses are already reporting that the Windows NT version of the Explorer interface won't be compatible with what Windows 95 uses. In addition, the system policies are already incompatible, making it difficult for you to write an application that reads data directly from these files (thank goodness all the printer calls are the same). I'm almost positive that you're going to run into problems between the Windows NT Server and the Windows NT Workstation as well. In other words, don't take anything for granted when you write printer add-ons that access system data directly.

- Hardware Abstraction Layer—This particular Windows NT element appeared in the architecture section where I told you what it does. Now, how does this little feature change the face of printing under Windows NT? Just think for a moment about some of the tricks you tried to get away with under Windows 3.x and how they just barely work under Windows 95. Calling an interrupt or trying to interface with a VxD just won't work under Windows NT because there is a brick wall in your way called the hardware abstraction layer. Any kind of direct hardware interaction is completely severed because of this layer and it has to be. You can't be sure that an application you write will actually run on an Intel platform. Someone could try to run it on something else. That's why the hardware abstraction layer is there—to protect you, the programmer, from the vagaries of the hardware.

Creating Standard Reports

Now that we have some of the architectural details out of the way, let's take a look at some implementation. There are two ways to access the printer in Delphi: custom print routine and ReportSmith. You use a custom print routine for non-database applications like our text editor in Chapter 6 or the graphics primitive demonstration in Chapter 7. ReportSmith is a database management report tool. You use it when you want to create a report that uses tables.

This section covers the first type of printer access—when you need to create output from a non-database application. Since we already have a simple application that's partially completed, I'll use the text editor from Chapter 6 in this section. It already has some of the elements that you'll need to access the printer in place. For example, it includes a Print and a Print Setup menu entry on the File menu.

I think that you'll find there are two tasks you have to perform before you can actually print a report. The first task is to paginate the text area. You have to know where one page ends and another be-gins to provide full printer functionality for the user. The other task is to reconcile any user specified formatting features. For example, if your application allows the user to include headers and footers, then you'll need to add them into the pagination routine. The position of alternative text like foot-notes is also important. Some people will want them at the end of the document while others will want them to appear on the same page where they're mentioned. You'll also need to consider things like margins when printing, or you'll end up with a report that doesn't fit on the paper—much less provide the margins that the user will want.

Note: I wanted to provide the source code for the editor-only and print-enabled versions of the editor as separate files. You'll find the original version in the COMMDLG.DPR file. The version that includes printer additions is in the PRINTER.DPR file.

We'll begin by adding one more entry to the File menu. I added a Page Setup option right after the Print Setup option. Figure 8.3 shows what the Page Setup dialog looks like for this example. There are several controls on this page including: two edit controls for the header and footer, four edit controls for the margins, four up/down controls, and a pushbutton. I also used two group boxes to group the various controls together and some labels as shown in the figure. Table 8.1 provides a list of the controls and any changes I made to their parameters. Notice that I didn't associate the up/down controls with their associated edit controls. There's a good reason for this. I wanted to allow the user to change the margin size by 0.1 inch. If you associate an up/down control with an edit control, you're forced to make changes in whole integer increments. Adding the controls in pairs and some synchronization code to the OnChange or OnExit events takes care of the problem as we'll see later in this section.

Figure 8.3.
The Page Setup dialog allows the user to specify the margins, a header, and a footer.

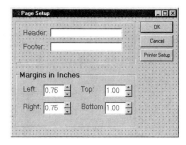

Table 8.1. Page Setup Dialog Control Settings.

Object	Property	Setting
PageLeft	Text	.75
	Height	28
PageRight	Text	.75
	Height	28
PageTop	Text	1.0
	Height	28
PageBottom	Text	1.0
	Height	28
UpDown1	Position	7
	Max	85
	Height	28
UpDown2	Position	7
	Max	85
	Height	28
UpDown3	Position	10
	Max	110
	Height	28
UpDown4	Position	10
	Max	110
	Height	28

One of the things that users of the 16-bit version of Delphi will need to change before creating the Page Setup dialog are the up/down controls. You can simply remove them and the synchronization code to make this example work. Of course, you'll also have to change the print routine in Listing 8.1 to look at the edit controls rather than the up/down controls as a source of margin settings. You can use the code found in the TPageSetup.PageLeftExit procedure in Listing 8.2 as an example of how to convert the print routine to 16-bit operation.

Unlike other tasks that a user can perform with your application, printing takes time—a lot of it if you have a slow printer. Using the Print Manager does allow Windows to spool the printer output to disk, but it can still take a lot of time to get the job done. With this in mind, I also added a Printer Status dialog to the program. It includes an Abort pushbutton that the user can click on to end the printing process. The setup for this dialog appears in Figure 8.4. As you can see, this is a very simple dialog. I didn't do much more than change the control captions as shown in the figure and add some code to the Abort pushbutton. Note that I did add a separate page number label to the dialog to make it easier and faster to update.

Figure 8.4.
The Print Status dialog tells the user which page the program is printing and allows him to abort the print job.

Tip: There is a problem with communication between the 16-bit version of Delphi and Print Manager; when the user aborts a print job, your application handles the process correctly, but the spooled file will remain. Hopefully Borland will fix this problem soon. In the meantime, you can clear the print job from Print Manager using the AbortDoc(Printer.Handle) Windows API call. Simply make the call before you use the Printer.Abort method to abort the printing process in your application.

There's a peculiar limitation with the Rich Text Edit control as of this writing. It appears that it doesn't support the full set of rich text macros. For example, I read an RTF created by Word for Windows into the sample editor, then saved it again without making any changes. The file lost about half its size. This file had also contained a /PAGE entry. That's the entry you'll see for a hard page. Delphi's Rich Text Edit control not only ignored the /PAGE directive by not displaying a page break on-screen, it removed the /PAGE entry from the file. The bottom line is that you'll need to be very careful about the level of support you expect from any applications you write. You'll probably need to subclass the control and add extra capabilities if you need anything more than the basics I showed you in Chapter 6.

Unfortunately, the loss of the /PAGE directive also adversely affects your ability to quickly paginate a document. You'll need to use some other control character throughout the document as a new page character. I suggest using the same character you find in text documents—ASCII character 12.

Now that you have some idea of what the additional form looks like, let's take a look at the code changes that our older module requires to implement our printing example. I've only included the functions that changed from the editor example in Chapter 6. Look at the various listings in that chapter—there's one listing for each dialog box type in the editor. You'll also need to add "Procedure PrintDocument;" to the public section of the unit. Make sure you add the appropriate Uses entries to the Implementation section as well (Delphi will remind you if you don't). Notice that we've also changed the code for both the File | Print menu command and SpeedButton4.

Listing 8.1. Creating a standard report.

```
procedure TForm1.Print1Click(Sender: TObject);
begin
    {Call on our print procedure.}
    PrintDocument;
end;

procedure TForm1.PageSetup1Click(Sender: TObject);
var
    sLeft, sRight, sTop, sBottom: String;   {Margin storage variables.}
    sHeader, sFooter: String;             {Header and footer storage.}
    iUD1, iUD2, iUD3, iUD4: Integer;         {Up/Down Control Settings.}
begin
    {Store the current page setup values.}
    sLeft := PageSetup.PageLeft.Text;
    sRight := PageSetup.PageRight.Text;
    sTop := PageSetup.PageTop.Text;
    sBottom := PageSetup.PageBottom.Text;
    sHeader := PageSetup.HeaderText.Text;
    sFooter := PageSetup.FooterText.Text;

    {Store the current Up/Down control position settings.}
    iUD1 := PageSetup.UpDown1.Position;
    iUD2 := PageSetup.UpDown2.Position;
    iUD3 := PageSetup.UpDown3.Position;
    iUD4 := PageSetup.UpDown4.Position;

    {If the user cancelled the printer margin setup.}
    if PageSetup.ShowModal = mrCancel then

        {Restore the values to their previous settings.}
        begin
         PageSetup.PageLeft.Text := sLeft;
         PageSetup.PageRight.Text := sRight;
         PageSetup.PageTop.Text := sTop;
         PageSetup.PageBottom.Text := sBottom;
         PageSetup.HeaderText.Text := sHeader;
         PageSetup.FooterText.Text := sFooter;

         {Restore the Up/Down Control Position settings.}
         PageSetup.UpDown1.Position := iUD1;
         PageSetup.UpDown2.Position := iUD2;
```

continues

Listing 8.1. **continued**

```
            PageSetup.UpDown3.Position := iUD3;
            PageSetup.UpDown4.Position := iUD4;
            end;
end;

procedure TForm1.SpeedButton4Click(Sender: TObject);
begin
     {Call on our print procedure.}
     PrintDocument;
end;

procedure TForm1.PrintDocument;
var
     iLineCount: Integer;      {Line Counter.}
     iStartLine: Integer;      {The print starting line.}
     iEndLine: Integer;         {The print ending line.}
     iCharCount: Integer;      {Character Counter.}
     iLineOffset: Integer;      {An offset into the first selected line of text.}
     iEndOffset: Integer;      {An offset into the last selected line of text.}
     iCurrentPos: Integer;      {Current position on printed page.}
     iCurrentChr: Integer;      {Current character within document.}
     iYPos: Integer;            {Current cursor position on printer canvas.}
     iLeftMargin: Integer;      {Left page margin.}
     iRightMargin: Integer;      {Right page margin.}
     iTopMargin: Integer;      {Top page margin.}
     iBottomMargin: Integer;      {Bottom page margin.}
     iXPrintFactor: Integer;      {Inches to Pixels X axis conversion.}
     iYPrintFactor: Integer;      {Inches to Pixels Y axis conversion.}
     iFooterPosit: Integer;      {Footer position on page.}
     fWordWrap: Boolean;         {Current word wrap status.}
     iSelS, iSelL: Integer;      {Selection saving variables.}
begin

     {If the user has selected specific text, the enable the selection
      option of the print dialog.}
     if RichEdit1.SelLength > 0 then
          PrintDialog1.Options := [poSelection, poPageNums];

     {if the user selected a print option, then act on it.}
     if PrintDialog1.Execute then
          begin

               {Save the current text selection.}
               iSelS := RichEdit1.SelStart;
               iSelL := RichEdit1.SelLength;

               {Get the inch to pixel conversion factors.}
               iXPrintFactor := GetDeviceCaps(Printer.Handle, LOGPIXELSX);
               iYPrintFactor := GetDeviceCaps(Printer.Handle, LOGPIXELSY);

               {Convert the values in the page setup dialog to pixels.}
               iLeftMargin := (PageSetup.UpDown1.Position * iXPrintFactor) Div 10;
               iRightMargin := (PageSetup.UpDown2.Position * iXPrintFactor) Div 10;
               iTopMargin := (PageSetup.UpDown3.Position * iXPrintFactor) Div 10;
               iBottomMargin := (PageSetup.UpDown4.Position * iXPrintFactor) Div 10;

               {Initialize our positioning variables.}
```

```
iCurrentChr := 0;
iStartLine := 0;
iLineCount := 0;
iLineOffset := 0;
iCurrentPos := iTopMargin;
iYPos := iLeftMargin;

{Set the document title in Print Manager.}
if Length(SaveDialog1.Filename) > 0 then
    Printer.Title := SaveDialog1.Filename
else
    Printer.Title := 'Untitled Document';

{Open the printer for use.}
Printer.BeginDoc;

{Check to see if there's a header to print.}
if Length(PageSetup.HeaderText.Text) > 0 then
    begin

        {Use the default text characteristics.}
        Printer.Canvas.Font.Assign(RichEdit1.DefAttributes);

        {Send it to the printer and update our positioning variable.}
        Printer.Canvas.TextOut(iYPos, iCurrentPos, PageSetup.HeaderText.Text);
        iCurrentPos := iCurrentPos +
Printer.Canvas.TextHeight(PageSetup.HeaderText.Text) + 20;
        end;

    {See if there's a footer to print.}
    if Length(PageSetup.FooterText.Text) > 0 then
        begin

        {If so, change our bottom margin to make space for it.}
         iBottomMargin := iBottomMargin +
Printer.Canvas.TextHeight(PageSetup.FooterText.Text) - 20;

        {Calculate the footer position.}
         iFooterPosit := Printer.PageHeight -
Printer.Canvas.TextHeight(PageSetup.FooterText.Text) - iBottomMargin;
        end;

    {See if the user wants to print all the text.}
    if PrintDialog1.PrintRange = prAllPages then
        begin

        {Select the first character in the edit area.}
        RichEdit1.SelStart := 0;

        {Select the last line of the edit area.}
        iEndLine := RichEdit1.Lines.Count;
        end;

    {See if the user selected specific text to print.}
    if PrintDialog1.PrintRange = prSelection then
        begin
        with RichEdit1 do begin {Use our edit control.}
```

continues

Listing 8.1. continued

```
              {Find the right starting line.}
            while (iCurrentChr + Length(Lines[iStartLine])) < SelStart do
              begin
                {The length of a line is equal to the text it contains
                    and the end of line characters.}
                iCurrentChr := iCurrentChr + Length(Lines[iStartLine]) + 2;
                iStartLine := iStartLine + 1;
                end;

            {Find the starting position within the selected line.}
            iLineOffset := SelStart - iCurrentChr;

            {Initialize our end of selected area variables.}
            iEndLine := iStartLine;
            iCharCount := iCurrentChr + Length(Lines[iEndLine]) + 2;

            {Find the right ending line.}
            while (iCharCount + Length(Lines[iEndLine + 1]) + 2) < (SelStart + SelLength)
do
              begin
                {The length of a line is equal to the text it contains
                    and the end of line characters.}
                iCharCount := iCharCount + Length(Lines[iEndLine]) + 2;
                iEndLine := iEndLine + 1;
                end;

            {Modify our character counter so that it points to the real end of line.}
            {iCharCount := iCharCount - iLineOffset + Length(Lines[iEndLine]) + 2;}

            {Find the ending position within the selected line.}
            if iCharCount > (SelStart + SelLength) then
                iEndOffset := SelStart + SelLength - iCurrentChr
            else
                iEndOffset := SelStart + SelLength - iCharCount;

          end; {with RichEdit1 do begin}
      end; {if PrintDialog1.PrintRange = prSelection then}

    {Turn off word wrap so that we can get true line lengths.}
    fWordWrap := RichEdit1.WordWrap;
    RichEdit1.WordWrap := False;

    {Display the page printing and abort dialog, allow it to process messages.}
    PrintStatus.Show;
    PrintStatus.SetFocus;
    Application.ProcessMessages;

    {See if everything we need to print is on a single line.}
    if not ((iStartLine = iEndLine) and (iEndOffset > iLineOffset)) then
        begin

    {Print the entire or selected contents of the document.}
    for iLineCount := iStartLine to iEndLine do
        begin

            {Print each line, one character at a time.}
            for iCharCount := iLineOffset to Length(RichEdit1.Lines[iLineCount]) do
```

```
begin

  {Select a single character.}
  RichEdit1.SelStart := iCurrentChr + iCharCount;
  RichEdit1.SelLength := 1;

  {Reset iLineOffset to 0 if we needed selected a midpoint in the first
   line of text.}
  iLineOffset := 0;

  {Determine its characteristics.}
  Printer.Canvas.Font.Assign(RichEdit1.SelAttributes);

  {Send it to the printer if the user hasn't aborted printing.}
  if not Printer.Aborted then
     Printer.Canvas.TextOut(iYPos, iCurrentPos, RichEdit1.SelText)
  else
     begin
      {If the user did abort, exit this procedure.}
      RichEdit1.WordWrap := fWordWrap;    {reset word wrap}
     exit;
      end;

  {Update our canvas positioning variable.}
  iYPos := iYPos + Printer.Canvas.TextWidth(RichEdit1.SelText);

  {If we're at the end of the printable area, but not at the end
   of the line of text in the document.}
  if iYPos > Printer.PageWidth - iRightMargin then
     begin

       {Reposition ourselves at the beginning of the next line.}
       iCurrentPos := iCurrentPos +
Printer.Canvas.TextHeight(RichEdit1.Lines[iLineCount]);
       iYPos := iLeftMargin;
       end;
     end;

{Once we reach the end of the line, go to the next line of the print
 canvas and update our character counter.  Make sure you always add
 2 to the character counter value for the end of line characters.}
iCurrentChr := iCurrentChr + Length(RichEdit1.Lines[iLineCount]) + 2;
iCurrentPos := iCurrentPos +
Printer.Canvas.TextHeight(RichEdit1.Lines[iLineCount]);
iYPos := iLeftMargin;

{If we've come to the bottom of the page, go to the next page.}
if iCurrentPos > Printer.PageHeight - 20 then
  begin
   {If the user hasn't aborted the procedure.}
   if not Printer.Aborted then
     begin

     {Use the default text characteristics.}
         Printer.Canvas.Font.Assign(RichEdit1.DefAttributes);

     {Set the positioning variable at the bottom of the page.}
     iCurrentPos := iFooterPosit;
```

continues

Listing 8.1. continued

```
                          {Print the footer.}
                   Printer.Canvas.TextOut(iYPos, iCurrentPos,
PageSetup.FooterText.Text);

                          {Go to the next page.}
                   Printer.NewPage;

                          {Print the header.}
                   Printer.Canvas.TextOut(iYPos, iCurrentPos,
PageSetup.HeaderText.Text);
                   iCurrentPos := iCurrentPos +
Printer.Canvas.TextHeight(PageSetup.HeaderText.Text) + 20;
                       end
                else
                   begin
                      RichEdit1.WordWrap := fWordWrap;    {reset word wrap}
                      Exit;
                      end;
                PrintStatus.CurrentPage.Caption := IntToStr(Printer.PageNumber);
                iCurrentPos := iTopMargin;
                end;
         end;
         end;

         {If the user printed a selection of text instead of the entire document,
          check to see if we have a remainder of a line to print.}
         if (PrintDialog1.PrintRange = prSelection) and (iEndOffset > 0) then
            begin

            for iCharCount := iLineOffset to (iEndOffset - 1) do
                begin
                {Select a single character.}
                RichEdit1.SelStart := iCurrentChr + iCharCount;
                RichEdit1.SelLength := 1;

                {Determine its characteristics.}
                Printer.Canvas.Font.Assign(RichEdit1.SelAttributes);

                {Send it to the printer if the user hasn't aborted printing.}
                if not Printer.Aborted then
                   Printer.Canvas.TextOut(iYPos, iCurrentPos, RichEdit1.SelText)
                else
                   begin
                   {If the user did abort, exit this procedure.}
                   RichEdit1.WordWrap := fWordWrap;    {reset word wrap}
                   exit;
                   end;

                {Update our canvas positioning variable.}
                iYPos := iYPos + Printer.Canvas.TextWidth(RichEdit1.SelText);
                end;

            {Reset our canvas positioning variable.}
            iYPos := iLeftMargin;
            end;

      {Check to see if there's a footer to print.}
```

```
         if Length(PageSetup.HeaderText.Text) > 0 then
            begin

              {Use the default text characteristics.}
              Printer.Canvas.Font.Assign(RichEdit1.DefAttributes);

              {Set the positioning variable at the bottom of the page.}
              iCurrentPos := iFooterPosit;

              {Send it to the printer.}
              Printer.Canvas.TextOut(iYPos, iCurrentPos, PageSetup.FooterText.Text);
            end;

          {Close the printer.}
          Printer.EndDoc;

          {Hide the printing dialog.}
          PrintStatus.Hide;

          {Turn word wrap back on.}
          RichEdit1.WordWrap := fWordWrap;

          {Restore the original text selection.}
          RichEdit1.SelStart := iSelS;
          RichEdit1.SelLength := iSelL;

       end; {if PrintDialog1.Execute then}

end;
```

The actual print routine is very lengthy. I split it up into sections using a lot of comments to make the various component parts easier to understand. You'll notice that this particular routine handles printing all the text and a selected portion of text. All you would need to do is look at the selected portion part of the code to add the capability to print specific pages. Instead of having to write a line offset based on a particular selection, you would find the requested page and use that line offset as the starting point for the print routine. In essence, you would need to add one more section for finding a particular iStartLine and iEndLine value based on page number.

Tip: If you go through the list of functions that Delphi provides, you'll notice that there aren't any functions provided for checking the status of the printer or its capabilities. Even the Printer object supplied with Delphi lacks this feature. You have to rely on the Windows API if you want to determine a device's status. I use the GetDeviceCaps function in Listing 8.1 to determine the printer's resolution. You can use this function to determine the capabilities of most devices attached to your system. Another function to look at is the DeviceCapabilities function. It offers some information that the GetDeviceCaps function won't. You'll also find that this function provides a few unique Windows 95 capabilities. For example, you can determine if a printer will support enhanced metafiles directly by using the DC_EMF_COMPLIANT capability request.

Note: The GetDeviceCaps function in Windows NT provides a lot more features than those found under Windows 3.x. For example, the VREFRESH option allows you to determine the refresh rate of the display. Windows 95 supports some, but not all, of the Windows NT additions to the GetDeviceCaps function.

The code for allowing the user to change the margins and add a header and footer is a lot shorter. You'll find it in Listing 8.2. Most of it takes care of keeping the edit and the up/down controls in sync by monitoring specific events for both controls. I also added a short piece of code that allows the user to open the printer configuration dialog.

Listing 8.2. Adding margins to a standard report.

```
unit Print2;

interface

uses Windows, SysUtils, Classes, Graphics, Forms, Controls, StdCtrls,
  Buttons, ExtCtrls, ComCtrls;

type
  TPageSetup = class(TForm)
    OKBtn: TButton;
    CancelBtn: TButton;
    Bevel1: TBevel;
    HeaderText: TEdit;
    FooterText: TEdit;
    Label1: TLabel;
    Label2: TLabel;
    GroupBox1: TGroupBox;
    PageLeft: TEdit;
    PageRight: TEdit;
    PageTop: TEdit;
    PageBottom: TEdit;
    Label3: TLabel;
    Label4: TLabel;
    Label5: TLabel;
    Label6: TLabel;
    Button1: TButton;
    UpDown1: TUpDown;
    UpDown2: TUpDown;
    UpDown3: TUpDown;
    UpDown4: TUpDown;
    procedure Button1Click(Sender: TObject);
    procedure UpDown1Changing(Sender: TObject; var AllowChange: Boolean);
    procedure UpDown2Changing(Sender: TObject; var AllowChange: Boolean);
    procedure UpDown3Changing(Sender: TObject; var AllowChange: Boolean);
    procedure UpDown4Changing(Sender: TObject; var AllowChange: Boolean);
    procedure PageLeftExit(Sender: TObject);
    procedure PageRightExit(Sender: TObject);
    procedure PageTopExit(Sender: TObject);
    procedure PageBottomExit(Sender: TObject);
  private
```

```
    { Private declarations }
  public
    { Public declarations }
  end;

var
  PageSetup: TPageSetup;

implementation

uses Print1;

{$R *.DFM}

procedure TPageSetup.Button1Click(Sender: TObject);
begin
    {All we need to do is display the dialog, Windows takes care of the rest.}
    Form1.PrinterSetupDialog1.Execute;
end;

procedure TPageSetup.UpDown1Changing(Sender: TObject;
  var AllowChange: Boolean);
begin
    {We don't want an actual integer change, we want a tenth change.}
    PageLeft.Text := IntToStr(UpDown1.Position Div 10) + '.' + IntToStr(UpDown1.Position
Mod 10);
end;

procedure TPageSetup.UpDown2Changing(Sender: TObject;
  var AllowChange: Boolean);
begin
    {We don't want an actual integer change, we want a tenth change.}
    PageRight.Text := IntToStr(UpDown2.Position Div 10) + '.' + IntToStr(UpDown2.Position
Mod 10);
end;

procedure TPageSetup.UpDown3Changing(Sender: TObject;
  var AllowChange: Boolean);
begin
    {We don't want an actual integer change, we want a tenth change.}
    PageTop.Text := IntToStr(UpDown3.Position Div 10) + '.' + IntToStr(UpDown3.Position
Mod 10);
end;

procedure TPageSetup.UpDown4Changing(Sender: TObject;
  var AllowChange: Boolean);
begin
    {We don't want an actual integer change, we want a tenth change.}
    PageBottom.Text := IntToStr(UpDown4.Position Div 10) + '.' +
IntToStr(UpDown4.Position Mod 10);
end;

procedure TPageSetup.PageLeftExit(Sender: TObject);
var
    sValue: String;      {Current value of our edit control.}
    iNewPosit: Integer;     {New up/down control position.}
begin
    {We need to keep the up/down control in sync with the edit box.  Change
     the position to match what we have in the dialog.}
```

continues

Listing 8.2. continued

```
    {First we need to make sure the user added a decimal point.}
    if Pos('.', PageLeft.Text) = 0 then
        PageLeft.Text := PageLeft.Text + '.0';

    {Get the integer portion}
    sValue := Copy(PageLeft.Text, 1, Pos('.', PageLeft.Text) - 1);

    {See if there's an integer value, then multiply by 10 to convert to
     positional value.}
    if Length(sValue) > 0 then
        iNewPosit := StrToInt(sValue) * 10;

    {Get the 10ths value.}
    sValue := Copy(PageLeft.Text, Pos('.', PageLeft.Text) + 1, 1);

    {See if there's a 10ths value and add it to our position.}
    if Length(sValue) > 0 then
        iNewPosit := iNewPosit + StrToInt(sValue);

    {Store the new position.}
    UpDown1.Position := iNewPosit;
end;

procedure TPageSetup.PageRightExit(Sender: TObject);
var
    sValue: String;    {Current value of our edit control.}
    iNewPosit: Integer;    {New up/down control position.}
begin
    {We need to keep the up/down control in sync with the edit box.  Change
     the position to match what we have in the dialog.}

    {First we need to make sure the user added a decimal point.}
    if Pos('.', PageRight.Text) = 0 then
        PageRight.Text := PageRight.Text + '.0';

    {Get the integer portion}
    sValue := Copy(PageRight.Text, 1, Pos('.', PageRight.Text) - 1);

    {See if there's an integer value, then multiply by 10 to convert to
     positional value.}
    if Length(sValue) > 0 then
        iNewPosit := StrToInt(sValue) * 10;

    {Get the 10ths value.}
    sValue := Copy(PageRight.Text, Pos('.', PageRight.Text) + 1, 1);

    {See if there's a 10ths value and add it to our position.}
    if Length(sValue) > 0 then
        iNewPosit := iNewPosit + StrToInt(sValue);

    {Store the new position.}
    UpDown2.Position := iNewPosit;
end;

procedure TPageSetup.PageTopExit(Sender: TObject);
var
```

```
    sValue: String;    {Current value of our edit control.}
    iNewPosit: Integer;    {New up/down control position.}
begin
    {We need to keep the up/down control in sync with the edit box.  Change
     the position to match what we have in the dialog.}

    {First we need to make sure the user added a decimal point.}
    if Pos('.', PageTop.Text) = 0 then
        PageTop.Text := PageTop.Text + '.0';

    {Get the integer portion}
    sValue := Copy(PageTop.Text, 1, Pos('.', PageTop.Text) - 1);

    {See if there's an integer value, then multiply by 10 to convert to
     positional value.}
    if Length(sValue) > 0 then
        iNewPosit := StrToInt(sValue) * 10;

    {Get the 10ths value.}
    sValue := Copy(PageTop.Text, Pos('.', PageTop.Text) + 1, 1);

    {See if there's a 10ths value and add it to our position.}
    if Length(sValue) > 0 then
        iNewPosit := iNewPosit + StrToInt(sValue);

    {Store the new position.}
    UpDown3.Position := iNewPosit;
end;

procedure TPageSetup.PageBottomExit(Sender: TObject);
var
    sValue: String;    {Current value of our edit control.}
    iNewPosit: Integer;    {New up/down control position.}
begin
    {We need to keep the up/down control in sync with the edit box.  Change
     the position to match what we have in the dialog.}

    {First we need to make sure the user added a decimal point.}
    if Pos('.', PageBottom.Text) = 0 then
        PageBottom.Text := PageBottom.Text + '.0';

    {Get the integer portion}
    sValue := Copy(PageBottom.Text, 1, Pos('.', PageBottom.Text) - 1);

    {See if there's an integer value, then multiply by 10 to convert to
     positional value.}
    if Length(sValue) > 0 then
        iNewPosit := StrToInt(sValue) * 10;

    {Get the 10ths value.}
    sValue := Copy(PageBottom.Text, Pos('.', PageBottom.Text) + 1, 1);

    {See if there's a 10ths value and add it to our position.}
    if Length(sValue) > 0 then
        iNewPosit := iNewPosit + StrToInt(sValue);

    {Store the new position.}
```

continues

Listing 8.2, continued

```
    UpDown4.Position := iNewPosit;
end;

end.
```

There's one thing that should really become obvious as you look through this code. Delphi lacks the ability to handle real numbers effectively. This results in a lot of extra code to convert our edit control entries into something that the up/down controls can understand. Fortunately, the actual amount of extra code in this case is minimal, but you'll want to use DLLs or other methods of handling real numbers if you have a lot of calculations to perform.

Our final bit of code takes care of the needs of the printer status dialog. It appears in Listing 8.3. Delphi's inherent capabilities make what could be a rather long and arduous task simple—a mere three lines of code in this case. You'll see the other half of the abort code throughout the TForm1.PrintDocument procedure in Listing 8.1. In most cases you'll want to return the display to it's pre-print condition, then simply exit the print routine if the user decides to abort the print job.

> **Warning:** Attempting to write to the printer after you execute a Printer.Abort command could have unusual results when the Print Manager tries to interpret your request. Using the Abort method tells Windows that you no longer need the printer, so Windows gets rid of the printer handle you were using. If you try to write to the printer again, you'll be using an invalid printer handle and Windows will—as a minimum—raise an exception. Always monitor the Aborted parameter of the Printer object to make sure the printer handle is still usable. Never use the EndDoc method after using the Abort method.

Listing 8.3, Stopping a print job.

```
unit Print3;

interface

uses
  Windows, Messages, SysUtils, Classes, Graphics, Controls, Forms, Dialogs,
  StdCtrls, Printers;

type
  TPrintStatus = class(TForm)
    Label1: TLabel;
    CurrentPage: TLabel;
    AbortPrinting: TButton;
    procedure AbortPrintingClick(Sender: TObject);
  private
    { Private declarations }
  public
    { Public declarations }
```

```
    end;

var
  PrintStatus: TPrintStatus;

implementation

{$R *.DFM}

procedure TPrintStatus.AbortPrintingClick(Sender: TObject);
begin
    {Abort Printing}
    Printer.Abort;

    {Tell the user that printing is aborted.}
    MessageDlg('Printing aborted', mtInformation, [mbOK],0);

    {Close the dialog.}
    Close;
end;

end.
```

You could do a variety of other things with this baseline printer routine. For example, the header and footer only allow text entry at the moment. You could add the capability of printing the filename, page number, or other information in the header and footer. Another way to improve the print routine would be to allow the user to format the header and footer text. I currently use the default text attributes in the routine. Adding formatting capability wouldn't involve much more than using the same routines that we used to format the text in the edit area (see Listings 6.2 and 6.4 in Chapter 6), so I didn't include the required code here.

Using ReportSmith

The previous section should have demonstrated one thing to you: Creating a full-fledged print routine under Delphi can become a complex undertaking. Positioning characters and keeping track of all the required printer canvas elements can become quite involved. Trying to find errors in all this code is even more difficult. It doesn't take too much to imagine what that task would be like if you also had to take the needs of a remote database into account when writing your routine. Fortunately, there's an easier way. ReportSmith is the Delphi way to access your printer when it comes to database specific reports. Sure, you could write a blow-by-blow description of how you want things to appear, but using ReportSmith makes the job a lot faster and easier.

New Features

Before I look at the various implementation details of using ReportSmith, let's take a look at what ReportSmith version 3.0 (supplied with the 32-bit version of Delphi) can do for you. The following paragraphs look at these new features and explain what they can do for you. Obviously this isn't a complete feature list, it only tells you what changed since version 2.5 appeared on the scene.

• Fully 32-bit—Speed is always a major cause for concern. A print routine has to be faster than most parts of an application because each moment that the user has to wait seems like an eternity. 32-bit routines under Windows 95 and Windows NT enjoy many special privileges—not the least of which is the ability to use threads of execution. Both operating systems are designed to allow a process to execute in the background instead of taking up precious user time. Another 32-bit feature that the database programmer will love is the flat address space this environment provides. You aren't limited to 64 KB strings any more. For that matter, you'll find improved capacity in all variables.

• Windows 95 Common Controls—I've already shown you how to use a few of these controls in examples in this book. For example, the up/down control (one of my personal favorites) used in the Page Setup dialog in this chapter is an example of a Windows 95 common control. You'll find a complete description of all the Windows 95 common controls in Chapter 1. Look in the section entitled "Support for Windows 95 UI Controls." Using these new common controls in your ReportSmith reports has obvious advantages. For one thing, using these controls makes it a lot easier for the user to get the job done quickly.

• Long Filenames and UNC (Universal Naming Convention)—Anyone who uses Windows 95 or Windows NT for very long will become completely hooked on long filenames. It must have taken me all of about five minutes to get hooked myself. Users have complained for years about the limitations of trying to name a file using the DOS 8.3 naming convention. What you may not have spent a lot of time with in the past is UNC. Networks, like Novell's NetWare, use UNC to make drive mappings almost invisible to the user. In other words, you no longer have to remember a string of long pathnames because the network drive uses a universal naming convention—the one that you've used all along on your machine. So, what does UNC do for the programmer—it means that you can avoid a lot of configuration problems because you can specify one path for your network data and applications.

• Delphi Data Connection—I always wondered how long it would take Borland to implement this feature. It seemed strange to me that you couldn't really get Delphi and ReportSmith to work together without a lot of extra work. You'll still find that you need to do a few special things to get these two products to work together, but the task is far from difficult now. I provide you with a step-by-step procedure for creating a Delphi to ReportSmith connection in the section entitled "Getting ReportSmith and Delphi to Talk," in this chapter.

• CTLib Native Connection—Providing this new connection type will allow you to access some types of databases, like Sybase, more quickly.

- Improved Data Access Performance—Part of the speed increase you'll notice during data access is a direct result of the improved data drivers supplied with Delphi. However, I'd be remiss in not mentioning the improvements that other vendors have made to their ODBC drivers as well. Added to these improvements is the 32-bit programming environment; ReportSmith 3.0 uses 32-bit ODBC, not the 16-bit environment used with previous versions. Suffice it to say that you'll get access to your data faster under the new version of ReportSmith, but that it's for a lot more reasons than the work that Borland has put into making ReportSmith better.

Getting Connected

It always helps to know what kind of connections a product supports before you use it. In this case I'm referring to which data formats that ReportSmith supports. (Actually, it's not so much the format of the data, but the language of the server that you need to worry about the most.) The following list tells which formats that the 3.0 version of ReportSmith can connect to. Most of the old choices are still there along with a few new ones. Notice that Delphi 1.0 is absent from the list since it's a 16-bit product and ReportSmith 3.0 can only access 32-bit products—you'll need to reconcile any needs from the older version of Delphi with the newer version of ReportSmith before you upgrade.

- 32-bit ODBC 2.0
- AS/400 (ODBC)
- DB2
- dBASE
- Delphi 2.0
- Informix
- Interbase
- MS SQL Server
- Paradox
- Sybase (including System10 via CTLib)
- Terradata (ODBC)
- Oracle Text (ASCII)

You'll notice that our list of supported connections doesn't include ODBC 1.0. That's because ODBC 1.0 is 16-bit. Borland decided not to include a "thunk" layer in ReportSmith to support these older applications. That means you'll have to upgrade all your ODBC drivers to the 2.0 specification and re-create all your connections. Both Delphi and ReportSmith can detect old 1.0 connections and notify you of their presence. They can also help you migrate the connections, but not without the required drivers. The bottom line is that you should install all the ODBC drivers you need, even if you currently have a version of that driver installed.

Fortunately both Windows 95 and Windows NT make it easy for you to determine which of your ODBC drivers are 16-bit and which are 32-bit. All you need to do is open the Control Panel. If you see a 32-bit ODBC applet, then you know you have some 32-bit drivers installed. All you need to do is open this applet and click on the Drivers pushbutton to see which drivers are 32-bit. (All the drivers in the dialog box are 32-bit; any other drivers on your machine are 16-bit or improperly registered.) Click on the Drivers pushbutton to display a list of current drivers as shown in Figure 8.5. The drivers list also provides you with the means to determine which version of the driver you're using and what files it requires (at least which main files it requires—you may have to do a little more research in some cases to get a complete file list). All you need to do is click on the driver name and then the About pushbutton. Never confuse the driver version with the ODBC version. All of your 32-bit drivers will be ODBC 2.0 compliant; all your 16-bit drivers will be ODBC 1.0 compatible. Figure 8.6 shows you a typical ODBC driver About dialog.

Tip: Delphi supports both direct and either ODBC or IDAPI connections for some database products. Always use the direct connection as the first choice since its the fastest way to access your data. Choosing IDAPI second has the advantage of fewer configuration issues to worry about and a higher probability of making the connection without error. IDAPI connections are usually faster as well. Use ODBC connections as a last resort since you have to rely on several pieces of software working in concert to make the connection.

Figure 8.5.
The 32-bit ODBC applet
will provide you with a list of
32-bit drivers installed on
your system.

Figure 8.6.
An ODBC driver's About
dialog can tell you a lot about
the driver you're using and
aid in some types of
troubleshooting.

Looking Ahead: I'll show you how to create ODBC connections in Chapter 12. You'll see how easy it can be to access data stored in any supported database file. Of course, you'll have to have a 32-bit ODBC driver to make the connection.

Getting ReportSmith and Delphi to Talk

One of the ways that ReportSmith 3.0 improves on the services provided by its predecessor is that it can share a table with Delphi. The level of integration between the two products is also improved from the previous version. These two features work hand-in-hand to make it easier for the programmer to create some truly spectacular reports in a modicum of time.

We reviewed the new Delphi database controls in Chapter 1. One of those new controls allows you to place a ReportSmith report right on a Delphi form. All you need to do to access it during design time is to double-click on it. Before you can do much work with the form though, you'll need to create a database. ReportSmith works with database tables as a source of information.

Getting Delphi and ReportSmith to talk with each other isn't quite as easy as sticking a couple of controls on a form and adding a bit of code to make them work. You need to create the actual connection between them. Use the following procedure if you want Delphi and ReportSmith to share the same data source.

1. Create the Delphi form that you'll use to access the report. It could be a menu or perhaps a data entry form of some type. You will need to add a combination of active TTable or TQuery objects like those shown in Figure 8.7 to start the connection process. If you want to create a Delphi database, you'll also need to add a Database control. The Database control provides a receptacle for one or more tables.

Figure 8.7.

Creating a connection between Delphi and ReportSmith starts with a form—just like most Delphi tasks.

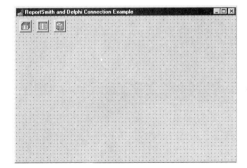

2. Once you define a query or a table, you can do something with the data it contains. Place a TReport control from the Data Access page on the form as shown in Figure 8.7.

3. Double-click on the TReport control. This will launch ReportSmith into the design environment. You'll see a dialog similar to the one show in Figure 8.8. Notice that ReportSmith automatically asks which report that you want to open.

Figure 8.8.

ReportSmith automatically asks which report you want to open when you start it.

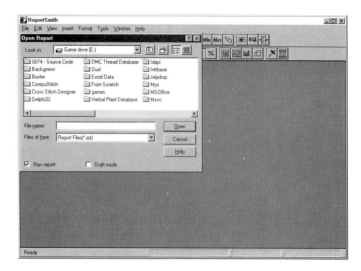

4. Click on Cancel to close the Open dialog. Click the New Report button on the far left of the toolbar. You'll see a dialog similar to the one shown in Figure 8.9. ReportSmith currently supports four report types—you may see more types available in the future. The pictures of the form types make it pretty clear how you would use each type.

Figure 8.9.

You can create four basic report types using ReportSmith.

5. Double-click on the type of report you want to create. ReportSmith will display the dialog shown in Figure 8.10. This is the dialog where you decide what types of information will go into your report.

Figure 8.10.

The Report Query-Tables dialog allows you to choose the sources for the information your report will contain.

Note: Some database managers use the term database to refer to tables. When ReportSmith talks about a table, it is referring to a single data set from within a database. A Microsoft Access database may contain multiple tables—you would choose one or more of those tables as a source of information. In some cases—like DBF files—a table and a database are almost synonymous since a database can only contain a single table. In this case, you would supply the name of the single table file that contains the information you want to output in the report.

6. Click on the Add Table button. You'll see a Select Table To Be Added dialog similar to the one shown in Figure 8.11. The actual appearance of this dialog changes depending on the data source you choose and whether you have already made a connection to the server.

Figure 8.11.
The Select Table To Be Added dialog allows you to choose which data source you want to use, then select from one of the tables available from that data source.

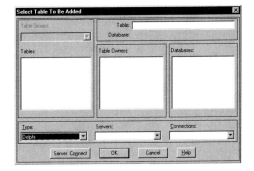

7. Select Delphi from the Type drop-down list in the lower left corner of the dialog. Click on the Server Connect button. You should see a list of available tables if there are any to choose from. One of the tables in the list should match the name of the TTable control that you added to your Delphi form.

8. Choose the name of the TTable control. If you have more than one TTable control on the form, then choose one or more of them for your report. Click on OK to close the Select Table To Be Added dialog. Click on Done to close the Report Query Tables dialog. Delphi will display an icon showing that it's communicating with the data server for at least a few moments, then display the data on-screen. This is the point where you actually start to design the report.

9. Rearrange and format the data that ReportSmith retrieved from the TTable control. I'll show you some of the things you can do with a report in the next section of the chapter.

10. Use the File | Save command to save the report. You might be tempted to use a long filename, but I usually keep the name short in the Delphi source code. Of course, you'll want to make the name as descriptive as possible.

11. Use the File | Exit command to leave ReportSmith and return to the Delphi IDE.

12. Add the name of your new report to the TReport Report Name property. You'll need to add a button or a menu to the form to use the new report. Assuming that the name of your TReport control is Report1, you would add "Report1.run;" to the OnClick event of the button or to the code associated with the new menu entry.

Delphi won't start the design portion of ReportSmith when the user decides to print the report at runtime. There's a runtime version of ReportSmith in a separate directory. Delphi executes this runtime version of the product and supplies the name of the report.

Creating a ReportSmith Report

The previous section spent some talk showing you how to create a connection between Delphi and ReportSmith. Let's use that information to create a simple Delphi database example. You'll start out with the same form you saw in Figure 8.7. That's where you define the first three elements we'll need to make this example work: a database, a table, and a report. You can't create any kind of Delphi database program without at least one of each of these components. The following procedure will take you through the steps required to create a ReportSmith report. In this case we want to create a report listing the names, addresses, and identification numbers of all the employees in your company.

Note: I'm going to use one of the sample databases found in your \RptSmith\Demos directory for the purposes of this example. You may want to check for the EMPLOYEE.DBF file stored there before you start the example in this section.

1. The first thing you'll need to do is create the form shown in Figure 8.7. Make sure you add a Database, Table, and Report control to it for right now.

2. Before you can make the TTable control do anything, you have to define a database for the form. To do that, double-click on the TDatabase control. You'll see a Database dialog similar to the one shown in Figure 8.12.

3. I've already filled out the form shown in Figure 8.12 so you would know what entries to make. Make sure you type the path to the RptSmith directory on your machine. I provided the path to my directory as an example. Notice that I unchecked the Login Prompt check box. You won't need this dialog unless you're using some form of security with your DBMS. Check the box if the user will need to log in to the DBMS before your application can retrieve any information.

4. Click on OK to close the dialog.

Figure 8.12.
The first step in creating your database report is to define a database connection using the Database dialog.

5. Set the Database1 Connected Property to True if Delphi doesn't do it automatically. Connecting to the database allows you to access the data it contains. You'll need to access the field names at minimum sometime during the setup process. For example, ReportSmith needs to know them before it can place any fields on your new report.

6. Select Table1 (our TTable control). Set the following property values: Database Name to EMPLOYEE, Table Name to EMPLOYEE, Table Type to ttDBase, and Active to True. Make sure you set the Active property last; otherwise, you'll get an error message from Delphi.

7. Double-click on the Report1 control to start ReportSmith. We're finally ready to start creating the report. I'm not going to list every detail of the creation process here; look in the previous section for detailed instructions.

8. Create a new Columnar report type. Click on the Add Table pushbutton. Select the Delphi table type and click on Server Connect. You should see a Select Table To Be Added dialog similar to the one shown in Figure 8.13.

Figure 8.13.
This time the Select Table To Be Added dialog contains the name of the table we described in the previous steps.

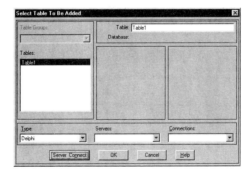

9. Click on OK, then Done to close the dialogs. ReportSmith will query the database server, then display a default report like the one shown in Figure 8.14. You could execute this report as it is from within Delphi. We'll add a few bells and whistles to it though before saving it. The first thing you'll want to do is make the header a little more aesthetically pleasing.

Figure 8.14.

This default ReportSmith
report is ready to execute
even though we haven't
done anything to it.

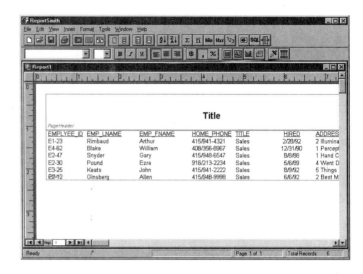

10. Click on the Title entry of the report, then click on it again. Don't double-click, because that won't allow you to edit the actual title text. I changed the title in my report to ABC Corporation. Now we need a little more room in the header for additional text.

11. Click anywhere in the header area but the title. Use the sizing bars you see to increase the header height. We'll need the extra space to put more than just the company name in the title area.

12. Click on the Text tool, then on the header area. Positioning isn't important immediately, but getting the text in the right area will save you a bit of time later. Unlike a word processor where you select the character attributes before you type the text, you type the text, then select the character attributes in ReportSmith. My second heading reads "Current Employee List."

Tip: ReportSmith highlights the area taken by a particular object on the ruler. You can use this highlighted area as a positioning aid when putting a report together.

13. Select the Arial font, a point size of 10, and the bold attribute for your new text. Beside these identifying pieces of information, I usually like to see a page number and current date on each page of my reports.

14. Use the Insert | Field command to display the Insert Fields dialog. Select System Variables from the first drop-down box. You should see a dialog similar to the one shown in Figure 8.15. The Insert Fields dialog will also allow you to add data fields from your table, derived fields, report variables, and summary fields. ReportSmith provides all the system variables as a default and reads all the data field entries from the tables you select. The other three field types are defined as needed.

Figure 8.15.
The Insert Field dialog will allow you to add page numbers and dates to your reports.

15. Click on Page Number, then on the Insert pushbutton. The mouse cursor shape will change to an Object cursor. Position the page number somewhere within the header. Repeat this step for the Date object. Click on Done to close the Insert Field dialog. Now it's time for a little more formatting.

Tip: You can also drag and drop the fields you need.

16. I added a text field with "Page:" in the upper right corner of the header followed by the page object. The upper left corner contains another text field containing "Date:" followed by the date object. Your header should look like the one in Figure 8.16. You'll also notice that the zoom factor of my display has changed. Clicking the third zoom control on the toolbar will allow you to see the entire width of the print area without scrolling. This view also shows you what our next step is—the data runs off the end of the page so we'll have to reduce its size. We'll change the report headings at the same time.

Tip: You can use the Tools | Alignment command to display a dialog that allows you to align various elements on your report. All you need to do is click on the objects that you want to align, then on the alignment tool that displays the form of alignment that you want to perform. Make sure that the first object you select is the one that you want to use as the alignment object—the one that all the other objects will change to match.

17. Click on the EMPLOYEE_ID heading and change it to ID. Change the font attributes to a point size of 12 and bold. Remove the underline. Once you change the name of the field, you can reduce its size so it takes the minimum space required to display all the employee IDs. Let's turn our attention to the next two fields. The employee name fields could be combined to save a lot of space on the report.

18. Select both the EMP_LNAME and EMP_FNAME fields at the same time. Use the Edit | Cut command to remove them. Now that we've gotten the old fields out of the way, let's add a new combined field. We'll have to create a derived field first to make everything work.

Figure 8.16.
Our finished header should
provide everything the user
will need to identify the
report.

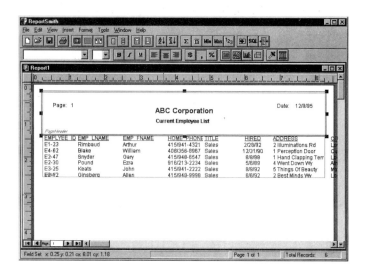

19. Use the Tools | Derived Fields command to display the Report Query-Derived Fields dialog shown in Figure 8.17. Notice that I've already filled in the name of our new combined employee name field.

Figure 8.17.
The Report Query-Derived
Fields dialog is the first stop
in creating a new query or
looking up an existing one.

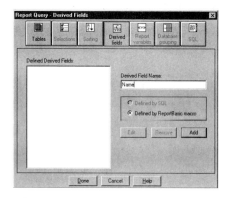

20. Click the Add pushbutton to add the derived field to the list. Adding the derived field to the list also displays the Choose A Macro dialog shown in Figure 8.18. We'll have to create a macro to define the contents of the derived field. I think you'll find that ReportSmith uses a BASIC-like language—strange when you consider it's used with a Pascal language product. I already provided the name and description for our new macro in the dialog.

Figure 8.18.

The Choose A Macro dialog
lists the dialogs you've
already defined and allows
you to create new ones.

21. Click on New to create the new macro. You'll see a dialog similar to the one shown in Figure 8.19. ReportSmith provides a point and click interface for building macros. I find it's very handy in reducing the time required to create an application (and the programmer's learning curve as well). This dialog contains the macro we'll need to combine the two employee name fields into one. There are a few important items to note about the macro. First, you can't use field names directly in the macro; ReportSmith requires that you convert them in some way first. In this case I simply convert them to a string using the Fields function. Notice that we also have to assign the result of the macro to the derived field. That's the last step in the conversion process.

Figure 8.19.

ReportSmith uses a BASIC-
like syntax for its macro
language.

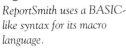

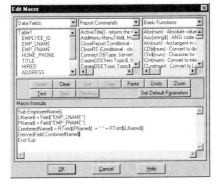

Tip: Don't let the simple appearance of ReportSmith fool you. It provides a fairly complete programming environment that includes standard Windows interface elements like dialog boxes. Since ReportSmith does provide this complete programming environment, it almost always pays to manipulate the report data using macros within the report, rather than manipulate the data within Delphi and pass the query results to the ReportSmith report.

22. Once you complete the macro, click on OK to save it. Click on OK to close the Choose A Macro dialog and Done to close the Report Query-Derived Fields dialog. ReportSmith will display a communication message as it updates the new derived field from the database. You'll see a new Name column appear at the end of the report.

23. Move the Name field between the ID and HOME_PHONE fields by clicking on it, then dragging it to the new position. All the other fields will automatically reposition themselves as needed.

24. Make the rest of the column headings aesthetically pleasing using the procedure in step 17. Your report should look similar to the one in Figure 8.20. Notice that all the fields now appear within the border of the detail area.

Figure 8.20.

The final version of the ReportSmith report looks aesthetically pleasing and required little coding to produce.

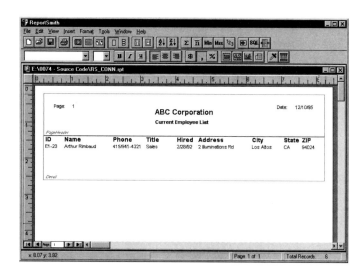

Note: It'll look as if there's only one detail line in the report now. In fact, if you run the report right now, that's all you get. The rest of the detail lines will reappear when you run the report. ReportSmith needs to reconnect to the database to obtain all the appropriate values for the derived field we just created.

25. Use the File | Save command to save the report. I saved it as RS_CONN.RPT. Exit ReportSmith. Now it's time to complete our Delphi program and test the report out. The first thing we need to do is tell the TReport control where to look for the report.

26. Select the Report1 ReportDir property. Either type the path to your report file or use the Select Directory dialog that you can display by clicking on the ellipses. Enter the report filename in the ReportName property. Now all we need is a way to run the report when the program is active.

27. Add a pushbutton to the form (you could also add a menu and add a Print entry to it). Add "Report1.Run;" to the pushbutton OnClick event and set the Report1.Preview property to True. This second step tells Report1 to show itself in the foreground.

28. Run the Delphi application. Press the pushbutton and you'll see the runtime version of ReportSmith start. It will display a communication icon for a few moments—or longer depending on the size of the database, the number of tables you used, and the complexity of the report. Once ReportSmith updates the report's data, it'll display a screen similar to the one in Figure 8.21 as it outputs the data to the printer.

Figure 8.21.
The runtime version of ReportSmith allows you to output a report from within Delphi.

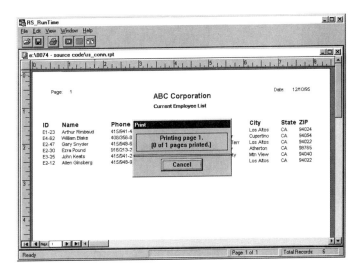

It doesn't take long to figure out that ReportSmith is a lot easier to use than writing a printing routine by hand. However, there are times that you'll need one or both—it all depends on what kind of data you need to output to the printer. As previously stated, ReportSmith excels at producing reports from databases. You could probably use this feature to your advantage by using databases in your Delphi applications more often.

Looking Ahead: We only took the briefest of looks at the database management capabilities of Delphi in this chapter. We'll examine this issue in several other chapters as well. Chapter 12 is the place to look for specifics on general database programming under Delphi. If you need to add some OLE capabilities to your database management application, take a look at Chapter 10. Look at Chapter 13 if you need some specifics on network programming—especially in regard to NetWare. I'll include some database specifics in that chapter as well. We'll also look at ReportSmith in these chapters. You can't get much out of a database without creating reports to view the data.

Summary

This chapter provided you with a complete look at methods for printing under Delphi. We began with an overview of the architecture. Knowing how things work can save you a lot of time in planning, implementing, and debugging your application. It also helps you communicate with the user a lot better when it comes time to install your application in the field.

Sending the data produced by your application can be one of the most time-consuming parts of any application. Windows makes the job even harder because you have to keep track of all those proportional fonts while you output data or you'll run out of space on the page. Delphi does its part to make creating printed output a little easier, but you'll still need to rely on the Windows API to get part of the job done.

We also looked at ReportSmith, the Borland supplied utility for creating print jobs when your data resides in a database. Creating a report with ReportSmith is a lot easier that writing one by hand as long as you don't need to perform a lot of data manipulation. As soon as you have to start deriving fields, add dialog boxes to ask users question, or perform other types of processing, you'll run into ReportSmith's BASIC-like macro language. While it's not a big obstacle, using the macro language could prove frustrating—not to mention time-consuming—for the programmer who knows Pascal and not much else. You'll want to set some time aside to learn ReportSmith's programming language before you tackle your first big report. Fortunately, the prompts and other aids the IDE provides make the learning curve less steep.

9

Miscellaneous Windows Services

The term miscellaneous is a little misleading when talking about Windows services (API function calls). You won't find a "miscellaneous" entry anywhere in the Windows API help file. I'm not really talking about miscellaneous functions, but those services that didn't get pigeonholed somewhere else. It's the miscellaneous services that you'll probably use most often within Delphi since it does a reasonably good job of taking care of the rest of your needs using visual components.

Unlike the other API areas that we've visited so far in this section of the book, I can't really point to a specific area of Windows and show you where the miscellaneous services are located. You'll find groups of miscellaneous functions in the LZExpand and Version areas of the Windows API. However, even the mainstream groups contain some miscellaneous functions. For example, you'll find a few miscellaneous services in the Windows area of the API. The EnumThreadWindows function falls into this category. It doesn't really operate on a window directly; it merely helps you list them. Supplemental functions are miscellaneous in nature. They provide a useful service, but you can't really pigeonhole them. As you can see, the miscellaneous services come from a variety of areas and perform a variety of tasks.

An Overview of the Miscellaneous Services

I mentioned two of the miscellaneous function groups in the previous section. The LZExpand function group allows you to decompress files that were compressed using Microsoft's COMPRESS.EXE or a compatible file compression utility. I'll tell you a lot more about these functions in the "Compressing and Decompressing Files" section of this chapter. The following sections tell you about the miscellaneous services that I use most often. There are other functions hidden throughout the Windows API. Just reading through the API becomes like a treasure hunt in many cases. You never know what new treasure in the form of unexpected Windows functionality you'll find laying around.

Note: You're going to see a lot of seemingly duplicate functions when using some functions under Windows 95 and Windows NT—functions that don't seem to appear in the on-line help. For example, the LZ32.DLL file contains two GetExpandedName function entries: GetExpandedNameA and GetExpandedNameW. The A version of the function uses ANSI 8-bit characters. The W version of the function uses the newer unicode 16-bit characters. Using 16-bit characters allows you to implement foreign language character sets like Chinese. From this point on, I'll just refer to a single function—GetExpandedName in the case of this example—to avoid lot of needless duplication. Just remember to remove the "A" or "W" from the end of an external function if you can't find a function by that name in the on-line help.

The Version Function Group

The Version function group contains entries that most programmers will need to implement a setup program for their application. For example, you can use the GetWindowsDir function to determine where the user has Windows installed. The VerInstall function makes fast work of moving compressed files from the installation CD or floppy to the user's hard drive. You'll find the 16-bit version of these functions in VER.DLL and the 32-bit version in VERSION.DLL in your SYSTEM directory. Table 9.1 contains a complete list of these functions. I also included two of the functions that Windows 3.x provides, but neither Windows 95 nor Windows NT do.

Table 9.1. Version Function Group Listing.

Function	Description
GetFileResource	Use this function to copy a resource into a buffer. This is a Windows 3.x specific function; you can't use it under Windows 95 or Windows NT.
GetFileResourceSize	This function returns the size of a resource. This is a Windows 3.x specific function; you can't use it under Windows 95 or Windows NT.
GetFileVersionInfo	You need to use this function in combination with the GetFileVersionInfoSize function. It returns version information about a specified file. The Delphi documentation will tell you that this call only works with 32-bit file images. If you use the Windows unit and don't want to deal with the idiosyncrasies of thunking, that's true. However, you can add a call to the 16-bit DLL and still determine version information for 16-bit files. I was happy to see that the Windows 95 version of the files contained the thunking functions you'll need to get the job done.
GetFileVersionInfoSize	There are two outputs from this function. It begins by telling you whether Windows can retrieve version information from the specified file. It then tells you the size of the buffer required to hold the information. You need the buffer size to create a buffer to hold the information you'll get from the GetFileVersion function.
GetSystemDir	Use this function to get the path of the Windows system subdirectory.
GetWindowsDir	Use this function to get the path of the Windows directory.
VerFindFile	More installation programs should use this particular function. It would resolve some of the difficulties that users experience when one

continues

Table 9.1. continued

Function	Description
	application copies its system files to the application directory and another uses the Windows SYSTEM directory. This function determines where to install a file based on what's currently installed on a user's machine. You supply it with input like the current Windows directory and where you intend to put related files. The first thing it does is determine if there is another copy of this file on the user's machine. If not, there are a lot of other criteria it checks, like the status of certain flags you provide. The function returns its recommendation of where you should install the new file.
VerInstallFile	I find that this particular function saves more work than it creates. For one thing, it automatically decompresses any files compressed using the Windows compression scheme. It also checks to see that the installed file got copied to the right directory and didn't get corrupted in any way. You can use the VerFindFile function to locate the proper directory for shared files. However, I've also hand-input the information that this function requires without any negative results.
VerLanguageName	This function doesn't have a single thing to do with files; it converts a Microsoft language identifier into a string. For example, if you supply this function with a value of $0401, it will return Arabic as the language. Figuring out what language the user has installed lets you customize your application. In an ever growing international market, multiple language support is becoming a given, not an added feature. Making the support automatic only enhances the user's view of your application.
VerQueryValue	You use this function with the GetFileVersionInfo function. It returns version information about a specific file resource. For example, you can retrieve the file and product version information. You could also use the function to retrieve a pointer to a table of language and character set identifiers.

Windows and Screen Savers

Another set of miscellaneous functions has to do with screen savers under Windows. I'm talking about the default Windows screen saver handling, not something like Berkeley's After Dark here. Screen savers are an important feature of Windows. Not only can you use them to save a display from burning in, but as part of your security strategy. You could create a special company-wide screen saver that incorporates the features that your security plan requires. For example, you could add a feature that requires users to change their password at specific intervals. You could also include some type of monitoring to tell the system administrator when the user leaves a sensitive application open when the computer is inactive. All that your application would need to do is look for a specific application name in the list of global tasks currently running on the host machine. If you create your own screen saver or use a standard screen saver throughout the company, you could also add a Lock pushbutton to the applications you create. A screen saver is just another form of DLL. You can call external DLLs using at least two different methods with Delphi. All you would need to do is add an external call to the screen saver's ScreenSaverProc function and use the WM_ACTIVATE message. Screen savers are also just plain fun to write—as witnessed by the deluge of screen savers available on the market today. Table 9.2 contains a complete list of the screen saver functions.

Tip: You can change the extension of a screen saver, file SCR, to DLL and read all the functions that the screen saver supports using Windows 95 View utility as shown in Chapter 5. Change the name back to SCR to use it as a screen saver again. You perform a similar change when creating your own screen saver. Compile it as a DLL, then give it an SCR extension when you want to test it.

Table 9.2. Screen Saver Function Group Listing.

Function	Description
DefScreenSaverProc	Windows provides some default screen saver handling functions—you don't have to take care of every potential event. This function allows you to call the default screen saver function. It works much like the PostMessage we talked about in Chapter 5. You'll need to provide the same things for this function that you would any other message function: a window handle, a message, a wParam, and an lParam.
DlgChangePassword	This function calls the dialog used to change the screen saver password. As with the DefScreenSaverProc, you would pass it a window handle, a message, a wParam, and an lParam. Normally the ScreenSaverConfigureDialog function calls this function, but you could call it as a separate function within your screen saver. There's only one documented message associated with this function, DLG_CHANGEPASSWORD, defined as 0x2000.

continues

Table 9.2. continued

Function	Description
DlgGetPassword	Normally the DlgChangePassword function uses this function to retrieve a screen saver's password. Your application could also use it for the same purpose. You need to supply four variables: A window handle, a message, a wParam, and an lParam. There's only one documented message associated with this function, DLG_ENTERPASSWORD, defined as 0x2001.
DlgInvalidPassword	This function displays a dialog that warns the user they typed an invalid password. Normally it gets called by the DlgGetPassword function. As with all the other Dlg functions to date, this one requires a window handle, a message, a wParam, and an lParam as input. There's only one documented message associated with this function, DLG_INVALIDPASSWORD, defined as 0x2002.
HelpMessageFilterHookFunction	The ScreenSaverConfigureDialog function calls this function when the user presses the F1 key. In most cases you'll want to let the default screen saver procedure handle help—unless your screen saver provides some special services that require additional help information. The calling parameters include a hook identifier (a Windows specific code that tells how to process the message), a virtual key code (the key the user would press to display help), and a pointer to a help message to use this function.
RegisterDialogClasses	Use this function to register any non-standard Windows classes required by your screen saver's configuration dialog box. It allows you to override some of the standard Windows screen saver configuration behavior. You need to supply a handle to the non-standard window class procedure.
ScreenSaverConfigureDialog	Your application must support a screen saver configure dialog if you plan on letting the user change any settings. A specialty program could also use this dialog to prevent anyone from disabling the password requirement. This is the function that another application would call to display the configuration dialog.
ScreenSaverProc	This is the main entry point for a screen saver. It processes all the messages that Windows sends to it. Of course, this means the function must accept a window handle, a message, a wParam, and an lParam as input.

Accessing the Accessibility Features

Providing users with special needs access to your application may be a major concern when designing your application. Windows NT and Windows 95 provide full access to these functions. The Explorer interface used by the current version of Windows 95—and soon by Windows NT as well—provides additional capabilities that you might find useful. There are only two accessibility functions. I describe them both in the following sections.

Using GetSystemMetrics

The GetSystemMetrics function allows you to determine the size and shape of various system objects like cursors. One of the nice things about this function is that you only have to tell it what you want, then wait for it to return what you requested. You don't have to provide any other kind of input like flags or handles. Fortunately, there are a lot of other useful functions in here as well. For example, Windows 95 supports more than one booting mode. You can determine the boot mode used for this session by checking the SM_CLEANBOOT metric. This comes in handy if you don't want someone to run your application when they used the Fail Safe boot mode. (Booting in this mode usually means that the system has experienced a failure of some kind.)

> **Note:** I'm only covering the more interesting functions here. GetSystemMetrics actually does return many bits of useful graphic information. For example, you can use it to retrieve the size of the client window. However, Delphi makes using this function unnecessary by providing the Rectangle method. You can use this method to determine the size of a client window or various types of image components as I did in Chapter 7 (see Listing 7.3).

Boot mode is only one interesting system metric that GetSystemMetrics can retrieve. There's a function call named SM_DEBUG that tells you that the debug version of USER.EXE is installed. You could use this particular call to enable specific troubleshooting aids in your application. In other words, you could hide your debugging tools from a user, but keep them in place for finding errors later on. It's extremely unlikely that anyone but another programmer would have the debug version of USER.EXE installed on their machine.

We initially brought up this particular function because it tells you about accessibility functions. The SM_SHOWSOUNDS function does just that. It tells you that the user wants you to show the system sounds rather than actually send them to the speaker. This particular function isn't only useful for the hearing impaired. Think about a crowded office where the "really neat" sounds you added to an application would be distracting. Sure, the user would still like the pleasure of "hearing" the sounds, but the user can't afford to disturb others. When someone enables the Show Sounds feature of Windows, then you shouldn't only show the sounds in text, but turn off the speaker as well.

Warning: Some of the GetSystemMetrics functions are only usable in Windows 95. Others only appear with Windows NT. You can use still other functions with any version of Windows. To add to the confusion, the new Explorer equipped version of Windows NT may support some of the Windows 95 functions even if they're only marked Windows 95. Always verify that a function you intend to use will actually run in the environment that plan to use it in. I've experienced some unpredictable results when using a Windows 95 specific function under Windows NT and vice versa.

Using SystemParametersInfo

There's a second function that'll allow you to determine the state of the accessibility features. SystemParametersInfo provides even more interesting functions than GetSystemMetrics does. For example, you can use the SPI_GETACCESSTIMEOUT parameter to determine accessibility timeout length. The SPI_GETFILTERKEYS parameter will tell you all about the user settings for the feature. You can also use the SPI_HIGHCONTRAST parameter to find out whether the user wants a high contrast display. There are some situations where you may want to alter the colors that you use for some system components in this situation. There are quite a few other accessibility feature parameters that you can use, I simply provided these as a sample of what you'll find— SystemParametersInfo has a parameter for each accessibility feature that Windows 95 supports.

Warning: Some of the SystemParametersInfo functions are only usable in Windows 95. Others only appear with Windows NT. You can use still other functions with any version of Windows. To add to the confusion, the new Explorer equipped version of Windows NT may support some of the Windows 95 functions even if they're only marked Windows 95. Always verify that a function you intend to use will actually run in the environment that plan to use it in. I've experienced some unpredictable results when using a Windows 95 specific function under Windows NT and vice versa.

Unlike GetSystemMetrics, the SystemParametersInfo function does require some additional input. You have to tell it what parameter you want it to get (obviously). Depending on the parameter, you may also need to provide an unsigned integer, a pointer to a structure or other variable, or a user profile update flag. Fortunately, Delphi defines all the structures you need. All you have to do is find out which ones they are by checking the API reference supplied with the product.

Like GetSystemMetrics, the SystemParametersInfo function seems to provide some features that aren't consistent with its name. For example, the SPI_GETANIMATION parameter will retrieve the animation effect associated with particular user actions under Windows 95. I found it interesting that you can use the SPI_GETGRIDGRANULARITY parameter to determine the size of the spacing grid used on the desktop. There are other "graphics" oriented parameters in here as well like the SPI_GETBORDER parameter that tells you the sizing factor for the border of each window.

SystemParametersInfo doesn't just retrieve information about your system; you can set the various parameters as well by using a different parameter. For example, while the SPI_HIGHCONTRAST parameter tells you when the high contrast accessibility feature is set, you can use the SPI_SETHIGHCONTRAST parameter to turn it on. In fact, you'll find that there's some type of SET parameter for every type of information this function will retrieve, including the screen saver. I found that you could turn the screen saver on using the SPI_SETSCREENSAVEACTIVE parameter. This is a lot easier than trying to call the screen saver using an external function. Unfortunately, this parameter only appears to work under Windows 95 for the moment.

Note: The SPI_SETSCREENSAVEACTIVE will only work with Windows 95 specific screen savers. There are also some Windows NT and Windows 3.x files that will work. It won't work with third party screen savers like After Dark at all since these screen savers use a different activation method.

Now that you have a better idea of what the SystemParametersInfo function can do for you, let's look at a practical application. Figure 9.1 shows a form containing two timers and a pushbutton. The first timer, Timer1, has its Enabled property set to False. The second timer is set for a 2000 interval and has its Enabled property set to False. I also changed the caption of the form and pushbutton as shown.

Figure 9.1.

This example shows a simple application lock method that will help minimize security risks at the workstation.

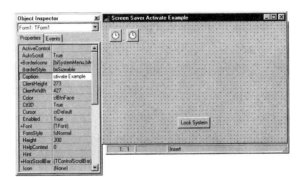

Once you create the form, you'll need to add some code to it. Listing 9.1 shows the code for this particular example.

> **Note:** You'll find that this function takes a few seconds to activate the screen saver under Windows 95. Run it, then wait for a few seconds. Make sure you don't touch the keyboard or mouse in the interim.

Listing 9.1. Using the SystemParametersInfo function.

```
unit ScrnAct1;

interface

uses
  Windows, Messages, SysUtils, Classes, Graphics, Controls, Forms, Dialogs,
  ExtCtrls, StdCtrls;

type
  TForm1 = class(TForm)
    Button1: TButton;
    Timer1: TTimer;
    Timer2: TTimer;
    procedure Timer1Timer(Sender: TObject);
    procedure Button1Click(Sender: TObject);
    procedure Timer2Timer(Sender: TObject);
  private
    { Private declarations }
  public
    { Public declarations }
  end;

var
  Form1: TForm1;

implementation

{$R *.DFM}

procedure TForm1.Button1Click(Sender: TObject);
begin

    {Turn Timer1 on.  The timer will activate the screen saver.}
    Timer1.Enabled := True;
end;

procedure TForm1.Timer1Timer(Sender: TObject);
const
    fScreenOn = 1;              {A value of true enables the screen saver.}
var
    uiTimeSaver: Integer;    {Old timeout value.}
    ptrTimeSaver: ^Integer;    {Old timeout pointer.}
begin

    {Initialize the pointer.}
    ptrTimeSaver := @uiTimeSaver;

    {Once the timer interal elapses, turn on the screen saver.}
    SystemParametersInfo(SPI_SETSCREENSAVEACTIVE, fScreenOn, NIL, 0);
```

```
   {Get the current timeout value.}
   SystemParametersInfo(SPI_GETSCREENSAVETIMEOUT, 0, ptrTimeSaver, 0);

   {Save the value for future use and active the secondary timer.}
   Timer2.Tag := uiTimeSaver;
   Timer2.Enabled := True;

   {Set the interval to 1 second so it goes on immediately.}
   SystemParametersInfo(SPI_SETSCREENSAVETIMEOUT, 1, NIL, 0);

   {Turn Timer1 back off.}
   Timer1.Enabled := False;

end;

procedure TForm1.Timer2Timer(Sender: TObject);
begin
   {Use value stored in our timer tag property to restore the screen saver
    timeout value.}
   SystemParametersInfo(SPI_SETSCREENSAVETIMEOUT, Timer2.Tag, NIL, 0);

   {Set the secondary timer off.}
   Timer2.Enabled := False;

end;

end.
```

As you can see, the code makes heavy use of the SystemParameterInfo function. There are several things you should notice about the way I used it. You'll need to provide pointers to variables in your application from time to time; SystemParameterInfo never passes data to your application directly. Even though DLLs can use variables, you can't access them without using a procedure. It's common for a DLL to ask for a pointer to a variable in your application. Using this technique allows you to exchange a lot of information with the DLL without having to pass many variables on the command line.

Note: There are many situations where you can use an address instead of a pointer parameter within Delphi. For example, you could replace the pointer in the GETSCREENSAVETIMEOUT call with an address like this: SystemParametersInfo(SPI_GETSCREENSAVETIMEOUT, 0, @uiTimeSaver, 0);. Either method is equally acceptable in most cases.

Notice how I stored the current screen saver time interval in the Timer2.Tag property. Most components have a Tag property for this very reason. I had to make sure that Timer2 would wait a reasonable amount of time for the screen saver to activate before I reset the timeout value back to its original value. Since I have the screen saver set to 1 second, waiting 2 seconds is sufficient in most cases.

Accessing Low Level Routines

The first thing we've got to talk about is what constitutes a low level routine. Think about low level routines as those functions that you can't directly access in Delphi and you're on the right path. All of the functions that I've told you about so far in this chapter are low level routines. They aren't part of Delphi—you'll find them in a Windows DLL somewhere. In most cases you'll find the DLL in the Windows SYSTEM directory, but there isn't anything stopping you from using DLLs in other locations as well. In fact, you can literally access any documented DLL on your system. If you know what parameters the function in a DLL requires, then you're halfway to adding the functionality of that DLL to your application.

There are two different ways to access low level routines in Delphi: external declaration or loading the DLL into memory. The first method has the advantage of being easier to implement. It's also the most common way to access a DLL since it allows Windows to take care of loading the DLL and unloading it later. This is also the faster of the two access methods. The second method does enhance an application's use of memory. You only load the DLL if you actually need it and you can choose the time to load it. For example, you could load all needed DLLs at the same time that Windows is loading your application. Sure, the user would see a longer load time, but then every other operation would be fast—at least faster than if you had to load the required DLL from disk.

Using an External Declaration

Using an external declaration is the easier and faster method of using a DLL. All you need to do is declare the function, then add the key word External, a module name, and an index or function name within the module. Listing 9.2 shows a typical example of how to create external declarations for your application. In this case I created a unit for the LZ functions since Delphi doesn't support them (at least as of this writing). I'll describe the functions in full detail in the section entitled "Compressing and Decompressing Files," in this chapter. Notice that the 32-bit version of the DLL provides calls for both the ANSI and Wide versions of some LZ functions. It's also important to note that I added "Uses Windows;" to the Interface section of the unit. Using the Windows unit will greatly reduce the amount of work you'll need to do—you'll have access to all the predefined Windows structures and variable types.

> **Tip:** Spend some time in the Windows unit before you start your own external declaration unit. You'll be surprised at how many Windows specific data types that it contains. I use the Windows variable type declarations so that the types shown in my external declarations unit match those in the API documentation, avoiding any confusion for any programmers that follow after me.

Listing 9.2. Creating an external declaration file.

```
unit LZFuncs;

interface

uses Windows;

{Define some error codes.}
const
LZERROR_BADINHANDLE = -1;    {invalid input handle}
LZERROR_BADOUTHANDLE = -2;    {invalid output handle}
LZERROR_READ = -3;                {corrupt compressed file format}
LZERROR_WRITE = -4;            {out of space for output file}
LZERROR_GLOBALLOC = -5;           {insufficient memory for LZFile struct}
LZERROR_GLOBLOCK = -6;            {bad global handle}
LZERROR_BADVALUE = -7;            {input parameter out of acceptable range}
LZERROR_UNKNOWNALG = -8;       {compression algorithm not recognized}

{Define the function interface.}
function GetExpandedNameA(const lpszSource: LPCSTR; lpszBuffer: LPCSTR) :DWORD; stdcall;
function GetExpandedNameW(const lpszSource: LPWSTR; lpszBuffer: LPWSTR) :DWORD; stdcall;
procedure LZClose(hFilename: Integer); stdcall;
function LZCopy(hSource: Integer; hDestination: Integer) :DWORD; stdcall;
function LZInit(hSource: Integer) :Integer; stdcall;
function LZOpenFileA(lpszFilename: LPCSTR; var lpOFStruct: TOFStruct; wStyle: WORD)
:Integer; stdcall;
function LZOpenFileW(lpszFilename: LPWSTR; var lpOFStruct: TOFStruct; wStyle: WORD)
:Integer; stdcall;
function LZRead(hSource: Integer; lpBuffer: LPSTR; cbRead: Integer) :Integer; stdcall;
function LZSeek(hSource: Integer; lOffset: LONGINT; iOrigin: Integer) :LONGINT; stdcall;

implementation

{Tell Delphi where to find the functions.}
function GetExpandedNameA; external 'LZ32.DLL' name 'GetExpandedNameA';
function GetExpandedNameW; external 'LZ32.DLL' name 'GetExpandedNameW';
procedure LZClose; external 'LZ32.DLL' name 'LZClose';
function LZCopy; external 'LZ32.DLL' name 'LZCopy';
function LZInit; external 'LZ32.DLL' name 'LZInit';
function LZOpenFileA; external 'LZ32.DLL' name 'LZOpenFileA';
function LZOpenFileW; external 'LZ32.DLL' name 'LZOpenFileA';
function LZRead; external 'LZ32.DLL' name 'LZRead';
function LZSeek; external 'LZ32.DLL' name 'LZSeek';

end.
```

You'll notice that I made the LZCopy call a procedure rather than a function. That's because it doesn't return a value. There are a few Windows API calls that won't return a value, yet Pascal always requires a return value from a function call. Using the procedure format shown in the listing is the standard method for getting around this situation.

Note: The Windows unit provided by Borland normally declares three versions of each function. The first two are as shown in the source code. One calls the ANSI version of the function and the other calls the Wide character version. The third function is a generic form that follows the Windows 3.x convention of not appending an "A" or "W" to the function name. I prefer not to include the generic function calls since you can never be certain that your implementation exactly reflects that found in Windows 3.x. It's better to provide the precise function name actually used by the Windows API if at all possible.

There are some cases where you'll want Windows to fill a structure with information and return it to you. That's why I added the VAR keyword to the LZOpenFileA and LZOpenFileW definitions. You'll need to exercise some caution in this regard. Only use VAR if you want Windows to actually do something with the structure you pass.

Note: Delphi will give you a really strange error code of BCWDBK32 Error(1) if you try to access a 16-bit DLL using the new 32-bit version. (Yes, your program will compile just fine because Delphi doesn't know whether the DLL is 16-bit or 32-bit until it attempts to load the DLL into memory.) If you have to access a 16-bit DLL, then you'll need to create a wrapper function for it using a 32-bit C compiler; then access the 32-bit DLL from within Delphi. I recommend that you avoid this course of action if possible since writing a wrapper function is no small undertaking. The wrapper function will have to "thunk" the 32-bit call to a 16-bit call. In essence, your wrapper function will have to translate the 32-bit call into its 16-bit counterpart.

Getting the Address of and Loading the DLL

The second method of using external routines found in DLLs is to get the name of the DLL, then load it. You'll use two function calls to implement this method—one of the reasons I suggest you don't use it. The first call, LoadLibrary, loads the library from disk into memory. It requires a pointer to a filename as input. It returns a handle to the library if you successfully load it.

Note: You can unload a DLL when you don't need it any more using the FreeLibrary function. Windows automatically frees any DLLs that you don't unload when you close your application, so you won't normally need to use the FreeLibrary function. The one time you'll find it comes in handy is when the machine you're working with is short on memory. Freeing the DLL could give you the memory you need to perform some task.

Once you load the library, you use the handle that LoadLibrary returned to access specific functions within the DLL. The GetProcAddress function accepts a library handle and the name of a procedure it contains as input. As an alternative, you can provide the index value of the function you want to access. The only problem with using an index value is that GetProcAddress could return an invalid, non-null address if the DLL doesn't number its functions consecutively. Using a name ensures you get the address of the function you really want. GetProcAddress returns the address of the procedure in memory. You use the address to call the DLL function.

Note: The spelling and capitalization of the name you specify when calling GetProcAddress must match the function name used in the DLL itself. Windows treats "Function" differently from "FUNCTION". As far as it's concerned, they are two different functions. The problem of capitalization is another reason to use the other external method of accessing the function.

There's one advantage to using this method of accessing a DLL function. If you use the external function method described in the previous section and Windows can't find the requested DLL or function within the DLL, it will raise an exception. The exception will stop the current thread of execution. Using this method allows you to recover from the error—your application can continue to run, it just won't have access to the desired DLL. One place where this might be helpful is if you provide ancillary modules with your application like a spelling checker. The user might request a spelling check even if the spelling checker isn't loaded. The result is that your application would search for the spell check DLL and not find it. You could display a message stating that the spelling checker isn't loaded, then continue regular processing.

Compressing and Decompressing Files

One of the more useful miscellaneous routines is the ability to compress and decompress files as needed. The decompression routines appear in LZEXPAND.DLL (16-bit) and LZ32.DLL (32-bit). The compression program, COMPRESS.EXE, is provided with most Microsoft programming products. You use the data compression library functions to get the job done. Most of them start with the initial letters LZ. The following paragraphs tell you about this group of functions.

Note: Windows 3.x provides several functions that neither Windows NT nor Windows 95 support. The CopyLZFile (Windows 3.x) and LZStart (Windows 3.x) functions are replaced by the LZCopy function. You'll find that LZOpenFile has replaced the LZDone (Windows 3.x) function. Are these exact replacements? The Windows 95 replacements for these older functions aren't direct replacements. What Microsoft did was combine the older functions with the new ones. In essence, the new functions save some time and effort for the programmer.

- GetExpandedName—Most programmers compress files using the -R option of the COM-PRESS utility. You can use this feature to determine the uncompressed name of a file. The GetExpandedName function returns the expanded filename, which you could then place in a list box or as part of a prompt.

- LZClose—You use this function to close a file that you opened with the LZOpen function. Never use a standard file close when working with a compressed file. The only thing you need to supply when using this function is the handle returned when you called the LZOpen function.

- LZCopy—This is the function you call to decompress (or simply copy) a file. It requires two file handles—a source and a destination as input. You can use either the LZInit or LZOpenFile function to obtain the needed file handles. This function automatically decompresses files for you if they were compressed using the Microsoft COMPRESS.EXE utility.

- LZInit—Use this function to create a handle for a new uncompressed file. You can't use this file handle with any other functions than those found in this section. All you need to provide this function is the handle of the source file.

- LZOpenFile—You need to open a compressed file using this function before you can use it. The function accepts the compressed file's name, a file structure, and an opening method as input. Windows allows you to use a variety of opening methods—you don't even have to keep the file open if you don't want to. There's an EXIST opening method that simply checks to see if the file is there.

- LZRead—Would you like to keep a lot of documentation handy, but don't want to waste the space required? This is the LZ function to use in that case. You can open a compressed file, then use this function to read its contents. I find this really handy for opening a compressed text file, reading the required information from it, then closing the file again. A text file normally compresses rom 50% to 80% depending on a number of factors. Even at a 50% compression rate, the disk savings could be considerable for a large file. You must supply the file handle that LZOpenFile returned, a pointer to a local buffer, and the number of bytes you want read as parameters. The function returns the number of bytes read or an error number.

Tip: You can use file compression as a psuedo-encryption technique. Most users are used to seeing Windows compressed files with an underscore in place of one of the characters in the extension. The LZ functions don't care what the file extension is; the underscore is used as a programmer convention. Using a different extension would allow you to use compressed text files, yet keep their contents hidden from the user. (Obviously this technique has limitations and some advanced users will likely figure out that the file is merely compressed, not encrypted.)

- LZSeek—Use this function to find a specific spot within the compressed file (the function works as if the file were decompressed). It allows you to move the file pointer a specific number of bytes from the current file pointer position, the beginning, or the end of the file. The function takes a file handle (returned by LZOpenFile), the number of bytes you want to move the file pointer, and a starting position as input. It returns the new file pointer position or an error number.

Peter's Principle: When Using Windows Compress Won't Work

It may appear that the file compression utility provided with Windows will work in every circumstance. Nothing could be further from the truth. Sure, there are a lot of places you can use it and save the user—and yourself—time and grief learning to use a third party compression product.

However, those third party products have a lot to offer. I find that the vast majority of them provide much higher compression ratios than the Windows supplied product, but this isn't the real issue. The real issue is that the COMPRESS.EXE program will only compress one file at a time. Unlike a ZIP file, or any other compressed file format for that matter, you can only place one file in the compressed file. This means that you'll still end up with the same number of files that you did before you compressed them, they'll just take a little less room.

The single file limitation obviously reduces the number of places where you can use the Windows supplied compression utility. You couldn't use it to create one compressed file for file transmission over a modem—limiting its use in manual operations. (This doesn't limit its usefulness one iota when it comes to automated transfer routines where the program can automatically track the names of the files you need to transfer.)

COMPRESS.EXE is a DOS application. Calling it from within a Windows application will certainly seem like a kludge to some users. You'll obviously want to avoid this impression if you want the user to see your program as a polished application. (You could, as an alternative, come up with a Windows version of COMPRESS.EXE—using the LZ routines would still save you the trouble of creating the requisite decompress routines.)

Once you consider these limitations, it becomes pretty obvious that you'll need to use a third party product in many circumstances. Any time you want the user to interact with the compressed file in some way, you should consider using a third party utility unless the entire purpose of using the compressed files is to work with single files. For example, you could add a routine that would allow a user to decompress a single file using the setup portion of your application. I've found this feature particularly helpful if one of the files for a particular application becomes corrupted or accidentally gets erased.

So, now that you know what these functions do, it should be somewhat obvious how you would use them. You can use file compression for a lot more than installation programs—the use to which Windows puts this particular set of functions. They come in very handy for archiving data to floppy or even to a hard drive. You could also use them in tandem with a communication program to reduce data upload and download times. By incorporating these routines into your application you could make the process of compressing and decompressing the data seamless to the user.

Tip: By this time you may be wondering why you wouldn't use one of the third party utilities on the market to compress and decompress files. Most of them do a far better job of compressing data than the utilities supplied with Windows, so using them would seem the best course of action. There are two reasons for using the routines built into Windows: cost and availability. You'll never know if the people using your application have the third party utility you decide to use installed on their machine. The Windows utilities have to be there so you don't need to worry about finding them when you need them. Third party utilities also cost money—the Windows routines are free for the asking.

Now that you have a better idea of why you would want to use these functions, let's take a look at a sample application. Figure 9.2 shows the form we'll use for this example. Table 9.3 provides a list of the components and the properties you'll need to modify. This is one of the few times where it's actually inconvenient to use a common dialog. Our example contains the components needed to search for a file: TDriveCombo, TDirectoryList, and TFileListBox. Another set of the same components allows you to tell the program what destination directory to use. The destination directory side includes an edit component that allows you to specify a new filename. You can select a file from the file list box if you simply want to overwrite an existing file. I've also added a component that shows the expanded name for a file—which assumes that you've selected a compressed file. (The filename shown here will be the same as the filename shown in the file list box if you select an uncompressed file.) There are several buttons along the side that allow you to try out several of the LZ functions. Use the Read button if you want to view the contents of a compressed file. The Copy button decompresses a file and places it in the directory you specify—this is a handy utility in those situations where a file gets corrupted or accidentally erased. The Exit button allows you to exit the program. In essence, this program will allow you to view or expand compressed files one at a time. It's a utility that I wish Microsoft had included with Windows—but they didn't decide to do so for whatever reason.

Figure 9.2.

This form is the starting point for an application that allows you to expand files compressed using COMPRESS.EXE (or a compatible utility).

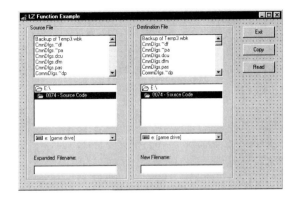

Table 9.3. Form1 Component Listing and Parameter Modifications.

Object	Property	Setting
ExpandedName	Enabled	False
SourceDrive	DirList	SourceDir
SourceDir	FileList	SourceFile
DestDrive	DirList	DestDir
DestDir	FileList	DestFile

We'll also need a form to use for reading the contents of files. I designed the form in Figure 9.3 for this purpose. As you can see, it simply contains a TRichEdit component and a pushbutton. I chose the TRichEdit component for flexibility purposes. You could just as easily use a standard TMemo component in its place. The only property I changed in this case was the ScrollBars property to ssBoth.

Figure 9.3.

The File Read Dialog allows you to view the contents of a file.

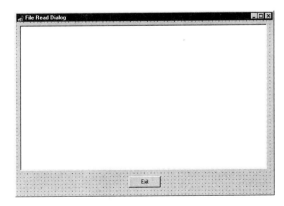

The code for this example appears in Listings 9.3 and 9.4. It contains two units, one for each form. You'll also need the LZFuncs unit shown in Listing 9.2 to make this example work.

Listing 9.3. Compressing and decompressing files (main form).

```
unit Extern1;

interface

uses
  Windows, Messages, SysUtils, Classes, Graphics, Controls, Forms, Dialogs,
  StdCtrls, FileCtrl;

type
  TForm1 = class(TForm)
    ExitProgram: TButton;
    GroupBox1: TGroupBox;
    SourceFile: TFileListBox;
    SourceDir: TDirectoryListBox;
    SourceDrive: TDriveComboBox;
    ExpandedName: TEdit;
    Label1: TLabel;
    GroupBox2: TGroupBox;
    DestFile: TFileListBox;
    DestDir: TDirectoryListBox;
    DestDrive: TDriveComboBox;
    Label2: TLabel;
    NewFilename: TEdit;
    Copy: TButton;
    Read: TButton;
    procedure ExitProgramClick(Sender: TObject);
    procedure SourceFileChange(Sender: TObject);
    procedure CopyClick(Sender: TObject);
    procedure ReadClick(Sender: TObject);
  private
    { Private declarations }
  public
    { Public declarations }
  end;

var
  Form1: TForm1;

implementation

uses LZFuncs, Extern2;

{$R *.DFM}

procedure TForm1.ExitProgramClick(Sender: TObject);
begin
    {Leave the application.}
    Halt;
end;

procedure TForm1.SourceFileChange(Sender: TObject);
var
```

```
    sSource: String;          {Source String}
    sBuffer: String;          {Expanded Name String}
    lpSource: LPCSTR;          {Source String Pointer}
    lpBuffer: LPCSTR;          {Expanded Name String Pointer}
begin
    if Length(SourceFile.Filename) > 0 then
        begin
         {Get the source filename.}
         sSource := SourceFile.Filename;

         {Set the length of the buffer equal to the source.}
         SetLength(sBuffer, 255);

         lpSource := PCHAR(sSource);
         lpBuffer := PCHAR(sBuffer);

         {Get the expanded filename.}
         GetExpandedNameA(lpSource, lpBuffer);

         {Store the expanded filename.}
         ExpandedName.Text := sBuffer;
        end;
end;

procedure TForm1.CopyClick(Sender: TObject);
var
    hFileHandle: HFILE;        {Handle of opened file.}
    hLZFile: HFILE;         {Special LZ source file handle.}
    hLZDestFile: HFILE;        {Special LZ destination file handle.}
    OpenBuffer: TOFSTRUCT;   {Source File Open Structure.}
    DestBuffer: TOFSTRUCT;    {Destination File Open Structure.}
    wStyle: WORD;            {File Opening Method.}
    sSource: String;          {Name of file to open.}
    lpSource: LPCSTR;          {Pointer to filename to open.}
    sDestination: String;    {Name of destination file.}
    lpDestination: LPCSTR;    {Pointer to destination filename.}
    sReadString: String;     {Read buffer.}
    lpReadString: LPCSTR;     {Pointer to read buffer}
    sPascalString: String;    {Pascal string.}
    cbRead: Integer;         {Number of bytes read from file.}
begin

{Check for a source filename.}
if length(SourceFile.Filename) = 0  then
    begin
    MessageDlg('Select a source filename.', mtError, [mbOK], 0);
    Exit;
    end;

{Check for a destination filename.}
if length(NewFilename.Text) = 0 then
    {Check to see if the user supplied a new name.}
    if length(DestFile.Filename) = 0 then
        begin
        MessageDlg('Select a destination filename.', mtError, [mbOK], 0);
         Exit;
         end
```

continues

Listing 9.3. continued

```
        {The user has selected an existing file to overwrite.}
        else
            begin
            sDestination := DestFile.Filename;
             lpDestination := PCHAR(sDestination);
             end
else
        {The user wants to use a new file.}
        begin
        sDestination := DestDir.Directory + '\' + NewFilename.Text;
        lpDestination := PCHAR(sDestination);
        end;

{Initialize our read string.}
SetLength(sReadString, 128);
lpReadString := PCHAR(sReadString);

{Get the filename.}
sSource := SourceFile.Filename;
lpSource := PCHAR(sSource);

{Open the file for reading.}
wStyle := OF_READ;

{Open the file.}
hFileHandle := OpenFile(lpSource, OpenBuffer, wStyle);

{If we opened the file successfully, then read from it.}
if (hFileHandle < 0) then
        begin

        {Display an error message and exit if we weren't successful.}
        MessageDlg('There was an error opening the file.', mtError, [mbOK], 0);
        Exit;
        end
else
        begin
        {Initialize the file.}
        hLZFile := LZInit(hFileHandle);

        {Check for errors.}
        if hLZFile < 0 then
            begin
            MessageDlg('Error creating file memory structure.', mtError, [mbOK], 0);
            LZClose(hFileHandle);
            Exit;
            end;

        {Open our destination file.}
        wStyle := OF_CREATE;
        hLZDestFile := LZOpenFileA(lpDestination, DestBuffer, wStyle);

        {Check for errors.}
        if hLZDestFile < 0 then
            begin
            MessageDlg('Error creating destination file.', mtError, [mbOK], 0);
            LZClose(hFileHandle);
```

```
        Exit;
        end;

    {Copy the file.}
    cbRead := LZCopy(hLZFile, hLZDestFile);

    {Display an error message if the file copy is unsuccessful.}
    if cbRead < 0 then
        MessageDlg('Error copying file.', mtError, [mbOK], 0);

    {Close the files.}
    LZClose(hFileHandle);
    LZClose(hLZDestFile);

    {Clear the new filename.}
    Newfilename.Text := '';
    end;
end;

procedure TForm1.ReadClick(Sender: TObject);
var
    hFileHandle: HFILE;         {Handle of opened file.}
    hLZFile: HFILE;        {Special LZ file handle.}
    OpenBuffer: TOFSTRUCT;    {File Open Structure.}
    wStyle: WORD;             {File Opening Method.}
    sSource: String;         {Name of file to open.}
    lpSource: LPCSTR;         {Pointer to filename to open.}
    sDestination: String;    {Name of destination file.}
    lpDestination: LPCSTR;    {Pointer to destination filename.}
    sReadString: String;     {Read buffer.}
    lpReadString: LPCSTR;    {Pointer to read buffer}
    sPascalString: String;    {Pascal string.}
    cbRead: Integer;         {Number of bytes read from file.}
begin

{Check for a source filename.}
if length(SourceFile.Filename) = 0  then
    begin
    MessageDlg('Select a source filename.', mtInformation, [mbOK], 0);
    Exit;
    end;

{Initialize our read string.}
SetLength(sReadString, 128);
lpReadString := PCHAR(sReadString);

{Initialize our destination filename.}
SetLength(sDestination, 128);
lpDestination := PCHAR(sDestination);

{Get the filename.}
sSource := SourceFile.Filename;
lpSource := PCHAR(sSource);

{Open the file for reading.}
wStyle := OF_READ;
```

continues

Listing 9.3. continued

```
{Open the file.}
hFileHandle := OpenFile(lpSource, OpenBuffer, wStyle);

{If we opened the file successfully, then read from it.}
if (hFileHandle < 0) then
    begin

    {Display an error message and exit if we weren't successful.}
    MessageDlg('There was an error opening the file.', mtError, [mbOK], 0);
    Exit;
    end
else
    begin
    {Initialize the file.}
    hLZFile := LZInit(hFileHandle);

    {Check for errors.}
    if hLZFile < 0 then
        begin
          MessageDlg('Error creating file memory structure.', mtError, [mbOK], 0);
          LZClose(hFileHandle);
          Exit;
          end;

    {Display our FileRead form.}
    FileRead.Show;

    {Get the expanded filename.}
    GetExpandedNameA(lpSource, lpDestination);
    sPascalString := StrPas(lpDestination);

    {Clear the text area and display the current filename.}
    FileRead.RichEdit1.Lines.Clear;
    FileRead.Caption := 'Currently Reading: ' + sPascalString;
    {FileRead.RichEdit1.Lines.Add('');}

    {Initialize cbRead}
    cbRead := 128;

    while cbRead = 128 do
        begin

        {Read the file.}
        cbRead := LZRead(hLZFile, lpReadString, 128);
        sPascalString := StrPas(lpReadString);

         {Add the text to our rich text edit control.}
         FileRead.RichEdit1.Lines.Add(sPascalString);
          end;

    {Close the file.}
    LZClose(hFileHandle);
    end;
end;

end.
```

Listing 9.4. Compressing and decompressing files (file read form).

```
unit Extern2;

interface

uses
  Windows, Messages, SysUtils, Classes, Graphics, Controls, Forms, Dialogs,
  StdCtrls, ComCtrls;

type
  TFileRead = class(TForm)
    ExitForm: TButton;
    RichEdit1: TRichEdit;
    procedure ExitFormClick(Sender: TObject);
  private
    { Private declarations }
  public
    { Public declarations }
  end;

var
  FileRead: TFileRead;

implementation

{$R *.DFM}

procedure TFileRead.ExitFormClick(Sender: TObject);
begin
    {Hide the form once the user gets done with it.}
    FileRead.Hide;
end;

end.
```

There are a few tricks of the trade hidden in this code. For example, look at the technique I needed to use when sending the filename to Windows. You'll always have to create a separate variable for holding the address of the filename string. Notice that I also used the PCHAR function instead of @. These two functions produce different results—results that Windows will definitely notice.

I also change the name of the File Read dialog to match the uncompressed name of the file the dialog is displaying. It's a simple matter to call the GetExpandedName function to retrieve the filename. Notice that I have to translate the null terminated string produced from the call to Windows to a Pascal string. You'll get an error message otherwise. The RichEdit1 component also requires this translation. According to the Delphi documentation you no longer need to use the StrPas function to perform string translation. This wasn't a fact at the time of this writing—you still need to use the old translation technique.

File opening is a little less than straightforward as well. You need to open the source file using the standard OpenFile function, then initialize a decompression structure using LZInit. The destination file requires the use of the LZOpen function along with the OF_CREATE style. The LZOpen function returns a special file handle. You can only use it with LZ functions.

> **Tip:** I've used the actual DLL names in my code. However, Delphi doesn't currently support wide character strings. You could use the old function names in your external definition unit. That way, you could easily transfer files between the 16-bit and 32-bit versions of Delphi with little change.

Now that we have the two forms put together and some code to go with them, let's take a look at one of the features this application provides. Figure 9.4 shows how you could use the Read feature of this program to look at the contents of a file without decompressing it to disk. I find this very handy for README and other files I tend to clear off my hard drive. Some of them can take huge amounts of space and I hardly ever need to look at them. This utility makes it very convenient for me to take a look when I need to.

Figure 9.4.
The LZ function example provides some essential services that you'll need long after you learn the techniques in this book.

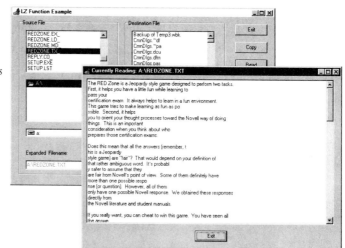

Summary

We've spent some time looking at functions that probably won't make headline news in this chapter. They're the little sideline functions that get glossed over all too often—yet provide useful services that every programmer needs.

I began by providing you with an overview of the miscellaneous functions that Windows provides. We obviously didn't look at the whole API, but I did alert you to the more interesting choices that you'll find buried in your C/C++ documentation. (Interestingly enough, Delphi also comes with a fairly complete copy of the Windows API—the paraphrased version as I like to look at it.)

We then looked at the methods you would need to use to access some of the lower level routines. Admittedly, you won't use these functions every day, but isn't it nice to know how to access them when you do? I look at these functions as the type of thing you keep in your tool chest, but don't really pay much attention to for the most part.

File compression and decompression isn't as big a deal as it used to be with the newer modems on the market today. You can usually send a large file at a decent rate of speed even with a 9600 baud modem, the low end model in today's computing environment. However, there are times when a compressed file is still the way to go. A user will never complain too much if you make an application faster by reducing the time it takes to transfer data from one point to another.

III

Putting Delphi to Work in Applications

10

Using Delphi with OLE

It used to be that you had a choice about implementing DDE (dynamic data exchange) and OLE object linking and embedding) in your application. No longer—OLE 2.0 compliance is a requirement to obtain a Windows 95 logo from Microsoft. Of course, if you implement OLE, you may as well implement DDE as well.

Fortunately, Delphi provides a wealth of both DDE and OLE components that you can simply plug into your application. Adding a little code makes them active. Obviously, the amount of code you'll add depends on the type of application and the level of functionality you intend to provide.

Dephi's components are aimed at the application level. In other words, you'll have to perform some fancy footwork if you want to create either a DDE or an OLE server. The type of OLE server you decide to create is also important—the most difficult implementation is a shell extension (which we'll get into later).

Since DDE and OLE are such important topics in the world of Windows 95 and Windows NT, I decided to devote an entire chapter to it. We'll start at the ground floor of DDE and work our way through several varieties of OLE servers and clients. I'll also take you on a tour of the OLE section of the registry. You'll need a good handle on everything that goes on inside the registry if you intend to create complex OLE applications.

 Even Windows 3.x adds OLE and DDE entries to the registry. The Windows 3.x registry is far less complex, though, than the one used with Windows 95. This chapter will concentrate on the Windows 95 version of the registry. However, you can still learn a lot about implementing OLE in your applications even if you use the 16-bit version of Delphi.

Delphi and DDE

Before OLE arrived on the scene, applications exchanged data through the Clipboard using DDE. There are actually two parts to DDE—implementation and macro language. The implementation part of the specification has been largely replaced by OLE. Only older applications still use DDE as their major form of data exchange in a manual data transfer. However, the macro portion of DDE is still alive and well. All you need to do is look at some of the entries in the registry or even scan some through the file associations you create using Explorer to see that DDE is still there. Figure 10.1 shows just one example of what I mean. These are the DDE entries required to start Word for Windows when you decide to double-click on a DOC file in Explorer.

It doesn't take much to figure out that if you want to provide automated access to your application's files, then you'll need to provide some kind of DDE server support. DDE client support comes into play for two reasons. You might want to use it as part of your internal OLE support. If your application sports a macro programming language, then it should also support DDE. The people who use your application will probably need to modify some bit of data that another application owns. They'll need DDE to modify that data by remote control.

Figure 10.1.
DDE is still alive and well
when it comes to macro
programming like the file
association shown here.

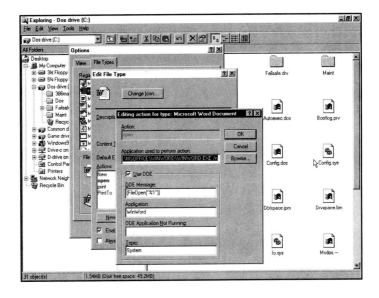

Peter's Principle: DDE Versus VBA (and Other DDE Killers)

Some people—like Microsoft for example—are claiming that DDE is going to be dead soon. In fact, Microsoft acts as if it's already dead—they should probably take a look at Explorer for a few minutes to figure out that their own products still use it. DDE is not dead today, nor is it likely to simply disappear tomorrow. Not only would you break a lot of applications on the market, but DDE is about the only way to automate certain Windows functions like file associations for the moment.

The problem isn't that DDE is so great no one wants to get rid of it—ask anyone who has spent sleepless nights trying to get a DDE macro to work about how wonderful it is to use—the problem is one of standardization. Just about every major application on your machine will support DDE in one form or another. In fact, a lot of the smaller utility programs on my machine support it. You can use this feature to control another application by remote control. The DDE macro tells the other application which menu choices you want to do, just as if you were there pressing the required keys. If you want to load a file into your spreadsheet from within your word processor—DDE will let you do it. However, DDE goes a lot further than simple things like loading files; you can use almost all of the macro language components of some applications through DDE—it's that powerful.

More than a few vendors recognized the limitations of DDE long ago. For one thing, it's not only difficult to read a DDE macro, but you have to know the macro languages for two applications. That's where VBA comes in. Visual BASIC for Applications (VBA) is Microsoft's answer to the DDE question. It provides the same interface no matter which application you use. Not only that, but you can fully document a VBA macro—something that isn't all that doable with DDE.

Not everyone is buying the VBA solution though and that's causing problems. Microsoft wants everyone to think that VBA will replace DDE. The only problem is that Lotus thinks the same thing about Lotus Script and Corel thinks the same thing about PerfectScript. As you can see, there's no end to the list of potential candidates to re-place DDE.

The bottom line is that unless you feel very lucky, VBA (or any other DDE alternative for that matter) just isn't a safe bet today. You could find yourself reworking your application to meet user needs later if you implement one of these solutions today. The safe route is to add DDE capabilities to your application, and then think about supporting one of these other tools as an added feature. I think that you'll probably agree with the rest of the industry for the moment though. DDE is the way to go—anything else is going to be a waste of time until everyone agrees on a standard replacement.

DDE Clients

There are two types of DDE implementation: clients and servers. (Most applications provide both.) You need to understand how a client interacts with a server as a first step to understanding DDE as a whole. The client is literally the user end of the DDE process. It's the part that a user will interact with when creating a DDE macro. A user provides macro steps that your application will read and act upon. You'll need to know how to work with DDE macros as a first step to creating your own DDE client applications. Once you get the user perspective down, you can use that knowledge to create a client application that reads the user macros and performs the required client tasks. The second type of DDE implementation, which appears in the next section, is to understand DDE from the server perspective. A server accepts the macro input from the client and acts upon it.

The following sections take you through the two phases of a DDE client implementation. We first take a look at the user perspective by looking at the way one application implements DDE macros. You'll want to spend some time looking at other applications to learn about different DDE imple-mentation approaches before you decide on an approach for your own application.

Tip: Various applications have different needs when it comes to DDE. For example, a text processor may not need to work with graphics very much. Its perspective of DDE will probably be different from that taken by a graphics application or a spreadsheet. The best way to make sure your application does what it needs to do is to spend time looking at other applications of the same type.

Understanding the User Perspective

Let's look at DDE a bit from a user (or client) perspective. There are some significant problems with using DDE. The most significant of these is that it creates a static link, much like the one you get using cut and paste. The fact that it provides a stable macro language that you can use to open files and perform other fancy maneuvers from the command line doesn't change much.

DDE is a messaging protocol. It sends a message from one application to another and asks it to do something. Originally, DDE was supposed to provide the means to open another application and copy some data to the Clipboard. You could also get it to do other chores such as printing files. A DDE macro contains part DDE and part application macro language. This is another problem with using it. Not only do you need to learn the native language of the application you're using and DDE itself, but you also have to learn the macro language for the server application. Needless to say, DDE didn't get the kind of reception that Microsoft originally hoped it would. DDE is simply too hard for the average user to even consider using. In fact, even some programmers find it difficult to use (unless they use it on a regular basis).

Just to give you an idea of how difficult DDE can be to understand, here's a short macro that I created for Lotus 1-2-3. DDE is anything but user-friendly. I've seen low-level languages that provide more information than this does. All this application does is place a copy of LEAVES.BMP in a Word document. The amazing thing is that I actually got this to work. In essence, Lotus 1-2-3 is controlling Word.

```
{LAUNCH "D:\WIN\WINWORD\WINWORD"}
{DDE-OPEN "WINWORD","SYSTEM"}
{DDE-EXECUTE "[InsertObject .IconNumber = 0, .FileName = ""D:\WIN95\LEAVES.BMP"",
.Link = 1, .DisplayIcon = 0, .Tab = ""1"", .Class = ""Paint.Picture"",
.IconFilename = """", .Caption = ""LEAVES.BMP""]"}
{DDE-EXECUTE "[CharLeft 1, 1]"}
{DDE-EXECUTE "[EditBookmark .Name = ""DDE_LINK1"", .SortBy = 0, .Add]"}
{SELECT A1}
{LINK-CREATE "LINK1";"Word.Document.6";"Document1";"DDE_LINK1";"Picture";"Automatic"}
{LINK-ASSIGN "LINK1";"A:A1"}
```

The first line of this mini-application launches Word for Windows. DDE sends a message to Explorer, telling it to start Word. Once Explorer completes this task, it sends a completion message back to the DDE server. The next line opens Word as a DDE server. Even though Word is running, the DDE server won't know it exists until it gets a message from your application. The third, fourth, and fifth lines are the most difficult to understand. The short version is that they tell Word to insert a copy of LEAVES.BMP into the current document. (By the way, these three lines are actually a single line of DDE code—you wouldn't type them as separate lines in the actual macro.) The sixth line tells Word to highlight the image, just like you would by clicking on it with the mouse. The seventh line creates a bookmark. Now, you might wonder why we would do all this just to assign a bookmark to an object we embedded in Word, but you'll find out in a second. The eighth line places the Lotus 1-2-3 cursor in the upper-left corner. The next line is very important. It assigns the object we created in Word to a link in Lotus 1-2-3. The final line makes that link a reality.

By now you're asking yourself why I would go through all that trouble just to link a .BMP file to a Lotus 1-2-3 worksheet. To answer that question, you'll have to experiment a little. I think you'll find it pretty tough to create the same kind of link that the DDE procedure performs without performing this procedure manually. Just try it sometime. OLE just doesn't provide all the features you'll need to create every type of link you'll need and it certainly doesn't allow you to create those links as part of a macro or program (OLE automation should change that in the future, but it isn't here today). The automatic method allows me to place logos in my worksheets with a minimum of effort. As you can see, learning DDE is a requirement if you plan to create automated links in macros and other types of programs.

Implementing a DDE Client

A user normally doesn't need to worry about the vagaries of DDE programming when using OLE. On the other hand, programmers regularly do worry about DDE programming and use it to take care of certain needs. You'll find that DDE is more than just a quaint tool that someone added to Windows as an afterthought; you'll need to work with the Clipboard and perform a variety of other activities.

Now, let's take a closer look at what you would need to do to make a similar conversation take place in your Delphi application. The first thing you'll need to do is add two components—a TDDEClientItem and a TDDEClientConv. These two components perform all the tasks you'll need DDE to do for you. Think of the TDDEClientConv component as a mouth; it performs the task of talking to the server application. The TDDEClientItem component is the brain; it gives the TDDEClientConv component something to talk about.

Just like any other conversation, you start a DDE conversation by attracting someone's attention. In this case we'll want to talk to another application. Once you get their attention, you need to tell them what you want to talk about. The DDEService property of the TDDEClientConv component tells Windows which application you want to talk with. The DDETopic property tells what you want to talk about. Simply thinking about a conversation doesn't actually start it. You use the SetLink method to tell Windows to start the conversation. A second method, OpenLink, gets used if you use the ddManual connection mode. In most cases you won't need to worry about using the OpenLink method because you'll use the ddAutomatic connection mode.

Tip: Every DDE server provides one standard topic named SYSTEM. Just like the weather, you can always start a conversation about the system. Using the SYSTEM topic as a starting point allows you to find out what other topics the server supports. I'll show you how this works later in this section of the chapter.

Once you decide who to talk with and what you want to talk about, you have to talk about the particulars of the topic. The Text property of the TDDEClientItem component is where these particulars will appear. If you want to say something to the server, you place a message in the Text property. When the server wants to talk to your application, it will likewise place something in the Text property. You'll know that the server had something to say because Delphi generates an OnChange event every time the contents of the Text property changes.

> **Note:** Delphi places a 255 character limit on the length of a line of text (unless you use the new long string capability). You'll need to use the Lines property to create multiple lines of text if you have more than 255 characters to send to the server. Delphi uses a similar process when the server sends more than 255 characters to your application. This means you'll always have to use the Lines.Count method to see how many lines of text the server sent.

At this point you might wonder how the server knows that there is information that it needs to see in TDDEClientItem.Text property. It doesn't know—you have to tell it. Just like any other conversation, your mind thinks about what it wants to say, then your mouth says it. In this case you'll use one of the following TDDEClientConv methods to talk to the server application.

- ExecuteMacro—Use this method to send a single line of text to the DDE server. The null terminated line of text contains macro instructions for the server. This is the way you tell the server to do something by remote control. The method includes a wait flag, which allows you to either wait around until the server gets done performing the task you asked it to do or allows you to execute another instruction immediately.

- ExecuteMacroLines—This method does the same thing that the ExecuteMacro method does, except it allows you to use more than one line of text. You supply a TStrings object in place of the single line of text.

- PokeData—Conversations consist of more than instructions, you might need to provide the other person with some information as well. Likewise, you might need to provide server with some data in addition to the instructions you provide. That's the purpose of this method. You tell the server what kind of information you're supplying using an Item parameter, then what information is using the Data parameter. Unlike the ExecuteMacro method, there isn't a flag that allows you to wait until the server accepts the data you provide.

- PokeDataLines—You'll use this method when you have more than 255 characters of information to send to the server. It accepts a TStrings object in place of a null terminated data string. All of the data you provide must pertain to the same item; you can't use this method to send multiple items worth of data using a single call. You have to make a single call to either PokeData or PokeDataLines for each item of data you need to send to the server.

I mentioned previously that every DDE server supports at least one topic named SYSTEM. You can usually request items from the SYSTEM topic that tell you about other topics that the server supports—the exact number and type of topics vary from server to server. Use the RequestData method of the TDDEClientConv component to perform this task. Every server that supports multiple topics does provide three SYSTEM topic items that you can request as shown below.

- SysItems—Requesting this item returns a list of all items in the SYSTEM topic. In other words, you'll still use the SYSTEM topic, but you can discuss other items within that topic.

- Topics—Use this item to get a list of available topics. You would supply one of these other topics in place of the SYSTEM topic the next time you started a conversation with the DDE server.

- Formats—Sometimes you need to know what kind of data that the server supports before you make a PokeData or a PokeDataLines call. This item returns a list of all the Clipboard formats supported by the server application.

Now that you have some of the basics of DDE client conversations down, let's take a look at a simple DDE client application. I like to have a variety of programming test tools at my disposal, so I created this utility to test DDE conversations outside a normal application environment. It will also provide information about the server you want to use, making it easier to start a conversation. You'll find that some applications implement DDE differently than others. These differences can make an otherwise simple programming exercise quite complex. Using this utility will help you design a DDE macro that works. You can use a consistent language that isn't dependent on a particular application's implementation of DDE. Simply copy the working macro into your application and test it out. You'll probably need to do a little tweaking, but you'll find that it's a lot less work to get things to work this way.

We'll start out with the form in Figure 10.2. Notice that I've used Delphi's built-in DDE components: TDDEClientConv and TDDEClientItem. I added a few pushbuttons: Exit Program, Copy Macro, Test Macro, and Information. You can use the Copy pushbutton to copy any macros you create to the Clipboard—making it a lot easier to test DDE connections using the utility and then transferring them to Delphi or an application program macro. The Test Macro pushbutton sends the contents of the TMemo component to the DDE server. You'll see the result in a Result dialog. The Information pushbutton brings up another dialog that asks what kind of information you want to request. I could have implemented a lot of these functions through the Windows API and increased the functionality of the utility program. However, since I didn't want to try to handle DDE and the Windows API at the same time, I let Delphi do as much of the work as possible.

Note: Figure 10.2 shows a typical macro and specifies the locations of files on my machine. You'll probably need to change these locations to match your machine configuration.

Figure 10.2.
This simple application form contains several DDE components that will allow us to do some work as a DDE client.

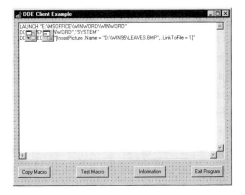

I needed several supplementary forms to make this example work. They appear in Figures 10.3 through 10.5. The DDE Server Information dialog allows the user to input the information required to launch a DDE server. For the purposes of working with Delphi (and many other programming platforms) you'll need the path and filename of the server application, the name of the server, and the topic you want to discuss. The name of the server application and the registry name for the server don't always match. Make sure you use the name as it appears in either Explorer or the Registry. I also added a blank for the program's exit macro in this form. Most applications use either [FileExit] (as shown in the figure) or [Quit]. The Information Type Selection dialog is used with the Information button. It allows you to select from one of the three standard types of information. You may want to modify this dialog and its associated code to extend the functionality of this utility later. However, I think you'll get everything you need from these general requests. The Results form displays the result of the query. Remember that the Memo component on Form1 holds our macro code. You need a separate dialog to display the results of both the Information and Macro pushbuttons. This form also contains an Exit pushbutton, but it isn't functional when using the Information function.

Figure 10.3.
The DDE Server Information dialog allows you to define the parameters needed to launch a DDE server.

Figure 10.4.
Use the Information Type Selection dialog to define the type of information you want to retrieve about the DDE server.

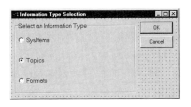

Figure 10.5.

The Results form displays the results of all queries you make with this utility— including the output of any macros.

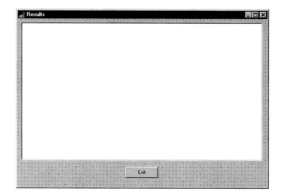

Once you get the forms together, it's time to create some code to make them work. There are two major sections of code for this example and they both appear in the DDECli1 unit. The first bit of code makes the Information button work; the second piece of code makes the Macro button work. There are also short sections to implement the Exit and Copy pushbuttons. You'll find all the code required to implement the DDE client in Listing 10.1.

Listing 10.1. Code to implement DDE client.

```
unit DDECli1;

interface

uses
  Windows, Messages, SysUtils, Classes, Graphics, Controls, Forms, Dialogs,
  StdCtrls, DdeMan;

type
  TForm1 = class(TForm)
    DdeClientConv1: TDdeClientConv;
    DdeClientItem1: TDdeClientItem;
    TestMacro: TButton;
    ExitProgram: TButton;
    Macro: TMemo;
    Information: TButton;
    CopyMacro: TButton;
    procedure ExitProgramClick(Sender: TObject);
    procedure InformationClick(Sender: TObject);
    procedure TestMacroClick(Sender: TObject);
    procedure CopyMacroClick(Sender: TObject);
  private
    { Private declarations }
  public
    { Public declarations }
  end;

var
  Form1: TForm1;

implementation
```

```
uses DDECli2, DDECli3, DDECli4;

{$R *.DFM}

procedure TForm1.CopyMacroClick(Sender: TObject);
begin
    {Select the entire length of the memo field for copying.}
    Macro.SelectAll;

    {Copy the text to the clipboard.}
    Macro.CopyToClipboard;
end;

procedure TForm1.TestMacroClick(Sender: TObject);
var
    iSelStart: Integer;     {Starting point for selecting text.}
    iSelLength: Integer;    {Length of selected text.}
    sServerName: String;    {Server application name and location.}
    sDDEName: String;       {DDE Server Name.}
    sDDETopic: String;      {DDE Topic.}
    iLineCount: Integer;    {Current macro line within Memo control.}
    sMacroText: String;     {Pascal string version of the macro text.}
    pcharMacro: PCHAR;      {Null terminated macro string.}
    sItemText: String;      {Pascal string version of the item text.}
    pcharItem: PCHAR;       {Null terminated item string.}
    sDataText: String;      {Pascal string version of the data text.}
    pcharData: PCHAR;       {Null terminated data string.}
    sItem: String;
begin
    {Make sure the user has input a macro.}
    if Macro.Lines.Count = 0 then
    begin
        MessageDlg('You must type a macro.', mtInformation, [mbOK], 0);
        Exit;
        end;

    {Parse the first line to see if it includes an open statement.  If not,
     display the Information dialog so that the user can open a DDE server.}
    if Pos('LAUNCH', UpperCase(Macro.Lines[0])) = 0  then

                            {Display the Server Information form.}
        if DDEServerInfo.ShowModal = mrCancel then
        Exit

            {If the user selected OK, then load the variables.}
            else
            begin
                sServerName := DDEServerInfo.ServerName.Text;
                sDDEName := DDEServerInfo.DDEName.Text;
                sDDETopic := DDEServerInfo.DDETopic.Text;
                end

    {If the first line did contain a useful command.}
    else
    begin

                        {Parse the LAUNCH command.}
                sServerName := Macro.Lines[0];
```

continues

Listing 10.1. continued

```
                iSelStart := Pos('"', sServerName) + 1;
                iSelLength := Length(sServerName) - iSelStart;
                sServerName := Copy(sServerName, iSelStart, iSelLength);

        {Update our dialog in case we need it later.}
        DDEServerInfo.ServerName.Text := sServerName;

            {See if the next line is a DDE-Open command}
        if Pos('DDE-OPEN', UpperCase(Macro.Lines[1])) = 0 then

            {Display the Server Information form.}
        if DDEServerInfo.ShowModal = mrCancel then
    Exit

            {If the user selected OK, then load the variables.}
        else
        begin
                    sServerName := DDEServerInfo.ServerName.Text;
                    sDDEName := DDEServerInfo.DDEName.Text;
                    sDDETopic := DDEServerInfo.DDETopic.Text;
            end;

        {Parse the DDE-Open command.}

        {Get the DDE Server Name first.}
        sDDEName := Macro.Lines[1];
        iSelStart := Pos('"', sDDEName) + 1;
        iSelLength := Length(sDDEName) - iSelStart;
        sDDEName := Copy(sDDEName, iSelStart, iSelLength);
        sDDETopic := sDDEName;
        iSelLength := Pos('"', sDDEName) - 1;
        sDDEName := Copy(sDDEName, 0, iSelLength);

        {Get the DDE Topic next.}
        iSelStart := Pos('"', sDDETopic) + 1;
        iSelLength := Length(sDDETopic) + 1 - iSelStart;
        sDDETopic := Copy(sDDETopic, iSelStart, iSelLength);
        iSelStart := Pos('"', sDDETopic) + 1;
        iSelLength := Length(sDDETopic) + 1 - iSelStart;
        sDDETopic := Copy(sDDETopic, iSelStart, iSelLength);

        {Store the DDE Topic and Name for later use.}
        DDEServerInfo.DDEName.Text := sDDEName;
        DDEServerInfo.DDETopic.Text := sDDETopic;
        end;

    {Tell Delphi where to find the application if it's not active.}
    DDEClientConv1.ServiceApplication := sServerName;

    {Now that we have some data to work with, let's open the application.}
    if DDEClientConv1.SetLink(sDDEName, sDDETopic) then
    begin

        {Get the name of the item we're working with.}
        DDEClientConv1.OpenLink;
        DDEClientConv1.RequestData(DDEClientItem1.DDEItem);
        sItem := DDEClientItem1.DDEItem;
```

```
{Start parsing the remaining lines of the macro.}
for iLineCount := 2 to Macro.Lines.Count do
begin

    {See if this is a macro execute line.}
    if Pos('DDE-EXECUTE', UpperCase(Macro.Lines[iLineCount])) > 0 then
    begin

{Parse the DDE-Execute command.}
sMacroText := Macro.Lines[iLineCount];
iSelStart := Pos('"', sMacroText) + 1;
iSelLength := Length(sMacroText) - iSelStart;
sMacroText := Copy(sMacroText, iSelStart, iSelLength);

        {Send the macro text to the server.}
pcharMacro := PChar(sMacroText);
if not DDEClientConv1.ExecuteMacro(pcharMacro, False) then
MessageDlg('Error in DDE Macro', mtError, [mbOK], 0);
        end;

    {See if this is a data poke line.}
    if Pos('DDE-POKE', UpperCase(Macro.Lines[iLineCount])) > 0 then
    begin

        {Get the DDE Item first.}
        sItemText := Macro.Lines[iLineCount];
        iSelStart := Pos('"', sItemText) + 1;
        iSelLength := Length(sItemText) - iSelStart;
        sItemText := Copy(sItemText, iSelStart, iSelLength);
        sDataText := sItemText;
        iSelLength := Pos('"', sItemText) - 1;
        sItemText := Copy(sItemText, 0, iSelLength);

        {Get the DDE Data next.}
        iSelStart := Pos('"', sDataText) + 1;
        iSelLength := Length(sDataText) + 1 - iSelStart;
        sDataText := Copy(sDataText, iSelStart, iSelLength);
        iSelStart := Pos('"', sDataText) + 1;
        iSelLength := Length(sDataText) + 1 - iSelStart;
        sDataText := Copy(sDataText, iSelStart, iSelLength);

        {Send the Item and Data text to the server.}
        pcharItem := PChar(sItemText);
        pcharData := PChar(sDataText);
        if not DDEClientConv1.PokeData(pcharItem, pcharData) then
        MessageDlg('Error in DDE Data', mtError, [mbOK], 0);
        end;

    end; {for iLineCount := 2 to Macro.Lines.Count do}

    {Close the conversation.}
    DDEClientConv1.CloseLink;
end; {if DDEClientConv1.SetLink(sDDEName, sDDETopic) then}

end;
```

continues

Listing 10.1. continued

```
procedure TForm1.InformationClick(Sender: TObject);
var
sInfo: PCHAR;              {Requested Information Holder.}
    fMore: Boolean;        {Request additional information?}
begin
                         {Display the Server Information form.}
    if DDEServerInfo.ShowModal = mrCancel then
    Exit;

    {Open the requested server.}
    with DDEServerInfo do
    begin

        {Tell Delphi where to find the application if it's not active.}
        DDEClientConv1.ServiceApplication := ServerName.Text;

        {Establish a DDE link to the server.}
        if DDEClientConv1.SetLink(DDEName.Text, DDETopic.Text) then
    begin
            {Set the data request loop variable.}
            fMore := True;

            {Keep doing this until the user is finished.}
            while fMore do
            begin

            {If we're successful in establishing a link, select a data type.}
            if GetInfoType.ShowModal = mrCancel then
            Exit;     {Exit the procedure.}

            {Once we get an information type, get the Results form ready.}
            ResultsForm.Show;
            ResultsForm.ResultData.Clear;

            {Request the specified data.}
            case GetInfoType.TypeSelect.ItemIndex of
            0:      begin
                        sInfo := DDEClientConv1.RequestData('SYSITEMS');
                        ResultsForm.ResultData.Lines.Add(StrPas(sInfo));
                    end;

                1:    begin
                        sInfo := DDEClientConv1.RequestData('TOPICS');
                        ResultsForm.ResultData.Lines.Add(StrPas(sInfo));
                    end;

                2:    begin
                        sInfo := DDEClientConv1.RequestData('FORMATS');
                        ResultsForm.ResultData.Lines.Add(StrPas(sInfo));
                    end;
            end; {case GetInfoType.TypeSelect.ItemIndex of}

            {Ask the user if he wants to see more information.}
            if MessageDlg('Display more information?', mtConfirmation, [mbYes,
mbNo], 0) = mrNo then
                fMore := False;
```

```
              {Hide the result form.}
              ResultsForm.Hide;

            end; {while fMore do}
        end; {if DDEClientConv1.SetLink(DDEName.Text, DDETopic.Text) then}
    end; {with DDEServerInfo do}

  {Close the requested server.}
  sInfo := PChar(DDEServerInfo.ShutdownCmd.Text);
  if not DDEClientConv1.ExecuteMacro(sInfo, False) then
    MessageDlg('Warning, DDE server did not shut down.', mtError, [mbOK], 0);
  DDEClientConv1.CloseLink;

end;

procedure TForm1.ExitProgramClick(Sender: TObject);
begin
{Exit the program.}
  Halt;
end;

end.
```

The Information button is very general in nature; you could use it with literally any application and learn about the way that application reacts when you request information. You may even find out that the application provides topics that either don't appear in the vendor documentation or are so poorly documented that you didn't know they existed. You'll notice that a lot of the code in this section relates to string manipulation, a constant concern in Delphi since it uses Pascal strings and the rest of Windows tends to use the null terminated C string. The central command is the RequestData method. I provide three different data requests in this example; you could easily extend that number to take some types of specialty topics into account.

The Macro Execute button implementation required me to make some assumptions about the DDE environment; you'll obviously have to make similar assumptions when you implement DDE. The first assumption is that you wouldn't want to use anything other than DDE macro commands. I also had to assume that the first two statements would contain the LAUNCH and DDE-OPEN commands. Once you establish a conversation, you can use any combination of DDE-EXECUTE and DDE-POKE commands required to perform a task. Some type of parsing logic will be needed for a standard DDE implementation.

There are three commands (and a lot of string manipulation) at the core of the Macro Execute button code. You already saw the SetLink method used in the Information code to establish a conversation with the server. We use the same sort of implementation here. The only difference is the way that I obtained the required parameters. I implemented the DDE-EXECUTE macro command using the ExecuteMacro method. All you really need to do is send a null terminated string to the server telling it what macro command that you want to execute. I found that there are some limitations on what macro commands that an application will allow you to use. You'll need to experiment a little to find a formula that works in your particular situation. The final macro command, DDE-POKE, was implemented using the PokeData method. In this case you must supply both a DDE item and a data value to make the command work. A DDE topic normally refers to a specific document or spreadsheet. An item refers to a particular piece of that topic, like a cell in a spreadsheet or a field in a database. The data, of course, is what you want to put in that item. In most cases DDE will limit you to strings.

Warning: You'll notice that both the InformationClick and TestMacroClick procedures contain implicit CloseLink method calls. I don't leave this detail up to the user because it's important to always close a DDE link before you exit your application. The reason for my caution is simple: Windows will behave in an unpredictable manner if you leave the DDE link open and exit the client application (or prematurely close the server application for that matter). Windows 95 is a little better about catching open DDE links than Windows 3.x was, but it'll still freeze up the user's machine on occasion. Machine freezes are the least of your worries though. I've seen some rather bizarre problems that could result in data loss or show up later on—after the user has forgotten all about your application—as problems with applications that aren't even associated with your program. The very least that you can expect is a loss of system memory and resources. Once you close your application, Windows can't get to the memory used by the DDE link—it's gone until the user shuts Windows down and reboots the machine.

The only supplementary form code that I needed to provide was for the Exit button in the Results form. This code appears in Listing 10.2. It's relatively short code whose whole purpose is to hide the form.

Listing 10.2. Supplementary forum code.

```
procedure TResultsForm.HideFormClick(Sender: TObject);
begin
    {Hide the results form.}
    ResultsForm.Hide;
end;
```

Now that we've gotten some forms and code to make them work together, let's take a look at what it'll do for us. The Information button is the one to look at first. I use it to figure out what topics the server will support. I also find that it comes in handy for determining what the server calls a document (in most cases I need the name of a blank document, but there are cases like spreadsheets where I need the name of an existing document). The Sever Information dialog will appear first—its sole function is to establish communication with the server application for you. All you need to do is fill out the four blanks and click OK. Once you fill out the required information, the example program will open the server application for you, then display an Information Type Selection dialog. Figure 10.6 shows the result of getting the SysItems information for Word for Windows. Notice the difference between it and the same data for Excel (see Figure 10.7).

Figure 10.6.
The SysItems display will tell you which topics that Word will support.

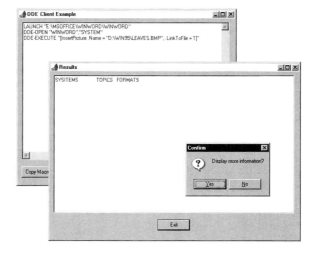

Figure 10.7.
It doesn't take long to figure out that Excel supports many topics that Word doesn't.

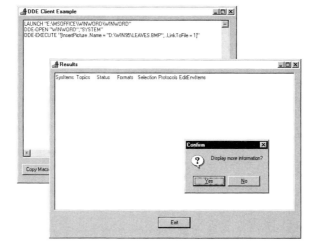

Tip: There is an easy way to figure out what to put in the blocks of the Server Information dialog. Use the View | Options command of Explorer to display the Options dialog. Select the File Types page. Double-click on the file association for the application you want to use. For example, I used Microsoft Word Document for Word. You should see an Edit File Type dialog. At this point I usually double-click on the Open action. You'll see the Editing Action Type dialog. The Application Used to Perform Action field is the first blank of the Server Information dialog. You'll find the information for the second blank in the Application field. The third blank's information appears in the Topic field.

Notice that the program automatically asks if you want to view another type of SYSTEM informa-tion. All you need to do is click on Yes and the program will automatically display the Information Type Selection dialog again without closing the server. I wasn't too surprised by what the Topics selection showed me for Excel (see Figure 10.8) when I opened a multiple sheet worksheet file. There's one topic for each of the sheets. You'd need to access each sheet as a separate topic, then select an item within that sheet before you could send any data to Excel. Fortunately, you can normally pro-vide an extended Item definition to get around this problem (sheet name, then row and column within the specified sheet).

Figure 10.8.
Excel always provides a System topic along with one topic for each sheet in an open file.

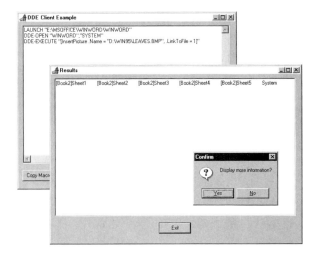

The Formats option of the Information Type Selection dialog won't tell you much more than the vendor documentation. However, it'll tell you which DDE formats that the application supports. There is a difference in some applications—you can import some types of data, use others as part of OLE, but the application may allow you to use only a subset of those formats in a DDE exchange. Figure 10.9 shows the formats that Excel supports, a rather substantial number in comparison to some products.

Figure 10.10 shows the result of using a relatively short and simple macro (along with the macro itself). In this case I started Word for Windows, established communication with it, then told it to insert a picture object (LEAVES.BMP) into the current document. This tells you something about DDE that some people may forget. DDE isn't OLE, but you can use it within the OLE setting. I cre-ated an OLE object by remote control in Word using a DDE macro. The bottom line is that you shouldn't count DDE out of the picture when you create OLE applications.

Figure 10.9.

Excel supports an array of non-native data formats including Rich Text Format and SYLK. Notice that it only supports WK1 format in a DDE setting.

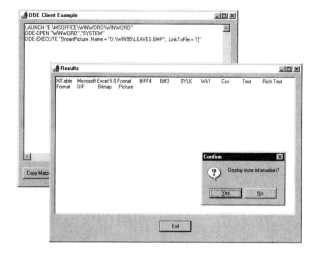

Figure 10.10.

This short DDE macro creates an OLE object in Word for Windows by remote control.

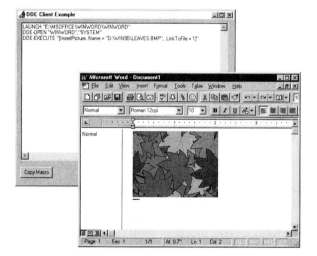

DDE Servers

Implementing the client end of the DDE picture is only half the story; you'll normally need to implement the DDE server end as well. I find that most applications simply pass the DDE command to whatever mechanism takes care of macros. In other words, the server normally supports the same commands as a DDE server as it does when you write a macro for it. The exception to this rule is high end products that use one language for macros and another—totally different language—for standard programming.

You create a DDE server in Delphi using two components. The TDDEServerConv component performs the same service as the TDDEClientConv component—it establishes and maintains contact. The TDDEServerItem component contains two properties that you'll need to work with for a minimum implementation. You'll fill the ServerConv field in with the name of the TDDEServerConv component. The Text property will contain the data sent to your application by the client.

The TDDEServerConv component handles the ExecuteMacro event. This is the event you'll need to define for things like standard macro statements or when the client application requests data.

Let's take a quick look at an example of how a server would work. I created a quick form like the one shown in Figure 10.11 for this example. It has a TMemo component that's used to display messages from the client. The other two components are a TDDEServerConv and a TDDEServerItem component. You'll need both to receive both macros and data from a client application.

Figure 10.11.
Our DDE server application provides a simple form for displaying messages.

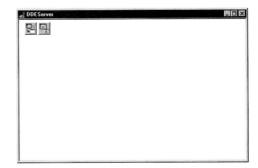

I've attached a short procedure to every event that the TDDEServerConv or TDDEServerItem component might intercept. In fact, you'll see that they're all used on a regular basis for very specific events. Listing 10.3 shows the code for this example.

Listing 10.3. Code for the example.

```
unit DDESrv1;

interface

uses
  Windows, Messages, SysUtils, Classes, Graphics, Controls, Forms, Dialogs,
  DdeMan, StdCtrls;

type
  TForm1 = class(TForm)
    System: TDdeServerConv;
    SysItems: TDdeServerItem;
    ClientInput: TMemo;
    procedure SystemOpen(Sender: TObject);
    procedure SystemExecuteMacro(Sender: TObject; Msg: TStrings);
    procedure SystemClose(Sender: TObject);
    procedure SysItemsChange(Sender: TObject);
```

```
  procedure SysItemsPokeData(Sender: TObject);
private
  { Private declarations }
public
  { Public declarations }
end;

var
  Form1: TForm1;

implementation

{$R *.DFM}

procedure TForm1.SystemOpen(Sender: TObject);
begin
  {The client triggers this event every time it wants to open
   the server for use.}
  ClientInput.Lines.Add('Client requested contact.');
end;

procedure TForm1.SystemExecuteMacro(Sender: TObject;
  Msg: TStrings);
begin
  {This is where you would normally use some type of macro
   messaging scheme. It could be as simple as sending the
   macro command to the application's macro processor. You
   could also choose to implement the commands right here.}
  ClientInput.Lines.Add('Command: ' + Msg.Strings[0]);
end;

procedure TForm1.SystemClose(Sender: TObject);
begin
  {This event gets called if the client application gets
   terminated or if it explicitly closes the DDE session.}
  ClientInput.Lines.Add('Client closed DDE Conversation.');
end;

procedure TForm1.SysItemsChange(Sender: TObject);
begin
  {Every time the client or some part of the server application
   changes the TDDEServerItem.Text property, this event gets
   called.}
  ClientInput.Lines.Add('Item Text Change: ' + SysItems.Text);
end;

procedure TForm1.SysItemsPokeData(Sender: TObject);
begin
  {This event only gets called if the client pokes data into the
   server.}
  ClientInput.Lines.Add('Item Data Change: ' + SysItems.Text);
end;

end.
```

I wrote a quick macro to test the responses of this server application. You can see the results in Figure 10.12. Every time the client takes an action, the server reacts to it. Notice how the data from the client gets passed to the server through either the DDE item component or the Msg parameter of the SystemExecuteMacro procedure.

Figure 10.12.

As this display shows, the client parses then sends macro commands or data to the server, which then reacts to it.

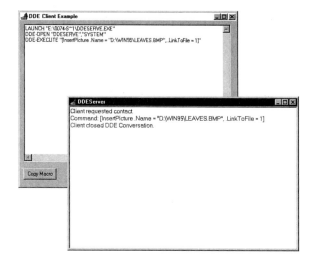

Compound Documents: The Microsoft Strategy

Once you get past DDE, you start getting into OLE. The previous sections showed that DDE and OLE are intertwined in ways that most people don't expect. We need to look at a bit of terminology before going much further. You need to speak the language of OLE to really understand it. The following list defines some of the terms you'll see in this chapter (and those that follow).

- Client: This term refers to the application that holds the linked or embedded object. For example, if you place a spreadsheet object in your word processed document, the word processor becomes the client.

- Server: The server is the application that the client calls to manipulate an object. Embedded or linked objects are still in the native format of the application that created them. A client must call on the originating application to make any required changes to the object's content. What you really have is two applications working together to create a cohesive document.

- Compound document: This is a document that contains one or more objects. Every OLE document is considered a compound document. We'll take a better look at what this means a little later in this chapter.

- Object: An object is a piece of data that you move from one application to another in its native format. You can create objects from any data if the originating application supports

OLE. This is the big difference between an object and cutting and pasting. You can do a lot more with an object because it contains intelligence that a simple piece of text does not.

- The Object menu: We'll take another look at how to use this particular OLE menu later. Suffice it to say that this is the menu you use to change the contents of an OLE document, convert it, or perform any other operations that the object allows.

- Container: An object that holds other objects. Visualizing a folder, such as the ones used by Explorer, will give you a good idea of what a container represents. However, instead of simply holding files like a folder does, an OLE container can hold any kind of object.

The User Perspective of OLE

Now that you have some idea of what these OLE terms mean, we can take a look at some actual examples. It's important for a programmer to take a user eye view of things before starting to write code. How often have you seen a program that's so difficult to use no one discovers the really neat features it provides? A really good programmer can almost always provide an application that provides a superior set of features. However, a user doesn't see features, he sees ease of use.

Let's take a look at an example of how a user would view OLE. I used Microsoft Paint and WordPad for my example so that you could follow along if you want to. It isn't really necessary to do so; the important thing is that you understand the process from the user perspective.

The first thing I did was double-click on a .BMP file—Honeycomb—in the main Windows folder. Then I opened a copy of WordPad. You should see something similar to Figure 10.13. There isn't anything particularly special about these two applications, but they do both support OLE 2. This will allow me to show you some of the object handling features that you need to include in your application. Remember that you'll need OLE 2 compliance to get a Windows 95 logo for your application. It's important to know the difference between OLE 1 and OLE 2 for starters, then see how Microsoft implemented OLE 2 support in an application they designed. That'll give you the clues you need to design a great application without getting mired in too many details. (Believe me, the OLE specification will allow you to get mired in as much detail as you want, so it's important to look at other applications as a means for filtering out the things you really don't need.)

Use the Edit | Select All command in Paint to select the entire image, and then right-click on it. You should see the object menu shown in Figure 10.14. Notice that you can't drag and drop this image because Paint doesn't support that particular OLE 2 feature. If it did support drag and drop, you could simply right-click on the object and drag it where you wanted it to go in WordPad. You'll need to keep features like this in mind when you design your application. Microsoft didn't add drag and drop support to Paint because it's a small utility and few people will really need that feature. Before you bloat your application with needless code, it's important to consider whether a user will really need a specific OLE 2 feature.

Figure 10.13.
*Using OLE starts with
something as simple as
opening two applications.*

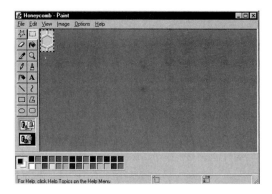

Figure 10.14.
*This object menu contains
options that allow you to
place the object on the
Clipboard.*

The object menu in Paint allows you to cut or copy the image. Notice the number of other editing options this menu contains. You might want to make note of what is available and compare it to the WordPad object menu later. For right now, select the Copy option. Doing so will place a copy of the object on the Clipboard. About this time you should hear some sirens going off in your head. OLE and DDE both use the Clipboard as a method for transferring data between applications. From a programming perspective, this means that you'll be able to at least partially reuse some of the coding techniques you learned when using DDE. (In fact, we'll see in just a bit that Delphi makes use of this fact in the way that it implements its OLE components.)

> **Note:** There's another design decision hidden in this part of the example. OLE 1 applications always provide a Paste Special command to paste objects from the clipboard into the current document. In fact, you could still use the Edit | Paste Special command in place of the object menu when working with WordPad (or other applications that provide this feature). OLE 2 compliance doesn't necessarily mean implementing every bell and whistle in the specification. The type of object menu you choose to provide—if any—should be more a matter of user need than anything else. We'll also get into another OLE 2 innovation in this chapter—the Insert | Object command and associated dialog.

Click on WordPad to bring it forward. Right-click anywhere within the window. You should see an object menu similar to the one in Figure 10.15. Notice how this menu differs from the one we saw in Paint. Each object menu will have features that are unique to that application. A graphics application needs menu entries to help it manipulate graphic images. A word processor needs a set of options that allow the user to manipulate text. It's not too surprising, though, that the three most common Object menu items are: Cut, Copy, and Paste. We'll see later that the menu items that appear on most object menus are actually embedded in the registry as verbs—actions that you can perform with the object. Delphi programmers have other, less painful, options at their disposal for defining these menu entries if they want to (we'll also cover this topic later in the chapter).

Figure 10.15.
The WordPad object menu differs from the one found in Paint because it needs to perform different work.

Select the Paste option from WordPad's object menu. You'll see a copy of the graphic image in WordPad, as shown in Figure 10.16. There are some things you should see here that you'll need to consider when writing your OLE application that are apparent in this image. The first thing you should notice is the sizing handles around the image. The presence of sizing handles tells you that the application is maintaining the graphic object separately from the text elements in memory. The sizing handles allow you to increase or shrink the object as needed. This means that you'll need to manage an object differently than either graphics or text in your application. In other words, you can't simply place it in the drawing area using the Lines.Add method or by drawing it on the canvas. Dynamically creating image components to place in the drawing area will help you out in this regard. A lot of users will need the ability to resize objects, especially when it comes to embedding graphics. For example, when I need to draw a logo, I usually draw it very large. That way, I can get it done quickly without worrying too much about detail. When I paste the logo into a document, I shrink it to the size I really need it to be. Voilà—instant detail. As you shrink the graphic, it actually gains some amount of detail you normally wouldn't get if you drew the image that size.

Figure 10.16.
The pasted object always provides sizing handles when you select it.

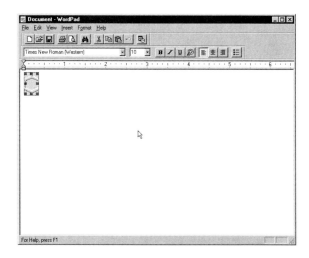

Now that the image is stored in WordPad, go ahead and close Paint. We can always open it back up if we need it later. If you right-click on the graphic object, you'll see a menu similar to the WordPad object menu that we saw earlier. Notice the two bottom options, Bitmap Image Object and Object Properties. Highlight Bitmap Image Object to display a submenu.

There are two options here: Edit and Open. The difference between them is distinct. Select Edit if you want to perform in-place editing. The Open option actually opens a copy of Paint with which you can edit the graphic. Fortunately, Delphi makes it easy (as we'll see when we get to the programming example) to implement both editing methods. To see what I mean, select Edit now. You should see a display similar to the one in Figure 10.17. You should notice quite a few changes. For one thing, there's a hatched box around the object. This is an OLE 2 way of telling you which object you are currently editing. Also notice that the toolbar and menus changed to match those of Paint. This is what I mean by in-place editing. The window didn't change, but the tools did to meet the editing needs of the object.

Figure 10.17.
In-place editing is one of the new OLE 2 features.

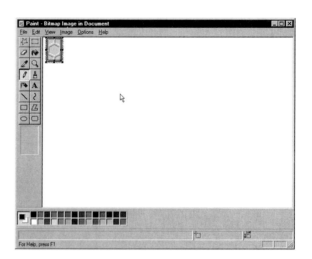

You can click anywhere outside the object to restore the original WordPad menu and toolbar. This time, let's select the Open option to see what happens. You should see a display similar to the one in Figure 10.18. This figure provides you with some visual cues. The most obvious is the fact that you're editing the graphic object outside WordPad using the originating application. The method you use is largely dependent on personal taste since the end result of using either method is the same. The advantage of using the in-place method is that you remain in the same window all the time. This tends to increase efficiency and reduce the chance of losing your train of thought. The Open method has the advantage of returning you to the native editing environment. If I chose to edit one of my logos instead of opening it, I would have to perform in-place editing on a much smaller version of my original picture. Of course, I could always resize it to its original state, but that would be as inefficient as any other method—perhaps more so. Notice also that the object is hatched over in WordPad. This is another visual cue telling you which object you're editing externally.

Figure 10.18.
The Open option produces
an entirely different result
than Edit does.

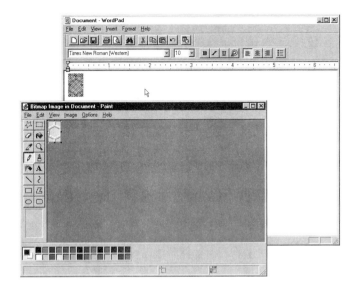

Exit Paint and return to WordPad. Notice that the Exit entry on the File menu now says Return to Document. If you provide OLE server capabilities in your application, you'll also need to make a similar change to your application's menu. The visual cue provided by the new menu entry tells the user that he's updating an object, not a new data file.

Now it's time to see what that other WordPad object menu entry contains. Right-click on the graphics object and select the Object Properties option. You should see the Bitmap Image Properties dialog, shown in Figure 10.19. This is a Windows 95 specific feature and you can't access it using a Delphi component (at least as of this writing); you'll need to access it directly from the Windows API. About the only interesting entry on the General page from the user's perspective is the Convert button. You'd need to implement this button as part of a DLL. Windows 95 uses the convert routine in a number of places, not the least of which is the Context menu inside Explorer. In essence, the convert routine is a shell extension—which I'll discuss in a separate area of the chapter. Clicking on the Convert button displays another dialog with a list of conversion options. This option allows you to convert the graphic object from one file type to another. This page also displays the file size and type.

Figure 10.19.
The General page of the
Bitmap Image Properties
dialog provides access to
the Convert dialog.

Click on the View tab. You'll see the View page of the Bitmap Image Properties dialog, shown in Figure 10.20. This page has several interesting entries. The first is the radio button that determines whether the image is displayed as a graphic or an icon. You can make your machine run faster and use less memory if you select the icon option. Using an icon means that Windows doesn't need to load the actual image or the application required to support it unless you decide to edit it. Windows will suggest a default icon, but you can use the Change Icon button to select another. Normally you'll grab this icon from the server's EXE file.

Figure 10.20.
The View page of the Bitmap Image Properties dialog allows you to change the appearance of the object.

The bottom part of this dialog is fairly interesting too, even if you can't select it at the moment. It allows you to select a precise scale to use when displaying your graphic. The .BMP format and application used to display it doesn't support the scaling option in this particular case. Close WordPad; we don't need it anymore for now. You don't have to save the image unless you want to.

Clients and Servers

Now that we've taken a quick tour of the mechanics of OLE, let's start to talk about some theory. There are many different ways of looking at OLE from both the user and application standpoint. For example, the act of data transfer involves two different kinds of application: A server and a client.

Every application that supports OLE is either a client, a server, or a combination of both. A client always acts as a container for objects that it receives from a server. The client doesn't need to know what to do with those objects—that's the server's responsibility. It's the client's responsibility to store the objects in such a way that it can retrieve them intact later. The client establishes contact with the server and requests the data it needs. The server normally places this data on the Clipboard. We're not talking about data in the same sense as DDE offered here; we're talking about data objects. An object has properties and you can interact with it in more than one way. That fact differentiates a dynamic data object from the static data offered by DDE.

You might have noticed in all our examples I have used Paint as the server and WordPad as the client. The reason is simple: Paint can't function as a client; it offers itself only as an OLE server. You'll need to make the same decision when you create your application. Microsoft chose to make

Paint an OLE server and not a client because it's unlikely that anyone would use Paint as a container to put objects together to create a final document—they'd probably use a word processor or desktop publishing application to perform that task. On the other hand, it is entirely possible that someone would use Paint as a server. Anyone who wanted to place a logo contained in a BMP file into their word processed document could use Paint and get perfectly acceptable results.

The distinction between client and server is important because it affects the way you use an application. More than that, limitations of OLE support necessarily limit an application's value for creating a finished product. Consider what would happen if you tried to use a graphics program to create a poster, but it didn't support OLE as a client. Would you simply settle for cut and paste if there were a chance that you would need to modify the chart frequently? Therein lies the dilemma for the programmer—it's a question of code bloat versus user need. It isn't always necessary to make your application both a client and a server; it's really a matter of how you expect a user to interact with your application.

Whether your application is a client or a server is an important consideration for another reason as well. It takes a lot of time and effort to fully implement OLE. For one thing, if your application is a server and it uses nonstandard data formats (like the forms used in a database application), you'll need to create your own data handlers and register them with the Clipboard. Obviously you'll need to check the input from other applications as well. If your application can't handle a particular data format, you'll need to find a way to provide this information to the user. (It's really irritating to use an OLE server that simply ignores anything it doesn't understand.) Another server issue is whether you plan to support all the data formats that your application can use, or simply the native formats that it produces.

Servers can become mired in other problems as well. What happens when the user accesses your application using DDE? Do you allow them to access the OLE capability provided by your server using a DDE macro? Word does this; we saw it in the DDE macro at the beginning of this chapter. All I did was create an OLE link, select the object, put it on the Clipboard, and copy it to a specific area of my spreadsheet. Think about all the work involved in implementing a DDE client and a DDE server; now add the code required to implement OLE as well, and you will easily see why adding full OLE support is no small issue.

Unfortunate as it may seem, Borland didn't add OLE server support to the 16-bit version of Delphi. If you program in that environment, the TOLEContainer component will only provide support as an OLE client. Does this mean that you're stuck—that there isn't any way to add OLE to your application? Not exactly. You can still create an OLE server using Delphi 1.x, but you'll have to do it using Windows API functions. There's one way to reduce your workload. Microsoft provides an OLE SDK. You can order it for about $50.00 from Microsoft by calling (800)227-4679. What you'll get is a book and a CD that's just packed with specifications and other materials you'll find very handy when creating your application.

Linking Versus Embedding

There are some issues that the programmer has to resolve when it comes to linking and embedding—the two things you can do with a data object in Windows. Both types of OLE object implementation have pluses and minuses that a user needs to consider. For example, a user will need to weigh the convenience of the automatic updates that a link will provide versus the data permanence provided by embedding. Of course, they'll also need to decide how any links they create will get updated—automatically or as a manual operation.

What you, the programmer, need to worry about is how to implement these two object insertion techniques and still make OLE easy from a user perspective. For example, there's a standard dialog used for inserting an object. The dialog provided by Delphi allows the user to select between an existing file and creating a new file—its the same dialog you'll see in a lot of other OLE 2 compliant applications under Windows. How you react to the changes that the user makes to this dialog is a programming consideration similar to the one we faced in Chapter 6 when we talked about common dialogs. Unlike the common dialogs, however, you have less flexibility in the way that you react to user input. It's no longer a matter of one programmer's method of implementing a dialog—we're talking about two or more applications working together to produce a specific result.

There are also Object menus to consider. Do you provide a different Object menu for a linked object than an embedded object? Some applications seem to use the same or a slightly modified version of the same Object menu in both cases.

You'll also need to consider the object itself. When the user creates a link to a document, he is, in essence, creating a pointer to that file on disk. As with most links to files, OLE uses a path as needed to locate the file. In fact, if you create an OLE object under Delphi that contains a static link, you'll see the path as part of the ObjItem property. The link works fine as long as you don't move the document. The second you do move the document, you break the links. Of course, you can always reestablish the links, but that's a waste of time when not moving the file in the first place would require a lot less work.

OLE 1 had a significant problem in this regard because it noted the location of the linked file in precise terms—just like the precise location of executable files are noted in the AUTOEXEC.BAT Path statement. Any movement of the file at all resulted in broken links that the user had to fix. OLE 2 takes a different approach. Instead of using a precise location, it uses a relative direction. For example, if two files are in the same directory, you won't see any path information at all. As long as the two files stay in the same directory, OLE 2 doesn't care where they appear on the hard drive. If the linked file should appear in a subdirectory under the container file, you would see only the subdirectory name as part of the path. I think you get the idea—relative paths make it harder to break OLE links, but not impossible.

Embedding is a lot simpler from a programmer perspective, especially when you consider the way that Delphi creates OLE objects. All you need to do in this case is store the object itself within the confines of the container (compound file). The problem here is a matter of creating a new file type that supports OLE. Remember the text editor in Chapter 6? That program assumed that the user could output either a text or RTF file. The text option is no longer available if you want to save embedded objects. You'll probably find that you need to create an enhanced version of the TRichEdit component to make the RTF option work. (I recently tried using the native TRichEdit component to save an OLE object, but it didn't work as of this writing. The same component wouldn't read an RTF file created by Word that contained an OLE object.)

Kinds of OLE Services

There are three different kinds of OLE services you can perform using Delphi: inserting, pasting, and dropping. You insert an OLE object using the Insert | Object menu of an application. Most applications allow you to either create a new OLE object or to embed or link an existing document in its entirety. You can't select a subset of a document using this method.

You'll normally allow a user to paste an OLE object using the Copy | Paste Special command of an application. This method takes whatever OLE object it finds on the Clipboard and pastes it into an application. A user would select this method if he needed either all or part of an existing document.

Dropping is new to OLE 2. Both the client and the server have to support dropping or it won't work. Essentially the user takes an object from a source like Explorer and drops it on the client application. This comes in handy if the user needs to grab a lot of different files from various sources and put them together into one document.

Of these three OLE service types, the user is always going to expect to find the pasting technique. This particular method has been around since OLE 1 and it answers a need the other two methods don't. You have to provide pasting services if you want to allow the user to insert a partial document into your OLE container.

The insertion technique is most popular in spreadsheet and word processing applications. It won't work with a database manager in some cases since you'll probably want to use an entry form in place of a browse for adding data. The obvious exception to this rule is if you want to insert a graphic or other object in a BLOB (binary large object) field.

Application Interoperability

Every programmer has nightmares about troubleshooting a bug for weeks, only to find out that the problem wasn't in their code; it was in the way their application interacted with another application. Getting two applications to work together might not always be as easy as it seems. We've already seen a lot of different ways that two applications can differ in their implementation of OLE, and this barely scratches the surface. For the most part, we've looked at the standard ways that two applications can deviate. The following list gives you some ideas of what to look for when you can't get your objects to work properly.

- Neither application is a server. Remember that you must have a server and a client to make OLE work. One application must communicate needed changes to the other. The server then makes any required changes to the object and hands it back. The whole purpose of OLE is to maintain this kind of communication.

- Data corruption has ruined one or more OLE files. This isn't very common, but it does happen. One of the reasons for this particular kind of corruption is old data files. I've seen applications overwrite newer versions of OLE files with old ones. Even though the application can use the older files, other applications might not be able to. It's usually a good idea to record the time and date stamps on your OLE files. That way, you can always check for this special form of data corruption.

- One program provides 32-bit services and the other 16-bit. This problem isn't supposed to happen. I've seen it only once or twice, and when it did occur, I couldn't get the problem to repeat after I rebooted my machine. What exactly happened is debatable. If you do find that two programs that normally talk to each other with ease are suddenly hostile toward each other, it might be time to reboot the machine and see if clearing memory helps. You'll most definitely have problems with Delphi if you try to use the wrong DLL to implement an OLE task. Always use a 32-bit OLE DLL for Delphi 2.x and a 16-bit DLL for Delphi 1.x.

- Corrupted entries in the registry prevent the application from working correctly. I'll cover the registry entries at the end of this chapter. The bottom line is that if you have so much as a punctuation mark wrong, the registry will balk and your OLE connection won't work. Now, think what'll happen as you test your application. The chances of getting an improper registry entry are pretty good. Make sure that a problem you have is really a bug and not some errant entry in the registry. Fortunately, Delphi keeps these problems to a minimum.

- Old entries in the registry are confusing the application. The registry is a lot better organized than the WIN.INI and SYSTEM.INI files used by Windows 3.x, and you'll definitely find it easier to maintain, but there are still times when you might have to remove an entry manually. Some applications get confused when they run across these old OLE entries and end up trying to use the wrong files or settings.

- Your network doesn't fully support OLE links. Some networks require the use of special software when creating OLE 2 links. LANtastic falls into this category. As long as you use Artisoft's procedures, you should maintain good OLE connections. Other networks, such as the Microsoft network supplied with Windows 95, use OLE without any additional software. A third category of network software seems to have trouble maintaining links. Banyan falls into this category. Unfortunately, all this assumes that you create exactly the same drive mappings every time you log on to the network. As an experiment, I tried a setup in which the user needed to use her old CD-ROM only occasionally. She didn't want to load the real-mode drivers every day because the driver lowered system stability. The days she didn't have the CD-ROM connected, all her OLE links worked fine. On the days it was connected, none of the OLE links would work. We finally traced the problem to changes in the drive mapping when the CD-ROM drive was active.

This is just a sample of the types of problems you could encounter with a common setup. Add to these problems a vendor who doesn't fully support the OLE 1 or OLE 2 standard. I actually ran into one piece of software that ended up providing some strange cross of support between the two standards (and I don't think this vendor was alone). These support problems only make the situation worse. If every application supported OLE perfectly, you could probably get past the other problems I listed in this section. The combination of faulty support and less-than-adequate linking mechanisms does paint a grim picture for the user. It would be easy to point a finger and say that the vendor was totally at fault. Yet anyone who has tried to read the OLE standards, much less follow them, will attest to the level of difficulty involved.

Before you get the idea that all is lost with OLE, let me inject a dose of reality. I wanted you to be aware of all the problems you might find. In most cases, I don't have any substantial problems with OLE that I didn't cause myself. Sure, there are times when I would like to be able to do more than the applications I'm using will allow, but these are inconveniences; they don't make OLE unusable. The best thing you can do when using OLE is to thoroughly check everything before you make a huge commitment in time and energy to a specific solution. It always pays to check for potential pitfalls, but this is especially true of a technology as new and complex as OLE.

Differences Between OLE 1 and OLE 2

Microsoft introduced OLE 1 as part of Windows 3.x. It provided a basic set of linking and embedding features that users soon outgrew. One of the biggest problems was the huge amount of memory that OLE required to create more than one or two links with other applications. The lack of speed was also a major concern.

OLE 2 is supposed to remedy some of these problems and provide much more functionality to boot. The following list gives you an idea of all the improvements Microsoft made in OLE 2. Some of these improvements are programmer specific—others affect both the programmer and the user.

> **Tip:** Most of these new features require that both applications support OLE 2. At the very minimum, the client must support OLE 2 in order to make any of the features work. Unfortunately, it's not always easy to determine what level of support an older application provides. The Windows 95 registry contains complete information on every OLE server on your machine. Even Delphi registers its applications there. We'll look at the registry near the end of this chapter. Looking in the registry can provide important clues as to the type and level of OLE support that an application provides.

- Visual editing: One of the problems with OLE 1 was that the user's train of thought got disrupted every time he needed to make a change to an object. The reason is simple: OLE 1 loaded a copy of the server and displayed the object in the originating application's window for editing. OLE 2 allows visual (or in-place) editing. Instead of opening a new window, the host merely overlays its toolbar, menu structure, and controls with those of the client. The user simply sees a change in tools, not a change in applications. As a result, the transition between documents is less noticeable.

- Nested objects: OLE 1 allowed you to place one object at a time in the container document. An object couldn't become a container; all the objects existed as a single layer within the container. OLE 2 treats every potential container as just that—a container. It doesn't matter how many containers you place inside a container or how many ways you stack them. To get a better idea of how nesting will help you, look at the way Windows 95 implements folders. You can treat OLE 2 container objects the same way.

- Drag and drop: You used to cut or copy an object in the server application and then place it in the client using the Paste Special command. This option still works. However, OLE 2 provides a new method of creating links to other documents. You can simply grab the object and move it wherever you want. It becomes linked wherever you decide to drop it.

- Storage-independent links: OLE 2 allows you to create links to other documents, even if they aren't physically located on the local drive. It implements this using an LRPC (Light Remote Procedure Call) mechanism. Unfortunately, this linking mechanism has limitations. For example, you'll find that it works fine with some peer-to-peer networks, but it works only marginally with other network types. The next revision of OLE is supposed to fix this problem by supporting RPCs (Remote Procedure Calls).

- Adaptable links: Many users screamed for this feature. If you moved any of the files required to create a compound document under OLE 1, all the links got destroyed, and you had to re-create them. This older version stored the full path, including drive, to the linked data. OLE 2 stores only enough path information to maintain the link. If you create links between two files in the same directory, you can move these two files anywhere on the drive, and OLE 2 can maintain the link. The only criteria for maintaining a link under OLE 2 is that the relative path remain the same.

- OLE automation: Everyone knows about Visual Basic for Applications (VBA), right? This is the new programming language that Microsoft is trying to get everyone to support. OLE automation is part of VBA. VBA defines a standard interface for talking with the server application. This allows the client application to send commands to the server that will change the contents of an object indirectly. OLE automation is the direct descendent of the DDE macro language that many applications still use. The big difference from the user's perspective is that DDE macros were difficult to write and very prone to error. VBA is the native language of the application and is consistent across platforms. The surprising thing is, even though many applications support the VBA interface right now, none of them support it as a programming language. In essence, no one has fully implemented this feature yet. Obviously, the 16-bit version of Delphi doesn't support OLE automation. You must use DDE with this product. On the other hand, you'll find that the 32-bit version of Delphi does support OLE automation.

- Version management: Have you ever received a document from someone, only to find that part of it wouldn't work with your software? OLE 2 can store the application name and version number as part of the link. If an application developer implements this feature correctly, a server (or client, for that matter) will detect an old version of a file and ask if you want to update it. This means that you'll never have an old file sitting around just waiting to make life difficult. Unfortunately, except for a few Microsoft applications and one or two other vendors, this feature is largely unimplemented right now. Hopefully, the Windows 95 version of products will incorporate it. (As of this writing, the 32-bit version of Delphi doesn't support this feature.)

- Object conversion: Your friend uses Excel and you use Lotus 1-2-3, yet you need to share OLE documents containing spreadsheets. One of you could go through the inconvenience and expense of changing to the other person's application and document format, but OLE 2 can probably solve this problem without such a change. Object conversion allows Excel to act as a server for a compound document containing a Lotus 1-2-3 object. All you need to do is select the Convert option from the Object menu. At least, that's how it's supposed to work. Real life is a bit different. Conversion will work only if the other application already supports that data format. Of course, when you think about it, this restriction makes sense.

- Optimized object storage: Remember the screaming about memory I told you about at the beginning of this section? This feature is part of the cure. It allows the linked documents to stay on disk until needed. That way, Windows doesn't need to load every application and data file required to support the compound document. In most cases, Windows uses a buffer-zone technique. A word processor might keep the applications and objects required for the preceding, current, and next page in memory. The rest of the objects stay on disk, greatly reducing the memory footprint of a compound document in some cases. You'll find the functions for implementing this feature in the STORAGE.DLL file in your SYSTEM directory.

- Component object model: This is a new standard interface that Windows provides for component object. Essentially, this is Microsoft's way of making 16-bit and 32-bit application OLE conversations transparent. This is also the feature that's responsible for allowing OLE 1 and OLE 2 applications to live together. You'll find the calls for the component object module in COMPOBJ.DLL. Windows issues a pointer to a list of functions when you create an object using one of these DLL calls. It helps to think of a component object as a special VCL—the only difference is that it only contains functions, not data fields or properties.

With all the changes to OLE 2, you might think that there would be compatibility problems. OLE 1 and OLE 2 can mix freely on your machine. Not only does Windows provide features in the common object module to help this along, but you'll find that there are separate entries in the registry for OLE 1 and OLE 2 (we'll talk about these entries at the end of the chapter.) Each application has a set of OLE 1 and OLE 2 entries in the registry; an OLE capable application uses the OLE 1 settings when talking to an OLE 1 application or the OLE 2 settings when talking to an OLE 2 application. The important thing to remember here is that OLE takes a least-common-denominator approach. Everything's tied to the application that has the fewest capabilities. This means that if you had four OLE 2 applications and one OLE 1 application, everything would be tied to the level of support provided by the OLE 1 application.

OLE Components

I've already talked about two of the OLE specific files in this chapter: STORAGE.DLL and COMPOBJ.DLL. You'll probably see a whole group of other files in your \SYSTEM directory that provide support for OLE. The following list provides some details on the tasks each file performs. You can use this list if you ever run into a problem with corruption or if you would simply like to know what level of support you can expect from a certain application. The presence or absence of these files might indicate problems with your installation as well. Missing OLE files means you won't get the kind of support needed to make your system work efficiently.

- OLE2.DLL: If you see this file, you know that some part of the Windows installation on your machine supports the OLE 2 standard. Windows 95 always installs this file. This dynamic link library (DLL) provides some base functions.

- OLECLI.DLL: This file contains all the basic client code your application needs. Your application uses this file as a base for building its own client features.

- OLESRV.DLL: This file contains all the basic server code your application needs. Like the client code, this DLL won't provide everything. Your application uses it as a basis for building its own set of features.

- OLE2CONV.DLL: This file provides the generic routines a program needs to convert an object to the client program's native format.

- OLE2DISP.DLL: Every OLE client application uses this DLL to help it display the objects it contains.

- OLE2NLS.DLL: Most versions of Windows provide National Language Support (NLS). This program helps OLE keep pace with the rest of Windows in providing support for other languages.

- OLE2.REG: You can import this registry file into your registry to install OLE 2 support. In most cases, your application will do this automatically, so you don't need to worry about it. The only time you'll need to use it is if you can't get OLE 2 to work and discover that the registry doesn't contain the correct entries.

- MCIOLE.DLL: Sounds require special handling under Windows. Unlike with most objects, you don't display a sound. This special DLL provides the support an application needs in order to handle a sound object.

- OLE32.DLL: A whole group of OLE files in the \SYSTEM directory has "32" somewhere in their names. These files provide the same services as their 16-bit counterparts to 32-bit applications.

- MFCOLEUI.DLL: C programmers need every bit of help they can get. They use something called Microsoft Foundation Classes to make their workload a little lighter. This file (and any with similar names) provides the C interface to OLE. If you see a file with "MFC" in its name, you know one of your applications uses the Microsoft Foundation Classes.

Using an OLE Container

The TOleContainer component appears on the same System VCL tab as I mentioned earlier when talking about the DDE components. Essentially you use this component to add OLE container abilities to your application. Each OLE container can store one item. In the case of a database management application that shows one OLE item at a time, this is probably going to be enough. Other applications, like text editors, will probably require you to create the OLE containers dynamically using the same methods that I've shown you throughout the book. The big difference here is managing those containers. I think you'll find that using an array or some type of pointer system will allow you to keep track of all the containers in your application a little easier than creating them one at a time. (For an example of how to create an array of components dynamically, look at the CD player code shown in Listing 11.7 in Chapter 11. You could also create a list of object pointers similar to the message list I created in Chapter 15 for the SendKeys() function example.)

The new version of TOleContainer provided with Delphi 2.0 is much improved over its predecessor. In the past you had to take care of all the structures that OLE required. Delphi now takes care of this for you automatically. In addition, it takes care of some of the low-level tasks like registering your data formats with the Clipboard. Of course, it only registers the "standard" formats. You'll still need to register any esoteric formats yourself, but at least you have less work to do in this regard. I was also happy to see the inclusion of so many standard dialogs in this version. The only dialog that you'll need to create yourself is one that can manage link information. Obviously this has to be a custom dialog that takes your method of managing more than one OLE container into account.

Let's take a look at a simple OLE container example. Figure 10.21 shows the form we'll start with. It includes a menu, a TRichEdit component, and a TOleContainer component. I used a simple Exit entry for the File menu, inserted the Edit menu template, and added a single Object entry to the Insert menu. The figure shows the modifications I made to the Edit menu—I simply removed the entries I didn't plan to use for this example. You'll probably leave them in when writing an editor application. Notice also that I changed the OLE container Align property to alBottom so that it would follow the bottom of the form when I resized it. The rich text edit component's Align property is set to alClient. This allows you to double- or right-click within the OLE container to see the effect of various edit commands and then return to the application by clicking on the rich edit component area.

> **Tip:** Delphi 2.0 doesn't provide a default Insert menu template. You'll probably want to create one of your own based on other applications on your machine. In most cases you'll want to add pictures and sounds as standard menu entries. Applications like Microsoft Word and Excel provide good examples of the kinds of entries you'll find on a typical Insert menu.

Figure 10.21.
Our OLE container example begins with a simple editor style window and associated menu.

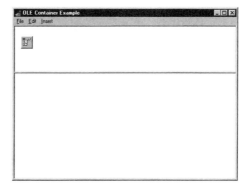

You'll need to add the code found in Listing 10.4 to make the most of the functions in the menu work. I'll cover the requirements for listing link information in just a moment. The code contains all the required functions in the order they appear on the menu. Notice that I included a special function to change the Edit menu options depending on the current status of particular user selections.

Listing 10.4. Code to add.

```
unit OLECont1;

interface

uses
  Windows, Messages, SysUtils, Classes, Graphics, Controls, Forms, Dialogs,
  StdCtrls, ComCtrls, Menus, OleCtnrs, Clipbrd;

type
  TForm1 = class(TForm)
    MainMenu1: TMainMenu;
    File1: TMenuItem;
    Exit1: TMenuItem;
    RichEdit1: TRichEdit;
```

```
    Insert1: TMenuItem;
    Object2: TMenuItem;
    OleContainer1: TOleContainer;
    Edit1: TMenuItem;
    Object1: TMenuItem;
    Links1: TMenuItem;
    N1: TMenuItem;
    PasteSpecial1: TMenuItem;
    Paste1: TMenuItem;
    Copy1: TMenuItem;
    Cut1: TMenuItem;
    procedure Exit1Click(Sender: TObject);
    procedure Object2Click(Sender: TObject);
    procedure PasteSpecial1Click(Sender: TObject);
    procedure Paste1Click(Sender: TObject);
    procedure Object1Click(Sender: TObject);
    procedure Edit1Click(Sender: TObject);
    procedure Links1Click(Sender: TObject);
    procedure Copy1Click(Sender: TObject);
    procedure Cut1Click(Sender: TObject);
  private
    { Private declarations }
  public
    { Public declarations }
  end;

var
  Form1: TForm1;

implementation

uses OLECont2;

{$R *.DFM}

procedure TForm1.Exit1Click(Sender: TObject);
begin
    {End the application.}
    Application.Terminate;
end;

procedure TForm1.Edit1Click(Sender: TObject);
begin
    {Determine if there is any data on the clipboard to paste.  If so, enable
     our two paste options.}
    if Length(Clipboard.AsText) > 0 then
        begin
        Paste1.Enabled := True;
        PasteSpecial1.Enabled := True;
        end;

    {Determine if the user has selected the OLE container.  If so, enable the
     Copy option.}
    if (Form1.ActiveControl = OleContainer1) and (OleContainer1.State <> osEmpty) then
        begin
        Copy1.Enabled := True;
        Cut1.Enabled := True;
        end;
```

continues

Listing 10.4. continued

```
end;

procedure TForm1.Cut1Click(Sender: TObject);
begin
    {Copy the contents of the object to the clipboard.}
    OleContainer1.Copy;
end;

procedure TForm1.Copy1Click(Sender: TObject);
begin
    {Copy the object to the clipboard.}
    OleContainer1.Copy;
end;

procedure TForm1.Paste1Click(Sender: TObject);
begin
    {Paste a new object.}
    OLEContainer1.Paste;
end;

procedure TForm1.PasteSpecial1Click(Sender: TObject);
begin
    {Display the Paste Special dialog.}
    if OleContainer1.PasteSpecialDialog then

        {Determine whether the object is linked or embedded.}
        if OleContainer1.Linked then
            begin

            {Enable our link and object menu items.}
            Links1.Enabled := True;
            Object1.Enabled := True;
            end
        else

            {Enable our object menu item}
            Object1.Enabled := True;
end;

procedure TForm1.Links1Click(Sender: TObject);
begin
    {Display the links dialog box.}
    OLELinkInfo.ShowModal;
end;

procedure TForm1.Object1Click(Sender: TObject);
begin
    {Display the object properties dialog.}
    if Form1.ActiveControl = OleContainer1 then
        OleContainer1.ObjectPropertiesDialog;
end;

procedure TForm1.Object2Click(Sender: TObject);
begin
    {Display the Insert Object dialog.}
    if OLEContainer1.InsertObjectDialog then
```

```
        {Determine whether the object is linked or embedded.}
        if OleContainer1.Linked then
            begin

            {Enable our link and object menu items.}
            Links1.Enabled := True;
            Object1.Enabled := True;
            end
        else

            {Enable our object menu item}
            Object1.Enabled := True;
end;

end.
```

I think you'll find most of the functions fairly easy to understand since the new TOleComponent takes most of the work out of creating new containers. One of the problems with the current TOleContainer component is a lack of error trapping. Delphi will raise an exception if you try to use most of the methods provided with the component when the component is empty. Part of the task then is to ensure that you don't do anything with the container until the user fills it. That's why I start with all the Edit menu options disabled and enable them when certain events take place.

Notice especially the technique required to determine if the Clipboard has any data on it. Trying to paste a blank Clipboard to your OLE container usually results in some kind of an exception. Fortunately, the method for determining the current container state is easy. All you need to do is check the output of the State method. If the container is empty, you'll get a return value of osEmpty.

Now let's take a look at the second form for this example. Figure 10.22 shows components I used to create it. The basic form is a standard dialog box. I needed some way to display the link information when the user selected the Edit | Links command. Since there's only one object in this example, I used a combination of edit and list box components to display the information. Table 10.1 contains a list of the components and the changes you'll need to make to them. I considered several alternatives to this approach. For example, you could use a string grid to display the information for more than one linked OLE container. Obviously the list of OLE verbs associated with a particular object would require special processing in this case since the list is provided as part of a TStrings object.

Figure 10.22.
Displaying the link informa-
tion is an important part of
managing OLE links.

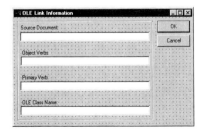

Table 10.1. OLE Link Information Dialog Component Settings.

Object	Property	Setting
edSourceDoc	TabStop	False
	ReadOnly	True
lbObjectVerbs	TabStop	False
edPrimaryVerb	TabStop	False
	ReadOnly	True
edOleClassName	TabStop	False
	ReadOnly	True

Once you get the form together, you can add the code in Listing 10.5 to make it work. As you can see, there isn't anything mysterious about this code. All I do is list some properties provided as part of the TOleComponent.

Listing 10.5. Code to add.

```
unit OLECont2;

interface

uses Windows, SysUtils, Classes, Graphics, Forms, Controls, StdCtrls,
  Buttons, ExtCtrls, Grids, OleCtnrs;

type
  TOLELinkInfo = class(TForm)
    OKBtn: TButton;
    CancelBtn: TButton;
    Bevel1: TBevel;
    Label1: TLabel;
    Label2: TLabel;
    Label3: TLabel;
    Label4: TLabel;
    edSourceDoc: TEdit;
    edPrimaryVerb: TEdit;
    edOleClassName: TEdit;
    lbObjectVerbs: TListBox;
    procedure FormShow(Sender: TObject);
  private
    { Private declarations }
  public
    { Public declarations }
  end;

var
  OLELinkInfo: TOLELinkInfo;

implementation
```

```
uses OLECont1;

{$R *.DFM}

procedure TOLELinkInfo.FormShow(Sender: TObject);
begin

    {Fill in the OLE link information.}
    edSourceDoc.Text := Form1.OleContainer1.SourceDoc;
    lbObjectVerbs.Items := Form1.OleContainer1.ObjectVerbs;
    edPrimaryVerb.Text := lbObjectVerbs.Items[Form1.OleContainer1.PrimaryVerb];
    edOleClassName.Text := Form1.OleContainer1.OleClassName;

end;

end.
```

It's time to look at the application in action. If you try the various menu options out, you'll find that they work much like the ones in the application programs I showed you before. In fact, you'll probably be surprised at just how similar. Microsoft provides the three different dialog boxes as part of the OLE support for Windows. Figure 10.23 shows the special OLE Link Information dialog that we created previously. Notice that it lists both of the verbs provided with this particular link.

Figure 10.23.
The OLE Link Information dialog provides some of the particulars about the selected object.

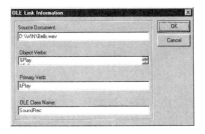

There are a few hidden goodies provided with Delphi's support for OLE. For one thing, if you right-click on an object, you'll see context menu. It's not as fancy as the one provided with applications like Word for Windows, but it's more than adequate to the task. You'll also find that double-clicking on an OLE object performs the default action for that object. Delphi also supports in-place editing. If you choose the Edit option from the Object Context menu, the server application will take over your application's menu and tool bars. It even supplies the tools bars if you didn't.

OLE Automation Controller

I find it amazing that some companies are determined to confuse whatever issues they can by changing the terms we use to refer to things. Take an OLE automation controller, for example. I think you'll quickly recognize that it's not something new—it's merely an extension of the OLE client we've used in the past. So why go with a new term for this rather old idea? Your guess is as good as mine. Suffice it to say that an OLE automation controller combines the usefulness of OLE with a consistent macro language that you can use to control the server from a client. If this sounds a lot like DDE, you're partially right. We'll take a look at the differences as the example in this section progresses.

DDE uses a rather arcane set of client macros to execute a particular set of steps on the server. An OLE automation controller gets rid of a lot of these extra elements. All you really need to do is start a conversation with an OLE automation server and then use its language to do whatever you need to do. I had previously mentioned that OLE automation uses a standard language set. That's not precisely true, although it could be true sometime in the future. All of the automation servers that I know right now use some form of Basic. In fact, if you need to work with any Microsoft product, you will indeed use a standard language. My concern at the moment is that as other vendors either accept or reject OLE automation as the way to go in the future, they'll try to inject a few proprietary language elements into the picture. The result will be the mess we've seen in the past with DDE— a really strange set of esoteric commands to get something really basic done.

You're probably going to see any number of really complicated ways of using an OLE automation controller in the future. What I thought I'd do in this chapter is show you the basics—not a basic example, but a simple one. Figure 10.24 shows the form for this example. I placed the changes you'll need to make to the components in Table 10.2.

Figure 10.24.
This example uses the memo component to display application information.

Table 10.2. OLE Automation Controller Form Component Settings.

Object	Property	Setting
Memo1	TabStop	False
	ScrollBars	ssVertical
	TabOrder	0
pbTest	Caption	'Test'
OnClick	pbTestClick	
pbExit	Caption	'Exit'
	OnClick	pbExitClick

I made the code for this example fairly simple, but it does illustrate the four things you'll need to do within any OLE automation controller application: start the server, retrieve information, perform tasks, and close the server. Listing 10.6 shows the code you'll need. Notice that I separated the four types of automation tasks with comments.

Listing 10.6. Code needed for the example.

```
unit OLEAutC1;

interface

uses
  Windows, Messages, SysUtils, Classes, Graphics, Controls, Forms, Dialogs,
  StdCtrls, OleAuto;

type
  TForm1 = class(TForm)
    Memo1: TMemo;
    pbTest: TButton;
    pbExit: TButton;
    procedure pbExitClick(Sender: TObject);
    procedure pbTestClick(Sender: TObject);
  private
    { Private declarations }
  public
    { Public declarations }
  end;

var
  Form1: TForm1;

implementation

{$R *.DFM}

procedure TForm1.pbExitClick(Sender: TObject);
begin
    {Exit the application}
    Application.Terminate;
end;

procedure TForm1.pbTestClick(Sender: TObject);
var
    MSWord: Variant;    {Our OLE Automation Server.}
begin
    {Every OLE automation conversation starts by creating a variant type
     variable and assiging an OLE object to it.  You start the converstation
     by launching the application server, not the application itself.}
    try
        MSWord := CreateOleObject('Word.Basic');
    except
        MessageDlg('Could not start Microsoft Word.', mtError, [mbOK], 0);
        Exit;
    end;
```

continues

Listing 10.6. continued

```
    {Clear the memo control before we use it.}
    Memo1.Clear;

    {Once you open the application for use, you can query it for information.  This
    section shows just a few of the things you can ask Word.}
    try
        {Some environmental settings.}
        Memo1.Lines.Add('Operating System Envionment: ' + MSWord.AppInfo(1));
        Memo1.Lines.Add('Word Version Number: ' + MSWord.AppInfo(2));
        Memo1.Lines.Add('Math Coprocessor Installed: ' + MSWord.AppInfo(13));
        Memo1.Lines.Add('Mouse Installed: ' + MSWord.AppInfo(14));
        Memo1.Lines.Add('Available Disk Space: ' + MSWord.AppInfo(15));
        Memo1.Lines.Add('Word Language: ' + MSWord.AppInfo(16));
        Memo1.Lines.Add('');

        {Some display settings.}
        Memo1.Lines.Add('List Separator: ' + MSWord.AppInfo(17));
        Memo1.Lines.Add('Decimal Separator: ' + MSWord.AppInfo(18));
        Memo1.Lines.Add('Thousands Separator: ' + MSWord.AppInfo(19));
        Memo1.Lines.Add('Currency Symbol: ' + MSWord.AppInfo(20));
        Memo1.Lines.Add('Clock Format: ' + MSWord.AppInfo(21));
        Memo1.Lines.Add('A.M. String: ' + MSWord.AppInfo(22));
        Memo1.Lines.Add('P.M. String: ' + MSWord.AppInfo(23));
        Memo1.Lines.Add('Time Separator: ' + MSWord.AppInfo(24));
        Memo1.Lines.Add('Date Separator: ' + MSWord.AppInfo(25));
        Memo1.Lines.Add('');
    except
        MessageDlg('Word can''t supply the requested information.', mtError, [mbOK], 0);
        Exit;
    end;

    {Up until this point, Word hasn't appeared on the Task Bar—Take a look.}
    MessageDlg('Take a look at the Task Bar, Word doesn''t appear there.  Let''s display
it.', mtInformation, [mbOK], 0);

    {Now let's display Word so we can see it.}
    try
        MSWord.AppShow;                 {Display the program.}
        MSWord.FileNew;                 {Open a new document.}
        MSWord.Insert('Hello World');   {Add some text.}
        MSWord.EditSelectAll;           {Select the entire document.}
    except
        MSWord.AppMinimize;
        MessageDlg('Error in Word BASIC Macro.', mtError, [mbOK], 0);
        Exit;
    end;

    {Give the user a chance to save the file.}
    try
        MSWord.FileSave;        {Display the File Save dialog.}
    except
        MSWord.AppMinimize;
        MessageDlg('Received error because you didn''t save the file.', mtError, [mbOK],
0);
    end;


    {Time to close the application and exit this procedure.}
```

```
    try
        MSWord.FileClose;
    except
        MSWord.AppMinimize;
        MessageDlg('Received error on closing Word.', mtError, [mbOK], 0);
    end;

end;

end.
```

You should notice several things about the pbTestClick procedure right away. First is the use of a Variant variable type. Previous versions of Delphi didn't provide this variable type since Pascal is a strongly typed language. This new variable type allows one variable to receive a variety of information input. The same variable can accept bitmaps or text. This flexibility is essential for an OLE automation application since you never know what kind of information the server will send.

The second feature you should notice about this code is that I've encapsulated every bit of contact with the server in a try…except structure. This is an important part of programming an OLE automation application. Just like any Delphi application, errors will raise an exception you can trap. For that matter, you can even trap specific exception types (although I didn't do that here to keep the code easy to read). You have to provide user-friendly feedback to the user and act on any errors that the server might encounter. You'll find that this is one of the big areas where OLE automation differs from DDE—you always get detailed feedback from the automation server.

Notice the level of interaction in this example as well. I'm mixing the two applications together as if they were a single unit. Contrast this with our DDE example earlier in the chapter. Using OLE automation makes your application feel as if it were one unit, not two applications having a conversation.

Let's take a look at our program in action. Figure 10.25 shows the results of the first part of the code. Notice that I've listed quite a few application specific settings. This is one of the things you'll need to decide on if you write an OLE automation server. Word makes just about every piece of information accessible, making it easy for you to determine its current status before you try to do something. I only show some of the more interesting pieces of information; Word provides a lot more bits of information through its BASIC language.

Figure 10.25.
The first part of our program queries Word about its current status.

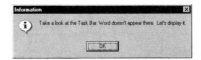

Another feature of OLE automation that makes it different from DDE is that you can't see the server. I purposely placed a message in the application so you could take a look for yourself. Word isn't anywhere on the Task Bar. You won't find it on the task list either. The only part of the application that's active at the moment is the automation server.

Of course, you can always make the application active. That's what I do in the next phase of the program as shown in Figure 10.26. Notice the first statement in this section, the MSWord.AppShow method. This is where you tell Word that you want to see the application interface. I then add some text and select it. Word would disappear from view again here, but I keep it in view by telling it to display the File Save dialog.

Figure 10.26.
You don't have to keep the server application in the background; you can usually force the server to display itself.

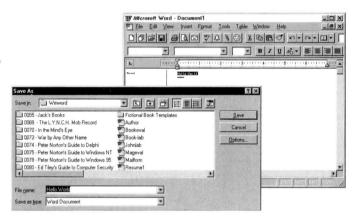

If you were to click Cancel in the File Save As dialog, Windows would return an error message to the application—it wouldn't display the error message itself. Contrast this to DDE where every application displays its own error messages. So, how does this help you? First, it allows your application to handle any error trapping. You even get to do it using standard Delphi programming techniques. Second, it'll help when it comes time to implement network OLE. Consider what would happen if an error occurred when using a remote application with DDE. How would the user recover from such an error? Handling the error locally means that you don't have to worry about what to do with an error when one does occur.

The last section of this program takes care of closing our server. In this case I only need to use Word's FileClose method. As with every other aspect of using OLE automation, the server will tell you if an error occurs when it shuts down. For example, Word will send an error message if you close it down without saving a file. The type of exception that Delphi returns tells you how to react to the situation. Since we really don't want to save the sample file I created, I simply display an error message saying that Word experienced problems shutting down.

OLE Automation In-Process Servers

Creating an OLE automation in-process server is a little more complex than the OLE automation controller we looked at in the previous section. You'll probably want to experiment with a very simple application and only one or two automation commands at first, then move on to something a little more complicated. I follow this three-step process in creating an in-process server shell.

- Write the application. You need a completely finished and debugged application to start the process. I'd suggest something very simple for your first project—in our case I'll show you a random string generator. The bottom line is that you'll want to pick a simple form of whatever kind of application you eventually want to create.

- Decide on an automation interface. Make sure you figure out the commands that you want to react to at the very beginning of the process. I usually pick something that provides me with some type of feedback that I can see instantly and save some of the more esoteric commands for later. You can add additional commands later, but try to stick with your original plan until you create a working OLE automation server. I usually start with one or two simple commands to test the lines of communication, then add commands as needed.

- Use Delphi's built-in features to create an automation server registry function shell—this also includes the automation unit that you'll use later to create an interface for your application. You have to tell the Windows registry that your application exists before you can use it. I'll show you how to do this in a few seconds; it's actually a lot easier than you might think since Delphi does some of the work for you. The only time you need to start working with the registry by hand is if you want to do something beyond the normal OLE automation functions.

- Add the interface commands to the automation unit. The last step is to add stub functions to call your automation commands. These stub functions define how your server will react to client application requests. In essence, the stub will call the real function within the automation server.

Let's start with the server application. Figure 10.27 shows the form we'll use for this example. All I've done is add two single line edit components and a couple of pushbuttons to the form. Notice that I added an up/down component as well so that I can use the mouse to change the string size during testing. You don't have to add this feature if you don't want to. Make sure you do associate the up/down component with the single line edit that controls string length.

Figure 10.27.
Our Automation Server uses a simple set of components to create random strings.

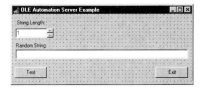

Once you get the form completed, add the code shown in Listing 10.7. The code itself is pretty easy to figure out. Notice that I did keep the string generation function separate from the pushbutton event handler code. I find that this reduces the amount of problems I have creating an interface to the server later.

Listing 10.7. Code to add.

```
unit OLEAutS1;

interface

uses
  Windows, Messages, SysUtils, Classes, Graphics, Controls, Forms, Dialogs,
  StdCtrls, ComCtrls;

type
  TForm1 = class(TForm)
    edLength: TEdit;
    Label1: TLabel;
    UpDown1: TUpDown;
    Label2: TLabel;
    edRandom: TEdit;
    pbTest: TButton;
    pbExit: TButton;
    procedure pbExitClick(Sender: TObject);
    procedure pbTestClick(Sender: TObject);
  private
    { Private declarations }
  public
    function CreateRandomString(iStringLength: Integer): String;
  end;

var
  Form1: TForm1;

implementation

{$R *.DFM}

procedure TForm1.pbExitClick(Sender: TObject);
begin
    {Exit the application.}
    Application.Terminate;
end;

procedure TForm1.pbTestClick(Sender: TObject);
var
    iStringLength: Integer;        {Length of the random string.}
begin
    {Get the length of our string.}
    iStringLength := StrToInt(edLength.Text);

    {Call our string generator.}
    edRandom.Text := CreateRandomString(iStringLength);

end;

function TForm1.CreateRandomString(iStringLength: Integer): String;
var
    iCount: Integer;               {Loop counting variable.}
    iCharValue: Integer;           {Current character value.}
begin
    {Start the random number generator.}
    Randomize;
```

```
    {Create a string of the specified length.}
    for iCount := 1 to iStringLength do
        begin
        {Create a string a character at a time.}
        iCharValue := Random(25) + 65;
        Result := Result + Chr(iCharValue);
        end;

end;

end.
```

Take some time to check the application out. Make sure it's fully functional before you take the next step. Obviously testing won't require much work in this case.

Once you have a functional application, it's time to add the OLE server capabilities to it. The first thing you'll need to do is add another unit. Select the Automation Object entry from the New page of the New Items dialog. Delphi will display a dialog similar to the one shown in Figure 10.28. I filled mine out as shown in the figure. The various entries you make here will affect the automatic entries that you'll see in the registry later. The OLE Class Name field is the name the client application will supply later to start the server. The Instancing field determines whether Windows will start additional copies of your server for each application that requests its services—a multiple instance selection starts one copy no matter how many applications need to access the server. Selecting single instance will start one copy of the server for each application, but it also reduces the number of problems you'll have trying to create a bullet proof interface.

Figure 10.28.
The Automation Object Expert dialog determines how other applications will interface with your server.

Once you fill out the Automation Object Expert dialog, click on OK and you'll see a new unit added to your application. This unit will contain everything needed to register your application as an automation server. What you'll need to do is add interface function or procedure stubs. Listing 10.8 shows the new unit.

Note: Make sure you add the OleAuto entry to the USES statement. There are some cases where Delphi doesn't do this for you automatically and you'll need it to make the application work.

Listing 10.8. **The new unit.**

```
unit OLEAutS2;

interface

uses
  OleAuto, OLEAutS1;

type
  TRandomString = class(TAutoObject)
  private
    { Private declarations }
  automated
    function CreateString(iStringLength: Integer): Variant;
  end;

implementation

function TRandomString.CreateString(iStringLength: Integer): Variant;
begin
  Result := Form1.CreateRandomString(iStringLength);
end;

procedure RegisterRandomString;
const
  AutoClassInfo: TAutoClassInfo = (
    AutoClass: TRandomString;
    ProgID: 'OLEAutoS.RandomString';
    ClassID: '{1D832740-648B-11CF-8C70-00006E3127B7}';
    Description: 'A Random String Generator';
    Instancing: acSingleInstance);
begin
  Automation.RegisterClass(AutoClassInfo);
end;

initialization
  RegisterRandomString;
end.
```

Notice the TRandomString.CreateString function. I provide a return type of Variant because this is an OLE automation server interface function. It's also important to note that I placed the forward reference for the function in the Automated section of the class declaration. As you can see though, the function itself is a mere stub that calls the real function in my main unit.

Everything you need to create a server is done. However, I do add one additional line of code to my project unit as follows: if Automation.ServerRegistration then Exit. It appears right before the form creation statement. The main purpose of this code is to prevent the application from starting when I register it with Windows. So, now that we've gotten a full-fledged server together, it's time to compile one last time. Once you have the server compiled, register it using the application name followed by: /REGSERVER. This tells the server to place the required entries in the registry and Windows who to call with automation requests.

Putting an application together to test the server is pretty simple. I started with the form shown in Figure 10.29. All it contains is a simple memo component and two pushbuttons. Listing 10.9 contains the source code for this example. The only thing I did here was start the server and call its one interface function several times.

Figure 10.29.

The OLE Automation Server Tester uses a very simple form to get the job done.

Listing 10.9. Source code for the example.

```
unit OLETest1;

interface

uses
  Windows, Messages, SysUtils, Classes, Graphics, Controls, Forms, Dialogs,
  StdCtrls, OleAuto;

type
  TForm1 = class(TForm)
    Memo1: TMemo;
    pbTest: TButton;
    pbExit: TButton;
    procedure pbExitClick(Sender: TObject);
    procedure pbTestClick(Sender: TObject);
  private
    { Private declarations }
  public
    { Public declarations }
  end;

var
  Form1: TForm1;

implementation

{$R *.DFM}

procedure TForm1.pbExitClick(Sender: TObject);
begin
    {Close the application.}
    Application.Terminate;
end;

procedure TForm1.pbTestClick(Sender: TObject);
```

continues

Listing 10.9. continued

```
var
    OLEAuto: Variant;          {Our automation server.}
    iCount: Integer;           {Loop counter variable.}
begin
    {Clear our memo control.}
    Memo1.Clear;

    {Start our server.}
    try
        OLEAuto := CreateOleObject('OLEAutoS.RandomString');
    except
        MessageDlg('Error Starting Server.', mtError, [mbOK], 0);
        Exit;
    end;

    {Add some random strings to our memo control.}
    for iCount := 1 to 25 do
        try
            Memo1.Lines.Add(OLEAuto.CreateString(iCount));
        except
            MessageDlg('Error Creating String.', mtError, [mbOK], 0);
            Exit;
        end;
end;

end.
```

Let's go ahead and test the server. Run the application and you'll see the server appear for a few moments, then disappear. Windows will only start it long enough to fulfill any application requests. You should see the results shown in Figure 10.30.

Figure 10.30.
The output from our OLE automation server program is a series of random strings.

OLE Automation Out-of-Process Servers

We've looked at how you can create an in-process server in the previous section. The short definition of an in-process server is that it provides the means to externally manipulate an application using a DDE-like macro language, but with a common interface and language. An out-of-process server shares this definition. So what makes an output-of-process server different? All those OLE specific DLLs on your hard drive are examples out-of-process servers. An out-of-process server resides in an external DLL—that's the first difference. You'll also find an out-of-process server as part of the shell extensions that Windows 95 provides, meaning that they exist outside the application they support—that's the second difference.

In essence, an out-of-process server is an OLE server, just like the one we created in the previous section, that resides in a DLL or other independent executable file. Obviously it's not quite that simple, but we can use this definition as a starting point for discussion in this chapter. We'll visit the differences between creating a Delphi DLL and an application in Chapter 15. Suffice it to say here that the basic logic you'll use is the same, but some of the interface elements are different.

The important consideration here is why you would use an out-of-process server in place of an in-process server. After all, creating an in-process server keeps all your code together and simplifies the process of using the server once you create it. There are several advantages to using a DLL—we'll cover them in Chapter 15. However, there are some advantages to using an out-of-process server that has nothing to do with its DLL heritage.

One of the most important advantages is that out-of-process servers are always more resource efficient than in-process servers. There are two reasons for this. First, an out-of-process server need not support an interface. The client application communicates directly with the business end of the code without any need for user interaction. Lack of an interface means that an out-of-process server uses less memory and processing cycles. Second, an out-of-process server also uses processing cycles more efficiently. It can run in the background as a separate task. Depending on the urgency of the information you need, you can always allow the user to perform other tasks in the foreground while he waits for the result of an out-of-process server call.

I find that out-of-process servers are also more flexible than in-process servers in several situations. You can't create a viable shell extension without an out-of-process server. (A shell extension allows you to create a new document from the Windows 95 context menu without opening the associated application. It also comes into play when you create a new object from the Insert | Object menu of a client application.) A shell extension must be memory efficient on most of the memory starved machines out there right now. I don't think the term "memory starved" is going to go away either— even when we all have 64 MB of RAM or more on our machine. It seems that you always need twice as much memory as you actually have to get the job done right. You'll also find that out-of-process servers share all the same flexibility advantages associated with DLLs.

There are also many disadvantages to using an out-of process server, most of which are associated with the fact that it's a DLL. I won't cover the DLL specific issues here—look in Chapter 15 for that information. From an OLE specific point of view, there's one big disadvantage that I feel we do need to cover here. Using out-of-process servers does present more than a few opportunities for program error. For example, what if a user upgrades his application, but for some reason the DLL that contains the out-of-process server doesn't get upgraded as well? You'll also find that you pay for the memory and processor cycle efficiency of an out-of-process server with a hit in speed. They just aren't as fast to use because you have to load them from a disk as a separate act. You also have to deal with the overhead of using a DLL, but I'll cover that problem later. Suffice it to say that you need to use the right tool for the job—in-process servers are good for one type of application, out-of-process servers for another.

Understanding the Windows 95 Registry

Now it's time to take a look at my least favorite part of OLE—the registry. You have to register your application before Windows will know what to do with it. (Fortunately, Delphi does most of the work for you—I've already explained just how much it does for you in the "OLE Automation In-Process Servers" section of this chapter.) This section doesn't give you a blow-by-blow description of every part of the registry. What it does provide is an overview of the registry as a whole, then a detailed description of the sections you'll need to work with to implement OLE.

The Windows 3.x registry was so simple that most people never gave it a second thought. About the only thing it contained were some file associations and a few OLE settings. You might have found a few bits and pieces of other information in there as well, but for the most part, even Windows ignored the registry. The lack of support for the Windows 3.x registry showed in the tools that Microsoft provided to manage it. About the only thing you could do with this version of the registry was edit the file associations. There wasn't much a developer could do to see how well his application was registered short of breaking out a hex editor and going through the registry one line at a time.

Along came Windows NT. This product contains a registry that is so complex that you need a four-year degree just to figure out the basics. (All you need to do is look at the Windows Resource kit for a few moments to realize just how complex the registry is.) The Windows NT registry contains every piece of information about everything that the operating system needs to know. This includes equipment settings, software configuration, network setup, and all the DLLs it needs to run applications. The tools for this version of the registry are also much improved from its predecessor. You can view all the various registry components using the editor that Microsoft provides. Not only that, but you can use the editor to modify more than simple file associations. The new version of RegEdit allows you to add and remove keys. You can also save specific keys out to disk for future reference. Suffice it to say, developers now have a tool that'll actually help them find problems in the way their application is registered with Windows. This added functionality should help reduce the problems that some users encounter trying to making OLE work.

Note: I'm going to concentrate my discussion on the Windows 95 registry in this chapter since both Windows 95 and Windows NT provide similar capabilities when it comes to OLE. The additional Windows NT registry entries are server and security specific.

Windows 95 uses a Windows NT-style registry. However, because Windows 95 is designed for workstation use and not as a file server, its registry is a bit less complex. You'll still see all the file associations that you did with Windows 3.x. The Windows 95 registry also contains all your equipment settings, software configuration information, and a list of DLLs to load. In essence, the registry has become the central repository of information for the Windows 95 operating system.

The Windows 95 registry also replaces two files that had bad reputations under Windows 3.x. Anyone who has spent time working with Windows 3.x knows about the fun of working with the SYSTEM.INI and WIN.INI files. The WIN.INI file holds Windows environment settings; it changes the way Windows interacts with the user. The SYSTEM.INI file contains hardware and device-driver configuration information; it changes the way Windows configures itself during startup. Of course, the distinction between these two files is somewhat blurred. For example, WIN.INI holds the serial port and printer configuration information.

These two poorly organized, cryptic files hold the vast majority of configuration information for the Windows 3.1 system. Every time the user adds an application to Windows 3.1, the application adds yet another heading or two and some additional entries to both files. On the other hand, when the user gets rid of an application, the entries don't go with it. They just sort of hang around and slow system performance. Some entries can even cause error messages or, in extreme circumstances, a system crash. Windows 95 still supports these rather archaic and difficult-to-understand files, but it prefers that applications use the new registry.

Note: Windows 95 copies the contents of SYSTEM.INI and WIN.INI into the registry whenever possible. The only reason that these two files exist is to meet the needs of Windows 3.x applications. You could remove both files from your hard drive if you didn't have any older applications to run. Of course, in reality, it'll be quite a while before you can get rid of either file.

You use the RegEdit utility to view and change the contents of the registry. It displays the registry in the format shown in Figure 10.31. Windows 95 uses two hidden files, USER.DAT and SYSTEM.DAT, to store the registry information, but RegEdit displays them as one contiguous file. Even though the RegEdit display might seem a bit difficult to understand at first, it's really not. The big difference between the registry and the Windows 3.1 alternative of SYSTEM.INI and WIN.INI is that the registry uses a hierarchical organization and plain English descriptions that you'll find easy to edit and maintain. Every application you add will add entries to this file, but the file's organization makes it easy for an application to remove the entries when you uninstall it. Even if you install an older application that doesn't understand the registry, you can still remove its entries with ease.

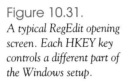

Figure 10.31.

A typical RegEdit opening screen. Each HKEY key controls a different part of the Windows setup.

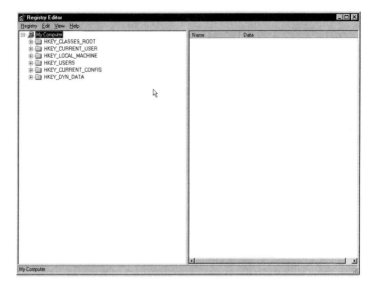

The Windows 95 registry uses two types of entries to maintain its organization: keys and values. Keys are a RegEdit topic. Think of a key as the heading that tells you what a particular section contains. Looking at all the keys provides an outline for a particular topic. The topics could range from the setup of each drive in the system to the file associations needed to configure the machine. The key at the top of the hierarchy usually contains generic information. Each subkey provides a little more detail about that particular topic. Keys always appear on the left side of the RegEdit window.

Values are the definition of a RegEdit topic; they describe the key in some way. Think of a value as the text that fills out the heading provided by a key. Values are like the text in this book, while keys are the headings that organize the text. A value can contain just about anything. For example, the value for a file association key can tell you which application Windows 95 will start when you double-click on a file that has that extension in Explore. A value could tell you which interrupt and I/O port settings a piece of hardware uses as well. Suffice it to say that you'll find the value you need using the keys, but you'll find the actual information you need by reading the values.

There are three types of values: binary, string, and DWORD. Usually, only applications use the binary and DWORD value types. Values usually store configuration data in a format that can't be understood by humans. Some applications use DWORD or binary values to store data. For example, you might find the score from your last game of FreeCell here. String values provide a lot of information about the application and how it's configured. Hardware usually uses string values as well for interrupt and port information. Values always appear on the right side of the RegEdit window.

Key entries also have a superset. I differentiate these particular keys from the rest because they are the major headings in the registry. During the rest of this discussion I refer to these special keys as *categories*. Think of categories as the chapter titles in a book. You need to go to the right chapter before you can find the right type of information. Information in one category might appear in the same order and at the same level in another category. The difference between the two is when Windows 95 uses the entries in one category versus another.

Categories are the six main keys under the "My Computer" key. Categories divide the registry into six main areas:

- HKEY_CLASSES_ROOT
- HKEY_CURRENT_USER
- HKEY_LOCAL_MACHINE
- HKEY_USERS
- HKEY_CURRENT_CONFIG
- HKEY_DYN_DATA

Each category contains a specific type of information. As you can see, the Windows 95 registry is much enhanced from its Windows 3.1 counterpart. Even though Windows 95 still has to use the infamous SYSTEM.INI and WIN.INI files for antiquated applications, the use of the registry for all other purposes does reduce the user's workload. Eventually, all applications will use the registry to store their configuration data. The following paragraphs provide an overview of the registry's categories.

HKEY_CLASSES_ROOT

There are two types of entries in the HKEY_CLASSES_ROOT category. The first key type (remember, a key is a RegEdit topic) is a file extension. Think of all the three-letter extensions you've used, such as .DOC and .TXT. Windows 95 still uses them to differentiate one file type from another. It also uses them to associate that file type with a specific action. For example, even though you can't do anything with a file that uses the .DLL extension, it appears in this list because Windows 95 needs to associate DLLs with an executable file type. The second entry type is the association itself. The file extension entries normally associate a data file with an application or an executable file with a specific Windows 95 function. Below the association key are entries for the menus you see when you right-click on an entry in the Explorer. It also contains keys that determine what type of icon to display and other parameters associated with a particular file type. Figure 10.32 shows the typical HKEY_CLASSES_ROOT organization.

Figure 10.32.

A typical HKEY_CLASSES_ROOT display. Notice the distinct difference between file extension and file association keys.

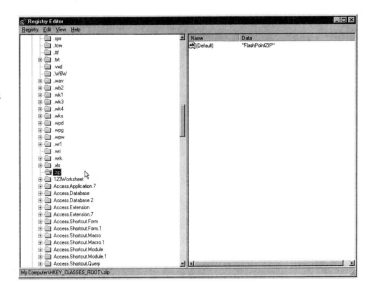

HKEY_CURRENT_USER

The HKEY_CURRENT_USER category contains a lot of "soft" settings for your machine. These soft settings tell how to configure the desktop and the keyboard. It also contains color settings and the configuration of the Start menu. All user-specific settings appear in this category.

The HKEY_CURRENT_USER category is slaved to the settings for the current user, the one who is logged into the machine at the time. This is differentiated from all the user configuration entries in other parts of the registry. This is a dynamic setting category; the other user-related categories contain static information. The registry copies the contents of one of the user entries in the HKEY_USERS category into this category and updates HKEY_USERS when you shut down.

This is the area where Windows 95 obtains new setting information and places any changes you make. As you can see from Figure 10.33, the keys within the HKEY_CURRENT_USER category are pretty self-explanatory in most cases. All the entries adjust some type of user-specific setting, nothing that affects a global element such as a device driver.

Figure 10.33.

*The
HKEY_CURRENT_USER
category contains all user-
specific settings.*

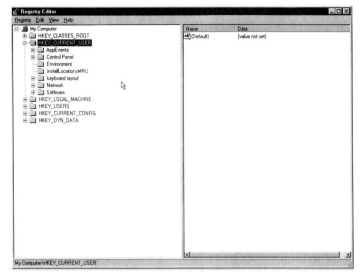

HKEY_LOCAL_MACHINE

The HKEY_LOCAL_MACHINE category centers its attention on the machine hardware. This includes the drivers and configuration information required to run the hardware. Every piece of hardware appears somewhere in this section of the registry, even if that hardware uses real-mode drivers. (Obviously, every detail of Windows NT hardware appears here since it doesn't allow the use of real mode drivers.) If a piece of hardware doesn't appear here, Windows 95 can't use it.

Note: Windows NT doesn't support plug and play, so the entries in this section don't quite match those used by Windows 95. I won't get into any details about these differences here since they won't affect you as a programmer unless you decide to write plug and play specific software—something that few of us will do in the near future.

A lot of subtle information about your hardware is stored in this category. For example, this category contains all the plug and play information about your machine. It also provides a complete listing of the device drivers and their revision level. This section might even contain the revision information for the hardware itself. For example, there's a distinct difference between a Pro Audio Spectrum 16+ Revision C sound board and a Revision D version of that same board. Windows 95 stores that difference in the registry.

This category does contain some software-specific information of a global nature. For example, a 32-bit application will store the location of its Setup and Format Table (SFT) here. This is a file that the application uses during installation. Some applications also use it during a setup modification. Applications such as Word for Windows NT store all their setup information in SFT tables.

The only application information that does appear here is global-configuration-specific like the SFT. Figure 10.34 shows a typical HKEY_LOCAL_MACHINE category setup.

Figure 10.34.

The HKEY_LOCAL_MACHINE category contains all the hardware and device-driver-specific information about your machine. It also contains the global application setup information.

HKEY_USERS

The HKEY_USERS category contains a static listing of all the users of this particular registry file. It never pays to edit any of the information you find in this category. However, you can use this category for reference purposes. The reason for this hands-off policy is simple: None of the entries here will take effect until the next time the user logs in to Windows 95, so you really don't know what effect they'll have until you reboot the machine. In addition, changing the settings for the current user is a waste of time since Windows 95 will overwrite the new data with the data contained in HKEY_CURRENT_USER during log out or shutdown.

One other problem is associated with using this category as your sole source of information. Windows 95 actually maintains multiple registries in a multiuser configuration—in some cases, one for each user who logs in to the system. Because of this, you never quite know where you'll find the information for a particular user. Windows 95 tracks this information, but it really is a pain for the administrator to have to do it as well. Besides, Microsoft thoughtfully provided a utility that helps the network administrator maintain the various registries. The Policy Editor utility enables the network administrator to maintain static user information with ease. Using the Policy Editor lets the network administrator bridge the various registry files on the system when each user provides his or her own Desktop configuration.

Figure 10.35 shows a setup that includes the default key. If this system were set up for multiple Desktops, each user would have a separate entry in this section. Each entry would contain precisely the same keys, but the values might differ from user to user. When a user logs in to the network, Windows 95 copies all the information in his profile to the HKEY_CURRENT_USER area of the registry. When he logs out or shuts down, Windows 95 updates the information in his specific section from the HKEY_CURRENT_USER category.

Figure 10.35.

Windows 95 creates one entry in the HKEY_USERS category for each user who logs in to the machine.

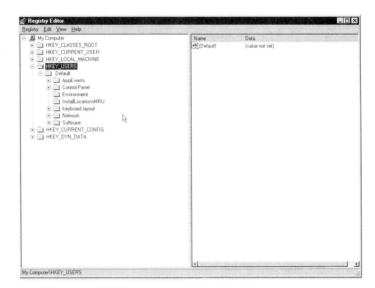

HKEY_CURRENT_CONFIG

The HKEY_CURRENT_CONFIG category is the simplest part of the registry. It contains two major keys: Display and System. Essentially, these entries are used by the GDI API (described later) to configure the display and printer.

The Display key provides two subkeys: Fonts and Settings. The Fonts subkey determines which fonts Windows 95 uses for general display purposes. These are the raster (non-TrueType) fonts that it displays when you get a choice of which font to use for icons or other purposes. Raster fonts are essentially bitmaps or pictures of the characters.

The Settings subkey contains the current display resolution and number of bits per pixel. The bits per pixel value determines the number of colors available. For example, 4 bits per pixel provides 16 colors, and 8 bits per pixel provides 256 colors. The three fonts listed as values under this key are the default fonts used for icons and application menus. You can change all the settings under this key using the Settings tab of the Properties for Display dialog box found in the Control Panel.

The System key looks like a convoluted mess. However, only one of the subkeys under this key has any meaning for the user. The Printers subkey contains a list of the printers attached to the machine. It doesn't include printers accessed through a network connection. Figure 10.36 shows the major keys in this category.

Figure 10.36.
The
HKEY_CURRENT_CONFIG
category echoes the settings
under the Config key of the
HKEY_LOCAL_MACHINE
category.

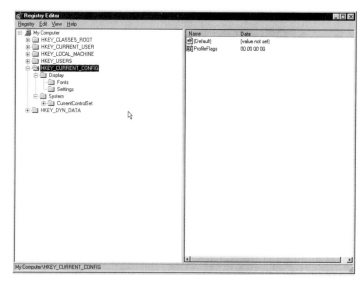

HKEY_DYN_DATA

The final category, HKEY_DYN_DATA, contains two subkeys: Config Manager and PerfStats. You can monitor the status of the Dynamic key using the Device Manager. The PerfStats key values appear as statistics in the System Monitor utility display. Figure 10.37 shows these two main keys and their subkeys.

Figure 10.37.
HKEY_DYN_DATA
contains registry entries for
current events. The values in
these keys reflect the current,
or dynamic, state of the
computer.

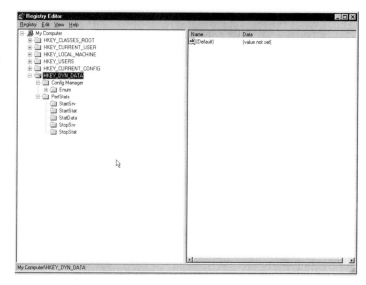

A Detailed Look at the OLE Part of the Registry

The previous section provides a whirlwind tour of the registry as a whole, now let's take a look at the OLE specific section. All the detail you need to know about OLE and the registry appears in the HKEY_CLASSES_ROOT category of the registry. It's the one you will probably change the most often as a programmer and a user. Don't let the deceptively simple appearance of this category fool you—it contains a lot more than the file associations of the past. In fact, the deeper you get into the registry as a programmer, the more you'll realize that it's actually a labyrinth of facts about an application's interface.

> **Tip:** You should always change your application file entries to make your working environment as efficient as possible. However, you should never change an executable file association. Changing an executable file extension such as .DLL could make it hard for Windows 95 to start your applications or could even crash the system. We'll look at the procedure for changing an application file association in the "Modifying File Associations" section of this chapter.

The following sections are going to show you the OLE part of the registry in detail. We'll explore the various types of information you can expect to find there. I'll also help you decrypt some of the entries that applications—including Delphi—make for you. Once you get a good idea of how the entries work, you'll know how to change the registry to meet your application's needs.

Special Extension Subkeys

Some file extensions such as .TXT provide a ShellX subkey (see Figure 10.38). In the case of .TXT and .DOC, the standard subkey is ShellNew (the most common key). The term ShellX means "shell extension." I like to think of it as an automated method of extending the functionality of Windows as a whole. When you right-click on the Desktop and look at the New option on the context menu, all the types of files you can create are the result of shell extensions. Even though ShellNew is the most common type of shell extension, a variety of other shell extensions are available. The actual number is limited only by your application vendor. For example, Microsoft Excel provides no less than three different shell extension entries for the .XLS file extension.

Figure 10.38.

The shell extension is a powerful OLE 2 feature that few applications implement.

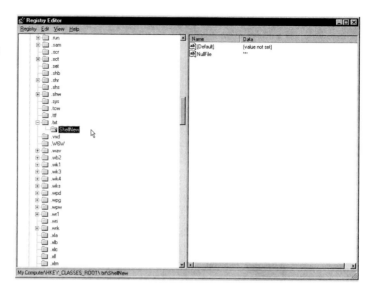

A shell extension is an OLE hook into Windows 95. Only an application that supports OLE 2 extensions can place a ShellX key into the registry. When you see this key, you know that the application provides some type of extended OLE-related functionality. For example, if you double-click on a shortcut to a data file that no longer exists, an application with the ShellNew shell extension will ask if you want to create a new file of the same type. (If you look at the values associated with ShellNew, there's always a NullFile entry that tells the shell extension what type of file to create.) This is one of the features of an out-of-process server that I mentioned previously. You can look at the other ShellX entries in the registry as a guideline for creating your own.

Tip: Sometimes a file type won't appear on the context menu even though the application provides support for it. Most of the time it happens with 16-bit applications that don't install correctly. You can use the shell extension behavior to create new files as if the context menu entry did exist. All you need to do is create a temporary file, place a shortcut to it on your Desktop, and erase the temporary file. (Make certain that the application provides a ShellNew shell extension before you do this.) Whenever you double-click on the shortcut, your application will create a new file for you. This behavior also works if you place the file shortcut in the Start menu folder.

There are other, more generic, shell extensions as well. For example, the * extension has a generic ShellX subkey. Below this you'll see a PropertySheetHandler key and a 128-digit key that looks like some kind of secret code. Actually, the 128-digit value *is* a secret code. It's a reference identifier for the DLL (a type of application) that takes care of the * extension. You'll find this key under the CLSID key. (CLSID stands for "class identifier.") The secret code is for the "OLE Docfile Property

Page." Looking at the value of the next key will tell you it exists in DOCPROP.DLL. This DLL provides the dialog that asks which application you want to use to open a file when no registry entry is associated with that extension.

> **Note:** Delphi provides one class identifier for you when you create a new automation object unit. This is part of the code that I showed in Listing 10.8. Notice the ClassID field in the AutoClassInfo structure. The Microsoft OLE 2 SDK provides a utility for creating class identifiers if you need one to add a shell extension or other entry to the registry. Don't try to create a class identifier on your own because you may inadvertently create one that conflicts with another application. Fortunately, the number of times you'll need to use more than one class identifier for an application is rare.

OLE 1 and OLE 2 Registry Entries

Windows 95 provides both OLE 1 and OLE 2 support; so do many of the applications. To show you just how organized the registry is, the OLE 1 and OLE 2 entries appear in different areas. You can always tell what kind of OLE support an application provides by checking its registry entries. If you see registry entries in one area of the registry, then you'll know that the application provides OLE 1 support. Registry entries in a second area of the registry show that the application provides OLE 2 support. In fact, the registry will often tell you more than the application's documentation does. You might find by looking at the registry that the application supports certain verbs. Think about a verb in OLE just like you would in a sentence; it represents some type of action that you can perform using the OLE capabilities of the application. I'll tell you a little more about verbs later on. Windows always places OLE 1 support information in the file association area. (I'll show you where the OLE 2 support appears in the registry after we look at OLE 1.) Figure 10.39 shows a typical setup, but the actual setup varies between applications. Table 10.3 describes the various entries in this area (plus a few not supported by this particular application). The OLE support provided by each application on your machine will probably differ from the one shown in the figure; this is only a sample for you to look at right now.

Figure 10.39.
*Windows places OLE 1
support in the file association
area of the registry.*

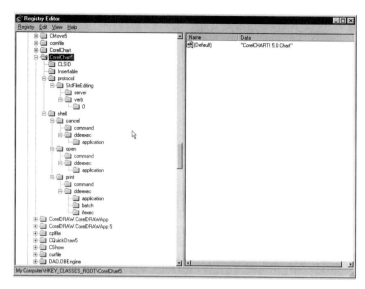

Table 10.3. OLE 1 Entries in the Windows Registry.

Entry	Description
CLSID	This is actually part of the OLE 2 entry even though it appears in the OLE 1 section. It's a pointer to an entry in the CLSID section of the category. C programmers use a special application to generate this 128-digit "magic number." If you look for this number under the My Computer | HKEY_CLASSES_ROOT | CLSID key (as we'll do in just a bit), you'll find the OLE 2 entries for this file association.
Insertable	Normally you won't see any value associated with this key. A blank value means that Windows can place this file association in the Insert Object (or equivalent) dialog provided by many applications, such as Word for Windows. Some OLE 1 objects aren't insertable for a variety of reasons.
Protocol	This is a header key (think of it as a heading in a book, a means to group like information together in one place). Underneath it you'll find all the standard actions that this OLE 1 application can perform. The only supported function in most cases is a standard file edit.
StdFileEditing	This key is another header. In this case it's the heading for all the keys that will define a particular action—standard file editing.
Server	You'll find the name of the application Windows will call to service any OLE 1 calls for this file association. The string always includes the application's name, extension, and path. If you ever run into a situation in which your OLE links worked yesterday but won't work

Entry	Description
	today, check this value to make certain the path matches the actual application location.
Verb	Several verbs are associated with an OLE 1 object. Each verb defines a specific action that the server will perform. This key doesn't have a value associated with it; its sole purpose is to organize actual verb entries. A client application can use only the verbs that are defined for a specific server.
	−3 = Hide, 0, 1 — This verb allows the client application to hide the server window. The first number after the verb is a menu flag. The second number is the verb flag. As a user, you don't need to worry about either value as long as you supply the values shown here (or use the settings provided by the vendor).
	−2 = Open, 0, 1 — This verb allows the client to open the server in a separate window rather than allow it to take over the client window.
	−1 = Show, 0, 1 — A client would use this verb to display the server window in its preferred state. The whole idea of a state can get to be quite complex. Think of it as the way the window looks, and you'll have a pretty good idea of what to expect from a user's point of view.
	0 = &Edit, 0, 2 — Every server provides this verb. It allows the client to call the server to edit the object.
	1 = &Play, 0, 3 — The only time you'll see this verb is when you're looking at some form of multimedia object.
RequestDataFormats	This entry allows the server to define what data formats it supports for retrieval purposes.
SetDataFormats	This entry allows the server to define what data formats it supports for storage purposes.

While you're still looking at this OLE 1 entry, you'll notice that I didn't cover anything under the Shell key. Each of these entries defines an action you can perform on the file using Explorer. The shell key is a refinement of the same entry used for file associations by File Manager. The entries defined here will appear on the context menu for each file of that type.

Now it's time to look at the OLE 2 part of the registry. You'll find these entries under the HKEY_CLASSES_ROOT | CLSID key. Each of the 128-digit numbers here represent a specific class of information. Not all of entries under the HKEY_CLASSES_ROOT | CLSID key are OLE 2 entries, but some of them are. You'll also find that not every application supports OLE 2. Your first clue that CorelChart supports it is the CLSID entry in the OLE 1 section. (We talked about the HKEY_CLASSES_ROOT | CorelChart5 | CLSID key in Table 10.3 and you saw it in Figure 10.39.) The HKEY_CLASSES_ROOT | CorelChart5 | CLSID entry is a pointer to the OLE 2 entry under the HKEY_CLASSES_ROOT | CLSID key. Figure 10.40 shows this key for CorelChart—the same application I used to describe an OLE 1 registry entry. Table 10.4 describes these entries in detail. An application doesn't necessarily need to provide every entry that I describe in Table 10.4 in the registry. It depends on what OLE 2 features the application vendor decided to support. You can use these registry entries to determine the capabilities of your application, just like you can with OLE 1.

Figure 10.40.

Windows places OLE 2 support in the file association area of the registry.

Table 10.4. OLE 2 Entries in the Windows Registry.

Entry	Description
AuxUserType	This key is a heading for all the user type keys that follow.
2	The 2 AuxUserType always contains the short name for the application. A client can use this name in a list box to identify the object's owner.
3	This key contains the full name of the application that created the object. Like the 2 key, a client could use the 3 key value to provide an English application name for the object.

Entry	Description
DataFormats	This key is a heading for all the data format keys that follow.
GetSet	This key is a subheading for all the data formats the server can store and retrieve. For example, an OLE server like Word for Windows would support a DOC, RTF, and standard text format. Its OLE 2 entries would reflect this fact. Each entry below this one defines a specific format type.
n = format, aspect, medium, flag	Each of the sequentially numbered keys contains a different format. Format contains the type of format as a string. You might find some as easy to read here as "Rich Text Format" or as cryptic as "Embed_Source". In every case, this string tells you the name of the format that the application supports. The client displays this string (for get formats) in the dialog box where you select the format you want to use when performing a Paste Special command. Aspect tells the client what display orientation the object supports. This usually means portrait and/or landscape. You'll usually find a value of 1 here for portrait. Medium contains the supported format as a computer-readable number. Flag tells the client whether this is a get, set, or both format—a value of 1 is get, a value of 2 is set, and a value of 3 is both.
DefaultFile	This entry works much like GetSet, except it identifies the default file format for this particular object.
DefaultIcon	The value of this key tells the client which application icon to use when displaying the object as an icon.
InProcHandler	This key contains the name of the in process handler. In most cases, this is OLE2.DLL unless the application provides its own OLE 2 handler. (A handler is a special program that helps two programs communicate.)
Insertable	Normally you won't see any value associated with this key. A blank value means that Windows can place this file association in the Insert Object (or equivalent) dialog provided by many applications such as Word for Windows. Some OLE 1 objects aren't insertable for a variety of reasons.

continues

Table 10.4. continued

Entry	Description
LocalServer	Every OLE 2 object must have a server. This key contains the name of the server on the local machine. Since OLE 2 doesn't support RPCs (remote procedure calls), you'll always need a local server.
MiscStatus	This key contains the default value for all data format aspects.
ProgID	The program identifier is a pointer back to the file association that this class identifier belongs to. The file association is always a character string of some sort. It's the same string that you look for when you try to find the file association that goes with a file extension in the HKEY_CLASSES_ROOT category. For example, if you looked at the ProgID value for Corel Chart, you would see CorelChart5. That's the same value we see in Figure 10.39 as the first key for the file association.
Verb	Several verbs are associated with an OLE 2 object. Each verb defines a specific action that the server will perform. This key doesn't have a value associated with it; its sole purpose is to organize actual verb entries. A client application can use only the verbs that are defined for a specific server. See Table 10.3 for a list of verbs and their meanings.
InProcServer	This is a special form of OLE server. Instead of calling the application that created the object, the client calls a DLL to handle any necessary display or editing functions. This has the advantage of speed; a DLL is faster than calling the executable. However, the programmer has to do a lot more coding to make this kind of interface work.
TreatAs	When this key is present, it contains the CLSID for another file format. The client can treat the current file format like the specified file format. For example, if you looked at the Paintbrush Picture OLE 2 entry, you would find a TreatAs value with the same 128-digit value as a Bitmap Image. This tells you that Windows 95 uses the same application to service Paintbrush Picture files as it does for Bitmap Image files. A little more research would tell you that the OLE 2 server for Paintbrush Pictures is Microsoft Paint.

Entry	Description
AutoTreatAs	This key forces the client to treat the current file format the same way it would treat the file format specified by the CLSID. From a user perspective it works just like the TreatAs entry that I described previously.
AutoConvert	Some objects' context menus contain a Convert option. This key allows you to automatically convert the current file format to the one identified by CLSID. For example, Word for Windows allows you to convert many types of data to a format that it specifically supports. This conversion process changes the embedded or linked object into a Word for Windows object. In other words, it changes the data into something that Word might have created itself.
Convertible	There are two levels of subkeys below this one. The first level contains two keys, Readable and Writeable. Below them are keys that contain a list of readable or writeable file formats that you can convert this file format to. For example, you'll find that Word for Windows supports several formats including Word Document. The number of entries in this area usually varies by the number of file filters you install for the application. For example, if you install WordPerfect file support for Word for Windows, then you'll likely find an entry for it here. Remember though that these are OLE 2 entries. Even if an application supports another application's file format as part of a Save As option, it still might not support it for OLE purposes.
Interfaces	This key contains a list of interfaces supported by the server. The value for this key will eventually contain the names of other ways of accessing the OLE server (other than from the local machine), but there aren't any applications that support it right now. For example, this entry could contain the types of network protocols that the application supports.

Summary

This chapter has covered more than a little territory in a very short amount of space. There are a lot of issues in developing an OLE application and it's no wonder that many developers are confused about what to do. The bottom line though is that you can't develop for Windows 95 and ignore OLE. Microsoft has made OLE 2 compliance one of the items on their list of Windows 95 criteria.

I've provided you with a lot of ancillary information in this chapter. For example, if you never decide to write anything more extensive than a simple OLE application, you'll probably never need to worry about the registry. Delphi does a good job of making the appropriate entries as long as you don't go outside of the areas that it supports directly.

The second the user decides that he needs to "fix" the registry or you decide that your application needs to provide some special form of support, you'll need the registry information I've provided in this chapter. In fact, if you do decide to enhance your application's functionality, you'll probably want to spend some time with the OLE 2 SDK as well.

Finally, we did spend some time looking at DDE. Is this particular specification dead? It probably won't be for a very long time. I don't think that DDE will be with us forever though. Microsoft and other companies are working on ways to provide DDE-like performance with all the functionality of OLE. So, for today you'll still need to think about DDE when designing an application. Tomorrow you'll probably need to look at something else. The bottom line is that you'll probably want to keep DDE's demise in mind as you design your application and make it easy to remove when the time comes for a change.

11

Delphi and Multimedia Programming

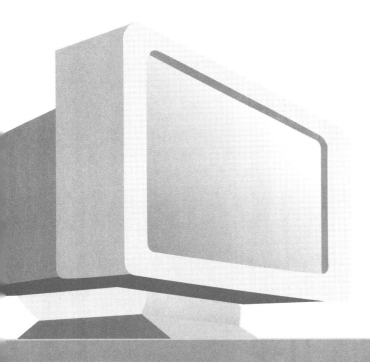

I was more than a little surprised when I starting working with Delphi's multimedia programming capabilities. Of all the programming capabilities that this product provides, I think you'll find multimedia programming the easiest to use. The differences between using Delphi and the Windows API directly are only amplified if you try to perform the same programming task using a language like C.

Lest you think that there isn't any programming involved at all, I'll tell you that you'll need to provide some code when it comes time to synchronize the various system elements. You'll also need to exercise some care when constructing your multimedia application. I found that it takes some planning to use all the features that Delphi provides in the most efficient manner possible.

I'm not going to cover every type of multimedia programming you'll ever run into in this chapter. What I plan to cover are the four major areas that most people will want to use in a standard application. Once you learn how to program these four areas, you'll find that the rest of the multimedia programming environment falls right into place.

We'll also spend some time looking at ways that you can improve the overall appearance of graphic multimedia elements. Again, we're not going to cover every potential artistic consideration here—there are entire books on design that'll help you in that regard—we'll cover things from the programmer's eye view of multimedia programming.

Peter's Principle: Programmer Efficiency—Using the Right Tool for the Job

There are a lot of situations where I combine DLLs that I've written in C/C++ with my Delphi applications. The reason is simple: I can get the job done faster using the C routines. C is the right tool for the job if you need to work with a lot of low level routines or perform extensive bit manipulation.

I've also used Delphi to access the Windows API directly when the native commands don't do everything I need them to (take a look at most of the chapters in the API section of this book and you'll see how). The Windows API often provides features that Borland chose to exclude from the VCL (look at the LZ functions in Chapter 9 for a specific example of excluded features).

However, there are times when I'd actually make more work for myself and wouldn't gain any functionality at all by using C to access them. The multimedia functions we'll look at in this chapter is one such case. Since Delphi provides everything I need to use, I won't need to access the Windows API directly either.

Programmer efficiency is often more a matter of using the right tool for the job than it is knowing the fanciest coding technique for getting the job done. Make sure you take the time to build skills using more than one programming language—each language is a new tool at your disposal and can make the difference between getting the job done fast or perhaps not at all.

Wave File Programming

Wave file programming is probably the easiest form of multimedia addition there is. It's also the best understood; it's been with us since before Windows 3.x came out. I still have more than a few DOS utilities for creating and playing wave (WAV) files.

The most common (and only as far as I know) method for playing wave files on your PC is through the sound board. In the past, you simply configured the IRQ, I/O port, and DMA settings of the sound board and left things at that. Sound boards today provide features that allow you to do more than just record and play wave files; they allow you to customize the way that they store and read those files. Windows 3.x hasn't really kept up with these latest developments. You'll find very few configuration options here. On the other hand, Windows 95 has changed the way that you need to view sound boards and the way they work with the system.

I'm going to take the time to look at configuration and setup options for your sound board under Windows 95. The first two subsections take care of that need. Once we get some theory out of the way, I'll show you how to program the sound board using Delphi's native capabilities. I think you'll find it surprisingly easy to produce a very polished application using this product.

Configuring Your Sound Board

There are all kinds of sound. You don't have to settle for the mediocre level of sound that Windows 3.x provided. Windows 95 provides the controls required to fully exploit the expanded capabilities that modern sound boards provide. All you need to do to start using these capabilities is to adjust the settings found in the Audio Properties dialog. To access this dialog, right-click on the Speaker icon on the Taskbar, and select Adjust Audio Properties. You should see a dialog similar to the one shown in Figure 11.1.

Figure 11.1.
The Audio Properties dialog allows you to make full use of the audio capabilities your system provides.

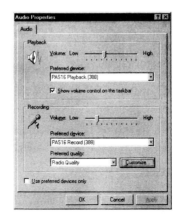

Note: You can also access the Audio Properties dialog by double-clicking on the Multimedia applet in the Control Panel. What you'll see is a tabbed dialog containing several pages worth of configuration settings. This particular applet also contains settings for video, MIDI, and CD music. Most important of all are the settings you can access on the Advanced page. These settings provide a multimedia specific subset of the settings you'll find in the Device Manager.

Windows 95 will always play back any audio using the full capability of the sound board you select. However, there's a lot of room to customize the recording of sound. Microsoft thoughtfully provided three default recording selections. Each selection reflects the kind of sound recording quality these settings will give you: CD, radio, or telephone.

The actual level of quality you get has to do with the frequency, or the number of samples of sound that Windows takes per second. The more samples it takes, the better the quality of your sample. Using stereo and 16-bit samples also improves the sound quality, as does the recording format. Before we go much further, let's define a few terms.

- Sample rate: The number of times per second that Windows samples the microphone input line. A higher setting means that you get more samples. More samples always provide a better playback.

- Sample size: Windows supports two sample sizes: 8-bit and 16-bit. A 16-bit sample allows you to record a broader range of values. This means that you can better differentiate between various sounds, resulting in a higher-quality recording.

- Format: There are many ways to store a sound, just as there are many ways to store graphics. Some formats take more space but preserve image quality better. Likewise, some audio formats are better than others at preserving sounds. You'll have to experiment to see which one sounds the best to you. Most recordings use the PCM (pulse-code modulation) format. Since this is the most common format, you'll probably want to use it when you need to exchange the recording with someone else, unless there's an overriding reason to do otherwise.

- Number of channels (mono or stereo): You probably already know the implication of this setting. A stereo recording uses two microphones to record the sound from different perspectives. During playback, a stereo recording has much greater depth than a mono recording of the same quality.

Now that you have some ideas of the ways you can customize sound under Windows 95, let's look at the dialog you use to do it. Click on the Customize pushbutton to see the Customize dialog, shown in Figure 11.2.

Figure 11.2.
Use the Customize dialog to change the way you record sound under Windows 95.

Notice that there are two comboboxes. One determines the recording format, and the other allows you to select from a variety of options, including the sample rate, sample size, and number of channels. Notice that this combobox also tells you the storage requirements for the sample in kilobytes per second. This is the number of kilobytes that the sample would consume for each second you recorded. Obviously, some formats can eat a lot of storage space quickly.

You can save any custom settings that you create using the Save As pushbutton. Windows will store the settings and present them later in the Preferred Quality listbox of the Audio Properties dialog.

So what's the best way to customize these settings? Remember that the better the quality, the higher the storage requirements. I tend to prefer stereo over mono recordings because the depth of sound can make up for a host of other problems. The trouble is if you have only one microphone. In that case, selecting stereo is a waste of disk space since you can record only one channel of information. Selecting 16-bit sound improves quality a great deal for a very small increase in storage size. You get a sample 2^{16} (65,536 possible combinations) versus 2^8 (256 possible combinations) for a mere doubling of disk space. Unless you're recording music, the highest sampling rate you need is 22,050 Hz. In fact, using 11,025 for simple voice recordings usually proves sufficient.

Tip: If your users ever complain that the sound coming out of their system just doesn't sound right, you may want to check the Multimedia applet in the Control Panel. There's an advanced page of multimedia settings beside the four pages described in this chapter. You'll want to check the basic settings first, then turn to this advanced page to see if the user has accidentally changed any settings in a way that adversely affected the sound quality. For example, the Wave Audio Devices dialog accessed through this dialog will allow you to change the amount of memory set aside for playing wave files. A larger cache could result in better audio performance.

Creating a Simple Wave File Player

We're actually going to end up creating a full-fledged multimedia viewer and recorder by the time we get finished with this chapter. I felt that the first step should be to get the wave audio portion of the program to work. Let's begin by creating the form shown in Figure 11.3. It contains the four file related controls you'll find under the System tab of the component palette: TFileListBox,

TDirectoryListBox, TDriveComboBox, and TFilterComboBox. I also added a standard TEdit control and several labels to make it easier to find what you need on the drive. The TMemo control isn't actually used right now, but we'll need it later on to display videos. I wanted to reserve space for it as part of the initial design process. The TTimer and TTrackBar controls work together to show you where you're at in the current multimedia file. I'll also show you how to use the TTrackBar control to change the current position within the multimedia file. The TMediaPlayer control is what will make using multimedia under Delphi so easy. Except for a few commands and parameter changes, you'll find that this control provides everything you need without a lot of programming. Finally, I added an Exit pushbutton. It looks a little lonely right now, but we'll change that as the chapter progresses. Once you get all the controls in place, you'll need to change some parameters as shown in Table 11.1.

Figure 11.3.
Our Multimedia Player and Viewer begins with this simple dialog.

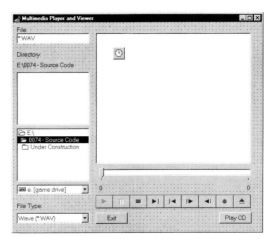

Note: The figure shows a Play CD button. We won't actually use that button right this second. I show you how to add a CD play function to it later in the chapter.

Table 11.1. Wave File Multimedia Programming Example Control Changes.

Object	Property	Setting
MCIFile	Text	*.WAV
	OnChange	MCIFileChange
	OnKeyPress	MCIFileKeyPress
FileListBox1	FileEdit	MCIFile
	Mask	*.WAV
	OnClick	FileListBox1Click

Object	Property	Setting
DirectoryListBox1	DirLabel	DirName
	FileList	FileListBox1
	OnChange	DirectoryListBox1Change
DriveComboBox1	DirList	DirectoryListBox1
FilterComboBox1	FileList	FileListBox1
	Filter	'Wave (*.WAV) | *.WAV | Video (*.AVI) | *.AVI | MIDI (*.MID) | *.MID | MIDI (*.RMI) | *.RMI | All (*.*) | *.*'
Timer1	Enabled	False
	Interval	125
	OnTimer	Timer1Timer
Memo1	TabStop	False
	ReadOnly	True
TrackBar1	Enabled	False
	Orientation	tbHorizontal
	TabStop	False
	TickMarks	tmBottomRight
	TickStyle	tsManual
	OnChange	TrackBar1Change
TrackLen	Alignment	taRightJustify
	Caption	' 0'
MediaPlayer1	Display	Memo1
	OnClick	MediaPlayer1Click
ExitApp	Hint	Exit Application
	Caption	Exit
	ParentShowHint	False
	ShowHint	True
	OnClick	ExitAppClick

Writing the playback portion of the code was easy—Delphi almost wrote it for me. Listing 11.1 shows most of the code for both the record and playback portions of this example. I've added a few bells and whistles to this example. The TrackLen label allows me to display the total length of the track in seconds. Notice how I used Timer1 to control the position of the pointer on TrackBar1. Every second, I tell the track bar to match its pointer position to that of the media player.

Note: As of this writing, there is a bug in the way that Delphi reads some types of wave audio files. It has to do with the sample rate of the file. Every wave file contains a sample rate and an average sample rate (we'll see how this works in a second). Delphi reads the sample rate field, but ignores the average sample rate field. The result is that you'll get an inaccurate track length reading on wave audio files that use two different settings—most generally a sound effect like a bell or a whistle. The SHRED.WAV file provided by Windows NT falls into this category. Try viewing it with both the built-in Windows media viewer and the viewer I just created with Delphi and you'll see the difference.

Listing 11.1. Code for the record and playback.

```
unit MCI1;

interface

uses
  Windows, Messages, SysUtils, Classes, Graphics, Controls, Forms, Dialogs,
  FileCtrl, StdCtrls, MPlayer, ExtCtrls, ComCtrls;

type
  TForm1 = class(TForm)
    FileListBox1: TFileListBox;
    DirectoryListBox1: TDirectoryListBox;
    DriveComboBox1: TDriveComboBox;
    FilterComboBox1: TFilterComboBox;
    MediaPlayer1: TMediaPlayer;
    Label1: TLabel;
    MCIFile: TEdit;
    Label2: TLabel;
    DirName: TLabel;
    ExitApp: TButton;
    TrackBar1: TTrackBar;
    Memo1: TMemo;
    Timer1: TTimer;
    Label3: TLabel;
    Label4: TLabel;
    TrackLen: TLabel;
    procedure ExitAppClick(Sender: TObject);
    procedure Timer1Timer(Sender: TObject);
    procedure MediaPlayer1Click(Sender: TObject; Button: TMPBtnType;
      var DoDefault: Boolean);
    procedure TrackBar1Change(Sender: TObject);
    procedure MCIFileChange(Sender: TObject);
    procedure FileListBox1Click(Sender: TObject);
    procedure MCIFileKeyPress(Sender: TObject; var Key: Char);
  private
    procedure OpenFile;
```

```
  public
    { Public declarations }
  end;

var
  Form1: TForm1;

implementation

uses
    WAV_Def;

{$R *.DFM}

procedure TForm1.ExitAppClick(Sender: TObject);
begin
    {Exit the application.}
    Halt;
end;

procedure TForm1.Timer1Timer(Sender: TObject);
begin
    {Change the trackbar position as needed.}
    Trackbar1.Position := MediaPlayer1.Position;

    {Check to see if we're at the end of the file.  If we are, then
     reset everything for the next file.}
    if Trackbar1.Position = Trackbar1.Max then
        begin
          Timer1.Enabled := False;
          Trackbar1.Position := 0;
          end;
end;

procedure TForm1.MediaPlayer1Click(Sender: TObject; Button: TMPBtnType;
  var DoDefault: Boolean);
begin
    {Select an action based on the button the user pressed.}
    case Button of

        {Start the pointer moving across the track bar.}
        btPlay: Timer1.Enabled := True;

    {Stop track bar pointer movement, but leave it in its current position.}
        btPause: Timer1.Enabled := False;

        {Check the recording status.  If we're recording, ask the user if they
         want to save the current media player contents.}
        btStop:
            begin
              if MediaPlayer1.Mode = mpRecording then
                  if MessageDlg('Save the recorded file?', mtConfirmation, [mbYes,
mbNo], 0) = mrYes then
                      MediaPlayer1.Save;
              end;

        {As with play, we need to start the pointer moving across the track
```

continues

Listing 11.1. continued

```
                bar.  In this case we also need to start recording the data coming
                into the sound board's Line In input.}
             btRecord:
                 begin
                  Timer1.Enabled := True;
                  MediaPlayer1.StartRecording;
                  end;
          end; {case button of}
end;

procedure TForm1.TrackBar1Change(Sender: TObject);
begin
     {Change the position of the multimedia player to match our pointer.}
     MediaPlayer1.Position := TrackBar1.Position;
end;

procedure TForm1.FileListBox1Click(Sender: TObject);
begin
     {Assign the filename to our edit box.}
     MCIFile.Text := FileListBox1.Filename;

     {Open the selected file.}
     OpenFile;
end;

procedure TForm1.MCIFileChange(Sender: TObject);
begin
     {Allow the user to enter a filename directly.}
     MediaPlayer1.Filename := MCIFile.Text;
end;

procedure TForm1.MCIFileKeyPress(Sender: TObject; var Key: Char);
var
     mBuffer: TFileStream;          {Pseudo contents for our new file.}
     WaveHeader: WavHeader;         {Wave file header record.}
begin
     {Check to see if the user pressed Enter.}
     if Key = #13 then
         try
             {If so, try opening the file.}
             OpenFile;
         except
             {If the file doesn't exist, then give the user an opportunity
              to create it.}
             on EMCIDeviceError do
                 begin

                    {If the user chooses not to create the file, then reset
                     our setup and exit.}
                    if MessageDlg('File Doesn''t Exist, Create it?', mtError, [mbYes, mbNo],
0) = mrNo then
                        begin
                         MediaPlayer1.Filename := '';
                         Exit;
                         end;

                    {If the user wants to create a new file, then perform
```

```
 the required setup.}
case FilterComboBox1.ItemIndex of
    {Wave Audio}
 0: MediaPlayer1.DeviceType := dtWaveAudio;

    {AVI File}
    1: begin
         ShowMessage('This record feature not implemented yet.');
          Exit;
       end;

    {MID MIDI File}
    2: begin
         ShowMessage('This record feature not implemented yet.');
          Exit;
       end;

    {RMI MIDI File}
    3: begin
         ShowMessage('This record feature not implemented yet.');
          Exit;
       end;
    end;

{Get the media player buffer ready for recording.}
mBuffer := TFileStream.Create(MCIFile.Text, fmCreate);

{Initialize the header to record 1 channel at 11025 samples
 per second and 44100 average samples.  Use byte alignment
 and an 8-bit data recording.}
InitWavHeader(WaveHeader, 1, 11025, 44100, 4, 8);

{Output the WAV header to a file.}
mBuffer.Write(WaveHeader, SizeOf(WaveHeader));

{Get rid of the file stream we previously created.}
mBuffer.Destroy;

{Open the media player.}
MediaPlayer1.Open;

{Start at the beginning of the buffer.}
MediaPlayer1.Position := 0;

{Set our track bar up.}
TrackBar1.Enabled := True;
TrackBar1.Max := MediaPlayer1.TrackLength[1];

{Display the actual track length in seconds.}
with TrackLen do
    begin
    Caption := IntToStr(MediaPlayer1.TrackLength[1] div 1000);
    Caption := Caption + '.';
    Caption := Caption + IntToStr(MediaPlayer1.TrackLength[1] mod
1000);

    Caption := Caption + ' Sec';
    end;
end; {on EMCIDeviceError do}
```

continues

Listing 11.1. continued

```
        end; {except}
end;

procedure TForm1.OpenFile;
begin

    {Open the multimedia file.}
    if (MCIFile.Text <> ") then
    MediaPlayer1.Filename := MCIFile.Text;
    MediaPlayer1.Open;

    {Set our track bar up.}
    TrackBar1.Enabled := True;
    TrackBar1.Max := MediaPlayer1.TrackLength[1];

    {Display the actual track length in seconds.}
    with TrackLen do
        begin
        Caption := IntToStr(MediaPlayer1.TrackLength[1] div 1000);
        Caption := Caption + '.';
         Caption := Caption + IntToStr(MediaPlayer1.TrackLength[1] mod 1000);
         Caption := Caption + ' Sec';
         end;
end;

end.
```

One of the things you should notice about this example is that recording also looks too simple. And it is—as long as you record over an existing file. All you have to do is open the existing file and tell the media player to start recording.

The problems start when you want to create a new file. Delphi doesn't know what to do if you tell it to start recording when there is no file loaded. How can it record a multimedia file when there aren't any parameters for it to use to create the recording? That's the question answered by the TForm1.MCIFileKeyPress procedure in Listing 11.1.

Look through the example carefully, and you'll see a couple of handy tips for handling file exceptions. First, I take control of the exception from Delphi. The Try...Except part of the procedure does the work for you. What you're telling Delphi is to try to open the file, and then if the file doesn't exist, perform the steps you provide to fix the problem. I find this type of procedure handy for all kinds of situations—especially on the network. What happens if two users want to use the same file at the same time? Are you simply going to allow your application to fail with some strange message that the user will never figure out? This procedure shows a way around this problem—it's easy to implement and will definitely make life easier for the user as well.

Once the procedure figures out that the user has entered the name of a non-existent file, it asks if the user wants to create the file. Notice that I only implemented a procedure for creating wave files. You can use the same techniques to add other file types as well. I wanted to keep the example short and easy to understand so I only implemented one case—the wave file. If users enter a non-existent filename and answers Yes when asked if they want to create the file, I create one for them.

Now it's time to look at the actual wave file format. You need to create a "blank" file for Delphi to use. Remember, you have to tell it what parameters to use when creating your file. In fact, you could probably extend this particular application to display a dialog that asks the user what parameters to use. I chose to hard code the file format. Listing 11.2 shows the wave file format and the initialization procedure you'll need to create the required record.

Listing 11.2. Wave file format and initialization procedure.

```
unit WAV_Def;

interface

uses
    Windows;

type
    {".WAV" file definition}
    WavHeader = record
        RIFF: array[1..4] of char;      {4 bytes 'RIFF'}
        FileLength: DWORD;              {4 bytes Length of the file - 8 bytes}
        WAVE: array[1..4] of char;      {4 bytes 'WAVE'}
        fmt: array[1..4] of char;       {4 bytes 'fmt '}
        InfoLength: DWORD;              {4 bytes Length of the 'Info' block 10h}
        Format: WORD;                   {2 bytes Format tag 01h}
        Channels: WORD;                 {2 bytes Number of channels (1=mono, 2=stereo)}
        SamplesSec: DWORD;              {4 bytes Samples per second}
        AveSampSec: DWORD;              {4 bytes Average samples per second}
        BlockAlign: WORD;               {2 bytes Block alignment (01/02/04)}
        BitsSample: WORD;               {2 bytes Bits per sample (08/16)}
        data: array[1..4] of char;      {4 bytes 'data'}
        DataLength: DWORD;              {4 bytes Data length}
        SData: array[1..40] of WORD;    {X bytes Sample data }
         end;

procedure InitWavHeader(var Header: WavHeader; Channels: WORD; Samples: DWORD;
                AverageSamples: DWORD; BlockAlign: WORD; BitsSample: WORD);

implementation

procedure InitWavHeader(var Header: WavHeader; Channels: WORD; Samples: DWORD;
                AverageSamples: DWORD; BlockAlign: WORD; BitsSample: WORD);
var
    iCounter: WORD;

begin
    Header.RIFF := 'RIFF';
    Header.FileLength := SizeOf(Header) - 8;
    Header.WAVE := 'WAVE';
    Header.fmt := 'fmt ';
    Header.InfoLength := $10;
    Header.Format := 1;
    Header.Channels := Channels;
    Header.SamplesSec := Samples;
    Header.AveSampSec := AverageSamples;
    Header.BlockAlign := BlockAlign;
```

continues

Listing 11.2. continued

```
    Header.BitsSample := BitsSample;
    Header.data := 'data';
    Header.DataLength := SizeOf(Header.SData);
    for iCounter := 1 to 40 do
        Header.SData[iCounter] := iCounter * 2;
end;

end.
```

The file format itself is pretty straightforward. However, there are a few Delphi problems that you need to worry about. First, it won't record over an empty file. You must provide some sample data in the file for Delphi to read. I use the for loop at the end of the procedure to take care of this need. Another problem is in 16-bit recording. I couldn't get Delphi to work with anything but 8-bit files. Hopefully Borland will have this problem fixed by the time you read this. Notice the use of constants in the wave file format. The header always begins with the key word RIFF, followed by the file length—the 8 bytes already consumed by the first two fields. Next you'll see WAVEfmt. The space after fmt is extremely important since the file won't work without it. The information part of the header is always 16 bytes long, so the InfoLength field will always contain $10. The procedure does need the number of channels (mono or stereo), sample rate, average sample rate, the block alignment, and the size of the sample (8 or 16-bits) as input. The data section of the file always begins with the key word "data" (note the lowercase), followed by the data length and the data itself.

Other Wave File Recording Methods

Delphi does come with a special multimedia unit named MMSYSTEM that you can use to create a wave file or perform certain types of low level tasks. All you need to do is add MMSYSTEM to the Uses clause of your unit.

The central function that the MMSYSTEM provides is MciSendCommand. It requires—not surprisingly—four parameters. You'll quickly find that this function acts just the same as the PostMessage function did in Chapter 5. What you're really doing is posting a special kind of message to the Windows multimedia system. The first parameter is the device identification (a handle to the device if you want to look at it that way). The second parameter is a message or command—what you want the device to do. The third (WORD) and fourth (long integer) parameters are variables containing any data needed to execute the command. The first variable always contains the flags used to adjust the way that the command works. For example, when using the MCI_CLOSE command you can choose to wait for the command to complete or simply send the command and continue with the current activity. Normally the second of these variables will contain a pointer to a data structure since multimedia requires a significant amount of configuration data. The most common data structure is MCI_GENERIC_PARMS.

Warning: You can usually depend on a device to support the MCI_GENERIC_PARMS and other generic MCI data structures. However, some specialty devices like videodisc players may require additional information that the generic structure doesn't provide. The extended information may affect the way the device reads or writes data. You may even find that the device won't work at all without this additional information. The only problem is that Delphi and the MCI system won't raise an error when this happens. You'll find that the device doesn't work as expected, but lacks the information needed to correct the problem. It's up to you as the programmer to know the needs of the device you want to access and provide the appropriate data structure. In most cases you'll find this information in a developer guide provided by the vendor. For example, Creative Labs and Media Vision both provide developer kits for their sound boards. You'd need this information to access advanced capabilities like voice.

So, now that you have an idea of how to send commands and messages, the next obvious question is what kind of things you can do. There really isn't a limitation when you think about it; all a device would need to do is add its command set to those supported by the MCI (media control interface) system. In fact, you'll find some device drivers do just that. We'll stick to the mainstream devices in this chapter though. Table 11.2 shows the more common MCI commands and describes their use. You'll find that you can perform the same types of commands using this low level method that you can using the Delphi classes. The difference is the level of control that you can achieve using this method. The trade-off is that you have to do everything manually. For instance, in our previous example we didn't have to do much to play a wave file. Using MCI commands would require a lot more work on your part to accomplish the same task.

Table 11.2. Common MCI Messages.

Command	Description
MCI_CLOSE	This message releases a device that you previously opened using the MCI_OPEN command.
MCI_COPY	I find that this particular message is very handy when it comes to wave files. It allows you to place a copy of the MCI element data on the clipboard, and then paste it somewhere else. You could easily use this as part of a DDE implementation. Support for this particular command is optional though, so you'll want to use the MCI_GETDEVCAPS command to verify that the device supports it.
MCI_CUT	You can use this command in the same way as the MCI_COPY command. The only difference is that this command removes the

continues

Table 11.2. continued

Command	Description
	data from the MCI element after placing it on the clipboard. Normally a device that supports the copy command will also support this command (the exception being read-only devices like CD-ROM drives).
MCI_DELETE	Use this command to permanently remove all or a specific range of data from an MCI element. Unlike MCI_CUT, the data isn't placed on the clipboard, so there isn't any way to undo this command. I prefer to use MCI_CUT whenever possible in place of this command so that I can provide the user with at least one level of undo at a very low cost in programming time.

Note: The MCI_DELETE command is the first time you need to decide which data structure to use. Unfortunately, the documentation is less than clear about this issue. If you decide to pass the MCI_NOTIFY flag, then you'll need to also provide a pointer to a MCI_GENERIC_PARMS data structure. On the other hand, if you decide to also add either the MCI_FROM or MCI_TO flags, you'll need to use the MCI_WAVE_DELETE_PARMS data structure instead. This data structure provides the contents of the MCI_GENERIC_PARMS data structure and the additional information needed to select a starting and ending place for the deletion process.

Command	Description
MCI_GETDEVCAPS	Unless you really need some of the extended information that this command could provide, you'd probably be better off using the Capabilities property of the media player control. This property will tell you what kinds of things you can do with a device. For example, you can determine whether the device is capable of recording new information. I do find that this command comes in handy for some of the more esoteric bits of information I need. For example, the MCI_GETDEVCAPS_HAS_AUDIO flag allows you to determine if the device has its own audio output.
MCI_INFO	You'll find this particular command very handy if you write applications for a large company or in other situations where you may need to support a multimedia application without really knowing the machine that it's installed on. It allows you to determine the characteristics of the hardware on a particular machine.

Command	Description

Tip: The one flag that I use the most with the MCI_INFO command is MCI_INFO_PRODUCT. It returns the hardware and driver information. All you need to do is display this information as part of the About dialog. When the user calls in with a problem, you can check the hardware by having him display the dialog and telling you the information it contains. I've run into more than one situation where an old driver or piece of hardware made an otherwise good application act like it was broken.

Command	Description
MCI_LOAD	This optional command allows you to load a file from disk. You can use it with devices like wave audio and MIDI, but not with a CD-ROM player.
MCI_OPEN	Before you can use any of the other commands in this table, you have to open a device. This particular command returns the device identifier (handle) that you'll need to use any of the other commands in the MCI_OPEN_PARMS data structure. Always send a device identification value of 0 when using this command—don't send the handle to the current window.
MCI_PASTE	This command works with the MCI_CUT and MCI_COPY commands. It takes the data on the clipboard and places it within the current MCI element. You could use this in the traditional way—a means to transfer data from one place to another—or you could use it to implement the second stage of an undo function. Simply copy the contents of the current MCI element to the clipboard before the user starts to edit it. Then, if the user decides to undo his edits, you can paste the original data back into the element. Obviously you'll need to monitor the clipboard in some way to make sure that another application doesn't overwrite your data. Otherwise, you could end up pasting garbage data into the MCI element.
MCI_PAUSE	You can use this function to pause a current MCI action. It works just like the pause button on the media player. The difference between this command and the MCI_STOP command is that this command leaves the device in a state where it's ready to immediately resume playing at the current position. MCI_STOP normally resets the position indicator to the beginning of the data area.
MCI_PLAY	In most cases this command reacts just like the media player's play button. On the other hand, this MCI command provides a lot more flexibility. Instead of simply playing the desired MCI element, it

continues

Table 11.2. **continued**

Command	Description
	allows you to set a variety of parameters that affect the presentation of the data. For example, you can tell an animation device to play the file or other data fast using the MCI_ANIM_PLAY_FAST flag. Want to see that animation in reverse? Simply use the MCI_ANIM_PLAY_REVERSE flag instead.
MCI_RECORD	Unlike the StartRecording method provided by the media player, this command doesn't require you to have an existing file. All you need is an open device. One of the ways to use this command is to create a blank file. All you need to do is open a device using MCI_OPEN, record some data using MCI_RECORD, and then save it using MCI_SAVE. The resulting file will work just fine with the media player. The only thing that you'll need to worry about is how much data you want to record. You use the MCI_TO flag and make an entry in the MCI_RECORD_PARMS data structure to define the size of the data area.

Note: One of the trade-offs of using the MCI functions is that you can't control some of the more esoteric recording parameters for an MCI device without making extra calls to the MCI_SET command (even then some parameters aren't fully supported). For example, there isn't any way to quickly change the number of channels or the bit size used to record wave file information. The benefit of using these functions are two-fold. First, you avoid having to rework your code every time someone decides to change the way that the MCI works. Borland will take care of that in such a way that your wrapper calls should work just fine. Second, you gain a certain level of ease using the MCI calls. You don't have to worry about the vagaries of the wave file format because the MCI calls take care of that for you.

Command	Description
MCI_RESUME	The need for this command might not seem obvious at first. After all, when you create an application using the media player, the user pauses the device by pressing the pause button, and then continues by pressing the pause button again. The MCI_RESUME command is the second press of the pause button. It allows the user to continue from the current position in the file. If you were to use the MCI_PLAY command in place of this one, the MCI device would start playing the data at the beginning, not the current position.
MCI_SAVE	You'll use this command to save any data recorded by the current device into a file. All you need to provide is the filename as part of the MCI_SAVE_PARMS data structure.

Command	Description
MCI_SET	There are so many flags for this particular command that there isn't any way for me to cover them here. You'll find that this is one of the more complex MCI commands that you'll use. There are some generic flags, like MCI_SET_AUDIO, that control which channels are on or off, and MCI_SET_TIME_FORMAT that allow you to change a device's time format. Other flags are very specific to the type of device you want to use. For example, the wave audio flags include settings for the number of channels and the sample rate. You'll find a combination of specific and generic data structures as well. The MCI_WAVE_SET_PARMS data structure works with wave devices while the more generic MCI_SET_PARMS data structure works with devices like CD-ROM drives.
MCI_STATUS	The media player will provide you with most of the same information that this command will. In essence, this command tells you all about the specified device. This includes things like whether it's playing or recording. You can also find out what track the device is playing and the total length of the media. Wave audio devices will tell you their current setup including parameters like sample rate and the format tag.
MCI_STOP	This command does the same thing as the stop button on the media player. You use it to stop the current device and return the position pointer back to the beginning of the data area.
MCI_SYSINFO	So far I've been telling you about device specific commands. This particular command will tell you about the MCI system itself. For example, you can find out how many devices are currently opened. You can also use this command to determine how many devices of a specific type are in the current machine and what name they appear under in either SYSTEM.INI or the registry.

Obviously this is just a small sampling of the messages that Delphi supports. You can find a complete list of messages by looking at the MCI command messages help topic in the MMSYSTEM.HLP file. Obviously some of these messages are so esoteric that you'll never use them with a standard machine; they answer the needs of sophisticated devices like videodisc players.

Tip: Creating your own wave file (or other media file) header is a time-consuming process. However, you'll find that this particular technique provides better flexibility than using the MCI system. For example, you can set the recording parameters of a particular file by simply filling out the header as shown in the example in Listings 11.1 and 11.2. Use the MCI message system you'd need to make several calls to the MCI system to accomplish the same goal.

Now that we've looked at this alternative to direct file access, let's take a look at a programming example. Figure 11.4 shows a sample data screen. All we're going to do in this example is find out what devices are currently open in the MCI system. Then we'll take a look at the specific device capabilities. The form consists of three buttons and a memo control—nothing too fancy. Table 11.3 tells you how to configure the controls on the form. Notice that I've disabled the Device Status pushbutton at the beginning. You need to query the system regarding the devices installed on the current machine before you can query a specific device.

Figure 11.4.
*This data screen will allow
you to detect the current
MCI system status and the
status of a specific device.*

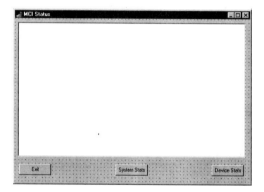

Table 11.3. Multimedia Device Status Example Control Changes.

Object	Property	Setting
pbExit	Caption	Exit
	OnClick	pbExitClick
pbSystem	Caption	System Stats
	OnClick	pbSystemClick
pbDevice	Caption	Device Stats
	Enabled	False
	OnClick	pbDeviceClick

We also need a small dialog like the one shown in Figure 11.5 to allow you to select a specific device. All I did was grab the standard dialog from the Gallery and add a label and a list box control to it. I did rename the list box control to lbDevList to make it easier to see in the code. Other than that, you won't need to make any other changes.

Figure 11.5.

The list box in this dialog contains the names of the devices on the current machine after you press the System Stats pushbutton.

Now that we've gotten the forms put together, let's take a look at some code to make them work. Listing 11.3 shows the source for this example. I didn't include the dialog box source since Delphi takes care of everything for you automatically when you design the form.

Listing 11.3. Source.

```
unit MCIStat1;

interface

uses
  Windows, Messages, SysUtils, Classes, Graphics, Controls, Forms, Dialogs, MMSYSTEM,
  StdCtrls;

type
  TForm1 = class(TForm)
    Memo1: TMemo;
    pbExit: TButton;
    pbSystem: TButton;
    pbDevice: TButton;
    procedure pbExitClick(Sender: TObject);
    procedure pbSystemClick(Sender: TObject);
    procedure pbDeviceClick(Sender: TObject);
  private
    { Private declarations }
  public
    { Public declarations }
  end;

var
  Form1: TForm1;

implementation

uses
    MCIStat2;

{$R *.DFM}
```

continues

Listing 11.3. **continued**

```
procedure TForm1.pbExitClick(Sender: TObject);
begin
    {Exit the application.}
    Halt;
end;

procedure TForm1.pbSystemClick(Sender: TObject);
var
    MCISysInfo: TMCI_SYSINFO_PARMS;    {System information structure.}
    fSysReq: WORD;                     {Information request flag.}
    sData: String;                     {String form of requested data.}
    lpszErrorMsg: PCHAR;              {Error message string.}
    fResult: WORD;                     {Error if not 0 return.}
    iDevices: DWORD;                  {Number of devices.}
    iCounter: Integer;                 {Counter for query loop.}
begin

    {Clear the memo display area and our device list.}
    Memo1.Clear;
    DevDialog.lbDevList.Clear;

    {Get the total number of devices.}
    fSysReq := MCI_SYSINFO_QUANTITY;

    {Get the data buffer ready.}
    MCISysInfo.lpstrReturn := @iDevices;
    MCISysInfo.dwRetSize := 4;

    {Get all the devices by using the GET_ALL_DEVICES_ID parameter.  It's
     currently broken, so I used the actual value of $FFFF instead.}
    fResult := MCISendCommand($FFFF, MCI_SYSINFO, fSysReq, LongInt(@MCISysInfo));

    {If the call wasn't successful, signal an error and exit.}
    if fResult <> 0 then
            begin
          lpszErrorMsg := PCHAR(sData);
          MCIGetErrorString(fResult, lpszErrorMsg, Length(sData));
        MessageDlg(sData, mtError, [mbOK], 0);
         Exit;
          end
    {Otherwise, let's display the number of devices.}
    else
        begin
        Memo1.Lines.Add('There are ' + IntToStr(iDevices) + ' devices.');
         Memo1.Lines.Add('');
         Memo1.Lines.Add('The devices include:');
         end;

    {Get the string data buffer ready.}
    SetLength(sData, 50);
    MCISysInfo.lpstrReturn := PCHAR(sData);
    MCISysInfo.dwRetSize := Length(sData);


    {Poll the MCI system once for each device.}
    for iCounter := 1 to iDevices do
        begin
```

```
{Get set up to request the device name.}
fSysReq := MCI_SYSINFO_NAME;
MCISysInfo.dwNumber := iCounter;

{Request the name of the current device.}
fResult := MCISendCommand($ffff, MCI_SYSINFO, fSysReq, LongInt(@MCISysInfo));

{If the call was successful, display the device name and add it to
 our device list.}
if fResult = 0 then
    begin
     Memo1.Lines.Add(IntToStr(iCounter) + ' - ' + sData);
     DevDialog.lbDevList.Items.Add(sData);
     end

{Otherwise, display an error dialog and check the next device.}
else
     begin
     lpszErrorMsg := PCHAR(sData);
     MCIGetErrorString(fResult, lpszErrorMsg, Length(sData));
     MessageDlg(sData, mtError, [mbOK], 0);
     end;

end; {for iCounter := 1 to iDevices do}

{Enable the device status pushbutton.}
pbDevice.Enabled := True;

end;

procedure TForm1.pbDeviceClick(Sender: TObject);
var
   MCIOpen: TMCI_OPEN_PARMS;     {The device open structure.}
   DParm: TMCI_GETDEVCAPS_PARMS;    {The device parameter structure.}
   DInfo: TMCI_INFO_PARMS;       {The device information structure.}
   fReq: WORD;                   {Information request flag.}
   sData: String;                 {String form of requested data.}
   lpszErrorMsg: PCHAR;          {Error message string.}
   fResult: WORD;                 {Error if not 0 return.}
   uiDeviceID: UINT;             {Device identifier.}
begin

   {Clear the Memo1 display area.}
   Memo1.Clear;

   {Display the device dialog.  If the user clicks on Cancel, exit the
    procedure.}
   if DevDialog.ShowModal = mrCancel then
       Exit;

   {Make sure the user actually selected a device.}
   if DevDialog.lbDevList.ItemIndex = -1 then
       begin
        MessageDlg('You must select a device from the list.', mtError, [mbOK], 0);
        Exit;
        end;
```

continues

Listing 11.3. continued

```
    {Open the requested device so we can determine its status information.}
    MCIOpen.lpstrDeviceType :=
PCHAR(DevDialog.lbDevList.Items[DevDialog.lbDevList.ItemIndex]);
    fReq := MCI_OPEN_TYPE;
    fResult := MCISendCommand(0, MCI_OPEN, fReq, LongInt(@MCIOpen));

    {Set up our text buffer.}
    SetLength(sData, 150);

    {See if there was an error.}
    if fResult <> 0 then
        begin
         lpszErrorMsg := PCHAR(sData);
         MCIGetErrorString(fResult, lpszErrorMsg, Length(sData));
         MessageDlg(sData, mtError, [mbOK], 0);
         Exit;
         end;

    {Save the device identifier.}
    uiDeviceID := MCIOpen.wDeviceID;

    {Display a header.}
    Memo1.Lines.Add('Device Type: ' +
DevDialog.lbDevList.Items[DevDialog.lbDevList.ItemIndex]);
    Memo1.Lines.Add('');

    {Get the device hardware and driver information.}
    fReq := MCI_INFO_PRODUCT;
    DInfo.lpstrReturn := PCHAR(sData);
    DInfo.dwRetSize := Length(sData);
    fResult := MCISendCommand(uiDeviceID, MCI_INFO, fReq, LongInt(@DInfo));

    {See if there was an error.}
    if fResult <> 0 then
        begin
         lpszErrorMsg := PCHAR(sData);
         MCIGetErrorString(fResult, lpszErrorMsg, Length(sData));
         MessageDlg(sData, mtError, [mbOK], 0);
         Exit;
         end;

    {Display the results and another header.}
    Memo1.Lines.Add('Hardware Information: ' + sData);
    Memo1.Lines.Add(' ');
    Memo1.Lines.Add('Device Capabilities:');

    {Check to see if the device can eject.}
    fReq := MCI_GETDEVCAPS_ITEM;
    DParm.dwItem := MCI_GETDEVCAPS_CAN_EJECT;
    MCISendCommand(uiDeviceID, MCI_GETDEVCAPS, fReq, LongInt(@DParm));

    {Display the results.}
    if DParm.dwReturn = 1 then
        Memo1.Lines.Add('Device can eject.')
    else
        Memo1.Lines.Add('Device cannot eject.');
```

```
{Check to see if the device can play.}
DParm.dwItem := MCI_GETDEVCAPS_CAN_PLAY;
MCISendCommand(uiDeviceID, MCI_GETDEVCAPS, fReq, LongInt(@DParm));

{Display the results.}
if DParm.dwReturn = 1 then
    Memo1.Lines.Add('Device can play.')
else
    Memo1.Lines.Add('Device cannot play.');

{Check to see if the device can record.}
DParm.dwItem := MCI_GETDEVCAPS_CAN_RECORD;
MCISendCommand(uiDeviceID, MCI_GETDEVCAPS, fReq, LongInt(@DParm));

{Display the results.}
if DParm.dwReturn = 1 then
    Memo1.Lines.Add('Device can record.')
else
    Memo1.Lines.Add('Device cannot record.');

{Check to see if the device can save.}
DParm.dwItem := MCI_GETDEVCAPS_CAN_SAVE;
MCISendCommand(uiDeviceID, MCI_GETDEVCAPS, fReq, LongInt(@DParm));

{Display the results.}
if DParm.dwReturn = 1 then
    Memo1.Lines.Add('Device can save.')
else
    Memo1.Lines.Add('Device cannot save.');

{Check to see if the device is a compound device.}
DParm.dwItem := MCI_GETDEVCAPS_COMPOUND_DEVICE;
MCISendCommand(uiDeviceID, MCI_GETDEVCAPS, fReq, LongInt(@DParm));

{Display the results.}
if DParm.dwReturn = 1 then
    Memo1.Lines.Add('Device is a compound device, it uses device elements.')
else
    Memo1.Lines.Add('Device is not a compound device.');

{Determine the device type.}
DParm.dwItem := MCI_GETDEVCAPS_DEVICE_TYPE;
MCISendCommand(uiDeviceID, MCI_GETDEVCAPS, fReq, LongInt(@DParm));

{Display the results.}
case DParm.dwReturn of
    MCI_DEVTYPE_ANIMATION: Memo1.Lines.Add('Device Type: Animation');
    MCI_DEVTYPE_CD_AUDIO: Memo1.Lines.Add('Device Type: CD Audio');
    MCI_DEVTYPE_DAT: Memo1.Lines.Add('Device Type: Digital Audio Tape');
    MCI_DEVTYPE_DIGITAL_VIDEO: Memo1.Lines.Add('Device Type: Video');
    MCI_DEVTYPE_OTHER: Memo1.Lines.Add('Device Type: Other');
    MCI_DEVTYPE_OVERLAY: Memo1.Lines.Add('Device Type: Video Overlay');
    MCI_DEVTYPE_SCANNER: Memo1.Lines.Add('Device Type: Scanner');
    MCI_DEVTYPE_SEQUENCER: Memo1.Lines.Add('Device Type: Sequencer (MIDI)');
    MCI_DEVTYPE_VIDEODISC: Memo1.Lines.Add('Device Type: Video Disk');
    {MCI_DEVTYPE_VIDEOTAPE: Memo1.Lines.Add('Device Type: Video Tape');}
    MCI_DEVTYPE_VCR: Memo1.Lines.Add('Device Type: Video Tape (VCR)');
```

continues

Listing 11.3. continued

```
            MCI_DEVTYPE_WAVEFORM_AUDIO: Memo1.Lines.Add('Device Type: Waveform Audio');
        end;

    {Check to see if the device has audio.}
    DParm.dwItem := MCI_GETDEVCAPS_HAS_AUDIO;
    MCISendCommand(uiDeviceID, MCI_GETDEVCAPS, fReq, LongInt(@DParm));

    {Display the results.}
    if DParm.dwReturn = 1 then
        Memo1.Lines.Add('Device has audio.')
    else
        Memo1.Lines.Add('Device does not have audio.');

    {Check to see if the device has video.}
    DParm.dwItem := MCI_GETDEVCAPS_HAS_VIDEO;
    MCISendCommand(uiDeviceID, MCI_GETDEVCAPS, fReq, LongInt(@DParm));

    {Display the results.}
    if DParm.dwReturn = 1 then
        Memo1.Lines.Add('Device has video.')
    else
        Memo1.Lines.Add('Device does not have video.');

    {Check to see if the device uses files.}
    DParm.dwItem := MCI_GETDEVCAPS_USES_FILES;
    fResult := MCISendCommand(uiDeviceID, MCI_GETDEVCAPS, fReq, LongInt(@DParm));

    {Display the results.}
    if DParm.dwReturn = 1 then
        Memo1.Lines.Add('Device uses files.')
    else
        Memo1.Lines.Add('Device does not use files.');

    {Close the device when we're done with it.}
    MCISendCommand(uiDeviceID, MCI_CLOSE, 0, 0);

end;

end.
```

Take a look at the pbSystemClick procedure. You'll notice that I obtained the names of the multimedia devices in two steps. The first step is to determine how many devices there are. If you look closely, you'll see that the variable I provided to retrieve the data isn't a string, but a DWORD. There's actually a good reason for this. The multimedia documentation tells you that the return value is a DWORD even though everywhere else it insists that this particular record element is a string—which, in fact, it is—except in this particular case. There's a lesson to be learned here: Read between the lines when it comes to the API documentation. Sometimes it'll appear that you need one data type when another data type will actually work better.

The second step in getting the system information is a loop. I simply query the device names one at a time by placing a number in the dwNumber record element. The multimedia documentation appears to tell you that you can grab all the device names in one call. That simply isn't true—you have to request them one at a time. It also doesn't tell you that the devices are sequentially numbered; that's another thing you'll need to learn through experimentation. Notice that in this case I do use a string to get the return value from the MCI system.

Warning: Never confuse the device number, like that provided for the dwNumber record element, with a device identifier. They're two separate items. The first is a simple pointer into a table of MCI devices. The second is an actual handle to an open device.

Now let's look at the pbDeviceClick procedure. I've performed four steps in this procedure. The first is to open the requested device. You need to grab this from the dialog. Notice that I perform several checks to make sure that the user actually selected something and that the device does indeed exist. There are times when a user will install a device and then later remove it and Windows becomes confused in the process. It'll tell you that the device exists because the device driver is still loaded. However, when you attempt to poll the device you'll get an error return. Once you poll the device for the first time, you can more or less depend on it being there.

Once you have the device open, you can perform any number of queries or use it to work with files. We explored just some of the things you can do with MCI commands in Table 11.2. In this case I use the MCI_INFO command to determine the hardware information for the device and the MCI_GETDEVCAPS to determine its capabilities. It's important to note that I had to make one call for each capability. Contrast this with the ease of checking a property value when using the media player control.

Note: As of this writing, there is an error in the MMSYSTEM library file. The MCI documentation states that you can check for a MCI_DEVTYPE_VIDEOTAPE device type. The MMSYSTEM file has this listed as MCI_DEVTYPE_VCR. That's why I commented out the line with the correct constant in the code and substituted the incorrect one in its place.

Tip: If you query the hardware information for a device using the MCI_INFO command and it returns a generic name like Sound, then the device is using the default Windows driver—not a vendor specific driver. Vendor specific drivers normally provide the name of the vendor and occasionally the version number of the driver.

The last step in our device query process is to close the device. You always have to close a device that you open with an MCI command. I've gotten a lot of strange results by leaving a device open when I exit an application. The very minimum you can expect to see is a loss of memory used by the device. Other symptoms include an inability to use the device from another application and error messages from Windows saying that the application won't respond. You'll also get messages from Delphi saying that it can't create the EXE file if you try to recompile the program. That's because Windows has control over the EXE file until it releases the device. Obviously it can't release the device—it becomes inaccessible once you exit the application. In most cases the only cure for this problem is to exit Windows and restart the machine.

Let's take a look at the application in operation. Figure 11.6 shows what happens when you press the System Stats pushbutton. This is the same list of devices that you'll find in SYSTEM.INI under Windows 3.x. Windows 95 may store some device definitions in the registry that don't appear in SYSTEM.INI, so using this call to determine the actual list of system devices becomes even more important.

Figure 11.6.
Pressing the System Stats pushbutton displays a list of devices available on the current machine.

Once you poll the system for the devices it contains, you can click on the Device Stats pushbutton, which displays the dialog shown in Figure 11.7. Notice that the dialog contains a simple list of the devices. Just click on a device type and then on OK, and you'll see results similar to the ones shown in Figure 11.8. This particular utility has practical value in that it allows you to quickly determine the capabilities of a device as you write a program for it.

Figure 11.7.
This simple dialog allows you to select a device that the program will then query regarding its capabilities.

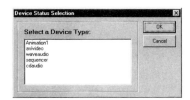

Figure 11.8.
The results of a device query
include its hardware
information as well as the
types of things you can do
with it.

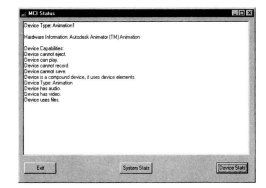

MIDI Programming Considerations

Once you get past the more or less standard wave file format, there is a whole world of MIDI (musical instrument digital interface) files to look at. There are two basic file extensions for these files—MDI and RMI. I'm not going to go into the intricate differences between the two file formats here; suffice it to say that the file extension is merely the tip of the iceberg. If you decide to get into MIDI programming, you need to take the sound board and Windows capabilities into consideration, as well as the instrument you decide to record from.

So, what precisely is a MIDI file and how does it differ from a waveform file? Think about the differences between a raster and a vector format graphic file and you'll be on the right track. A waveform file records the actual changes in amplitude of a waveform. The sampling rate determines how often the amplitude gets recorded. It's just like creating a graph. If you know the X and Y coordinates for each point on the graph, you can plot it. Drawing a line between the points completes the picture. That's precisely what happens with a waveform file.

A MIDI file, on the other hand, corresponds to a vector formatted graphic. It records the steps required to produce a sound and the instrument used to record them. Instead of recording a mere waveform pattern, a MIDI file tells the computer how to re-create the sounds that the original instrument made. That's why MIDI files are so much more complex than a waveform file is. It takes a lot more information to tell the computer how to reproduce a specific sound than to record the sound itself.

Fortunately, Delphi takes care of most of the work for you. It accesses the sequencer—the device that reproduces the MIDI sounds on your machine—and tells it what sounds to make. We could get into a long and very complicated discussion of how all this works, including the creation of instruments and the like; but that's really a topic for musicians, not programmers.

Note: At the time of this writing, I found that Delphi couldn't play some types of complex MIDI files, even though other Windows applications could. In other words, there are limitations in the types of files that you can use with native Delphi. Hopefully Borland will have this problem fixed by the time Delphi gets released. Even if they don't, you can always resort to using the Windows API directly if your application needs require the use of some of these complex files.

Native Delphi won't allow you to record to a MIDI device, even though the device does provide this capability. That's because it accesses the sequencer and assumes specific things about it. For one thing, Delphi assumes that there aren't any instruments attached to your machine—a prerequisite for recording MIDI music. About the only thing that the media player control will let you do is play MIDI files.

Even when it comes to playing a MIDI file there are some subtleties that you need to be aware of. Listing 11.4 shows a new procedure I developed to take care of the time differences between wave and MIDI files. Wave files store their length in milliseconds, so it's relatively easy to figure out how to display their length. On the other hand, MIDI files use a packed 4-byte number that contains hours, minutes, and seconds. Fortunately there are MCI macros included with Delphi to take care of a variety of time formats. All you need to do is detect the time format as shown in the sample code and perform the appropriate data manipulation using the macros.

Listing 11.4. **Procedure for time differences.**

```
procedure TForm1.GetTrackLength;
var
    liLength: LongInt;     {Total length of media in any number of formats.}
begin
    with TrackLen do

        {Determine what the current time format is so that we can process
          it correctly.}
        case MediaPlayer1.TimeFormat of

            {Wave files normally define their length in milliseconds.}
            tfMilliseconds:
                begin
                {Determine how many seconds of data the file contains.}
                Caption := IntToStr(MediaPlayer1.TrackLength[1] div 1000);
                Caption := Caption + '.';

                {Get the decimal portion of the time in seconds.}
                Caption := Caption + IntToStr(MediaPlayer1.TrackLength[1] mod 1000);
                Caption := Caption + ' Sec';
                end;

            {MIDI files use a 4-byte packed number containing hours, minutes
              and seconds.}
            tfHMS:
```

```
          begin

            {Store the media length in a variable.}
            liLength := MediaPlayer1.Length;

            {Use one of three MCI macros to determine the hours, minutes
             and seconds that the selection lasts.}
            Caption := IntToStr(MCI_HMS_HOUR(liLength));
            Caption := Caption + ':';
            Caption := Caption + IntToStr(MCI_HMS_MINUTE(liLength));
            Caption := Caption + ':';
            Caption := Caption + IntToStr(MCI_HMS_SECOND(liLength));
            end;
        end; {case MediaPlayer1.TimeFormat of}
end;

end.
```

Once you get this new procedure in place, you can call it whenever you need to display the total length of a particular media. You might want to change the procedure into a function and have it return a standard string containing hours, minutes, seconds, and tenths of seconds. I found that this particular format works fine though in most of the situations that I needed to use it with.

Video File Programming

There are a lot of different video formats and devices that you can access using Delphi. The world of video includes VCRs and videodiscs in addition to the variety of file formats that vendors have come up with over the years. However, most of them aren't in common use right now except in specialized situations like high level presentations and the like. There's one common video format though and that's the one I'll concentrate on in this section. The AVI format is being used for a variety of purposes. In fact, you'll find several AVI files in the \FUNSTUFF\VIDEOS folder of your Windows 95 disk.

Note: Unlike the audio settings discussed in this chapter, changing the video settings on the Video page of the Multimedia applet won't affect the way that Delphi displays a video file. These settings are designed to affect the way that Windows' built-in features display the video image. You'll need to use Delphi's built-in features to affect the size of the video. This also means that you'll need to provide within your application some controls for the user if you want to allow the user to change the appearance of the video display.

Delphi does provide access to a wide variety of add-on capabilities for video files. For example, you can play a video backward or at slow speed if you want. However, you won't find these capabilities as part of the media player control; you'll need to access them using MCI commands. We looked at some of these commands in Table 11.2, but you'll want to spend some time looking at the MCI documentation provided with Delphi to get a better idea of all the capabilities you can access. There are commands for controlling the size of the image area and even for cropping it. You can perform a wide range of tasks without ever leaving Delphi and using DLLs directly. Fortunately, all the commands work in the same way as the MCI commands I showed you in Listing 11.3.

MPEG Support

Motion pictures revolutionized the world, and now they'll revolutionize your PC. MPEG (Motion Pictures Experts Group) is a method of compressing VHS video into a very small format that will fit on a CD-ROM. VHS is the same format your VCR uses.

The technical term for the type of functionality that MPEG provides is a codec (coder/decoder). Think of a codec in the same way you would think of a modem. It allows you to send and receive video data using a standard medium. Instead of a telephone wire, you're using a CD-ROM drive. In place of digital data, you're receiving video images.

Windows 95 currently provides the capability to display VHS-quality images in a 640×480 window at 30 frames per second. That's about the same rate that you see on television. You're supposed to get this level of performance from a double-speed CD-ROM drive, but I have a quadruple-speed unit connected to my system and just barely get what I would call acceptable performance. I'm sure part of Microsoft's assumption is that you won't be running anything else when using the multimedia capabilities, but that probably isn't very valid. Most people will want to use this capability for training, which means that they'll probably have another application open.

Suffice it to say that if you want to fully exploit your machine's hardware capabilities to perform training, this is one way to do it. Make sure you get more than a minimal system if you plan to use the multimedia capabilities Windows 95 provides on more than an occasional basis, though. Otherwise, you'll probably be disappointed with the acceptable performance that low-end hardware will provide.

Video Programming Example

As with MIDI files, Delphi won't allow you to record AVI files (or any other video for that matter) without a lot of extra programming. A video recording program will require that you have the correct device attached to your machine, the correct driver installed, and at least a passing knowledge of the file format that you intend to use. You'll probably find that you need to use a combination of MCI commands and low level DLLs to get the job done. In any event, we'll take a look at the resources that Delphi does provide—playing a video file or accessing a device.

Videos add a new element that we haven't talked about in the past. The addition of a video display means that you have two elements to think about: pictures and sound. Our example program in Listing 11.1 already contains just about everything we'll need to display a video image. You will need to change the btPlay code as shown in Listing 11.5 to make the picture fit in our Memo1 control.

Tip: Never make your video display area too large. There are several things that will happen—none of them good from the user perspective. First, since it takes more time to display the image, your application will drop more of the display frames. Just how many frames it drops depends on the speed of your machine and the device used to store the video data. Suffice it to say that most video is recorded at 30 frames per second, which is just barely adequate to give the user the illusion of smooth animation. Second, a larger display tends to enhance the poor resolution found in most video recordings. A larger display area doesn't equate to more picture—you get the same picture—it's just spread out a lot more.

Listing 11.5. btPlay code.

```
{Start the pointer moving across the track bar.}
btPlay:
    begin
    Timer1.Enabled := True;
     MediaPlayer1.DisplayRect := Rect(0, 0, Memo1.Width, Memo1.Height);
     end;
```

Let's take a look at our new video capable version of the Multimedia Viewer. Figure 11.9 shows the viewer in action. Notice that the video fills the entire Memo1 display area. You could modify this program to display the video actual size. The only problem with this approach is that some videos would appear larger than others. You could also run into problems with cropping if the video happened to exceed the display area of the Memo1 control.

Figure 11.9.
Windows 95 provides several AVI files like this Welcome video that you can use to test your application.

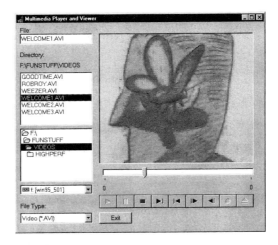

Accessing the CD-ROM Drive

The last type of multimedia device that we'll look at is the CD-ROM drive. This device is unique from others that we've looked at so far in this chapter because it doesn't use files. You still open the CD-ROM drive to use it, but you'll open it using a different technique than the other examples in this chapter.

The CD-ROM drive also has another difference. It uses tracks to store more than one multimedia element—in this case music. There are other device types that use this technique including video-discs. A videodisc can use a similar strategy called chapters to access particular data segments or to store more than one video per disc.

Since we've already explored most of the basics behind multimedia access at this point, let's dive right into the CD-ROM drive programming example and see how we implement these differences. The first thing we'll need to do is change the Multimedia Player and Viewer form by adding a new control to it. Figure 11.10 shows the updated form—it includes a new Play CD push button (now that Exit button doesn't look quite as lonely). Listing 11.6 contains the code that makes this pushbutton work.

Figure 11.10.
Our updated Multimedia Player and Viewer form includes a pushbutton that allows us to play CDs.

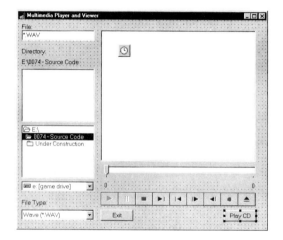

Listing 11.6. Pushbutton code.

```
procedure TForm1.pbPlayCDClick(Sender: TObject);
begin
    {Display the CD-Player dialog.}
    dlgCDPlay.ShowModal;
end;
```

As you can see, there isn't too much going on here. All the Play CD button does is display the CD Player dialog shown in Figure 11.11. I added this form to make it easier to perform CD-specific tasks like determining the number of tracks available. Notice the empty bevel control on this form. I'll show you how to fill it with buttons in just a few seconds. The form also contains three panel controls (disguised to look like edit controls) to display the current CD track and time. The OK and Cancel buttons are non-functional for the most part; their only purpose is to close the dialog when the user is done playing CDs. This dialog gets rounded out with the addition of a timer and a media player control. I'll show you the very different purpose for the timer in this example in a few seconds. Table 11.4 shows the various control settings.

Figure 11.11.
The CD Player dialog looks empty during the design phase, but that will change during runtime.

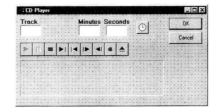

Table 11.4. Multimedia Device Status Example Control Changes.

Object	Property	Setting
Track	BevelInner	bvLowered
	BevelOuter	bvLowered
	Color	clWhite
	Font.Color	clRed
	Font.Height	10
	Font.Name	MS Sans Serif
	Font.Style	[fsBold]
Minutes	BevelInner	bvLowered
	BevelOuter	bvLowered
	Color	clWhite
	Font.Color	clBlue
	Font.Height	10
	Font.Name	MS Sans Serif
	Font.Style	[fsBold]
Seconds	BevelInner	bvLowered
	BevelOuter	bvLowered
	Color	clWhite
	Font.Color	clBlue
	Font.Height	10

continues

Table 11.4. continued

Object	Property	Setting
	Font.Name	MS Sans Serif
	Font.Style	[fsBold]
Timer1	Enabled	False
	Interval	250
	OnTimer	Timer1Timer
MediaPlayer1	OnClick	MediaPlayer1Click

Now that you've gotten the dialog set up and ready to go, let's take a look at the code required to make it work. Listing 11.7 contains the code required to create the CD Player dialog. Pay particular attention to the techniques I used to create the track buttons. You'll also want to take a look at the method for translating the CD time format since it differs from what you've seen so far.

Listing 11.7. CD Player dialog.

```
unit MCI2;

interface

uses Windows, SysUtils, Classes, Graphics, Forms, Controls, StdCtrls,
  Buttons, ExtCtrls, MPlayer, Dialogs, MMSYSTEM;

type
  TdlgCDPlay = class(TForm)
    OKBtn: TButton;
    CancelBtn: TButton;
    MediaPlayer1: TMediaPlayer;
    Label1: TLabel;
    Label3: TLabel;
    Label4: TLabel;
    Timer1: TTimer;
    Track: TPanel;
    Minutes: TPanel;
    Seconds: TPanel;
    Bevel1: TBevel;
    procedure FormShow(Sender: TObject);
    procedure FormClose(Sender: TObject; var Action: TCloseAction);
    procedure MediaPlayer1Click(Sender: TObject; Button: TMPBtnType;
      var DoDefault: Boolean);
    procedure Timer1Timer(Sender: TObject);
    procedure ChangeTrack(Sender: TObject);
  private
    { Private declarations }
  public
    { Public declarations }
  end;

var
```

```
        dlgCDPlay: TdlgCDPlay;
        aButtons: array[1..30] of TButton;    {An array of buttons.}

implementation

{$R *.DFM}

procedure TdlgCDPlay.FormShow(Sender: TObject);
var
    iCounter: Integer;                  {Track Counter Variable}
    iXPosit, iYPosit: Integer;          {Positioning variables.}
begin
    {Tell the media player that we want to open the CD drive.}
    MediaPlayer1.DeviceType := dtCDAudio;

    {Open the CD Player for use.}
    MediaPlayer1.Open;

    {Initialize our positioning variables.}
    iXPosit := 11;
    iYPosit := 107;

    {Create the pushbuttons.}
    for iCounter := 1 to 30 do
        begin
          aButtons[iCounter] := TButton.Create(dlgCDPlay);

          {Initialize the pushbutton settings.}
          aButtons[iCounter].Caption := IntToStr(iCounter);
          aButtons[iCounter].Left := iXPosit;
          aButtons[iCounter].Top := iYPosit;
          aButtons[iCounter].Width := 33;
          aButtons[iCounter].Height := 25;
          aButtons[iCounter].OnClick := ChangeTrack;
          aButtons[iCounter].Visible := True;
          aButtons[iCounter].Enabled := False;

          {Insert the control into our dialog box.}
          dlgCDPlay.InsertControl(aButtons[iCounter]);

          {Update the positioning variables.}
          iXPosit := iXPosit + 33;
          if iXPosit >= 341 then
              begin
                iXPosit := 11;
                iYPosit := iYPosit + 25;
                end;
        end;

        {Enable enough controls for the tracks on the CD.}
        for iCounter := 1 to MediaPlayer1.Tracks do
            aButtons[iCounter].Enabled := True;

end;

procedure TdlgCDPlay.FormClose(Sender: TObject; var Action: TCloseAction);
var
```

continues

Listing 11.7. **continued**

```
    iCounter: Integer;    {Track Button Counter}
begin
    {Close the CD-ROM drive before we exit.}
    MediaPlayer1.Close;
end;

procedure TdlgCDPlay.MediaPlayer1Click(Sender: TObject; Button: TMPBtnType;
  var DoDefault: Boolean);
begin
    {Select an action based on the button the user pressed.}
    case Button of

        {Start the timer display.}
        btPlay: Timer1.Enabled := True;

        {Stop the timer display.}
         btPause: Timer1.Enabled := False;

         {Stop the timer display and return it to its starting position.}
         btStop:
             begin
              Timer1.Enabled := False;
              MediaPlayer1.Position := 0;
              Track.Caption := '0';
              Minutes.Caption := '0';
              Seconds.Caption := '0';
              end;

        end; {case Button of}
end;

procedure TdlgCDPlay.Timer1Timer(Sender: TObject);
begin
    {Display the current position.}
    Track.Caption := IntToStr(MCI_TMSF_TRACK(MediaPlayer1.Position));
    Minutes.Caption := IntToStr(MCI_TMSF_MINUTE(MediaPlayer1.Position));
    Seconds.Caption := IntToStr(MCI_TMSF_SECOND(MediaPlayer1.Position));
end;

procedure TdlgCDPlay.ChangeTrack(Sender: TObject);
var
    iTrackNumber: Integer;    {Change To track number.}
begin
    {Get the desired track number.}
    iTrackNumber := StrToInt((Sender as TButton).Caption);

    {Select either the next or previous track based on the user's selection.}
    if iTrackNumber >= MCI_TMSF_TRACK(MediaPlayer1.Position) then
        while iTrackNumber > MCI_TMSF_TRACK(MediaPlayer1.Position) do
            MediaPlayer1.Next
    else
        while iTrackNumber < MCI_TMSF_TRACK(MediaPlayer1.Position) do
            MediaPlayer1.Previous;

    {Display the current position.}
    Track.Caption := IntToStr(MCI_TMSF_TRACK(MediaPlayer1.Position));
```

```
    Minutes.Caption := IntToStr(MCI_TMSF_MINUTE(MediaPlayer1.Position));
    Seconds.Caption := IntToStr(MCI_TMSF_SECOND(MediaPlayer1.Position));
end;

end.
```

While you may not have thought to use the array of buttons technique that I show in FormShow procedure, it does come in handy for situations like this. Instead of having separate names for each pushbutton, I can control them through an array reference. That makes the job of managing the active tracks a snap. You may be wondering why I don't provide a method for freeing the controls when I exit the application. Normally you would need to do that to prevent memory leaks. The dlgCDPlay.InsertControl(aButtons[iCounter]); call tells the whole story here. As soon as you insert a control into a form, the form takes responsibility for it. If you try to free the control, Delphi would raise an exception telling you that you had violated its memory space.

Now that you have the program ready to go, let's take a look at how it performs. Your CD Player dialog should look like the one in Figure 11.12 when it runs. Notice how well the buttons fit within the bevel control. You can use similar techniques to create buttons on the fly whenever you need them. There are some situations where such a technique is not only more memory efficient, but less confusing to the user. For example, you might run into a situation where the user needs access to a control only if a specific event occurs. You could create the pushbutton needed to implement that action on the fly.

Figure 11.12.
*Our CD Player dialog looks
complete at runtime thanks
to some dynamic control
creation.*

Summary

This chapter has taken you on a whirlwind tour of multimedia programming using Delphi. I've shown you how easy it is to play back any file using the media player control. We've also looked at some of the gotchas you'll experience when trying to record data using that same control.

One of the more important things that we looked at was the MCI system itself. Delphi provides more than one way to access multimedia, and it's important to remember that they're at your disposal. The media player will work fine in most cases, but we looked at a few places where the MCI commands will provide some added flexibility that you'll need to get the job done—especially when it comes time to troubleshoot a problem installation or determine the capabilities of the machine you're using.

We also took a look at a simple direct access method of programming a wave file. You can use a similar technique to record other multimedia file types. Obviously this isn't the route of choice if you can avoid it since it requires a very detailed knowledge of the file format. It also exposes your application to sudden failure when the vendor decides to change a particular file format. Borland will help you keep your Delphi application up-to-date by changing the internals of the controls you use without changing the interface.

12

Database Management Under Delphi

I usually loosely define a database as a collection of interrelated data. Delphi uses a more formal definition that includes specific forms of data that is managed by a database server of some type and appears in a specific type of file. Database management systems (DBMS) have become more than simple business tools; they've become the stuff of business itself. I can't think of too many businesses that don't make use of a DBMS in some way. From financial reports to a simple mailing list manager, DBMS are present in every facet of business.

There are those of you who probably think of a DBMS as that monster application that holds all the company contact information. Another popular view is the custom database used to hold a mailing list or other special information. However, these are pretty limited views of what a database is and what it can do for you. Occasionally DBMS hide themselves in other applications. For example, most spreadsheets contain simple flat file database management functionality. You'd also be surprised at the number of DBMS you'll find in applications like word processors and even in places like cash registers.

I still remember an application I wrote for a company. They stored all their employee, inventory, and purchase information in cash registers connected to the main office via modem. Every night my program would download the cash register's data, sort it into specific data types, then store it in a variety of tables in the database. Fortunately the data was in ASCII format because the cash register seemed to store the information without much regard for order. The fact that the cash register was a very primitive form of PC didn't affect the fact that it stored information in a database. Most people would look at it as a device—a cash register. I looked at it as a DBMS, a place where a company stored its valuable information.

There are other hidden areas where DBMS dwell as well. Have you ever wondered how some applications keep track of the documents you produce or provide those handy lists of miscellaneous information like state abbreviations or ZIP codes? All of these little applications are also examples of DBMS. Unlike the cash register in my previous example, the only way you can access these DBMS is through the application.

What we're interested in is DBMS that provide a full set of data manipulation capabilities—the ability to add, change, delete, and view all the data that the DBMS manages. Delphi provides some fairly complex DBMS capabilities, not just the ability to retrieve information in a few simple formats, but the ability to move that data around and view it in a variety of ways. You can access everything from a mainframe database to the name and address file stored on your local hard drive as long as Delphi provides a native driver for it, or there's an ODBC driver lurking on your drive somewhere. In fact, more often than not you'll find that the hardest part of creating a database application with Delphi is figuring out the best way to access the data you need.

The main goal of this chapter is to show you how to access your data and create simple DBMS applications. I'm not going to get into the vagaries of certain types of optimization schemes or any intricacies like that. There are whole books written on the topic of DBMS security alone—optimization technique books could fill an entire shelf by themselves. Suffice it to say that we'll look at the mechanics of DBMS in this chapter along with the usual array of tips and techniques for making Delphi work better for you.

> **Looking Ahead:** There's more to DBMS applications than just data access and presentation—the two topics we'll concentrate on in this chapter. You also need to worry about printing. We covered that topic in the ReportSmith section of Chapter 8, "Printer Magic." Working with LANs is part of the DBMS scene as well. We'll cover that topic in Chapter 13, "Delphi on a LAN." You'll want to look at Chapter 10, "Using Delphi with OLE," if your DBMS supports BLOBs (binary large objects) or OLE in any way. It doesn't take too long to figure out that DBMS application programming covers a wide range of topics. It's not just limited to a few small areas of programming like some types of utility programming are.

Data Access Components

Data access is what creating a DBMS is all about. You have to have a way to get to all that data your business has been accumulating. An inventory is only as good as the DBMS used to access it. If you can't get up-to-date stock status, then why enter the information into the DBMS at all? More importantly, just accessing the data isn't enough; some databases are so large that it would take you months to find a single item. Reducing the size of the data so that you can view it in a variety of ways is also important. So, just how do you gain access to your data in Delphi? The Data Access component tab of the Component Palette is all you need in most cases. The only requirement is that the database you want to access must support ODBC, IDAPI, or provide some type of native Delphi driver.

Figure 12.1 shows the group of data access components provided by Delphi. I think you'll agree that it's a very short list of items. In fact, I originally felt that there had to be some hidden components or missing elements when I first viewed this part of the component palette. However, after having worked with Delphi for a while I can tell you that this set of components is all you'll need to access the data (we'll talk about manipulating it in the next section). Table 12.1 provides a complete description of each component. Amazingly enough, you'll find that you use at least three of them for even the simplest of data access situations.

Figure 12.1.
*Delphi's data access
components are few in
number and straightforward
to use.*

Table 12.1. Delphi Data Access Component Description.

Component	Description
TDataSource	A data source works much as its name implies—it's the place where you gain access to the information you need. While a database is a repository for all the related information and a table contains a single type of information, the data source actually retrieves it for you. A data source can be a table, query, or stored procedure, all of which are part of the database. Think of a database as a person that you talk to and the data source as the telephone you'll use to call them. When you call the person you want to talk to, you'll ask them about a particular subject (a query, table, or stored procedure). That's the purpose of a data source in Delphi; it's the part of Delphi that allows you to talk to the DBMS.
TTable	Some people have gotten the terms table and database confused over the years; they use the two terms incorrectly or interchange them as if they were the same thing. Some vendors, like Ashton-Tate, only made the situation worse when they refused to use standard terminology in their documentation. A table is a single grouping of related information. Databases typically hold one or more tables—a database is a collection of all the information related to a data set. Tables normally hold one set of data. For example, you might place the names, addresses, and telephone numbers of all your employees in one table. Another table might hold individual instances of an employee's pay record, the amount they receive each pay period. The two tables are related by an employee name or other identifying information, but they don't contain the same type of information. The database containing these two tables might represent all of the company's payroll information. In other words, the database contains all of the tables that are related to company payroll. I always like to think of a database as the person I ask a question of and a table as the topic that I want to talk about.
TQuery	If a database is the source of answers to questions and the table contains the answer to the question, this component is the question itself. A TQuery component allows you to ask the database or other data source a very precise question and retrieve only the information you need. In the past people would grab an entire table or even the database itself when they needed to get some piece of information. Networks aren't built to maintain that kind of traffic—especially if you have several hundred users asking questions. Using a

Component	Description
	query reduces the amount of time it takes to answer the question and network traffic at the same time. Delphi's queries all use SQL (structured query language). SQL is a very standard way to talk with a data source. We'll take a look at the methods that Delphi provides for using SQL efficiently a bit later in this chapter.
TStoredProc	We had talked about DDE in Chapter 10 as a remote control method for performing specific tasks—a remote control macro of sorts. You're going to run into situations where a DBMS doesn't reside on a DOS or local machine—a source of information that you could potentially manipulate using OLE automation or DDE. A database could reside on a mainframe or other difficult-to-access source. Stored procedures are macros for data sources. They get stored on the data server—which could be a file server, mainframe, or even your local PC—and use the server's native language. Most DBMS use SQL for their stored procedures. So what good is a stored procedure? Think of it as an enhanced form of query. Stored procedures often let you reduce the size of the data set or perform some types of calculations before you retrieve the data. Some of the biggest advantages of Stored Procedures are the same as using procedures in code. For example, they help you eliminate code duplication and enforce both industry and company standards. They also reduce your workload because you only change the code in one place if a query needs to change.
TDatabase	The TDatabase component is the method that Delphi uses to control access to the information—it provides the mechanical link between your application and the data server so to speak. For example, the TDatabase component is responsible for initiating transactions like a commit or a rollback. It also takes care of things like logging into the database for those DBMS that provide security—most large DBMS do. You don't have to add a TDatabase component to your application to access the data; Delphi will create a virtual TDatabase component if it needs to. However, adding the component will give you an added level of flexibility.
TSession	I found this particular component a bit confusing when I first looked at the name. Fortunately, the purpose for the component is very clear. Think about a TSession component as the overlord of all the database related activities for an application and you'll be started in the right direction. You can't dynamically create a TSession component—you need to add this component at design time. Delphi does automatically create one TSession component called Session that you can access without adding a component to your application. This component provides access to the session's properties and

continues

Table 12.1. **continued**

Component	Description
	methods. For example, the Databases property will tell you the names of all the databases opened by the current application. One of the methods that you'll find really handy is GetStoredProcNames—which returns a list of the stored procedures provided by the database server. For the most part, you'll find that you use the TSession component as a means to control the overall DBMS picture, not individual databases, data sources, or tables. The main purpose for the TSession component is to allow you to maintain multiple database sessions within one application. In other words, you could theoretically log in to the database using more than one user name or multiple copies of one name.
TBatchMove	The TBatchMove component comes in handy for a variety of tasks. Any time you need to move data from one location to another, this component is the one you should think about using. It greatly reduces the amount of work that you'll need to do when it comes to updating the company's main database from a satellite office or grab last year's equipment inventory so that you can verify any changes in equipment this year. I also find that the TBatchMove component comes in handy as a pseudo-import routine. You can move data between two different database products that Delphi supports—and it supports more than a few through ODBC and native drivers. In essence, you're exporting the data from one format and placing it in another.
TUpdateSQL	There are times when you only want to read the data in a table—you really don't need to edit it. Normally you'd use a read-only dataset for this purpose to reduce network traffic. A read-only dataset gets cached on the local machine. However, if you're using that table for reference purposes, wouldn't it be nice to have the most current data at your disposal? That's what this component is all about. The TUpdateSQL component allows you to access Delphi's cached update support to update the read-only dataset and the information you see as a result.
TReport	We've already looked at this component once in Chapter 8. It allows you to execute a ReportSmith report from within Delphi using the runtime files.

There's something you should notice about the components I've described so far. All of them can react to the database without going through a TDataSource component. Data Access components can access the data directly. A Data Control or QuickRpt component always requires a connection to a data source. Let's look at the example again in Chapter 8. You'll notice that all I needed was a TDatabase, TTable, and TReport component to get the job done. That's because a TReport component can access the data directly. In this case it's because ReportSmith is an external application, but the same thing would apply to any Delphi component.

Figure 12.2 gives you a little better perspective of how the Data Access components work together to create a connection from your application to the data server. It also shows how this connection enables you to use the Data Control and QuickRpt components described in the next two sections of the chapter. Always remember that Data Control and QuickRpt components need a connection to the data source when you write an application.

Figure 12.2.
The Data Access Compo-
nents work together to help
your application access a
database and manipulate its
contents using the Data
Control and QuickRpt
components.

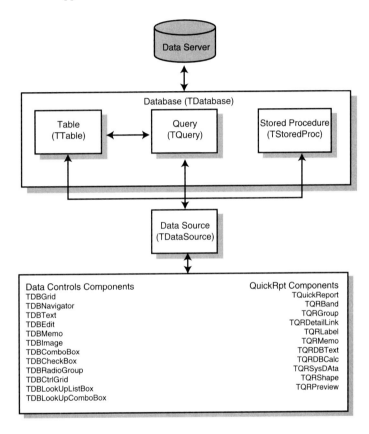

We've already taken a good look at the TReport component in Chapter 8, but we haven't looked at the TBatchMove component. Figure 12.3 shows the connection between a TBatchMove component and the other required Data Access components. You always have to have a TTable component as a destination for a batch move. However, you can use a TTable, TQuery, or TStoredProc component as a source. The availability of all these data sources allows you to create extremely flexible data import and export routines.

Figure 12.3.

Batch moves can use a variety of sources, but only one type of destination—TTable components.

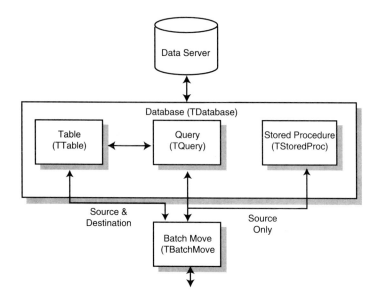

Peter's Principle: Making Use of a TTable Filter

Delphi has a number of new features—in fact, there are so many new features that I really think the average developer will feel a bit overwhelmed. Mind you, I'm not saying that any of them should have been left out, but some of them will confuse developers who are used to the 16-bit way of doing things.

Take a look at the TTable filter as an example. Developers used to the 16-bit way of doing things will certainly remember the SetRange method. The developer would define an index to sort out the values he was looking for, then define the range in which those records appeared. It took a bit of effort and slowed the application down a little, but the SetRange method did get the job done.

The new TTable component contains a Filtered property and an OnFilterRecord event. Setting the Filtered property to true tells the TTable component to call the OnFilteredRecord event that allows you to process the records. One of the parameters for an OnFilteredRecord event is Accept. To set a filter you set Accept equal to some condition. The short version of this is: Accept := FieldName = Value. You can use the normal Boolean operators to separate multiple field arguments. Using this method has a certain advantage—you don't have to index the table. For that matter, you don't have to use a table at all—you can search for records based on a query instead.

Using the TTable filter capability isn't the right choice all the time, however. Even though it allows you as the developer to get by with less code and may reduce the amount of network traffic, the user will have to pay the price. Once you set up a range, the time between records is minimal since they're all contiguous. The records in a filter condition aren't in any particular order—so the user will probably see a longer delay between records.

Another, somewhat hidden, problem is that the records could literally appear in just about any order on the user's display. That makes a filter less than ideal for a browse where the user is looking for specific information unless you take time to order the data properly first. In essence, the TTable filter capability is a new tool that will greatly speed your application development, but you shouldn't make it the only tool that you use. Fortunately, you can get around the ordering problem by using a TQuery instead of a TTable component.

Data Control Components

Before you can create an application, you need to know what kinds of components that Delphi places at your disposal. In this case a component provides a method for displaying or otherwise manipulating the data found in a table. All of these components are on screen controls; we'll cover the QuickRpt components used to print data in the next section. We took a brief look at these components in Chapter 8 when I introduced ReportSmith. Let's take a more formal look at them now.

Figure 12.4 shows the Data Controls you'll find on the Component Palette. I think you'll find that most of them act the same as their common component counterparts with a DBMS twist. For example, the TDBEdit component is a standard edit with a database connection. You would use it to create custom forms. A TDBGrid component allows you to create a database browse display. Table 12.2 describes all of these components in detail.

Figure 12.4.

There are specialized versions of most of the common Delphi components designed to work with DBMS.

Table 12.2. Delphi Data Controls Description.

Component	Description
TDBGrid	This component displays a grid—like a spreadsheet display—on screen. You can use it to create database browse displays. There are two common types of browses. The first one is used to work with a single table. Normally you would use this type of display to search for data, then display a detail form to allow the user to see all the

continues

Table 12.2. continued

Component	Description
	data at once. The second type is part of a one to many form. You would use the TDBGrid component to display the records in the secondary data that are related to the current record in the primary database.
TDBNavigator	You'll find that the vast majority of your applications will need to use a TDBNavigator component. The default configuration contains 10 pushbuttons, which you can limit using various properties that the object provides. The main purpose of this component is to allow you to move from one record to the next. Three of the pushbuttons—edit, delete, and insert—allow you to modify one or more table records. The Post pushbutton makes a change permanent—most DBMS call this action a commit. Likewise, the Cancel pushbutton returns a record to its former state. A majority of DBMS calls this a rollback. Finally, you can use the Refresh pushbutton to update the contents of whatever components are attached to the TDBNavigator component.
TDBText	Any time you want to create a custom form that shows one record at a time, you'll need one or more of these components. In essence, they display any textual data that a table might contain. The user can't edit the information that this component contains. The advantage of using the component is that it's data aware—which means that the component automatically updates its contents as you move from record to record.
	A TDBText component consumes a lot more memory than a TLabel component consumes. Always use a TLabel component if you need to display simple, non-changing text. For example, headings and data tags should use TLabel components in place of a TDBText component.
TDBEdit	A TDBEdit component allows you to display text information from a table, query, or stored procedure. You can use all the standard editing techniques with this particular component. The big difference is that it's data aware—the contents of the component will change as you move from record to record in the table.
	There are situations where you'll need to provide an edit component for non-changing data that still gets inserted into the table. For example, you might want to place the current date in one of the table fields. This would happen with a payroll entry or other one-to-many fields. Using a TEdit component in this situation will save

Component	Description
	you quite a bit of memory, yet doing so won't compromise the integrity of your database in most cases.
TDBMemo	Like all the other editing components discussed so far, the TDBMemo component is data aware—its contents will change as you move from record to record. In just about every other way, the TDBMemo component behaves like the TMemo component. There is one interesting feature with this particular component. It provides the AutoDisplay property that determines whether Delphi automatically displays any BLOBs that the TDBMemo might contain. You can set this property to false to reduce the level of network traffic and the screen update times for users of your application. The LoadMemo method allows you to update the TDBMemo manually. All you would need to do is attach this method to an Update pushbutton on the form.

The TDBMemo component does provide some features other than data awareness that might make it attractive in some situations. However, it does use a lot more memory than either the TMemo or the TRichEdit components do. The most memory efficient of the three is TMemo, followed by TRichEdit. Only resort to using a TDBMemo if you need its data aware or BLOB handling features.

Note: Just like any other memo component, TDBMemo won't display graphic images. This runs contrary to what most people look at as a BLOB, but it's the way that Delphi works. You must use a TDBImage component if you need to display a graphic BLOB on screen.

TDBImage	Use this component if you need to display an image from a table. The BLOB handling capabilities of the TDBImage component do make it possible to handle more than straight graphics. For example, Delphi will handle graphic OLE objects embedded in a database BLOB field.

While the TDBImage component doesn't consume many more system resources than a TImage component, it does consume some. With this in mind, you'll probably want to use a TImage component whenever possible. For example, you could use it to display a company logo. You could also use it during data entry in conjunction with a list box. The user would select the desired image by selecting it from the list box. The TImage component would show what the image looks like.

continues

Table 12.2. continued

Component	Description

Tip: A TDBImage or TImage components make perfect examples of a situation where a double click could perform a special task. If I have five or less images for the user to select from—like I would if the database were used to store specific categories of data and I used the image to show the category—then I allow the user to double click on the component to change the image. Some users find this more intuitive than selecting the proper image from a list box.

Component	Description
TDBListBox	I often use this component to display lists of semi-static information for the user. For example, I would probably use it to display a list of states in a mailing list DBMS. The advantage of storing the list of appropriate entries as a table in the database is that you can actually reduce the data storage requirements for some types of data. For example, you could store the state information in a single character instead of using two. If you needed to add another state, country, or other type of semi-static information, you would simply modify the table holding the data—one time. The user would immediately see the new entry the next time they used your application.
	Think about the other possibilities as well. For example, if you stored a list of data in your application and used a standard TListBox component to display it, you would have to update your application every time you wanted to add a new item to the list. Using configuration files to solve the problem is somewhat messy to say the least. Besides, using configuration files leaves that list at the mercy of the user—who knows when he'll erase it by accident.
	Another reason to use this approach is speed of update. What would happen if you displayed a certain type of semi-static information one way, then the boss told you to change it? Normally you'd need to verify that you had changed every entry in the table besides updating your user procedures and application to reflect the change. Using a table and TDBListbox combination would allow you to make one change to the database—every entry relies on this one so they would all get updated immediately.
TDBComboBox	This component works just like its counterpart, the TComboBox component. It allows the user to either select a value from a predefined list, or type a new value in the edit box. The major

Component	Description

difference between the two components is that the TDBComboBox is data aware.

I've actually found little use for this particular component. Normally if you want to limit a user's selection to a range of choices you would use a TDBListBox. On the other hand, if you want to allow them to add new values, then a TComboBox is actually more memory efficient. Use this component only if you want to allow the user to change the contents of a lookup table within the database. Obviously this would be limited to an administrator form in most cases.

TDBCheckBox

Use this component for Boolean values that you need to store in the database. If the box is checked, the entry is true. This component provides the same capabilities as the TCheckBox component. The big difference is that it's data aware.

TDBRadioGroup

This component represents another way to implement a short list of items like the category list that I mentioned previously. Obviously you would have to limit the number of choices—making the use of this particular component very limited.

Database tables normally store large quantities of information, not just five or six values. It's true that you could use a table to store something like a short list of categories if for no other reason than ease of updating the list as needed later. However, if the list really is so short and stable that a radio group will work, you should probably consider using the standard TRadioGroup component and storing the list of options locally. Obviously, there is a great number of exceptions to this rule, most of which I've already mentioned in the TDBListBox entry in this table.

TDBLookUpListBox

Using a lookup table in your application used to require some coding. Not any more. This component allows you to add a lookup table to your application and not do much more than define a few simple properties. The contents of the list box are defined by the ListField and ListSource properties. The master database field that it affects is defined by the DataSource and DataField properties. You keep the master and lookup tables in sync using the KeyField property.

continues

Table 12.2. **continued**

Component	Description

> **Tip:** You can make it appear that your application has an edit component with a spin button by setting the RowCount property of the TDLookUpListBox component to 1. What the user will see is an edit box with a double arrow on the right side.

TDBLookUpComboBox	The TDBLookUpComboBox component works precisely the same way as its counterpart, the TDBLookUpListBox component. You use the same fields to create a link between the master and lookup tables. The only difference is that a combo box will provide a drop-down list.
TDBCtrlGrid	Imagine for a moment that you want to create a label preview screen for your application. This component will allow you to do just that. It displays a combination of a custom form and a browse at the same time. You define one version of the display, then Delphi replicates it as needed. This component even provides a row and column property so that you can display the labels in the same format that they'll appear in on paper. Of course, this isn't the only use for this particular component (you could use it for a custom browser or any number of other applications), but it's the first one that came to mind as I looked at it for the first time.

I didn't mention it in the preceding paragraphs, but most of these components require two entries before they'll display any information for you: A source and a field name. The source is the name of the Data Source component that we talked about in the previous section. The field name is the name of the data field within the selected table.

Some of the components listed in this table, as well as those in the next section (QuickRpt), provide the capability to use more than one field type. The 32-bit version of Delphi provides three: Data, Calculated, and Lookup. The data field is one that exists naturally in the table. All you have to do is read it. A calculated field is derived from an existing field. It requires you to provide some type of equation or function definition.

The lookup field is one of the nicer additions to Delphi. You used to use code to create a link between the lookup table and the data table. For example, you would have to create some type of relationship between a table containing the names of states and the table that actually contained those states as data. Delphi 2.0 changes that by allowing you to define a non-coded lookup field within certain types of components.

So what's the secret to all this? It's the Field Editor. Any component that uses the Field Editor can also use these three types of fields because they're standard issue. Borland also provided many other updates to the Field Editor that we'll explore within the various examples in this chapter.

QuickRpt Components

Quick reports are completely new for Delphi 2.0. This set of components provides that halfway point between completely writing a print routine by hand—like we did in Chapter 8—and using an external product like ReportSmith. Sure, ReportSmith will actually provide you with more tools than you'll find on the QuickRpt component list, but you have to carry around a lot of baggage to use it. Not only that, but calling an external routine to process a print job seems like a bit of a kludge from the user's perspective.

Before we get much further, let's take a look at the QuickRpt components and what they can do for you. Figure 12.5 shows the QuickRpt components you'll find on the Component Palette. As with the Data Control components, I think you'll find that some of them act the same as their common component counterparts with a printing twist. For example, the TQRLabel component is a standard label used to output data to the printer. You would use it to display any constant information on the report like a date or title. Some of the components are even extensions of the Data Control components. For example, the print output version of a TDBText component is a TQRDBText component. They do the same thing, but on different mediums. On the other hand, the TQRPreview component is strictly meant for printing—you wouldn't use it on a form for any reason. Table 12.3 describes all of these components in detail.

Figure 12.5.
The QuickRpt components are new to Delphi 2.0. They allow you to create reports within Delphi without resorting to ReportSmith.

Table 12.3. **Delphi Data Controls Description.**

Control	Description
TQuickReport	This is the main quick report component. It handles all the printing and data tasks. To use this component, drop it on to a form and set its DataSource property to the TTable or TQuery component containing the data you want to print. Add other components like TQRBand and TQRDBText to format the output. The two main methods that you'll use with this component are Preview and Print.

continues

Table 12.3. continued

Control	Description
	To use the first one you'll need to add a TQRPreview component to your form. The Preview display also provides the ability to print the data once the user has looked at it.
TQRBand	Essentially, a band is a single type of data in a report. I got used to seeing this term in conjunction with graphic application print routines. Corel Draw uses this term as it prints various layers and areas of the current drawing. You set the band's type by changing the BandType property. There are a variety of band types including: title, detail lines, groups, footers, and headers. What the TQRBand component does is separate your data into usable areas. It doesn't actually display any data, that's taken care of by other QuickRpt components.
TQRGroup	Think of a TQRGroup component as special type of display component. It doesn't display data directly like an edit component would, but it does provide data to the report whenever specific group information is required. To use this component you define a data source and data field, just like you would any other display component. A change in the data field value signals the end of the group. Once you define these two properties, you have to tell Delphi where to place the group information. That's where the HeaderBand and FooterBand properties come into play—they tell Delphi where to place the information you provided. You normally couple a TQRGroup component with a TQuery to produce a master/detail report. The main reason to use the TQRGroup component is when you need to create reports with more than two layers of grouping. If you need multiple levels of detail, then the TQRDetailLink component is the best one to use.
TQRDetailLink	You would use the TQRDetailLink report to create a master/detail report with multiple detail tables at the same level. This is the second method for producing master/detail reports (the TQRGroup component is the first). This component works by coupling a TQRDetailLink component with a detail group band. You specify the name of the master table as the data source for the TQRDetailLink. Quick report will print one group for each record in the master table.
TQRLabel	This is a standard label, but designed for printer output instead of the screen (you'll still see the contents of the label in design mode). It allows you to display column headings and other non-changing data.

Control	Description
	If you want to display data from a table, then you'll need to use the TQRText component.
TQRMemo	This is a standard memo component, but designed for output to a printer. There's one important consideration when using this component: Unlike the display, printed output can't make use of scroll bars. This means that any text your TQRMemo component can display on screen, also won't appear in the printed report. Since this component always takes the same amount of space—even if the text in the memo field doesn't fill it—you have to weigh the size of the component itself with the amount of data you expect to print. Obviously this isn't the best way to display text, but it does work. Unlike other database related components, you don't fill a TQRMemo component with data by specifying a data source and a data field. This component uses the TStrings property to determine what data it'll display. Obviously this isn't a data aware component, so you need to use it with care.
TQRDBText	The TQRDBText component is probably the one that you'll use the most to display data. Its functionality is similar to that of the TDBText component—except that it outputs data to the printer instead of the display. You specify the data that the component will print using the DataSource and DataField properties.
TQRDBCalc	You'll find this particular component in groups and footers for the most part. It allows you to either display a total value for a particular field or count the number of entries that a detail area contains. For example, what if you wanted to print a report that shows the total travel expenses on a regional basis for your company. You could display the travel expenses for each employee, then add this component to each group to display the total expenses for that group. As with other data aware components, the DataSource and DataField properties tell the TQRDBCalc component what to calculate. The ResetGroup property tells it when to reset its counter.
TQRSysData	I find this particular component very handy. In one component I have the ability to display the current date or time, the report title or page number, or any number of system parameters. Of special interest to me was the detail count property. I could use it to place a number to the right or left of each line of detail data. The only property that

continues

Table 12.3. continued

Control	Description
	you really need to worry about when using this component is Data, which defines what type of data you'd like to see.
TQRShape	Business reports of the past usually eschewed any form of graphics for the clarity of text. That's changing. No longer are presentations boring lectures filled with endless tables of statistical information. A good presenter uses graphics (and multimedia if necessary) to dress up a presentation now. Delphi's QuickRpt components won't allow you to make any dramatic changes to your report, but the TQRShape component will allow you to add just a bit of pizzazz when used properly. This component places a shape like a circle or square in your report. This may seem a trifle limited—and it is—but you can always use these shapes to define specific types of data. For example, you could use shaded circles to define one type of statistical information and shaded squares another. The actual level of shading might be used to define the level of data. For example, you might use a dark square to define a high sales line of a report or a clear square to define something at the low end. You could also use these graphics primitives to create simple bar graphs or pie charts. Maintain the width of a set of squares, but vary their height and you can create a bar chart. The Brush parameter not only allows you to select color, but brush style (diagonal, cross, horizontal, and so forth).
TQRPreview	I felt that this was probably the most polished part of quick report. It allows you to display the current report on screen. The user can move from page to page or send the report to the printer. There's even a scaling factor included so that you can zoom in on a section of the report. We'll see how all this works in just a bit.

Now that you've gotten a chance to look at the QuickRpt components, you may ask yourself why you would even want to use them. Some of the components, like TQRShape, are a bit limited in their appeal. On the other hand, I really feel that the TQRPreview component is very well thought out and very usable even without any ancillary code attached to it. (I doubt that many programmers will complain that quick reports does too much work for them.) Here's the one major reason to use a quick report instead of an external report: You get an integrated package when you finish. There aren't any runtime versions of anything to distribute to your client. Everything that they need is in your application.

There's a second reason that'll appeal to you as a programmer. You might want to take another look at the somewhat esoteric code in Chapter 8. We used it to create a calculated field. Custom reports just take too long to create, yet ReportSmith expects you to learn BASIC before you can get any useful work done. It doesn't take too long to figure out that you'll probably save time using quick reports, despite its current limitations, for all but the most complex reports.

I wouldn't be surprised if Borland made Quick Reports their major reporting component in the next update of Delphi. It provides the one thing that I wish the first version had: A fast way to create a report without learning a new programming language. Just think of the time you'll save at the outset by using the QuickRpt components in place of ReportSmith.

Using Database Desktop

Now that we've looked at the components that Delphi gives you to work with, let's take a look at one of the more important utilities. Just about every database programming job requires your to use a combination of existing and new data. Wouldn't it be nice if you could look at all the sources of data using one utility? Database Desktop provides that capability and more. If you can view it with Delphi, then you can modify it with Database Desktop (which is written in Delphi after all).

Figure 12.6 shows how Database Desktop will appear when you first start it up. The first thing you'll notice is three speed bar buttons. The first will open any table that Delphi supports natively. In other words, it'll support any of the standard file types that you requested during the installation process. The second button will open a query into those same sources of information. The third, and most interesting of the three, is the SQL button. You can use it to open a variety of SQL specific sources.

Figure 12.6.
Database Desktop allows you to create and edit tables from a variety of sources.

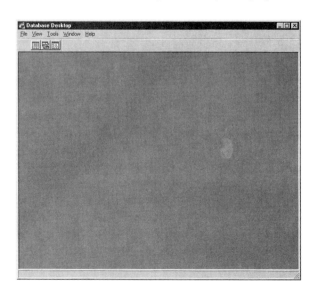

A Quick Look at Opening Standard Tables

Let's take a quick look at a simple example of what Database Desktop can do. For this example I grabbed some data from the \RPTSMITH\DEMOS folder on my drive. However, you can use any source of data you see fit to follow along. I'll be looking at both Xbase (DBF) and Paradox (DB) files.

1. Open Database Desktop, then click on the Open Table speed button. You'll see a standard File Open dialog like the one shown in Figure 12.7. Database Desktop will provide you with a list of standard drivers to choose from in the Files of Type field. Notice the Alias field at the bottom. We'll get into this field in a second; just remember that it's there for the moment.

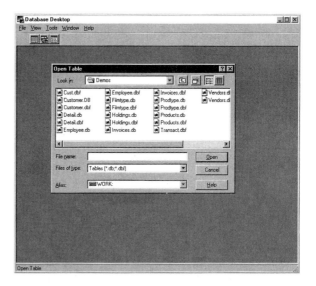

2. Choose a file from one of the standard types listing in the Files of Type field. I chose the CUSTOMER.DB files in the \RPTSMITH\DEMOS folder. You'll see a display similar to the one shown in Figure 12.8. Notice how the speed bar has changed. The first three buttons allow you to cut, copy, and paste data. I'll talk about the rest of the buttons throughout the rest of this section.

3. Click on the Restructure (the fourth) speed bar button. You should see a display similar to the one shown in Figure 12.9 if you're using a Paradox table—the dBASE dialog looks slightly different. This is the display you'll use to reconfigure a table. However, this display does a lot more than that. Notice the area on the right side of the dialog. The Table Properties combo box allows you to select a table property (I'll discuss this in the Understanding the Restructure Dialog section). The edit fields are specific to the property you

select (Validity Check is the default property for Paradox, Indexes is the default for Xbase). If you click on the combo box and scroll through the list of properties, you'll see that this dialog affects just about every aspect of the table and the data it contains. In essence, this dialog allows you to perform a lot of the setups required to use the table within Delphi—without spending a lot of time programming. Now let's talk about the Field Roster—the table that grabs nearly two-thirds of the display area.

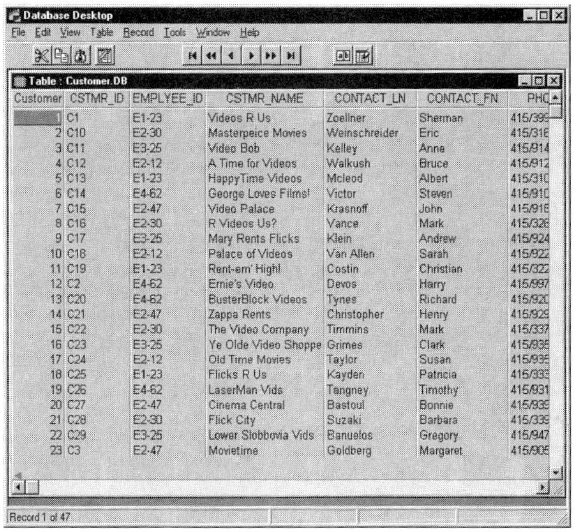

Figure 12.8.
Database Desktop changes the speed bar once it loads a file. Notice that you can now modify the table's data or structure as needed.

Figure 12.9.
The Restructure dialog allows you to do a lot more than simply redefine the database structure; it allows you to perform some of the setups required to use it within Delphi.

4. Click on the number 1 in the first column and drag it down one space. Notice that Database Desktop moves the field associated with that number to the new position. You can use this feature to reorganize a table. So, why would you want to do this? For one thing, I normally place all my key fields first so that they always appear at the beginning of the list. You should have also noticed that the mouse cursor changed to a double arrow as you moved the field—if you didn't move the field again. Database Desktop will normally provide you with some visual cue that tells you what a particular action will accomplish.

Tip: If you still need some additional cues, there is a box directly below the table structure. It tells you what you can do with a particular field or edit box.

Note: You can add a new field to the table by pressing the Insert key when any of the columns in the Field Roster are selected. Pressing Ctrl-Delete will remove a field.

5. Move the field back to its original position—we don't want to change the way any of the example programs are supposed to work.

6. Click once, then a second time on the Field Name column of the table. Notice that the cursor changes to an edit cursor. Database Desktop allows you to change the name of an existing field. Obviously you'll want to exercise some caution here since any applications you create to use this table will depend on that field name staying the same.

7. Right click on the Type column. (Another method of doing this is to click on the column and press the spacebar.) You should see a context menu similar to the one shown in Figure 12.10 if you've opened a Paradox table (the Xbase context menu will look slightly different). The contents of this context menu change automatically to match the type of table that you're looking at. The Type context menu allows you to choose a new type for an existing field.

8. Click on the Size column. There aren't any tricks here, you just enter a number. However, what if you forget the size limit for a particular field type—something that's very easy to do if you work with a variety of table types in one application? You should see a size limitation tip in the same box where you've seen all the tips so far. Desktop Database won't leave you in the dark when it comes to modifying the size of the field.

9. Click on the DEC column if you have an Xbase table open. This column is only active when you select a numeric or a float field. It determines how many characters appear after the decimal point. So, if you have a number that's 15 characters long and contains 7 characters after the decimal point, you'll see 7 characters before the decimal point since the decimal point counts as a character.

Figure 12.10.
Database Desktop automatically displays the field types for the table type that you are editing.

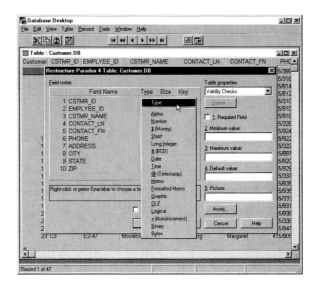

10. Double click on the Key column if you have a Paradox table open. Notice that Database Desktop inserts an asterisk next to the field that you clicked on. This column tells Delphi which fields are primary keys. It uses this information to help you during the application design process.

11. Click on Cancel to close the Restructure dialog. There are a few other minor controls that I want to show you quickly, but they aren't nearly as important as the Restructure dialog. I'm not going to discuss the database navigator since we've already covered that topic in this chapter.

12. Reduce the size of one of the fields so that you can't see all of it. All you need to do is place the mouse cursor on the line between two fields, wait until it changes into a double arrow, then drag the line one way or another.

13. Click on the next to the last button on the speed bar—this is the Field View button. The Field View button allows you to look at fields, like memo fields, that are too long for the display area. Notice that you can scroll through the field, but that any other keys that you press get ignored. I really like this safety feature. It allows me to really get a good look at the data in a particular field without worrying about changing its contents.

14. Click on the last button—the Edit Data button. Now if you type anything in the selected field, Database Desktop will change its contents. Notice how Database Desktop depressed both the Field View and the Edit Data buttons. It also added an insertion cursor to the field. Always verify that you have the right button pushed before selecting a field.

15. Select the File | Exit command to exit Database Desktop. You may see a dialog asking if you want to save the changes you made to the current table. Tell Database Desktop no (unless you really do want to make the changes). We'll talk about some of the other features it provides in the next two sections.

As you can see, Database Desktop is more than just a handy utility. I think you'll find it indispensable. The more types of data that your application has to handle, the easier it becomes to use this one utility to make any required modifications. Obviously there's another reason to use this utility. The data you save will directly impact your Delphi application—the table properties entries you make in the Restructure dialog will show up as you add components to your Delphi application.

Using Other Sources of Data

Database Desktop does provide a lot more than meets the eye. The main event—as I call it—doesn't appear on the speed bar; it appears on Tools menu. It also appears on the File Open dialog. I have found that I use the Alias Manager more often than not to open a database because a lot of my client data is in Access or other ODBC compliant databases. Using the Alias Manager allows you to access these tables and still make the required Restructure dialog settings.

I'm not going to show you how to make all the required entries to access the data in this section—I'll take care of that in the "Accessing DBMS Through ODBC" and "Using the BDE Configuration Utility" sections that follow this one. The process isn't too involved, but you need to take it one step at a time.

For right now, I'll assume that you already have an ODBC data source defined (or you can simply follow along with this example and see how to make the appropriate connections in Database Desktop). I'll walk you through the process of viewing data through an ODBC connect—in this case an Access database.

1. Open Database Desktop.
2. Click on the Open Table speed button. You'll see the same File Open dialog as you saw in Figure 12.7.
3. Click on the Alias combo box and you'll see a list of available aliases like the one shown in Figure 12.11. You define these aliases using the BDE Configuration utility (or the Database Desktop Alias Manager). An alias in this case is a predefined connection that you've created. Notice that the symbol for an ODBC connection is completely different than the one used for a standard connection.
4. Select the ODBC connection—in this case it's ODBC_Access1. You should see a Database Information dialog like the one shown in Figure 12.12. This dialog allows you to log into the database server. I've used the Admin account for Access for the purpose of this example. Normally you would enter your user name and password.

Note: You'll normally have to have administrator equivalent access to a database to modify its structure and perform a variety of other tasks. If you can't access a particular database, you may need to ask the database administrator for additional rights.

Figure 12.11.

The Alias combo box will display a list of predefined connections to tables or databases.

Figure 12.12.

The Database Information dialog usually asks for a user name and password—which Database Desktop passes on to the database server to gain access to the database.

5. Once you enter the appropriate data in the Database Information dialog, click on OK. Database Desktop will display an SQL cursor as it gains access to the database. Once it does establish a connection, you'll see a list of tables in the File Open dialog.

6. Double click on one of the tables to open it. You should see an open table, just like we saw in the previous section.

There's one thing you need to know about some types of ODBC connections. While you can view and even edit the data in the database using Database Desktop, you can't use the Restructure dialog. The reason is simple: The table that you want to modify isn't under Delphi's direct control. You're going through a server to access the data. To get around this problem you'll need to modify the table and its access rules using the utilities provided with the database server.

Understanding the Restructure Dialog

Now that we've looked at most of the mechanics of using the Database Desktop utility, let's look at the kinds of things you can modify using the Restructure dialog. Figure 12.9 shows what this dialog looks like when using a Paradox table—the Restructure dialog for tables created using other DBMS will look slightly different. What we're interested in here are the items listed in the Table Properties combo box. Obviously different DBMS require different types of Table Properties. These properties allow you to change the way that Delphi interacts with the table in particular and the database as a whole. Table 12.4 describes the various Table Properties for both Paradox and dBASE IV and their use. (Other Xbase languages will use properties similar to the ones you'll use for dBASE IV.)

Table 12.4. Restructure Dialog Table Properties Description.

Property	Description
Validity Checks	This property allows you to define the individual data entry limitations for each field in the table. For example, you can define the minimum and maximum value that the user can enter. This could prevent the user from making some types of data entry mistakes. The Default Value field often gets overlooked and it shouldn't. Think of this field as your opportunity to show the user how to make a proper data entry. There are some situations where this isn't important—like a last name, and others where it is—like an account or stock number. The Picture field can really help out when it comes to complex data field entries. You literally define a character by character map of the data that you want entered into that field in the table. I talk more about pictures in the Using Pictures to Verify Data Entry section that follows.
Table Lookup	I've talked about lookup tables quite a few times in this chapter so far. Selecting this property allows you to create a lookup table automatically. All you need to do to use it click on the Define pushbutton. I'll talk about this property a bit more in the Creating Lookup Table Links section that follows.
Secondary Indexes	Paradox differentiates between primary and secondary indexes. The primary index is the one that you choose using the Key field of the Field Roster area. You won't run into too many situations where the user will want to look at their data in only one way. That's where this particular table property comes into play. It allows you to define a secondary index. Every table has one primary index—the one that it uses to order the table in almost every situation. A secondary index gets used for lookups, browses, and print routines. I'll talk about this property a bit more in the Defining Secondary Indexes section that follows.
Referential Integrity	This particular property could mean a lot of things to a lot of people—especially if you're a relational purist like some folks out there. I'm not going to tell you all the grizzly details when it comes to referential integrity; there are entire tomes on the subject. However, for the purposes of our discussion, let's look at referential integrity as

Property	Description
	a lock-stepped relation between two tables, a master and a slave. For a slave to hold a record, there must be a corresponding record in the master. When you delete the record in the master, all the related records in the slave also get deleted. I'll cover the method for using this particular property in the Adding Referential Integrity section that follows.
Password Security	It's important to protect your data. Then again, if you're the only one using that data in a small business, there aren't too many dangers from other people looking at your data. It's pretty obvious when you set up an SQL server that more than one person will use the data, so security becomes an issue. You'll find that all SQL DBMS on the market provide a password screen for just that reason. Paradox provides password security as an option. That's what this particular property is all about. You select this property, then click on Define to display a Password Security dialog. Simply type the password you want to use in the two fields provided and then click on OK. That's all it takes to add a password to your table.

Warning: I can't think of a single Xbase product that comes with built-in security. You normally need to use a combination of hand programmed security screens and network security to protect your data. This means you'll need to exercise some extra care when using an Xbase product in a large database environment. Does this mean that Xbase products are inherently unsafe? Some people think so; others have used Xbase products without problems for years. I personally prefer the built-in security provided by products like Access and Paradox, but I've used Xbase on more than one project as well. Security is always a head's-up event. Built-in security just doesn't cut it by itself; the programmer always has to take an active hand in security.

Table Language	Language is a funny thing. When you talk to most people about language, they think about French or German. In this case we're not talking about language as much as we're talking about the characters used to represent the language. Selecting this property, then clicking on the Modify pushbutton will allow you to change the character set (code page) used to display the data in the table. It won't magically change the words in the table from one language to another.

continues

Table 12.4. **continued**

Property	Description

> **Tip:** Selecting the code page for your application may only be one step in the process. Most operating systems require you to load the required code page into memory during the boot process. The operating system has to know how to interpret the character codes produced by your application before it can display them on screen. You may also experience some problems using DBCS (double-byte character set) characters if your operating system doesn't provide the proper level of support. Languages that use more than 26 characters, like Chinese, require DBCS support.

Property	Description
Dependent Tables	This particular property doesn't allow you to change anything. What it does do is display all the tables that depend on the current table for referential integrity. In other words, if you look at this property and see a filename listed, then you know that this is a master table to that detail table.
Indexes	dBASE doesn't differentiate between primary and secondary indexes. It allows you to switch between indexes as needed. However, the principle of defining an index is the same as Paradox—you choose which fields you want to use to create the index. I'll talk about this property a bit more in the Defining Secondary Indexes section that follows.

Using Pictures to Verify Data Entry

I mentioned a Picture field for the Validity Checks property. A picture can do a lot more than just verify that the data a user enters is correct, it can actually help him enter a correct value. Database Desktop doesn't leave you out in the cold when it comes to defining your own picture. You'll notice an Assist pushbutton at the bottom of the dialog when the Validity Checks property is selected. If you click on this pushbutton you'll see a dialog similar to the one shown in Figure 12.13.

The first thing you need to understand is how a picture gets created and what that long list of characters represents. Table 12.5 shows the various characters used to create a picture. Notice that the actual character set is fairly simple, it's the implementation of those characters that can get quite complex.

Figure 12.13.

The Picture Assistance dialog can help you create a data entry picture for each field in a table.

Table 12.5. Validation Picture Character Set.

Character	Description
#	Numeric digit
?	Any letter (A through Z) (uppercase or lowercase)
&	Any letter (convert to uppercase)
~	Any letter (convert to lowercase)
@	Any character (a character is anything you can type, contrasted to a letter that is an alphanumeric character from A through Z)
!	Any character (convert to uppercase)
;	This is a semicolon. It tells Delphi to interpret the next character as a literal, not as a special picture-string character. For example, if you needed to add an actual # to a picture—like #123, then you'd have to precede it with a semicolon.
*	This is an asterisk. You follow it with a number followed by the type of character in brackets. For example, *3{#} means three numbers in a row.
[abc]	Brackets always indicate optional characters. In this case we're looking at optional characters a, b, or c. You can also use this with groups of picture elements.
{a,b,c}	This is another method for indicating optional characters. Notice that we're using curly brackets this time in place of the square brackets in the previous example.

So, how would you use this character? Say you want to define a telephone number that looks like 619/555-1234. You'd create a picture like this *3{#}/*3{#}-*4{#}. Delphi would expect the user to enter three numbers, then it would automatically add a slash. The user would continue by adding three more numbers; Delphi would add the dash. Finally, the user would add four numbers to complete the entry.

Once you create a picture, you can ask Database Desktop to check it for errors by pressing the Verify Syntax pushbutton. Use the Restore Original pushbutton if you make a mistake and need to start over again.

I found the next section of this dialog very handy. You can't always be sure that you'll get the expected result from a picture, even if the syntax is correct. Database Desktop provides the Sample Value field so that you can test your picture once you verify that the syntax is correct. You'll see messages right below the Test Value pushbutton that will lead you through the testing process. You can press the Test Value pushbutton at any time to see if a partial value is accepted.

Borland also helps you along with some predefined pictures. All you need to do to see them is click on the Sample Pictures combo box. Select a picture, then read the comment to make sure it'll do what you want. To use the picture simply click on the Use pushbutton. If you decide that you no longer need a picture, select it, then click on the Delete From List pushbutton.

Saving your own pictures is easy. All you need to do is create a picture, verify the syntax, test it to make sure it'll do what you want it to, then click on the Add to List pushbutton. Database Desktop will display a dialog similar to the one in Figure 12.14. All you need to do to complete the process is add a comment and click on OK.

Figure 12.14.

The Save Picture dialog allows you to save pictures that you can use later in other projects.

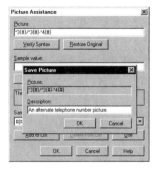

Creating Lookup Table Links

Lookup tables come in handy for a wide variety of data entry and data verification purposes. For example, I always use a lookup table for the state field of a mailing list manager. They almost always appear in applications where I have to categorize something. Using a lookup table enables me to maintain a superior level of flexibility in the application—all the administrator has to do is update the table when new categories (or other lookup items) are needed.

As I previously mentioned, the Restructure dialog provides access to a lookup table definition dialog. It appears in Figure 12.15 as the Table Lookup dialog and allows you to define a link between the existing table and the lookup table. You access this dialog by selecting Table Lookup in the Table Properties field of the Restructure dialog, then pressing Define. There's a simple procedure to follow whenever you want to define a lookup. The following steps will show you how I do things—you can modify them as needed for your particular situation. (I'm assuming that you've already gotten the Table Lookup dialog open.) I decided to use the CUSTOMER.DB table in the ReportSmith DEMOS directory as my starting point, but this procedure will work fine no matter what table you start with.

Figure 12.15.

The Table Lookup dialog allows you to define lookup table links for your application.

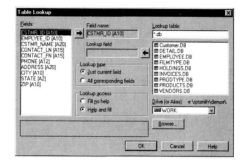

1. Select a source of information using the Alias field. Delphi doesn't restrict you to using the current directory or database, but I usually find that I do for the special lookup tables connected to the current project. Notice that a directory substitutes for a database when using some types of files like Xbase DBF files.

> **Tip:** Always store common lookup tables in one database or directory. For example, I maintain a list of common lookup tables for Xbase in a LOOKUP directory on my drive. These tables might include lists of states, common categories, and standard abbreviations for things like computer terms. Using this technique allows you to update the lookup table values for all your projects by modifying a single table. It also reduces data replication and associated problems that most database developers would prefer to avoid.

2. Click on the table that you want to use as a lookup table. In this case I chose EMPLOYEE.DB.
3. Click on the right pointing arrow next to the Lookup Field field. You'll see the key field for the selected table. In my case it was EMPLOYEE_ID.
4. Find the field that matches the key field in the current table, highlight it, then press the left pointing arrow next to the Field Name field. Your dialog should look like the one in Figure 12.16.

Figure 12.16.
Defining a lookup table is as easy as telling Database Desktop which table and field to use.

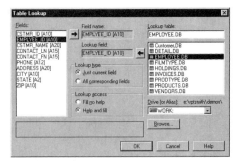

Note: Database Desktop always chooses the first field in a lookup table as the one to use when creating a link. If you can't access the field that you need, then open the lookup table and use the Field Roster in the Restructure dialog to move the appropriate field to the top of the list.

5. Select a Lookup Type. The default setting of Just Current Field allows you complete control over which data gets selected. The All Corresponding Fields option selects all the fields in the master table that match fields in the lookup table. This option can backfire on you unless you're very sure of how the two tables are structured. I normally use this option with special purpose lookup tables like the one I use to store the names of states (it only has two fields: one containing the abbreviation and another containing the full name).

6. Select a Lookup Access. The Help and Fill option does two things. First, it automatically fills the master table field that you select with the information in the lookup table. Second, it provides help to the user—a message stating what kinds of entry are acceptable. The second option only fills the master table; it doesn't provide any form of assistance to the user.

7. Click OK to complete the process. You'll see three new entries on the Restructure dialog as shown in Figure 12.17. The first is a list box that contains the names of any lookup tables used with the current table. The second is an Erase pushbutton, which allows you to remove any lookup table connections that you no longer need. The third is a Modify pushbutton that allows you to change the link.

Note: The lookup table information will only appear when you select the affected field. If you change the highlight in the Field Roster to another field, Database Desktop will display a define button, but nothing else. Notice also that it disables the Define pushbutton once you define a lookup table link for a particular field. Obviously you can't define more than one lookup table link for a field.

Figure 12.17.
The Restructure dialog
automatically updates itself
to show any new lookup
table connections that you
create.

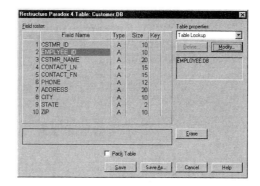

I view lookup tables as one of the essential methods of reducing database bloat in an application. Everyone wins when the developer thinks ahead and uses lookup tables whenever appropriate. The user wins in data entry speed and reduced ambiguity—there isn't any doubt as to what values are acceptable. The developer wins because he doesn't have to redefine the same data for every project. The network administrator wins because long sequences of characters get reduced to a simple code, saving an immense amount of space on disk and reducing network traffic as well. The database administrator wins with fewer user calls and a lower number of data entry errors.

Defining Secondary Indexes

Secondary indexes (or simply indexes when you're talking about Xbase) come in handy for a variety of purposes. However, I normally view them as a means of ordering data to meet the user's needs in browse, print, and lookup routines. A secondary index allows a user to view his data in a variety of alternate ways. For example, a mailing list manager normally maintains the master table in last name order. However, to meet postal requirements, you might have to print labels out in ZIP code order. A user may also want to view his data by city or state to target a specific group of people.

Database Desktop provides a quick method of defining any secondary indexes that you may need. Simply select the Secondary Index (Indexes for Xbase tables) property on the Restructure dialog, then click the Define pushbutton. You'll see a Define Secondary Index dialog similar to the one shown in Figure 12.18 for Paradox or Figure 12.19 for Xbase. Since the actual procedure for creating the index is different for both products, I'll cover them separately in the following sections.

Figure 12.18.
The Define Secondary Index dialog (Paradox) allows you to order a table in more than one way by creating a secondary index.

Figure 12.19.
The Define Index dialog (Xbase) allows you to order a table in more than one way by creating a new index.

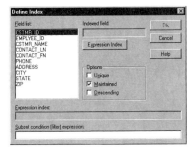

Creating a Paradox Index

All you need to do to use this dialog is click on the field you want to use from the Fields list box, then the right pointing arrow. The field name will appear in the Indexed Fields list box. To remove a field from the list you simply select its entry in the Indexed Fields list box and press the left pointing arrow. Database Desktop uses the order that the fields appear in the Indexed Fields list box as the criteria for ordering the information. You can move fields around by selecting a particular field name, then pressing the up or down Change Order arrow.

You can create a variety of special effects using the check boxes in the Index Options group. A Unique index only contains unique values—which prevents a user from entering more than one type of an indexed item. For example, if you decided that there could be only one entry of each customer name in a file, you might use their name as an index and specify the unique option. Case-sensitive indexes allow the user to dictate precise search criteria because Search becomes a different value from "SEARCH." Some DBMS store their indexes in separate files—you can choose whether you want to load them or not. If you don't load the file, then the DBMS doesn't keep it up to date. The tradeoff is that you do save some program execution time because the DBMS has one less index to maintain. Delphi assumes that you want to maintain an index in ascending order unless you tell it otherwise—the Descending check box allows you to do just that.

Warning: Unique indexes can be a two-edged sword. On the one hand they assist the database administrator in maintaining table integrity by disallowing duplicate entries. On the other hand, they can prevent the user from making a legitimate entry unless the programmer fully figures out the ramifications of a unique index beforehand. Consider what would happen if you had two customers with the same name and used name as a unique index. Would your client be willing throw away a perfectly good customer because of a lack of flexibility in your indexing scheme? It always pays to think ahead when using any of the index options that a particular DBMS supports.

Once you define the index, Database Desktop will normally ask you what name you would like to save it under using the dialog shown in Figure 12.20. This isn't a filename; it's the name that you'll use to refer to the index later on.

Figure 12.20.
The Save Index As dialog
allows you to save an index
for future use.

Note: When creating a Paradox index, the Save Index As dialog box only appears if you create an index that's case-insensitive or based on more than one field. Never give an index the same name as a field.

Once you do define the index, it appears in the list box directly below the Table Properties field as shown in Figure 12.21. Notice that you can modify or erase the secondary index if you want to. I named my index Temp since I don't plan to keep it in this case. However, there's another good reason for keeping a Temp index in your table—you can use it to create ad-hoc indexes later.

Creating an Xbase Index

dBASE IV uses MDX—maintained index files to store the indexes you create. Other index types include NDX and IDX. You'll also find a few other formats floating around like the NTX index used by the Clipper Xbase derivative. For the purposes of this book, we'll always use the MDX index when creating an index. It's the most versatile and the newest of the various index formats available. I normally don't use the NDX format for anything but temporary or ad-hoc indexes (we'll see how Database Desktop creates them for you in a bit).

Figure 12.21.

Database Desktop maintains a list of any secondary indexes you create.

Unlike Paradox, there's no differentiation between indexes in an Xbase MDX file—the first index in the list loaded indexes is always the one that has control over the order of a browse or printout. Xbase maintains the other indexes that it loads, but doesn't use them to order the data.

You can create an index for Xbase using one of two methods. The first method is the easier. The first thing you need to do is select Expression Index using the pushbutton in the center of the dialog. (It toggles between two states.) You would use the index field state if you wanted to use the exact contents of a particular field to index the table. Next, double click on a field in the Field List and click on OK. You'll see a Save Index As dialog like the one shown in Figure 12.22. There are two things you should notice about this dialog. First, the Index Tag Name field is enabled. If you store an index in an MDX file, it's called an index tag since there's more than one index in the file. The second thing you should notice is that there's a field name automatically entered in the dialog. Database Desktop always suggests the field name as the index tag name if you're using a single field. I recommend that you stick with the field name to make it easier to figure out where the index came from later. dBASE IV doesn't provide you with a very long tag name area—only 10 characters—so using the field name makes sense.

Once you click OK in the Save Index As dialog, you'll see it added to the list of indexes in the Restructure dialog as shown in Figure 12.23. This list won't show any of the NDX files that you create, which is just another reason not to use them if at all possible. You can erase or modify an index once you highlight it.

Figure 12.22.
The Save Index As dialog
allows you to save any new
indexes that you create.

Figure 12.23.
The Restructure dialog shows
all of the index tag names
contained in the MDX file
associated with the current
table.

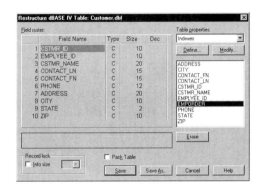

Previously, I told you that there is a second method for creating Xbase indexes. You aren't restricted to a single field or even to using fields in an index. Xbase allows you to use a combination of fields and functions in an index expression. The way to start this process is to select the Index Field option by clicking the pushbutton in the middle of the Define Index dialog. Double clicking on a field will place it in the Expression Index field. You use the + sign to concatenate fields together.

So, how do you use an index expression? I normally reserve them for those occasions when I want to create a special means of displaying the data—especially in browses or printed output. For example, you could use the expression: Upper(CONTACT_LN) + Upper(CONTACT_FN) to create an index that orders the data by last name, then first name. Adding the Upper() function allows you to make the index case-insensitive.

There are several other things you can do with a dBASE IV index. The Subset Condition (Filter) Expression field of the Define Index dialog allows you to specify a condition for choosing specific records from the table. For example, if you wanted to see all the customers in Wisconsin, you would add a filter expression like: STATE = 'WI'. There are a few things you need to know about filters. First, a filter must always evaluate to true or false. Second, since a filter is a Boolean expression, you can use relational operators like: .AND., .OR., and .NOT. to combine various expressions.

dBASE makes a differentiation between maintained and non-maintained indexes. Any index it finds in an MDX file is always maintained. The MDX file is associated with a specific table and automatically loads when it loads. dBASE also maintains any other indexes that you load into memory. These indexes can appear in an NDX or IDX file—Database Desktop supports the NDX file—that's the file it uses if you decide to create a non-maintained index.

Beside choosing whether or not to maintain an index, you can create a variety of other special effects using the check boxes in the Options group. A Unique index only contains unique values—

allowing the user to find the first in a series of like items. Delphi assumes that you want to maintain an index in ascending order unless you tell it otherwise—the Descending check box allows you to do just that.

Adding Referential Integrity

Referential integrity—I could probably open every can of worms on the planet if I wanted to. I've read more than a few texts on the subject, most of which are highly technical, detailed discourses on database theory. You, as a developer, need to know some theory, but I'm sure you don't want to get buried in it. The easiest way to view referential integrity is as an algebraic proof. Anything you do to one side of the equation, you have to do to the other—anything you do to the master table, you have to do to the detail tables as well. I find this particular definition works just fine for my needs, you'll probably find it works for you as well. The bottom line is that if you have some key value in your detail table that doesn't match up with a value in your master table, then how do you access it? And, if you can't access a value, then your database is corrupt. It's just that simple.

Database Desktop provides the means for you to maintain referential integrity within your database. However, to make referential integrity work you have to do some prior setup. Let's take a look at the data in our \RPTSMITH\DEMOS directory again. There are two related tables in there that I'll use in the following procedure. However, you could follow the same procedure for any two tables in your database. My master table is EMPLOYEE.DB; the detail table is CUSTOMER.DB. Each employee will interact with 0, 1, or more customers.

Tip: Many of the theoretical database management books you'll read use the following acronyms: referential integrity (RI), primary key (PK), foreign key (FK), and entity relationship (ER). I'm going to spell all the terms out in my discussion. Sometimes there are just a few too many acronyms in the computer industry—even for me.

1. Open Database Desktop.
2. Verify that the working directory points to the \RPTSMITH\DEMOS directory (or your current work directory) using the File | Working Directory command and entering the correct path in the Set Working Directory dialog.
3. Load the EMPLOYEE.DB (or your master) table.
4. Open the Restructure dialog.
5. Set the primary key to the EMPLYEE_ID field by double-clicking on the Key column in the Field Roster.
6. Click on Save to save the primary key.
7. Open the CUSTOMER.DB (or your detail) table.

8. Open the Restructure dialog.

9. Double-click on both the CSTMR_ID and EMPLYEE_ID fields to set them up as a primary key.

10. Select the Referential Integrity option in the Table Properties field. Click the Define pushbutton. You'll see a dialog similar to the one shown in Figure 12.24. Notice that it lists all the tables in the current working directory on the right side and all the fields from the current table on the left side.

Figure 12.24.
The Referential Integrity dialog allows you to set up the data entry rules for a master/detail table set.

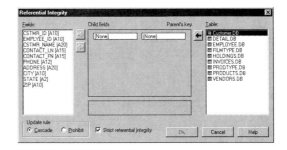

11. Double-click on the EMPLYEE_ID field. Notice that Database Desktop adds the field name to the Child Fields entry in the dialog. (Most database management texts call the child field a foreign key.) You should also notice that it adds a copy of the table name to the list of tables.

12. Double-click on the EMPLOYEE.DB table. Your dialog should now look like the one in Figure 12.25. Notice that Database Desktop automatically selected the primary key in the EMPLOYEE.DB table that you defined previously.

Figure 12.25.
The completed Referential Integrity dialog shows the relationship between the two tables.

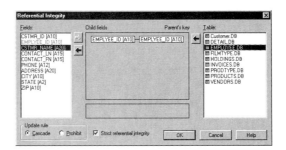

13. Click OK. Database Desktop will display the Save Referential Integrity As dialog shown in Figure 12.26.

14. Type Employee ID and click on OK. Your Restructure dialog should now show a referential integrity rule like the one shown in Figure 12.27.

Figure 12.26.
The Save Referential Integrity As dialog allows you to save the current referential integrity rule.

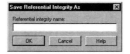

Figure 12.27.
Database Desktop tracks the referential integrity rules that you create.

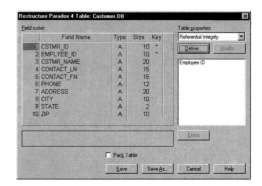

15. We really don't need to save these modifications so click on Cancel to clear them.

16. Reopen the EMPLOYEE.DB table.

17. Open the Restructure dialog and clear the primary key entry that you made previously.

18. Click on Save to save the change.

19. Close Database Desktop using the File | Exit command.

That's all there is to it. The mechanics of defining appropriate referential integrity rules are fairly simple. Figuring out the relationships between the various tables in your database could become quite cumbersome if you don't perform some prior planning. You'll definitely want to draw the relationships out—either by hand or using some of the entity relationship (ER) CAD programs like ERWin that are available on the market.

Accessing DBMS Through ODBC

Creating an ODBC source is a two-step process when using Delphi. The first step involves the data server and Windows. You have to tell both of them that some application is going to use a particular database as a source of information. So how do you do this?

You'll find a 32-bit ODBC applet in your Control Panel if there are any 32-bit ODBC drivers on your machine. Likewise, the ODBC applet contains 16-bit drivers. Delphi 1.0 (the 16-bit version) can only use 16-bit ODBC sources. Delphi 2.0 can only use 32-bit sources (at least as of this writing). This means you'll have to obtain the right kind of driver for your particular application and the source of data you want to tap.

I'm going to show you how to create a link to an Access database in this example. However, you can use the same procedure for any DBMS that supports ODBC. Only the name of the table and the DBMS specific definition procedure will change. If you don't have a 32-bit Access ODBC driver installed on your machine, you can still follow along and see how to get the job done.

1. Open the Control Panel, then the 32-bit ODBC applet. (Use the ODBC applet if you're running 16-bit Delphi, the process for designing a data source is virtually the same.) You should see the Data Sources dialog shown in Figure 12.28. Notice that the screenshot shows a Microsoft Access 7.0 Database source. You should see a similar source in your dialog.

Figure 12.28.
The Data Sources dialog shows the current ODBC sources you have defined.

2. Click the Add pushbutton. You should see an Add Data Source dialog like the one shown in Figure 12.29. Notice that Access is the only driver listed in this dialog even though there were two data sources listed in the Data Sources dialog. This tells you that the other data source was actually a database source that I had already defined for some other purpose.

Figure 12.29.
The Add Data Source dialog tells you which ODBC drivers you have installed.

3. Highlight the Access data source, then click on OK. You should see the ODBC Microsoft Access 7.0 Setup dialog shown in Figure 12.30. Every ODBC driver uses a different display for configuration purposes—the exact format depends on the needs of the ODBC driver. You'll need to check the vendor documentation to see what types of information you need to provide to create the ODBC connection. Access makes it fairly easy for you to define a data source by providing a variety of point and click responses.

4. Type a data source name in the Data Source Name field. In my case I typed Sample Database. Obviously you'll want to type something a little more descriptive for your database—usually a name that describes its purpose or the type of data it contains.

Figure 12.30.
*The ODBC Microsoft
Access 7.0 Setup dialog is
where you tell Access which
database you want to access
from another application.*

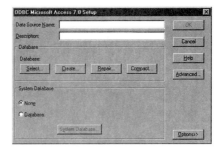

5. Type a description for the data source in the Description field. I typed 'This is some sample data.' for this example. Make sure the description you type amplifies the data source name, not merely reiterates what the name would tell the user.

6. Click the Select pushbutton. The ODBC driver will open a Select Database dialog. It works and acts just like a File Open dialog.

7. Choose the database you want to use, then click on OK. In my case I chose 'My Database.MDB' as the database.

8. Click on OK. You'll see a new data source added to the Data Sources dialog. Notice that it includes the name of the ODBC driver in parenthesis after the entry.

9. Click Close to close the ODBC dialog. You now have a new data source to use with Delphi. All you need to do to use it is define the entry using the BDE Configuration utility. I'll describe how to use it in the next section.

Both the 32-bit ODBC and ODBC applets provide a few additional pushbuttons in the Data Sources dialog that you need to know about. If you need to change the information for a data source that you defined, highlight the data source and click on Setup. Likewise, if you're done using a data source, you can simply highlight it and click on Delete.

It always helps to know something about the ODBC driver you're using, especially if you get into trouble trying to make it work. You can find out about the driver by clicking on the Drivers pushbutton to display the Driver dialog. Highlight the driver that you want to learn about and click on About. You'll see an About dialog similar to the one in Figure 12.31. Click on OK to remove the dialog once you've finished looking at it.

Figure 12.31.
*The ODBC driver About
dialog can tell you a lot about
the driver you're using—
including the version number
in most cases.*

I don't always track everything that's going on with the ODBC drivers on my machine. There are two exceptions to this rule: Development time and debugging time. I need to know what's going on as I develop a new application. The only good way to do that with ODBC is to log the activity that takes place. The same thing holds true when I'm debugging the application or the user reports a problem that I can't solve using an application's built-in troubleshooting capabilities. To track the activity of a data source all you need to do is turn tracking on. Highlight the data source you want to track, then click the Options pushbutton. You'll see a dialog similar to the one in Figure 12.32.

Figure 12.32.
The ODBC Options dialog allows you to trace ODBC calls—a valuable trouble-shooting tool.

All you need to do to turn tracking on is to click on the Trace ODBC Calls check box, then click on OK. Pressing the Select File pushbutton displays a Select ODBC Trace File dialog (which looks just like a File Open dialog). Simply select the file you want to use in place of the default SQL.LOG file, then click on OK. You can define a new log file name in place of selecting an existing one. The Stop Tracing ODBC Calls Automatically check box should stay checked. Otherwise, you'll find that your log just keeps getting bigger and bigger as Windows keeps logging events into the file. Checking this option allows you to monitor the events for one debugging session. You have to recheck the Trace ODBC Calls check box to restart logging for the next debugging session.

Using the BDE Configuration Utility

You'll use the BDE (Borland Database Engine) Configuration Utility to define all the data sources for your Delphi application. It provides the connection information that your application needs to access the database. Think about BDE as the lowest level of database access in your application— the physical connection between your application and the host DBMS. This section isn't going to explore every detail of the BDE Configuration Utility—its main purpose is to show you how to create a connection.

When you load the BDE Configuration Utility, it opens to the drivers page shown in Figure 12.33. The first time you open it, you'll see a list of the drivers you installed during the installation process. (I happened to install the dBASE, Paradox, and Interbase drivers in this case.) These are all the default drivers that you can use—the DBMS sources that you won't need to define since BDE defines them during the installation process for you.

Most people find that defining ODBC sources is one of the most difficult things to do, and for good reason. Defining a standard source of information doesn't involve much more than a few simple directory entries. To create an ODBC requires two steps—defining the ODBC source, then the data source.

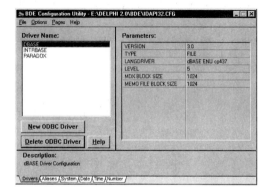

Figure 12.33.
The BDE Configuration Utility normally opens to the Drivers page when you start it.

I'm going to describe the ODBC process in this section. However, I'll describe it in two steps. The first step—defining an ODBC source—is ODBC specific. You can ignore it for Delphi supported sources of data. (There are situations where you may need to use this technique for sources other than ODBC like some types of SQL sources.)

Look in the second section to see how to define the data source. I'll be using the same ODBC example, but you'll get enough information to define just about any source. Obviously the exact entries will change from source-to-source, but you'll get an idea of what's involved.

Defining an ODBC Source

We looked at the first phase of defining an ODBC source in the previous section. You need to determine whether the driver is actually present by looking at the ODBC or 32-bit ODBC applet in the Control Panel before you can use it. Then you need to tell the ODBC driver which database you want to use. You have to configure the ODBC driver and Windows first, then BDE. Look in the section entitled "Accessing DBMS Through ODBC" if you need further details.

Once you get Windows and the ODBC driver taken care of, you need to tell BDE about the driver you want to use. You always have to have the driver installed before you can define any aliases for it. The following procedure will show a generic method of adding an ODBC driver. In this case I'll add the Access 7.0 driver to my BDE list. You can use a similar procedure for other types of drivers.

1. Open the BDE Configuration Utility if you haven't already done so and select the Drivers page.

2. Click on New ODBC Driver. You'll see a dialog similar to the one in Figure 12.34.

Figure 12.34.
The Add ODBC Driver dialog allows you to define a new ODBC driver for BDE.

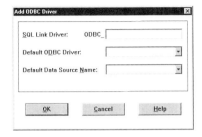

3. Type in the name of the driver (or database) in the SQL Link Driver field. I always use the application name to make it easy to identify the driver later. However, you can use whatever name you like. This is the identifier that all the other Delphi utilities will use to identify the driver; so make the name easy to recognize.

4. Select the Default ODBC Driver from the drop down list provided. In my case I selected Microsoft Access Driver (*.MDB). The BDE Configuration Utility will normally supply an entry for the Default Data Source Name.

5. Change the Default Data Source Name, if necessary, by selecting a new option from the drop down list.

6. Click on OK to save the driver definition. You should see the new driver name added to the Drivers page.

That's all there is to it. Adding new ODBC drivers doesn't have to be difficult. All you need to do is follow a few simple steps and make sure that the driver is available. It always pays to make sure you perform the proper Control Panel setup before you attempt to work with Delphi itself.

Defining a Data Source

You'll spend a lot more time defining data sources than you will adding drivers. Adding a driver is a one-time process—adding data sources can happen over and over again for the same driver. One thing is certain, the BDE Configuration Utility should always be your first stop when it comes to defining data sources. Defining a data source first makes using the other Delphi database utilities a lot easier.

Let's take a look at what you'll need to do to add a new data source. I'm going to show you an ODBC data source. Adding other data sources will require different types of information from you, but the basic process is the same.

1. Open the BDE Configuration Utility if you haven't already done so and select the Aliases page.

2. Click on New Alias. You'll see a dialog similar to the one in Figure 12.35. It's important to know that this dialog is the starting point for every alias you'll define—it doesn't matter which type of driver you intend to use.

Figure 12.35.

The Add New Alias dialog allows you to add a new blank alias to the Aliases page of the BDE Configuration Utility.

3. Type a name in the Sample Alias Name field. I used AccessMyDatabase for this example since it describes the kind of data source I plan to create. Make sure you create an equally usable data source name. This is the name that you'll see in the other Delphi utilities, so the choice of name is important.

Tip: I always add the name of the DBMS application to the data source name. The reason is simple, adding the application name makes it easier to determine which DBMS controls the data. I follow this by the name of the database or table. This makes it easier to find the physical source of data later. You could add other modifiers to make the name even more meaningful if necessary. For example, adding the purpose of the data source is handy. The one thing you'll want to be careful of making is that name too long. Remember that you'll have to refer to the data source by name throughout your application.

4. Select the Alias Type (driver name) from the drop down box. Note that BDE uses Standard to refer to some types of DBMS sources like Paradox and dBASE IV. In my case I chose ODBC_Access since I plan to use an Access ODBC source.

5. Click on OK to complete the process. The BDE Configuration Utility will add another entry to the Alias Names field.

This isn't the end of the process, but it is the end of the section that's the same for all DBMS. From this point on you'll need to work with the configuration requirements for a specific driver. You'll find that most drivers require at least a path and database name entry. Some, like the Standard type, will only ask for a path. In essence, the directory (folder in Windows 95 terms) acts as the database. The individual files within the directory are the tables that you'll choose from in the various Delphi utilities.

I'm going to complete the process that I started in the previous procedure. We'll finish defining the Access ODBC data source. The following procedure shows the minimal number of entries that you'll need. Then I discuss some of the alternative entries you could make.

1. Highlight the alias name. In my cases it's AccessMyData.

2. Select the Path field. Type the path to your data. I stored my sample data locally—
   E:\DATA.

3. Select the Database field. Type the name of the database you want to use. In my cases it's My Database.MDB.

4. Select the User Name field. Normally you wouldn't enter anything here since this is the name that all the Delphi utilities will display when they display the password dialog. I always put a name in to save time during the development process, then remove it once the application becomes active (once I make it available for everyone to use). The Alias page of your BDE Configuration Utility should look similar to Figure 12.36. Notice that I have one other data source defined so far.

Figure 12.36.
The BDE Configuration Utility will display all the aliases you define on the left side of the dialog. The right side shows the parameters for the highlighted alias.

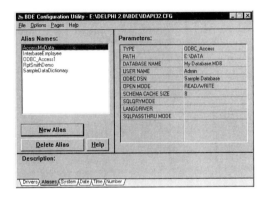

There are four other entries in the Parameters group of the dialog: SCHEMA CACHE SIZE, SQLQRYMODE, LANGDRIVER, and SQLPASSTHRU MODE. Each of these entries provides additional information that you really don't have to define unless you want to set up special conditions. In most cases Delphi will know what to do with the data once you define a source as I showed in the previous steps.

The SCHEMA CACHE SIZE parameter allows you to change the performance characteristics of your application. A schema defines the structure and characteristics of a table. This field tells Delphi how many table schemas to cache. Every SQL schema cache consumes memory. Adding more caches than the default will reduce table load time if you have more than 8 tables. On the other hand, you can free up memory and improve overall application performance by reducing the number when you use less than 8 tables.

The SQLQRYMODE parameter allows you to define the source of SQL information. This entry is only important when you have both a local and server SQL source—the two sources that you can choose from. In most cases you'll want to retain the default NULL setting.

Use the LANGDRIVER parameter to change the default character set for a database. Changing this setting only changes the characters (via a code page) that Delphi uses to display information—it doesn't change the words in the table itself. You can override this setting within the Database Desktop utility. (I covered Database Desktop in an earlier section of this chapter.)

Finally, the SQLPASSTHRU MODE parameter affects the way that Delphi interacts with the database. There are three pass through modes: NOT SHARED, SHARED AUTOCOMMIT, and SHARED NOAUTOCOMMIT. The default setting is SHARED NOAUTOCOMMIT. Use the NOT SHARED setting if you want exclusive access to the database. This would come in handy for some types of maintenance actions or if you needed to perform updates to the table structures. The SHARED AUTOCOMMIT mode allows you to share the database with other people. Delphi automatically commits any changes you make. The advantage to this mode is that you don't have to manually commit the data. The disadvantage is that you can't easily provide the user with an undo mode in the data entry screen. The last mode, SHARED NOAUTOCOMMIT, allows you to share the database with everyone, but any changes made by an individual user won't show up until you commit them. Not only does this mode come in handy if you want to provide an undo feature, but you can use it for a number of batch processing modes.

Using Database Explorer

Database Explorer is a new utility for Delphi 2.0. It allows you to explore databases much like Explorer allows you to view folders and files within Windows 95 (and the new version of Windows NT when it appears on the market). Database Explorer is more than that though, it's a method for actually defining a database and everything that goes with it (except for things like stored procedures—you have to create those separately).

> **Tip:** Since Database Explorer interacts with the BDE, just like the BDE Configuration Utility, you can use it in place of the utility to add new aliases. Each tool has its advantages. I find that the BDE Configuration Utility is extremely fast to use, but it doesn't tell me much about the database I'm using. Database Explorer provides a lot of information about the database I'm using, but it can get to be quite time consuming to use.

When you initially start Database Explorer, you'll see a window similar to the one shown in Figure 12.37. There are two pages: Databases and Dictionary. The Databases page will hold information about the databases you add. This includes things like tables and indexes. We'll get into the precise contents a little later since they vary. The Dictionary page helps you manage the organization of the database. It allows you to define the structure of the tables and perform a variety of other maintenance-type actions.

Now that I've gotten you introduced to Database Explorer, let's take a look at some of the things you can do with it. The following sections explore some, but not all, of the tasks you can perform with Database Explorer. I've concentrated on those tasks that you'll need to perform in order to create basic applications and modify the database as needed during the design process.

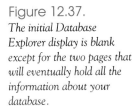

Figure 12.37.
The initial Database
Explorer display is blank
except for the two pages that
will eventually hold all the
information about your
database.

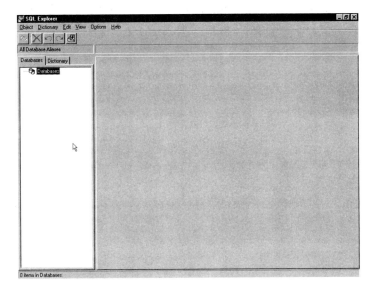

Adding Databases

You can't do much with Database Explorer until you add a database to it, so that's the first task we'll tackle. The following procedure provides you with a generic procedure you can use to add a database. In this case I added the ReportSmith demonstration directory (remember that a standard database is actually a directory containing DBF or DB files) to the list.

1. Right click on the Databases icon. You'll see the context menu shown in Figure 12.38. Every Database Explorer object provides a context menu that you can use to perform actions. I find that the context menu is a lot faster than using the standard menu in most cases. It's also a lot more intuitive than the speed bar in some cases as well.

2. Select New from the context menu. You'll see the New Database Alias dialog shown in Figure 12.39. The Database Driver Name field normally contains the name of a specific driver. However, if you decide to access standard files like dBASE IV or Paradox tables, you'll use the Standard driver.

Tip: Database Explorer automatically inserts any aliases you create into the BDE Configuration Utility. In other words, you don't have to define the alias twice. Use Database Explorer or the BDE Configuration Utility, not both, when defining aliases. You'll have to resort to the BDE Configuration Utility to use ODBC drivers since you have to define a new driver type. However, you can use the Database Explorer once the driver is defined.

Figure 12.38.
Database Explorer provides a context menu for every object you'll interact with.

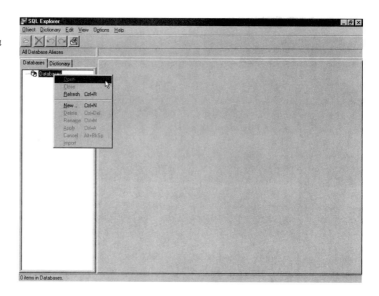

Figure 12.39.
The New Database Alias dialog allows you to select the database type for the database you want to use.

3. Select the driver that you want to use from the drop-down menu and click on OK. In this case I chose the Standard driver since I planned to access a directory containing Paradox and dBASE IV tables.

4. Database Explorer will display a new database on the left side of the Databases window. Notice that the name is selected and there is an edit cursor next to the database name.

5. Rename the database by typing a new name. I chose RptSmithDemo in this case since it's the path to my data. You could, however, use just about any name that's appropriate. For example, I often use the name of the database driver followed by the name of the database. In the previous section I showed how to create an Access ODBC entry using the BDE Configuration Utility. I used AccessMyDatabase as the alias name for that database. The name you use here will appear as the alias throughout all the Delphi utilities and within your application.

Tip: You can always rename the alias if you want to as long as the database is closed. Simply highlight the database name, then click on it a second time. Database Explorer will highlight the database name and follow it with an edit cursor. Just type in the new name and press Enter.

6. Select the Path field on the right side of the display. Type in the path to the directory containing the data. In my case I typed in E:\RPTSMITH\DEMOS.

7. Right click on the RptSmithDemo database entry and select Apply from the context menu. This completes the alias entry. If the alias information is correct, Database Explorer will retrieve all the information about the database you defined. If the information isn't correct, you'll see an error message. Now that you have an alias defined, we can open the database for use.

8. Click on the plus sign next to the RptSmithDemo database entry. You'll see a Tables entry. Click on the plus sign next to this entry as well. This will open the database and display a list of database objects like the ones shown in Figure 12.40. Notice that the database icon changes color to tell you that it's open. You have to use the Close option on the context menu to close the database when you're finished using it.

Figure 12.40.
Once you complete defining the alias, you can open the database and see the objects it contains.

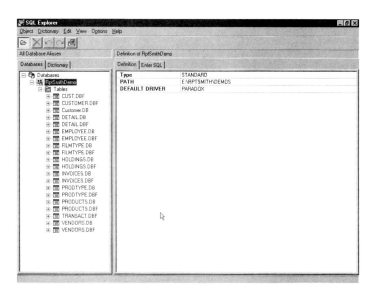

Obviously our example database doesn't contain much—only tables. However, you can use the same process to create a connection to an Interbase database. Figure 12.41 shows the types of information you can collect from an Interbase database. I used about the same procedure to create this database entry as I did for the example. The only difference was the server specific information required to make a connection. (You'll also need to provide a password for the database, the default password for the SYSDBA is: "masterkey". The password is case sensitive, so make sure you use lowercase characters. If this password doesn't work, look at the READIB file in your IntrBase directory to find out what the new default is.) In this case I had to provide the local server name and the path to the EMPLOYEE.GDB database.

Figure 12.41.

Creating an Interbase connection isn't much different from any of the other alias definitions we've done so far in the chapter.

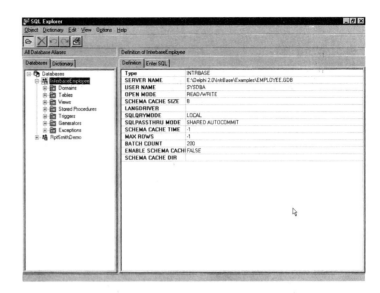

Tip: You'll need to do three things to make sure you can create a reliable connection with the local Interbase server. First, always make sure you install the Interbase SQL Link. You do this by selecting the SQL Links option in the Installation Components and Sub-Components dialog of the Setup program, then clicking on the Interbase Link option within the Select Subcomponents dialog. It may appear that you only need this link for the remote server, especially when the local Interbase Server Manager utility can log into the server and make a connection without any problem. Second, never provide a server name in the Server Name field on the Definition page of Database Explorer. I found this extremely confusing at first, but it became apparent that I only needed the server name when accessing a remote host. Put the path and filename of the database you want to open in this field instead. Finally, set the SQLQRYMODE field to LOCAL. This entry tells Database Explorer to use the local server and not look for a remote host. (See Figure 12.41 to see how I accessed the EMPLOYEE.GDB database.)

Creating a Data Dictionary

A data dictionary does for databases what any dictionary will do for the human language—it defines one or more databases in precise terms and tells you what those terms are. In the case of a database dictionary, the words are databases. For definitions you'll find things like table structures and index definitions as well as any stored procedures and queries. Data dictionaries should be a common component of any DBMS, especially when you consider how easy they make it to manage the structure and resources of a database. Unfortunately, most DBMS don't provide this feature. Database

Explorer provides what I would term an adequate database dictionary—it allows you to perform the majority of the tasks that you'll need to do to create an application.

Before you can create a data dictionary, you have to tell Database Explorer what database to use. This means that you'll have to create a database entry using the procedure in the previous section. The following procedure shows you a generic method for creating a data dictionary. You can use this method with any open database within Database Explorer (in other words, defining the alias within the BDE Configuration Utility, then trying to access it from Database Explorer won't work). I use a separate directory to hold my database dictionary. If you want to store your dictionary in the same database as your data, skip steps 1 and 2.

Tip: You don't have to contaminate your production databases with data dictionary information. I usually set aside a directory on my local drive, then create a database entry for it in Database Explorer. Since you can place as many databases as you want within one dictionary, I usually try to group my dictionaries by functional area or project. For example, I maintain a dictionary named GenericDataDictionary. It contains all of the generic databases that I'll include with a project. For example, a database used to store application configuration information would fall into this category. Obviously a project dictionary would contain all the custom databases for a specific project.

1. Create a data dictionary directory on your local hard drive. I used the name \DATADICT for this example. You can use any name that you want. Remember that you can use long filenames to make the dictionary name readable and help you remember its purpose later. This directory is where you'll find all the definitions for your data later. It's just as important to maintain the integrity of this database as any other that you're working with.

2. Add a new database entry for the data dictionary folder. Using the Standard driver will make the entry as simple as adding the path to the directory. I named my new entry SampleDataDictionary since I'm using it to hold sample data.

3. Click on the Dictionary page on the left pane of the Database Explorer window. Highlight Dictionary, then right click on it. Select New from the context menu. You'll see the Create a new Dictionary dialog shown in Figure 12.42. Notice that the InterbaseEmployee name is already entered in the Database field. Database Explorer also adds the name of a table to the Table Name field. This table gets added to the database and it contains all of the data dictionary information that you define. Using this technique allows Database Explorer to maintain the data dictionary and the database as one unit.

4. Type SampleData (or some other appropriate name) in the Dictionary Name field. Select SampleDataDictionary in the Database field. Type a description in the Description field. Make sure you provide enough information so that you know why you created the dictionary later.

Figure 12.42.

The Create a new Dictionary dialog allows you to define the dictionary name and the database to use as a source of information.

5. Click on OK to complete the process. Database Explorer will probably take a few minutes to create the dictionary—especially if you want to place the data dictionary in an SQL database on a remote server. Once Database Explorer completes the task, it'll display a dictionary entry like the one in Figure 12.43 on the right side of the display. Now that we have the dictionary defined, let's add some actual data to it. You have to add the databases that you previously defined one at a time.

Figure 12.43.

Once you create a new data dictionary, you'll see a description of it in the right pane of Database Explorer.

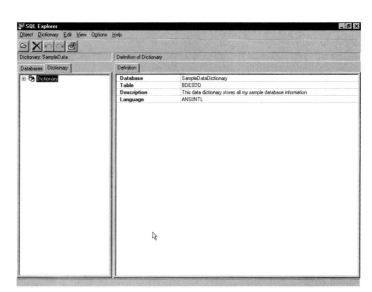

6. Use the Dictionary | Import from Database command to display the Import Database dialog shown in Figure 12.44. This is where you tell Database Explorer which database you want to include in the data dictionary.

Figure 12.44.

The Import Database dialog allows you to select a database for import into the data dictionary.

7. Select the first database you want to import. I selected the InterbaseEmployee database that I defined earlier. Notice that the list doesn't provide room for you to type in a new database name. You have to define the database before you can import it. You also need to decide whether you want to import the system tables at this point. Normally the system tables only contain data that the DBMS can use—importing tables of this type is a waste of time and tends to clutter your dictionary.

8. Click on OK to complete the action. If the DBMS you want to query provides password protection, Database Explorer will display a dialog asking you to enter a password. Once you provide a password and user name, Database Explorer will take a few minutes to query the database server about the database you want to import. Make sure you allow extra time for remote servers since all the information for your data dictionary has to travel over network lines.

9. Repeat steps 7 and 8 for any other databases that you want to include in your dictionary. I included the RptSmithDemo database as well.

10. Open the data dictionary. You'll see a list of imported databases like the ones in Figure 12.45.

Figure 12.45.
The end result of importing databases is to have all the data sources you need grouped in one area and easy to access.

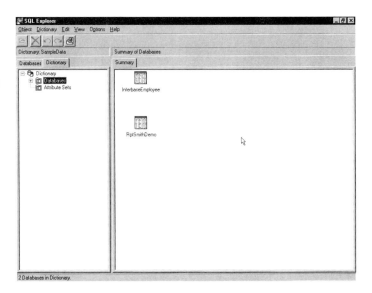

Now that you've gotten a data dictionary, what do you do with it? I'll answer that question in the next section. All you can really do right now is explore the contents of the various databases and make structural modifications. I'll show you in a few moments the actual power behind Database Explorer—attributes.

Defining Attributes

Attributes are one of the biggest reasons to use the data dictionary provided with Database Explorer. Defining attributes for the various fields in your program is easy because you really don't have to do it; Delphi does it for you. The connection between Delphi and Database Explorer is through the Fields Editor.

It's actually easier to show you how this works. Let's take one of the tables in the RptSmithDemo database that we added to the data dictionary in the previous section. Currently if you look at the attributes for this table in Database Explorer, you'll see a blank page. (To look at the attributes work your way through the Database Explorer hierarchical view until you see RptSmithDemo | EMPLOYEE.DB | Fields | HOME_PHONE | Attribute Sets.) If you look at any of the other fields you'll see the same thing—there aren't any attributes. The reason I specifically mentioned HOME_PHONE is that we'll define some attributes for it in a second.

So, now that you've verified that there aren't any attributes for the EMPLOYEE.DB let's define some. The first thing you'll need to do is open Delphi and create a simple database application. My form only contains one table, EMPLOYEE.DB. I used the Database Form Expert to create the basic program. Check out the section in this chapter entitled "Using the Database Form Expert" if you need some help getting this done. Once you get the simple program up and running, follow the procedure below to define some attributes. Just like everything else I've shown you so far in the chapter, I tried to make this procedure as generic as possible so that you could use it in a variety of situations.

1. Select the Table1 (or any other TTable or TQuery) component. This is the component that provides the link to the EMPLOYEE.DB (or other) table.

2. Right click on the Table1 component to display the context menu. Select the Fields Editor entry. You'll see the dialog shown in Figure 12.46. All the Fields Editor looks like is a list of fields that you've selected from the current table (which may not even include all the fields that the table contains).

Figure 12.46.
The Fields Editor doesn't look like much more than a list of the fields in your table.

3. Highlight the desired field (in this case I chose HOME_PHONE). Right click on the field entry to display the context menu shown in Figure 12.47. Notice all the attribute entries on the list. I'll go through the most important of these in this procedure, but you really need to spend some time learning to use them properly. Let's set up some attributes for the HOME_PHONE field, then save them to the data dictionary.

Figure 12.47.
*The Fields Editor context
menu is where you'll use the
attribute sets defined in the
data dictionary.*

4. Select the EditMask property of the HOME_PHONE field in the Object Inspector. The Fields Editor will automatically select the proper component in the Object Inspector for you, all you need to do is edit the attributes you want to change.

5. Click on the ellipses in the EditMask property and you will see the Input Mask Editor dialog shown in Figure 12.48. Notice that there are few default masks provided. You can use any of these or create your own mask. The reason for using a mask is that you can prevent the user from entering invalid data into the table. This doesn't mean that the data is correct, simply that it won't corrupt the table even if it is incorrect.

Figure 12.48.
*The Input Mask Editor
allows you to define an input
mask for a field—preventing
the user from entering invalid
data.*

6. Type in the following input mask: '!999/000-0000;1;_' (don't add the single quotes), then click on OK to save it. This change modifies the current field; it doesn't save the edit to your data dictionary. It's important to remember that Delphi doesn't automatically assume that you want to save the attributes you define to the data dictionary.

7. Highlight the DisplayLabel property of the HOME_PHONE field and change it to Phone.

8. Make sure that the HOME_PHONE field is still selected in the Fields Editor, then right click on the field to display the context menu.

9. Select the Save Attributes entry. You'll see the Save HOME_PHONE Attributes dialog shown in Figure 12.49. The Fields Editor will provide a default Attribute Set Name for you. I normally save the original settings as Default, making it easier to figure out which attribute set is the normal setting when I'm in Database Explorer.

Figure 12.49.
The Save Attributes dialog allows you to save the attributes you've defined for a particular field to the data dictionary.

10. Type Default, then click on OK to save the attributes. So, what happens if you want to use more than one edit mask for your phone number? The data dictionary allows you to save more than one attribute set for each field.

11. Select the EditMask property of the HOME_PHONE field again. Click on the ellipses to display the Input Mask Editor shown in Figure 12.48.

12. Select the default Phone entry. Notice that the input mask changes to '!\(999\)000-0000;1;_'.

13. Click on OK to save the change. If we tried to use the Save Attributes entry of the Fields Editor context menu this time, we'd overwrite the original settings. This time I'll show you how to save an alternate attribute set.

14. Right click on the HOME_PHONE field in the Fields Editor. Select the Save Attributes As entry. Notice that the Fields Editor displays the same dialog we saw in Figure 12.49. The big difference this time is that the Based On field has Default in it. Once you define a default setting, you can simply modify the attributes it contains as needed.

15. Type AlternatePhone1 in the Attribute Set Name field, then click on OK to save the setting. Now that we have two attribute sets defined for the HOME_PHONE field, let's use the Default attribute set again.

16. Right click on the HOME_PHONE field in the Fields Editor. Select the Associate Attributes entry. You'll see the Associate Attributes dialog shown in Figure 12.50. Notice that this dialog contains both the attribute sets that we previously defined. If we had defined another set from within the data dictionary, it would show up here as well. You don't necessarily have to use the Fields Editor to create attribute sets; the Database Explorer utility also provides the means to create them by hand.

Figure 12.50.
The Associate Attributes dialog allows you to retrieve previously stored attributes from the data dictionary.

17. Select Default from the list of attribute sets, then click on OK. The Table1HOME_PHONE EditMask property will revert to its original setting.

Now that we've gone through all this work to define some attributes for the HOME_PHONE field of the EMPLOYEE.DB table, you're probably asking yourself what we accomplished. If you're like me, you really hate to do the same thing twice. Even if it is a simple point and click task, defining all the attributes for every field in your database every time you use it has to be one of the most boring ways to spend an afternoon that I can think of. What if you could define them once, then have Delphi do it for you? That's what this is all about. Now that we've recorded the attributes for the HOME_PHONE field you'll never need to do it again.

So, what do these attribute sets look like in the data dictionary? If you open Database Explorer and select the Attribute Sets folder, you'll see two attribute sets like the ones shown in Figure 12.51. In addition, the HOME_PHONE field of the EMPLOYEE.DB file contains an entry pointing to the Default attribute—the one that we selected last. This was just a simple example; Delphi provides very complete control over the appearance of your data using the data dictionary in this way. Even more important is the fact that it does so in a data independent fashion. You don't have to learn six ways to create edit masks—all you need to know is the Delphi method of doing things.

Figure 12.51.
The Database Explorer data dictionary shows the results of the attribute sets we defined using the Fields Editor.

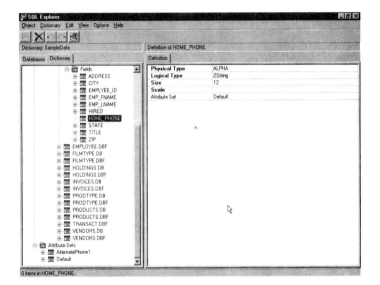

Building a Form Using Native Capabilities

Delphi provides a lot of native capabilities that you can use to create forms. You could actually build a form by hand like we did in Chapter 8, or you can use the faster methods that Delphi provides. I usually use one of two methods to start every database project. In actuality, I use one of them more often than not. The Database Form Expert can provide a significant productivity boost if you use it correctly. However, I'd be remiss in saying that this expert is complete. For one thing, you can only build forms that use two tables with it. Yet, even with this failing, using the Database Form Expert can at least get you started in the right direction—a major plus when you think about the problems in starting an application from scratch.

Once I get a basic form built, I usually resort to a variety of hand coding techniques. Hand-coding probably isn't the right term to use at this point though; it's really more like drag and drop with a little glue code thrown in for good measure. I'm going to show you one method of building an application without a single line of code in the next section. Will this application knock your socks off? Probably not since it's a simple editor. However, the fact remains that such an application would have been impossible in years past. I still remember spending an hour or two writing my first Windows Hello World program in C—Delphi's RAD (rapid application development) is a far cry from those days.

Using the Database Form Expert

I think that the easiest way to start just about any database form is to use the Database Form Expert. This is a new feature for Delphi 2.0 that I think is really going to help most developers get a fast start on their applications. I don't think that most developers are going to use the result as the final product though and I'll show you why in the next few paragraphs. For starters, let's take a look at what you need to do to use the Database Form Expert.

I'm assuming at this point that you have already defined your database source using either the BDE Configuration Utility or Database Explorer. If you're using Database Explorer, make sure you take the extra time needed to create a data dictionary. I cover the techniques for doing this in the Database Explorer section of this chapter. The same section goes over all the reasons for using a data dictionary, so I won't bore you with the details here again.

Once you have data source defined, it's time to start Delphi. Remember that we're going to look at an application created using automated means this time around. I've tried to make this procedure as generic as possible, but you'll need to substitute the names of the tables you want to use when you start your own application.

1. Create a new application, then remove Form1 from the project by clicking on the Remove File From Project speed bar button and selecting the Form1 entry. We'll be creating a new Form1 using the Database Form Expert.

2. Use the Database | Form Expert command to start the Database Form Expert. You'll see dialog shown in Figure 12.52. The first two design criteria you need to decide is whether this form will contain one or two tables and whether you'll use TTable or TQuery components. Normally you'll need to use a TQuery component if you want to display a limited data set from an SQL database. Always use the TTable component for a standard database type like dBASE or Paradox.

Figure 12.52.
The Database Form Expert
begins by asking you what
type of application you want
to create.

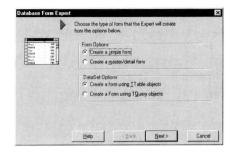

3. Accept the default settings of Create a Simple Form (one table) and Create a Form Using TTable Objects by clicking on Next. You'll see what appears to be a File Open dialog like the one in Figure 12.53. There is at least one thing you should notice about this dialog. The Drive or Alias Name combo box allows you to select one of the databases you defined using the BDE Configuration Utility or Database Explorer. You could select a table directly from the drive, but this wouldn't be the most efficient method available. I always use an alias when programming a database application since it allows me to use the data dictionary provided by Database Explorer. Note that you have to use an alias to access remote data or ODBC sources like Access.

Figure 12.53.
You can use either a drive or
an alias when choosing a
data source—the alias
method is a lot more efficient
from a programmer
perspective.

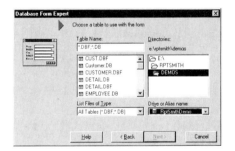

4. Select an alias in the Drive or Alias Name combo box, then select the table that you want to use. I chose the RptSmithDemo alias that I created earlier and the EMPLOYEE.DB table.

5. Click on Next to complete the table selection. You should see the dialog shown in Figure 12.54. It allows you to choose from the list of fields in the table that you selected.

6. Select all the fields by clicking on the double right pointing arrow. All the fields for the current table should appear in the right pane of the dialog. Any fields that appear in the right pane will also appear on the initial form. You need to select all the fields you intend to use, even if those fields won't appear in the final application (you can turn off the visible property or simply delete them if you wish). Key fields are especially important if you plan to use more than one table in the form.

Figure 12.54.
This dialog allows you to
choose one or more fields
from the currently selected
table.

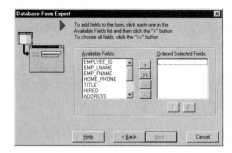

7. Click on Next to complete the field selection process. You should see the dialog shown in Figure 12.55. This dialog allows you to choose the orientation of the data. Delphi will display it in a grid, across the form in a horizontal direction, or down the form vertically. Delphi always includes the field name as a label next to the TDBEdit component that contains the data for that field. Normally I use the grid view for browses. The other views come in handy for detail editing.

Figure 12.55.
This is the dialog you use to
select the orientation of your
data.

Note: If you were designing a two table form, the Database Form Expert would repeat steps 4 though 7 for the second table at this point. You would also need to define a relationship between the key fields of the two tables.

8. Accept the default orientation of Horizontal by clicking on Next. You'll see the dialog shown in Figure 12.56. The Database Form Expert supports both the traditional approach of leaving the Data Access components on the form and the Delphi 2.0 approach of using a data module. I'll talk about data modules in the section entitled "The TDataModule Approach in this chapter."

9. Select the Form and Data Module options since I'll show you how to add some other features to this program later. Click Finish to complete the process. Delphi will work for a few seconds, then display a form similar to the one in Figure 12.57.

Figure 12.56.

The final step in creating a database form using the Database Form Expert is to decide where the Data Access components will appear.

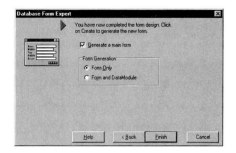

Figure 12.57.

You can run the final product of the Database Form Expert, but it lacks some important features.

10. Click on the Run button. Once Delphi saves the unit and application for you, it will run the application automatically. Notice that you can move from record to record, delete, add, and edit the table. You can also jump to the beginning or end of the table using the jump pushbuttons.

There you have it, the only application that I'll present in this book that doesn't require any code. Is this the end all of applications? Not by a long shot. There are so many holes in it right now that no one in their right mind would implement it. However, it does show the direction that programming is taking. Delphi does a lot of the drudge work for you so that you can concentrate on the actual task of writing an application without getting mired in detail.

What's Missing in this Application?

There's a lot missing from the application that I created in the previous section—that it works at all is pretty amazing, but it's not what I would call a production application. For one thing, there isn't any menu attached to this application. Sure, I've created a utility or two in the book that didn't provide a menu, but I always provide some means of ending the program. This application doesn't provide that feature.

Database applications have to provide a few other features as well. For one thing, you didn't have to provide any kind of a password to get into this application. What would happen on a network if anyone could access any data in any manner that they wanted? The resulting chaos would result in some nightmarish results that no one would appreciate. Suffice it to say, you'll need to add security to this application before it would work properly.

You'll also notice that I can't output my data to the printer. This may not be a big deal in a utility program used to view graphics, but it is a big deal with a database application. The sole purpose for using a database in the first place is to provide an easy method of manipulating and viewing your data. Obviously this application provides on-screen viewing, but it lacks the very necessary printed output. Just think about the usefulness of an inventory control database that wouldn't output receipts when someone purchases a product.

I'm going to take care of the first two problems in this section of the chapter. You'll want to spend some time looking at the other chapters in this book for some of the common menu entries that most people would expect to find in a database application. For example, Chapter 8 showed how to create a ReportSmith printout (we'll see a Quick Report example near the end of this chapter). Chapter 6 showed you how to use the common dialogs that Windows provides. A user would expect to find some type of search functionality provided with a database application along with a means for saving changes to the data (in most cases all you need to do is a commit—something that could be performed automatically by the DBMS—negating the need for this feature).

The first thing I did was add a TMenu component to the form. I added a File main menu entry and an Exit entry. Normally you'd also provide a Help main menu entry along with any required Edit entries. In this case I just wanted to give the user an easier way to exit the program. I also changed the size of the form and rearranged it as shown in Figure 12.58. I changed the name of the form to EmpEdit and changed the caption as shown. I also had to add some code to implement the File | Exit command, which appears in Listing 12.1.

Figure 12.58.
The modified form looks nicer and is a lot easier to use. The addition of a menu makes it easier for the user to exit the program.

Listing 12.1. Implementing the File | Exit command.

```
procedure TEmpEdit.Exit1Click(Sender: TObject);
begin
    {End the application.}
    Application.Terminate;
end;
```

Once you get the form updated, it's time to add a password dialog. I was happy to see that Borland provides this as part of Delphi. All you need to do is use the File | New command, then select a Password dialog from the object repository. I didn't modify the password dialog at all for this example, but I did want to show you how to integrate it into the application.

The first thing you'll want to do is ensure that the password dialog gets displayed first. Use the Project | Options command to display the Project Options dialog. The Main Form combo box on the Forms page will allow you to make the PasswordDlg form the first one that executes.

You'll also need to provide some method for displaying the EmpEdit form once you check the password. Make sure you add the EmpEdit unit name (I used FileWiz2) to the Uses section of the PasswordDlg unit (I used FileWiz3). Since I use a MessageDlg to display an error message if the user provides the wrong password, I also add the Dialogs entry in the main Uses statement for the unit. Listing 12.2 shows the code you'll need to add to complete the process. Note that I'm not actually checking for a real password right now. The simple check I added is representative of what you might do along with some other code to retrieve a password from a network database or other file. You could implement that process in a variety of ways (some of which we'll get into in Chapter 13 on LANs). Needless to say, this probably isn't the most comprehensive way to address the limitations of the original application, but it is a step in the right direction.

Listing 12.2. Completing the process.

```
unit FormWiz3;

interface

uses Windows, SysUtils, Classes, Graphics, Forms, Controls, StdCtrls,
  Buttons, Dialogs;

type
  TPasswordDlg = class(TForm)
    Label1: TLabel;
    Password: TEdit;
    OKBtn: TButton;
    CancelBtn: TButton;
    procedure CancelBtnClick(Sender: TObject);
    procedure OKBtnClick(Sender: TObject);
  private
    { Private declarations }
  public
    { Public declarations }
  end;

var
  PasswordDlg: TPasswordDlg;

implementation

uses FormWiz2;

{$R *.DFM}
```

continues

Listing 12.2. continued

```
procedure TPasswordDlg.CancelBtnClick(Sender: TObject);
begin
    {End the application if the user selects Cancel.}
    Application.Terminate;
end;

procedure TPasswordDlg.OKBtnClick(Sender: TObject);
begin

    {If the user enters the correct password.}
    if Password.Text = 'MASTER' then
       begin
       EmpEdit.Show;          {Display the edit form.}
        PasswordDlg.Hide;     {Hide the password dialog.}
        end

    {Otherwise, display an error message an exit the program.}
    else
       begin
       MessageDlg('Incorrect Password, Terminating Application', mtError, [mbOK], 0);
       PasswordDlg.Close;
       Application.Terminate;
        end;
end;

end.
```

The TDataModule Approach

This is one of the new database management features provided by Delphi 2.0. It's a new form-like class that acts as a container for Data Access components. The advantage of using a TDataModule is that you can create data modules—a centralized location for all your Data Access components—by placing non-visual Data Access components in a TDataModule like the one shown in Figure 12.59. Notice how it looks almost like a standard form—one quick look at the Object Inspector will tell you that looks are deceiving.

Figure 12.59.
The TDataModule looks almost like a form, but its purpose is to act as a central storage place for non-visual database components.

The biggest reason to create data modules is that they enable you to separate the business rules (like how to filter records, the tables you want to use, and other database access mechanics) embedded in data access components from the presentation components (like Data Access and QuickRpt components) contained in forms. This separation of data access from data presentation provides you with a bit more flexibility when it comes to creating complex application. You can use form linking and visual form inheritance to access the data module's database components from forms that contain data aware components.

> **Tip:** You don't have to limit your TDataModule components to database specific items. You can add components like TDDEConv and TDDEClient to it as well. The only requirement is that the component you place in the data module not provide some type of visual feedback. You may even consider using this module for non-database specific programs as a method for keeping non-visual elements from cluttering the form in design view.

So, how do you use this new feature? Simply use the File | New | DataModule command to create a new data module. What you'll see looks like a new form with the background set to white. Just place all the data access components you need inside the new data module. Once you get this done, it's easy to access the data from all the forms in your application using this centralized repository. All you need to do is use the File | Use Unit command to link the form to your data module.

One of the more important things to consider when using a data module is the creation order of the components. You need to verify that the master-detail (or primary and secondary) relationships between tables remain intact when the form gets created. Always create the master table Data Access components first, then those for any detail tables.

As with any other form that you create, you can save a TDataModule form to the repository. This comes in handy if you use the same data definition for more than one application. You could create one data module and inherit from it as needed.

> **Peter's Principle:** Component Overkill Can Be Fatal
>
> Every time you create a new component it consumes some amount of memory. The exact amount depends on just what types of information the component needs to store. If you add enough components to a Delphi application, you'll find that the memory requirements become so high that no one can use your application.
>
> So, how does this relate to the new TDataModule component? I find that many programmers just have to stick every new bell and whistle provided by a programming language into their application. The TDataModule, like anything else in Delphi, will consume memory. If you use it with a small utility type application or perhaps even a moderately sized mailing list manager, you'll find that you've wasted the memory.
>
> The TDataModule is designed to relieve some of the memory problems that developers of large applications have experienced. If you're designing a multi-module accounts program,

then the TDataModule can probably save, rather than cost, you precious memory and application programming time. Obviously you'll need to make some decision as to when a component is valuable or not, but always consider the amount of memory you'll use to add that component to your application and ask yourself if the component is carrying its own weight.

Quick Reports—the Way to Go When Speed is Important

I quickly reviewed the QuickRpt components at the beginning of this chapter. Using the Quick Report feature of Delphi 2.0 is quick and easy. I thought I'd have to at least do a little coding to use it, but found that the most time consuming part of the process was dropping the components on a form and getting them lined up.

The sample application we started in the previous section still needs a print routine to make it complete. The first thing you'll need to do is add a new form to your application. We're not going to do anything fancy with it. In fact, we're not even going to display it. The whole purpose of this form is to act as a canvas for our report. I started by adding a TQuickReport component and a couple of TQRBands. The first band will act as a title area for the report—you'll need to set its BandType property to rbTitle. The second band contains the detail section—the data that we want to send to the printer. Set the BandType property for this band to rbDetail. The title band contains two TQRSysData and one TQRLabel components. I used one of the system data components for the date, the other for the current page. The label holds the report title. I then added the appropriate TQRDBText components to the detail band. The end result appears in Figure 12.60.

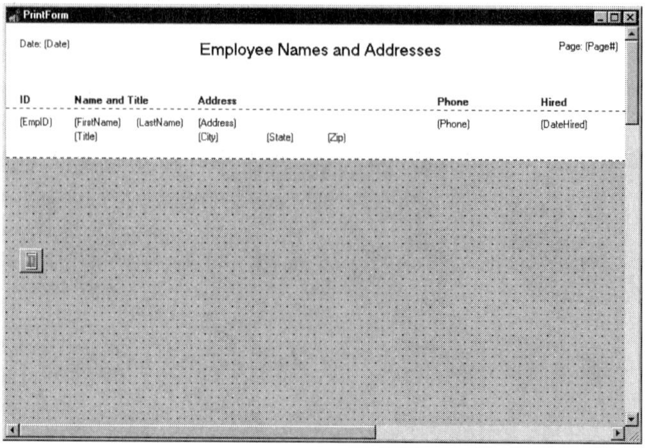

Figure 12.60.
The Quick Report in this example begins with a form filled with the data that we want to display.

Once you get the form complete, save it, then reference it in the Uses section of the EmpEdit unit (FormWiz2). You'll need to add a couple of new menu items to the File Menu on this form. The code for these menu items appears in Listing 12.3. Notice that we don't have to do too much, just tell the Quick Report to either preview or print itself.

Listing 12.3. Code for new menu items.

```
procedure TEmpEdit.PrintPreview1Click(Sender: TObject);
begin
    {Display the report on screen.}
    PrintForm.QuickReport1.Preview;
end;

procedure TEmpEdit.Print1Click(Sender: TObject);
begin
    {Send the report to the printer.}
    PrintForm.QuickReport1.Print;
end;
```

Now that we've gotten the report together (almost seems too easy, doesn't it), let's take a look at it in action. Figure 12.61 shows what happens when you select the Print Preview option from the File menu. As I said at the beginning, the whole process of creating a Quick Report seems almost too easy.

Figure 12.61.
The Print Preview display of our Quick Report is very functional and easy to use.

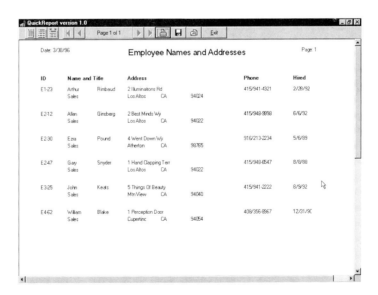

So, what are the advantages of using Quick Report? I find that it's a lot easier to keep everything coordinated. Not only that, but I don't have to break out the ReportSmith manual every time I want to do something. Creating a report this way also means that you don't have to distribute external report files or worry that the user will accidentally erase a report when you least expect it. The overall appearance of your application is improved as well because it doesn't look "glued" together. Everything is in one neat package—something that the user is sure to notice.

The disadvantages are fairly easy to figure out too. ReportSmith has a definite edge when it comes to getting everything aligned. I found I had to get the print preview function working first, then run the application whenever I wanted to see what the report really looked like. I also mentioned some limitations to the master detail reporting scenario at the beginning of the chapter. You'll find that ReportSmith has fewer of these as well.

Summary

It may seem like we've covered a mountain of information in this chapter, and we have. It's also true that this only represents the tip of the iceberg. Delphi is capable of doing a lot more than I've told you about—this chapter simply fills you in on the highlights. You should probably view this chapter as an overview of what's possible, what Delphi can do to make your database programming job just a bit easier.

Our whirlwind tour did cover quite a bit of ground. The first area I covered was the components that Delphi provides for creating a database application. We looked at three sets of components: Data Access, QuickRpts, and Data Control. The Data Access components give you access to the database itself. Use the Data Control components to create forms and other types of database editing objects. QuickRpts will allow you to access your data and output it to the printer.

Delphi also provides a wealth of utilities and I gave you an overview of them all. Remember that these tools will do a lot more than what I provided in this chapter—we simply covered the things that you would need to know to create an application. For example, you'll find that Database Explorer provides a lot more tools that'll help you maintain the database attributes—we didn't even go into the procedure for creating your own dictionary-wide attributes—something you'll want to learn about if you spend a lot of time writing database applications.

Finally, we also looked at some of the tools and techniques that Delphi provides for actually writing applications. I showed you two techniques for creating data entry forms and we spent a little time looking at writing a Quick Report. I think that you'll find that the Database Form Expert is a great way to get started on an application, but that it falls short on anything but the most rudimentary database form. Obviously, it's better to get any kind of help you can with a project—the Database Form Expert represents a major step in the right direction.

13

Delphi on a LAN

Unlike a lot of programming languages out on the market today, Delphi is equally useful for database management (DBMS) as it is for utility programs (and every program type in-between). So far in this book I've shown you quite a few examples of both application categories. Later I'll even show you how to create DLLs in Delphi so that you can share its programming capabilities with other languages. It's easy to see that the scope of applications you can create with this particular product eclipses a lot of the competition.

Let's focus on the native networking capabilities of Delphi for a second. Normally you would see a discussion of network related topics woven into the rest of the chapters with a DBMS programming language like FoxPro or Visual Objects. These products are designed with large network-based DBMS in mind. Since Delphi doesn't really fall into that niche, I decided to cover network programming separately. It's important to realize that as a general purpose language, Delphi has a lot more (and a lot less) to offer the programmer as far as networking is concerned.

The lot more part comes in the form of flexibility. You can use a variety of third party products with Delphi—even the products designed for use with full-fledged DBMS programming languages. It's also possible to directly interact with the network support that Windows provides using the API. There are a variety of DLLs in the SYSTEM folder that contain the basics needed to perform just about any kind of network access. In fact, you don't even have to be limited to a LAN or a WAN. With the proper programming, you could theoretically build in access to the Internet using point-to-point protocol (PPP).

The lot less part comes in actual Delphi support. You won't find any handy components provided that allow you to access the NetWare bindery or perform some bit of magic with the WinSock interface provided by Windows 95 and Windows NT. Delphi is, after all, a general purpose language, and there are limits to what it does provide. Just about any form of direct network interaction under Delphi is manual. Sure, Delphi will take care of logging on to a DBMS server if you write a DBMS application, but the level of supports ends there.

There are several things I'm going to talk about in this chapter—most of which relate to using Delphi on a network in a general way. I do plan to look at the network architecture that Windows provides. As always, I feel the best place to start learning about how something works is from the theoretical point of view. I'll put that theory into practice when I show you how to use the network related functions in the Windows API. We'll also spend some time looking at the types of things you need to think about when writing a network application. I'll also show you some examples of how to add network specific features like administrator support to your application and what to do about the network operating system (NOS) itself. Finally, we'll take some time to look at NetWare—the NOS that many of you will use for serious network applications.

An Architectural Overview of Windows 95 Networking

This section of the chapter looks at the hows of network support under Windows 95. What you can expect, and why do things work the way they do? These are just some of the questions I'll answer here. I chose to cover Windows 95 in this case since Windows NT uses a very similar architecture—anything you learn for Windows 95 will work equally well with Windows NT.

Note: There are some obvious areas where Windows NT will differ from Windows 95. For one thing, you can't use any kind of a real mode network operating system (NOS) with Windows NT—it just won't work with this operating system. I also can't imagine using a 16-bit NOS like LANtastic with Windows NT; it just doesn't make sense in that environment. You'd give up too much of the stability and reliability that NT is supposed to provide by exposing it to a 16-bit NOS. Suffice it to say that if you've made the investment to move the NT, then there's also good reason to use a 32-bit peer-to-peer NOS or a client/server architecture like NetWare.

Before we become too embroiled in some of the details of actually using Windows 95's network capabilities, I'd like to spend a little time looking at its architecture. Figure 13.1 shows the Windows 95 network architecture. Notice that a request can follow two discrete paths. Windows 95 provides a 32-bit protected-mode path for any network that it supports directly. It'll use a real-mode path for drivers that it doesn't support. Both paths end up at the NIC driver. The following list describes the individual components.

- 16-bit thunk API: Windows 95 provides full network support using 32-bit code. However, there are a lot of 16-bit applications to support out there as well. This module replaces the standard 16-bit API with calls to the 32-bit API. It has to provide thunk support in order to do this. We've looked at the thunk process before (in the "Getting 16-Bit and 32-Bit Applications to Work Together" section of Chapter 5), so I won't go into it again here.

- 32-bit API: All application requests start at this module. I won't go into details about the API, but Microsoft has gone to great lengths to reorganize and simplify it. A user won't notice these details—except in the way that they affect network performance—but they'll make a definite impact on the effort required to program. The API translates one application request into one or more standardized network requests. Quite a few files are involved in creating the network API under Windows 95. The two most prominent are NETAPI.DLL and NETAPI32.DLL. Loading NETAPI32.DLL also loads NETBIOS.DLL, which provides most of the low-level functionality that the API requires.

Figure 13.1.
An overview of the Windows
95 network architecture.

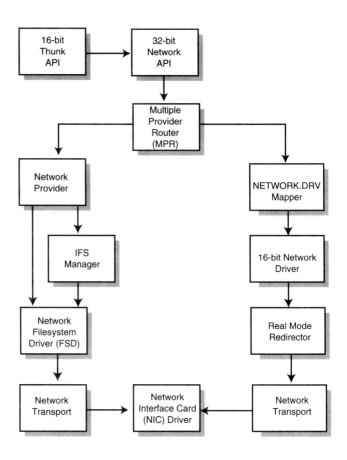

- Multiple provider router (MPR): You can use more than one protocol with Windows 95. In fact—theoretically, at least—you should be able to mix and match protected-mode and real-mode drivers on the same network. The current Windows 95 implementation will always allow you to perform the first function. For example, you can mix NetBEUI and IPX/SPX on the same network. However, it usually won't allow you to do the second without some restrictions. For example, you can't mix LANtastic with a Microsoft network, but you can mix it with NetWare in some cases. All network protocols require a network provider. The whole function of the MPR is to accept network requests from the API and send them to the appropriate network provider (NP). Part of each request states which NP to use. This is how the MPR knows which one it should send the request to. However, some requests are generic. For example, a request for the status of the entire network falls into this category. In that case, the MPR calls each NP in turn to fulfill the application request. In still other cases, a request might not include enough information for the MPR to know which NP to use to fulfill the application requirement. In this case, the MPR will "poll" the NPs to see if one of them can fulfill the request. If none of the installed NPs can, the MPR returns an error message. You'll find that the MPR functions appear in the \SYSTEM folder in MPR.DLL. This DLL gets loaded when Windows 95 executes MPREXE.EXE during startup. An intermediate file, MPRSERV.DLL, performs the actual loading process. Interestingly enough, loading this set of DLLs also loads ADVAPI32.DLL. The MPR uses the functions in this DLL to view the contents of the registry to determine which NPs and other network resources are available. The MPR also loads MSPWL.DLL. This module checks for your password and performs other security-related activities. There's also a path from the MPR to NETWORK.DRV. This path becomes active when you use a real mode driver in place of a Windows 95 specific NP. The MPR can't poll the real mode driver or perform any of the other NP specific tasks that I previously described. NETWORK.DRV provides the NP services that Windows 95 requires. I describe this particular part of the network a little later in the chapter.

- Network Provider (NP): The Network Provider performs all the protocol-specific functions that an application requires. It'll make or break connections, return network status information, and provide a consistent interface for the MPR to use. An application will never call the NP; only the MPR performs this function. Even though the internal structure of NPs varies, the interface that they provide doesn't. This mechanism allows Windows 95 to provide support for more than a single protocol. The code used by the MPR can remain small and fast because none of the NPs require special calls. If an NP can't fulfill a request because of a limitation in the network protocol, it simply tells the MPR that the required service is unavailable. The NP also keeps the IFS Manager up-to-date on the current connection status. This is how Explorer knows when you've made a new drive connection.

- IFS Manager: When the IFS (installable file system) Manager obtains new status information from the NP, it calls the Network File System Driver (FSD) to update file and other resource information. For example, when the NP tells the IFS Manager that it has made a new drive connection, the IFS Manager calls on the Network FSD to provide a directory listing. The same holds true for other resource types, such as printers. Besides this function, the IFS Manager performs its normal duties of opening files and making other file system requests. The MPR doesn't know what to do with a path name, so it passes such requests through the NP to the IFS Manager to fulfill. Of course, applications also access the IFS Manager in other ways. The only time that the MPR becomes involved is if a network-specific request also requires its intervention.

- Network File System Driver (FSD): Each server on the network could use a unique file system. For example, if you make a connection to an OS/2 server, you could require access to an HPFS drive. NetWare and other client/server networks all use special file systems that the vendor feels will enhance performance, security, reliability, and storage capacity. Since Windows 95 understands nothing about HPFS or any other special storage system, it needs a translator. The Network FSD performs this task. It translates the intricacies of a foreign file system into something that Windows 95 can understand. A Network FSD is usually composed of a file system-specific driver and VREDIR.VXD. The second file provides the Windows 95 interpretation of the file system specifics. Normally there's only one Network FSD for each NP. However, there's nothing to enforce this limit. An NP might require access to both an FAT and an NTFS Network FSD for a Windows NT Server. If so, both drivers will get installed when you install network support. The IFS Manager will also call on the Network FSD for support. While the NP usually makes requests for network status or connection information, the IFS Manager takes care of application needs such as opening files and reading their contents. These two modules— NP and IFS Manager—work in tandem, each fulfilling completely different roles.

Note: You might wonder why Microsoft didn't combine the NP and the IFS Manager into one module. After all, from this discussion it appears that the IFS Manager is simply part of an access strategy for network drives. Remember to take the whole picture into account. The IFS Manager also works with local drives. In addition, combining the modules would have produced a lot of replicated code. In essence, using two separate modules to access the drive status information and content is the only way to get the level of flexibility that network requests require with the minimum amount of code.

- Network transport (NT): I placed a single module called Network Transport (NT) in Figure 13.1. Actually, this module is made up of many smaller modules and drivers. The number of pieces in an NT is determined by the complexity of your setup and the require- ments of the protocol. The smallest NT could consist of a mere four drivers. For example, you could create an NT for the NetBEUI protocol using the following files: VNETBIOS.VXD, NETBEUI.VXD, NDIS.VXD, and NE2000.SYS. These are just the drivers, but let's take a quick look at them.

  VNETBIOS.VXD virtualizes access to the protocol. This is the reason that more than one virtual machine running on your system can access the network drives at the same time. NETBEUI.VXD performs the task of talking with the NDIS (network driver interface specification) module. It takes protocol-specific requests and translates them into smaller, standardized network requests. NDIS.VXD translates each Windows 95-specific request into a call that the NIC driver can understand. Finally, the NIC driver talks to the NIC itself. The driver can take things such as port addresses and interrupts into account— everything needed to talk to the NIC. Of course, the NIC converts your request into an electrical signal that appears on the network.

  The NT requires other files as well. For example, NDIS30.DLL provides the actual API support for NDIS.VXD. You'll find that NETBIOS.DLL performs the same function for VNETBIOS.VXD. In essence, it takes a lot of different modules to create one transport. The reason for all these files is fairly easy to understand. For example, what if you wanted to use a different NIC? All you need to do is change the NIC driver, not any of the protocol-specific files. What if you wanted to use two different levels of NDIS support

(Windows 95 does support two)? You would add an additional driver and its support files to the equation. Rather than going into too much additional detail, let's close the book on the NT for now. All you need to know is that the NT takes care of the "transportation" details for your network installation.

- Network interface card (NIC) driver: I make special mention of this part of the NT here for a reason. This particular driver is hardware-specific. It has to communicate with the NIC on a level it can understand. That's the first problem—trying to find a driver that provides a standard Windows 95 interface yet talks with the NIC installed in your machine. The second problem is that there can be only one driver. I mentioned earlier that there was a chance that a real-mode and a protected-mode network could coexist, but that it wouldn't happen in a lot of cases. Here's the reason why: If you can't load a Windows 95-specific NIC driver because it interferes with a driver that the real-mode product requires, you're faced with a decision of which network to use.

Tip: Even if you've invested in a real-mode networking product such as LANtastic, the performance and reliability increase that you'll get from a Microsoft Network running under Windows 95 might make it worth the effort to switch. Of course, you have to consider the trade-offs of making that decision versus the loss of features. Windows 95 doesn't provide many of the features that people switched to other networks to get. For example, Artisoft provides a DDE Link Book that helps you make OLE links to other machines. You'll also find that the Windows 95 mail and scheduling features are inadequate when compared to products like Artisoft Exchange. In addition, there's a very good chance that vendors such as Artisoft will eventually provide Windows 95-specific solutions to replace their current product. (Artisoft recently sent me a brochure stating that they were going to provide a Windows 95 version of their product.) Even if you decide not to switch, it might be beneficial to see if the real-mode network vendor can provide the required Windows 95 NIC driver to allow you to use multiple networks.

- NETWORK.DRV: The reason for this file is simple. You need to have an NP to gain access to a network under Windows 95. When you install the LANtastic client in the Network applet, this is one of the files that gets installed. It provides the interface to your real-mode network that Windows 95 requires in order to use the network. In this case, the NP also acts as a mapper—a module that maps the Windows 95-specific calls to something that the 16-bit driver will understand. It also provides a thunk layer to translate the 32-bit requests into their 16-bit equivalents. Remember that you still need to install the old 16-bit Windows version of the network drivers. In the case of LANtastic, you'll need the LANTASTIC.386 and LANTNET.DRV files from your distribution disks.

- 16-bit network driver: As I mentioned in the preceding paragraph, you'll still need a Windows driver for your real-mode network. Otherwise, there's no magical way that

Windows 95 will be able to talk to it. There has to be a framework for discussion before a discussion can take place. The 16-bit network drivers typically translate any requests into something that the real-mode redirector can understand. They then ask Windows 95 to make the transition to real mode so that the redirector can do its job.

> **Tip:** In some cases it's nearly impossible to get a good real-mode network installation under Windows 95. Some of the problems include the real-mode network setup program over-writing Windows 95-specific files, and the use of undocumented Windows 3.x features. A few setup programs also require Program Manager to complete their installation, so you might want to start a copy of Program Manager before you begin. I've found that the best way to get a good real-mode network installation under Windows 95 is to install a copy of Windows 3.x first, install the real-mode network there, and then install the copy of Windows 95 over the Windows 3.x installation. It seems like a roundabout way of doing things, but it'll ensure that you'll have a minimum of problems.

- Real-mode redirector: This network component translates your requests into network calls. It works with the real-mode network transport to create an interface with the NIC. Essentially, it performs about the same function in real mode that the IFS Manager and Network FSD do in protected mode.

This might seem like a lot of work just to create a workstation, but that's only half the picture on many peer-to-peer installations. Once you get past being a workstation, you have to take care of network requests as well. I'd like to show you how Windows 95 provides peer-to-peer network services. The next section does just that. We'll look at Windows 95's peer-to-peer support from a server level. We'll also look at a lot of the implementation details. For example, how do you share your printer or local hard drive with someone?

Peer-to-Peer Support

Peer-to-peer networks represent the easiest and least expensive way to get started in networking. Everyone starts with a workstation, just like you would normally need in any business environment. However, you can't share resources on stand-alone workstations; you need to connect them in order to do that. In the past, the standard method for sharing resources was to buy additional machines (called servers) and place the common components there. The investment in hardware and soft-ware for a full-fledged network can run into tens of thousands of dollars—prohibitively expensive for many companies (even though they still make the investment) and out of reach for others. Peer-to-peer networks take a different route. One or more workstations also act as servers. In fact, if you work things right and the network is small enough, everyone will probably have access to everyone else's machine in some form. This means that, except for the NICs and cabling you'll need, a peer-to-peer solution under Windows 95 is free for the asking.

Windows 95 provides peer-to-peer networking capabilities right out of the package. All you need to do is install an NIC in each machine, run some cable, and add a few drivers to your setup. Of course, once you get everyone set up, you'll want to install a few extra utilities, such as a centralized calendar and e-mail.

I was actually a little disappointed with the network utility feature set that Microsoft decided to provide for Windows 95. Exchange is a wonderful e-mail system. However, past versions of WFW came with Schedule+. Windows 95 doesn't provide this feature, and almost everyone will notice. Microsoft plans to introduce a Windows 95-specific version of Schedule+ as part of Office 95. Of course, this brings up another problem—that of incompatibility between the old and the new version of Schedule+. No matter which way you look at it, Schedule+ will become a thing of the past unless you're willing to perform a major upgrade of all your PCs at the same time—something I doubt that most businesses could do even if they wanted to and had the required resources. I see a definite third-party opportunity here. People will still need a centralized calendar for planning meetings, and with Schedule+ gone, some third-party vendor will fill the gap.

Peter's Principle: Grabbing a Piece of the Past

You don't have to do without Schedule+ in your new Windows 95 installation if you still have the files from your old version of WFW lying around. Even though that version of Schedule+ won't work with Exchange, you can still share information with other people on the network by copying the required files to your drive. Here are the files you should copy to your \WIN95 folder:

*.CAL
DEMILAYR.DLL
MSCHED.DLL
MSMAIL.INI
MSREMIND.EXE
SCHDPLUS.EXE
SCHDPLUS.HLP
SCHDPLUS.INI
TRNSCHED.DLL

You'll also need to copy the following files to your \SYSTEM folder:

AB.DLL
FRAMEWRK.DLL
MAILMGR.DLL
MAILSPL.EXE
MSSFS.DLL
STORE.DLL

If the new version of Microsoft Mail doesn't exactly meet your specifications, you can still use the old version under Windows 95. Simply copy these files to your \WIN95 folder:

MSMAIL.EXE
MSMAIL.HLP
MSMAIL.PRG

You'll also need to copy VFORMS.DLL to your \SYSTEM folder.

Once you copy all these files, make any required changes to the .INI files. For example, you'll want to change the directory names so that they match the new location. The only problem I've detected with this arrangement so far is that Schedule+ won't remember your password. This is a small price to pay for using an old and familiar utility program.

A Little History

Before we delve into all the details of how Windows 95 supports peer-to-peer networking, let's take a brief look at the history of this networking system. Apple actually introduced peer-to-peer networking in a covert manner in 1985. They included AppleTalk in every Macintosh sold. Most people didn't realize that they were actually using a network when they printed a document using the LaserWriter.

Peer-to-peer networking continued to be a cult classic in the years that followed. Many companies wouldn't recognize peer-to-peer networking as much more than a kludge or a poor man's network. Novell's NetWare used a client/server model that mimicked the big iron (mainframes) that corporations were used to using. It was comfortable using a network operating system that provided the look and feel of something substantial. In the PC world, many people thought it was client/server or nothing at all.

Note: Don't get me wrong. I'm not saying that peer-to-peer networking is the end-all solution for everyone. However, it's a very good solution for those on a limited networking budget who need to connect anywhere from two to 10 workstations. You might even want to look at it for workgroup connections (the very reason that Microsoft came out with Windows for Workgroups). You can combine the benefits of a client/server network with those of a peer-to-peer network under Windows 95. Although I would probably set an upper limit of 10 workstations for a peer-to-peer network, it might also work for larger numbers of workstations if the network load were very light.

A group of companies began distributing peer-to-peer networking solutions for the PC. One of the biggest contributors to this ground swell of alternative networking technology was Artisoft, which still sells LANtastic today. Other vendors contributed products such as 10Net and TOPS. The Software Link even marketed a processor-sharing operating system for the 80386 called PC-MOS/386.

This solution and others allowed people to share system resources without having to purchase a file server to do it. In addition, the cost of a peer-to-peer network operating system was a lot lower because these vendors faced stiff competition from Novell.

I'm not sure whether Novell helped or hindered the expansion of peer-to-peer networking with its introduction of NetWare Lite in 1991. This product was designed not to interfere with Novell's client/server product. As a result, NetWare Lite wasn't well-designed or implemented. It couldn't even compete with other peer-to-peer products such as LANtastic. However, the introduction of a peer-to-peer networking product by a major vendor such as Novell at least put this type of networking on some people's agenda for the first time.

Things started to change for the better in the peer-to-peer market when Microsoft introduced Windows for Workgroups at the 1992 fall COMDEX trade show. This show of support by Microsoft legitimized the use of peer-to-peer networking for some corporate applications. Of course, Microsoft didn't go so far as to say that you could use it for more than a few people. Still, it was a step in the right direction.

So, has everyone bought into the peer-to-peer networking technology? Not by a long shot, and I doubt that peer-to-peer networking will ever take over the market. However, using a solution such as Windows for Workgroups or Windows 95 in the right place could make a big difference for a very small cost. Windows 95 goes a long way toward making dual solutions—a combination of client/server and peer-to-peer networking—a viable solution.

A Look at the Architecture

We've already taken a detailed look at what it takes to provide workstation support under Windows 95. However, what happens if you also want to act as a server? Providing server support means that your machine must accept requests from other workstations, process those requests, and return the requested information. Figure 13.2 shows the Windows 95 peer-to-peer network server support. The following list describes each component in detail.

- Microsoft Share User Interface (MSSHRUI): This module responds to external requests from the user for network resource configuration. Every time you right-click on a resource and tell Windows 95 that you want to share it, this module fields that request. It works with the access control module to set password protection. An interface to the MPR and ADVAPI32.DLL allows the MSSHRUI to set the proper entries in the registry. You'll find it in the MSSHRUI.DLL file in your \SYSTEM folder.

- VSERVER: The central point of all activity for the server is the virtual server driver, VSERVER.VXD. As with all the other drivers in this chapter, you'll find it in your \SYSTEM folder. This component provides direct access of all local resources to network requesters through the Network Transport. It works with the IFS Manager and access control modules to limit access to shared resources and to ensure that any access is performed properly. Each access to shared system resources is maintained in a separate thread. This means that access by one requester need not interfere with any other request. In addition, a single requester can make multiple requests. Of course, the number of actual requests is usually limited by the protocol settings you provide.

Figure 13.2.

An overview of the Windows 95 server architecture.

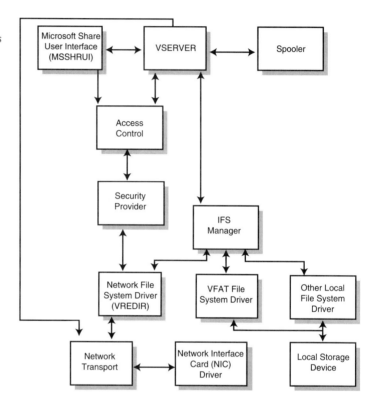

- Spooler: If you grant someone access to your printer, VSERVER will send any requests for print services to the spooler module. This module works just like it would for a local print request. As far as it's concerned, the request originated locally. There are three spooler-specific files in your \SYSTEM folder: SPOOLSS.DLL, SPOOL32.EXE, and WINSPOOL.DRV.

- Access control: Windows 95 uses this module for a variety of purposes, not just network access control. For example, Windows calls on this module to verify your initial logon password, even if you don't request access to a network afterward. Unlike the other modules discussed so far, the access control module makes use of .PWL (password list) files on your drive as well as registry entries to verify and set security. You'll find access control in the SVRAPI.DLL file in the \SYSTEM folder.

Tip: You can get around a potential security problem by removing user access to all of the .PWL files on your drive. If a user erases one of these files, it becomes a lot easier for him to override any security you provided. In addition, you can erase a user's .PWL file to give him access to Windows 95 if he forgets his password. Unfortunately, this means that you'll also have to perform the setup required to re-create that .PWL file.

- Security provider: There are a number of sources for this module. In fact, even if you choose to install a Microsoft Network, you can still choose between the Microsoft Network client and the Windows 95 Login module as a security provider. The Microsoft Network client is a network specific security provider that may include features that the Windows 95 Login module (a generic dialog box) may not provide. You can always access the Windows 95 Login module, even if the network isn't running. The advantage to using it is that the Login module will always be available, even if you change the network setup or remove it altogether. The security provider performs two tasks. First, it's the module that asks you for a password. Second, it combines the user's login name and the password provided to verify any network requests.

- VFAT file system driver (FSD) and other local file system driver: VFAT (virtual file allocation table) isn't a new file system—at least it's not new from the ground up. It's probably best to look at VFAT as the remodeled version of the FAT file system—the upgrade that Microsoft should have done long ago but didn't. VFAT includes support for things like long filenames. However, the basic structure of the file system is the same as the one that was used in the past. VFAT can't provide two important features that these new file systems can: reliability and improved access speed. If either one is of higher importance than compatibility with old applications, you might want to look at Windows NT or OS/2 in place of Windows 95. (Obviously if you want to program in Delphi, then Windows NT is probably your only other alternative unless you want to stick with the 16-bit version of the product.)

Note: You'll find a big difference between Windows NT and Windows 95 when it comes to the FSD. Windows 95 doesn't support the HPFS (high performance file system) or NTFS (Windows NT file system). These are high performance, high reliability file systems based on a completely different model than the FAT file system used. On the other hand, Windows NT supports both of these systems through an FSD. However, it doesn't support the Windows 95 VFAT system. The common file system between these two products is the old FAT (file allocation table) system that's been present from the days of DOS. The reason that this consideration is so important is that you might be tempted to use some of the new VFAT API features that Microsoft provides as part of Windows 95. Using these features directly would make your code less portable. The solution is to work with files in an FSD independent way—which allows maximum portability.

- IFS Manager, Network FSD, Network Transport, and NIC driver: I talked about these modules at the beginning of this chapter.

Understanding the server capabilities that Windows 95 provides is pretty straightforward from a conceptual point of view. However, once you get past theory, implementation becomes another story altogether. The problem isn't due to a poor plan, but due to all the compatibility issues that come into play. Fortunately for the user, the design of the server capabilities makes all these details fairly seamless.

 # Windows NT as a Server

Those of you using Windows NT probably realize that there are two versions of the product: Workstation and Server. You'll find the typical peer-to-peer networking capabilities in the workstation version of the product. The server version provides a lot more muscle for those situations where peer-to-peer connectivity won't do the job. Let's take a look at some of the differences between the two versions so that you can get a better idea of what to expect if you develop an application using the workstation version of the product.

Talking about Windows NT in a generic sense starts to break down when you start looking at networks because of the different thrust of the two versions. Windows NT Server is actually closer to a client/server model like the one provided by products like NetWare—not the peer-to-peer model used by products like Windows 95 or Windows for Workgroups. It provides all the tools needed to manage a large network along with the need to buy network connections on a per user basis.

Some of the network administration tools include user security and administration—any NOS would need these kinds of tools. Windows NT also adds tools needed to perform other types of network management tasks like changing your network's TCP/IP properties using the Dynamic Host Configuration Protocol (DHCP) Manager and Windows Internet Name Service (WINS) Manager. The DHCP Manager creates IP addresses for client workstations dynamically from a pool of addresses. Normally you would assign a user a static IP address, which could lead to conflicts somewhere along the way. The WINS Manager makes it easier for a user to use the network by assigning names to IP addresses. Instead of looking at a bunch of numbers and trying to figure out whom they belong to, the WINS Manager would assign the client a name like Joe's Computer. Other administration tools include: Network Client Administrator (creates disks for installing the network software) and Remote Boot Manager (configures diskless workstation clients).

Unlike NetWare—which uses the file server as the center of the universe—Windows NT Server uses a domain as the central point of a user's attention. A user can log in to the domain and have full access to the network whether that network consists of one or one hundred file (or other) servers.

Using a single domain would have some obvious drawbacks if your network consisted of a thousand workstations and six of seven servers spread across several states. An administrator can create multiple domains when a network gets too large or complex—providing several benefits for the user as well as enhancing security. For example, most WAN connections are notoriously slow. Putting each LAN within the WAN into a separate domain tends to reduce WAN traffic and makes the network look faster to the user.

Multiple domains could create some problems from the user perspective in some cases. What if the user is a manager who has to look at several satellite offices? Logging in and out of multiple domains to get the job done could become tiresome to say the least. If a user needs access to more than one domain in a network, then the administrator can create a trust relationship for her on more than one domain by adding her ID to that domain's list of users. This feature allows the user to make all the needed connections without logging in and out of domains.

Windows NT Server also provides a host of other features not found in the workstation version (or with products like Windows 95). For example, the server version supports RAID (redundant array of inexpensive disks) level 5 and disk mirroring—two techniques for reducing the chance of data loss on a file server. You'll also find advanced features like directory replication (the workstation version can receive replicated files, but it can't distribute them). You'll also find features like symmetrical multiprocessing (SMP)—the ability to use more than one processor in a machine.

Do any of these differences affect you as a Delphi programmer? Yes, you'll see a definite difference in application performance when running your program on a multi-processor Windows NT server versus a workstation. Do any of these differences have to affect your style of programming or the types of features you need to include? That's really a matter of what kind of application you want to create. You might find the directory replication feature especially handy for some types of database management work—especially if you need to keep several offices synchronized. This particular feature allows every replicated copy of a directory to reflect changes made in the master directory in a matter of seconds. Most programmers will never need to interact with the special network features that Windows NT Server provides. However, it always pays to know that those features are available, just in case the company you're programming for needs them.

Login Scripts

Any programmer who has spent any time at all writing applications for a network environment discovers the joys of writing login scripts. A network administrator may have a good idea of how to create a generic script for a user, but writing a script that answers the needs of a specific application program usually falls under the programmer's purview.

You may wonder why a programmer would even worry about a login script in the first place. The short answer is connections—login scripts usually establish the connections that applications require to get the job done. It's important to make certain that the user can connect to your application properly. That connection will make it possible for him to use your application to its fullest capability with the least number of trouble calls. That's why it's important to know what kind of capabilities the operating system provides when it comes to login scripts.

Windows 95 provides several support mechanisms for login scripts. The best support is for Novell's NetWare, but the same principles hold true (for the most part) with any other NOS (network operating system) that Windows 95 supports. This support doesn't extend to real-mode networks such as LANtastic. You'll need to perform any login script requirements as a call from AUTOEXEC.BAT before you enter Windows 95. In most cases, this means running STARTNET.BAT for LANtastic. Check the vendor documentation for any requirements for using a login script with your real-mode network. You'll usually follow the same procedure that you did prior to installing Windows 95.

Now that we have the real-mode networks out of the way, let's look at the kind of support you can expect for supported networks such as NetWare. The first thing you'll need to do is disable any AUTOEXEC.BAT or other batch files that you used to use under Windows 3.x. You don't need to log into the network before entering Windows 95. Any workstations that use NetWare must have an account on the server before you try to install Client for NetWare.

Note: I was surprised to find that the protected-mode Client for NetWare Networks isn't under the Novell entry of the clients listing. You'll find it in the Microsoft list of clients. Novell didn't supply the protected-mode client NetWare—Microsoft did. If you install either of the entries from the Novell listing, you'll be using real-mode drivers. Not only will this reduce performance and cause some level of system instability, but it'll also remove many of the positive benefits of using an integrated approach to networking. For example, you won't be able to use a single login screen for both NetWare and Microsoft; you'll have to enter them separately. Always try the protected-mode drivers first, just to see if they'll work with your system setup.

Once you get Client for NetWare installed, select it in the Primary Network Logon field of the Network Properties dialog. You access this dialog by right-clicking on the Network Neighborhood icon and selecting the Properties option. The first time you run Client for NetWare, you will see two login dialogs. The first dialog will log you into a preferred server. The second login dialog will take care of the Windows 95 security requirement. As long as the user name and password for NetWare and Windows 95 are the same, you'll see this dual login dialog only once. The next time you log in, you'll see only one dialog that will take care of both login needs.

To enable login script processing on the NetWare server, you need to check the Client for NetWare Networks Properties dialog, shown in Figure 13.3. This dialog has three fields. The one that you're interested in is a checkbox that'll enable login script processing. You'll also see fields for the preferred server and the first network drive.

Figure 13.3.
The Client for NetWare
Networks Properties dialog
allows you to enable login
script processing.

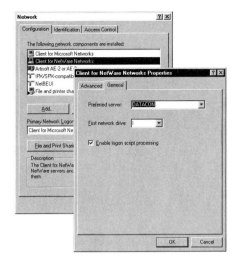

Tip: You can reduce your need to use the MAP command (or anything similar) by using the persistent mapping capability available using Explorer or the context menu of Network Neighborhood. Using the native Windows 95 capability means less chance of error if an individual workstation's configuration changes.

Enabling login script processing allows an administrator to maintain the pre-Windows 95 security policy on the server. It also provides a means for creating automatic drive mapping and other NOS-specific features. You'll need to check the documentation that came with your network to see exactly what types of script file processing you can perform.

Note: Windows 95 doesn't currently support the NetWare 4.x NDS style of login script processing out of the box. (There are, however, several update files on the WINDOWS forum on CompuServe that you can use to modify the way that Windows 95 works with NDS.) You must use the bindery-style login scripts provided by NetWare 3.x and below. This means placing your NetWare 4.x server in bindery emulation mode. The system login script for a NetWare server is stored in NET$LOG.DAT, and you edit it using the SYSCON utility. You'll find script file in the \PUBLIC directory. The individual user scripts will appear in their \MAIL directory.

You'll need to make any changes to a NetWare login script using the SYSCON utility shown in Figure 13.4. There are two different kinds of scripts that you can use. The script that I recommend programmers to change is the individual use script. You access it by selecting the User Information option of the Available Topics menu, selecting the desired user name, and then selecting the Login Script option from the User Information menu. What you'll see is an editor screen like the one shown in Figure 13.5.

Figure 13.4.
The SYSCON utility allows you to change a variety of system wide and user specific parameters including the login script under NetWare.

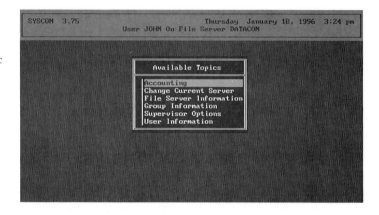

Figure 13.5.
This editor style window allows you add drive mapping and searches to an individual user's login script.

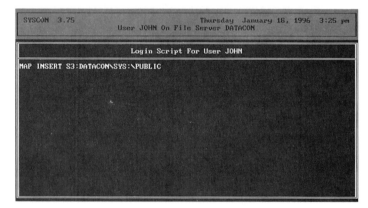

Warning: The Windows 95 protected-mode script processor can't run TSRs. The TSR will start in a separate virtual machine, which will terminate with an error when the script file processing completes. This lack of TSR processing in your script files means that you'll have to come up with a different way to install backup agents and other files that you normally install using the login script. In most cases, you'll need to install such files as part of the AUTOEXEC.BAT or within a DOS session after you start Windows 95.

Two Additional Areas of Support

Any discussion of networking with Windows has to include two other features that you'll probably see a lot of in the future. Both Windows NT and Windows 95 provide remote procedure call (RPC) and Windows Sockets (WinSock) support. (The next version of Windows NT is rumored to include network OLE as well.) I'm not going to tell you every detail about these features, but I did want to provide you with an overview of what they can do for you. The following sections will do just that.

Remote Procedure Calls (RPC) Support

Remember near the beginning of this chapter when we talked about network transports and the way Microsoft implements them? I mentioned then just how complex a network transport could get if you added a few features. Remote procedure calls (RPCs) are a somewhat new concept for Windows 95. They're implemented as a network transport mechanism using named pipes, NetBIOS, or WinSock to create a connection between a client and a server. RPC is compatible with the Open Software Foundation (OSF) Data Communication Exchange (DCE) specification.

So what does RPC do for you? OLE uses it, for one. Actually, OLE uses a subset of RPC called light RPC (LRPC) to allow you to make connections that you couldn't normally make. We discussed this whole issue in detail in Chapter 10, so I won't talk about it again here. However, OLE is only the tip of the iceberg. There are other ways that RPC can help people who use your applications.

Think about it this way. You're using an application that requires any number of resources in the form of DLLs, VxDs, and other forms of executable code. Right now, all that code has to appear on your machine or in a place where Windows will be certain to find it. What this means is that every time a network administrator wants to update software, he has to search every machine on the network to make sure the job gets done completely. What if you could "borrow" the DLL from someone else's machine? That's what RPCs are all about. An RPC lets your application grab what it needs in the form of executable code from wherever it happens to be.

You won't find a lot of RPC support in Windows NT or Windows 95 right now, but there's one way to see how it works. If you're running a Windows NT network, Microsoft provides a remote print provider utility in the \ADMIN\APPTOOLS\RPCPP folder. Installing this utility will allow a Windows 95 client to administer printer queues on Windows NT Servers. Using this print provider, a Windows 95 client can obtain complete accounting and job status information from the Windows NT Server.

Windows Sockets (WinSock) Support

Windows sockets (WinSock) started out as an effort by a group of vendors to make sense out of the conglomeration of TCP/IP protocol-based socket interfaces. Various vendors had originally ported their implementation of this protocol to Windows. The result was that nothing worked with anything else. The socket interface was originally implemented as a networked interprocess communication mechanism for version 4.2 of the Berkeley UNIX system. Windows 95 will require all non-NetBIOS applications to use WinSock if they need to access any TCP/IP services. Vendors may optionally write IPX/SPX applications to this standard as well. Microsoft includes two WinSock applications with Windows: SNMP (simple network management protocol) and FTP (file transfer protocol)—both of which were originally designed to work with the Internet.

Before I go much further, let me quickly define a couple of terms used in the previous sentence. We looked at what a protocol was previously. It's a set of rules. TCP/IP is one common implementation of a set of rules. Think of a socket as you would the tube holder found in old televisions and radios. An application can plug a request (a tube) for some type of service into a socket and send it to a host of some kind. That host could be a file server, a minicomputer, a mainframe, or even another PC. An application can also use a socket to make a query to a database server. For example, it could ask for last year's sales statistics. If every host uses a different sized socket, then every application will require a different set of tubes to fit those sockets. WinSock gets rid of this problem by standardizing the socket used to request services and make queries.

Besides making the interface easier to use, WinSock provides another advantage. Normally, an application has to add a NetBIOS header to every packet that leaves the workstation. The workstation at the other end doesn't really need the header, but it's there anyway. This additional processing overhead reduces network efficiency. Using WinSock eliminates the need for the header, and the user sees better performance as a result.

Sockets are an age-old principle (at least in the computer world), but they are far from out-of-date. The WinSock project proved so successful that Microsoft began to move it to other transports. For example, Windows 95 includes a WinSock module for both the IPX/SPX and NetBEUI transports. You'll use the IPX/SPX module if you use the protected mode NetWare interface that Microsoft provides. (This is the NetWare client that appears in the Microsoft area of the Select Network Client dialog—you access it through the Network Properties dialog.)

Of course, WinSock is really a stopgap measure for today. In the long term, companies will want to move from the client/server model for some applications and use a distributed approach. This will require the use of a remote procedure call (RPC) interface instead of WinSock. We've already looked at the implications of RPC in this chapter.

So what does it take to implement WinSock on your system? A group of five files in your \SYSTEM folder are used to implement WinSock. The following list tells you what they are and what tasks they perform.

- WINSOCK.DLL: This 16-bit application provides backward compatibility for older applications that need it. For example, an application such as Ping would use this DLL.
- WSOCK32.DLL: 32-bit applications use this DLL to access the WinSock API. It provides support for newer socket applications such as TelNet.
- VSOCK.VXD: Windows uses this driver to provide both 16-bit and 32-bit TCP/IP and IPX/SPX WinSock support. It provides virtualized support for each virtual machine, enabling Windows to perform more than one WinSock operation at a time. This is the general driver used for both protocols. If Microsoft added more WinSock interfaces later, they would all require this file for interface purposes.
- WSTCP.VXD: TCP/IP requires a protocol-specific driver. This file provides that support.
- WSIPX.VXD: IPX/SPX requires a protocol-specific driver. This file provides that support.

Accessing the Network Part of the Windows API

Now that we've gotten past all the architectural details for a network, let's look at some of the things you can do with the various network specific calls in the Windows API. Finding a list of these calls is easy; all you need to do is search under 'NET' in the Windows API help file. You'll see an entire list of network specific calls you can use.

One of the first things that I like to have in a network utility is the ability to find out what servers are available. After all, what good is it to try to make a connection if the server isn't listening to you? The NetServerEnum call is the one that you use to get the name of the servers on the network. (You can also use a combination of the WNetEnumOpen and WNetEnumResource calls to get not only the file server list, but a list of other resources as well.) One of the advantages of using the NetServerEnum function is that you can specify a server type. Table 13.1 shows the types of servers that the Windows API supports. You can also specify a starting location for the server search. Normally you'll want to use the current workstation as the starting point, but you could specify another domain (server in the case of NetWare) to start from. Once you have the server information, you can use the NetServerGetInfo call to retrieve some information about the server or the NetServerSetInfo call to change its setup—at least to a limited degree.

Tip: You'll find direct support for all the WNet calls in the WINDOWS.PAS file provided with Delphi. Any Net calls (like NetServerEnum) will require you to create a separate module. We've looked at the process for creating separate API call units in the past. For example, Chapter 9 shows you how to access the LZ API calls. Using the WNet calls whenever possible will obviously save you some time and effort as long as those calls will get the job done. In some cases you'll still find it more efficient to create your own separate module.

Table 13.1. File Server Types Supported by the Windows API.

Server Constant	Description
SV_TYPE_WORKSTATION	Returns a list of all LAN Manager workstations.
SV_TYPE_SERVER	Returns a list of all LAN Manager servers.
SV_TYPE_SQLSERVER	This constant returns a list of any server running Microsoft SQL Server.
SV_TYPE_DOMAIN_CTRL	The primary domain controller. In most cases this refers to a Windows NT server containing the master user records.
SV_TYPE_DOMAIN_BAKCTRL	Provides a list of all backup domain controllers. Every domain has a primary domain controller that contains the master copy of the user records. Every other domain controller has a replicated copy of the user records.
SV_TYPE_TIMESOURCE	Returns a list of any server running the timesource service.
SV_TYPE_AFP	Returns a list of all Apple File Protocol servers.
SV_TYPE_NOVELL	Returns a list of all Novell NetWare servers—both 3.x and 4.x. This particular constant is a bit misleading since Novell used to provide UnixWare as well (they sold their interest in the product in 1995). Use the XENIX option to obtain a list of any UnixWare servers.
SV_TYPE_DOMAIN_MEMBER	Use this option to obtain a complete list of all domain members. This includes both servers and workstations—along with any peripheral members.
SV_TYPE_PRINT	Returns a list of any server providing print queue services. In most cases this is going to be a dedicated print server on larger networks—especially when using Novell NetWare.

Server Constant	Description
SV_TYPE_DIALIN	Returns a list of any server running the dial-in service.
SV_TYPE_XENIX_SERVER	Returns a list of all XENIX servers. It should also provide a list of any UNIX servers. There may be situations where you won't get a complete listing—it all depends on the type of UNIX server and the connections that Windows provides to it.
SV_TYPE_NT	Provides a list of all Windows NT servers.
SV_TYPE_WFW	Provides a list of any server running Windows for Workgroups.
SV_TYPE_POTENTIAL_BROWSER	Returns a list of any server that can run the browser service.
SV_TYPE_BACKUP_BROWSER	Returns a list of any server running a browser service as backup.
SV_TYPE_MASTER_BROWSER	Returns the name of the server running the master browser service.
SV_TYPE_DOMAIN_MASTER	Returns the name of the server running the domain master browser.
SV_TYPE_DOMAIN_ENUM	Use this constant to obtain a complete list of all accessible domains.
SV_TYPE_ALL	Returns a list of all accessible servers, even if there isn't a current connection to it.

Obviously I could extend this chapter out by a couple of hundred pages if I talked about every call that you have at your disposal. Let's look at the way that you would use those calls instead. This example will show you how to get a list of servers and display them on a memo field. Microsoft stores the network information in a hierarchical format so you can use recursive calls to obtain a complete list of the network resources.

The first thing you'll need is the form shown in Figure 13.6. It's fairly simple form—containing only two pushbuttons and a memo component. The only property I changed was to add a vertical scroll bar to the memo component. Otherwise, the components use the default settings.

The interesting part of this example is the way that I implemented the code required to parse the network hierarchical tree. Listing 13.1 shows the source for this example. Notice that I used the WNet API calls in this example since Delphi supports them directly.

Figure 13.6.
This form is the first step in creating the network information browser.

Listing 13.1. **Example source.**

```
unit NetBrws1;

interface

uses
  Windows, Messages, SysUtils, Classes, Graphics, Controls, Forms, Dialogs,
  StdCtrls;

type
  TForm1 = class(TForm)
    Memo1: TMemo;
    pbExit: TButton;
    pbResources: TButton;
    procedure pbExitClick(Sender: TObject);
    procedure pbResourcesClick(Sender: TObject);
    function ParseNetTree(PNetBuffer: PNetResource):DWORD;
  private
    { Private declarations }
  public
    { Public declarations }
  end;

var
  Form1: TForm1;

implementation

{$R *.DFM}

procedure TForm1.pbExitClick(Sender: TObject);
begin
    {End the application.}
    Application.Terminate;
end;

procedure TForm1.pbResourcesClick(Sender: TObject);
begin
    {Clear the memo field.}
    Memo1.Lines.Clear;

    {Start looking for resources.}
    ParseNetTree(NIL);
end;
```

```
function TForm1.ParseNetTree(PNetBuffer: PNetResource):DWORD;
var
    hEnum: THandle;                         {Server enumeration handle.}
    NetBuffer: array [1..3] of TNetResource;          {An array of resources.}
    dwBufferLen: DWORD;                     {Length of the buffer.}
    dwCount: DWORD;                         {Resource item count.}
    fResult: DWORD;                         {Results of function calls.}
    iCount: Integer;                         {Loop counter.}
begin
    {Get the buffer length.}
    dwBufferLen := SizeOf(NetBuffer);

    {Initialize the item counter.}
    dwCount := $FFFFFFFF;

    {Obtain a Windows Network enumeration handle}
    fResult := WNetOpenEnum(RESOURCE_GLOBALNET, RESOURCETYPE_ANY, 0, PNetBuffer, hEnum);
    if fResult <> NO_ERROR then
        begin

          {Determine whether we're at the end of our hierarchy.}
          if fResult = ERROR_NOT_CONTAINER then
              begin
               Exit;
               end

          {If this is an actual error, display a message and exit.}
          else
              begin
               ShowMessage('An Open Error Occurred: ' + IntToStr(fResult));
               Exit;
               end;
        end;

    {Continue doing this until we run out of resources to check.}
    while fResult = NO_ERROR do
    begin

    {Get the current network resources.}
    fResult := WNetEnumResource(hEnum, dwCount, @NetBuffer, dwBufferLen);

    {Display the results.}
    if fResult = NO_ERROR then
        begin
         Memo1.Lines.Add('Scope: ' + IntToStr(NetBuffer[1].dwScope));
         Memo1.Lines.Add('Type: ' + IntToStr(NetBuffer[1].dwType));
         Memo1.Lines.Add('Display Type: ' + IntToStr(NetBuffer[1].dwDisplayType));
         Memo1.Lines.Add('Usage: ' + IntToStr(NetBuffer[1].dwUsage));
         Memo1.Lines.Add('Local Name: ' + NetBuffer[1].lpLocalName);
         Memo1.Lines.Add('Remote Name: ' + NetBuffer[1].lpRemoteName);
         Memo1.Lines.Add('Comment: ' + NetBuffer[1].lpComment);
         Memo1.Lines.Add('Provider: ' + NetBuffer[1].lpProvider);
         Memo1.Lines.Add('');
        end;

    {Check the results of our query.}
    if fResult <> NO_ERROR then
```

continues

Listing 13.1. continued

```
               {If an actual error occurred, display a message and exit.}
               if (fResult <> ERROR_NO_MORE_ITEMS) or (fResult = ERROR_NOT_CONTAINER) then
                  begin
                  ShowMessage('An Enumeration Error Occurred: ' + IntToStr(fResult));
                  Exit;
                  end

               {Otherwise, if we're at the end of our item list, exit.}
               else
                  begin
                   Exit;
                   end

         {If an error hasn't occurred, then look for the next item.}
         else
             ParseNetTree(@NetBuffer[1]);

         end; {while fResult = NO_ERROR do}

         {Close the enumeration handle.}
         WNetCloseEnum(hEnum);
end;

end.
```

There are several things you should notice about this example. The first item is the amount of checking I do for errors. This isn't just so that the program will fail gracefully—in fact, it'll have to fail somewhere along the way to complete its task. There are two kinds of errors that actually help you determine when you're at the leaf node of the hierarchy. The ERROR_NO_MORE_ITEMS constant tells you that you're at the last item in a particular level of the tree. It's the error code that stops the main while loop in this example. The ERROR_NOT_CONTAINER constant is the one that tells you that you're at the bottom of the tree. The last item on the network isn't a container—it can't hold any additional elements.

There are two kinds of leaf nodes that you'll run into (at least on most networks): printers and drives. The highest level of the hierarchy normally contains the network driver. You'll see a server or domain name at the next level. A third level usually contains a list of additional servers or the leaves of the network—the drives and printers that a user can actually use.

Tip: There is a bug in the current version of Delphi (or perhaps in Windows itself) where you need to allocate an array of three TNetStructure structures to fill one. Otherwise, the WNetEnumResource call will return an error code saying that the structure isn't large enough. That's why I used: NetBuffer: array [1..3] of TNetResource in the VAR area of the ParseNetTree function.

The second thing you should notice about our example code is the method I use for enumerating the resources. Essentially you're asking the resource to identify itself when you enumerate it. There are three steps that you'll use to perform this task in most cases.

1. Open a network resource enumeration handle using the WNetOpenEnum function call. There are two ways to open a handle. If you provide a value of NIL for the NETRESOURCE structure value, then Windows will return a handle for the very first level of the network hierarchy. In most cases this handle references the network drivers. Supplying a pointer to NETRESOURCE structure opens a handle to the items that the container referred to in the structure holds. That's why I used the following syntax in my recursive call: ParseNetTree(@NetBuffer[1]). I'm passing the NETRESOURCE structure returned by the previous call to WNetEnumResource to the next level of the hierarchy search.

2. Poll the network resources using the WNetResource call. You'll need to supply variables for every parameter you provide. The Windows API can (and probably will) modify every one of the values you provide so supplying a number won't work. The NETRESOURCE structure that this call fills is important for two reasons. First, it provides you with information about the current network resource. Second, you can use this structure in subsequent calls to determine what network resources this resource contains. Obviously, only container elements like network drivers and file servers fit into this category.

3. Close the network resource enumeration handle using the WNetCloseEnum function call. Just like any other handle you open, Windows can't deallocate the memory it uses if you exit the application before you close the handle. This kind of error can be very difficult to find, so it pays to spend a little time making sure you have all the bases covered.

Tip: Whenever I write a piece of code to open a handle—it doesn't matter what kind of handle it is—I immediately write the corresponding code to close it. I then place the code that does whatever I want to do with that handle between the open and close calls. If you follow this procedure, you'll find that you forget to close handles a lot less often.

Now that we have some working code, let's see the application in action. Figure 13.7 shows a typical display. In this case you're looking at the first level of a NetWare network—the network driver. Even though the figure doesn't show all of it, the next level is the file server (the network drives and printer appear below the server level).

Obviously this is only the tip of the network iceberg—the very starting point of the types of things that you can expect to do. The combination of Net and WNet functions provided as part of the Windows API allows you to do a variety of things including logging off and on the network. You could use some of these functions to make it possible for an administrator to move from LAN-to-LAN on a WAN or to obtain information about the users currently logged into the network. We'll see just how to use some of these features in the remaining sections of this chapter.

Figure 13.7.

The Network Browser will
parse your network tree and
display information about
each resource that it finds.

Creating Administrator Specific Application Features

As far as a Delphi programmer is concerned, the network or database administrator is the center of the networking universe. (The only exception to this rule is if you become an operating system or network utility programmer.) There's only one good reason to add networking features to an application—the network administrator needs some special functionality that the default Windows setup can't provide.

If you take a good look at the features that Windows 95 and Windows NT provide for the user, it doesn't take too long to figure out that they're pretty complete. How often do you find yourself going to the network itself for anything but administration purposes? Logging into the network is pretty much automatic—Windows asks for your password when you boot the operating system. When set up correctly, Windows even takes cares of re-creating the connections you need. Viewing those connections is made easy by Explorer. The bottom line is that a user has little need for added functionality in most cases.

So, what types of things would an administrator be interested in seeing in an application? There are probably a lot of features that you could add—the administrator might even use them all if he spends his entire day using your application. However, I find that there are two features I end up adding more often than not to the applications I create. The first is status information. The network or database administrator has to know what's going on with the network at all times. Otherwise, disaster could come knocking at the door and find the administrator ill-prepared to deal with the situation.

A second feature usually falls into the category of user administration—a rather broad area that could encompass all kinds of things—not just the administration of user needs for a specific application. The question you need to ask yourself in this situation is if there is an adequate tool to get the job done that's at the administrator's fingertips. Trying to re-create the tools that the NOS vendor has already supplied is not only a waste of time and effort, but your utility may not work as well as the one provided. The most common set of user related tools that an administrator needs are security related. Assigning rights to specific users, removing rights from others, and determining who can do what takes up most of an administrator's time. This is the one area you should always at least consider providing in your application—some type of security monitoring or administrator feature.

System Security and the Administrator

About now many of you are asking what kind of an administrator would need to access security, but wouldn't use the tools provided by the NOS to do so. There are actually a few good answers to this, but one situation almost always comes to mind when I think about security under Windows. What if the person administering the application isn't a network administrator—someone with the training to work with the NOS itself? Say that person is a workgroup manager or other individual who doesn't need the whole network picture—just enough information to maintain the application they're responsible for managing. You'll find yourself in that situation a lot more often than you might think. Large companies with a lot of small workgroups fall into this category a lot. The network administrator doesn't have the knowledge needed to administer the application correctly, but he doesn't want the workgroup manager crawling around the network either.

So, what do you need to know about system security to make it work under Delphi? Windows 95 and Windows NT both use a similar setup, so one security module will work with both of them in some cases. (In other cases you'll definitely want to use a separate module for Windows NT to make better use of its enhanced security capabilities—see note below for details.) I've shown you that there are objects lurking beneath the surface of Windows several times in the book so far. For example, look at the architectural overview in Chapter 5. Microsoft even refers to various Windows components like dialogs and icons as objects in Windows 95 (the new Windows NT will probably address icons and dialog boxes as objects too).

> **Note:** Windows NT does support a lot more Windows security API calls than Windows 95 does because its security is a lot more robust. In fact, you'll find that your ability to manage security when using Windows 95 is severely hampered by its lack of Windows NT security feature support. For example, you can't use the GetUserObjectSecurity call under Windows 95. Most of the access token calls that I describe in the next section won't work either. The best way to figure out if a call is supported or not is to test it out. If you get ERROR_CALL_NOT_IMPLEMENTED (value 120) returned from the call, then you know that you can only use it under Windows NT.

Knowing that everything is an object makes security a bit easier to understand—at least it's a starting point. However, objects are just a starting point. Users are the other part of the security equation. An object is accessed by a user—so security in Windows is a matter of comparing the object's protection to the user's rights. If the user has sufficient rights, then he can use the object. The Windows documentation refers to an object's level of protection as a security descriptor. This is the structure that tells the security system what rights a user needs to access the object. Likewise, the user has an access token—another structure that tells the security system what rights a user has in a given situation. Figure 13.8 shows both of these structures.

Figure 13.8.
Access tokens define the user's rights, while security descriptors define the protection level for a process.

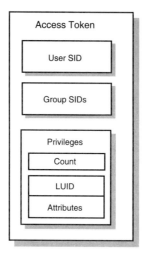

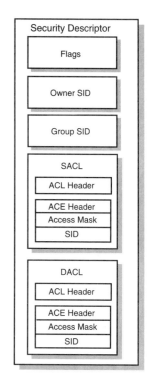

Understanding Access Tokens

You'll find that there are two of ways of looking at a user's rights under Windows—both of them related to objects in one form or another. The user's access token has a security identifier (SID) to identify users throughout the network—it's like having an account number. The user token that the SID identifies tells what groups the user belongs to and what privileges the user has. Each group also has a SID so the user's SID contains references to the various group SIDs that he belongs to, not a complete set of group access rights. You would normally use the User Manager utility under Windows NT to change the contents of this access token.

So, what is the privileges section of the access token all about? It begins with a count of the number of privileges that the user has—not the groups he belongs to, but the number of special privilege entries in the access token. This section also contains an array of privilege entries. Each privilege entry contains a locally unique identifier (LUID)—essentially a pointer to an object—and an attribute mask. The attribute mask tells what rights that the user has to the object. Group SID entries are essentially the same. They contain a privilege count and an array of privilege entries.

> **Tip:** Now would probably be a good time to look at the Windows API help file provided with Delphi and see what kind of SID and TOKEN related API calls that you can find. Examples of SID related calls include: CopySID and AllocateAndInitializeSID. You'll also find that the OpenProcessToken and GetTokenInformation calls are essential to making security work right under Delphi.

Using Access Tokens

Let's talk for a few seconds about the Token calls that the Windows API provides since they are the first stepping stone that you'll need to know about when it comes to security. To do anything with a user's account—even if you want to find out who has access to a particular workstation—you need to know about tokens. As I previously stated, tokens are the central part of the user side of the security equation. You'll almost always begin a user account access with a call to the OpenProcessToken call. Notice the name of this call—it deals with any kind of a process—user or otherwise. The whole purpose of this call is to get a token handle with specific rights attached to it. For example, if you want to query the user account, you need the TOKEN_QUERY privilege. (Your access token must contain the rights that you request from the system, which is why an administrator can access a token, but other users can't.) Any changes to the user's account require the TOKEN_ADJUST_PRIVILEGES privilege. There are quite a few of these access rights, so I won't list them all here.

Once you have an access token handle, you need to decide what to do with it. If you decide you want to change a user's privilege to do something, you need the LUID for the privilege you want to change. All of these appear in the WINDOWS.PAS file with an SE_ attached to them. For example, the SE_SYSTEM_PROFILE_NAME privilege allows the user to gather profiling information for the entire system. There are some SE values that aren't related to users (like the SE_LOCK_MEMORY_NAME privilege that allows a process to lock system memory). You get the LUID for a privilege using the LookupPrivilegeValue call. Now you can combine the information you've gotten so far to change the privilege. Most generally you'll use the AdjustTokenPrivileges call to make the required change.

Querying the user's account (or other access token information) is fairly straightforward. You use the GetTokenInformation call to retrieve any information you might need. This call requires a token class parameter, which tells Windows what kind of information you need. For example, you would use the TokenUser class if you wanted to know about a specific user. You'll also need to supply an appropriate structure that Windows can use for storing the information you request—which obviously differs based on the token class you request.

Understanding Security Descriptors

Now let's look at the security descriptor. Figure 13.8 shows that each security descriptor contains five main sections. The first section is a list of flags. These flags tell you the descriptor revision number, format, and ACL (access control list) status.

The next two sections contain SIDs. The owner SID tells who owns the object. This doesn't have to be an individual user; Windows allows you to use a group SID here as well. The one limiting factor is that the group SID must appear in the access token of the person changing the entry. The group SID allows a group of people to own the object. Of the two SIDs, only the owner SID is important under Windows. The group SID is used as part of the Macintosh and POSIX security environment.

The final two sections contain ACLs. The security access control list (SACL) controls Windows auditing feature. Every time a user or group accesses an object and the auditing feature for that object is turned on, Windows makes an entry in the audit log. The discretionary access control list (DACL) controls who can actually use the object. You can assign both groups and individual users to a specific object.

> **Note:** There are actually two types of security descriptors: absolute and self relative. The absolute security descriptor contains an actual copy of each ACL within its structure. This is the type of security descriptor to use for an object that requires special handling. The self relative security descriptor only contains a pointer to the SACL and DACL. This type of descriptor saves memory and reduces the time required to change the rights for a group of objects. You would use it when all the objects in a particular group require the same level of security. For example, you could use this method to secure all the threads within a single application. Windows requires that you convert a self relative security descriptor to absolute format before you can save it or transfer it to another process. Every descriptor you retrieve using an API call is of the self relative type—you must convert it before you can save it. You can convert a security descriptor from one type to another using the MakeAbsoluteSD and MakeSelfRelativeSD API calls.

An ACL consists of two types of entries. The first entry is a header that lists the number of access control entries (ACEs) that the ACL contains. Windows uses this number as a method for determining when it has reached the end of the ACE list. (There isn't any kind of end of structure record or any way of determining a precise size for each ACE in the structure.) The second entry is an array of ACEs.

Warning: Never directly manipulate the contents of an ACL or SID since Microsoft may change their structure in future versions of Windows. The Windows API provides a wealth of functions to change the contents of these structures. Always use an API call to perform any task with either structure type to reduce the impact of changes in structure on your application.

So, what is an ACE? An ACE defines the object rights for a single user or group. Every ACE has a header that defines the type, size, and flags for the ACE. Next comes an access mask that defines the rights that a user or group has to the object. Finally, there's an entry for the user's or group's SID.

There are four different types of ACE headers (three of which are used in the current version of Windows). The access allowed type appears in the DACL and grants rights to a user. You can use it to add to the rights that a user already has to an object on an instance by instance basis. For example, say you wanted to keep the user from changing the system time so that you could keep all the machines on the network synchronized. However, there might be one situation—like daylight savings time—where the user would need this right. You could use an access allowed ACE to give the user the right to change the time in this one instance. An access denied ACE revokes rights that the user has to an object. You can use it to deny access to an object during special system events. For example, you could deny access rights to a remote terminal while you perform some type of update on it. The system audit ACE types work with the SACL. They define which events to audit for a particular user or group. The currently unused ACE type is a system alarm ACE. It'll allow either the SACL or DACL to set an alarm when specific events happen.

Tip: Now would be a good time to look though the Windows API help file to see what types of access rights that Windows provides. You should also look at the various structures used to obtain the information. Especially important are the ACL and ACE structures. Look for the ACE flags that determine how objects in a container react. For example, check out the CONTAINER_INHERIT_ACE constant that allows subdirectories to inherit the protection of the parent directory.

Using Security Descriptors

Understanding what a security descriptor is and how the various structures it contains interact is only one part of the picture. You also need to know how to begin the process of actually accessing and using security descriptors to write a program. The first thing you need to understand is that unlike tokens, security descriptors aren't generalized. You can't use a standard set of calls to access them. In fact, there are five classes of security descriptors, each of which uses a different set of descriptor calls to access the object initially. (You have to have the SE_SECURITY_NAME privilege to use any of these functions.)

- Files, Directories, Pipes, and Mailslots—Use the GetFileSecurity and SetFileSecurity calls to access this object type.

Note: Only the NTFS file system under Windows NT provides security. The VFAT file system provides it to a lesser degree under Windows 95. You cannot assign or obtain security descriptors for either the HPFS or FAT file systems under either operating system. The FAT file system doesn't provide any extended attribute space, one requirement for adding security. The HPFS file system provides extended attributes, but they don't include any security features.

- Processes, Threads, Access Tokens, and Synchronization Objects—You need the GetKernelObjectSecurity and SetKernelObjectSecurity calls to access these objects. All of these objects, even the access tokens, are actually kernel objects. As such, they also have their own security descriptor for protection purposes.
- Window Stations, Desktops, Windows, and Menus—The GetUserObjectSecurity and SetUserObjectSecurity calls allow you to access these objects. A window station is a combination of keyboard, mouse, and screen, the hardware you use to access the system. Desktops contain windows and menus, the display elements you can see on screen. These four objects inherit rights from each other in the order shown. In other words, a desktop will inherit the rights of the window station.
- System Registry Keys—This object type requires use of the RegGetKeySecurity and RegSetKeySecurity calls. Notice that these two calls start with Reg, just like all the other registry specific calls that Windows supports.
- Executable Service Objects—The QueryServiceObjectSecurity and SetServiceObjectSecurity calls work with this object. For some strange reason, neither call appears with the other security calls in the Delphi help file. You'll need to know that these calls exist to find them. An executable service is a background task that Windows provides—like the UPS monitoring function. You'll find the services that your system supports by double-clicking the Services applet in the Control Panel.

Once you do gain access to the object, you'll find that you can perform a variety of tasks using a generic set of API calls. For example, the GetSecurityDescriptorDACL retrieves a copy of the DACL from any descriptor type. In other words, the descriptors for all of these objects follow roughly the same format—even though the lengths of most of the components will differ. One reason for the differences in size is that each object will contain a differing number of ACEs. The SIDs are different sizes as well.

The next step in the process of either querying or modifying the contents of a security descriptor is to disassemble the component part. For example, you could view the individual ACEs within a DACL or a SACL by using the GetACE API call. You could also use the owner and group SIDs for a variety of SID related calls (we discussed these calls in the access token section of the chapter). Suffice it to say that you could use a generic set of functions to manipulate the security descriptor once you obtain access using a specific procedure.

In essence, any security descriptor access will always consist of the same three steps: getting the descriptor itself, removing a specific component part, and then modifying the contents of that component. To change the security descriptor you follow the reverse process. In other words, you use a call like AddACE to add a new ACE to an ACL, then SetSecurityDescriptorSACL to change SACL within a descriptor, and finally save the descriptor itself using a call like SetFileSecurity (assuming that you want to modify a file object).

Peter's Principle: ACEing Security in Windows

I spent some time thinking about the way that Windows evaluates the ACEs in the DACL and came up with a few potential problem areas—problems that the Windows utilities take care of automatically, but which you'll need to program around in your application to derive the same result. (The SACL has the same potential problem, but it only affects auditing so the effect is less severe from a system security standpoint.)

Windows evaluates the ACEs in an ACL in the order in which they appear. At first this might not seem like a very big deal. However, it could become a problem in some situations. For example, what if you want to revoke all of a user's rights in one area, but her list of ACEs includes membership in a group that allows access to that area? If you place the grant access ACE first in the list, the user would get access to the area—Windows stops searching the list as soon as it finds the first ACE that grants all the user's requested rights (or an ACE that denies one of the requested rights). Granted rights are cumulative. If one ACE grants the right to read a file and another the right to write to it and the user is asking for both read and write rights, then Windows will view the two ACEs as granting the requested rights. The bottom line is that you should place all your deny ACEs in the list first, to prevent any potential breach in security.

You also need to exercise care in the ordering of group SIDs. Rights that a user acquires from different groups that he belongs to are cumulative. This means that if a user is part of two groups, one that has access to a file and another that doesn't, he'll have access to the file if the group granting the right appears first on the list.

Obviously, you could spend all your time trying to figure out the best arrangement of groups. As the number of groups and individual rights that a user possesses increases, the potential for an unintended security breach does as well. That's why it's important to create groups carefully and limit a user's individual rights.

Other Security Concerns

There are two other concerns when you look at security under Windows 95 or Windows NT. The first deals with a client's ability to access data it isn't supposed to when accessing data through a server. (I'm not talking about a file server here, but some type of DDE or other application server.) Think about it this way: What if a client didn't have rights to a specific type of data, but it accessed it through a DDE call to a server that did have the required rights? How could the server protect itself from being an unwilling accomplice to a security breach?

Windows provides several API calls that allow a server to impersonate a client. In essence, the calls allow a server to assume the security restrictions of the client in order to determine whether the client has sufficient rights to access a piece of data or a process. For example, a Word for Windows user might require access to an Excel data file. He could gain access to that file using DDE. In this case the server would need to verify that the Word for Windows user has sufficient rights to access the file before it sends the requested data. A server might even find that the client has superior rights when it uses this technique. The bottom line is that the server's only concern is for the protection of the data, resources, and environment that it manages.

There are three different types of communication supported by this set of API calls: DDE, named pipes, and RPCs. You need to use a different API call for each communication type. For example, to impersonate a DDE client you would use the DDEImpersonateClient call. There are some limitations to the level of impersonation support that Windows currently provides. For example, it doesn't currently support TCP/IP connections, so you'd have to resort to using other methods to verify that a user has the proper level of access rights in this case.

The other security concern is protecting the server itself. When a user calls Excel from within Word for Windows, what prevents him from doing something with Excel that damages the server itself? Ensuring that security concerns are taken care of isn't difficult to do with files and other types of named structures since the file server automatically attaches a security descriptor to these objects (a DDE server like Excel wouldn't need to do anything in this case because the file is under the control of the file server). However, many of the DDE or application server's private objects aren't named and require special protection. Windows also provides API calls to help a server protect itself. For example, the CreatePrivateObjectSecurity call allows the server to attach a security descriptor to any of its private objects—say a thread or other process. The security descriptor would prevent anyone other than the server from accessing the private object.

Accessing Network Resources and Security Using Delphi

Accessing network resources—like drives and printers—is where the example in this section starts. We'll take a look at how you can provide a set of management features in your application for the manager who needs to keep those under him happy, but doesn't need full access to the network. I'll show you how to perform the two basic tasks that I previously mentioned—viewing the current network status and changing any network configuration items as needed. Of course, you'll still have to hone this example to meet the custom requirements of the application you're creating. Remember, the whole purpose here is to provide a limited set of administration tools for the person who doesn't really need (or perhaps even want) full network administration capabilities.

We'll also look at how to use some of the system security features. I won't give you every detail on every call that Windows provides, that could quite possibly require an entire book by itself. What I'll show you is how to use an access token to enable or disable a user's ability to change the system clock. Notice that you can still read the system time; you just can change its value.

Note: The current Delphi documentation shows that the WNetConnectionDialog function only accepts the RESOURCETYPE_DISK constant as input. You can also use the RESOURCETYPE_PRINT constant with this function as shown in Listing 13.2. Unfortunately, there doesn't appear to be any way to invoke the option to log in as another user without using the Shutdown menu under either Windows 95 or Windows NT.

Let's begin with the form shown in Figure 13.9. All that we have here is a memo and five pushbutton components. The only change I made to any of the component configurations was to add scroll bars to the memo component. I also changed the Form1 BorderStyle property to bsDialog.

Figure 13.9.
This form is the central area for a network management application—you could easily attach it to another application as an administrator function that gets enabled or disabled as needed.

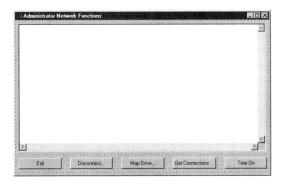

The first part of this example concentrates on system resource selection. You'll need some method to select the resource you want to either connect to or disconnect from. (The same dialog gets displayed when you want to display the various system connections.) Figure 13.10 shows the Resource Type Selection dialog I created for this purpose. All it contains is the default OK and Cancel buttons. I substituted a radio group for the standard bevel component. The radio group contains two TStrings property elements: Disk and Printer.

Figure 13.10.
This dialog allows you to
either connect or disconnect
two different resource types:
printers and disk drives.

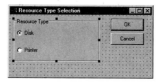

Once you get these two forms put together, it's time to add some code to make them work. You won't need to do anything for the resource selection dialog—Delphi automatically adds all the code you need to make it work. The code to make the pushbuttons on Form1 do something appears in Listing 13.2. Most of the functions are pretty straightforward, but the pbAccess component will require a bit of explanation.

Note: The pbAccess pushbutton only works under Windows NT. Windows 95 lacks most of the support you'll need to perform any useful work, so I chose to include a more robust Windows NT example in this particular situation. If you run the example under Windows 95, the program will report an error number 120—which means that Windows 95 doesn't support the call.

Listing 13.2. **Code for pushbuttons.**

```
unit NetAdmn1;

interface

uses
  Windows, Messages, SysUtils, Classes, Graphics, Controls, Forms, Dialogs,
  StdCtrls;

type
  TForm1 = class(TForm)
    pbDisconnect: TButton;
    pbExit: TButton;
    pbDriveMap: TButton;
    pbConnection: TButton;
    Memo1: TMemo;
    pbAccess: TButton;
    procedure pbExitClick(Sender: TObject);
    procedure pbDriveMapClick(Sender: TObject);
    procedure pbDisconnectClick(Sender: TObject);
    procedure FormShow(Sender: TObject);
    procedure pbConnectionClick(Sender: TObject);
    procedure pbAccessClick(Sender: TObject);
  private
    { Private declarations }
  public
    { Public declarations }
  end;
```

```
var
  Form1: TForm1;

implementation

uses NetAdmn2;

{$R *.DFM}

procedure TForm1.FormShow(Sender: TObject);
var
    sUserName: String;      {The current user's name.}
    dwNameSize: DWORD;      {Length of the user name buffer.}
    lpszName: PCHAR;        {User name pointer.}
begin
    {Size our user name string.}
    SetLength(sUserName, 80);
    dwNameSize := Length(sUserName);
    lpszName := PCHAR(sUserName);

    {Get the current user's name.}
    WNetGetUser(NIL, lpszName, dwNameSize);

    {Display the user name as part of the form caption.}
    Form1.Caption := 'Administrator Functions for: ' + sUserName;
end;

procedure TForm1.pbExitClick(Sender: TObject);
begin
    {End the application.}
    Application.Terminate;
end;

procedure TForm1.pbDriveMapClick(Sender: TObject);
begin
    {Display the resource selection dialog.  If the user clicks on Cancel, then
     exit the procedure.}
    if dlgResource.ShowModal = mrCancel then
        Exit;

    case dlgResource.rgSelect.ItemIndex of

        {Display a drive connect dialog.}
        0: WNetConnectionDialog(Form1.Handle, RESOURCETYPE_DISK);

        {Display a printer connect dialog.}
        1: WNetConnectionDialog(Form1.Handle, RESOURCETYPE_PRINT);

        end;

end;

procedure TForm1.pbDisconnectClick(Sender: TObject);
begin
    {Display the resource selection dialog.  If the user clicks on Cancel, then
     exit the procedure.}
```

continues

Listing 13.2. **continued**

```
    if dlgResource.ShowModal = mrCancel then
        Exit;

    case dlgResource.rgSelect.ItemIndex of

        {Display a drive disconnect dialog.}
        0: WNetDisconnectDialog(Form1.Handle, RESOURCETYPE_DISK);

        {Display a printer connect dialog.}
        1: WNetDisconnectDialog(Form1.Handle, RESOURCETYPE_PRINT);

        end;

end;

procedure TForm1.pbConnectionClick(Sender: TObject);
var
    iCount: Integer;          {Loop counter variable.}
    sLocalName: String;         {Local resource name.}
    lpszLocalName: PCHAR;    {Pointer to local resource name.}
    sRemoteName: String;     {Remote resource name.}
    lpszRemoteName: PCHAR;     {Pointer to remote resource name.}
    dwRemoteSize: DWORD;     {Size of the remote name buffer.}
begin
    {Initialize the remote name variables.}
    SetLength(sRemoteName, 1024);
    lpszRemoteName := PCHAR(sRemoteName);
    dwRemoteSize := Length(sRemoteName);

    {Display the resource selection dialog.  If the user clicks on Cancel, then
     exit the procedure.}
    if dlgResource.ShowModal = mrCancel then
        Exit;

    {Clear Memo1 before we put new information in it.}
    Memo1.Lines.Clear;

    case dlgResource.rgSelect.ItemIndex of

        {Display a list of drives connected to the workstation.}
        0:   begin
            for iCount := 65 to 90 do
                begin
                    sLocalName := chr(iCount) + ':';
                    lpszLocalName := PCHAR(sLocalName);
                    WNetGetConnection(lpszLocalName, lpszRemoteName, dwRemoteSize);
                    Memo1.Lines.Add(sLocalName + ' ' + sRemoteName);
                    end;
            end;

        {Display a list of peripheral devices connected to the workstation.}
        1:   begin

            {Get the parallel connections.}
            for iCount := 1 to 9 do
                begin
```

```
                sLocalName := 'LPT' + IntToStr(iCount) + ':';
                lpszLocalName := PCHAR(sLocalName);
                WNetGetConnection(lpszLocalName, lpszRemoteName, dwRemoteSize);
                Memo1.Lines.Add(sLocalName + ' ' + sRemoteName);
                end;

          end;

      end; {case dlgResource.rgSelect.ItemIndex of}

end;

procedure TForm1.pbAccessClick(Sender: TObject);
const
    {Token specific privileges.}
    TOKEN_ASSIGN_PRIMARY      = $0001;
    TOKEN_DUPLICATE           = $0002;
    TOKEN_IMPERSONATE         = $0004;
    TOKEN_QUERY               = $0008;
    TOKEN_QUERY_SOURCE        = $0010;
    TOKEN_ADJUST_PRIVILEGES   = $0020;
    TOKEN_ADJUST_GROUPS       = $0040;
    TOKEN_ADJUST_DEFAULT      = $0080;

    {Standard Privileges}
    SE_ASSIGNPRIMARYTOKEN_NAME   = 'SeAssignPrimaryTokenPrivilege';
    SE_AUDIT_NAME                = 'SeAuditPrivilege';
    SE_BACKUP_NAME               = 'SeBackupPrivilege';
    SE_CHANGE_NOTIFY_NAME        = 'SeChangeNotifyPrivilege';
    SE_CREATE_PAGEFILE_NAME      = 'SeCreatePagefilePrivilege';
    SE_CREATE_PERMANENT_NAME     = 'SeCreatePermanentPrivilege';
    SE_CREATE_TOKEN_NAME         = 'SeCreateTokenPrivilege';
    SE_DEBUG_NAME                = 'SeDebugPrivilege';
    SE_INC_BASE_PRIORITY_NAME    = 'SeIncreaseBasePriorityPrivilege';
    SE_INCREASE_QUOTA_NAME       = 'SeIncreaseQuotaPrivilege';
    SE_LOAD_DRIVER_NAME          = 'SeLoadDriverPrivilege';
    SE_LOCK_MEMORY_NAME          = 'SeLockMemoryPrivilege';
    SE_MACHINE_ACCOUNT_NAME      = 'SeMachineAccountPrivilege';
    SE_PROF_SINGLE_PROCESS_NAME  = 'SeProfileSingleProcessPrivilege';
    SE_REMOTE_SHUTDOWN_NAME      = 'SeRemoteShutdownPrivilege';
    SE_RESTORE_NAME              = 'SeRestorePrivilege';
    SE_SECURITY_NAME             = 'SeSecurityPrivilege';
    SE_SHUTDOWN_NAME             = 'SeShutdownPrivilege';
    SE_SYSTEM_ENVIRONMENT_NAME   = 'SeSystemEnvironmentPrivilege';
    SE_SYSTEM_PROFILE_NAME       = 'SeSystemProfilePrivilege';
    SE_SYSTEMTIME_NAME           = 'SeSystemtimePrivilege';
    SE_TAKE_OWNERSHIP_NAME       = 'SeTakeOwnershipPrivilege';
    SE_TCB_NAME                  = 'SeTcbPrivilege';
    SE_UNSOLICITED_INPUT_NAME    = 'SeUnsolicitedInputPrivilege';

var
    hToken: THandle;             {Handle of Access Token}
    liLUID: TLargeInteger;       {Locally Unique Identifier}
    NewState: TTokenPrivileges;  {New privilege level of token.}
    OldState: TTokenPrivileges;  {Old privilege level of token.}
    dwOldState: DWORD;           {Size of the token privilege structure.}
```

continues

Listing 13.2. continued

```delphi
    dwAccess: DWORD;            {Desired level of token access.}
    dwError: DWORD;            {Error number for current call.}
begin
    {Open the access token.  If there is an error, display the error number and
     exit.  An error value of 120 indicates that the function isn't supported on
     the host machine.}
    dwAccess := TOKEN_ADJUST_PRIVILEGES or TOKEN_QUERY;
    if not OpenProcessToken(Form1.Handle, dwAccess, @hToken) then
        begin
          dwError := GetLastError();
          MessageDlg('Error Number ' + IntToStr(dwError) + ' occured.', mtError, [mbOK],
0);
          Exit;
          end;

    {Get the LUID for the system time access token.}
    if LookupPrivilegeValue(NIL, SE_SYSTEMTIME_NAME, liLUID) then
        begin
          dwError := GetLastError();
          MessageDlg('Error Number ' + IntToStr(dwError) + ' occured.', mtError, [mbOK],
0);
          Exit;
          end;

    {Define the new privileges that we want.  Notice that the pbAccess button caption
     switches between states to indicate the current security level.}
    if pbAccess.Caption = 'Time Off' then
        begin
            NewState.PrivilegeCount := 1;
          NewState.Privileges[0].LUID := liLUID;
          NewState.Privileges[0].Attributes := SE_PRIVILEGE_ENABLED;
           pbAccess.Caption := 'Time On';
           end
    else
        begin
            NewState.PrivilegeCount := 1;
          NewState.Privileges[0].LUID := liLUID;
          NewState.Privileges[0].Attributes := SE_PRIVILEGE_USED_FOR_ACCESS;
           pbAccess.Caption := 'Time Off';
           end;

    {Change the set time access token.}
    AdjustTokenPrivileges(hToken, False, NewState, SizeOf(TTokenPrivileges), OldState,
dwOldState);
        begin
          dwError := GetLastError();
          if not dwError = ERROR_SUCCESS then
             begin
             MessageDlg('Error Number ' + IntToStr(dwError) + ' occured.', mtError,
[mbOK], 0);
             Exit;
              end;
          end;

end;

end.
```

> **Note:** The TForm1.pbAccessClick procedure contains a list of constants in the current example. This may change by the time you read this. As of this writing, Borland had no intention of adding the constants needed to use access tokens even though the WINDOWS.PAS file contains the necessary function call declarations.

Now that we've gotten all the pieces together, let's take a look at how the program performs. I'll start out with the Disconnect and Map Drive pushbuttons. The first thing you'll see when you press either of these pushbuttons is the Resource Type Selection dialog that you saw in Figure 13.10. Selecting the Disk option will display a dialog similar to the one in Figure 13.11 that allows you to map a drive. Notice that this is the same dialog you see when you select the Map Network Drive pushbutton in Explorer. (As you can see, not all the common dialogs actually appear in the common dialog DLLs.) Likewise, when you decide to map a new network printer, the program displays a Capture Printer Port dialog (surprisingly, Microsoft didn't include this functionality in Explorer). Neither of these dialogs require much work on your part; Windows takes care of all the details for you. Essentially, all you need to do is display the appropriate dialog.

Figure 13.11.
Mapping a drive is fairly easy—all you need to do is display the Map Network Drive dialog, and Windows takes care of the rest.

The Disconnect pushbutton displays the Disconnect Network Drive dialog shown in Figure 13.12 when you select the Disk option on the Resource Type Selection dialog. Notice that Windows lists all the drives that you currently have mapped. The printer dialog works in a similar manner to this one. Windows even includes error trapping when you call the dialog. Figure 13.13 shows the error message the user will receive if she tries to disconnect from a printer or drive and there are no connections available.

Figure 13.12.
Disconnecting a drive is just as easy as mapping one—just display the dialog and let Windows do the work.

Figure 13.13.
Windows automatically provides a certain level of error trapping when it comes to system resources like printer and drive connections.

Sometimes you'll need to know what resources you have available on the current machine. That's what the Get Connections pushbutton does for you. It displays a list of either the drive or the printer connections in the Memo1 component. Notice that I had to query each drive and printer separately. You'll need to create some kind of loop structure to do this. Figure 13.14 shows the output for the drive display.

Figure 13.14.

Getting a list of your current resource connections requires a bit of additional work since you have to query each connection separately.

Just in case you haven't noticed by now, your name appears in the caption area of the form as shown in Figure 13.15. I did this by using another WNet call to determine the current user's name when I first displayed the form. Look at the TForm1.FormShow procedure to see how I got the job done. You could use the same technique as part of a security program—even if you didn't want to work with the vagaries of the lower level Windows NT security functions, your application could maintain its own access database and grant user functions based on user name. By the way, this is one of the few security related functions that do work properly under both Windows 95 and Windows NT.

Figure 13.15.

In addition to displaying the user's login name, the WNetGetUser() API call can help you implement an internal security database for your application.

Now it's time to look at the security section of the program. I saved it for last because it's the most complicated part of the program. The first thing you'll notice if you press the Time On pushbutton is that the caption changes to Time Off. I like using dual state pushbuttons in situations like this because they give the user an added level of input by telling the current state of the application.

Normally I would have added some code to predetermine the current state of the time setting access token, but I left it out to simplify the application in this case.

The first thing I do in this procedure is get a handle to the access token. I request both the adjust and query privileges. There is also a constant for requesting all security access to a token. The problem with using it is that your application will take a performance hit because Windows will have to decide what privileges to give you. It can also hide errors in your application. You might find out somewhere along the way that you were modifying some token attribute that you really didn't want to modify if you request too many privileges. (The same thing applies to any kind of security access—only request the rights that you actually need to perform a specific task.)

The second thing that I did in this case was get the LUID for the SE_SYSTEMTIME_NAME privilege for the local machine using the LookupPrivilegeValue API call. The initial NULL value tells Windows that I want to deal with the local machine. You can also provide a value here if you want to access another machine on the network. Of course, you'll need to have the correct rights to that machine to get this call to work.

Once I have all the information I need from Windows, I can create a token privileges structure. Notice that the first parameter tells how many privileges I want to change. You could use this parameter to change a group of features. The Delphi structure only permits you to change one privilege at a time—the number that you'll be changing in most situations. If you do run into a situation where you need to change more than one attribute, make sure you use the existing Delphi structure as an example. The only thing you need to change is the number of array elements that the structure contains. Make sure that you always use a zero based array.

The final step is to adjust the token privileges. You'll need the token handle you received from Windows in the first step of the procedure and the structure you created in the third step to make the call. Notice that the error trapping I used for this API call is different from the rest in this procedure. The reason for the difference is fairly simple—AdjustTokenPrivileges always returns a value of True—there isn't any way to test for success unless you actually call the GetLastError() function. If you see a value of ERROR_SUCCESS returned, then the call was successful.

NetWare Specific Programming Considerations

There isn't any doubt about it—Windows NT has made inroads into networking areas once firmly held by Novell's NetWare. Does this mean that NetWare is simply going to disappear tomorrow? Don't hold your breath—NetWare is still the leading NOS for large networks and that isn't going to change any time in the near future.

Novell has made NetWare into one of the most flexible NOSs out there by adding the ability to dynamically load and unload pieces of the operating system. The NOS pieces are called NLMs (NetWare Loadable Modules) and there are more of them than most people realize. For example, you can load a NLM that helps you back up your system—that's not too surprising. Nor is it very surprising that there are NLMs that help you interface with a UPS or other equipment connected to the file server.

What most people don't realize is that there is a wealth of non-traditional NLMs as well. I've looked at some NLMs that allow you to inventory your network. I'm not talking about just the file server here, I'm talking about the workstations as well. All it takes is an NLM at the file server and an agent (a TSR) at the workstation. In fact, these inventory NLMs provide a lot more than just a list of equipment. At least one of the products that I tested will give the network administrator constant updates on the status of every workstation on the network.

NLMs don't end here—we've only just begun. There are also application level NLMs. You would use an NLM if you wanted to add a DBMS to your server. Oracle is just one example of a company that puts out NLM version of their DBMS. When a user accesses the file server, she can also access the DBMS that it supports. Putting the DBMS on the file server has certain advantages. For one thing, it reduces the likelihood of data damage because the NOS and the DBMS are working side-by-side. You'll also gain the benefits of centralized control of your data.

Okay, so there are a ton of different NLMs that you can use with NetWare—how does that affect you as a Delphi programmer? There are two ways that NLMs could affect your application. Novell markets the SDK required to write NLMs. This SDK shows you how to create NLMs using a standard C compiler and calls into the various API elements that Novell provides as part of NetWare. You can also use the SDK to access existing NLMs on the network or communicate with the file server. Say you want to write an application that directly interacts with the bindery. You could write most of the functionality you need using Windows, but there are some areas that Windows just won't help you with. For example, just try to change the trustee assignments using Windows API calls—it's not going to happen in some situations.

Suffice it to say that there are options outside of Windows when you really need them under NetWare. There might be situations where you need an additional layer of monitoring or some special network features that will require direct contact with the NetWare servers on your system. Knowing that NLMs and an SDK to create them exists is one of the first steps in expanding your network grasp beyond what Delphi can provide by itself.

Summary

This chapter has covered more than a little ground. First we looked at the overall network architecture provided by Windows 95 and Windows NT. Both operating systems provide similar features, but Windows NT is definitely more robust than Windows 95 is. Obviously the server version of

Windows NT provides the most features of all. We also looked at how both operating systems provide support for a variety of features like WinSock and RPCs. Both of these features are in their infancy today, but you'll be working with them almost exclusively sometime in the near future. (In fact, the network OLE promised for Windows NT will most certainly need to use RPCs to get the job done.)

The next few sections of the chapter looked at the capabilities that Windows provides for accessing the network. We discussed the types of information you could garner and some of the problems you might run into. I showed you two different applications in these sections. The first showed how to parse the network hierarchy to determine what resources are available. The second showed some of the features you could add to a network administrator specific section of your application.

Finally, we looked at Novell's NetWare. This is still the most popular network on the market, so a knowledge of some of its intricacies is always helpful. It's important to know what kind of network you're dealing with, but I have always felt that accessing the NOS in a generic way provides greater flexibility in your application. After all, you can't always guarantee what type of network your users will have. Using generic functions helps you protect the investment you've made in your application in the form of programming time.

Overall, network programming takes on many faces under Delphi because Delphi is a general purpose language. You might create a utility program with it one day—a full-fledged database manager the next. It's that difference that sets Delphi apart from some of the special purpose programming languages you may have used in the past. You pay for the extra flexibility that Delphi provides with the need to access the Windows API directly when it comes time to talk to the network.

14

Packaging Your Application

Packaging an application—sounds like you're going to shrink-wrap it and send it off to the store. From a programmer's perspective, packaging has nothing to do with stores, but it does have everything to do with how well an application is received by the user. When you look at something in a store, it's the package that grabs your attention. What's inside only gains your attention after you pick the package up. If a user installs your application and sees that the setup program provides everything he needs, he'll be a lot more likely to start using your application with a good attitude—something I consider crucial to the success of an application.

Packaging also has a lot to do with an application's ease of use and the user's ability to install it quickly. Imagine for a moment a car that wasn't packaged correctly. Sure, it comes with directional signals, but there isn't any light on the dash to tell you which way you're going. The engineer knows which way they work, so why bother to install them? You wouldn't buy a car like this and neither would anyone else. That's what an application without a good help file is like to a user who didn't design it. You may as well just tell him to guess about how to use the application because he'll never think to look at the README or other file you placed on the disk with a modicum of instructions.

Obviously there are other packaging concerns that everyone doesn't have to deal with. For example, an in-house programmer probably wouldn't worry as much about really neat graphics—someone distributing an application as shareware or commercially probably would need to worry about those factors. However, everyone should make their application look aesthetically pleasing because appearance affects the user's attitude toward the application. I've found that attitude is about half the battle in getting a user up and running with a program. Anything you can do to improve the user's attitude also benefits you by reducing service calls and the like.

A complete application also includes an install program that you can use to test the setup as a whole. Here's another scenario to think about. One programmer I know of decided to simply send out a batch file and a disk full of application files as a package. He never even bothered to test the application since it was only going to be used in-house. It didn't take too long before the programmer started getting a rash of calls from disgruntled users. It seems that he forgot to add a crucial file to the disk and the users who were actually able to figure out the batch file couldn't get the program to work. No one ever liked that application—even after the programmer added a nice looking interface, an install program, and fixed the bugs. The problem wasn't with the program; it was with the user's attitude toward the program. First impressions are crucial to a program's success.

As far as I'm concerned, it doesn't matter who will use your application; you have to package it correctly before you send it out the door. Anything less is going to be an exercise in frustration to both you and the user alike. No one wants to buy half a car—likewise, no one wants half an application. Take the time to package it correctly.

I'd be remiss in my duties to you as a writer then if I didn't at least take a few minutes to tell you about packaging an application. That's what this chapter is all about. We'll take a look at what I consider the two most important factors in the first impression that a user develops for the application you write: installation program and help files. I'll also take a look at some of the special factors that programmers should look at in various environments. For example, an in-house programmer will probably have a few concerns not shared by someone developing shareware.

Creating Help Files

One truism that I've found about programmers as a whole is that they hate to write documentation—and that's fairly straightforward when compared to writing help files. I've run across a few help files that are so difficult to use that I stick with the paper documentation instead. Help files should be as well constructed and easy to use as your application.

You're going to spend some time writing help files—there just isn't any way around it. The bigger your application, the larger and more complex the help files you'll need. In fact, I usually set aside one help file development hour for every four hours I spend programming. You might be able to get by with less than that, but probably not much less. The good part about creating a good help file is that you can usually use it as the basis for the application's manual. Some people I know of use a single file for both purposes.

There are quite a few ways to design a help file and even some tools to help you out. What I'd like to talk about first are the ways to design a help file. Organization is one of the first things you'll need to tackle. The way that you organize a help file can make it either easier or more difficult to use. For example, a help file that's task oriented will help a user get specific tasks done more quickly—assuming of course, that you know precisely what tasks they intend to perform with your application. On the other hand, a menu oriented help file can make searching for specific items faster. I always begin by writing an outline of what I want the help file to contain. The outline reflects the specific orientation that I plan to pursue when writing the help file. This helps me organize it from the very beginning and focuses my thoughts on each segment of the help file as I write it. The following list provides some of the organizational techniques that I've used in the past.

- Menu Flow—The menu flow technique starts with the menu system and works down from there. I simply list all of the menu items in hierarchical format. Once I have all the menu items listed, I start listing any dialogs. Each dialog gets listed in order along with the various controls that it contains. Finally I list the main window and any components it contains. Using this organizational method has the advantage of fast access to specific program features. The disadvantage is that I'm not telling the reader how to accomplish something, just what a specific item is used for. This type of help file works very well with utility programs because most readers will have a good idea of what to do when they buy the application. I also find that it works well with configuration modules in which the questions I'm asking are pretty straightforward, but the reader may need a little additional help answering them.

- Task—Most users that I've talked to really don't care about the latest "gee whiz" feature in a program. All they know is that they have to get a particular job done. This is especially true of people who crunch numbers all day or perform some of the more mundane office chores in a company. They don't have time to figure out how to do something—you have to tell them. That's where this kind of help file is most useful. You work out a list of the kinds of tasks that the reader will perform, and then explain each one in detail. I usually start out with an explanation of the task itself—what will the user accomplish. Then I provide a procedure to get the job done. I think you'll find that this particular technique works well with data entry or other programs that have a fixed number of tasks to perform. Once you start getting into the free-wheeling world of the word processor or other general purpose application, you need to take a different approach.

- Generalized Menu/Task—There are times when you'll write an application that could perform a variety of tasks. For example, a word processor isn't used for just one purpose—it fulfills several. If you wrote hard and fast rules for accomplishing tasks in this case, you'd be doing the reader and yourself a disservice. What I usually do is provide a very generalized assortment of task explanations that demonstrate how to use product features, but not how to accomplish specific tasks. I also provide an overview of the menu system rather than a detailed look. That way the user gets a general feel for what the application can do without absorbing too many preconceived ideas from the developer. I do follow this up with ample use of cloud help—that's the little balloons that appear near a control when you place the mouse cursor on top of it for a few seconds.

- Reference—Compilers and applications that provide their own macro language often include a reference type help file. In this case you're not looking at the program from a physical perspective, but from a control perspective. It doesn't really pay to do much more than list the macro commands for a word processor in alphabetical order because there isn't any way to know how the user will use them. I normally describe the command, tell what each parameter will do, then provide some kind of example of how to use the command. Obviously you can also add other information like hints and version specific differences. One type of tip that users find helpful is the kind that says "If you want to do X, then use this command; otherwise, use command Y—it's more efficient."

- Tutorial—This is a special purpose help file. I only use it with applications designed for novices. In essence, you'll use a help file to teach someone how to use your application. I find that this kind of help file is effective in places where the user may not have had much previous experience using the application. A minimal amount of experience with the computer and operating system is essential to making this type of help file work. Data entry applications are one of the situations where I find this type of help file useful. I normally provide a short, task oriented text section, followed by some type of question and answer section. An interactive help session where the user works with a mock up of the real application is also helpful. You can use help file macros to make this kind of situation work. The help file actually monitors user input for correct responses. This type of help file is unfortunately difficult to put together and provides little benefit to the user over the long haul. You'd probably be better off trying to convince a company to hire a trainer or two instead of taking the time to put one of these together.

- Functional Area—Some applications lend themselves to this kind of help file organization because of the way that they're used. CAD and other drawings fall into this area because you can group the things that they do into functional areas. A CAD program provides commands for drawing, others that control the color palette, and still others that allow you to manipulate the drawing size and shape. Grouping like items in this case is going to help the user find what he needs quickly. The reason is simple: When the user is creating the drawing, he'll look for drawing commands. Later, as he embellishes his work of art, he'll want to know about color and texture related commands.

Once you create an outline, you have to fill it in with some meaningful text. There are a few rules that I follow here as well. The first is to try to keep a help section down to one screen. A user won't want to page up and down in the help file as he looks for that critical piece of information. In a lot of cases you can break a large piece of the help file into subtopics—making the file easier to read. In today's computing environment you'll probably want to keep a single screen down to what you can see at 800 × 600 resolution. Even though many of us have larger displays, I know of more than a few people who still use these smaller displays.

There are some obvious exceptions to the one screen rule. For example, you don't want to divide a procedure into subtopics. It's really annoying to get a help file that works this way. It'll have instructions like "create a mail merge file—see help topic 3A for instructions on how to do this." The fact that this type of procedure exists is manifested in all the satire built around this particular kind of problem in such everyday pieces of equipment as the stereo. I know you've all heard expression "This reads like stereo instructions."

You'll also want to exceed a single screen help topic if there isn't any way to conveniently break it into parts. Make sure that the screen reads well without the subtopics. What I normally do is place amplifying information in the subtopic area. That way an advanced user can look at a single help screen and get the information they need.

Peter's Principle: The Importance of a Glossary

Those of us who spend each and every hour of the work week immersed in programming or other computer related activities learn even the most arcane terms rather quickly. A new term is something to spice up the day, not a hindrance to communication. In fact, I'm often surprised at just how many terms I learn without even realizing it.

On the other hand, most users look at the computer as a mere acquaintance—something they use to do their job, and nothing more. (A good friend of mine even says that she's computer hostile—how's that for a descriptive term?) For the typical user a new term is an insurmountable obstacle to getting their work done. Help files filled with undefined jargon are worse than no help file at all. The user can read the file, but they don't really understand what it means.

Let's face it, there isn't any way to completely avoid jargon when writing a help file. We're working in an industry that seems to invent yet another new term (and sometime even more) every day. You should do your best to avoid jargon when writing a help file, but it's physically impossible to avoid the use of standard computer terms.

I normally script my help files before committing them to final form. In other words, I create an outline, then fill in the blanks. What I'm really talking about is a simple form of book. Then I have one or two people who haven't seen the file before read it and write down any terms they don't understand. Picking non-technical types is the best way to go because you'll get better input from someone who isn't immersed in the technology. I take the list of "unknown" words from each reader and define them. Now I have a glossary that's hand-tuned to the user's needs, or at least closer to those needs than something I would have put together.

The last step in the process is to add hot links from every occurrence of an unknown word in the text to its entry in the glossary. If a user doesn't know what a term means, all he needs to do is click on the hot link. Windows Help will take him to your glossary entry.

The entire process that I've just described could be best termed as building a script. You're creating what amounts to a book, but not in book form. One topic doesn't necessarily flow into the next as it would in a book. (It's really irritating to see a help file that is written as a book—you'll get screens that introduce a topic, but don't really lead anywhere.) Each topic is designed to stand on its own merit. Of course, adding continuity between topics in a help file will always make it easier to use.

Creating a script is about half the process of building a help file. Another third of the process is to convert that script into something that the Windows Help system can use to display information to the users of your application. You'll need to break the outline up into screens and add hypertext links as required. Some help compilers also require the equivalent of a make file—creating it is the final sixth of the process. The make file tells the compiler which script files to include in the help file and can add optional features like buttons.

The following sections are going to take you through the process of creating a help file from your script. Once you accomplish that task, we'll look at what you need to do to add context sensitive help to your Delphi application. That's that last part of the help file creation process. You want to make sure everything else is in place before you actually start adding the help file to your application.

Using the Microsoft Help Compiler and RTF Files

I'm not going to go through the entire Microsoft Help Compiler reference in this chapter. I think you'll find that the help file provided with the compiler is pretty well designed as a programmer's reference. What we'll look at is a simple example of how you could put together a help file using a standard word processor and the help compiler.

Note: It doesn't matter which word processor you use—you could even use a programmer's editor if you'd like. The only requirement to use the Microsoft Help compiler is that the script file be in RTF format. Fortunately RTF is really an ASCII file containing special formatting commands. We talked about this topic in the Color section dialog of Chapter 6 when I described the output of the TRichEdit component. Since TRichEdit doesn't support the full RTF command set, you can't build an editor in Delphi to write your help files unless you subclass the component and add the missing commands.

The Microsoft Help Compiler requires a minimum of two files: the help script and a make file. I normally use Microsoft Word to create the help script since it provides full RTF support and it's my word processor of choice when writing. The first thing I do is separate the various help file sections. You do this by adding a hard page break before each new section. The page break is symbolized as the \page statement in an RTF file.

Adding one or more footnotes to each heading comes next. Footnotes are used for a variety of hyperlink functions. For example, the search words for your index will come from this source. You'll also use footnotes to define links between words in the glossary and the help file. Table 14.1 shows a partial list of footnotes. I find that these are the footnotes I use most often. You should also check the documentation for the Microsoft Help compiler for additional ideas—there are times where those alternatives to the standard footnote come in handy. So, what do you type in the footnote? You have to add one of several things depending on the footnote types. For example, when using the # footnote you add the name of a hyperlink. Make sure you read the text that follows each footnote in the table to learn about any requirements for using them. It's extremely important to create unique names for each of your footnotes. Descriptive names are also essential since you'll have to remember what those names mean later. One thing that you need to remember is that hyperlink names, like variables, don't contain spaces. Footnotes are symbolized by the <footnote type>{\footnote <text>} RTF file statement.

Table 14.1. Standard Footnote Styles for the Microsoft Help Compiler.

Footnote Type	Purpose
*	You'll eventually end up with a lot of RTF files on your machine, and you may not want to include all of the topics they have in every help file. For example, I have one help file that I include with a communication program that talks about on-line courtesy. It's very generic and most users find it helpful when trying to figure out the various acronyms that they see on-line. It appears in an RTF file of general topics. While I wouldn't want to include that topic in a utility program, the general file does have topics I do want to include. This footnote defines a build tag. It works in concert with the help project (HPJ) file that I'll describe later. The help compiler looks at the list of help topics you want to include, then looks at the build tags in the RTF file to find them. You must include this footnote as the very first footnote for a topic. Build tags are case insensitive, but I still type mine in uppercase so that any future changes to the way that Microsoft handles help files won't break mine. A typical build tag in an RTF file looks like this: *{/footnote BUILD_TAG}.
#	This is a topic identifier footnote. Think of this as a label used by a GOTO statement. Whenever you "call" this topic identifier using a technique I'll describe in just a bit, Windows Help changes the focus to this particular footnote. This is the first half of a hyperlink within the help file. You can use hyperlinks for a variety of tasks including menus and to create links to a glossary. Topic identifiers are case insensitive, but I still type mine in uppercase so that any future changes to the way that Microsoft handles help files won't break mine. One example of this kind of footnote in an RTF file is: #{\footnote SOME_LINK}.
$	Use this footnote type to create a topic title. The topic title appears in the gray area above the help text in the help window. You'll also see the topic title in the Topics Found and the History dialog boxes. This footnote accepts any kind of text. For example, you could use ${\footnote This is a title.} as a topic title.
+	There may be times when you want to create a sequence of help topics to allow the user to move from one area of the help file to another with relative ease. For example, a lengthy procedure may be inconvenient to use if you make it fit in one window. One alternative to this is to break the procedure into window-sized elements, then allow the user to browse from one window to the next. Adding the browse-sequence identifier footnote to an RTF file does just that. It activates the two browse buttons >> and << in the help window. Windows will allow you to use

Footnote Type	Purpose

any identifier for a browse sequence—it sorts the identifiers in alphabetical order to determine which sequence to display next—but I usually use a page numbering sequence. For example, +{/footnote Page:1} would be the first page in a sequence. The only limitation to using sequences is that you can only have one per topic.

Note: You have to enable the browse buttons by adding a BrowseButtons macro to the HPJ file. Windows Help looks for this macro as part of the help file initialization process. I'll show you how to add it in the Creating the Make File section of the chapter.

Tip: The browse-sequence identifier is one of the handier help file footnotes because you can use it to break up long sections of text without causing any confusion for the user. I also find it essential when I need to display a multi-page graphic like a hierarchical chart. For example, one of the help files I created contained a complete hierarchical chart of all the Novell forums. Since the chart required more than one page, I used a browse sequence to make it easy for the user to move from one area to the next. You could also use this feature in a reference type help file to move from one command to the next. The applications for this particular footnote are almost unlimited.

K | The search capability of your help file depends on the keyword footnote. You define one or more descriptive words for each topic and subtopic in your help file. I always err on the side of too many, rather than too few keywords. The keywords you define appear in the Index page of the Search dialog if you're using the Windows 95 interface. A keyword can contain any sequence of characters including spaces. Windows also preserves the case of your keywords—making it easier for you to come up with descriptive terms that the user can identify easily. One topic can also have more than one keyword; just separate them with semicolons. There's a flaw in the DOS version of the help compiler, HC31, that you need to compensate for when using this footnote. You'll need to add an extra space between the footnote and the next character in the RTF file or it won't appear in the help file. In addition, if your keyword begins with a K, then you'll need to precede it with an extra space or a semicolon. One example of a keyword footnote might be: K{/footnote Control;Exit Pushbutton;Leaving the Program}. In this case the user could find the same help topic using three different routes.

continues

Table 14.1. continued

Footnote Type	Purpose

> **Tip:** You'll find it easier to build a comprehensive, yet consistent help file if you maintain a sorted list of keywords as you build the RTF files. Make sure that you use the same keyword in every place a topic appears. For example, if you say "Control" in one place, then don't use the plural form or a different term in another place. A user can adapt to a help file that's consistent—it's when the help file uses terms inconsistently that you start running into problems.

Footnote Type	Purpose
@	What would a program be without comments? You couldn't figure out what you did during the previous build the next time you needed to add a new feature. As you can tell by looking at the examples in this book, I like to add a lot of comments. I've found that comments are an essential part of any programming effort. Help files can get quite complex. You could easily forget why you added a macro or did something in a particular way between editing sessions. The author-defined comment footnote solves this problem. It's like adding comments to your help file. The only difference is that you won't see the comment in most cases until you open the footnote for viewing (assuming, of course, that you're using a standard word processor to create the file). A typical author-defined comment footnote looks like this: @{/footnote This is a comment.}. Needless to say, since the help compiler ignores this footnote, you can include any kind of text within it.

What I usually do at this point is compile a list of the topic identifier (#) footnotes I've created. Armed with this list, I can go through the rest of the help file and create the appropriate hyperlinks. Just how do you go about doing this? When you look at a standard help file and see the green text that signifies a hyperlink, what you're looking at is a double underline (/uldb in an RTF file) or a strikethrough (/strike in an RTF file). So, the first part of creating a hyperlink is to double underline or strikethrough the text that you want the user to see as green text. Right after the double underline, add the topic identifier of the hyperlink in hidden text (use the /v statement in an RTF file). This is the same identifier that you typed in the # footnote.

It's at this point where you will probably need to decide a variety of things. For example, do you want to add graphics to your help file? A few graphics in the right places can go a long way toward making your help file truly user friendly. Some people like to add sound or other multimedia. Unless you're proficient at using this mediums, I'd probably avoid them for the first few projects. You'll also need to decide what types of things to include in your make file. The following sections provide you with the details of completing your help file. I'll spend some time talking about the various options you have and what I normally do with specific types of help files.

Adding Special Effects to a Help File

There are a variety of enhancements you can add to a help file. One that I usually add are graphics. For example, you can grab a screen shot of your application, then define hot spots on it with the Hotspot Editor utility (SHED.EXE). (Microsoft makes the SHED.EXE file available for download from several of its programming language specific forums on CompuServe.) You can use BMP, DIB, WMF, and SHG graphic formats with the Hotspot Editor. Files containing hot spots always use the SHG extension. Unfortunately, Delphi doesn't include the Hotspot Editor—you'll need to get a copy as part of buying a Microsoft (or other) product that supports it. I would have liked to see Borland provide some tool that's at least similar to the Hotspot Editor, but they didn't.

> **Tip:** One of my favorite graphic additions to tutorial style help files are Answer buttons. These are pushbuttons that I create as a graphic image. The user reads the question, answers it, then presses the Answer pushbutton to see if they made the correct response. You can also use this technique to simulate a variety of other application controls—the Windows Help utility doesn't provide very much help in this regard. It does, however, provide the {BUTTON [LABEL], Macro1[: Macro2: ... : MacroN]} macro that allows you to create a standard pushbutton. Label contains the caption you want to see on the pushbutton. The macro parameters allow you to attach one or more macros to the pushbutton.

Let's take a look at the Hotspot Editor. Figure 14.1 shows a typical view. I've already opened a screen shot of the example program we'll use later to test the help file out. In this case we're looking at a picture of the main form. I plan to add hot spots for each control to make it easy for the user to find out about the application. Remember that you can't use the Hotspot Editor to create a new drawing—you'll need some type of graphics application to do that. The whole purpose of using the Hotspot Editor is to add places where the user can point and expect something to happen. Every time you see the cursor change from a pointer to a pointing hand in a help file, you're seeing the effect of using the Hotspot Editor.

Figure 14.1.

The Hotspot Editor won't allow you to create a new drawing, but it does add hot spots to existing ones.

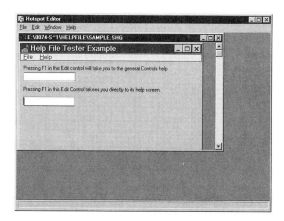

Creating a new hot spot is as easy as dragging the mouse. All you need to do is create a box like the one shown in Figure 14.2. The area within the box is the hot spot.

Figure 14.2.
Creating a hot spot is as easy as dragging the mouse—a square shows where the hot spot will appear.

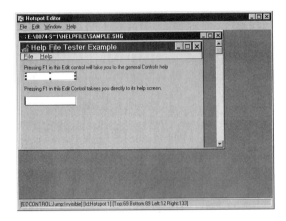

Once you create a hot spot, you need to define it. Just double-click on the hot spot, and you'll see the Attributes dialog box shown in Figure 14.3. There are only three mandatory entries in this dialog: Context String, Type, and Attribute. A context string works just the same as the double underlined (or strikethrough) text in the previous section. It acts as the second half of a hyperlink. When the user clicks on the hot spot, Windows Help will transport them to the place in the help file that you've defined. You can choose to make the box surrounding the hot spot visible or invisible. I normally make them invisible and can't say that I've seen anyone else do otherwise. There are three different types of hot spots. The following paragraphs tell you where they're used.

Figure 14.3.
The Attributes dialog is where you define what will happen when the user clicks on the hot spot.

> **Tip:** You can define a standard set of hot spot attributes using the Edit | Preferences command. What you'll see is a dialog that allows you to define a default Context String, Type, and Attribute. You can also use this dialog to define a default Hotspot ID.

- Jump—Windows Help will replace the contents of the current window with whatever help topic is pointed at by the context string. A jump moves the user from one area of the help file to another. I find that this type of hot spot works well for icons that tell the user what other kinds of information they can find on a given topic. You could use it to create a "See

Also" icon. I also use this type of jump when creating links between a multi-page hierarchical chart. Hot spots allow the user to jump directly from one place to another without using the Browse buttons. This is also the kind of jump that I use with controls pictures used to simulate the real thing in an application.

- Pop-up—You'll find that this kind of a jump is used most often with control descriptions or other pictorial type hot spots. The help topic associated with the hot spot is displayed in a pop-up window. Since the user doesn't leave the picture, they can easily select other controls to look at. I also use this in tutorial type help files in the question and answer section. The Answer button displays a pop-up window containing the answer to a question.

- Macro—There are times where you won't want a picture to display a help topic. The macro type of hot spot allows you to play back a predefined macro. I'll show you examples of macros in the "Creating the Make File" section of this chapter. You'll find that macros are a powerful (and underused) feature of Windows Help. You can even use macros to call programs or reprogram the way that Windows help works.

Tip: The Microsoft help compiler provides a lot of predefined macros. For example, you can use the SetPopupColor macro to change the color of a pop-up window. Attaching these macros to a button or menu will give the user a specific level of control over the help window and enhance their ability to use it. One way to combine a macro with a bitmap is to create a bitmap of colored squares. When the user clicks on a colored square, the color of the help windows changes to match it.

There are several other entries on the Attribute dialog that you need to know about, but don't necessarily need to change. The first is the Hotspot ID field. It tells the Hotspot Editor how to identify this particular hot spot. I'll show you in a second how this comes into play for you as a programmer. The other four entries define the bounding box for the hot spot. You can use these entries to fine-tune a box's position or size. I find that using the sizing controls is a lot faster and easier for the most part. The users probably won't notice if the hot spot is a pixel or two off—all they'll care about is that the hot spot is there for their use.

You may find that you need to redefine a hot spot somewhere along the way. Hot spots are easy to find if you make them visible, but I've already noted that most people don't. So, how do you find a hidden hot spot on a complex drawing? The Edit | Select command provides the answer. It displays the Select dialog shown in Figure 14.4. Notice that this dialog lists the various hot spots in the current drawing by hot spot identifier, not by context string. Selecting a particular hot spot will display its context string though so that you can be sure you have the right one without actually going to that location on the drawing. Along with the context string, the Select dialog displays the jump type and attribute information. I wish that Microsoft had added bounding box information to this dialog as well, but there's sufficient information to allow you to find what you need in most cases.

Figure 14.4.
*The Select dialog allows you
to find a specific hot spot
quickly.*

After you get all the hot spots defined, you may be tempted to save your graphic using the current name with the File | Save command. I always save it with an SHG extension using File | Save As. For some reason the Hotspot Editor doesn't insist that you do this. However, if you don't, you'll find that you've overwritten your drawing with information that some drawing programs can't read. Since you can't modify your drawing within the Hotspot Editor, you're stuck with an image that you can't change. I always retain the original drawing in its pristine state so that I can modify it later.

Now that you have a drawing (or other multimedia element), how do you add it to your help file? Microsoft has defined a set of commands that allow you to add graphics or other elements to your help file. The same commands allow a certain level of control over the placement of these graphics, but I find that the positioning mechanism is crude at best. Table 14.2 shows a complete list of the commands you'll need to add multimedia elements to your help file.

Tip: You can add a T (for transparent) to the three graphics commands listed below. This changes the background color of the image to match that of the help window. For example, the {BMRT FIGURE.BMP} command would display a bitmap named figure on the right side of the screen and change its color to match that of the help window. Windows Help only allows you to use this feature with 16-color graphics.

Table 14.2. Multimedia Element Help Commands.

Command	Description
{BMR <Filename>}	Displays a graphic on the right side of the display window. You must provide a full filename and extension. Windows help recognizes bitmaps (BMP, DIB, and WMF files), multiple hot spot bitmaps (SHG files), and multiple resolution bitmaps (MRB files). Unfortunately, you can't use PCX files within a help file.
{BMC <Filename>}	Displays a graphic in the center of the display window.
{BML <Filename>}	Displays a graphic on the left side of the display window.

Command	Description

Tip: You can specify more than one bitmap within a single command to compensate for differing display capabilities of the machines that use your help file. Windows help chooses the bitmap that most closely matches the color capabilities of the machine and displays it. For example, the command {BMR CAT016.BMP;CAT256.BMP;CAT024.BMP} might allow three different computers display bitmaps in 16-, 256-, and 24-bit colors. You can further enhance the flexibility of your help file by using MRB files to compensate for differences in resolution. The positive side of this approach is that you gain a lot of flexibility in your ability to display detailed information to those users who have a machine capable of displaying it. The downside is that this approach greatly increases the size of the help file and its corresponding memory requirements.

Command	Description
{MCI_LEFT [<Options>,] <Filename>}	Displays a media control interface (MCI) file on the left side of the display. There is a mistake in the Microsoft Help Workshop help file that says you can only use this option with AVI files like those provided on the Windows 95 CD. The current version of Windows Help supports all MCI formats including WAV, MID, and AVI files. Sticking with these three formats is probably a good idea though, unless you know that the target machine supports other formats. You can also specify one or more options with this command including: EXTERNAL, NOPLAYER, NOMENU, REPEAT, and PLAY. The EXTERNAL option keeps the file outside the help file, reducing the amount of memory that the help file consumes when the user loads it. The downside of this option is that you must include the multimedia file as a separate item. Normally Windows Help displays a multimedia player when it displays the file—you can use the NOPLAYER option to prevent this. This option would come in handy if you wanted to automatically play or repeat a multimedia file. The NOMENU option allows you to display a play bar without the menu button, effectively keeping the display elements of the play bar but removing the user's ability to control playback. The REPEAT option tells Windows Help to automatically repeat playing the file when it finishes playing the first time. The PLAY option automatically plays the file—a handy feature for splash screens.
{MCI_RIGHT [<Options>,] <Filename>}	Displays an MCI file on the right side of the display.

> **Note:** If you don't see everything you want in regard to multimedia capability, Microsoft also provides a special help statement you can use to further enhance a help file. The {EW*x* <DLLName>, <WindowName>, <Data>} statement allows you to access routines in an external DLL. We'll cover DLLs in Chapters 15 and 16. The *x* in EW*x* specifies left (l), right (r), or center (c) placement of the output from the DLL. WindowName contains the name of the current help file window—it's the $ footnote we covered earlier. The Data parameter allows you to send data to the DLL for processing.

It doesn't take long to figure out that you aren't very limited when it comes to including bells and whistles in your help file. Just about anything you can include in an application will also go into a help file. There are some obvious things you'll need to consider though before you go overboard in making your help file look like someone's idea of a nightmare. A little multimedia goes a long way. Use graphics and sounds only where they really fit—where they can enhance the appearance of your help file.

You'll also need to consider memory consumption when writing your help file. Windows Help loads an entire help file when the user tries to access it. One of the ways to reduce the memory load on the machine is to use a lot of external files—you can break the help file into pieces and store any multimedia externally. In the end though, a modicum of restraint when using graphics and sounds in your help file is what you'll need to make it efficient as well as fun to use.

Creating the Make File and Compiling Your Help File

Creating a set of RTF files is probably the most time consuming part of writing a help file unless you plan to include a lot of "features" in it. Unlike the make (project) files you use when writing an application, the make file used with a help compiler usually contains more than just a list of files to compile.

I'm going to show you the manual method of creating a make file in this section of the chapter. The Microsoft Help Workshop utility provides a more automated method that I'll show you later in that section of the chapter. The reason for looking at the manual method first is that you'll need it when using the older DOS utility, HC31, to create help files. It's also handy to know what a make file contains so that you can hand tune some features like macros if necessary.

Let's begin by looking at a typical make file. Listing 14.1 contains a make file for the help file in this book. If I were using the DOS utility to write this help file, I'd have to add everything it contains by hand. The only difference is the comment at the top of the make file that says that the help compiler is maintaining the file for you automatically. We'll use the Microsoft Help Workshop to create an example for this book a bit later. I've included a variety of things here that you might include in a typical help file. We'll take a look at these items so that you can decide whether you want to use them.

Listing 14.1. Make file.

```
; This file is maintained by HCW. Do not modify this file directly.

[OPTIONS]
HCW=0
COMPRESS=12 Hall Zeck
ERRORLOG=HELP.LOG
LCID=0x409 0x0 0x0 ;English (United States)
REPORT=Yes
CONTENTS=CONTENTS
TITLE=A Sample Help File for Delphi
COPYRIGHT=1996 Some Company
HLP=.\ExmplHlp.hlp

[FILES]
.\SAMPLE.rtf
.\GLOSSARY.rtf

[MAP]
CONTENTS=1          ; Main help file menu.
CONTROLS=2          ; Controls bitmap shortcut.
EDCONTROL=4          ; Shortcut to our edControl information.
EDDIRECT=5          ; Shortcut to our edDirect control information.
GLOSSARY=3          ; Glossary window shortcut.

[WINDOWS]
main="A Sample Help File for Delphi",(0,0,640,480),60672,(r14876671),(r12632256),f3; This
is the main window.
glossary="Sample Help - Glossary",(50,50,640,480),53508,(r14876671),(r12632256),f3; The
direct glossary help window.

[CONFIG]
CB("glossary", "&Glossary", "JI(`EXMPLHLP.HLP>glossary', `GLOSSARY')") ; Add a Glossary
button to the display.
CB("controls", "C&ontrols", "JI(`EXMPLHLP.HLP>main', `CONTROLS')")    ; Add a jump to
the controls bitmap button.
RegisterRoutine("USER", "EnableMenuItem", "uuu")       ; Enable (or disable) a menu
item.
RegisterRoutine("USER", "GetSubMenu", "u=uu")             ; Get the name of a submenu.
RegisterRoutine("USER", "GetMenu", "u=u")         ; Get a menu name.
RegisterRoutine("USER", "GetActiveWindow", "u=")         ; Get the active window name.
RegisterRoutine("USER", "DrawMenuBar", "u")           ; Instruct Windows Help to draw a
menu bar.
EnableMenuItem(GetSubMenu(GetMenu(GetActiveWindow()), 1), 0, 1027)       ; Disable the
Copy option of the Edit Menu.
DrawMenuBar(GetActiveWindow())             ; Redraw the menu when we're through.
```

As you can see, the make file can look a bit overwhelming the first time you view one. It helps to take the file one section at a time. For example, if you look at the FILES section, you'll see it contains a list of the script (or topic in Microsoft parlance) files used to create the help file. Let's take a closer look at the first section.

The OPTIONS section of the make file tells you how the help compiler will compile the file. Most of the entries here are self explanatory. For example, the COPYRIGHT statement appears in the

About Box of Windows Help when the user loads the help file. The COMPRESS statement defines whether the help compiler compresses the file and what technique it'll use to do so. The HCW statement is Microsoft Help Workshop specific—you wouldn't include it when using the DOS help compiler.

You'll use the MAP section to define the help context property settings that Delphi will ask you for (we'll take a look at this in just a bit). Each word here has to appear as a topic identifier (# footnote) in one of the script files. Associating a number with each jump that you want to export makes the topic accessible from a control. All the user needs to do is select the control and press F1 to get help on that particular control.

There is more than one way to display the data in your help file. I usually display main topics in their own window. You'll notice that there are two windows listed in the WINDOWS section. The first is the main window that I always display. The second is a special window for the glossary. If the user presses the Glossary button on the speed bar, she'll see this window. It allows the user to look up a word without losing her current position in the help file. Obviously I don't display this window every time the user accesses the glossary. If she hot links to the glossary by clicking on a highlighted word in the help file, the glossary gets displayed in the main window—not a separate window. In this case the user can simply press the Back button on the speed bar to return to her former position.

The CONFIG section is the one that will take the most amount of explanation in this case. You'll find that this is probably the section where you'll spend the most time when creating your make file because it offers the greatest amount of flexibility. There are three different events taking place in my make file: button creation, function registration, and a set of Windows API calls. Obviously you could add any number of events to your file, but let's take a look at this fairly simple example.

I begin by creating two new buttons. The first button is the Glossary button I told you about before. Notice that I have to use two different macro calls to get the job done. The first call creates the button. I tell the help compiler that I want to call this button "glossary." I want to use the word Glossary for my button label, and I want the G underlined. This button is going to provide a jump to the identifier returned by the JI macro call. The JI macro call requires three parameters even though it looks like only two. The "EXMPLHLP.HLP>GLOSSARY" parameter actually provides two pieces of information. First, I'm telling the JI macro what help file to look into. Second, I'm telling it what window to use to display the help topic that I'm going to jump to. The second parameter provides the name of a topic identifier—remember that's a # footnote.

The second task I need to perform is to register some DLL functions with Windows Help. You can use just about any DLL function that you want as long as you register it first. Registering a DLL function is always a three-step process. First you need to tell Windows Help what DLL to look in. Windows Help always assumes that the DLL is in the SYSTEM directory, so you'll need to either place the DLL there if it isn't already or provide path information. I usually move the DLL since there isn't any way to know in advance where the user will place the DLL if you don't. The second bit of information is the name of the function you want to use within the DLL. Make sure you use the same capitalization that the DLL uses—I've had strange results when I didn't in the past. Finally, you need to tell Windows help what kind of parameters that function will look for. That's what the "u=uu" is all about when I register the GetSubMenu function. In this case I'm telling Windows Help that the GetSubMenu function requires two unsigned numbers as input and returns an unsigned number as output. There are four types of values that you can specify: unsigned number (u), signed number (i), string (s), or unknown (v). The equals sign (=) always delimits the input values from the output value.

Now that I've gotten some Windows API calls registered, I can make some changes to the help display. (You could do anything that the routines that you register will allow.) In this case I disable the Edit | Copy command. You can still see it, but it's grayed out. I find there are a lot of things you can do to spruce up your help files using this technique. Notice that I use the DrawMenuBar function to redraw the menu bar when I'm done. If you don't do this, then there's a good chance that any menu changes you make won't show up.

About the only thing you have left to do now is compile the help file. If you're using the DOS version of the help compiler (HC31.EXE), you'll want to make sure you specify a log file as part of the CONFIG section options. That's what the ERRORLOG=HELP.LOG statement is for in my make file. It allows me to view the errors in my help file using a text file. Unfortunate as it may seem, the DOS version of the help compiler is command-line driven and doesn't provide anything in the way of an interface. If you don't specify a log file, you'd better be prepared to read fast. All you need to do to use the help compiler is type: HC31 <MAKEFILE>.HPJ. Make sure you append the .HPJ to the end of the make filename or the help compiler won't be able to find it. The help compiler will display a series of dots as it creates the help file. When you see the DOS prompt return, you know the help file is done.

Using the Microsoft Help Workshop

Early Windows programmers had a lot to learn to complete even the smallest projects. The tools that we had to use were difficult to use and even a small program required a lot of coding. DOS was present in force during those early days, but as compilers increased in functionality, DOS all but disappeared. However, DOS was still present until very recently when it came to creating help files. I really hated using a DOS utility to create my help files, but it was about all I had to use until the latest Windows 95 compilers came around. Even the third party products I used to create the help file required some level of interaction with the dreaded HC31 command line utility. The fact that they hid the actions of the help compiler really didn't change much.

Microsoft has changed all that recently. No longer will you need to rely on a DOS application to build your Windows help file. The Microsoft Help Workshop allows you to create help project files (another name for a help make file that we visited in the previous section) and compile them from within Windows. Figure 14.5 shows a typical view of the Microsoft Help Workshop.

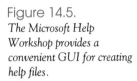

Figure 14.5.

The Microsoft Help Workshop provides a convenient GUI for creating help files.

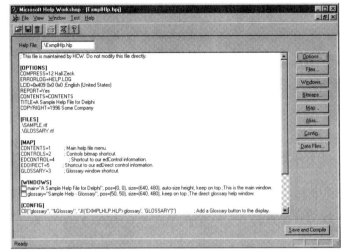

Note: Even if you use the Microsoft Help Workshop, you'll still need an editor that produces RTF files. I'm not quite sure why Microsoft left this feature out of an otherwise phenomenal improvement in help compiler technology, but it did. I still use Microsoft Word to create my RTF files, then reference them from within the make file I create using the Help Workshop.

Let's look at how this tool can help reduce the complexity of creating that make file we looked at in Listing 14.1. (I'll assume that you've already created some RTF files containing a help script.) The first step is to create a new project. Simply use the File | New command to display the New dialog shown in Figure 14.6. Select Help Project and click on OK to complete the action. As you can see from Figure 14.5, I've already created a new help project. It starts out as a blank page that you fill in with the characteristics of your help file.

Warning: The files you'll create using the Microsoft Help Workshop aren't compatible with those created using the older DOS utilities I described in the previous sections. You have to decide on a single application strategy. I think that the new Help Workshop makes life a lot easier for the developer, but only if you work with 32-bit operating environments. If you still need Windows 3.x compatibility, then you need to use the DOS utility versions of the help compiler.

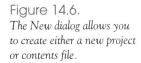

Figure 14.6.
The New dialog allows you to create either a new project or contents file.

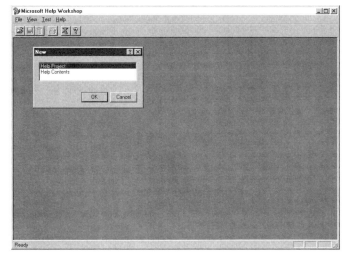

Defining a Project's Options

Once I have a new project to work with, I usually start defining at least some of the project options. For example, you should at least have some idea of what you want to call your help file and what type of copyright information to add. I always use the contents topic as my main topic, so adding that entry at the beginning is a good idea as well. All you need to do is click on the Options button and you'll see the Options dialog shown in Figure 14.7. Notice that I've already defined some general options in this case. All of these options should look familiar since I described them as part of the make file discussion in the previous section. (You'll find that the options on the Compression page look pretty familiar too—they define the type of compression you'll use to reduce the size of your help file.) Some programmers may feel at this point that they won't get much benefit out of using this tool, especially if they have a lot of predefined files sitting around on disk. It's important to remember that this dialog provides a simple form for you to fill out—no longer do you need to remember what statements to use to accomplish a specific task.

Figure 14.7.
The Options dialog allows you to define the general options for your help project.

The Sorting page of the Options dialog contains two areas. The first area determines the language of the help file. Language makes a difference in the way that things are sorted since everyone's alphabet is slightly different. You'll also find two options in this dialog. The first allows you to ignore non-spacing characters. For example, the "^" that appears over ê would affect the sort order if you didn't select this option. The second option tells the help compiler to ignore any symbols in the help file when sorting. This comes in handy if you want to create a non-specialized index for a data entry program or other general application. On the other hand, it would actually get in the way when creating an index for a reference help file. Consider the fact that many C functions begin with an underscore. Ignoring those underscores would make the function more difficult to find.

Figure 14.8 shows the Files page of the Options dialog. Notice that there are a lot of entries here that I've talked about before. You can change the name of the help file by changing the contents of the Help File field. Normally the help compiler uses the name of the project file as a basis for naming the help file. The Log File field contains the name of a log file. Fortunately (as we'll see later) this particular option isn't really required with the new help compiler. I still use a log file to keep track of the status of various help file projects, but it's an option now.

Figure 14.8.
The Files page of the Options dialog allows you to define the RTF files you'll use to build the help file.

One of the most important fields on this page is the Rich Text Format files list box. You'll find a list of the files for the current help project here. Clicking the Change button next to the field displays the Topic Files dialog shown in Figure 14.9. This is where you add and remove topic files from the list in the FILES section of the project file. Notice the two check boxes at the bottom of this dialog. They're important because they control how the help compiler reacts to your RTF files. The first option allows the help compiler to automatically implement any changes you make to the RTF files during the next compile. If you leave this box unchecked, the help compiler will ignore any changes. The second option is important if you use a double byte character set (DBCS) within your help file. This option changes the way that the help compiler works with your file and allows it to preserve the special characters. (This feature is mainly used by languages with complex character sets like Chinese.)

Figure 14.9.
The Topic Files dialog allows you to add and remove RTF files from your project—it also determines how the help compiler reacts to those files.

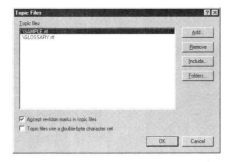

Tip: Another way to access the Topic Files dialog is to click on the Files button on the main Window shown in Figure 14.5.

There are a couple of other options on the Files page of the Options menu. One of them is the Contents file. If you're creating a project from scratch, then Help Workshop will fill this in for you automatically when you create the contents page. The reason for this entry is if you already have a contents page that you want to use with the current project. The TMP Folder field only comes into play when your help file gets over 8 MB in size. It allows you to specify something other than the current directory for the temporary files that Help Workshop creates when it compiles your help file. In most cases you won't need to change this entry unless the current drive is short on disk space. The final field, Substitute Path Prefix, comes into play if you move the files used to create the help file and don't want to change all the path information in the project file.

Windows 95 help files offer something that you won't find in those of its predecessors—full text search. That's the database created when you select the Find page of the Help Topics dialog. It allows you to search an entire help file word-by-word. The FTS page of the Options dialog contains an option to generate this file when you compile the help file. Since Windows 95 generates this file anyway, I normally leave this option blank. The GID file that the help compiler creates takes up a lot of room on the distribution disks and increases compile time by a considerable margin for large files.

You'll want to spend some time learning to use the Macros page shown in Figure 14.10. This is where you can define keyword macros to use on a file-wide basis. Not only that, but these macros appear on the Index page of the Help Topics dialog when the user tries to search for a particular topic. Clicking on the Add pushbutton on this page displays a Keyword Macros dialog containing three fields. The first field contains the name of the macro. The second field contains the macro itself. The third field contains a string that tells Help Workshop how to display the macro on the Index page. I use this particular entry when I have more than one help file, but want to display a particular keyword file-wide. For example, I often place the glossary and list of acronyms in a separate file, then using the JI macro to create a file-wide jump to them. The keyword macro is the method I use to do this. The user never even realizes that she has loaded another file—it's that transparent.

Figure 14.10.
The Macros page of the
Options dialog allows you to
add visible macros to the help
file.

I had previously talked about the * footnote with regard to build tags. The Build Tags page of the Options dialog is where you make use of this feature. I had covered this topic pretty well previously, so I won't go into detail again here. The main idea is to provide Help Workbench with a list of build tags that you want to include in a help file. Even if an RTF file contains other topics, it won't include them in the help file if you don't include that topic's build tag. If you leave this page blank, then Help Workbench assumes that you want to include all of the topics in all of the RTF files you've included as part of the final help file.

The Fonts page of the Options dialog is your first chance to customize the look and feel of your help file. I normally don't use this page to control the appearance of the help file and rely on the formatting capabilities of my word processor instead. However, if you're creating an RTF file using a text editor, this particular feature can save you some time. The Character Set field allows you to select a particular character set for your help file—the default is ANSI. You can also choose from several different language types like Arabic. The Font in WinHelp Dialog Boxes field is where you define a default font type. Click on the Change pushbutton and you'll see a Font dialog with three fields. The first defines the font name, the second the font point size. The third field defines the character set you'll use with dialog boxes. The list box below the Font in WinHelp Dialog Boxes field allows you to change the general fonts used within the Windows help file. It allows you to substitute one font for another. The Add pushbutton displays an Add/Edit Font Mapping dialog which contains two groups of three fields. The three fields are precisely the same as the ones used in the Font dialog that I just described. The only problem with using this particular page is that it doesn't work if your word processor overrides the settings—something that generally happens if you use a product like Word for Windows.

Defining Windows

Defining options is only the first phase of creating a project file. Once you have the options in place you need to define some windows to display your data in. I always create one window called main. It's the main window that my application will use.

Creating a window is fairly simple. All you need to do is click on the Windows pushbutton in the main window (refer to Figure 14.5) to display the Window Properties dialog shown in Figure 14.11. The first page you'll need to look at is the General page shown in the figure. Click on the Add pushbutton on this page, and you'll see an Add a New Window dialog with two fields. The first field contains the name of the window. The second field contains the window type. There are three window types that Help Workbench can create: procedural, reference, and error message. There is very little difference between the procedural and reference windows. They're both auto-sizing and contain the three system buttons. The big difference between the two is their placement on-screen—which you can override with the settings I'll show you next. The error message window differs from the other two in that it doesn't include the three system buttons. It looks somewhat like a dialog in appearance.

Figure 14.11.
The Window Properties dialog is where you'll define the main and ancillary windows used to display the data in your help file.

The Title Bar Text field determines what Windows Help places on the title bar. This entry doesn't affect the appearance of the topic title area of the help window. The Comment field allows you to place a comment next to the entry in the project file—something that I always take advantage of. There are also three attribute check boxes. Help Workbench may disable one or more of these check boxes depending on the situation. For example, you can't make the main help window auto-sizing. If you do make an ancillary window auto-sizing, then you can't choose to maximize it when it opens. Most procedural windows default to staying on top. This is a handy feature if you want to keep help available to a user as they try to work with an application.

> **Tip:** I normally turn the Auto-Size Height feature off to provide better control over the appearance of a window on-screen. The options on the Position page that we'll look at next allow you full control over the appearance of your help window on-screen.

Figure 14.12 shows the Position page of the Window Properties dialog. The name of this page is a little deceiving because it provides a little more functionality than you might initially expect. There are fields: Left, Top, Width, and Height that control the size and position of your window. I normally position my first help window in the upper left corner and use a size of either 640 × 480 or

800×600 depending on the capabilities of the target machine for my application. This may seem a bit small, but the user can always resize the window as needed. Trying to find a help window on an older display when the programmer positions it near one of the edges is frustrating to say the least. I really like the Adjust for User's Screen Resolution option on this page because it prevents the help window from becoming totally hidden when the user has a low resolution display.

Figure 14.12.

The Position page of the Window Properties dialog allows you to control the size as well as the position of your help window.

There's one very special feature on this page, and you may not notice it at first. Look at the Auto-Sizer pushbutton. Clicking on this button displays the example window shown in Figure 14.13. If you change the window's position, the Left and Top field values also change. Resizing the window changes the value of the Width and Height fields. This graphic method of changing the window size will definitely reduce the number of times you have to recompile the help file to take care of aesthetic needs.

Figure 14.13.

The Auto-Sizer pushbutton displays this pseudo-window that you can use to size and position the real thing.

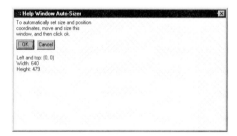

Windows 95 defines a lot of default buttons that you can add to your help file. There are situations where you may not want to add all of them. For example, the browser buttons aren't all that important if you don't define a browse (+ footnote) in one of your RTF files. The Buttons page shown in Figure 14.14 allows you to define the buttons used with your help window. All ancillary procedure and reference windows lack both the Contents and Index buttons. Main windows contain both of these buttons as a default as well as the Print and Back buttons. On the other hand, a main window won't allow you to select the Help Topics button. Unlike all the other window types, an error message window has no restrictions. You can include any of the default buttons that you like on it.

Figure 14.14.

The Buttons Page of the
Window Properties dialog
allows you to add default
buttons to your help window.

Tip: You can get around the Help Workbench imposed limitations on buttons for the main help window by clicking the No Default Buttons check box. This check box only appears for the main window, which means that you can't override the restrictions for ancillary procedure and reference windows.

The next page that you'll want to look at is the Color page. This contains two fields: non-scrolling area color and topic area color. Each has a Change button. All you need to do is click on the Change button to display a color palette. Selecting a different color from the palette changes the appearance of the help window.

The final page is the Macros page shown in Figure 14.15. The main window always uses the macros in the CONFIG section of the project file as a default. All of the macros you see in this section are self-executing—that's why the macros in the CONFIG section are added to the main window. You want those macros to execute when the main windows opens. Adding a new macro to the main window always adds it to the CONFIG section of the help project file. Adding macros to other windows changes the way those windows appear in comparison to the main window. For example, if you add a browse to one of the ancillary windows, you might need to add a macro or two here to set up any conditions not taken care of by the default browse button selection on the Buttons page. Each of these ancillary windows will have their own special CONFIG-<window name> section in the help project.

Figure 14.15.

The Macros page of the
Windows Properties dialog
allows you to add self-
executing macros to the
windows.

> **Tip:** Another way to access the Macros dialog for the main window is to click on the Config button on the main Window shown in Figure 14.5.

Mapping Help Topics

I've already expressed the importance of this particular part of creating a help project file. If you don't map the topic identifiers in your help file to a help context number, then you can't attach context sensitive help to the controls in your application. You'll see how this works in the "Adding Context Sensitive Help to Your Application" section that follows.

Clicking on the Map pushbutton displays a Map dialog like the one shown in Figure 14.16. This is where you define the relationship between a topic identifier and a particular context number. Notice that I've already defined a few in this case. The topic identifier is set equal to a help context number. It's followed by a comment the describes the entry.

Figure 14.16.

Mapping topic identifiers to help context numbers makes your help file accessible to an application.

There are any number of ways to keep the context numbers straight. I usually start at one and count up from there until I reach the last topic identifier for small help files. Large help files require something a bit more complex though or you'll find yourself reusing numbers. I normally use a three- or four-digit number in this case. The first two numbers are the position of the control or menu item described by the help context within the application. For example, the File menu is normally 01 and the Edit menu is 02. A description of the File | New command would receive a help context number of 0101 since the New option is usually the first one on the File menu. I assign a value of 0001 to the first non-application topic. For example, the glossary would fall into this category. The first two numbers for a control on the form of an application would be one greater than the last menu item. I use the tab order for the last two numbers since it's unlikely that a label or other non-active component would ever appear in the help file.

It's easy to add a new map entry. Simply click on Add, and you'll see the Add Map Entry dialog shown in Figure 14.17. This dialog contains three fields: the topic identifier, the mapped numeric value (help context number), and a comment. Fill out the three fields and click on OK to add a new map to the project.

Figure 14.17.
The Add Map Entry dialog contains the three fields needed to add a map to the help project file.

Compiling Your Help File

Once you get a help project file put together, it's time to try to compile it. All you need to do is click on the Save and Compile button at the bottom of the main window shown in Figure 14.5. The Help Workbench window will minimize while it compiles the help file. This allows you to work on something else—compiling a large help file can take a very long time. Once the compilation is complete, you'll see a dialog similar to the one shown in Figure 14.18.

Figure 14.18.
This compilation screen shows the current status of the help file and any error messages.

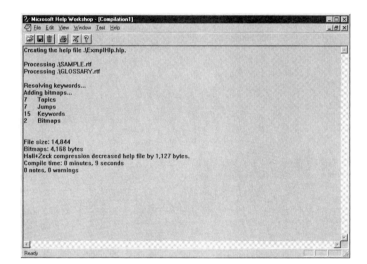

Adding Context Sensitive Help to Your Application

Creating a help file doesn't make it accessible to your application; you have to do a little work to accomplish that. There are two basic methods for adding help to an application. You can either define commands to get the job done, or you can add numbers to the Help Context properties of the various components used to create the application. In reality, you'll probably use a combination of these methods.

Let's take a look at a very simple application designed to test the help file we created in the previous sections. Figure 14.19 shows the form we'll use in this case. All it contains is a menu, two labels, and two single line edits. The menu contains two main entries: File and Help. The File menu contains a single entry, Exit. The Help menu is derived from the Help template provided with Delphi. Table 14.3 shows the changes I made to the two single line edits.

Figure 14.19.
Our Help File Tester
consists of a simple form with
a few components and a
menu.

Table 14.3. Help File Tester Form Control Settings.

Object	Property	Setting
edControl	HelpContext	2
edDirect	HelpContext	5

There's something worthwhile noting about the context settings I chose and the names of the two edit components. One of these edit components will take you directly to its context sensitive help when you select it and press F1. In the other case, I chose to make life a little more interesting. You'll end up at a screen shot of the application. Each of the components has a hot spot defined for it. Click on the hot spot, and you'll end up at the context sensitive help for that control. I find that expert users like the direct method best because it allows them to find the one answer they need quickly. A novice user is still exploring his environment. He likes the second method because it gives him the opportunity to check out the other controls on the application as well. There isn't any right or wrong answer here; both the direct and indirect methods are perfectly legitimate. What you need to do is tailor the type of context sensitive help to the needs of your user.

Once you have the form put together, you can add some code to the menu entries to make them active. Listing 14.2 contains the code for this example. Pay special attention to the two different methods I used to access the help file.

Listing 14.2. Example code.

```
unit HelpTst1;

interface
```

```
uses
  Windows, Messages, SysUtils, Classes, Graphics, Controls, Forms, Dialogs,
  Menus, StdCtrls;

type
  TForm1 = class(TForm)
    MainMenu1: TMainMenu;
    File1: TMenuItem;
    Exit1: TMenuItem;
    Help1: TMenuItem;
    SearchforHelpOn1: TMenuItem;
    Contents1: TMenuItem;
    Label1: TLabel;
    edControl: TEdit;
    Label2: TLabel;
    edDirect: TEdit;
    procedure Exit1Click(Sender: TObject);
    procedure Contents1Click(Sender: TObject);
    procedure SearchforHelpOn1Click(Sender: TObject);
  private
    { Private declarations }
  public
    { Public declarations }
  end;

var
  Form1: TForm1;

implementation

{$R *.DFM}

procedure TForm1.Exit1Click(Sender: TObject);
begin
    {Exit the application.}
    Application.Terminate;
end;

procedure TForm1.Contents1Click(Sender: TObject);
begin
    {Display the help contents.}
    Application.HelpJump('CONTENTS');
end;

procedure TForm1.SearchforHelpOn1Click(Sender: TObject);
begin
    {Display a search dialog using a Windows API command.}
    Application.HelpCommand(HELP_FINDER, 0);
end;

end.
```

Borland has attached several special help related methods to the Application object. In this case I used the HelpJump method in the Contents1Click procedure. This allows me direct access to one of the topic identifiers that I had previously defined in the help file. You should probably use this technique whenever possible because it self-documents the link between your application and the help file.

The second special help method is used in those situations where you don't have either a topic identifier or a help context number to use to access a help file feature. The Index button falls into this category. How do you display a list of help topics if you can't access the topic? Fortunately, there's a combination of Delphi method and Windows API that you can use here. The SearchforHelpOn1Click procedure uses the HelpCommand method. In this case we make a call to the HELP_FINDER Windows API call. There are a lot of these API calls that you can use to get a variety of effects. In some cases you'll also need to supply some data. I didn't in this case, so the second parameter of the HelpCommand method is blank.

We only have one more thing to do to make this application work. A Delphi application doesn't just know which help file to use; you have to tell it. Use the Project | Options command to display the Project Options dialog. Select the Application page, and you'll see the Help File field entry shown in Figure 14.20. This is where you tell Delphi which help file to use. Clicking on the Browse button will display a File Open type dialog that you can use to select the help file.

Figure 14.20.

The Application page of the Project Options dialog allows you to add a help file to the current application.

Let's see how the application works. If you try the Help | Contents command, you'll see a dialog similar to the one in Figure 14.21. This dialog contains a menu-like structure the user can use to learn more about specific areas of the application. There are a lot of graphics you could add here, but I usually go for something simple. Notice that this display also contains the Glossary and Controls buttons that we defined in the help project file. You'll also notice that the Edit | Copy command is disabled.

Selecting the Help | Search for Help On command displays the dialog shown in Figure 14.22. This is the standard Help Topics dialog used by Windows 95. If you look at applications like Word for Windows, you'll notice that there are additional pages in this Help Topics dialog. The CONFIG section of the help project file is the key here. You need to register the Windows API functions required to add the page, then construct a macro to do it. Notice that the Index page displays all of the keywords that I defined as part of the RTF files. If a keyword gets used more than once, then clicking on the Display pushbutton will display a Topics Found dialog the user can use to select a specific area of help. The names listed here are the topic titles ($ footer) that you defined for each header. Hopefully looking through here and comparing what you see to the RTF files will help you understand how the various footer types are interrelated.

Figure 14.21.
The Help | Contents command takes you to a standard menu window.

Figure 14.22.
The Help | Search for Help On command displays this standard Help Topics dialog.

Try selecting the first edit control and pressing F1. You'll see a window like the one shown in Figure 14.23. The interesting thing about this particular display is the way that I defined hot spots for the screen shot. There are two types: a jump and a pop-up. Click on the menu, and you'll see a pop-up. Click on either of the two edit controls, and you'll go to the context sensitive help associated with that control.

The final display I want to show you is a direct jump. Select the second edit control and press F1. You'll see a help window similar to the one in Figure 14.24. Notice that you didn't go to the Controls page this time—you went directly to the context sensitive help page in the file.

Figure 14.23.

Using screen shots in a help file allows you to create both jumps and pop-ups as a means for explaining the function of a control or other object.

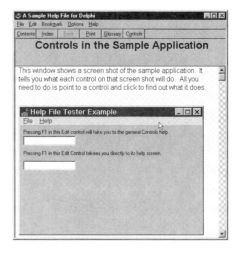

Figure 14.24.

Direct jumps to a context sensitive help page is the best choice for an expert user.

Using InstallShield Express Lite

Just about every programming language available today comes with some kind of installation utility. Some are better than others. I still like the full customization I got out of the Visual Basic setup program. Even though the setup program defaulted to something very simple, you could always get what you wanted by modifying the program as needed. It was written in Visual Basic—a concept I really liked at the time.

InstallShield is a nice product, but the Express Lite version provided with Delphi is a trifle limited. In fact, I probably wouldn't be too far off base in saying that it's about as bare bones as you can get and still meet the basic needs of an installation utility. On the other hand, this version of InstallShield is extremely easy to use—I was able to put an installation program together in a relatively short amount of time. It also provides a full graphic interface, making it even easier to use. (From this point on I'll simply refer to the Delphi product as InstallShield for the sake of simplicity.)

Note: As of this writing, the InstallShield Express Lite utility doesn't get installed automatically, so you may have to install it from the CD before reading this section. Just look in the \ISXPRESS\DISK1 directory of your CD for the Setup program.

What I'm going to show you right now is how to create a simple installation program for the example in the previous section. It contains two files: the executable and the help file. The following procedure will take you through the steps I followed to get the setup program put together. You can use this basic set of steps as a starting point for any application. Obviously, the more complex your application, the longer it'll take to put the setup program together.

1. Open the InstallShield program. The first thing you'll see is the Welcome to InstallShield Express dialog shown in Figure 14.25.

Figure 14.25.
You'll begin every project with this Welcome to InstallShield Express dialog unless you choose to keep it hidden.

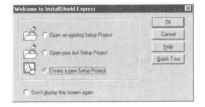

2. Select the Create a New Setup Project radio button, then click on OK. InstallShield will display the New Project dialog shown in Figure 14.26. This is where you'll start defining the new project. You'll need to provide a Project Name as a minimum; placing the new project in its own directory is also a good idea. I filled the dialog out as shown in the figure.

Figure 14.26.
The New Project dialog is where you start defining the project parameters.

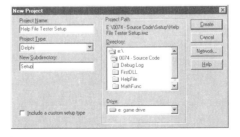

3. Click on Create to create the new project. What you'll see next is the Setup Checklist shown in Figure 14.27. This is where you'll define all the project parameters. What we'll do is go through the parameters you need to define for any project. You'll also want to check out some of the other parameters provided on this sheet.

Figure 14.27.
The Setup Checklist sheet is where you'll perform all data entry required to create the setup program.

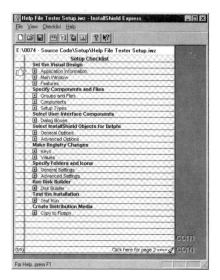

4. Select the Set the Visual Design group on the Setup Checklist. You'll see a Set the Visual Design dialog like the one in Figure 14.28. The only entry that you have to change here is the Application Executable field on the App Info page. This tells InstallShield which file to install as the executable. If you look on the Features page, you'll see a single entry for an automatic installer. InstallShield checks this box by default. You can also change the appearance of the main window for the setup program on the Main Window page. For example, you could add a logo instead of the default text Main Title. By default, InstallShield uses the Project Name you provided when you created the setup program in step 2.

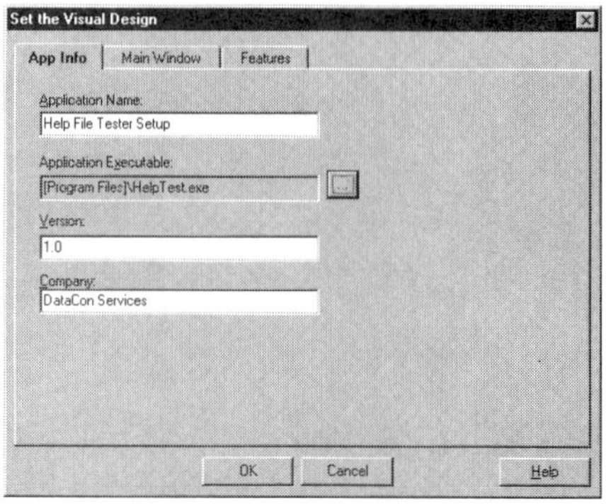

Figure 14.28.
The Set the Visual Design dialog is where you'll change the appearance of your setup program's main window.

5. Click on OK to complete the action. What you'll see now is a set of check marks next to each item you completed on the Setup Checklist as shown in Figure 14.29. Notice that the check marks are displayed in groups to make it easy for you to associate a particular check mark with a configuration dialog box.

Figure 14.29.
InstallShield provides plenty of visual feedback to show you where you are in the installation process.

6. Select the Specify Components and Files group next. You'll see the Specify Components and Files dialog shown in Figure 14.30. This is where you'll add any other files that belong with the application. In my case I have a help file, so I'll need to add at least that entry. Notice that InstallShield has already added the executable file for you.

Figure 14.30.
The Specify Components and Files dialog helps you add other files to your project.

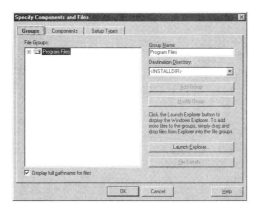

7. Type the name of a new group in the Group field. In my case I typed Help Files since that's what I was adding to the setup program. You'll also need to select a location for this group of files. I chose the default <INSTALLDIR> selection. Other default options include the Windows directory, the Windows system directory, the program file directory, and the common file directory.

8. Click on Add Group to make the new group permanent. What you'll see is a new group. The reason that I didn't add the help file to the Program Files group is that you normally wouldn't force the user to install help to use the application. Placing help in a separate group allows you to create more than one installation type.

9. Click on the Launch Explorer button to open a copy of Explorer. Find the files you want to add to the new group. In my case I needed to find the EXMPLHLP.HLP file. Make sure you can see both the Specify Components and Files dialog and your files in Explorer.

10. Drag the files from Explorer to the group entry. What you'll see during the drag is a sheet of paper with a plus sign attached it. When you drop the files onto the group, you'll see them added one at a time. The other two pages for this dialog are somewhat superfluous. The Components page allows you to add other components—the basic building blocks of a setup program. The Setup Types page allows you to create more than one type of setup. The default setup installs all the files that you've told the InstallShield you want to install. I'll show you in a bit how you can increase the number of installation options.

11. Click on OK to complete this part of the setup.

12. Select the Select User Interface Components group. You'll see a dialog like the one shown in Figure 14.31. This is where you'll decide which dialogs that user will see during the installation process. In most cases the options on this dialog will work fine. However, I normally disable the Billboards option unless I'm creating an application for commercial distribution.

Figure 14.31.
The Select User Interface Components group is where you'll decide what screens the user will see.

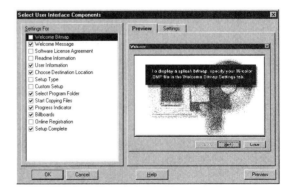

> **Tip:** If you want to allow the user more than one setup choice, choose the Custom Setup option on the Select User Interface Components dialog. You'll need to go back to the Specify Components and Files group. Open the Components page. You'll need to define some additional components to make the custom selections work. All you need to do is type the name of a component, a description, and click the Add Component pushbutton. Add two components—one for each installation option. Once you define a component, add one or more of the groups to it. Open the Install Type page. Now you'll see the compact and custom options added to the installation options. Add the components that you defined to each option. When the user starts the installation, one of the screens they'll see will allow them to select a custom, typical, or compact installation.

13. Click OK to close the dialog and go to the next section of the setup.

14. Select the Select InstallShield Objects for Delphi group, and you'll see the dialog shown in Figure 14.32. I won't need any of the Delphi features shown here with my applications. You'll probably need to add one or more of them if you create a database specific applica-tion. Notice the Advanced page. InstallShield uses this page to tell you when it detects special file needs on the part of your application. In most cases you won't see anything here.

Figure 14.32.
The Select InstallShield Objects for Delphi dialog allows you to add specific Delphi features to your application.

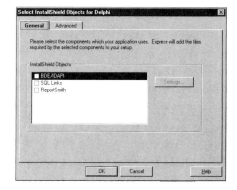

15. Click on OK to complete this part of the setup. I usually skip the Make Registry Changes part of the Setup Checklist unless I need to register an application in some special way. Delphi's OLE registration normally takes care of any application needs I have. I also skip the Specify Folders and Icons section unless I want to change the default icon used for the application. In most cases you'll take care of this need as part of the application writing process.

16. Select the Disk Builder group. You'll see a dialog similar to the one in Figure 14.33.

Figure 14.33.
Disk Builder is the last stop before you create the final setup disks.

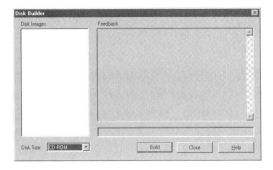

17. Select the disk size that you want to use from the Disk Size drop down box. In most cases the 1.44 MB size will work fine. I was happy to see that the options included 2.88 MB disks and CD-ROM. A lot of larger applications are going out on CD-ROM now, making this an essential setup program feature.

Tip: Corporate users will want to select the CD-ROM options more often than not. Using this option allows you to place the setup program on the network drive, then allow everyone to upgrade from the setup directory. This reduces the need to run around the office with a set of installation disks for your latest creation.

18. It will take a while for the Build option to complete, even with a small application. Fortunately, InstallShield gives you plenty of feedback during the process. Figure 14.34 shows the final set of build messages. It also shows the success message that you'll see when you create a setup program.

Figure 14.34.
Once the InstallShield Build option completes, you'll get a success message like the one shown here.

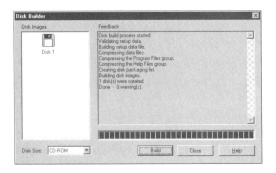

19. Click on Close to complete this part of the process.

That's about all there is to using the InstallShield Express Lite setup utility. You'll find that you end up with a very fast and easy method for creating professional setup programs using this method. Of course, I only skimmed the surface in this chapter; you'll probably want to add other features like splash screens when you create your setup program. The most important aspect of this whole process as far as I'm concerned is that the user ends up with a friendly way to install an application. InstallShield certainly provides plenty of help in that department.

Summary

By now you should have a pretty good idea of why packaging is so important. In this chapter I've shown you the two parts of packaging that I feel are most important: the installation program and the help file. Neither of these items will affect the way your program works—they're add-ons that give your application that finished feel.

However, the effect of these two items on the user are important. A user's attitude toward your application affects how fast they learn it and how they approach it. Giving the user a good first impression of the program you build, even if you aren't going to distribute it commercially, is extremely important.

Help files and installation programs affect every kind of application on the market today. However, that's where the commonality in development environments ends. There are a lot of other packaging considerations for the programmer as well. We visited a few of these concerns. However, I feel that we really only touched on them. You'll want to spend some time looking through this chapter again and then adding the material I've provided. It's always important for a programmer to develop a complete plan for packaging a complete application. As I said at the beginning of this chapter—no one wants to buy half a car. Likewise, no one wants to use an application that's only partially packaged.

IV

Enhancing Delphi

15

Creating Your Own DLLs Using Delphi

I spent a lot of time in Chapter 3 introducing you to some of the features that make Delphi so easy to use. One of those features was the ability to save forms and components as reusable parts you could bolt together to create a basic application—off-the-shelf components so to speak.

This chapter is going to tell you about another, more traditional, way to reuse code under Windows— the DLL. The DLL has been around from the earliest days of Windows. DLLs represent one of the major differences from a programmer's perspective between working in Windows and DOS. We'll start by looking at what a DLL is and what it means to use as a programmer. Then we'll spend some time exploring DLLs from a Delphi perspective.

> **Looking Ahead:** While you can create DLLs in Delphi, it's not the only language that supports them. There are certain advantages to creating DLLs in C; like speed and, in some cases, code size. (Some developers are still debating the speed issue, but I've found that a well-written C DLL generally beats Delphi in the speed category.) We'll explore this issue in Chapter 16.

What Is a DLL?

A dynamic link library (DLL) is a special kind of a library of object files. Just like the libraries you used under DOS, a DLL contains object modules that get linked into your application. Under DOS you had to link these object modules during link time—that is, every executable contained a copy of the object modules. DLLs get linked into your application at run time—every EXE shares a single copy of the DLL in memory.

> **Note:** The object modules I'm talking about here aren't objects in the OOP programming sense of the word. What I'm referring to are the OBJ files that a compiler creates. You use a library manager to place these OBJ files into a LIB file under DOS. Under Windows you follow a different process. The DLL contains entry points to executable code in the form of function calls. You'll see other differences as well as this chapter progresses.

There are quite a few advantages to this approach. First, using a DLL instead of a LIB reduces memory use if more than one application needs the object modules it contains. All the applications that require the functions in a DLL use a single copy of that DLL. A DLL, unlike a LIB, provides re-entrant code. In other words, you can execute the code more that once. By the way, this is where the "dynamic link" portion of DLL comes in. You're dynamically linking the library into your application at run time instead of statically linking it at link time.

DLLs are more efficient from another perspective as well. Under DOS your entire application— libraries included—loaded at run time. A program that uses a DLL only needs to load itself.

Windows loads the DLLs when the application calls for them. In other words, if a user doesn't require a particular feature, then the DLL associated with that feature doesn't get loaded into memory.

Updates are also easier with DLLs. When you change a LIB file under DOS you have to relink all the programs that depend on it. Under Windows you only need to compile and link the DLL—any application that uses the DLL will automatically use the updated code when you run it. This difference alone should make the eyes of many DOS programmers light up. In fact, these three advantages of DLLs are so good, that there are a few products on the market that create a DOS version of the DLL now.

So far I've introduced you to a lot of differences between DLLs and LIB files. However, there are other, deeper, differences that really make a difference in the way that you view a DLL. One of the differences is that every 16-bit DLL has a main entry point (function) named WEP (Windows Entry Point). 32-bit DLLs can also have a main entry point, but it doesn't have to have a specific name. This is the function that Windows calls on when it loads the DLL. The purpose of this function is to perform any required setup for the DLL. There's another function that Windows calls when it unloads the DLL. The purpose here is to perform any required clean-up. I'll go into the specifics of the initialization and exit routines later; right now all you need to know is that they exist.

There are differences between 16-bit and 32-bit DLLs as well. I'll use the Viewer utility that comes with Windows 95 and the latest version of Windows NT to show you some typical examples. Figure 15.1 shows the 16-bit version of the OLECLI.DLL. Figure 15.2 shows the 32-bit version of the same file (OLECLI32.DLL). As you can see, the two files are quite different. The first thing you'll notice is differences in the header information. Some of the differences are obvious. For example, a 16-bit DLL will have a 16-bit characteristic, while a 32-bit DLL will use a 32-bit characteristic. Other differences are less noticeable at first. A 32-bit DLL requires an Entry Point Address entry because it doesn't have to use a specific name for its entry point procedure. 16-bit DLLs do use a specific name so you won't find an address to it in the header.

Figure 15.1.
This is the 16-bit version of the OLE client DLL.

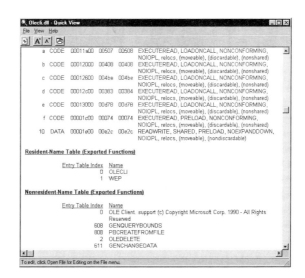

Figure 15.2.
This is the 32-bit version of
the OLE client DLL.

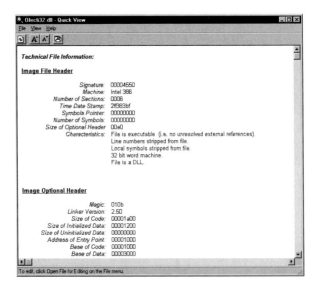

Tip: The Viewer utility provides an excellent method for browsing through the files in your SYSTEM folder. I've done so on several occasions and found out a lot more about DLL structure as a result. More than that, scouting around in your SYSTEM folder might help you turn up DLLs that you didn't know about, or undocumented functions within the DLLs that you do know about.

Obviously this overview is merely the tip of the iceberg. There are a lot of other things you'll need to consider as well. For example, when do you use a DLL to store code versus creating a component or other object for the Gallery (Object Repository)? The answer to this question can get quite thorny because there's a certain amount of overlap between the two. DLLs and the Gallery are two separate tools to help you become more productive with Delphi. It's important that you use each tool for its intended purpose. You'll find that DLLs are a convenient way to distribute executable code and reduce your debugging efforts at the same time. DLLs are also useful when you need to distribute the same code to a number of applications or if you want to create a method for automatically updating parts of an application that change on a frequent basis. I wouldn't replace the Gallery with a DLL though. The Gallery is there to hold objects—non-executable code—for you. These objects are the forms, dialogs, and other components you'll use to bolt an application together. I always use the Gallery for those items that are unique to an application. In other words, you can store part of the application, but not all of the application. An object in the Gallery usually requires some level of customization—a DLL is complete by itself.

PCHAR Versus Pascal Strings

The fastest way to transfer string data between various Delphi applications is using a Pascal string. After all, that's what the language uses as a native format. However, using strings in a DLL can cause a lot of problems. There are two things you need to realize about Windows. First, most of the DLLs you'll find use C as their basic language—that means they use C formatted strings. Second, if you want to use your DLL with other languages, those languages will probably expect to provide C formatted strings as parameters.

The PCHAR type string does cause a little extra work in Delphi, but not much. Essentially you're looking at a null terminated string instead of what Pascal uses. I've shown you more than a few examples of how you can convert your strings from one format to another so far in the book. Every time I used a Windows API call that required string input, I had to convert the strings to PCHARs.

Delphi doesn't force you to conform though. You can always use short or long strings in your DLL. The limiting factor when using long strings though is that your DLL can no longer stand on its own. You'll need to provide the DELPHIMM.DLL when distributing your DLL. Delphi also requires that you add ShareMem to your USES statement. It must appear as the first unit. The ShareMem unit translates Pascal strings into something the rest of Windows can understand.

So, whether you want to or not, your DLL will eventually use PCHAR type strings somewhere along the line. I find that the overhead associated with using the DELPHIMM.DLL with my applications is unacceptable—you probably will too. The way to avoid this overhead is to restrict yourself to PCHARs in a DLL.

Creating a DLL Using Delphi

I don't want to spend a lot of time in this chapter beating you over the head with theory. I think that a few example programs will help you get started creating a DLL and using it within an application. The first thing you need to do is create the DLL itself. DLL code is different in several ways from that used in an application.

Let's begin this example with a new DLL. You do that by opening the New Items dialog shown in Figure 15.3 and selecting the DLL entry. Delphi will create what looks like an application without any forms for you. That's because DLLs don't necessarily use forms—they could contain functions for calculating the monthly payment for a loan or a scientific calculation. The first rule you need to remember is that DLLs don't have a main form—a DLL is a collection of executable code modules, not an application.

Figure 15.3.
You'll find the start for a DLL on the New Items dialog (use the File | New command to access it).

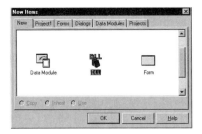

Now you need to decide what you want the DLL to do. In this case I'm going to add the About Box that I created in Chapter 3 (see the section entitled Adding a New Template for details). Figure 15.4 shows what the About Box looks like. I want to create the About Box using a DLL. That way if someone has more than one of my applications on their machine, they only pay for the About Box code once. Using this technique will also make it easier for me to update the About Box for all my applications to meet changing copyright or other needs.

Figure 15.4.
This example dialog will display an About Box like this one.

If I tried to compile the DLL right now, nothing would happen. I wouldn't even be able to access my About Box from outside of the DLL. An application knows nothing about the dialog contained in my DLL, so it can't access it. Unlike other situations where I use a form, I can't access it using a simple File | Use Form command. You'll also find that trying to directly access the methods associated with an object won't work—I'll explain why in just a bit. So, how do we gain access to our DLL? Listing 15.1 provides the answer.

Listing 15.1. Gaining access to DLL.

```
unit SmDLL1;

interface

uses Windows, SysUtils, Classes, Graphics, Forms, Controls, StdCtrls,
  Buttons, ExtCtrls;

type
  TAboutBox = class(TForm)
    Panel1: TPanel;
    ProgramIcon: TImage;
    ProductName: TLabel;
    Version: TLabel;
```

```
    Copyright: TLabel;
    OKButton: TButton;
    procedure OKButtonClick(Sender: TObject);
  private
    { Private declarations }
  public
    { Public declarations }
  end;

function ShowAboutBox:Integer;

var
    AboutBox: TAboutBox;

implementation

{$R *.DFM}

procedure TAboutBox.OKButtonClick(Sender: TObject);
begin
    {Close the About Box}
    AboutBox.Close;
end;

function ShowAboutBox: Integer;
begin
    {Create the About Box}
    AboutBox := TAboutBox.Create(AboutBox);

    {Display the About Box}
    AboutBox.ShowModal;

    {Return a result}
    Result := mrOK;

    {Destroy the dialog when we're through.}
    AboutBox.Free;
end;

end.
```

There are several important things you should notice about this source code when compared to the application code I've provided throughout the book. First you should see that I declared a stand-alone function in this unit. You can't access a method of an object—only stand-alone functions are accessible from a DLL.

The second thing you should look at is the function itself. The first thing I do is create the form. Notice that I don't declare a variable for the form—that's done at a global level. However, unlike an application, a DLL doesn't have any way to create the form until it's called. Look at the project file for an application and compare it to this code. The first thing that an application does is create the main form. The main form allows us to call other forms in the application. A DLL doesn't have a main form so we have to create everything manually.

Once you create a form, you use the same methods as usual to display it. Our function also returns a result. In this case there's only one result that it can return since there is only one pushbutton for the user to press. You could use standard techniques for checking the return value of a dialog though—DLLs are no different from applications in this regard.

The last step doesn't look like much, but it's extremely important. If you create something in Delphi, you're also responsible for destroying it. In this case I started by creating an About Box. I have to end the function by freeing it. This releases the memory that I used and prevents memory leaks in an application.

Now that you've had a good look at the source for the About Box, let's look at the project source shown in Listing 15.2. I usually don't present this part of a project because Delphi creates it automatically. In this case you'll have to do some work. Notice the "exports" part of the project file. The function names you place here are the ones that someone can access outside the DLL. If you want to keep a function private, then don't put it here. As I said previously, you can't put methods of objects in this area—only functions and procedures are valid.

Listing 15.2. Project source.

```
library SmallDLL;

uses
  SysUtils,
  Classes,
  SmDLL1 in 'SmDLL1.pas' {AboutBox};

exports
    ShowAboutBox;

begin
end.
```

Note: Use the Project | Build All command to create your DLL instead of pressing the Run button. You can't run a DLL from within Delphi. The only way to fully test a DLL is to build it, then call it from an application.

Tip: I usually build the code for a DLL as an application first. Once the code is tested, I use cut and paste techniques to create the DLL. This may seem like a lot of extra steps, but it actually saves time since you can't run a DLL from within Delphi.

So, what does our DLL look like from the outside? Figure 15.5 shows the results of the program we just created. Even though the DLL contains two functions, all you can see is the one that we exported, the method used to close the About Box when you click on OK is nowhere to be seen.

Figure 15.5.
A Delphi DLL will contain a list of exported functions along with some of the more familiar entries you'll see in any DLL.

Accessing the DLL from Delphi

Creating a DLL is only part of a program. We need to write an application to access the DLL. Using a DLL requires a bit of special handling on the part of application. You have to build a linkage between the application and the DLL. I've already covered this subject pretty well when it comes to the Windows API in Chapter 9 (see Listing 9.2 for details). However, creating a separate unit is probably more suited to a DLL with a lot of functions. Let's take a look at how we can use our single function DLL.

The first thing you'll need to do is create an application with a form. Figure 15.6 shows the simple form I created for this example. All it contains is two pushbuttons: One to test the DLL and another to exit the program. I could have provided something more substantial, but I wanted to keep the code fairly simple.

Listing 15.3 contains the code required to make this particular example do something. As you can see, there are a few twists in this case that I haven't shown you before. The first thing you'll notice is the CONST section of the code. It contains a simple constant we can use to access the DLL. You really don't have to use this technique, but I find it less error prone than constantly referencing the DLL filename.

Figure 15.6.

Testing our DLL requires a simple form with two pushbuttons.

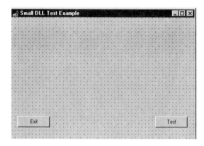

Listing 15.3. Showing the CONST section.

```
unit SDLLTst1;

interface

uses
  Windows, Messages, SysUtils, Classes, Graphics, Controls, Forms, Dialogs,
  StdCtrls;

const
    {A constant to hold the DLL filename.}
    SmallDLL = 'SMALLDLL.DLL';

type
  TForm1 = class(TForm)
    pbTest: TButton;
    pbExit: TButton;
    procedure pbTestClick(Sender: TObject);
    procedure pbExitClick(Sender: TObject);
  private
    { Private declarations }
  public
    { Public declarations }
  end;

{Declare the exported function in our DLL.}
function ShowAboutBox: Integer; external SmallDLL name 'ShowAboutBox';

var
  Form1: TForm1;

implementation

{$R *.DFM}

procedure TForm1.pbTestClick(Sender: TObject);
var
    fResult: Integer;    {Result of our DLL call.}
begin
    {Use the exported function in our DLL to display an about box.}
    fResult := ShowAboutBox;

    {Display a result.}
```

```
    if fResult = mrOK then
        ShowMessage('User pressed OK')
    else
        ShowMessage('Return type undetermined.');
end;

procedure TForm1.pbExitClick(Sender: TObject);
begin
    {End the application.}
    Application.Terminate;
end;

end.
```

Notice that the ShowAboutBox function declaration is somewhat different from what you'd use in a normal application. In this case we have to tell Delphi that the function appears in an external file. You need to include the filename (or a constant containing the filename) and either the ordinal value or the name of the function in the external DLL. There are advantages to using names in place of ordinal numbers. The number of a function may change when you compile it; the name probably won't.

The pbTestClick procedure used to test the DLL is fairly simple. The active code consists of a single line. You don't even have to pass any values to the DLL in this case. The return value tells which button the user pressed. In this case there's only one button so you'll always get a return value of mrOK. I display a dialog telling what kind of value we got back. If the return type doesn't match mrOK, then an error occurred and you'll need to debug the application.

Passing Data Between the DLL and Delphi

The previous example in this chapter showed you a very short and very limited example of a DLL. You can call it, expect it to do something for you, then return a result. However, DLLs commonly need to provide a little more interaction with the application than that. Just think about all the API functions that we've talked about to date that require long lists of input values (parameters) or a pointer to a structure. Both of these methods represent a means for exchanging information between an application and its associated DLL.

> **Tip:** Making incremental changes in a DLL, as we've done in this chapter, is one way to reduce the amount of time you spend debugging it. Start with a simple DLL that works, then embellish it one step at a time. You'll find that DLL programming is a little more exacting than application program and requires additional patience to complete.

The first thing that you need to decide then is what kind of data transfer method you'll use. Standard parameters like numbers are a lot easier to use than structures from several perspectives. For one thing, it takes a bit more processing (and typing) time to work with the values inside a structure. This isn't too big a deal, but I find it's an important one for programmers who are constantly looking at yet another method for getting code written faster. Another problem with structures is that you need to initialize them properly to make them work. It's another nit-picky observation, but one worth considering. The bottom line is that I normally use parameters for a short list of input values.

Using parameters does become cumbersome when you start reaching the four or five input value point. Who really wants to have a single line of code that extends more than 80 or so characters? Of course, you could always reduce the size of your parameter names and finally the function name itself to conserve space, but that's a little counterproductive when you think about it. Either way you look at it, the code becomes difficult to read at some point and you'll want to reduce its length and improve its readability by using a structure in place of parameters. The strength of a structure is that you can initialize its members once, then change only the structure member you need to during successive calls.

You probably noticed in our previous example that the About Box lacked a program name or version number (all it has is place holders that show Product Name and Version). Let's change that example so that it allows us to display both a product name and a version number. We'll pass the program name and version number as strings to the program. I'm going to use PCHAR strings in this example so that it follows the industry standard. Make sure you spend some time reading the PCHAR Versus Pascal Strings section in this chapter to understand why. Fortunately, none of the forms require change, so I'll start out with the source code changes. Listing 15.4 shows the new DLL code that we'll use to process the input from our application.

Listing 15.4. New DLL code.

```
unit SmDLL1;

interface

uses Windows, SysUtils, Classes, Graphics, Forms, Controls, StdCtrls,
  Buttons, ExtCtrls;

type
  TAboutBox = class(TForm)
    Panel1: TPanel;
    ProgramIcon: TImage;
    ProductName: TLabel;
    Version: TLabel;
    Copyright: TLabel;
    OKButton: TButton;
    procedure OKButtonClick(Sender: TObject);
  private
    { Private declarations }
  public
```

```
    { Public declarations }
  end;

function ShowAboutBox(lpszProgName, lpszVersion: PCHAR): Integer;

var
    AboutBox: TAboutBox;

implementation

{$R *.DFM}

procedure TAboutBox.OKButtonClick(Sender: TObject);
begin
    {Close the About Box}
    AboutBox.Close;
end;

function ShowAboutBox(lpszProgName, lpszVersion: PCHAR): Integer;
begin
    {Create the About Box}
    AboutBox := TAboutBox.Create(AboutBox);

    {Assign the program name string.}
    if lpszProgName = '' then
        AboutBox.ProductName.Caption := 'Sample Program'
    else
        AboutBox.ProductName.Caption := lpszProgName;

    {Assign the version string.}
    if lpszVersion = '' then
        AboutBox.Version.Caption := '0.0'
    else
        AboutBox.Version.Caption := lpszVersion;

    {Display the About Box}
    AboutBox.ShowModal;

    {Return a result}
    Result := mrOK;

    {Destroy the dialog when we're through.}
    AboutBox.Free;
end;

end.
```

The two big changes in our DLL code are the forward reference and the ShowAboutBox function. You'll find that error trapping in a DLL is very important. However, providing a substitute value if the user doesn't provide one is even more important. Most programmers at least hope that a DLL call will work to the point that they can figure out what went wrong. Descriptive error return values, message boxes, or substitute values are an important part of the communication between yourself and the programmer using the DLLs you create. In this case I go the substitute value route because the About Box provides visual feedback that the programmer can use.

There's another important feature of the ShowAboutBox function. I have to communicate with the About Box in some way. Normally, all I'd need to do is reference the component within the About Box and assign a value to one of its properties. You'll notice that I need to do a little more work this time. You're actually accessing the About Box from the outside, not the inside as you would within an event procedure. The difference is slight, but important to remember.

Now that we have a new and improved DLL, let's take a look at what we need to do to the application that uses it. Listing 15.5 shows the modified source code for this example.

Listing 15.5. Modified source code.

```
unit SDLLTst1;

interface

uses
  Windows, Messages, SysUtils, Classes, Graphics, Controls, Forms, Dialogs,
  StdCtrls;

const
    {A constant to hold the DLL filename.}
    SmallDLL = 'SMALLDLL.DLL';

type
  TForm1 = class(TForm)
    pbTest: TButton;
    pbExit: TButton;
    procedure pbTestClick(Sender: TObject);
    procedure pbExitClick(Sender: TObject);
  private
    { Private declarations }
  public
    { Public declarations }
  end;

{Declare the exported function in our DLL.}
function ShowAboutBox(lpszProdName, lpszVersion: PCHAR): Integer; external SmallDLL name
'ShowAboutBox';

var
  Form1: TForm1;

implementation

{$R *.DFM}

procedure TForm1.pbTestClick(Sender: TObject);
var
    fResult: Integer;          {Result of our DLL call.}
    sProdName: String;         {Product Name}
    lpszProdName: PCHAR;       {Null Terminated Product Name}
    SVersion: String;          {Program Version Number}
    lpszVersion: PCHAR;        {Null Terminated Program Version Number}
```

```
begin
    {Initialize our strings.}
    sProdName := Form1.Caption;
    lpszProdName := PCHAR(sProdName);
    sVersion := '1.0';
    lpszVersion := PCHAR(sVersion);

    {Use the exported function in our DLL to display an about box.}
    fResult := ShowAboutBox(lpszProdName, lpszVersion);

    {Display a result.}
    if fResult = mrOK then
    ShowMessage('User pressed OK')
    else
    ShowMessage('Return type undetermined.');
end;

procedure TForm1.pbExitClick(Sender: TObject);
begin
    {End the application.}
    Application.Terminate;
end;

end.
```

You'll notice two changes in this version of the source. The first is the forward reference. I like the way that Delphi works in this regard. Unlike C, where you could shoot yourself in the foot by providing the wrong value or not enough of them, Delphi provides additional safeguards. It's pretty difficult to cause data type errors with Delphi once you get the external function declaration right.

Now let's look at the pbTestClick event procedure. About the only thing we needed to do here was add the program name and version number strings. Notice how I used the caption of the main form as my program name. I find that this is the best way to take care of this string since I normally create applications using a template. The only thing I end up changing is the version number from program to program.

> **Tip:** You could eliminate the need to change the About Box display code for an application at all by placing the version number of the program in the Tag property of the main form. Delphi provides the Tag property for your own internal use. One way to use the property to your advantage is by storing something that you don't want to track in the application code. The program's version number fits into this category.

Once you get all the new code in place, it's time to take a look at the program's output. Figure 15.7 shows the new About Box. There are still a few limitations to this DLL. For one thing, you might want to provide a different copyright statement in some cases. Adding another string to the function would take care of that problem. You might also want to change the placement of the dialog.

Again, adding some additional parameters would take care of the problem. However, as you add more and more flexibility to your DLL function it becomes more cumbersome to use. The solution? Create several versions of the About Box call that allow different levels of customization. That way you can use a short call in most cases and only resort to a longer call when needed to display the About Box in some special way.

Figure 15.7.
Our improved About Box DLL includes a program name and version number.

Advantages to Using a Delphi DLL

Before I get into some of the more complex ways you can use a Delphi DLL, let's take a look at some of the advantages to using one. It's important to realize that the one tool fits every situation approach to programming is probably a dead-end. Somewhere along the line you'll find a DLL need that Delphi doesn't take care of properly—or perhaps doesn't take care of as well as some other language could. The following paragraphs talk about the advantages of using Delphi to create DLLs.

- No or Reduced Learning Curve—This is one of the more obvious benefits of using Delphi. Since you already know the language and use it to write applications, your learning curve to write DLLs is practically non-existent. However, I've already shown you that there are some small differences between using Delphi for applications and DLLs. You'll want to at least exercise some extra care when writing DLLs in Delphi. Make sure you understand the problem fully, then write the DLL to match. I find that it's the little things like form or data access that cause me the most grief when writing a DLL in Delphi.

- Native Data Types—Unlike C, where you have to translate the data type to something that Delphi understands, using a Delphi DLL means there is little if any chance of confusing one data type for another. An integer in your DLL is the same as the one used in your application. The only exception to this rule is strings. While you could use the String data type, it means including some extra baggage with your DLL. You might find the extra baggage worthwhile, but I usually use the PCHAR data type instead.

- Support for Delphi Specific Features—Our DLL examples in this chapter show one of the biggest reasons for using Delphi instead of another language to write a DLL. You have the option of using all the Delphi templates and components that you've created within the DLL. I used an About Box form that I created for application use within my DLL—you don't have that option if you use a language like C to write your DLL. This means that all the time you invest in creating those objects for your applications will also pay dividends when creating DLLs.

- Reduced Support Problems—Using another language to write a DLL means that you accept the limitations and benefits of using that language. In some cases you'll find that those benefits far exceed any problems you'll encounter in using the language—C provides speed and code size benefits that Delphi will find hard to beat. In other cases you'll find that using a Delphi DLL, while not as fast or efficient, is the way to go because you encounter fewer problems. Inter-language compatibility bugs can be some of the most difficult to locate and fix. Finger pointing between vendors is one of the biggest causes of the difficulty. Even if you do manage to locate the problem, in some cases there isn't any fix. For example, when writing DLLs in C for some specialty database languages, I found that I had to pass everything as a string. There was something about the way that the DBMS handled numbers that mangled them when passed to the C DLL.

- Reduced Resource Requirements—Hard disk space and machine memory aren't unlimited quantities. Have you ever tried to run two programming language products at the same time? Most machines just don't have the resources required to get the job done. The only solution is to open one product, work for a while in it, then open the other product and perform any tasks you need to do there. This constant switching back and forth takes its toll on programmer productivity.

I probably haven't covered every advantage here, but these are the major ones. Don't get the idea though that Delphi is the perfect solution. C still maintains definite advantages over Delphi in some areas. You may find that creating DLLs in some specialty languages, especially when it comes to database management, is a definite plus as well.

Creating a SendKeys() Function Using a Delphi DLL

I promised to show you how to create your own SendKeys() function during our discussion in Chapter 5. That's the point of this section of the chapter. The first thing I'd like to do though is tell you why such a function is even important. Beside the obvious benefit of showing you another DLL programming technique, a SendKeys() function can help you when it comes time to talk with another application that doesn't support all the modern features that we've come to expect from Windows application. This feature is important enough that products like Word for Windows and Visual Basic still include it as part of their feature set. (Delphi doesn't provide this feature as of this writing.) In sum, a SendKeys() function allows you to control another application by emulating keystrokes—you can use it in place of sending messages. As far as the other application is concerned, a user is typing away at the keyboard. Only your application knows that you're controlling it remotely.

> **Tip:** The WH_JOURNALPLAYBACK hook is only half the story in this case. You can also simplify macro creation by using a WH_JOURNALRECORD hook. This is the function that the original Windows macro recorder used to keep track of your keystrokes. You'd probably find this function at work today in any application that provides a macro recorder feature.

So, what special programming technique are you going to learn? The process of creating hooks is an important part of learning to work with the Windows API. There are a lot of different kinds of hooks at your disposal, but the example in this chapter will show you how to create a JournalPlayback hook. Chapter 5 goes through all of the theory behind creating a Windows hook, so I won't go into those details again here.

> **Note:** Unlike our previous DLL example, you can't build a journal playback hook procedure within your application to test it. There are two reasons for this. First, a journal playback hook is a system level routine—it must reside within a DLL. Second, look at a journal hook as a sort of TSR. You can't test something designed to work outside the application from within the application. The whole purpose of this routine is to allow you to take remote control of another application. Fortunately, the bulk of this example isn't the journal hook. You can test the macro parsing functions from within your Delphi application and then add the journal playback hook routines later on.

Building this DLL will require several steps. There are actually three sections that we'll look at. The first section takes care of parsing the macro—the string of characters that you want to send to the other application. There are two parts to the parsing process: figuring out what character the user wants to send and creating appropriate messages. The second section creates the journal playback hook. The journal playback function is the third section. Listing 15.6 shows the code required to make this DLL work.

Listing 15.6. Required code.

```
unit SendKey1;

interface

uses
    Windows, Messages, Classes, SysUtils;

const

    {Error messages returned by this DLL.}
    ERROR_SUCCESS = 0;
    ERROR_HOOK = 1;
    ERROR_SPECIAL_CHARACTER = 2;
```

```
    ERROR_CLOSING_BRACE = 3;
    ERROR_OTHER = 4;

    {The amount of time Windows should wait before processing a message.}
    NO_WAIT = 0;

procedure CreateMessage(siKeyCode: SHORT; iMessageType: Integer);
procedure KeyPress(siKeyCode: SHORT; fControl, fUp: Boolean);
function OutputMessages(code: Integer; wparam: WPARAM; lparam: LPARAM): LRESULT stdcall;
function ParseMacro(sMacro: String): LRESULT;
function SendKeys(lpszMacro: PCHAR): LRESULT stdcall;
function SendMessages: LRESULT;
procedure SimulateKeyPress(siKeyCode: SHORT; fAltKey, fShiftKey, fCtrlKey: Boolean);

var
    MsgList: TList;        {A list of keystroke messages to send}
    MsgBuffer: TEventMsg;  {A single message in the message list}
    iMsgNum: Integer;      {Current message number.}
    hNextHook: hHook;      {Handle to next hook procedure in line.}

implementation

procedure CreateMessage(siKeyCode: SHORT; iMessageType: Integer);
var
    pMessage: PEventMsg;   {A pointer to an event message.}
begin
    {Create an new message.}
    New(pMessage);

    {Fill the message with information.}
    with pMessage^ do
    begin
        Message := iMessageType;
        ParamL := MakeWord(siKeyCode, MapVirtualKey(siKeyCode, 0));
        ParamH := 1;
        Time := GetTickCount;
    end;

    {Add the message to our message list.}
    MsgList.Add(pMessage);
end;

procedure KeyPress(siKeyCode: SHORT; fControl, fUp: Boolean);
begin

    {If we're passing a control key, then generate a control key message.}
    if fControl then

        {Determine whether we want to press the key or release it.}
        if fUp then
            CreateMessage(siKeyCode, WM_SYSKEYUP)
        else
            CreateMessage(siKeyCode, WM_SYSKEYDOWN)

    {Otherwise we need to generate a standard message.}
    else
        if fUp then
            CreateMessage(siKeyCode, WM_KEYUP)
```

continues

Listing 15.6. continued

```
            else
                CreateMessage(siKeyCode, WM_KEYDOWN);
end;

function OutputMessages(code: Integer; wparam: WPARAM; lparam: LPARAM): LRESULT;
begin
    case code of

        {See if we need to pull the next message out of our list.}
        HC_SKIP:
            begin

                {Increment the message counter.}
                Inc(iMsgNum);

                {Check to see if we're at the end of the list.}
                if iMsgNum >= MsgList.Count then
                    begin

                        {If so, unhook our output function.}
                        UnHookWindowsHookEx(hNextHook);

                        {Free our message list.}
                        MsgList.Free;
                        end
                else

                    {Load the next message.}
                    MsgBuffer := TEventMsg(MsgList.Items[iMsgNum]^);

                {Return a result code.}
                Result := ERROR_SUCCESS;

                end;

        {Windows needs to know when we want to play back the next message
         if we receive this message.  What we'll do is tell it to play the
         next message in the message buffer as soon as possible.}
        HC_GETNEXT:
            begin

                {Place a pointer to the message in our lParam variable.}
                PEventMsg(lParam)^ := MsgBuffer;

                {Return a result code.}
                Result := NO_WAIT;

                end;

        {If we get any other message, it's the resposibility of the next hook.}
        else
            Result := CallNextHookEx(hNextHook, code, wParam, lParam);

    end; {case iMessage of}

end;

function ParseMacro(sMacro: String): LRESULT;
```

```
var
    iCurrentPos: Integer;      {Current processing position in string.}
    sSpecialKey: String;       {Special keystroke.}
    siKeyCode: SHORT;          {Scan code for regular keystroke.}
    fAltKey: Boolean;          {Was the Alt key pressed?}
    fShiftKey: Boolean;        {Was the Shift key pressed?}
    fCtrlKey: Boolean;         {Was the Ctrl key pressed?}
begin
    {Initialize our string position indicator.}
    iCurrentPos := 1;

    {Initialize the control key indicators}
    fAltKey := False;
    fShiftKey := False;
    fCtrlKey := False;

    {Parse the macro one character at a time until we complete it.}
    repeat

    {Look for control characters first.}
    if sMacro[iCurrentPos] = '^' then
        fCtrlKey := True
    else if sMacro[iCurrentPos] = '+' then
        fShiftKey := True
    else if sMacro[iCurrentPos] = '%' then
        fAltKey := True

    {Check for a special caracter next.}
    else if sMacro[iCurrentPos] = '{' then
        begin

        {Initialize the special character value.}
        sSpecialKey := sMacro[iCurrentPos];

        {Find the end of the special character.}
        while sMacro[iCurrentPos] <> '}' do
            begin

            {Increment the string pointer.}
            Inc(iCurrentPos);

            {Add the current character to the string.}
            sSpecialKey := sSpecialKey + UpperCase(sMacro[iCurrentPos]);

            {Check to make sure that we haven't gone past the
             end of the string.}
            if iCurrentPos > Length(sMacro) then
                begin
                Result := ERROR_CLOSING_BRACE;
                Exit;
                end;
            end;

        {Compare the input key and generate an output value.}
        if sSpecialKey = '{TAB}' then Result := VK_TAB
        else if sSpecialKey = '{ENTER}' then siKeyCode := VK_RETURN
        else if sSpecialKey = '{ESCAPE}' then siKeyCode := VK_ESCAPE
```

continues

Listing 15.6. continued

```
        else if sSpecialKey = '{ESC}' then siKeyCode := VK_ESCAPE
        else if sSpecialKey = '{BS}' then siKeyCode := VK_BACK
        else if sSpecialKey = '{BACKSPACE}' then siKeyCode := VK_BACK
        else if sSpecialKey = '{BREAK}' then siKeyCode := VK_CANCEL
        else if sSpecialKey = '{CAPSLOCK}' then siKeyCode := VK_CAPITAL
        else if sSpecialKey = '{CLEAR}' then siKeyCode := VK_CLEAR
        else if sSpecialKey = '{DEL}' then siKeyCode := VK_DELETE
        else if sSpecialKey = '{DELETE}' then siKeyCode := VK_DELETE
        else if sSpecialKey = '{DOWN}' then siKeyCode := VK_DOWN
        else if sSpecialKey = '{END}' then siKeyCode := VK_END
        else if sSpecialKey = '{HELP}' then siKeyCode := VK_HELP
        else if sSpecialKey = '{HOME}' then siKeyCode := VK_HOME
        else if sSpecialKey = '{INS}' then siKeyCode := VK_INSERT
        else if sSpecialKey = '{INSERT}' then siKeyCode := VK_INSERT
        else if sSpecialKey = '{LEFT}' then siKeyCode := VK_LEFT
        else if sSpecialKey = '{NUMLOCK}' then siKeyCode := VK_NUMLOCK
        else if sSpecialKey = '{PGDN}' then siKeyCode := VK_NEXT
        else if sSpecialKey = '{PAGEDOWN}' then siKeyCode := VK_NEXT
        else if sSpecialKey = '{PGUP}' then siKeyCode := VK_PRIOR
        else if sSpecialKey = '{PAGEUP}' then siKeyCode := VK_PRIOR
        else if sSpecialKey = '{PRTSC}' then siKeyCode := VK_SNAPSHOT
        else if sSpecialKey = '{PRINTSCREEN}' then siKeyCode := VK_SNAPSHOT
        else if sSpecialKey = '{RIGHT}' then siKeyCode := VK_RIGHT
        else if sSpecialKey = '{UP}' then siKeyCode := VK_UP
        else if sSpecialKey = '{F1}' then siKeyCode := VK_F1
        else if sSpecialKey = '{F2}' then siKeyCode := VK_F2
        else if sSpecialKey = '{F3}' then siKeyCode := VK_F3
        else if sSpecialKey = '{F4}' then siKeyCode := VK_F4
        else if sSpecialKey = '{F5}' then siKeyCode := VK_F5
        else if sSpecialKey = '{F6}' then siKeyCode := VK_F6
        else if sSpecialKey = '{F7}' then siKeyCode := VK_F7
        else if sSpecialKey = '{F8}' then siKeyCode := VK_F8
        else if sSpecialKey = '{F9}' then siKeyCode := VK_F9
        else if sSpecialKey = '{F10}' then siKeyCode := VK_F10
        else if sSpecialKey = '{F11}' then siKeyCode := VK_F11
        else if sSpecialKey = '{F12}' then siKeyCode := VK_F12

        {If the special character doesn't match anything, raise an
         error and exit.}
        else
            begin
            Result := ERROR_SPECIAL_CHARACTER;
            Exit;
            end;

        {Simulate pressing the key.}
        SimulateKeyPress(MakeWord(siKeyCode, 0), fAltKey, fShiftKey, fCtrlKey);

        {Reset the control key indicators}
        fAltKey := False;
        fShiftKey := False;
        fCtrlKey := False;

        end {else if sMacro[iCurrentPos] = '{' then)

    {If it isn't a special or control character, it must be a key press.}
    else
```

```delphi
    begin

      {Convert the character to a scan code.}
      siKeyCode := vkKeyScan(sMacro[iCurrentPos]);

      {Simulate pressing the key.}
      SimulateKeyPress(MakeWord(siKeyCode,0), fAltKey, fShiftKey, fCtrlKey);

      {Reset the control key indicators}
      fAltKey := False;
      fShiftKey := False;
      fCtrlKey := False;

    end;


  {Update the string position pointer.}
  Inc(iCurrentPos);

  until iCurrentPos > Length(sMacro);

  {Return a success message if we get to this point.}
  Result := ERROR_SUCCESS;
end;

function SendKeys(lpszMacro: PCHAR): LRESULT;
var
  sMacro: String;    {String version of our macro.}
begin

  {Initialize our string.}
  sMacro := lpszMacro;

  {Create a keystroke message list.}
  MsgList := TList.Create;

  {Parse the macro string and determine if there were any errors.}
  Result := ParseMacro(sMacro);
  if Result <> ERROR_SUCCESS then
      begin
      MsgList.Free;
      Exit;
      end;

  {Send the message list to the current application and determine if
   there were any errors.}
  Result := SendMessages;
  if Result <> ERROR_SUCCESS then
      begin
      MsgList.Free;
      Exit;
      end;

end;

function SendMessages: LRESULT;
begin
```

continues

Listing 15.6. continued

```
    {Grab the first message in the list.}
    MsgBuffer := TEventMsg(MsgList.Items[0]^);

    {Initialize our message counter.}
    iMsgNum := 0;

    {Set the JournalPlayback hook.}
    hNextHook := SetWindowsHookEx(WH_JOURNALPLAYBACK, OutputMessages, hInstance, 0);

    {Determine if we successfully set the hook.}
    if hNextHook = 0 then
        Result := ERROR_HOOK
    else
        Result := ERROR_SUCCESS;
end;

procedure SimulateKeyPress(siKeyCode: SHORT; fAltKey, fShiftKey, fCtrlKey: Boolean);
const
    MENU = True;
    NOT_MENU = False;
    KEY_UP = True;
    KEY_DOWN = False;
begin

    {Determine which control keys are pressed.}
    if fAltKey then KeyPress(VK_MENU, NOT_MENU, KEY_DOWN);
    if fCtrlKey then KeyPress(VK_CONTROL, NOT_MENU, KEY_DOWN);

    {Determine the shift status.}
    if (((Hi(siKeyCode) and 1) <> 0) and (not fCtrlKey)) or fShiftKey then
        KeyPress(VK_SHIFT, NOT_MENU, KEY_DOWN);

    {There are two routes to follow for normal keystrokes.  Either the user
     pressed Alt-Key for a menu item, or they simply pressed a regular key.}
    if fAltKey and (not fCtrlKey) then
        begin
        KeyPress(siKeyCode, MENU, KEY_DOWN);
        KeyPress(siKeyCode, MENU, KEY_UP);
        end
    else
        begin
        KeyPress(siKeyCode, NOT_MENU, KEY_DOWN);
        KeyPress(siKeyCode, NOT_MENU, KEY_UP);
        end;

    {Release the shift key.}
    if (((Hi(siKeyCode) and 1) <> 0) and (not fCtrlKey)) or fShiftKey then
        KeyPress(VK_SHIFT, NOT_MENU, KEY_UP);

    {Release the other control keys.}
    if fAltKey then KeyPress(VK_MENU, NOT_MENU, KEY_UP);
    if fCtrlKey then KeyPress(VK_CONTROL, NOT_MENU, KEY_UP);

end;

end.
```

The first thing you should notice is that the SendKeys() function is pretty short. The only thing that it does is create a message list, then call the other two routines needed to initialize the message playback process. I've used a PCHAR here as in the previous DLL example for compatibility reasons. You'll notice that I have to convert it to a standard Pascal string before I can use it. Another thing you should notice is that I don't free the message list unless there's some kind of error. The reason is simple: If you free the message list when the routine gets finished, it won't be around when Windows calls the journal playback routine. Unlike most applications, you don't want to free all the variables that you create in a hook routine. Only free the variables that the callback procedure won't use.

Before you can do anything else with a SendKeys() macro, you have to define the keystrokes that it will react to. That's the purpose of the ParseMacro function in Listing 15.6. This function defines all of the keystrokes we'll send from the current application to another application. There are three different keystroke types that the function will react to: control (or shift), special, and standard character. Notice that the shift keys include: a + for a Shift key, a % for the Alt key, and a ^ for the Control key. You could expand this to include a separate left and right shift key, but I chose to keep the example simple. Special keys are key words enclosed in curly braces {}. For example, {TAB} is the tab character. This follows the same convention used by Word for Windows and other products that support the SendKeys() function. The end result of this particular function is to create a virtual key code for each character type that the user enters. You'll find a complete list of virtual key codes in the Windows unit provided with Delphi. Notice the special error code I provide here for special key input. It's important to add features like this to a DLL. The return value tells the users specifically where to look in their code for problems.

The ParseMacro function calls a function called SimulateKeyPress. A virtual key is the first step in creating messages. Now it's time to create the message sequence. It takes a few minutes to figure out why this particular function is so complicated. When you press a key you don't often realize all the steps you're taking. For example, if you want to press Alt-T, you have to press the Alt key, then the T, release the T, then release the Alt key—a four step process. The fact that pressing and releasing the key is two separate steps is important to remember as well.

Each step in creating a key press requires a separate message. For example, pressing the Alt key is a separate message even though it might be part of the process of sending an Alt-T to an application. The KeyPress and CreateMessage functions work together to create these messages and place them within our MsgList variable. The first thing we need to do is determine what kind of message to create. There are four that are important in this case: WM_KEYUP, WM_KEYDOWN, WM_SYSKEYUP, and WM_SYSKEYDOWN. The first two send input to whatever control is currently selected in an application. For example, I'll show you a test utility in a few moments. The first thing I do is select a result window where all the key presses will appear. The second two messages tell the application that you're requesting some type of system function. For example, the user may want to select a menu entry. Obviously there are two different messages for key presses and key releases. The CreateMessage function takes the messages that KeyPress creates and adds them to our message list.

Tip: I used WinSight to record various keystrokes before writing this code. The result is what you see. You can use a similar analysis procedure for other kinds of procedures that you take for granted. Start WinSight, then use the Messages | Options command to select the type of message you want to monitor. For example, I monitored the WM_KEYUP and WM_KEYDOWN messages to figure out how various keystrokes appeared.

All of the work we just went through parsed the macro sent by a client application and created a message list from it. Now that we have a message list, we can initialize the journal playback hook that will send the keystrokes to a server. That's the work of the SendMessages function. It loads the first message into a message buffer, initializes the message counter variable, then sets the journal playback hook. Notice that I provide another special error message here just in case the function can't set the hook. At this point, we exit the DLL for the first time. It returns to the client application with either a success or error message.

Windows calls our DLL now. The OutputMessages function is our journal playback callback function. There are three different things that this function can do based on the message that Windows sends to it. The first (HC_SKIP) is to load a new message into the message buffer. The message buffer only holds one message at a time. This is also the message handler that's responsible for unhooking our journal playback function. Once we've loaded all the messages in the message buffer, there isn't any reason to keep the DLL hooked into memory. The second task (HC_GETNEXT) is to send the message to Windows for processing. A journal playback function only needs to provide a pointer to the message that Windows should send in the lParam. The wParam is undefined in this particular case. Notice that you have to tell Windows how long to wait before it processes the message. Always provide a value of 0 when using a journal playback hook to play macros of some type. The third task is to pass information on to the next hook in line. There might be several journal playback hooks installed on your machine at any given time. They all need access to the messages you're looking at since a journal playback hook is a system level hook.

There's one last interesting piece of information you should see in this listing. Notice that I added "stdcall" to the end of the two exported functions in this case: SendKeys and OutputMessages. The reason for OutputMessages is pretty simple. Since Windows will call this routine you need to provide a standard calling convention. I used the standard method for the sake of continuity with SendKeys. This is an important consideration if you plan to use your Delphi DLLs with other languages. They'll be expecting the standard calling convention when using your DLL.

Now that you've gotten a good look at the DLL source, let's take a quick look at the project definition. Listing 15.7 shows the project code for this example. As you can see, it uses the same format as the source for the previous DLL.

Listing 15.7. Project code.

```
library SendKey;

uses
  SysUtils,
  Classes,
  SendKey1 in 'SendKey1.pas';

exports
    SendKeys, OutputMessages;

begin
end.
```

Once you get your DLL completely built, you need to create an application to test it (unless you're braver than I am and choose to use an existing application). You could add this DLL to the DDE Client example in Chapter 10, but I chose the simplicity of a separate program to test it out. (You may want to add the DLL to the DDE Client example later to fill the capabilities of this utility out.) Figure 15.8 shows the form we'll use in this example. I set its Boarder Style property to bsSingle since we don't have to resize this form to use it. The form contains an edit box for your macro and a TMemo component result window. I set the Memo1 TabStop property to False so that the user wouldn't have to tab through it when testing a macro out. You'll also find two pushbuttons on the form. The first pushbutton allows you to test the macro; the second allows you to exit the program.

Figure 15.8.
The SendKeys( ) Function Tester allows you to try out your new DLL in relative security.

Once you get the form together, you can add the source code shown in Listing 15.8 to it. The actual implementation is fairly simple. All we do is declare the external function and pass a macro to it. I also provided some extended error trapping here based on the error codes that the DLL returns. This example illustrates the second alternative before to error trapping. You can't place dialog boxes in most places of the SendKeys( ) DLL without taking a chance of it freezing the machine. This is especially true once you set the journal playback hook since Windows won't accept any keyboard or mouse input until you unhook the journal playback routine. There's one item to note: Since I made the SendKeys function a stdcall, you have to add stdcall to its external call in the testing program as well.

Listing 15.8. **Source code to add.**

```
unit SKTest1;

interface

uses
  Windows, Messages, SysUtils, Classes, Graphics, Controls, Forms, Dialogs,
  StdCtrls;

const
    SendKey = 'SENDKEY.DLL';

type
  TForm1 = class(TForm)
    Memo1: TMemo;
    Label1: TLabel;
    Edit1: TEdit;
    Label2: TLabel;
    pbTest: TButton;
    pbExit: TButton;
    procedure pbExitClick(Sender: TObject);
    procedure pbTestClick(Sender: TObject);
  private
    { Private declarations }
  public
    { Public declarations }
  end;

{Declare the exported function in our DLL.}
function SendKeys(lpszMacro: PCHAR): LRESULT stdcall; external SendKey name 'SendKeys';

var
  Form1: TForm1;

implementation

{$R *.DFM}

procedure TForm1.pbExitClick(Sender: TObject);
begin
    {End the program.}
    Application.Terminate;
end;

procedure TForm1.pbTestClick(Sender: TObject);
const
    {Error messages returned by the DLL.}
    ERROR_SUCCESS = 0;
    ERROR_HOOK = 1;
    ERROR_SPECIAL_CHARACTER = 2;
    ERROR_CLOSING_BRACE = 3;
    ERROR_OTHER = 4;
var
    lpszMacro: PCHAR;     {The macro string.}
    fResult: WORD;        {Result of the SendKeys() call.}
begin
    {Convert our edit box to a PCHAR.}
```

```
    lpszMacro := PCHAR(Edit1.Text);

    {Set the focus on our result window.}
    Memo1.SetFocus;

    {Call the external routine.}
    fResult := SendKeys(lpszMacro);

    {Check for an error.}
    if fResult <> ERROR_SUCCESS then
        case fResult of
            ERROR_HOOK: MessageDlg('Error setting hook.', mtError, [mbOK], 0);
            ERROR_SPECIAL_CHARACTER: MessageDlg('Error in special character.', mtError,
[mbOK], 0);
            ERROR_CLOSING_BRACE: MessageDlg('Closing brace on special character miss-
ing.', mtError, [mbOK], 0);
            ERROR_OTHER: MessageDlg('Unknown error in macro or program.', mtError,
[mbOK], 0);
        end;
end;

end.
```

Let's take a look at our new application. Figure 15.9 shows the result of running a simple macro. The macro appears in the edit window; the result in the result window. Notice that I had to add a shift character to the test even though it's capitalized in the macro. The reason is simple: Windows doesn't differentiate between a shifted and unshifted character. All it knows is that you requested a specific scan code. Make sure you keep this in mind for the characters above the number row. A dollar sign is actually a +4 (Shift-4) when using a SendKeys function.

Figure 15.9.
The finished SendKeys()
Function Tester allows you
try out various macros before
you commit to using them in
an application.

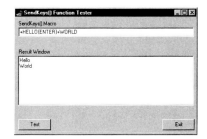

Summary

Obviously I haven't covered every kind of DLL that you'll ever write in this chapter. However, we have explored some of the mechanics of creating a DLL in Delphi. These examples give you the building blocks required to write DLLs of your own.

It's important to provide some form of feedback to the person using your DLL, even if that user is you. Nothing is worse than trying to write an application using several DLLs and not being able to figure out which one it is, much less the particular problem that's causing an error. I've shown you two methods of providing feedback in this chapter. The first method—using message boxes—is more automatic and user friendly. You can use it anywhere that a message box approach won't cause problems.

Standard DLLs don't provide feedback using message boxes. There are two reasons. First of all, imagine a user's surprise at seeing a foreign message box appear from nowhere on the screen. Second, using message boxes doesn't really provide a good method for the client application to respond to the error. Finally, some DLLs simply can't display a message box. A Windows hook routine is one type of DLL function that will experience problems if you use a message box approach to displaying error messages. In this case you have to resort to returning error codes and hoping that the client application responds appropriately.

16

Creating Your Own DLLs Using C

There's more than one way to create a DLL in Windows. You're going to want to spend some time looking at Chapter 15 (if you haven't already) because it shows the Delphi way to do things. Creating a DLL in Delphi is probably the easiest way for anyone reading this book to go for most DLL types. However, there are special circumstances that make C a better language for writing DLLs—that's what we'll cover in this chapter.

The first section of this chapter we'll spend some time talking about writing a C versus a Delphi DLL. I think it's important to weigh the various costs of following a route before you take it. It's especially important when designing something as long lived as a DLL. Obviously the biggest cost is knowing the C language—a prerequisite for following this particular route.

Note: This chapter isn't about learning C programming techniques. I'm assuming at least a basic knowledge of C in writing this chapter. If you haven't written in C before, you'll probably want to spend some time learning to use it before you delve into the intricacies of creating a DLL using that language. I'll also assume a generic C compiler for the most part—which means that you'll need to make any changes required to use the code in this chapter with your specific compiler. I'm using the Microsoft C compiler as a starting point and then testing that code with a Borland compiler to give it the widest possible appeal.

I added a special memory considerations section to this chapter. The reason is simple: Efficient memory use is the biggest reason to use C over Delphi for creating a DLL. Not that Delphi is any kind of a memory hog—quite the contrary; Borland has gone to great lengths to reduce the memory footprint of this latest version. However, when you need to get the very last ounce of memory out of a memory starved machine, there are a lot of ways that you can do it—including stripping as much as you can from the memory used by the DLLs in your program. It's important to remember throughout this chapter that I'm providing the most efficient way to do things; not necessarily saying that Delphi is inadequate in some way.

We'll also spend some time looking at the generic case C DLL. There are quite a few differences between a C DLL and the one that I showed you how to create in Chapter 15. Those of you who have created 16-bit DLLs will probably notice some differences with this 32-bit version as well. I did talk about some of these differences in Chapter 15, so you'll want to take a look at the introductory material. The bottom line is that DLLs in the 32-bit environment are easier to create. As with the generic Delphi DLL that I showed in Chapter 15, the purpose of this example is to show you the basics.

The last section will look at a financial function DLL. I consider functions of this type to be the best way to combine C and Delphi in an application. C is extremely efficient when it comes to writing short and fast DLLs that you'll access within a loop in your program. I consider Delphi far superior from a Delphi programmer's perspective for most other kinds of DLL programming.

Using C Versus Delphi to Build Your DLL

I can see people arguing the relative merits of C versus Delphi for quite some time to come after looking at the 32-bit version. The two products are extremely close in many ways. Delphi 1.0 was good, but the 2.0 version is better. That said, let's look at some of the ways that you could probably benefit from using C versus Delphi to create a DLL. It's important to keep these differences in mind when choosing a tool to get the job done.

- Speed—Someone from Borland will probably say that the difference between Delphi and C is small—perhaps even not noticeable, but the difference is there. Sure, you're not going to notice orders of difference in speed, but you'll notice a small amount of difference. So, does this small difference mean anything to you when compared to the time it'll take to create the DLL in C? When you execute a function from within in a loop it does. I've seen some fairly worthwhile speed increases when using C to create small loop functions. That's the key here—use C when you call a DLL function a lot.

- Memory—You'd think that memory wouldn't be a concern on today's workstations. A lot of them are coming with 16 MB or even 32 MB of memory standard. Memory is less of a problem on today's machines. However, your application may not have a new machine to run on. It may have to run on a machine that's two or three years old. These older machines are lucky to have 8 MB or 12 MB of memory installed—barely enough to run Windows 95, much less some high powered application. Memory is important and saving even small amounts of it can make the difference between using an application on an older technology machine and buying a new one. If you're part of a development project for a large company, memory conservation becomes even more important since replacing old machines often isn't an option.

- Compatibility—If you've spent any time looking at the examples in Chapter 15, you'll notice that I had to go through a few extra steps to make the Delphi DLLs work with other languages. The problem is that Pascal uses one calling syntax, the rest of Windows something else. This incompatibility even extends to strings. You have to use PCHAR variables in place of standard Delphi strings. Is this a big problem? No, but it does mean that you'll need to take a few extra steps writing a DLL with Delphi that you don't need to take with a C DLL.

- Extensibility—You're going to find a few situations where you can't create a function in Delphi that you can in C. These situations are extremely rare, but they do exist. For example, you can create a thunking layer using a C DLL. This would enable you to access a 16-bit DLL or even a favorite VBX. Obviously, the whole process of thunking is extremely complex. You'd have to explore every other possibility first before you took this extreme measure. I like to think of a C DLL as my option of last resort when it comes to needs like these.

- Flexibility—C doesn't do something for you that Delphi does automatically. Delphi creates an initialization routine for your DLL. That's normally a help since you really don't need an initialization routine for most programs. On the other hand, it can quickly become a problem if you do. I've only run into this situation a few times with hook routines (see Chapter 15 for an example of a journal playback hook routine). Suffice it to say that you really won't need to worry about this slight loss of flexibility very often.

- Low Level Access—As computer language products provide more and more in the way of functionality, the need for anyone to look at low level access to devices becomes a moot point. I still like to access one device directly, the math coprocessor. You can still get a speed boost from most math operations by accessing the math coprocessor directly (I'll show you how in the last section of this chapter). Even if you like the level of math speed you get from Delphi and really don't feel the need to test your assembler programming, knowing how to perform some types of low level access could come in handy. Delphi doesn't make this very convenient. For one thing, Borland took away the Inline function in this version. (If you look at some of the Delphi source, though, you'll see an ASM function that does about the same thing.) The reason I maintain my ASM code in C DLLs is two-fold. First, it's a lot faster using C for this purpose than Delphi. Second, keeping the "dirty" code in a C DLL keeps my Delphi code clean and portable.

If C is so great, then why don't I use it for every DLL? C isn't that great. It's going to take you a lot longer to write and debug a DLL in C than it will to write the same thing in Delphi. You'll also find that C doesn't provide as many ready-made tools for you. Things that you take for granted—like the VCL—just don't exist in C. That means a lot of extra work for you. The bottom line? You'll find that C is an important tool to add to your tool kit, but don't make the mistake of using it in places where it doesn't really fit.

DLL Programming Considerations

Our first example of how to create a C DLL and interface it with Delphi is very simple. All I'm going to do is create a function for calculating the value of the hypotenuse of a triangle. I chose this example because we really didn't work much with numbers in the previous chapter and I feel this is C's forte when compared to a Delphi DLL.

There are two files that you'll need to create for the C part of this example. The first appears in Listing 16.1. It only contains one function: TriCalc. In this case I accept two sides of a triangle as input and calculate the value of the hypotenuse as output. Notice I use double precision real numbers. The reason I do so is that the declaration is the same in both C and Delphi (as you'll see a bit later).

Note: Those of you coming from the 16-bit C environment should notice a few differences in the format and function declarations for the 32-bit environment. First, notice that I include a Microsoft specific storage class attribute: __declspec(dllexport). The alternative is to include an Exports section in your DEF file (this is what you'd need to do when using older versions of the Borland C compiler—the code shown compiles just fine with the 5.0 and above version of that compiler). You can also use the _export directive if your compiler supports it (as Borland C does). The TriCalc function doesn't require the Far, Pascal, or __Export modifiers used in the past either. I also dropped the 16-bit stub functions WEP and LibMain; you don't need them in the 32-bit environment. In essence, creating a 32-bit DLL is a much cleaner process than what you used in the 16-bit environment.

Listing 16.1. TriCalc.

```
#include <windows.h>
#include <math.h>
#include <stdlib.h>

__declspec( dllexport ) double TriCalc(double nSide1, double nSide2);
double TriCalc(double nSide1, double nSide2)
{
    // This function accepts two sides of a triangle as input
    // and computes the value of its hypotenuese.

    double    nHyp;    //Result value.

    // Use the sides to calculate the value of the hypotenuese.

    nHyp = (nSide1 * nSide1) + (nSide2 * nSide2);
    nHyp = sqrt(nHyp);

    return nHyp;
}
```

The second file defines the DLL parameters; it's the DEF file shown in Listing 16.2. There are a lot of things you can put in here. In fact, the contents vary slightly depending on which compiler you use. I'm using the Microsoft version of the DEF file in this case; all it contains is some memory parameters. The Borland version of the file would contain an Exports section that lists the TriCalc function as an exported function.

Listing 16.2. Defining the DLL parameters.

```
LIBRARY          FIRSTDLL
CODE             PRELOAD MOVEABLE DISCARDABLE
DATA             PRELOAD MOVEABLE SINGLE
HEAPSIZE         1024
```

The library also needs a MAK (make) file, but the C compiler will create it for you automatically so I won't include it here. Now that you've gotten all the code for the DLL together, use the appropriate Build menu option to create it. Some compilers will place the DLL in strange places. For example, the latest version of Microsoft C insists on placing the DLL in the RELEASE directory. You need to either copy the DLL to the SYSTEM folder or into the same directory as your Delphi code. Otherwise, the Delphi program we'll create next won't be able to find the DLL it needs.

Now that we have a DLL to test, let's build a Delphi application to test it. Figure 16.1 shows the form we'll use for this example. I made a few modifications to the components as shown in Table 16.1. All this form really contains is three labels: three single line edits, and two pushbuttons. The modifications are mostly cosmetic in nature, but they'll keep you from shooting yourself in the foot during testing.

Figure 16.1.

Our Simple C DLL Tester allows you to access the FIRSTDLL.DLL file we just created.

Table 16.1. Simple C DLL Tester Form Control Settings.

Object	Property	Setting
edSide1	TabOrder	0
	Text	'3'
edSide2	TabOrder	1
	Text	'4'
edHyp	TabStop	False
	ReadOnly	True
pbTest	Caption	'Test'
	TabOrder	2
	OnClick	pbTestClick
pbExit	Caption	'Exit'
	TabOrder	3
	OnClick	pbExitClick

Once you get the form configured, add some code to it as shown in Listing 16.3. As you can see, I kept the pbTestClick procedure simple so that the DLL access technique wouldn't be obscured. About the only thing that this function does is gather some information from the user, then display a result. Notice that I did include a width and decimals parameter for the STR function. If you don't include these parameters, Delphi will display the result in scientific notation.

Listing 16.3. **Code to add.**

```
unit FDLLTst1;

interface

uses
  Windows, Messages, SysUtils, Classes, Graphics, Controls, Forms, Dialogs,
  StdCtrls;

const
    FirstDLL = 'FIRSTDLL.DLL';

type
  TForm1 = class(TForm)
    pbTest: TButton;
    pbExit: TButton;
    Label1: TLabel;
    Label2: TLabel;
    Label3: TLabel;
    edSide1: TEdit;
    edSide2: TEdit;
    edHyp: TEdit;
    procedure pbExitClick(Sender: TObject);
    procedure pbTestClick(Sender: TObject);
  private
    { Private declarations }
  public
    { Public declarations }
  end;

{Declare the exported function in our DLL.}
function TriCalc(nSide1, nSide2: Double): Double stdcall; external FirstDLL name
'TriCalc';

var
  Form1: TForm1;

implementation

{$R *.DFM}

procedure TForm1.pbExitClick(Sender: TObject);
begin
    {Exit the application.}
    Application.Terminate;
end;
```

continues

Listing 16.3. continued

```
procedure TForm1.pbTestClick(Sender: TObject);
var
    nSide1, nSide2: Double;    {Two sides of triangle.}
    nHyp: Double;             {Calculation result.}
    sHyp: String;             {String version of result.}
    iCode: Integer;           {Result of string conversion.}
begin
    {Convert user input to numbers.}
    Val(edSide1.Text, nSide1, iCode);
    Val(edSide2.Text, nSide2, iCode);

    {Call the external routine.}
    nHyp := TriCalc(nSide1, nSide2);

    {Convert, then display, the results.}
    Str(nHyp:30:10, sHyp);
    edHyp.Text := Trim(sHyp);
end;

end.
```

The one thing that you'll want to take a close look at in this example is the way I access the C DLL. You shouldn't see any difference between it and the examples in Chapter 15. The only special requirement is that you use the StdCall calling convention.

So, what does our program look like in action? Figure 16.2 shows the results. You can easily calculate the hypotenuse for any triangle given two sides. I'll show you something a bit more useful in the next section of the chapter. My whole purpose in including this section was to acquaint you with the intricacies of creating a simple interface between C and Delphi. Like me, you probably found it easier than expected—which was Borland's intent all along.

Figure 16.2.

This is our first C to Delphi
interface example in action.

One of the things that does differentiate the output of some C compilers with that of Delphi is that the exported table isn't visible in Quick View. Figure 16.3 shows the example we just put together. Notice that there is an import table listing, but no export table listing. I view this as a small, but valuable, advantage for using C DLLs. If you really want to keep your exported functions a secret, you can do so using this technique. Obviously, this has disadvantages too, since the functions are hidden from everyone's sight, even your own.

Figure 16.3.
Some C compilers allow you
to hide your exported
functions from prying eyes,
as shown in this example.

Designing and Building Complex Math Functions

There are no two ways about it, C is still the fastest thing around (besides assembler) when it comes to math routines. Delphi has caught up to C in a lot of ways, but I don't think it'll ever quite catch up in this area. This section is going to look at three different kinds of complex math functions written in a combination of C and in-line assembler.

Note: I used both Microsoft and Borland C++ compilers to test the code in this section. There is one problem with both of them that you need to be aware of. Modern C++ compilers do something called name mangling as part of the compile and link process. The result is that you'll have problems using the resulting DLL in some situations. It's essential that you create a straight C DLL to make these examples work. Normally you'll find some environment settings that control the type of DLL the compiler produces. If you can't find an environment setting, then check your C++ compiler manual. Turning off name mangling is essential.

Creating the Math Routine DLL

Let's begin by designing a C DLL to perform three common financial calculations: annuity, compound interest, and simple interest. I even provide you with two different ways to get the job done (more about that later). Listing 16.4 shows the six functions we'll discuss in the next few paragraphs. What you should be interested in here is the technique I've used to create the functions. Obviously these are handy functions to have around as well, but that's secondary at this point.

Listing 16.4. Functions discussed in this section.

```c
#include <windows.h>
#include <math.h>
#include <stdlib.h>

__declspec( dllexport ) double CompInt(double nIntRate,
    double nCompPer, double nPrinciple)
{
    // Use this function to determine the intermediate results
    // of a compount interest calculation.  See the Delphi part
    // of the code to see how to use these interemediate results
    // to get a total amount.This function accepts three parameters
    // as input: interest rate, compounding periods per year, and
    // the amount of the original loan.  It returns the compound
    // value for one period.  In other words, the amount of a single
    // compounding period payment.  This is a compound interest
    // equation, so there is interest on the interest on the loan.

    double    nCompRes;   // Intermediate result.
    double    nRatePP;    // Interest rate per period.

    // Use the input values to calculate the future value of the principle.

    // Start by computing the amount of interest for each accounting period
    // in a year.

    nRatePP = nIntRate/nCompPer/100;

    // Calculate the return on our investment.for a single period.

    nCompRes = nPrinciple * (1 + nRatePP);

    return nCompRes;
}

__declspec( dllexport ) double SimpInt(double nIntRate,
    double nCompPer, double nPrinciple)
{
    // Use this function to determine the intermediate results
    // of a simple interest calculation.  See the Delphi part of
    // the code to see how to use these interemediate results to
    // get a total amount.This function accepts three parameters
    // as input: interest rate, compounding periods per year, and
    // the amount of the original loan.  It returns the simple
    // interest value for one period.  In other words, the amount
    // of a single simple interest period payment.  This is a simple
    // interest equation, so only the interest gets added each time.

    double    nRatePP;    // Interest rate per period.

    // Use the input values to calculate the future value of the principle.
```

```
    // Start by computing the amount of interest for each accounting period
    // in a year.

    nRatePP = nIntRate/nCompPer/100*nPrinciple;

    return nRatePP;
}


__declspec( dllexport ) double Annuity(double nIntRate,
      double nCompPer, double nPayment, double nValue)
{
    // Use this function to determine the intermediate results
    // of an annuity.  See the Delphi part of the code to see how to
    // use these interemediate results to get a total amount.  An
    // annuity measures the amount of money you can expect to get
    // by depositing a set amount of money each period and receiving
    // a set amount of interest.  This function accepts four inputs:
    // interest rate, compounding periods per year, and the payment —
    // amount of deposit—for each compounding period.  It also requires
    // the amount of the last calculation (0 if this is the first calculation).

    double    nRatePP;    // Interest rate per period.

    // Use the input values to calculate the intermediate annuity values..

    // Start by computing the amount of interest for each accounting period
    // in a year.

    nRatePP = nIntRate/nCompPer/100;

    // Calculate the return on our investment for this period.
    // This function is designed to be called as part of a loop from within Delphi.

    nValue = nValue * (nRatePP + 1);
    nValue = nValue + nPayment;

    return nValue;
}

__declspec( dllexport ) double mathCompInt(double nIntRate,
      double nCompPer, double nPrinciple, int nTotalPer)
{
    // This function accepts four parameters as input: interest rate,
    // compounding periods per year, the total number of compounding
    // periods, and the amount of the original loan.  It returns the
    // total cost of the loan.  In other words, the amount of the
    // load and the interest you would  need to pay.  This is a
    // compound interest equation, so there is interest on the
    // interest on the loan.

    double    nRatePP;        // Interest rate per period.
    double    nHundred = 100;    // Used with coprocessor.
    double    nOne = 1;        // Used with coprocessor.
    int    nCount;                // Loop counting variable.

    // Use the input values to calculate the future value of the principle.
```

continues

Listing 16.4. continued

```
     // Start by computing the amount of interest for each accounting period
     // in a year.

//    nRatePP = nIntRate/nCompPer/100;
     _asm
     {
     FLD    nIntRate    // Load the interest rate.
     FDIV   nCompPer    // Divide it by the componding period.
     FDIV   nHundred    // Divide it by 100.
     FADD   nOne    // Add 1 in preparation for next step
     FSTP   nRatePP    // Store the result.
     FLD    nPrinciple    // Load the result variable in preparation
               // for next step.
     }

     // Calculate the return on our investment.

     for (nCount = 0; nCount < nTotalPer; nCount++)
        {
//       nCompRes = nCompRes * (1 + nRatePP);
        _asm
        {
        FMUL    nRatePP    // We already loaded nCompRes in the previous
               // section and added 1 to nRatePP.
        }
        }

     // Store the result of our computation.

     _asm
     {
     FSTP    nPrinciple
     }

     return nPrinciple;
}

__declspec( dllexport ) double mathSimpInt(double nIntRate,
     double nCompPer, double nPrinciple, int nTotalPer)
{
     // This function accepts four parameters as input: interest rate,
     // compounding periods per year, the total number of compounding
     // periods, and the amount of the original loan.  It returns the
     // total cost of the loan.  In other words, the amount of the
     // load and the interest you would  need to pay.  This is a
     // simple interest equation, so the amount of interest is based
     // on the principle alone.

     double    nRatePP;        // Interest rate per period
     double    nHundred = 100;    // Used with coprocessor.
     int    nCount;            // Loop counting variable.

     // Use the input values to calculate the future value of the principle.

     // Start by computing the amount of interest for each accounting period
     // in a year.
```

```
//    nRatePP = nIntRate/nCompPer/100*nSimpRes;
    _asm
    {
    FLD     nIntRate    // Load the intrest rate.
    FDIV    nCompPer     // Divide by the number of compounding periods.
    FDIV    nHundred    // Divide by 100.
    FMUL    nPrinciple   // Multiply by the principle.
    FSTP    nRatePP    // Store the result.
    FLD     nPrinciple    // Load the result variable in preparation
                // for next step.
    }

    // Calculate the return on our investment.

    for (nCount = 0; nCount < nTotalPer; nCount++)
        {
//        nSimpRes = nSimpRes + nRatePP;
        _asm
        {
        FADD     nRatePP     // We already loaded nSimpRes in the previous
                // section.
        }
        }

    // Before we can convert our double, we need to perform one more
    // math coprocessor step.  We have to store the result of our
    // computation.

    _asm
    {
    FSTP     nPrinciple
    }

    return nPrinciple;
}


__declspec( dllexport ) double mathAnnuity(double nIntRate,
      double nCompPer, double nPayment, int nTotalPer)
{
    // This function accepts four inputs: interest rate, compounding
    // periods per year, total number of compounding periods, and the
    // payment—amount of deposit—for each compounding period. It
    // returns the total amount of the annuity at the end of the term.

    double    nRatePP;        // Interest rate per period
    double    nCount;          // Loop counting variable.
    double    nHundred = 100;   // Used with coprocessor.
    double    nOne = 1;        // Used with coprocessor.
    double    nResult = 0;    // Annuity Result

    // Use the input values to calculate the total annuity value..
    for (nCount = 0; nCount < nTotalPer; nCount++)
        {

        // Start by computing the amount of interest for each accounting period
        // in a year.
```

continues

Listing 16.4. continued

```
//    nRatePP = nIntRate/nCompPer/100;
    _asm
    {
    FLD    nIntRate    // Load the interest rate.
    FDIV   nCompPer    // Divide it by the componding period.
    FDIV   nHundred    // Divide it by 100.
    FADD   nOne    // Add 1 in preparation for next step
    FSTP   nRatePP     // Store the result.
    }

    // Calculate the return on our investment for this period.
    // This function is designed to be called as part of a loop from within VO.

//    nResult = nResult * (nRatePP + 1);
//    nResult = nResult + nPayment;
    _asm
    {
    FLD    nResult     // Load the result variable.
    FMUL   nRatePP     // Multiply by the incremental rate.
    FADD   nPayment    // Add the current payment.
    FSTP   nResult     // Store the result.
    }
    }

    return nResult;
}
```

Deciding on a Math Programming Technique

What we have in Listing 16.4 are two completely different ways of using C to your advantage. The first three routines are written in such a way that they provide intermediate results and use standard C calls. I find that this comes in handy when I need to show the user a lot of information. The disadvantage to this method is that you don't gain the full benefit of using C.

The second set of three routines provides Delphi with a finished result. In other words, given a specific set of input parameters, what can we expect as an output value? This is the type of function that you find in most spreadsheets. No intermediate response is asked for or given—we're only interested in the bottom line.

There's something else you should notice about the second set of three routines. I used the math coprocessor directly. Using C's _asm directive has some definite advantages in the speed area. Notice that I included the C counterpart to the assembly language instructions as part of the comments for these routines. I usually do that to help document what each section of code does in the native language of the compiler. That way, a programmer following behind me can quickly figure out what I was trying to accomplish. You can usually get an additional 10%–15% of speed out of an application by going this route. That's not too important if you only plan to use a routine a few times. However, if you're using it as part of a loop, the savings can really add up.

What are the disadvantages of the second route? Using the _asm directive means that you now need to know three languages: Delphi, C, and assembler. I know all three because I've used them for quite a few years. While having a few languages at your disposal gives you a lot of added flexibility in writing applications, most programmers have tossed assembler on the scrap heap in favor of more powerful languages. In addition, keeping up with three programming languages is, to say the least, a time consuming process. You might be better off using that time to hone your skills in other areas. It's a judgment call on your part. You need to decide whether the techniques I've just shown you provide enough of an application speed increase to justify the time you'll spend maintaining the required skills. I feel that it's worthwhile especially when writing real time applications like inventory control systems. On the other hand, I probably wouldn't waste my time for a batch processing application—speed isn't as critical an issue in this case. Obviously, you also have to weigh the cost in programmer productivity—writing assembler isn't the most time efficient way to write an application.

Note: Normally I place some type of error trapping in a DLL so that it provides user friendly feedback in the event of an error. There are two reasons why I don't provide that kind of feedback in this case. First, adding error trapping code would slow the routine down—negating part of the reason to use this kind of DLL in the first place. Second, the very nature of this kind of DLL makes it more difficult to monitor the input from within the DLL than without. The fact that this kind of DLL is normally used by its originator is another reason I don't include much in the way of feedback. Obviously this might not be true in your situation, so you need to weigh the needs of other people using your DLL accordingly. So, what does this lack of error trapping mean? You'll need to spend the time to check the values you want to use outside the loop where the DLL appears. This is the most efficient way to handle error trapping in this case.

Tip: You can reduce the burden of using assembler code in your DLLs by using it wisely. For example, in our example I only use the math coprocessor assembler calls—a very small and easily remembered subset of what's available to the programmer. Use a profiler to decide which sections of code need the extra speed enhancements that assembler can provide while reducing the burden of using it to a minimum.

Testing the Math Routines

Now that we have a DLL to test, let's write an application to test it. Figure 16.4 shows the main form we'll use in this example. I could have placed more than a menu on this form, but I wanted to reduce clutter in this case. We'll display the results of the various math calculations using other forms. All you need on this one is a simple menu. The File menu contains one entry, Exit. The figure shows the entries on the Math Function menu.

Figure 16.4.
The main form for our math function DLL tester contains a simple menu.

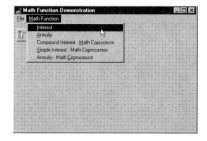

Listing 16.5 shows the code for this form. I had to add quite a bit of interface code to make this example work. Instead of creating a lot of forms with specific entries, I created two generic support forms. The added code in this listing allows me to customize those support forms to account for the kind of information they'll display. You could use a similar technique whenever you have a lot of different kinds of data to display that uses a similar format. This is especially handy for database management programs where the same form could serve as an editor for different tables with similar formats.

Listing 16.5. Code for the form.

```
unit MathDem1;

interface

uses
  Windows, Messages, SysUtils, Classes, Graphics, Controls, Forms, Dialogs,
  Menus, ExtCtrls;

const
  MathDLL = 'MATHFUNC.DLL';

type
  TForm1 = class(TForm)
    MainMenu1: TMainMenu;
    File1: TMenuItem;
    Exit1: TMenuItem;
    MathFunction1: TMenuItem;
    Interest1: TMenuItem;
    Annuity1: TMenuItem;
    InterestMathCoprocesor1: TMenuItem;
    AnnuityMathCoprocessor1: TMenuItem;
```

```
    SimpleInterestMathCoprocessor1: TMenuItem;
    procedure Exit1Click(Sender: TObject);
    procedure Interest1Click(Sender: TObject);
    procedure Annuity1Click(Sender: TObject);
    procedure InterestMathCoprocesor1Click(Sender: TObject);
    procedure SimpleInterestMathCoprocessor1Click(Sender: TObject);
    procedure AnnuityMathCoprocessor1Click(Sender: TObject);
  private
    { Private declarations }
  public
    { Public declarations }
  end;

{Declare the exported functions in our DLL.}
function CompInt(nIntRate, nCompPer, nPrinciple: Double): Double stdcall; external
MathDLL name 'CompInt';
function SimpInt(nIntRate, nCompPer, nPrinciple: Double): Double stdcall; external
MathDLL name 'SimpInt';
function Annuity(nIntRate, nCompPer, nPayment, nValue: Double): Double stdcall; external
MathDLL name 'Annuity';
function MathCompInt(nIntRate, nCompPer, nPrinciple: Double; nTotalPer: Integer): Double
stdcall; external MathDLL name 'mathCompInt';
function MathSimpInt(nIntRate, nCompPer, nPrinciple: Double; nTotalPer: Integer): Double
stdcall; external MathDLL name 'mathSimpInt';
function MathAnnuity(nIntRate, nCompPer, nPayment: Double; nTotalPer: Integer): Double
stdcall; external MathDLL name 'mathAnnuity';

var
  Form1: TForm1;

implementation

uses MathDem2, MathDem3;

{$R *.DFM}

procedure TForm1.Exit1Click(Sender: TObject);
begin
    {Terminate the application.}
    Application.Terminate;
end;

procedure TForm1.Interest1Click(Sender: TObject);
begin
    {Change the variable captions.}
    frmInterest.Label1.Caption := 'Interest Rate (%):';
    frmInterest.Label2.Caption := 'Compounding Periods/Year:';
    frmInterest.Label3.Caption := 'Principle:';

    {Configure the string grid.}
    frmInterest.StringGrid1.Cells[1, 0] := 'Compound Interest';
    frmInterest.StringGrid1.Cells[2, 0] := 'Simple Interest';
    frmInterest.StringGrid1.ColWidths[0] := 50;
    frmInterest.StringGrid1.ColWidths[1] := 155;
    frmInterest.StringGrid1.ColWidths[2] := 155;

    {Set the Calculate event procedure.}
    frmInterest.pbCalculate.OnClick := frmInterest.InterestCalculate;
```

continues

Listing 16.5. **continued**

```
    {Change our form caption and display it.}
    frmInterest.Caption := 'Compound and Simple Interest Calculation';
    frmInterest.ShowModal;
end;

procedure TForm1.Annuity1Click(Sender: TObject);
begin
    {Change the variable captions.}
    frmInterest.Label1.Caption := 'Interest Rate (%):';
    frmInterest.Label2.Caption := 'Annuity Periods/Year:';
    frmInterest.Label3.Caption := 'Payment Amount:';

    {Configure the string grid.}
    frmInterest.StringGrid1.Cells[1, 0] := 'Annuity Value';
    frmInterest.StringGrid1.ColWidths[0] := 75;
    frmInterest.StringGrid1.ColWidths[1] := 200;
    frmInterest.StringGrid1.ColCount := 2;

    {Set the Calculate event procedure.}
    frmInterest.pbCalculate.OnClick := frmInterest.AnnuityCalculate;

    {Change our form caption and display it.}
    frmInterest.Caption := 'Annuity Calculation';
    frmInterest.ShowModal;

    {Reset the number of columns.}
    frmInterest.StringGrid1.ColCount := 3;
end;

procedure TForm1.InterestMathCoprocesor1Click(Sender: TObject);
begin
    {Change the variable captions.}
    dlgIntCalc.Label1.Caption := 'Interest Rate (%):';
    dlgIntCalc.Label2.Caption := 'Compounding Periods/Year:';
    dlgIntCalc.Label3.Caption := 'Principle:';
    dlgIntCalc.Label5.Caption := 'Total Loan Amount:';

    {Set the Calculate event procedure.}
    dlgIntCalc.pbCalculate.OnClick := dlgIntCalc.CompoundInterest;

    {Change our form caption and display it.}
    dlgIntCalc.Caption := 'Compound Interest Calculation';
    dlgIntCalc.ShowModal;
end;

procedure TForm1.SimpleInterestMathCoprocessor1Click(Sender: TObject);
begin
    {Change the variable captions.}
    dlgIntCalc.Label1.Caption := 'Interest Rate (%):';
    dlgIntCalc.Label2.Caption := 'Compounding Periods/Year:';
    dlgIntCalc.Label3.Caption := 'Principle:';
    dlgIntCalc.Label5.Caption := 'Total Loan Amount:';

    {Set the Calculate event procedure.}
    dlgIntCalc.pbCalculate.OnClick := dlgIntCalc.SimpleInterest;
```

```
    {Change our form caption and display it.}
    dlgIntCalc.Caption := 'Simple Interest Calculation';
    dlgIntCalc.ShowModal;
end;

procedure TForm1.AnnuityMathCoprocessor1Click(Sender: TObject);
begin
    {Change the variable captions.}
    dlgIntCalc.Label1.Caption := 'Interest Rate (%):';
    dlgIntCalc.Label2.Caption := 'Annuity Periods/Year:';
    dlgIntCalc.Label3.Caption := 'Payment:';
    dlgIntCalc.Label5.Caption := 'Total Annuity Amount:';

    {Set the Calculate event procedure.}
    dlgIntCalc.pbCalculate.OnClick := dlgIntCalc.AnnuityCalculation;

    {Change our form caption and display it.}
    dlgIntCalc.Caption := 'Annuity Calculation';
    dlgIntCalc.ShowModal;
end;

end.
```

Most of this code is pretty straightforward. However, you'll want to pay special attention to the way that I handle the string grid. In one procedure, Interest1Click, I need three columns to display the required information. The other procedure, Annuity1Click, requires only two columns. The Annunity1Click procedure contains special code to handle this situation, freeing me from having to take care of it in two different places.

Using generic forms also means that you'll need to perform a little extra work with any push-buttons that the form contains. In this example I have a Calculate pushbutton. The frmInterest.pbCalculate.OnClick := frmInterest.AnnuityCalculate; line of code in the Annuity1Click procedure is one example of how I ensure the pushbutton does what the user expects it to. You'll want to check out the entries in the other procedures as well. In essence, the combination of con-figuration code and procedure assignment code allows me to take a generic form and make it into something quite specific. From the user's point of view you may as well use different forms. Of course, using multiple forms like this saves you a certain amount of memory. The cost is increased program-mer time. Using separate forms would make the job of writing the application faster from a program-mer perspective since you wouldn't have to customize each one individually.

Let's take a look at one of the generic forms we'll use to display data in this example. Figure 16.5 shows the generic form we'll use to display the individual calculation results for first three functions in our DLL. This comes in handy when you want to be able to pick points along the calculation route for analysis. For example, an insurance agent would use such a form to show a client what he'll earn during a given time period on an IRA or full life insurance policy. Remember, that the first three functions in our DLL used standard C code and returned an intermediate result for each step of the calculation. I started out with a standard form instead of a dialog in this case. It contains an assortment of single line edits, labels, and pushbuttons. The calculation results get displayed in the string grid. You'll also notice that I included an up/down control to make it easy to enter values in the Total Periods single line edit. Table 16.2 shows the changes I made to the various controls on this form.

Figure 16.5.

This generic form will display the intermediate results from the first three functions in the math DLL.

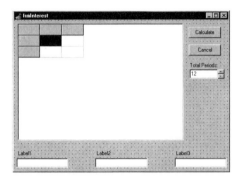

Tip: When creating a generic form or dialog, use its name as a caption. This allows you to see which form you're working with at a glance and reduces the chance that you'll make a mistake when modifying it. I find that this same idea works well when creating generic versions of forms or dialogs as templates.

Table 16.2. Generic Intermediate Result Form Control Settings.

Object	Property	Setting
frmInterest	BorderStyle	bsSingle
StringGrid1	ColCount	3
	DefaultColWidth	50
	RowCount	3
	Options	[goFixedVertLine, goFixedHorzLine, goVertLine, goHorzLine]
pbCalculate	Caption	'Calculate'
	Enabled	False
pbCancel	Caption	'Cancel'
	ModalResult	mrCancel
edPeriods	Text	'12'
UpDown1	Associate	edPeriods
	Min	12

Object	Property	Setting
	Max	360
	Increment	12
	Position	12
	Wrap	False
edVar1	OnChange	edVar1Change
edVar2	OnChange	edVar1Change
edVar3	OnChange	edVar1Change

Now that you've got a form put together, let's take a look at the code that makes it work. Listing 16.6 shows the code for this part of the example. Notice that we don't have any code for the two pushbuttons, at least not using the standard procedure names that Delphi assigns. I took care of the Cancel pushbutton by changing its ModalResult property. Pressing this pushbutton automatically closes the form and sends the result to the calling program.

Listing 16.6. More code for the example.

```
unit MathDem2;

interface

uses
  Windows, Messages, SysUtils, Classes, Graphics, Controls, Forms, Dialogs,
  StdCtrls, Grids, ComCtrls;

type
  TfrmInterest = class(TForm)
    pbCalculate: TButton;
    pbCancel: TButton;
    StringGrid1: TStringGrid;
    edVar1: TEdit;
    edVar2: TEdit;
    edVar3: TEdit;
    Label1: TLabel;
    Label2: TLabel;
    Label3: TLabel;
    Label4: TLabel;
    edPeriods: TEdit;
    UpDown1: TUpDown;
    procedure edVar1Change(Sender: TObject);
    procedure InterestCalculate(Sender: TObject);
    procedure AnnuityCalculate(Sender: TObject);
  private
    { Private declarations }
  public
    { Public declarations }
  end;
```

continues

Listing 16.6. continued

```pascal
var
  frmInterest: TfrmInterest;

implementation

uses MathDem1;

{$R *.DFM}

procedure TfrmInterest.edVar1Change(Sender: TObject);
begin
    {Enable the Calculate button if the user inputs three values.}
    if (Length(edVar1.Text) > 0) and (Length(edVar2.Text) > 0) and (Length(edVar3.Text) >
0) then
        pbCalculate.Enabled := True
    else
        pbCalculate.Enabled := False;
end;

procedure TfrmInterest.AnnuityCalculate(Sender: TObject);
var
    nInterest: Double;          {Interest rate.}
    nPayment: Double;           {Periodic payment amount.}
    nPeriods: Double;           {Annuity periods per year.}
    nTotalPeriods: Integer;     {Total number of periods.}
    iCount: Integer;            {Loop counter variable.}
    nValue: Double;             {Current annuity value.}
    sValue: String;             {Current annuity value as a string.}
    iCode: Integer;             {Val function return value.}
begin

    {Get the total number of periods and configure the string grid.}
    nTotalPeriods := StrToInt(edPeriods.Text);
    StringGrid1.RowCount := nTotalPeriods + 1;
    for iCount := 1 to nTotalPeriods do
        StringGrid1.Cells[0, iCount] := IntToStr(iCount);

    {Get the initial calculation values.}
    Val(edVar1.Text, nInterest, iCode);
    Val(edVar2.Text, nPeriods, iCode);
    Val(edVar3.Text, nPayment, iCode);
    nValue := 0;

    {Calculate the compound interest.}
    for iCount := 1 to nTotalPeriods do
        begin
          nValue := Annuity(nInterest, nPeriods, nPayment, nValue);
          Str(nValue:20:2, sValue);
          StringGrid1.Cells[1, iCount] := sValue;
          end;
end;

procedure TfrmInterest.InterestCalculate(Sender: TObject);
var
    nInterest: Double;          {Interest rate.}
    nPrinciple: Double;         {Loan prinicple.}
```

```
      nPeriods: Double;          {Compounding periods per year.}
      nTotalPeriods: Integer;    {Total number of periods.}
      iCount: Integer;           {Loop counter variable.}
      sValue: String;            {Current principle value.}
      iCode: Integer;            {Val function return value.}
      nSimpInt: Double;          {Simple interest value.}
begin

      {Get the total number of periods and configure the string grid.}
      nTotalPeriods := StrToInt(edPeriods.Text);
      StringGrid1.RowCount := nTotalPeriods + 1;
      for iCount := 1 to nTotalPeriods do
          StringGrid1.Cells[0, iCount] := IntToStr(iCount);

      {Get the initial calculation values.}
      Val(edVar1.Text, nInterest, iCode);
      Val(edVar2.Text, nPeriods, iCode);
      Val(edVar3.Text, nPrinciple, iCode);

      {Calculate the compound interest.}
      for iCount := 1 to nTotalPeriods do
          begin
            nPrinciple := CompInt(nInterest, nPeriods, nPrinciple);
            Str(nPrinciple:20:2, sValue);
            StringGrid1.Cells[1, iCount] := sValue;
            end;

      {Reset the principle value.}
      Val(edVar3.Text, nPrinciple, iCode);

      {Calculate the simple interest for one period.}
      nSimpInt := SimpInt(nInterest, nPeriods, nPrinciple);

      {Calculate the simple interest.}
      for iCount := 1 to nTotalPeriods do
          begin
            nPrinciple := nPrinciple + nSimpInt;
            Str(nPrinciple:20:2, sValue);
            StringGrid1.Cells[2, iCount] := sValue;
            end;
end;

end.
```

The Calculate pushbutton requires a bit more care. First of all, we can't enable it until all four of the single line edits contain some kind of data to send to the DLL. The edVar1Change procedure takes care of this need. Notice that I assigned it to the OnChange event of three of the single line edits. The forth single line edit always contains data of the right type, so there isn't any need to monitor it. In this case I check for the presence of text in each of the single line edits for the sake of simplicity. You'd probably want to check for the presence of numbers in a specific range. Second, the procedure that we need to follow when the user presses the Calculate pushbutton varies by the type of calculation we need to perform. I take care of this need in the MathDem1 unit that we looked at before. That's where the pushbutton OnClick event assignment that I talked about previously comes into play. The InterestCalculate procedure takes care of simple and compound interest calculations. The AnnuityCalculate procedure takes care of the annuity calculation.

There are a few generic items that we need to take care of in these procedures. I could have handled one of them as a separate procedure, but chose not to. Our string grid only contains three rows when we open the form—hardly enough to take care of the calculations that we'll perform. Notice that I change the number of rows to match the number of periods that the user selected, then fill the first column with appropriate numbers. You could add this code to the up/down control's OnChange event, but I chose to add it here as a matter of convenience. If you do decide to add it to the OnChange event, you'll also need to add a reference to the procedure to the form's OnShow event so that the string grid will contain the appropriate number of entries when Delphi displays it.

So, what does this form look like in action? Figure 16.6 shows the result of a simple and compound interest calculation. Notice that the form contains none of the lose threads that the design version contains. All of the labels are filled in and the dialog box itself has an appropriate title. I didn't bother to fill in most of these items during the design stage because I knew I would fill them in later as part of the program.

Figure 16.6.
A form showing the intermediate results of a compound and simple interest calculation.

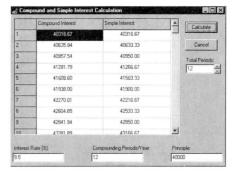

The second generic form for this example appears in Figure 16.7. I used a standard dialog as a starting point. Again, I didn't take a lot of time to make this form look pretty in the design stage because the program modifies it as needed. The form contains five single line edits, some labels, and an up/down control. Table 16.3 contains all the changes I made to the various controls on the form.

Figure 16.7.
This generic form will display the final results from the last three functions in the math DLL.

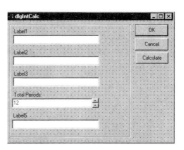

Table 16.3. Generic Final Result Dialog Box Control Settings.

Object	Property	Setting
edVar1	OnChange	edVar1Change
edVar2	OnChange	edVar1Change
edVar3	OnChange	edVar1Change
edPeriods	Text	'12'
UpDown1	Associate	edPeriods
	Min	12
	Max	360
	Increment	12
	Position	12
	Wrap	False
edResult	TabStop	False
	ReadOnly	True
pbCalculate	Caption	'Calculate'

Once you've got the form put together, we need to add some code to it. Listing 16.7 shows the code for this form. There are a few items that it contains that I've already talked about. For example, I use the same procedure to check the first three single line edits for some type of data. It's important to do this as part of the error trapping needed before you call the DLL.

Listing 16.7. Code for the form.

```
unit MathDem3;

interface

uses Windows, SysUtils, Classes, Graphics, Forms, Controls, StdCtrls,
  Buttons, ExtCtrls, ComCtrls;

type
  TdlgIntCalc = class(TForm)
    OKBtn: TButton;
    CancelBtn: TButton;
    Bevel1: TBevel;
    edVar1: TEdit;
    Label1: TLabel;
    pbCalculate: TButton;
    edVar2: TEdit;
    edVar3: TEdit;
    Label2: TLabel;
    Label3: TLabel;
    edPeriods: TEdit;
```

continues

Listing 16.7. continued

```
    Label4: TLabel;
    UpDown1: TUpDown;
    edResult: TEdit;
    Label5: TLabel;
    procedure edVar1Change(Sender: TObject);
    procedure CompoundInterest(Sender: TObject);
    procedure SimpleInterest(Sender:TObject);
    procedure AnnuityCalculation(Sender: TObject);
  private
    { Private declarations }
  public
    { Public declarations }
  end;

var
  dlgIntCalc: TdlgIntCalc;

implementation

uses MathDem1;

{$R *.DFM}

procedure TdlgIntCalc.edVar1Change(Sender: TObject);
begin
    {Enable the Calculate button if the user inputs three values.}
    if (Length(edVar1.Text) > 0) and (Length(edVar2.Text) > 0) and (Length(edVar3.Text) >
0) then
        pbCalculate.Enabled := True
    else
        pbCalculate.Enabled := False;
end;

procedure TdlgIntCalc.CompoundInterest(Sender: TObject);
var
    nInterest: Double;          {Interest rate.}
    nPrinciple: Double;         {Loan prinicple.}
    nPeriods: Double;           {Compounding periods per year.}
    nTotalPeriods: Integer;     {Total number of periods.}
    sValue: String;             {Current principle value.}
    iCode: Integer;             {Val function return value.}
begin

    {Get the total number of periods.}
    nTotalPeriods := StrToInt(edPeriods.Text);

    {Get the initial calculation values.}
    Val(edVar1.Text, nInterest, iCode);
    Val(edVar2.Text, nPeriods, iCode);
    Val(edVar3.Text, nPrinciple, iCode);


    {Calculate the compound interest.}
    nPrinciple := MathCompInt(nInterest, nPeriods, nPrinciple, nTotalPeriods);
    Str(nPrinciple:20:2, sValue);
    edResult.Text := Trim(sValue);
```

```
end;

procedure TdlgIntCalc.SimpleInterest(Sender: TObject);
var
    nInterest: Double;          {Interest rate.}
    nPrinciple: Double;         {Loan prinicple.}
    nPeriods: Double;           {Compounding periods per year.}
    nTotalPeriods: Integer;     {Total number of periods.}
    sValue: String;             {Current principle value.}
    iCode: Integer;             {Val function return value.}
begin

    {Get the total number of periods.}
    nTotalPeriods := StrToInt(edPeriods.Text);

    {Get the initial calculation values.}
    Val(edVar1.Text, nInterest, iCode);
    Val(edVar2.Text, nPeriods, iCode);
    Val(edVar3.Text, nPrinciple, iCode);

    {Calculate the compound interest.}
    nPrinciple := MathSimpInt(nInterest, nPeriods, nPrinciple, nTotalPeriods);
    Str(nPrinciple:20:2, sValue);
    edResult.Text := Trim(sValue);
end;

procedure TdlgIntCalc.AnnuityCalculation(Sender: TObject);
var
    nInterest: Double;          {Interest rate.}
    nPayment: Double;           {Periodic payment.}
    nPeriods: Double;           {Compounding periods per year.}
    nTotalPeriods: Integer;     {Total number of periods.}
    sValue: String;             {Current principle value.}
    iCode: Integer;             {Val function return value.}
begin

    {Get the total number of periods.}
    nTotalPeriods := StrToInt(edPeriods.Text);

    {Get the initial calculation values.}
    Val(edVar1.Text, nInterest, iCode);
    Val(edVar2.Text, nPeriods, iCode);
    Val(edVar3.Text, nPayment, iCode);

    {Calculate the compound interest.}
    nPayment := MathAnnuity(nInterest, nPeriods, nPayment, nTotalPeriods);
    Str(nPayment:20:2, sValue);
    edResult.Text := Trim(sValue);
end;

end.
```

The procedures in this unit are pretty short since the DLL does all the work for you. All of the code is used to either prepare data for input to the DLL or to display the result of the DLL's calculation. Notice that I use a separate procedure for simple and compound interest in this case. That's because the form design doesn't really lend itself to displaying more than one result.

Let's take a look at this form in action. Figure 16.8 shows the results of a compound interest calculation. Obviously this form lacks the appeal of the previous one when it comes to getting the intermediate results. However, I think you'll also notice that it's faster in displaying results. This is the kind of calculation that someone performing a "what if" analysis would need to use. The intermediate results aren't important, only the bottom line is.

Figure 16.8.

A form showing the final results of a compound interest calculation.

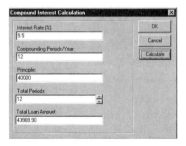

Summary

We've just taken a whirlwind tour of using a C DLL from within Delphi. I haven't even begun to show you everything you could potentially accomplish using C DLLs—that would take an entire book. The fact that most DLLs rely on C code will give you plenty of practice using them from within your Delphi applications. However, I wanted you to get more than that out of this chapter.

C DLLs represent the one way that you can actually improve Delphi's performance. Borland has done such a good job of writing Delphi that it's difficult to find areas where you can improve it by very much. I find that math routines are still a weak area and will probably remain so for the near future because of the way that Delphi handles calculations. Combining Delphi with C and assembler is one way to improve the speed of your application by a noticeable amount if it performs a lot of calculations. Certainly math and graphics applications fall into this category, but most text editors don't.

Even if you didn't get anything else out of this chapter, the C DLL examples should help you realize an application programmer's needs. A single language isn't enough to answer every programming situation you might encounter. For example, Delphi won't allow you to access 16-bit routines, no matter how much you need to access them. In some cases this means getting a 32-bit driver for an older piece of equipment. But what if the vendor doesn't provide a 32-bit driver? Will your company be willing to buy new equipment to gain the benefits of using Delphi? Using a C DLL to build a thunking layer to that 16-bit driver is a solution that Delphi doesn't offer. The bottom line is that there will always be something that another language will do better. Having more than one language in your tool kit is always a good idea.

17

Building a
Delphi VBX

Visual Basic eXtensions (VBXs) are what make that programming language easy to use. They're so popular, in fact, that just about every other programming language provides the means to use them—that is, every other 16-bit programming language. The reason for the popularity of VBXs is easy to understand. Instead of writing a lot of code or using an esoteric screen drawing application, the programmer need only grab a VBX from a toolbar (Component Palette to use the Delphi version of the term) and drop it on a form. Setting a few properties will make the control within the VBX active and a little code will make it do something when specific events occur. VBXs are also modular—opening a whole range of possibilities for third party vendors to expand the capabilities of Visual Basic (and every other programming language that supports VBXs).

Life was good and getting better until WIN32 came along—you could literally find a VBX that would do anything you asked of it. Microsoft chose not to use VBXs in its 32-bit strategy. The new tools of the day are OLE Custom eXtensions (OCXs). These Visual Basic extensions are really new forms of the VBX with an OLE twist. Needless to say, 32-bit language vendors are rushing to include OCX support in their products. By the time you read this, you'll probably be able to get an OCX to replace that aging VBX on your machine. Of course, there are a few problems with this strategy if you're a small consulting firm. How do you write off the cost of buying a whole new suite of tools just because Microsoft changed its strategy? A lot of folks are asking that question right now and I'll explore an answer to it in just a bit.

Like everyone else, Borland provides VBX support in Delphi 1.0 (16-bit) and OCX support in Delphi 2.0 (32-bit). They even include a few "free samples" samples with the Delphi package. You'll find your VBX or OCX samples on the appropriate tab of the Component Palette—Delphi 2.0 places them on the OCX tab. Just like everyone else, you can grab a VBX (or OCX) and stick it on a form. Voila, you have a functional control without any programming.

Looking Ahead: If you want to learn more about using OCXs with Delphi, take a look at Chapter 18, "Delphi and OCXs." I'll tell you how to use the samples provided as part of the package and provide some tips on how to use them efficiently. I was a bit surprised at the quality of the samples, but even more so at some of the gotchas that they came equipped with. OCXs represent one of the best ways to extend Delphi in a generic way—which isn't necessarily that bad.

Delphi also provides an alternative to the VBX and OCX question—something I feel is a lot better for a lot of reasons (more about these reasons later). The topic of this chapter is components. We've used them throughout the book, but haven't really discussed them from a programmer's perspective.

Looking Ahead: Appendix A, "A Guide to VBXs and OCXs," will provide you with a list of some of the more interesting VBXs, OCXs, and Delphi components offered by third party vendors. While it can't provide a complete list of everything, Appendix A will whet your appetite for additional information. I have a 55-page catalog of Delphi components sitting on my desk right now. The one for VBXs and OCXs is even larger. Suffice it to say that you owe it to yourself to explore the world of third party offerings out there. The time you save programming will more than make up for the cost of buying the add-on.

I'm going to tell you four things about components. First, we're going to spend a little time talking about what components really are. Next we'll take a look at the question of why components are better for the Delphi programming than either VBXs or OCXs in most cases. (I'll also give you a few reasons why components could cause problems for you along the way.) Once we finish looking at the theoretical side of components, we'll look at the whole question of libraries and what they mean to you as a Delphi user. Finally, I'll show you how to create new components and to maintain your current component list.

There's one final note of caution here. Obviously I can't cover in one chapter what Borland took an entire book to do. The *Component Writer's Guide* talks about some of the things you'll need to consider when writing a component for distribution—it comes in both book and help file format. However, even Borland probably didn't cover every detail about creating components either since they can become quite complex. What I want to try to do for you in this chapter is give you a first step—the one that you'll take by looking at the *Component Writer's Guide* right now is very long indeed. I feel that anyone can create simple components for their own use. However, once you get beyond that stage it's time to break out the heavy artillery. Look at this chapter as a beginning—a way to learn about components without getting mired in too much detail at first.

What Are Components?

Unless you spend some time reading the Delphi documentation, you might get the idea that components are some kind of built-in Delphi functionality—like the tools on the toolbar of a word processor. A component is far from that. Let's look at what a component really is from a programmer perspective.

What's the one thing that sets a VBX or OCX apart from a built-in feature? Its modularity, of course. The fact that you can add or remove VBXs as needed on a project by project basis makes them extremely flexible tools. Components also share this characteristic feature of the VBX and OCX. In fact, as far as modularity goes, they are actually a bit ahead of VBXs and OCXs. A VBX normally stores a lot of controls that you have to add or remove as a set. Many of the components you'll use are individual elements.

Another quality of a VBX is that it provides visual feedback to the programmer. When you place a pushbutton on a form, you know exactly what it'll look like when compiled. You don't have to guess about its location or what the user will see. Even non-visual VBXs like timers have a physical appearance in design mode. You don't have to guess whether you added one or two timers to the code, they're right there on the form to see. Needless to say, components also share this feature. We've seen throughout the book that both visual and non-visual components give the programmer instant feedback. Like a VBX, you don't have to guess where the component is, how many you've added, or what the user will see when they run your application.

A VBX (or OCX) is more than just a physical presentation like one of the templates we discussed in Chapter 3, "Building a Basic Program;" it's also compiled code. In Chapters 15 and 16, "Creating Your Own DLLs Using Delphi" and "Creating Your Own DLLs Using C," we discussed the idea of a DLL, which is a library of compiled functions. DLLs have one problem: You can't really interact with the functions they contain except through a function call interface. The benefit of using a DLL is code reuse—a feature that VBXs share. It's a combination of a physical presentation and code reuse that makes VBXs so popular. Components also provide this same level of duality. Using a component is like adding both a template and a DLL to your application at once.

Throughout this discussion I've described components by comparing them to VBXs and OCXs. They really aren't exactly alike. I wanted to explore the similarities between these two coding aids first so that you would get a better idea of what components really are. In the next section we'll look at the differences between these two coding aids. I'll answer the question of why you would want to use one in place of the other in certain cases.

Advantages of Using Components in Place of VBXs or OCXs

Using a RAD programming environment means using predefined controls whenever possible to reduce your programming load. Components are the Delphi way to add controls to your application. It's important to realize what kind of benefits you'll get by using them. I always like to look at the positive side of an issue first, so let's look at the reasons you would want to use a Delphi component in place of a VBX or OCX.

- Compatibility—Components are created with Delphi. We'll look at the exact process later, but the fact that they are should tell you something about their compatibility. Not only are there fewer problems with Delphi, but there are fewer problems with Windows. Just think about all those users who have VBXs on their machine. When they upgrade to a 32-bit programming language, they'll also have to buy new versions of their components. Delphi components usually don't have this problem; all your old components should work just fine. (Obviously you need the component's source code and you'll have to recompile it with Delphi 2.0 to make it work in that environment.)

- Source Code Availability—I won't say that this is a free or even necessary feature for most people, but it is available in more than a few cases. For a slight extra charge you can buy the Delphi source for your component from many vendors. Not only does this allow you to recompile the components when needed, but it allows you to study the coding techniques used by other people. I consider this particular feature alone worth the cost of using Delphi components in many situations.

- Delphi Specific Functionality—A VBX or OCX has to provide a generalized solution to any given problem since it's designed to work with more than one language. A component, on the other hand, can answer the specific needs of Delphi. You don't have to worry about whether a component will completely fix some problem with Delphi because it's specifically designed for that environment.

- Roll Your Own Accessibility—You can create your own components using Delphi—you can't create VBXs or OCXs as easily. I won't say that you can't do it at all, but the ease of creating a component in Delphi is almost ridiculous. I can't say the same thing when it comes to writing an OCX or VBX. You'll spend long hours trying to figure out how to get the job done, then a lot more hours trying to test the new VBX or OCX with a variety of language products. Suffice it to say, Delphi components are the way to go when you need to create a control for your own use.

- Visual Impact—Have you ever used an application that contains one or more forms that just don't fit? Chances are they were created using a VBX or OCX that didn't follow the rules—or simply followed a different set of rules than those of the language the rest of the application was created with. Using components keeps this from happening to a certain extent. Since you use Delphi components as the basis for new components, they all tend to look and feel alike—an important consideration from both the programmer and user perspective. Nothing's worse from a user's point of view than expecting one thing to happen and getting a totally different reaction. This includes the visual effect of the control they're using. If the control doesn't look like it's supposed to be part of the application, the user is going to be distracted.

- Enhanced Integration—A VBX or OCX is an outsider as far as Delphi is concerned. Sure, it sits there on your Component Palette looking just like any component you might use, but Delphi treats it differently. This schism between Delphi and the VBX or OCX you decide to use really isn't that big of a deal, but it could become one in some cases. Suffice it to say that anytime you can remove another potential area of conflict from your programming environment, it pays to do so.

Disadvantages of Using Components in Place of VBXs or OCXs

Now it's time to look at the disadvantages of using Delphi components in place of VBXs and OCXs. The following list tells you what you'll give up to use them. Obviously you'll have to weigh the cost of using a component versus the benefits you'll gain. If you're like me, you'll probably decide that the choice lies somewhere in the middle. There are times when a VBX or OCX really is the better choice and others when you'd be crazy for not picking a component solution.

Tip: You might find it difficult to figure out which items on the Component Palette are OCXs (VBXs) and which are Delphi Components. All you need to do is look at the SYSTEM folder of your Windows directory. You'll find a list of OCX files there. The OCX filenames will help you determine which Component Palette items are components.

- Price—I didn't do a formal survey of every product out there, but it appears that components are a little more expensive than VBXs and OCXs. I'm talking about components without the source code here. You'll always pay more for a component with source code.

- Multi-platform Usage—Let's face it, the only place you can use a component is with Delphi. The one VBX or OCX you buy will work with multiple programming languages. I use more than one language on a regular basis so a VBX or OCX looks pretty good in the cost department if I need a particular feature in more than one place.

- Vendor Stability—This is another one of those things that are a bit difficult to gauge. However, you've got to ask yourself whether a vendor will be around tomorrow to answer any questions you might have about a component. Since the market for VBXs and OCXs is larger than that for Delphi components, it usually attracts larger vendors. A large vendor has a better chance of being around tomorrow when you need to ask a question.

- Wider Availability—The reason that I have a Delphi component catalog sitting on my desk is that I can't find them at my local software store. Sure, not all the VBXs or OCXs appear there, but I can usually find a few. The wider availability of most OCX and VBX components means that you can shop around a bit more to get a better price. It also means that you have a better chance of actually finding the component you need.

- Greater Selection—There are more vendors producing VBXs and OCXs—there just isn't any other way to look at it. More vendors means greater selection.

- Multiple Application Use—Like a DLL, a VBX or OCX resides outside of the application. The application loads it at runtime. Depending on the licensing requirements of the product, more than one program could use the VBX or OCX at a time. This has the same effect as using a DLL, saving system memory. A Delphi component is compiled as part of the application. You load one copy of the component every time you load an application that uses it.

Removing and Installing Existing Components

Now that we've gotten all the theory out of the way, let's look at some actual implementation details. The first thing you'll want to know how to do is remove and install your own components. Delphi comes with a ton of components—some of which you may never use. I find that the tabs provided on the Component Palette keeps them separated, but there isn't any reason to clutter your desktop needlessly. Clutter may not seem like much of a problem when you start using Delphi, but it becomes progressively more difficult to ignore as you add your own custom components to the mix.

There are two different levels of adding and removing components. The first level simply removes them from the palette. The components are still available in the library, but they no longer exist on the Component Palette. This level of change isn't very permanent. You can always retrieve them from the library later. I'll show you how to do this kind of removal and installation in the following sections.

The second level is a bit more permanent. It actually removes or installs a component from the library. You can't retrieve a component you remove this way without reinstalling it. Obviously you'll want to use this option with care. The procedures for doing this appear in the "Using Libraries" section that follows this one.

Removing a Component from the Palette

Let's begin by looking that the method for removing a component from the palette. That's the part you actually see. The Component Palette is where you select components for use. This is the non-permanent method of removing components, so you can use it as needed without worrying too much.

> **Tip:** Fortunately, Delphi provides a fairly good component layout from the start. However, you might find that you use some components more often than others. For example, I use a combination of the components on the Standard and Win95 pages on a regular basis, so I created a new page that contains both. You can reorganize the Component Palette to better meet your needs by removing a component from one page and installing it on another. Delphi also allows you to create new pages as needed to create custom layouts.

1. Use the Component | Configure Palette command to display the Environment Options dialog shown in Figure 17.1. The pane on the right hand side of the dialog contains a complete list of the pages in the Component Palette. The right hand pane contains a list of the components on that page.

2. Click on either a page or a component entry. You have to do this even if the component or page you want to remove is already highlighted. Clicking on a page will remove the entire page and all the components it contains. Clicking on an individual component will allow you to retain the page and remove just that component.

3. Click on the Delete pushbutton. Delphi will remove the component or page without asking you.

Figure 17.1.
The Palette page of the
Environment Options dialog
allows you to change the
appearance of the Compo-
nent Palette.

4. Click on OK to complete the action. You'll see one less page or component.

Tip: You can reverse any changes you make in the Component Palette by pressing the Reset Default pushbutton on the Palette page of the Environment Options dialog. Delphi will display a dialog asking if you're sure. Just click on Yes to complete the action. If you only want to undo the current changes, then click on Cancel instead of OK when you exit the Environment Options dialog during the current editing session.

Adding a New Component Palette Page

I try not to change the default settings that Delphi provides unless there is a good reason to do so. What I do instead is create custom pages that contain the list of components that I use most often. If I find that the custom page doesn't work as anticipated, I can simply delete it and create a new one if desired. This allows me to maintain a base Delphi configuration that I can go back to with ease.

1. Use the Component | Configure Palette command to display the Environment Options dialog shown in Figure 17.1.

2. Click on the left pane, if necessary, to enable the Add pushbutton. The Add pushbutton only affects pages, not components.

3. Click on the Add pushbutton. You'll see an Add page dialog like the one shown in Figure 17.2.

Figure 17.2.
The Add page dialog allows
you to add a new page to the
Component Palette.

4. Type the name of a new component page, and then click on OK. Delphi will add the new page to the end of the component page listing in the left pane.

5. Use the up and down arrows to move the new page to the desired position. You can also use the arrows to move an existing page, bringing those that you use often to the front of the list.

Tip: I always place my custom configuration page at the very front for easy access. My custom configuration of default Delphi components appears first. A page containing components that I create appears next. Keeping Delphi components separate from those I create allows for easier management.

6. Add components to the new page using the technique described in the next section. You can remove any unneeded components using the procedure described in the previous section.

7. Click on OK to complete the action. Delphi will display the new page and associated components on the Component Palette.

Adding a Component to the Palette

Our last, non-destructive method of managing the Component Palette is to add new components to pages as needed. The first thing you need to remember is that a component must appear in a library before you can place it on a page. If the component doesn't appear in a library, you'll need to add it using the procedure in the following section first. Once a component appears in the library, you can always add it to the Component Palette.

1. Use the Component | Configure Palette command to display the Environment Options dialog shown in Figure 17.1.

2. Select the component page that you want to use as a source of a component. If the component doesn't currently appear on a page, then select the [Library] page. Remember that a component must appear in the library before you can add it to a page.

3. Click on the component you want to add to a page, then drag it to the new page. You'll see a component drag icon as shown in Figure 17.3 as you drag the component to its new location.

Note: Selecting a component on an existing page moves it from that page to the target page. Selecting a component on the [Library] page creates a copy of that component on the target page. Always select the [Library] page as a source if you don't want to modify the contents of the existing pages.

Figure 17.3.

The component drag icon
shows you that you're
copying a component from
the current page and
inserting it on a target page.

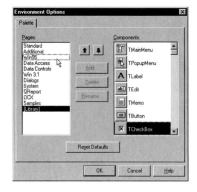

4. Select the target page and verify that the component was inserted properly.

5. Select the new component. Use the up and down arrows to move the new component to the desired position in the list. You can also use the arrows to move an existing component, bringing those that you use often to the front of the list.

6. Click on OK to complete the action. You'll see the new component on the specified page of the Component Palette.

Using Libraries

We saw in the previous section that you can hide components or move them around as needed on the Component Palette without too many problems. However, if you want to make any kind of permanent change, you need to do so at the library level. Think of a library as a container for storing components. You can keep different containers around for different tasks.

There is a very practical side to libraries. Since each component consumes some amount of memory when you load the library, there may come a time when you can't load all the components on your machine at once. When this happens, you'll need some way to manage multiple libraries. There are four different tasks associated with library management: Creating, rebuilding, inserting components, and removing components. The following paragraphs will show you how to perform all four tasks.

Creating a New Library

Before you can do much in the way of using libraries, you need to learn how to create one. I tend to take the simplest approach possible to getting any job done. Creating a new library doesn't have to be a time-consuming task. In fact, you can literally do it in a matter of seconds as long as you follow a few simple rules.

The first rule you need to observe is to never touch your baseline library—the CMPLIB32.DPR file that you received with Delphi. (The DPR file contains the project code—always retain a copy of the original. The DCL file is the compiled result.) Even if this library doesn't serve your purposes at all, you'll want to keep it intact so that you have a baseline library to use when creating others. Think of it this way: Delphi originally loads this library with all the default Delphi components. That's an advantage when you want to create a new library since you'll always have a list of the default components handy.

The second rule to follow is to create task oriented libraries and no more than you absolutely have to have. I have a library for utilities, another for database management work, and a third for multimedia. Each library is optimized to help me get a particular job done. Now that we've gotten a couple of ground rules down, let's look at creating a new library.

1. Use the Component | Install New command to display the Install Components dialog shown in Figure 17.4.

Figure 17.4.
The Install Components dialog allows you to perform a variety of component library related tasks.

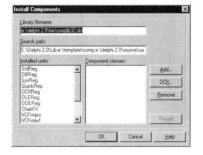

2. Type a new library name in the Library filename field.

Tip: Check the Show Compiler Progress option on the Preferences page of the Environment Option dialog. You can access this dialog using the Tools | Options command. The only way to verify that Delphi is actually creating a new library is to look for this dialog to appear. Otherwise, you might think that Windows is frozen since it takes quite a while to compile and link the library in some cases.

3. Click on OK. Delphi will display the Compiling dialog (if you selected the Show Compiler Progress option). Be patient, it'll take quite a while to create the new library in some cases.

4. Use the procedures in the "Removing a Module from a Library," and the "Inserting a Module into the Library" sections to create a custom configuration.

5. Rebuild the library using the procedure in the Rebuilding a Library section.

Once you build and customize a library, you can use it with any project as needed. Simply create a new application, then use the Component | Open Library command to display the Open Library dialog shown in Figure 17.5. Select the library you want to use from the list. That's the library Delphi will use for the current project.

Figure 17.5.
The Open Library dialog
allows you to choose which
library you want to use with
the current project.

Note: Always store your libraries in the BIN directory since that's where Delphi looks for them. Unlike components or templates, there's only one PAS and one DCL file associated with each library, so removing an old library is easy.

Rebuilding a Library

You might run into a situation where your library gets corrupted in some way. A simple disk error can do that. I placed this procedure in a separate area so that you could find it quickly when an emergency does happen (they invariably do at the worst possible moment). The following procedure takes you through the process of rebuilding a library.

1. Use the Component | Open library command to display the Open Library dialog shown in Figure 17.5. Select a library from the list and click on OK. You need to make sure you have the right library open before you rebuild it. (In most cases you will because you'll have just finished adding or removing components.)

2. Use the Component | Rebuild Library command to rebuild the library. Delphi will display the Compiling dialog (if you selected the Show Compiler Progress option). Be patient, it'll take quite a while to rebuild the library in some cases.

Removing a Module from a Library

There are going to be situations where merely reconfiguring your palette won't do the job. For one thing, every component that you load on the Component Palette consumes precious memory. Why pay the price for loading a component that you'll never use? It's easier to simply get rid of the component and reduce the memory footprint of Delphi in the bargain. Of course, the component really isn't gone. You can always add it back in from disk later.

Warning: The main Delphi component library is CMPLIB32.DPR, which you'll find in the Delphi BIN directory. Never modify this library file directly. Always create a new library to store your changes in. That way you'll always have a baseline library to use as a basis for comparison.

1. Use the Component | Open library command to display the Open Library dialog shown in Figure 17.5. Select a library from the list and click on OK. You need to make sure you have the right library open before you modify it.

2. Use the Component | Install New command to display the Install Components dialog shown in Figure 17.4. The pane on the left side shows the currently installed component modules. The pane in the right shows the components within those modules. One module can hold more than one component, although I usually limit myself to one component per module to make it easy to add and remove components. Delphi only allows you to remove complete modules. This means you'll have to create new modules if you want to use some components, but not others, in the current module setup.

3. Select the module that you want to remove. Make sure you scroll through the list of modules before you do so. You don't want to waste time by accidentally removing a needed component—even if you can install it again later.

4. Click on OK to remove the module.

5. Repeat steps 3 and 4 for all the modules you want to remove.

Tip: You can restore the original module list in a library at any time by clicking on the Revert pushbutton. This will remove any changes you made during the current session. Once you make the changes permanent, Delphi will disable the Revert pushbutton. You'll need to install the modules again before you can use them.

6. Click on OK to close the Install Components dialog and save your changes. Delphi will automatically rebuild your library. It'll display the Compiling dialog (if you selected the Show Compiler Progress option). Be patient, it'll take quite a while to rebuild the library in some cases.

Tip: If you don't need the entire contents of a particular module in a library, you can either create a wrapper for a new module by following the example units in the LIB directory or add an individual component from the SOURCE directory. The VCL subdirectory contains all of the standard Delphi components. The SAMPLES subdirectory contains the component examples provided with Delphi. This comes in handy in some cases. For example, you may want your library to include all of the standard dialogs, but none of the other components that module contains like the media player.

Inserting a Module into the Library

As you gain some expertise using Delphi, you'll find that there are times when you would have provided a different sort of control than Borland did. Unlike some programming languages, creating a new component in Delphi is relatively easy. Borland even provides an expert to make it easier for you to get the process started (more on that later). You may also want to buy third-party components. There are a lot more vendors than I originally imagined selling Delphi components. If you buy one of these packages, you'll need to install the new components into a library before you can use them. Whatever your reason for installing new components, it's an important part of managing your Delphi libraries. The following procedure takes you through the process of adding components or OCXs to your Delphi libraries.

1. Use the Component | Open library command to display the Open Library dialog shown in Figure 17.5. Select a library from the list and click on OK. You need to make sure you have the right library open before you modify it.

2. Use the Component | Install New command to display the Install Components dialog shown in Figure 17.4. The pane on the left side shows the currently installed component modules. The pane on the right shows the components within those modules. One module can hold more than one component, although I usually limit myself to one component per module to make it easy to add and remove components.

3. Click on the Add pushbutton. You'll see an Add Module dialog like the one shown in Figure 17.6. Notice the Browse button on the right side. This opens a File Open dialog you can use to search for modules on your machine.

Figure 17.6.
The Add Module dialog
allows you to add new
modules to a library.

4. Type the name of the module you want to add (or select it from the File Open dialog).

5. Click on OK to add the module.

6. Repeat steps 3 and 4 for all the modules you want to add.

7. Click on OK to close the Install Components dialog and save your changes. Delphi will automatically rebuild your library. It'll display the Compiling dialog (if you selected the

Show Compiler Progress option). Be patient, it'll take quite a while to rebuild the library in some cases.

Installing and Removing OCXs

Delphi allows you to use any OCXs that you have just as you would a component. The only difference is the way that you install them since an OCX requires a "wrapper" class within Delphi. I'm not going to go into the details of what that wrapper does right now since Delphi takes care of creating it for you automatically. Suffice it to say that the entire process is pretty much automated. About the only thing you really need to think about is the location of your OCXs. Normally they appear in the Windows SYSTEM folder or within the directory where you installed the OCX.

Note: You'll normally want to install your OCXs to the Windows SYSTEM folder if possible to reduce compatibility problems with Delphi and other applications. Most programs look for an OCX in their own directory first, then within the SYSTEM folder. Some programs will also look at other locations in the Windows path, but you can't count on this behavior.

1. Use the Component | Open library command to display the Open Library dialog shown in Figure 17.5. Select a library from the list and click on OK. You need to make sure you have the right library open before you modify it.

2. Use the Component | Install New command to display the Install Components dialog shown in Figure 17.4. The pane on the left side shows the currently installed component modules. The pane on the right shows the components within those modules. One module can hold more than one component, although I usually limit myself to one component per module to make it easy to add and remove components.

3. Click on the OCX pushbutton. You'll see an Import OCX Control dialog like the one shown in Figure 17.7. The list at the top of the dialog shows you which OCXs you have registered with Delphi. You must register an OCX before you can do it. The registration process creates an interface between Delphi and the OCX.

4. Skip this step if your OCX appears in the Registered Controls list. Click on the Register pushbutton to display the Register OLE Control dialog shown in Figure 17.8. This dialog looks and acts like a File Open dialog. All you need to do is find the OCX you want to use and click on Open. Once you open the OCX, you'll return to the Import OCX Control dialog shown in Figure 17.7. This is where you select the OCX you want to add to the library.

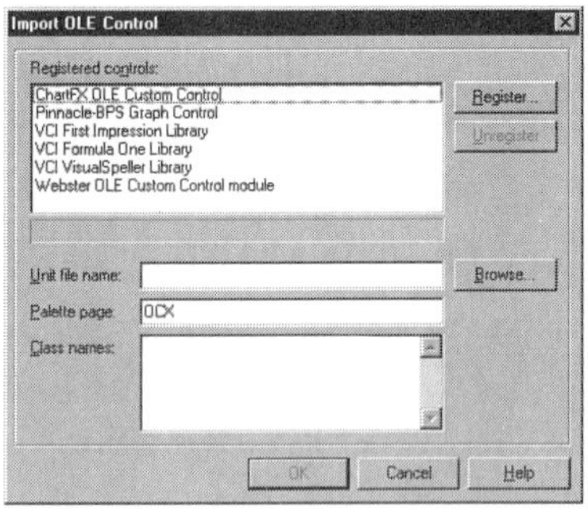

Figure 17.7.

The Import OCX Control dialog shows a list of all the OCXs you've registered with Delphi.

Figure 17.8.

The Register OLE Control dialog allows you to register a new OCX with Delphi.

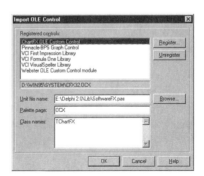

5. Select the OCX that you want to use from the Registered Controls list. Notice that Delphi fills in the Unit file name, Palette page, and Classes entries as shown in Figure 17.9. You can change these names, but I usually keep the ones that Delphi provides as a default. The Unit file name field tells Delphi where to automatically create the wrapper function required to use the OCX. The Palette page entry tells Delphi where to place the OCX entry—you can change this at any time using the Component Palette procedures that I provided at the beginning of this chapter. The Classes entry tells what components the OCX contains. Delphi normally uses the OCXs default name for each component preceded by a "T."

Figure 17.9.

Delphi automatically fills in the fields required to use a registered OCX, but you can change them if necessary.

6. Click on OK to add the module.

7. Repeat steps 3 through 6 for all the OCXs you want to add.

8. Click on OK to close the Install Components dialog and save your changes. Delphi will automatically rebuild your library. It will display the Compiling dialog (if you selected the Show Compiler Progress option). Be patient, it will take quite a while to rebuild the library in some cases.

Components and Delphi Classes

So far I've told you about component management from two points of view: The Component Palette and the library. Now it's time to look at what you would need to do to create a new Delphi component. The place to start creating a component is by looking at the current Delphi classes. The classes that Delphi provides fall into two categories: those that you use directly and those that act as the basis for other classes. If you look at the example components in the SOURCE and SAMPLES directories, you'll find that they are class descriptions and that they use base classes as a starting point. That's essentially what a component is—it's a new Delphi class.

Designing a component in Delphi doesn't have to be difficult or mind boggling. In fact, it should be fairly easy. Let's look at a typical scenario. You start subclassing a standard component on a frequent basis and see the need to create your own "super component." That's the starting point. All Delphi components are subclassed from an existing component. If nothing else, you can always subclass a component from the TComponent class (or any other base class for that matter). I always look at this as my starting point. I take a component that I normally create dynamically within an application, generalize it, then formalize it. That's what you'll need to do as well.

Once you have a debugged component to work with, you can make it a permanent part of the library. I always start with debugged code—a function that I've created specifically for subclassing a component is always a good starting point. The following procedure shows how you create a shell for your new component.

1. Close any existing forms and applications. You want to start out with a completely blank screen.

2. Use the File | New command to display the New Items dialog. Double-click on the Component object. Delphi will display the Component Expert dialog shown in Figure 17.10.

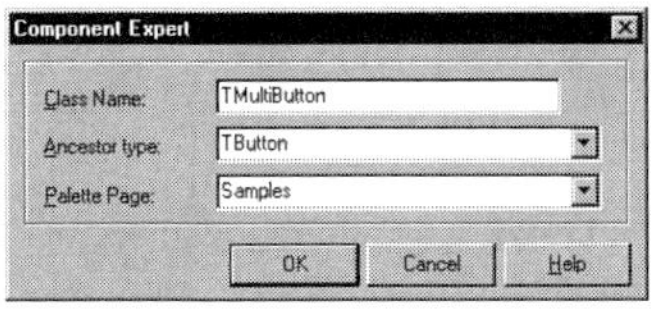

Figure 17.10.
The Component Expert allows you to create new components from existing code.

3. Type in a class name. I usually use the name of my function preceded by a "T." For example, if I create a pushbutton that allows a user to select between various states like on

and off, I would probably use a class name of TMultiButton. You have to select a class name that doesn't already exist.

4. Select a parent class from the Ancestor Type combo box. In my case I would select TButton since I'm creating a new type of pushbutton. There are times when the component you want to create doesn't really have an ancestor type. In that case you would select TComponent—the ancestor of all components in Delphi.

5. Select one of the Component Palette tabs in the Palette page combo box. I always place the components I create on a custom page. That way I can easily differentiate the custom components I create from those created by other people.

6. Click on OK to complete the process.

What you'll end up with is a component template that contains one predefined procedure named Register. The purpose of the Register procedure is to allow you to register a new component. It's the bit of information that Delphi needs to place your component on the Component Palette. You could leave things the way they are right now and simply compile the component shell. (You'll find out that you don't literally compile the shell as you would an application—you add the component to the library and Delphi compiles the library as a whole.) Delphi would allow you to register it as is. Obviously this isn't what you'll do, but you should try it out as a starting point to see what happens.

So, what would you do next? Components can get messy quickly if you don't take a structured approach to writing them. I usually take the component shell that Delphi provides and add two public methods: a constructor and a destructor. This is the starting point for every component you'll ever create since the component has to be able to create and destroy itself. Once you have a component that creates and destroys itself, you've added a certain margin of safety for testing it. Now you can start adding methods to change the way that the ancestor component works.

Every component on the Component Palette has a distinct icon associated with it. However, since you're not using a project file, you can't use the method that I introduced you to in the "Using Image Edit for Cursors, Icons, and Bitmaps" section of Chapter 4, "Adding Some Bells and Whistles." What you need to do is create a DCR (Delphi Component Resource) file using Image Edit. Give the DCR file the same name as your component PAS file. Create a new bitmap within the DCR with the same name as your component. For example, I created a bitmap called TMULTIBUTTON for the example in the next section.

Note: The component bitmap name must be in all uppercase or Delphi won't recognize it. You also need to keep Delphi's 24 × 24 pixel bitmap size limitation in mind when creating a component bitmap. Otherwise, Delphi will simply crop the bitmap when it displays your component on the Component Palette. All of the bitmaps provided with Delphi use 16 colors; you may want to observe the same limit.

Now you have a complete component. What you need to do next is add it to the library using the procedure that I talked about previously in "Inserting a Module into the Library." Delphi will try to compile the new component as part of the library rebuilding process. If it finds an error, it will display the first error point in an editor window. Fix the error, then use the Component | Rebuild Library command to try compiling the library again. Never use the Run button or try to compile the component in the normal way. Nothing bad will happen, but you won't succeed in adding the component to the library.

The final step in creating a new component is to test it out. Create a test application, add the component to it, and try to compile. Try all the features you've added out to make sure they work as anticipated. I usually build a few applications with the component to make sure there aren't any unforeseen interactions. You'll also want to test multiple copies of the component out to make sure the one instance of the component doesn't interfere with the others. It's important to test the component out on a variety of platforms if you intend to give the component to other people. You'll want to test the component on all the platforms that your applications appear on as a minimum.

Creating New Components Using Delphi

Let's take a look at the actual process of creating a component. I wanted to create something simple, yet useful for this example, so I chose a pushbutton modification. Listing 17.1 contains the source code for a multi-position pushbutton. If you select the On/Off mode, you can see the button switch states between on and off. I purposely designed this component so that you can extend it. For example, you could add the capability to allow other kinds of multi-position states. One option might include counting within a range of numbers. Obviously the actual number of permutations is somewhat limited, but the example will provide you with some important details of creating a component.

Listing 17.1. Source code for multi-position pushbutton.

```
unit MultiBtn;

interface

uses
  Windows, Messages, SysUtils, Classes, Graphics, Controls, Forms, Dialogs,
  StdCtrls, ExtCtrls;

type
  TMultiButton = class(TButton)
  private
    iCurrentState: Integer;              {Current button state.}
    iNumStates: Integer;            {Number of possible states.}
    fDefault: Boolean;               {User pick the default On/Off Mode?}
```

continues

Listing 17.1. continued

```
    procedure SetOnOff(Value: Boolean);
    function IsDefaultCaption: Boolean;
  protected
    { Protected declarations }
  public
    constructor Create(AOwner: TComponent); override;
    destructor Destroy; override;
    procedure Click; override;
  published
    property OnOff: Boolean read fDefault write SetOnOff stored IsDefaultCaption default
False;
  end;

procedure Register;

const
    {These three constants define the modal result values.  All of the stanard
     values are available plus two new values for the On and Off button values.}
    mrOn = mrNo + 1;
    mrOff = mrNo + 2;
    MultiBtnModalResults: array[-1..8] of TModalResult = (mrNone, mrOK, mrCancel,
        mrAbort, mrRetry, mrIgnore, mrYes, mrNo, mrOn, mrOff);

var
    {This array contains the two On/Off mode strings.  It could easily be
     changed to allow for other kinds of multivalue pushbuttons.}
    aDefaultStates: array [0..1] of String = ('On', 'Off');

implementation

procedure Register;
begin
    {Place the component on the Custom page of the Component Palette.}
      RegisterComponents('Custom', [TMultiButton]);
end;

constructor TMultiButton.Create(AOwner: TComponent);
begin
    {Always allow Delphi to create the component before you change it.}
    inherited Create(AOwner);

    {Initialize our state variables.}
      iCurrentState := 0;
      iNumStates := 0;
      fDefault := False;
end;

destructor TMultiButton.Destroy;
begin
    {Always clean up any dynamically created variables or other structures first,
     then call the inherited destroy method.}
      inherited Destroy;
end;

procedure TMultiButton.Click;
begin
    {Check to see if the user selected the On/Off mode.}
    if fDefault then
```

```
            {If they did, change the button state to its opposite condition. This
              includes changing the state indicator, the button caption, and the
              modal result that the button returns.}
            if iCurrentState = 0 then
                begin
                  iCurrentState := 1;
                  Caption := aDefaultStates[iCurrentState];
                  ModalResult := MultiBtnModalResults[mrNo + iCurrentState]
                  end
              else
                begin
                  iCurrentState := 0;
                  Caption := aDefaultStates[iCurrentState];
                  ModalResult := MultiBtnModalResults[mrNo + iCurrentState]
                  end;

      {Always call the inherited click method to process the user click.}
      inherited Click;
end;

function TMultiButton.IsDefaultCaption: Boolean;
begin
    {We have to check the current state of the caption before we store the
     new component. If the caption doesn't match the current state, then we
     need to reset the state variables.  In this case we need to reset the
     default indicator and the OnOff property value.  We also need to tell
     Delphi that we're storing something other than the default caption value.}
    if not (Caption = aDefaultStates[iCurrentState]) then
        begin
        fDefault := False;
        OnOff := False;
         Result := False;
         end;
end;

procedure TMultiButton.SetOnOff(Value: Boolean);
begin
    {Set the default indicator to the value of the OnOff property.}
    fDefault := Value;

    {If the user has selected the On/Off mode, then set up some state
     variables.  This includes the number of states—just in case there
     are more than two, the current state, the button caption, and the
     modal result value.}
    if fDefault then
        begin
        iNumStates := 1;
         iCurrentState := 0;
         Caption := aDefaultStates[iCurrentState];
         ModalResult := MultiBtnModalResults[mrNo + iCurrentState]
         end;
end;

end.
```

This example introduces some new constructs that I haven't shown you before. Look at the very beginning of the example. You'll notice that the class definition for a component is a lot different from the others in this book. I place the global component variables in the private declaration area. This encapsulates the variable within the component, but allows any method within the component to use the variable as needed.

Note: This example doesn't include any entries in the protected area because it doesn't need them. You would use this section for variable, procedure, or function declaration that you wanted to hide from the user, but make available to other component programmers. Any class derived from your class would contain the entries, but someone using your component to build a program wouldn't see them.

Notice that I included my create and destroy methods in the public area. Public declarations allow someone building an application to use the variable, function, or procedure, but they won't see them on the object inspector. Notice the key word "override" after each declaration in this section. Whenever you want to change a default component behavior, you have to override the existing behavior. The new behavior has to react in the same way as the old one, otherwise, you'll run into interaction problems. In fact, Delphi simply won't compile the component in most cases.

There is only one entry in the Published area in this example. Entries in this area appear on the object inspector, so you'll normally limit them to properties and events. A component can use as many or as few properties and events as it needs. Delphi automatically adds all of the entries from the ancestor class. Notice that I needed to create a new property for my component—in this case the property determines whether the user wants to create a special On/Off pushbutton or one of the standard type. A property declaration starts out looking like a variable declaration because that's what it is. However, you have to tell Delphi how to interact with that variable. There are four common interaction processes. First, you need to tell Delphi how to read the variable. The property is a Boolean type in this case so I tell Delphi to look at the value of my fDefault flag. Next, you need to add a write access method. In this case Delphi will provide you with a value that you have to add to the property in some way. You can also determine whether Delphi stores each property value. The "stored" part of the declaration has to contain either a Boolean value or the name of a function that returns a Boolean value. Finally, you can assign the property a default value as I've done in this case. Simply add the "default" key word followed by a value of the same type as the property.

Most of the code in this example is pretty straightforward. For example, the TMultiButton.Click procedure determines if the user has selected the special On/Off pushbutton mode. If so, it automatically switches the caption and modal result of the pushbutton to its opposite state. There's an important feature to notice here. I call the inherited Click method once I get done modifying the component's behavior. You have to do this if you want Delphi to provide standard processing. If I had left this call out, the pushbutton would've switched between states, but Delphi would have ignored any code in the user's Click procedure. The button would change states, but it couldn't do anything else.

There are times when you have to coordinate various component activities. For example, what if the user selects true in the OnOff property, that changes the caption of the pushbutton. Obviously, you have to decide on some way to handle the situation. I chose to add a stored function to my component named IsDefaultCaption. If the caption isn't the default one when the user goes to store the component, I automatically reset all the flags on the assumption that they really wanted to use a standard pushbutton—not the special On/Off variety.

> **Note:** Delphi normally stores the properties that you publish. You also have the option of storing private or protected properties, but Delphi doesn't do so automatically. Storing a property allows it to retain its value between editing sessions. Even though all published properties retain their value by default, you can use the "stored" keyword along with either true or false to change this behavior. A stored function allows you to define that true or false value based on how the user has set the component up or on other environmental factors.

As I previously mentioned, you always have to provide some method for setting new properties. In this case the SetOnOff procedure does the job. Notice that there is only one input variable called Value. This is the standard way that Delphi handles things. Value is always a string, so if your property reflects a numeric value, you'll need to convert it.

Now that we have a functional component, let's look at it in use. I started with the form shown in Figure 17.11. You should also take a peek at the Component Palette—it shows how the component will look once you add it to the display. Notice the new OnOff property on the Object Inspector. All this form contains is two of the TMultiButton components. I configured them in different ways so that you could see the functionality they provide. Table 17.1 contains a list of the property changes that I made. There are two special items of interest in the table. First of all, I defined my own special modal result settings so the ModalResult property contains a number instead of an actual string value. You could write some additional procedures to take care of this, but it's an aesthetic function that you'll find missing in a lot of components. Getting a number instead of a string really doesn't affect the functionality of the component, but it does make it more difficult to use. If you decide to market a component, you'll definitely want to add some code to take care of this particular issue. The second thing you'll notice is that the OnOff property is listed for MultiButton1, but not for MultiButton2. The reason is simple. The default state of the property is false. So, if the user decides to use the added functionality that my component provides, he needs to change the OnOff property value. That's why it gets listed where it does.

Figure 17.11.

Our simple component test form shows how you can use the On/Off multi-position component.

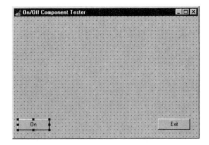

Table 17.1. On/Off Component Tester Form Control Settings.

Object	Property	Setting
MultiButton1	Caption	'On'
	ModalResult	8
	OnClick	MultiButton1Click
	OnOff	True
MultiButton2	Caption	'Exit'
	OnClick	MultiButton2Click

Let's add some code to our two pushbuttons. Listing 17.2 shows the very simple code I've provided for this test program. You'll want to keep the code to test your components simple at first, too. That way you can test specific actions. Once you know that the component works for the most part, you can increase the complexity of the test program to check for a variety of compatibility and interaction problems. Notice that I don't use the On/Off mode of the section TMultiButton component. It acts just like a normal pushbutton and provides an Exit function for this program. You'll want to check the normal actions of your components as well. It's important to know that you didn't break the default behavior in the act of adding new functionality.

Listing 17.2. Test program code.

```
unit CompTst1;

interface

uses
  Windows, Messages, SysUtils, Classes, Graphics, Controls, Forms, Dialogs,
  StdCtrls, MultiBtn;

type
  TForm1 = class(TForm)
    MultiButton1: TMultiButton;
```

```
    MultiButton2: TMultiButton;
    procedure MultiButton1Click(Sender: TObject);
    procedure MultiButton2Click(Sender: TObject);
  private
    { Private declarations }
  public
    { Public declarations }
  end;

var
  Form1: TForm1;

implementation

{$R *.DFM}

procedure TForm1.MultiButton1Click(Sender: TObject);
begin
    {Check the modal result of our pushbutton press.}
    case MultiButton1.ModalResult of
        mrNone: ShowMessage('Modal Result is None');
         mrOK: ShowMessage('Modal Result is OK');
         mrCancel: ShowMessage('Modal Result is Cancel');
         mrAbort: ShowMessage('Modal Result is Abort');
         mrRetry: ShowMessage('Modal Result is Retry');
         mrIgnore: ShowMessage('Modal Result is Ignore');
         mrYes: ShowMessage('Modal Result is Yes');
         mrNo: ShowMessage('Modal Result is No');
        mrOn: ShowMessage('Button is on.');
        mrOff: ShowMessage('Button is off.');
    end;
end;

procedure TForm1.MultiButton2Click(Sender: TObject);
begin
    {Exit the application.}
    Application.Terminate;
end;

end.
```

Figure 17.12 shows our test application in action. In this case I clicked on the pushbutton. It changed states from On to Off. The code within my test application checked the modal result property and determined that the pushbutton was off. It displayed a message to that effect. Notice that I check every other possible result in the code first, then check for my new result values. You'll need to do something similar to ensure that you don't accidentally overwrite a default value. In fact, part of my testing for this component included checking the other modal result values, just to make sure I didn't change a default behavior.

Figure 17.12.
The On/Off Component Tester shows off the new functionality of our modified pushbutton.

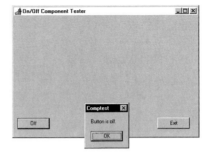

Creating Components to Access DLLs

The last part of our chapter is going to concentrate on accessing a DLL from within a component. There are actually more opportunities to do this than you might initially think. Take the math example we looked at in the previous chapter. You could easily encapsulate the functions provided by the MATHFUNC.DLL into several components. In fact, that's what our example is all about in this chapter. We'll take a look at what you'd need to do to create a component from the math function DLL we created previously.

I'm not going to go through the DLL code again. You can review it if you'd like by looking at Listing 16.3. This example even illustrates the coding technique that I talked about previously. Look at the Execute methods for each of the calculations and you'll see a modified version of the source in Listing 16.7. What I've done is create a different kind of shell for the code to work in. The single line edits that I used previously are now component properties. The logic has remained the same; only the variables are different.

Listing 17.3. DLL code.

```
unit MathStuf;

{$R-}

interface

uses
  Windows, Messages, SysUtils, Classes, Graphics, Controls, Forms, Dialogs,
  Menus, StdCtrls, ExtCtrls, ComCtrls;

type
  TCompInt = class(TComponent)
  private
    sTotalPeriods: String;    {Total number of intervals.}
    sCalcPeriods: String;     {Number of intervals in one year.}
    sInterest: String;        {Interest rate.}
    sPrinciple: String;        {Initial value of the investment.}
  protected
    { Protected declarations }
  public
```

```
    constructor Create(AOwner: TComponent); override;
    destructor Destroy; override;
    function Execute: String;
  published
    property TimeFrame: String read sTotalPeriods write sTotalPeriods;
    property Interval: String read sCalcPeriods write sCalcPeriods;
    property Interest: String read sInterest write sInterest;
    property Principle: String read sPrinciple write sPrinciple;
  end;

type
  TSimpInt = class(TComponent)
  private
    sTotalPeriods: String;    {Total number of intervals.}
    sCalcPeriods: String;     {Number of intervals in one year.}
    sInterest: String;        {Interest rate.}
    sPrinciple: String;       {Initial value of the investment.}
  protected
    { Protected declarations }
  public
    constructor Create(AOwner: TComponent); override;
    destructor Destroy; override;
    function Execute: String;
  published
    property TimeFrame: String read sTotalPeriods write sTotalPeriods;
    property Interval: String read sCalcPeriods write sCalcPeriods;
    property Interest: String read sInterest write sInterest;
    property Principle: String read sPrinciple write sPrinciple;
  end;

type
  TAnnuity = class(TComponent)
  private
    sTotalPeriods: String;    {Total number of intervals.}
    sCalcPeriods: String;     {Number of intervals in one year.}
    sInterest: String;        {Interest rate.}
    sPayment: String;         {Amount of payment for each interval.}
  protected
    { Protected declarations }
  public
    constructor Create(AOwner: TComponent); override;
    destructor Destroy; override;
    function Execute: String;
  published
    property TimeFrame: String read sTotalPeriods write sTotalPeriods;
    property Interval: String read sCalcPeriods write sCalcPeriods;
    property Interest: String read sInterest write sInterest;
    property Payment: String read sPayment write sPayment;
  end;

const
    MathDLL = 'MATHFUNC.DLL';

{Component registration procedure.}
procedure Register;

implementation
```

continues

Listing 17.3. continued

```delphi
{Declare the exported functions in our DLL.}
function MathCompInt(nIntRate, nCompPer, nPrinciple: Double; nTotalPer: Integer): Double;
stdcall; external MathDLL name 'mathCompInt';
function MathSimpInt(nIntRate, nCompPer, nPrinciple: Double; nTotalPer: Integer): Double;
stdcall; external MathDLL name 'mathSimpInt';
function MathAnnuity(nIntRate, nCompPer, nPayment: Double; nTotalPer: Integer): Double;
stdcall; external MathDLL name 'mathAnnuity';

procedure Register;
begin
  RegisterComponents('Custom', [TCompInt, TSimpInt, TAnnuity]);
end;

constructor TCompInt.Create(AOwner: TComponent);
begin
    {Create the component.}
    inherited Create(AOwner);

    {Initialize some variables.}
    sTotalPeriods := '24';
    sCalcPeriods := '12';
    sInterest := '9.5';
    sPrinciple := '1000';
end;

destructor TCompInt.Destroy;
begin
  inherited Destroy;
end;

function TCompInt.Execute: String;
var
    nInterest: Double;         {Interest rate.}
    nPrinciple: Double;        {Loan prinicple.}
    nPeriods: Double;          {Compounding periods per year.}
    nTotalPeriods: Integer;    {Total number of periods.}
    sValue: String;         {Current principle value.}
    iCode: Integer;         {Val function return value.}
begin

    {Get the total number of periods.}
    nTotalPeriods := StrToInt(sTotalPeriods);

    {Get the initial calculation values.}
    Val(sInterest, nInterest, iCode);
    Val(sCalcPeriods, nPeriods, iCode);
    Val(sPrinciple, nPrinciple, iCode);

    {Calculate the compound interest.}
    nPrinciple := MathCompInt(nInterest, nPeriods, nPrinciple, nTotalPeriods);
    Str(nPrinciple:20:2, sValue);
    Result := Trim(sValue);
end;

constructor TSimpInt.Create(AOwner: TComponent);
begin
    {Create the component.}
    inherited Create(AOwner);
```

```
    {Initialize some variables.}
    sTotalPeriods := '24';
    sCalcPeriods := '12';
    sInterest := '9.5';
    sPrinciple := '1000';
end;

destructor TSimpInt.Destroy;
begin
  inherited Destroy;
end;

function TSimpInt.Execute: String;
var
    nInterest: Double;         {Interest rate.}
    nPrinciple: Double;        {Loan prinicple.}
    nPeriods: Double;          {Compounding periods per year.}
    nTotalPeriods: Integer;    {Total number of periods.}
    sValue: String;          {Current principle value.}
    iCode: Integer;          {Val function return value.}
begin

    {Get the total number of periods.}
    nTotalPeriods := StrToInt(sTotalPeriods);

    {Get the initial calculation values.}
    Val(sInterest, nInterest, iCode);
    Val(sCalcPeriods, nPeriods, iCode);
    Val(sPrinciple, nPrinciple, iCode);

    {Calculate the compound interest.}
    nPrinciple := MathSimpInt(nInterest, nPeriods, nPrinciple, nTotalPeriods);
    Str(nPrinciple:20:2, sValue);
    Result := Trim(sValue);
end;

constructor TAnnuity.Create(AOwner: TComponent);
begin
    {Create the component.}
    inherited Create(AOwner);

    {Initialize some variables.}
    sTotalPeriods := '24';
    sCalcPeriods := '12';
    sInterest := '9.5';
    sPayment := '1000';
end;

destructor TAnnuity.Destroy;
begin
  inherited Destroy;
end;

function TAnnuity.Execute: String;
var
    nInterest: Double;         {Interest rate.}
    nPayment: Double;          {Periodic payment.}
    nPeriods: Double;          {Compounding periods per year.}
```

continues

Listing 17.3. continued

```
    nTotalPeriods: Integer;    {Total number of periods.}
    sValue: String;           {Current principle value.}
    iCode: Integer;           {Val function return value.}
begin

    {Get the total number of periods.}
    nTotalPeriods := StrToInt(sTotalPeriods);

    {Get the initial calculation values.}
    Val(sInterest, nInterest, iCode);
    Val(sCalcPeriods, nPeriods, iCode);
    Val(sPayment, nPayment, iCode);

    {Calculate the compound interest.}
    nPayment := MathAnnuity(nInterest, nPeriods, nPayment, nTotalPeriods);
    Str(nPayment:20:2, sValue);
    Result := Trim(sValue);
end;

end.
```

You'll notice a few changes from that DLL example, of course. First is the addition of the create and destroy methods. (You'll remember from the previous section that I always write create and destroy methods in pairs to keep from omitting one or the other by accident.) As with the previous example I call the inherited methods as part of the procedure. You'll also notice that I initialize the properties to specific values. I find that this prevents a lot of problems when the user doesn't fill all the values in, then calls the Execute method.

The second thing you should notice is that I've used a function format for the Execute method. This allows the user to call the method and get a return value immediately. You'll also find that it reduces the number of variables required to implement the method by one.

Let's take a look at a program to test these components. Figure 17.13 shows the form we'll use in this case. Notice that I've included the three components at the bottom of the form. They won't show up when you run the application (as I'll show later). I've also included some generic data entry fields and three output fields—one for each function. Table 17.2 contains a complete list of the modifications I made to the components.

Table 17.2. DLL Component Tester Form Control Settings.

Object	Property	Setting
GroupBox1	Caption	'Return Values'
edCompInt	TabStop	False
	ReadOnly	True

Object	Property	Setting
edSimpInt	TabStop	False
	ReadOnly	True
edAnnuity	TabStop	False
	ReadOnly	True
GroupBox2	Caption	'Input Values'
edPrinciple	Text	'1000'
edInterest	Text	'9.5'
edPeriods	Text	'12'
edTotalPeriods	Text	'24'
pbTest	Caption	'Test'
	OnClick	pbTestClick
pbExit	Caption	'Exit'
	OnClick	pbExitClick

Figure 17.13.

The DLL Component Tester form contains two sections, one for input and the other for output.

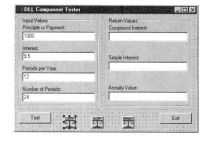

Now that we've gotten the form put together, let's add some code. Listing 17.4 shows the code for this example. All it really consists of are two procedures: one to test the components and another to exit the application. The component test procedure, pbTestClick, begins by initializing all the component properties. It then calls the component Execute methods and places the return values in the appropriate single line edit. Figure 17.14 shows the program in action. Notice that the components are nowhere to be seen.

Listing 17.4. Program in action.

```
unit DLLComp1;

interface

uses
  Windows, Messages, SysUtils, Classes, Graphics, Controls, Forms, Dialogs,
  StdCtrls, MathStuf;

type
  TForm1 = class(TForm)
    pbTest: TButton;
    pbExit: TButton;
    GroupBox1: TGroupBox;
    Label1: TLabel;
    edCompInt: TEdit;
    Label2: TLabel;
    edSimpInt: TEdit;
    GroupBox2: TGroupBox;
    edAnnuity: TEdit;
    Label3: TLabel;
    edPrinciple: TEdit;
    edInterest: TEdit;
    edPeriods: TEdit;
    edTotalPeriods: TEdit;
    Label4: TLabel;
    Label5: TLabel;
    Label6: TLabel;
    Label7: TLabel;
    CompInt1: TCompInt;
    SimpInt1: TSimpInt;
    Annuity1: TAnnuity;
    procedure pbTestClick(Sender: TObject);
    procedure pbExitClick(Sender: TObject);
    procedure DoCompCalc;
    procedure DoSimpCalc;
    procedure DoAnnuityCalc;
  private
    { Private declarations }
  public
    { Public declarations }
  end;

var
  Form1: TForm1;

implementation

{$R *.DFM}

procedure TForm1.pbTestClick(Sender: TObject);
begin
    {Test the components.}
    DoCompCalc;
    DoSimpCalc;
    DoAnnuityCalc;
end;
```

```
procedure TForm1.pbExitClick(Sender: TObject);
begin
    {Exit the Application.}
    Application.Terminate;
end;

procedure TForm1.DoCompCalc;
var
        sCompValue: String;
begin
    {Load the values into our components.}
    CompInt1.Principle := edPrinciple.Text;
    CompInt1.Interest := edInterest.Text;
    CompInt1.Interval := edPeriods.Text;
    CompInt1.TimeFrame := edTotalPeriods.Text;

    {Test the compound interest component.}
    sCompValue := CompInt1.Execute;
    Form1.edCompInt.Text := sCompValue;
end;

procedure TForm1.DoSimpCalc;
var
    sSimpValue: String;
begin
    {Load the values into our components.}
    SimpInt1.Principle := edPrinciple.Text;
    SimpInt1.Interest := edInterest.Text;
    SimpInt1.Interval := edPeriods.Text;
    SimpInt1.TimeFrame := edTotalPeriods.Text;

    {Test the simple interest component.}
    sSimpValue := SimpInt1.Execute;
    Form1.edSimpInt.Text := sSimpValue;
end;

procedure TForm1.DoAnnuityCalc;
var
    sAnnuityValue: String;
begin
    {Load the values into our components.}
    Annuity1.Payment := edPrinciple.Text;
    Annuity1.Interest := edInterest.Text;
    Annuity1.Interval := edPeriods.Text;
    Annuity1.TimeFrame := edTotalPeriods.Text;

    {Test the annuity component.}
    sAnnuityValue := Annuity1.Execute;
    Form1.edAnnuity.Text := sAnnuityValue;
end;

end.
```

Figure 17.14.
*Components represent
another way to use DLLs
within Delphi as shown in
this figure.*

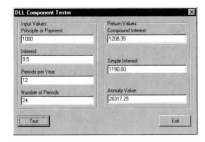

Summary

I've provided you with a whirlwind tour of components in this chapter. It covers three important areas: component management, library management, and component building. We haven't by any means exhausted the subject. Think of components as yet another way to save your debugged code into easily used objects.

18

Delphi and OCXs

OLE Control eXtensions (OCXs) are the big news for computer programmers today. (Most programmers shorten the term for OCX to simply OLE control or component.) For all intents and purposes, they're an updated version of the venerable VBX with an OLE twist. Both file types are special versions of a DLL—the file that we've explored in Chapters 15, "Creating Your Own DLLs Using Delphi," and 16, "Creating Your Own DLLs Using C."

Looking Ahead: Delphi comes equipped with several sample OCXs. However, these products represent a mere tip of the iceberg. I think you're going to see OCXs for just about every kind of application imaginable (and some that you might not even imagine) somewhere along the way. Just take a look at the OCXs I've already found in Appendix A, "A Guide to VBXs and OCXs." Add to that the VBXs that will soon be upgraded to OCX format and you have a wealth of code at your fingertips.

Some of the more unusual OCXs that I've found are used in the medical community for monitoring instruments. You'll find a variety of other scientific OCXs as well. For example, there's one company that is currently working on updating their scientific graphics program from a VBX to an OCX. It's important to realize that these "bottled" routines exist—a developer needs this kind of edge to make himself productive and efficient in a world that's becoming increasingly competitive for programmers.

There are other reasons for using OCXs though. You'll find that these tools are a convenient way to add debugged functionality to your application. The key word here is debugged. How much time do you spend finding those little bugs in your application? That time could probably be better used in more interesting pursuits like designing new applications.

We're going to look at OCXs from several vantage points in this chapter. By the time you get done reading it you should have a good idea of what makes an OCX special and how to use it when developing an application. We'll also look at some of the issues that Microsoft faced when putting the OCX specification together. For example, what is COM (component object model) and why is it important to you as a developer?

The one thing that you shouldn't expect from this chapter is a complete view of everything OCX. My intent is to give you an overview of some of the more important issues and provide a starting point for your own ventures into the world of OCXs. There are entire books written on this topic and most of them are works in progress. Suffice it to say that OCXs can be a complex topic if you want them to be—I prefer to start with the simple view of things and work my way toward the more complex areas. That's what this chapter provides—a starting point in your journey.

Peter's Principle: Future Shock—OCX on the Internet

I was recently looking through several of the trade presses and noticed the number of articles about OCX is on the rise. No longer is OCX just a way to expand an application on your local machine—Microsoft is also working on a network version (more on that later).

However, it wasn't the stories on network OLE that grabbed my attention most—I've been reading about that possibility for a while now. It was the recent stories on Microsoft's attempt to move OCXs to the Internet. What a user will be able to do is download an OCX, have it change their machine's configuration during the time that they are on-line, then the OCX will unload itself once they log off.

These "detachable objects" will make things like Internet terminals a workable reality. Microsoft is shooting for an optimal OCX size of about 50 KB. You'll use these new OCXs with Explorer 3.0, the next version of the browser that comes with products like Windows 95.

When will you see this new functionality? Microsoft currently plans to get the additions made to Explorer sometime this year. Office 97 will also include the ability to run OCXs—making it possible to use an OCX within products like Word for Windows. Obviously there's a lot more to putting OCXs on the Internet than that. Some of the early adapters of this technology are concerned about security. There's talk about adding a digital signature key or some other security measure to Internet terminals so that only authorized users can gain access to the OCXs. Of course, it will also take time for vendors to write the OCXs and incorporate them into Internet pages. Suffice it to say that this is a technology in the offing—only the future knows how far OCXs will go.

Programmers today should be looking at these doors of opportunity. When writing an OCX, you'll need to start considering where that OCX will actually get used. The location of an OCX will affect it more than you think. I doubt that Internet terminals will provide the same capabilities as a full-fledged desktop. What this means is that the OCX you create today will have to be even more flexible than before.

OLE—The OCX Difference

I've already spent some amount of time talking about OLE (object linking and embedding) in Chapter 10, "Using Delphi with OLE." You may want to take another look at that chapter if you have any remaining questions about OLE itself. Looking at Chapters 15 and 16 will be helpful if you really don't understand what a DLL is all about—we'll use DLLs for baseline comparison purposes in this section. What we're going to take a look at in this section is how OLE applies to components—in this case the OCX.

The VBX is a 16-bit component—Microsoft could have updated them to the 32-bit environment, but VBXs had some serious limitations. My short definition of a VBX is a DLL with a convenient interface. The most serious VBX limitation from a developer standpoint was a lack of OLE support. A VBX couldn't provide a full level of OLE support because of limitations in its design. So, my short definition of an OCX is a 32-bit DLL with a convenient interface and OLE support. I think that this definition is important because it puts the OCX in a perspective that most developers can understand.

Obviously my short definition is a bit limited. So, what does an OCX provide in addition to what my definition tells you about? Well, for one thing, an OCX differs from other OLE objects because it can fire events. This is part of the VBX connection that I alluded to in the previous paragraphs. When you define an OCX, you need to do more than simply create a DLL that also provides OLE capabilities. The following points will help you understand some of the more important developer issues.

- Display and Painting the Control—An OCX, like a VBX, gets painted on screen. More to the point, it displays some kind of representation of itself on the Component Palette. We saw how to do this as part of the Delphi component programming example in Chapter 17, "Building a Delphi VBX." An OCX has an additional consideration though. You must decide whether the component is going to provide active support (full interaction with its container) or inactive support (limited interaction with its container).

- ANSI or Unicode—There are two character set conventions used within Windows. The ANSI character set uses 8-bits—it's the character set that we've all come to know over the years. The Unicode character set uses 16-bits; it allows a developer to encode the characters used by any known language. Windows NT uses Unicode at the system level, but supports both character sets at the user level. If you want to provide the fullest possible language support for your OCX, then you need to use Unicode. Windows 95 doesn't support Unicode. You have to use the ANSI character set in this case. If you want your OCX to provide the greatest level of platform support, then ANSI is the way to go.

- Registration—You must register an OCX with Windows before you can use it. Some OCXs provide their own built-in function as part of a property page. However, it's not a requirement to provide a registration function within the OCX. If you decide to dispense with the registration function, you'll need to include REGSVR32.EXE (or an equivalent registration program) as part of the application package. Just pass the complete path and filename of the control (OCX file) as an argument to REGSVR32.

- Properties—Chapter 17 should have prepared you for this requirement as well. We created new properties for our Delphi components. In this case we treated properties much as you would variables in an application or as the parameters in a function call. However, the properties for an OCX have to provide additional functionality. You must define an interface that allows an application to interact with the control's automation interface. Without this support there is no OLE connection between the Delphi application and your OCX. As with any property, you can make this interface run-time only or read-only as required.

- Events—Fortunately, events for an OCX aren't much different than they are for any component. Obviously the orientation of some of those events will be toward resolving OLE issues, but the container that you create will take care of most of the communication needs.

- Methods—We saw how to add methods to a component in Chapter 17—OCXs aren't much different in this regard either. The difference in this case is that some of the methods will be OLE oriented. For example, you need to consider whether or not to add a Convert method for your component. Chapter 10 showed you that at least part of this functionality is part of the OLE container. However, you may find that you need to provide access to some of that functionality through component wrapper functions. (Anything that doesn't appear as part of the container's context menu is probably going to require some kind of wrapper.)

- Persistent Property States—You need to decide which properties are stored. This is where the STORED key word came into play when we developed the components in Chapter 17. In most cases you'll find that the OLE container takes care of many of the OLE specific issues for you. Anything that the container defines for you is going to be saved by the container automatically. The only time you need to worry about storing a property manually is when you define a new container element.

This isn't a complete list of considerations by any stretch of the imagination. To give you an idea of how mired in detail you can get, consider the fact that the OLE specification alone consumes the better part of a CD and that Microsoft includes a 600 page manual along with it. Add to that the complexities of creating a container (almost another book) and you have a situation where you can literally lose sight of the forest for the trees. I'm not going to get mired in detail in this chapter. What I do want to do is make you aware of the difference between a DLL, a VBX, and an OCX— that's what the list of developer considerations in this section is all about.

Understanding the Component Object Model (COM)

Before we go much further, I have to discuss a topic that has caused a lot of confusion for developers as they begin to use OLE and create their own OCXs. OLE uses something called the component object model (COM) to accomplish its work. COM is nothing more than a set of specialized functions and a specification on how to use them. Some of the documentation you'll read will refer to the functions as a common object library—I don't separate the two since you can't use one without the other.

The functions required to implement COM appear in COMPOBJ.DLL in your SYSTEM directory. Within this file are the various interface functions that you'll need to use to create any kind of an OLE application—including OCXs. (Look in Chapter 10 for the section entitled OLE Components for a list of additional OLE specific DLLs in your SYSTEM directory.) Delphi provides most (if not all) of the hooks you'll need to this DLL since it needs to use it as part of the OLE container and automation object features that it provides. It also initializes COM for you as part of the process of initializing the OLE container you'll need to use an OCX. Some of the documentation you'll read, especially the Microsoft documentation related to C++, will spend time talking about the process of initializing COMPOBJ.DLL before you can call any of the functions in OLE2.DLL. Normally this involves setting memory aside for the objects you'll create. You don't have to worry about this when using Delphi. It takes care of all the initialization for you. (Theoretically, most C++ compilers will also take care of this procedure as part of a wizard in the future if they don't do so already.)

The specification portion of COM is intertwined with the OLE 2 specification. You'll find it on the OLE 2 SDK. The COM part of the specification talks about the binary interface for OLE. In other words, COM expresses the lowest level of OLE functionality. You'll probably never need to work with COM directly as a Delphi programmer unless you create your own OCXs using C++. Even so, most C++ compilers attempt to hide some of the implementation details from the programmer through the use of Wizards or other program construction aids. (While it's theoretically possible to create an OCX using Delphi, you'll find the job is actually easier using C++ since Borland chose not to provide any OCX construction tools in this release.)

At this point you might wonder what benefits COM provides to you as the programmer and why you even need to know about it. Think about it this way. Every version of Windows has increased the size of the API by an order of magnitude. Considering the fact that Windows 1.0 started out with about 350 functions, trying to keep track of all those API functions could be quite a job for any programmer. What if there was a way to filter out just the instructions you needed to get a job done? That's what COM is all about for the programmer. When you look at a Windows object, what you're really seeing is a filtered version of the API. An OCX gives you access only to the functions you need and then only through methods and properties that are easily defined and understood. It would be easy for one vendor to implement this functionality in one way and another to use an entirely different approach. In fact, without COM, that's what you'd end up with. So, from a programmer's perspective, an OCX filters the set of Windows API functions into a manageable set while COM enforces one way to implement the filter. (Obviously, this is just one perspective of a much larger pie, but it's a useful one for the current discussion.)

Now, let's take another step forward in understanding the COM. Let's say there are two applications that need to talk with each other: one written in C and the other in Pascal. I purposely picked these two languages since they use inherently different implementations of everything including strings. We saw in Chapter 16 that a C DLL requires special handling when used under Delphi. The reason is simple: Pascal uses a different set of conventions than C does. COM makes these implementation differences transparent. An object-oriented interface isn't worried about those details. It promotes communication through properties, events, and methods. A Pascal property is the same as one implemented in C because both use the same standard for communication purposes. Even though the implementation of these programming constructs is strikingly different between the two languages, the interface that someone using a control created in the language sees is consistent.

Making all this work might seem like magic at first, but it really isn't all that difficult to understand. At the lowest level, an OCX registers itself with Windows. We looked at this registration process in Chapter 10 when we started looking at the registry and the way that your OLE application interacts with it. OCXs perform a similar registration that allows Windows to find it easily. What registration does is provide Windows with a method for communicating with the OCX. When your application requests to open a copy of the OCX, COMPOBJ.DLL creates an instance of the OCX called a component object. This is a special type of Windows object that uses its own class identifier. Once Windows creates the component object for you, it returns an object pointer to your application. What you get with this pointer is access to a table of functions (methods) that the OCX supports. You're communicating with the OCX through the COMPOBJ.DLL. This DLL provides all the translation required to make communication between your application and the OCX smooth.

I'd like to spend a little more time on the method that your application uses to request a copy of an OCX. Remember those 128-digit CLSID numbers in Chapter 10 in the registry discussion? I told you at that time that they were class identifiers. What I didn't tell you was that they are Windows' way to identify a particular Windows object. An OCX is a Windows object. Now, think about the OLE example I provided in that chapter. You saw the following code in the RegisterRandomString function.

```
procedure RegisterRandomString;
const
  AutoClassInfo: TAutoClassInfo = (
    AutoClass: TRandomString;
    ProgID: 'OLEAutoS.RandomString';
    ClassID: '{1D832740-648B-11CF-8C70-00006E3127B7}';
    Description: 'A Random String Generator';
    Instancing: acSingleInstance);
begin
  Automation.RegisterClass(AutoClassInfo);
end;
```

The ClassID constant appears in the CLSID section of the registry after you run this function. The Automation RegisterClass method creates the appropriate registry entry for you. Now let's look at the application's view of this. An application that wants to use the OLE server capabilities of the CreateRandomString function needs to call the server using the ClassID constant. Likewise, an OCX registers itself using a ClassID. When your application wants to create a copy of the OCX, it passes the ClassID to COMPOBJ.DLL. COMPOBJ.DLL takes this ClassID, looks up the associated OCX (a DLL in actuality), requests a pointer to its function (method) table, and returns the pointer to your application.

One of the other things that COMPOBJ.DLL has to do when you're using an OCX may not seem very obvious at first. An object can execute within another process' space in memory. This means that COMPOBJ.DLL has to provide a marshaling function. That is, it has to provide a method for a 16-bit and a 32-bit application to communicate with each other. We have already covered this topic at length in other areas of the book, so I won't go into it again here. The short story is that COMPOBJ.DLL has to provide a means for moving data between the boundaries of two processes.

I'll continue to refer to a specific object variable (i.e., a container for data) as a property throughout this chapter.

The need for a marshaling process isn't new. OLE 1 also had to provide this functionality. The difference between OLE 1 and OLE 2 in this regard is that OLE 1 uses an asynchronous marshaling technique—the call made by client process returns before the server process has a chance to complete it. This means that you have to block the current application until the server process is finished—an error ridden process to say the least (which means that you also have to provide error handling features in your application to take care of situations where the call isn't successful). OLE 2 uses synchronous calls. The client process' call returns when the server process completes the request, reducing the complexity of writing applications. You don't need extra error handling code because you know immediately whether the call was a success. In addition, you don't have to provide code to block the application.

So far I've discussed properties and methods—two of the elements that we commonly associate with a Delphi object. COMPOBJ.DLL provides the method for translating both of these items in a way that's transparent to the user of the object. Now it's time to look at the third element, events. Events don't require much translation since you can look at them as a message. All that COMPOBJ.DLL does when it sees a message is place that message in the client's messaging loop. Of course, it performs the marshaling required to make the message understandable first. Obviously, the 16-bit and 32-bit environments use different sized variables for the various parameters passed as part of a message.

Peter's Principle: The Importance of Network OLE

Right now an OCX has to reside on your machine for you to access it. That's because of a limitation of OLE, not a limitation with OCXs. As we saw in the preceding paragraphs, your application talks to the OCX through a communication layer in COMPOBJ.DLL. One of the hidden benefits to this approach is that only COMPOBJ.DLL needs to know where the OCX actually resides. The OCX could appear on your machine or on a server somewhere. Location, like interface, has become unimportant. (COMPOBJ.DLL knows the location of the OCX only because that location is part of the registration process.)

It's easy to see the benefits of this approach for a number of programming situations. For example, you could place one copy of the OCXs for a custom application on the file server. With this kind of setup, upgrading the application might become a matter of replacing one OCX in a central location. Think about the advantages for all the overworked network administrators out there right now.

The current OLE limitation is that it uses an LRPC (light remote procedure call) mechanism. This keeps communication tied to the local machine. Once Microsoft gets network OLE completed, you should be able to place an OCX anywhere. I say *should* because there isn't any way right now to determine if the current OCX standard will require changes to work with network OLE. Microsoft says that the current crop of OCXs will work, but we've heard that before with VBXs as well.

The bottom line for you as a developer is that network OLE represents a new door of opportunity that you couldn't open with a DLL or VBX. Centralized control over the OCXs that define your application would have a lot of benefits, the least of which is fewer support calls from users who overwrote your OCX with an older version of the same thing. With this in mind, it becomes even more important that you exercise some level of care when writing applications that use an OCX or when designing an OCX of your own. With network functionality coming to the market, what you should be looking at are the things that will prevent your OCX from working in that environment. For example, I can see a lot of problems with people who insist on adding path information to their code.

At this point I'm not quite sure about all the features that network OLE will bring. Let's just say that for a programmer, it'll add yet another layer of complexity to an already convoluted programming scenario, but that added complexity will also yield new opportunities.

I don't want you to get the idea that COM is a perfect solution in an imperfect world—it isn't. There are some distinct disadvantages to using this approach to programming. The one that you should recognize instantly is that there is at least one extra layer (and usually a lot more) of interface between you and the OCX. The immediate result of these extra layers is the performance penalty you'll experience. I find that OCXs are a lot slower than a DLL of similar capability.

Another problem occurs when you need to troubleshoot an errant application. When was the last time you found the documentation for anything perfect? There are always errors that make using a product less than intuitive. When you use a DLL, you know where the DLL resides and exactly how you're talking with it. There are a lot of different tools at your disposal for figuring out the problems you encounter using that DLL—even if you don't have the source code for it. You can't say the same thing about an OCX. Windows, in smoothing out interface problems and making the location of an OCX secret, has actually made your job of debugging and application harder.

As we get into the world of network OLE I'm sure that other problems are going to crop up. For example, how will your application handle a lost network connection—something we don't have to worry about now? As the tools for using OCX mature I'm sure some of these problems will go away. However, it's important to realize that while COM is a great idea, its implementation is still less than perfect.

Importing the Control

Registering an OCX with Delphi, then placing it on the Component Palette, is fairly easy. I've already provided this information in another chapter of the book, Chapter 17, but wanted to be sure you'd find a reference to it here as well. All you need to do is look at the section entitled "Installing and Removing OCXs." I included the information in that chapter instead of here to keep all the library procedures in one place. Make sure you also take a look at the "OCXs Are Not Created Equal— Read the Label Before Buying" principle in the "OCXs—The Wave of the Future" section of Appendix A. It contains valuable information on why some OCXs are a bit cantankerous when installed in Delphi.

Using OCX Controls in Applications

Now that we've gotten some of the technical details out of the way, let's have a little fun with the OCXs provided with Delphi. This section is going to visit the various components and show you what you can do with them.

Let's begin by looking at a simple form containing a TVCFormulaOne OCX component and a menu as shown in Figure 18.1. The menu contains several simple entries. There is a File | Exit command to allow the user to exit the application and a View | Graph command to display the graph form I'll describe later. At first glance, you might be tempted to think that an OCX provides the same functionality as other types of components. For one thing, it uses properties and events, just like any other component.

Figure 18.1.

The first form in our sample OCX application contains an OCX and a menu.

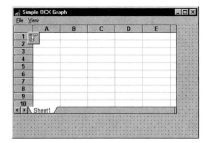

Remember that in the previous sections I mentioned that an OCX was much like a VBX with an OLE twist. I also told you that an OCX was descended from the venerable DLL that we've explored in the past. Now it's time to take a look at some of the OLE twist aspect of using an OCX. If you right click on the OCX, you'll expose a different kind of context menu than we've seen before. Look at the two additional entries shown in Figure 18.2.

If you click on the About entry, you'll see something similar to Figure 18.3. Why is this feature so important? Think about the various components and DLLs on your machine. Can you tell at a glance what version number they are or who produced them? No, it takes some detective work before you can figure these things out. The About Box of an OCX is the first difference that separates it from other types of add-in products.

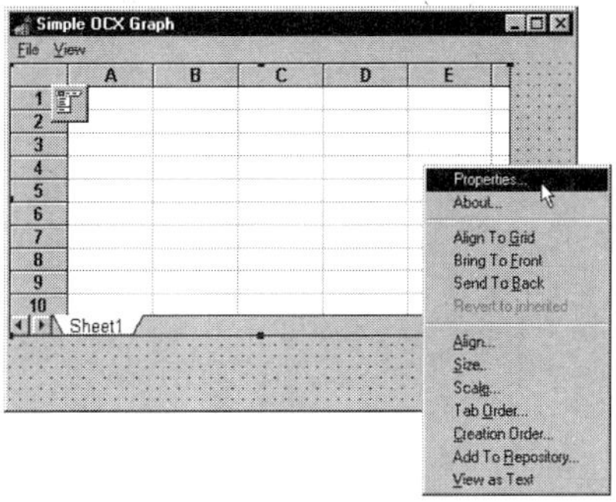

Figure 18.2.
An OCX provides additional context menu entries not provided by either Delphi components or DLLs.

Figure 18.3.
OCXs come with an About Box, something you won't find with most Delphi components or DLLs.

Obviously we could create an About Box for other types of components, but I think you'd find it difficult to add this feature to the context menu. Of course, even though an About Box is a nice feature, it's hardly worth all the hoopla that Microsoft would attach to OCXs. It's the properties page that makes the difference in OCXs. Figure 18.4 shows a typical example of this feature. In this case it's for the TVCFormulaOne component that we added to our sample application. Think of a property page as an extended example of some of the editors that you find provided with Delphi components. Anything you can add to a standard application, you can add to a property page. It's even possible to add other OCXs beside the standard list of components. You should start to see now why the OLE twist in an OCX is so important—it gives you an added level of functionality from the programmer perspective that you wouldn't have gotten otherwise.

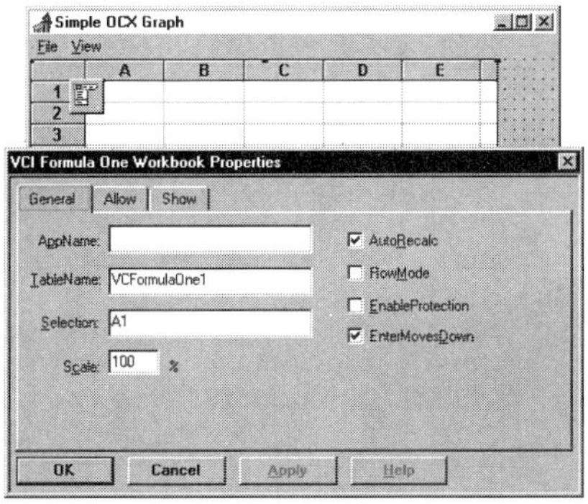

Figure 18.4.
The property pages provided with an OCX give it an added level of flexibility.

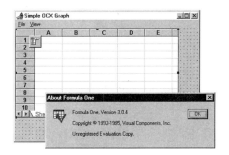

I wanted to keep this example simple enough to make some of the advantages of using an OCX easy to see. You'll find that the programs you create can and will make more extensive use of the OCX features that I present here. The one thing I wanted to do is define a link between the TVCFormulaOne component here and something else. In this case that something else appears in Figure 18.5. I defined another form; in this case it contains a TVCFirstImpression OCX component and another menu. The menu contains a simple File | Exit command designed to allow the user to exit the graphic. I also made the form background white so that the graph would show up better. Other than that, I haven't made a single change to the other properties.

Figure 18.5.
The second form in our sample application contains another OCX component.

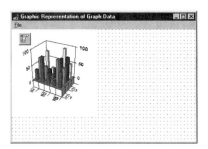

This is another area where we see an advantage to using an OCX. If you look at the context menu for this component you'll see the standard About and Properties entries for an OCX. However, when you select the Properties option, First Impressions will display a new menu. This one includes a Wizard selection (along with a lot of other entries). Select it and you'll see four pages worth of Wizard setup information as shown in Figure 18.6. There really isn't any limit to what you can add to an OCX in this regard—you can make them just as flexible as Delphi components. Lest you think that I've gone OCX happy, you should also spend some time looking at the help provided with these products. I think you'll find that most of it is very Visual BASIC specific; that's one of the costs of using an OCX versus a Delphi component. I found it relatively easy to use the help, but converting the example code to use it within Delphi did take a little time—something that you should consider when making your component choices. In most cases I think you'll find that OCXs provide a lot of programmer help in the form of menus and property pages. You pay for that assistance with a reduced level of assistance from the help files.

Once you've gotten the forms together, you'll need to add some code. Listing 18.1 contains the code for the first form. Listing 18.2 contains the code for the second form. As you can see, the code isn't all that complex. I simply wanted to show how the two forms would work together. Both of these products contain a lot more features than you'll see here.

Figure 18.6.

An OCX isn't necessarily limited to just a properties page; you can add features like Wizards if you'd like.

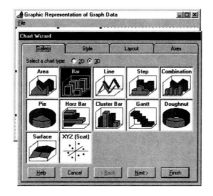

Listing 18.1. TVCFormulaOne OCX component.

```
unit OCXSprd1;

interface

uses
  Windows, Messages, SysUtils, Classes, Graphics, Controls, Forms, Dialogs,
  Menus, OleCtrls, VCFrmla1;

type
  TForm1 = class(TForm)
    VCFormulaOne1: TVCFormulaOne;
    MainMenu1: TMainMenu;
    File1: TMenuItem;
    Exit1: TMenuItem;
    View1: TMenuItem;
    Graph1: TMenuItem;
    procedure FormResize(Sender: TObject);
    procedure Exit1Click(Sender: TObject);
    procedure Graph1Click(Sender: TObject);
  private
    { Private declarations }
  public
    { Public declarations }
  end;

var
  Form1: TForm1;

implementation

uses OCXSprd2;

{$R *.DFM}

procedure TForm1.Exit1Click(Sender: TObject);
begin
{Exit the application.}
    Application.Terminate;
end;
```

continues

Listing 18.1. continued

```
procedure TForm1.Graph1Click(Sender: TObject);
var
    iRowCount: Integer; {Row loop counter.}
    iColCount: Integer; {Column loop counter.}
begin
    {Use the second form.}
    with Form2 do
    begin

    {Modify the data in the chart to match our data points.}
    for iRowCount := 1 to 5 do
        begin

        {Set the current row to match our row counter.}
        VCFirstImpression1.Row := iRowCount;
        VCFormulaOne1.SelStartRow := iRowCount;
        VCFormulaOne1.SelEndRow := iRowCount;
        for iColCount := 1 to 4 do
            begin

            {Set the current column to match our column counter.}
            VCFirstImpression1.Column := iColCount;
            VCFormulaOne1.SelStartCol := iColCount;
            VCFormulaOne1.SelEndCol := iColCount;

            {Set the data value.}
            VCFirstImpression1.Data := VCFormulaOne1.FormattedText;
            end;
        end;
        end; {with Form2 do}

    {Display the graph.}
    Form2.Show;
end;

procedure TForm1.FormResize(Sender: TObject);
begin
    {Change the size of the grid to match our display area.}
    VCFormulaOne1.Height := Form1.ClientHeight;
    VCFormulaOne1.Width := Form1.ClientWidth;
end;

end.
```

Listing 18.2. TVCFirstImpression OCX component.

```
unit OCXSprd2;

interface

uses
  Windows, Messages, SysUtils, Classes, Graphics, Controls, Forms, Dialogs,
  OleCtrls, VCFImprs, Menus;
```

```
type
  TForm2 = class(TForm)
    VCFirstImpression1: TVCFirstImpression;
    MainMenu1: TMainMenu;
    File1: TMenuItem;
    Exit1: TMenuItem;
    procedure FormResize(Sender: TObject);
    procedure Exit1Click(Sender: TObject);
  private
    { Private declarations }
  public
    { Public declarations }
  end;

var
  Form2: TForm2;

implementation

{$R *.DFM}

procedure TForm2.Exit1Click(Sender: TObject);
begin
    {Close the form.}
    Form2.Close;
end;

procedure TForm2.FormResize(Sender: TObject);
begin
    {Change the size of the grid to match our display area.}
    VCFirstImpression1.Height := Form2.ClientHeight;
    VCFirstImpression1.Width := Form2.ClientWidth;
end;

end.
```

As you can see, there aren't any deep dark secrets here. There are two FormResize procedures provided. Both of them do the same thing—they keep the OCX control size in sync with that of the
form. Unlike Delphi components, there isn't any automatic sizing feature provided with most OCXs.
The alternative is this simple procedure.

The main procedure appears in Listing 18.1—Graph1Click. It transfers the data from the grid OCX
to the graph OCX. I decided to show you this technique because most OCXs do provide a programming interface in place of what you might consider a foregone conclusion—OLE data transfer. These
controls provide the second option as well; you can create links between live data and the graph
OCX.

Let's take a look at this program in action. Figure 18.7 shows what the program will look like with
sample data entered in the grid and the graphic representation of that data displayed. The program's
currently hard coded for 5 rows and 4 columns of data. It only displays one graph type—a three-
dimensional bar chart. In a real application you'd add other options to allow the user to change the
graph type and range of data points.

Figure 18.7.

Our OCX example provides
you with an idea of what
these components are
capable of.

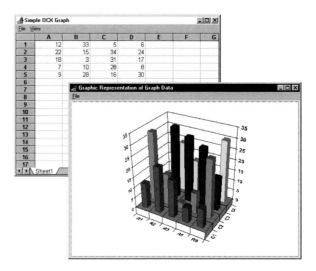

Creating Your Own OCX Using C++

Writing your own OCX doesn't have to be much harder than writing a Delphi component—at least not in theory. There are a few things you'll need to overcome before you dive right in though. First, you'll need to know a language like C++ to write an OCX. Borland didn't include the tools required to create an OCX as part of Delphi. That doesn't stop you from creating an OCX with Delphi, but I'd say that you'd find it a challenge to do so. Without the proper tools to write the OCX, you'd have to perform all of the initialization chores by hand—including the interface to COMPOBJ.DLL. Suffice it to say that this isn't a job that even an intermediate Delphi programmer would want to take on.

Note: The example in this section was developed using Microsoft Visual C++ version 4.0. It won't work with Borland C++ or any previous version of the Microsoft C++ product. Unfortunately, developing OCXs is a relatively new process and trying to create a generic example that works with everyone's product didn't prove viable. The example in this section will provide you with valuable hints and tips on developing your own OCXs no matter which programming language product you decide to use.

Note: I used the new Microsoft Developer Studio setup for this example. All the screen shots you see will reflect the Windows 95 orientation of that setup. If you choose to use the older interface, your screen shots won't match mine at all. There may be subtle differences even if you do use the Developer Studio interface, due to the variety of configuration options that this product provides.

Creating the Project

Let's begin with a new C++ project. However, unlike other projects you've created, you'll want to start with the OLE Control Wizard to create your workspace. To do that, use the File | New command to display the New dialog. Select the Project Workspace option and you'll see a dialog like the one shown in Figure 18.8. Notice the OLE Control Wizard entry in this dialog. That's the one you'll need to start the project. The Wizard provides you with an OCX framework that you can build on to create the final version of this example.

Figure 18.8.
Microsoft Visual C++ 4.0 offers several new workspace project types including the one you'll need to create an OCX.

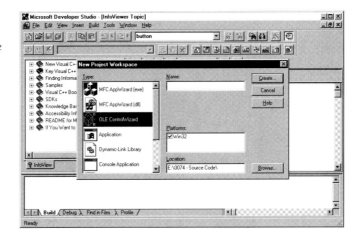

Note: I'm going to be talking about objects quite a bit in this section. Every object in this chapter is a Windows object (or a special form of it defined by COM). Some C++ programmers might get the idea that a Windows object is precisely the same as a C++ object. Since the COM uses a special form of Windows object, these same programmers might think that they won't run into any problems using any C++ object on hand to write an OCX. Nothing could be further from the truth. While you can use a C++ object to create a Windows object, there are limitations. There isn't space in this chapter to get into a full discourse of the intricacies of C++ programming—that's a topic that some authors take an entire chapter (or two) to cover as an overview—but I do want you to be aware that there are limits to what you can and should do when writing an OCX using C++. Following the example in this chapter is the best way to get started writing OCXs without running into problems. Once you get past the capabilities of the application I provide, you'll want to spend some time considering the differences between a C++ object and that used by Windows.

To get the project started, you'll have to type something in the name field. I used OCXExmpl for my project name. You'll also need to click on the OLE Control Wizard entry in the type field, then on the Create button. Microsoft Visual C++ will automatically select the Win32 option for you. It will also create a project directory.

What you'll see next is two dialogs worth of OLE Control Wizard screens. I accepted the defaults on both screens except for the subclass entry on the second page. You'll want to select the BUTTON class here if you want to create an example like this one. Otherwise, look through the list of available classes to determine what you want to use as a basis for your control. Notice that, like Delphi, you can choose to create your own basic class.

Once you click on the Finish button in the second Wizard screen, you'll see a New Project Information dialog. I usually look through the list of features presented here just to make certain the project contains everything I need. After I verify that the project setup is correct, I click on OK to get the project started. Visual C++ will churn your disk for a few moments, and then you'll see the project framework.

Modifying the Default About Box

Now that you've got a framework put together, it's time to start filling it out. I usually start by tackling the easy stuff first—who doesn't? The first thing you'll want to do is modify the About Box. Yes, Visual C++ creates one of those for you automatically—all you need to do is customize it. Getting access to the About Box is easy. Just use the View | Resource Symbols command to display the Resource Symbols dialog shown in Figure 18.9. Select the IDD_ABOUTBOX_OCXEXMPL entry, then click on the View Use pushbutton to display it. Figure 18.10 shows how I modified my version of the About Box for this example. You'll probably want to include additional copyright and company information in your About Box. Notice the variety tools that Microsoft provides for the dialog box. One of them is the custom control button. You can stick another OCX within the About Box or any other dialogs you create.

Figure 18.9.

The Resource Symbols dialog displays a list of all the symbol resources in your project.

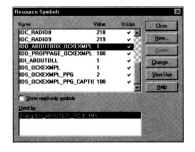

Figure 18.10.

The dialog editor looks like the one provided with Visual Basic—the difference is that you have to access it separately from the main editor screen.

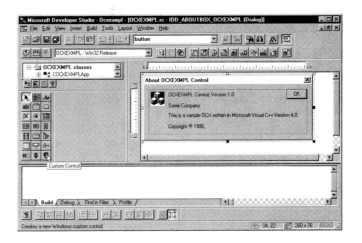

Adding Properties and Events

Customizing the About Box is fun, but let's get down to the business of creating an OCX. The first thing you'll want to do is make some of the button control properties and events visible to someone using the OCX. Unlike a Delphi component, there aren't very many properties visible when you first create a button. To make these various elements visible, you'll need to use the Class Wizard. Use the View | Class Wizard command to display the Class Wizard dialog shown in Figure 18.11.

Figure 18.11.

The Class Wizard dialog allows you to make properties and events visible to the OCX user.

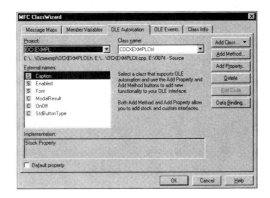

There are two different kinds of properties that we'll use in this example—Microsoft provides access to a lot more. The first type is a stock property. You'll find that things like the caption property that we all take for granted in Delphi aren't visible when you first create an OCX. Figure 18.11 shows a complete list of all the properties that we'll create in this example. The ones with an S are stock properties. The other kind of property that we'll create is a custom property. We've already done that in the Delphi component example. One of them is the OnOff property that we used to create an on-off switch in the multi-button example. We're going to do the same thing in this example so that you can see the differences and similarities between creating an OCX and a Delphi component. The properties with a C in Figure 18.11 are custom properties.

Creating a new property is fairly simple. All you need to do is click on the Add Property pushbutton to display the Add Property dialog shown in Figure 18.12. There are some important features to this dialog that you might not see at first. The External Name combo box contains a complete list of the default properties for the base class that you selected when creating the OCX. In this case you'll see things like the Caption property. To create a stock property, just select one of the items from this list and click on OK. Visual C++ will take care of the details for you in this case. We'll also need three custom properties: ModalResult, OnOff, and StdButtonType. To create these properties just type the names I've just mentioned into the External Name field. You'll need to select a Type as well. The Modal Result and StdButtonType properties are the long type, while OnOff is a BOOL.

Figure 18.12.
The Add Properties dialog allows you to create new properties for your OCX or make existing ones visible to the user.

All of the events we'll use in this example are stock—they come as part of the button base class. All you need to do is click on the OLE Events page to display the dialog shown in Figure 18.13. Adding a stock event is about the same as adding a stock property. Just click on the Add Event button to display the Add Event dialog. Select a stock name from the External Name combo box and click on OK to complete the process. Figure 18.13 shows all of the stock events I added to our example.

Figure 18.13.
The OLE Events page shows all the stock events added to our OCX programming example.

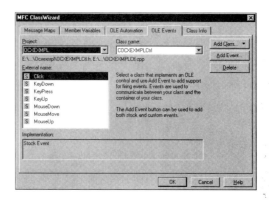

Defining the Property Page

Now it's time to add some functionality to our property page. You access it the same way that we did the About Box. In this case you'll select the IDD_PROPPAGE_OCXEXMPL entry in the Resource Symbols dialog. I decided to make use of the property page to diverge from our previous multi-button example a bit. What I did was add a method for defining standard button types to the page as shown in Figure 18.14.

Figure 18.14.
Our Property Page dialog will allow the user to create standard button type in addition to the multi-button.

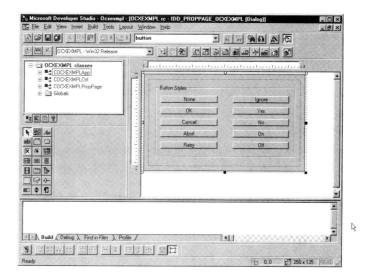

These are radio buttons. You'll need 10 of them. Double-clicking on a radio button will display the Radio Button Properties dialog shown in Figure 18.15. There are a few subtle changes you'll need to make to your radio buttons to make them look like mine. First, select the Style page and select the Push-like check box for each button. Now, we also need to place the radio buttons into a group. To do that you need to select the Group and the Tabstop check boxes on the first radio button in the group. Check only the Tabstop check box for all of the other radio buttons or you'll end up with ten groups of one button instead of one group of ten buttons. Visual C++ starts with the first button it sees that has the Group check box selected as the starting point for the group. The group continues with each radio button in tab order until Visual C++ sees the next one with the Group check box selected.

Figure 18.15.
The Radio Group Properties dialog allows you to change the visual presentation of the radio button as well as place the radio button in a group.

We have to do one more thing with the radio buttons in this dialog. To create an OLE connection between the radio buttons and the OCX control, you have to assign their output to an OLE property. Ctrl–double-click on the first radio button in the group to display the Add Member Variable dialog shown in Figure 18.16. The entries you make here are crucial because Visual C++ doesn't check them for errors and there isn't any way to select them from a list. In the Member Variable Name field, type m_stdButtonType. That's the internal name for one of the custom properties that we created earlier. Leave the Category and Variable Type fields alone. Type StdButtonType in the Optional OLE Property Name field. This is the entry that links the property page to your OCX control. Remember that C++ is case sensitive; capitalization is important.

Figure 18.16.
The Add Member Variable
dialog provides the means for
linking your property page to
the OCX.

Adding Some Code

Up to this point we haven't added a single line of code to our application. That's because we've been building a framework for the code. Now it's time to start adding code to the OCX. Listings 18.3 and 18.4 show you how to flesh out the OCXEXMPLCtl.CPP and OCXEXMPLCtl.H files.

Listing 18.3. OCXEXMPLCtl.CPP file.

```
// OCXEXMPLCtl.cpp : Implementation of the COCXEXMPLCtrl OLE control class.

#include "stdafx.h"
#include "OCXEXMPL.h"
#include "OCXEXMPLCtl.h"
#include "OCXEXMPLPpg.h"


#ifdef _DEBUG
#define new DEBUG_NEW
#undef THIS_FILE
static char THIS_FILE[] = __FILE__;
#endif


IMPLEMENT_DYNCREATE(COCXEXMPLCtrl, COleControl)
```

```
/////////////////////////////////////////////////////////////////////////
// Message map

BEGIN_MESSAGE_MAP(COCXEXMPLCtrl, COleControl)
    //{{AFX_MSG_MAP(COCXEXMPLCtrl)
    // NOTE - ClassWizard will add and remove message map entries
    //    DO NOT EDIT what you see in these blocks of generated code !
    //}}AFX_MSG_MAP
    ON_MESSAGE(OCM_COMMAND, OnOcmCommand)
    ON_OLEVERB(AFX_IDS_VERB_PROPERTIES, OnProperties)
END_MESSAGE_MAP()


/////////////////////////////////////////////////////////////////////////
// Dispatch map

BEGIN_DISPATCH_MAP(COCXEXMPLCtrl, COleControl)
    //{{AFX_DISPATCH_MAP(COCXEXMPLCtrl)
    DISP_PROPERTY_NOTIFY(COCXEXMPLCtrl, "OnOff", m_onOff, OnOnOffChanged, VT_BOOL)
    DISP_PROPERTY_NOTIFY(COCXEXMPLCtrl, "ModalResult", m_modalResult,
OnModalResultChanged, VT_I4)
    DISP_PROPERTY_NOTIFY(COCXEXMPLCtrl, "StdButtonType", m_stdButtonType,
OnStdButtonTypeChanged, VT_I4)
    DISP_STOCKPROP_CAPTION()
    DISP_STOCKPROP_ENABLED()
    DISP_STOCKPROP_FONT()
    //}}AFX_DISPATCH_MAP
    DISP_FUNCTION_ID(COCXEXMPLCtrl, "AboutBox", DISPID_ABOUTBOX, AboutBox, VT_EMPTY,
VTS_NONE)
END_DISPATCH_MAP()


/////////////////////////////////////////////////////////////////////////
// Event map

BEGIN_EVENT_MAP(COCXEXMPLCtrl, COleControl)
  //{{AFX_EVENT_MAP(COCXEXMPLCtrl)
  EVENT_STOCK_CLICK()
  EVENT_STOCK_KEYDOWN()
  EVENT_STOCK_KEYPRESS()
  EVENT_STOCK_KEYUP()
  EVENT_STOCK_MOUSEDOWN()
  EVENT_STOCK_MOUSEMOVE()
  EVENT_STOCK_MOUSEUP()
  //}}AFX_EVENT_MAP
END_EVENT_MAP()


/////////////////////////////////////////////////////////////////////////
// Property pages

// TODO: Add more property pages as needed.  Remember to increase the count!
BEGIN_PROPPAGEIDS(COCXEXMPLCtrl, 1)
  PROPPAGEID(COCXEXMPLPropPage::guid)
END_PROPPAGEIDS(COCXEXMPLCtrl)
```

continues

Listing 18.3. continued

```
//////////////////////////////////////////////////////////////////////////
// Initialize class factory and guid

IMPLEMENT_OLECREATE_EX(COCXEXMPLCtrl, "OCXEXMPL.OCXEXMPLCtrl.1",
  0xd8d77e03, 0x712a, 0x11cf, 0x8c, 0x70, 0, 0, 0x6e, 0x31, 0x27, 0xb7)


//////////////////////////////////////////////////////////////////////////
// Type library ID and version

IMPLEMENT_OLETYPELIB(COCXEXMPLCtrl, _tlid, _wVerMajor, _wVerMinor)


//////////////////////////////////////////////////////////////////////////
// Interface IDs

const IID BASED_CODE IID_DOCXEXMPL =
    { 0xd8d77e01, 0x712a, 0x11cf, { 0x8c, 0x70, 0, 0, 0x6e, 0x31, 0x27, 0xb7 } };
const IID BASED_CODE IID_DOCXEXMPLEvents =
    { 0xd8d77e02, 0x712a, 0x11cf, { 0x8c, 0x70, 0, 0, 0x6e, 0x31, 0x27, 0xb7 } };


//////////////////////////////////////////////////////////////////////////
// Control type information

static const DWORD BASED_CODE _dwOCXEXMPLOleMisc =
  OLEMISC_ACTIVATEWHENVISIBLE ¦
  OLEMISC_SETCLIENTSITEFIRST ¦
  OLEMISC_INSIDEOUT ¦
  OLEMISC_CANTLINKINSIDE ¦
  OLEMISC_RECOMPOSEONRESIZE;

IMPLEMENT_OLECTLTYPE(COCXEXMPLCtrl, IDS_OCXEXMPL, _dwOCXEXMPLOleMisc)

//////////////////////////////////////////////////////////////////////////
// COCXEXMPLCtrl::COCXEXMPLCtrlFactory::UpdateRegistry -
// Adds or removes system registry entries for COCXEXMPLCtrl

BOOL COCXEXMPLCtrl::COCXEXMPLCtrlFactory::UpdateRegistry(BOOL bRegister)
{
    if (bRegister)
        return AfxOleRegisterControlClass(
            AfxGetInstanceHandle(),
            m_clsid,
            m_lpszProgID,
            IDS_OCXEXMPL,
            IDB_OCXEXMPL,
            FALSE,                     //  Not insertable
            _dwOCXEXMPLOleMisc,
            _tlid,
            _wVerMajor,
            _wVerMinor);
    else
        return AfxOleUnregisterClass(m_clsid, m_lpszProgID);
}
```

```
///////////////////////////////////////////////////////////////////////
// COCXEXMPLCtrl::COCXEXMPLCtrl - Constructor

COCXEXMPLCtrl::COCXEXMPLCtrl()
{
  InitializeIIDs(&IID_DOCXEXMPL, &IID_DOCXEXMPLEvents);

  // TODO: Initialize your control's instance data here.
}


///////////////////////////////////////////////////////////////////////
// COCXEXMPLCtrl::~COCXEXMPLCtrl - Destructor

COCXEXMPLCtrl::~COCXEXMPLCtrl()
{
  // TODO: Cleanup your control's instance data here.
}


///////////////////////////////////////////////////////////////////////
// COCXEXMPLCtrl::OnDraw - Drawing function

void COCXEXMPLCtrl::OnDraw(
      CDC* pdc, const CRect& rcBounds, const CRect& rcInvalid)
{
  DoSuperclassPaint(pdc, rcBounds);
}


///////////////////////////////////////////////////////////////////////
// COCXEXMPLCtrl::DoPropExchange - Persistence support

void COCXEXMPLCtrl::DoPropExchange(CPropExchange* pPX)
{

  // Default actions on the part of the Class Wizard.
  ExchangeVersion(pPX, MAKELONG(_wVerMinor, _wVerMajor));
  COleControl::DoPropExchange(pPX);

  // Make all of our properties persistent..
  PX_Bool(pPX, "OnOff", m_onOff, FALSE);
  PX_Long(pPX, "OnOff", m_modalResult, mrNone);
  PX_Long(pPX, "OnOff", m_stdButtonType, 0);

}


///////////////////////////////////////////////////////////////////////
// COCXEXMPLCtrl::OnResetState - Reset control to default state

void COCXEXMPLCtrl::OnResetState()
{
  COleControl::OnResetState();  // Resets defaults found in DoPropExchange

  //Modify the Microsoft control to match Delphi property settings.
  COleControl::SetText("Button");
  COleControl::SetControlSize(75, 25);
}
```

continues

Listing 18.3. **continued**

```cpp
/////////////////////////////////////////////////////////////////////////////
// COCXEXMPLCtrl::AboutBox - Display an "About" box to the user

void COCXEXMPLCtrl::AboutBox()
{
  CDialog dlgAbout(IDD_ABOUTBOX_OCXEXMPL);
  dlgAbout.DoModal();
}


/////////////////////////////////////////////////////////////////////////////
// COCXEXMPLCtrl::PreCreateWindow - Modify parameters for CreateWindowEx

BOOL COCXEXMPLCtrl::PreCreateWindow(CREATESTRUCT& cs)
{
  cs.lpszClass = _T("BUTTON");
  return COleControl::PreCreateWindow(cs);
}


/////////////////////////////////////////////////////////////////////////////
// COCXEXMPLCtrl::IsSubclassedControl - This is a subclassed control

BOOL COCXEXMPLCtrl::IsSubclassedControl()
{
  return TRUE;
}


/////////////////////////////////////////////////////////////////////////////
// COCXEXMPLCtrl::OnOcmCommand - Handle command messages

LRESULT COCXEXMPLCtrl::OnOcmCommand(WPARAM wParam, LPARAM lParam)
{
#ifdef _WIN32
  WORD wNotifyCode = HIWORD(wParam);
#else
  WORD wNotifyCode = HIWORD(lParam);
#endif

  // TODO: Switch on wNotifyCode here.

  return 0;
}


/////////////////////////////////////////////////////////////////////////////
// COCXEXMPLCtrl message handlers

void COCXEXMPLCtrl::OnOnOffChanged()
{
  //If the programmer set the OnOff property true, take appropriate action.
  if (m_onOff)
  {
    COleControl::SetText("On");    //Change the caption.
    m_SetOn = TRUE;                //Set an internal caption flag.
    m_modalResult = mrOn;          //Set the modal result value.
  }
```

```
  else
  {
    COleControl::SetText("Button");      //Restore default caption.
    m_SetOn = FALSE;                     //Turn our caption flag off.
    m_modalResult = mrNone;              //Use the default modal result.
  }


  SetModifiedFlag();                     //Peform the default action.
}

void COCXEXMPLCtrl::OnClick(USHORT iButton)
{
  // See if the OnOff flag is set.  If so, change the caption and internal
  // caption flag.  The effect you should see from this code is a toggling
  // of the caption text.
  if (m_onOff)
  {
    if (m_SetOn)
    {
      COleControl::SetText("Off");
      m_SetOn = FALSE;
      m_modalResult = mrOff;
    }
    else
    {
      COleControl::SetText("On");
      m_SetOn = TRUE;
      m_modalResult = mrOn;
    }
  }

  // Call the default OnClick processing.
  COleControl::OnClick(iButton);
}


void COCXEXMPLCtrl::OnModalResultChanged()
{
  // We don't need to do anything here except set the modified flag.
  SetModifiedFlag();
}

void COCXEXMPLCtrl::OnStdButtonTypeChanged()
{
  // Change the modal result and button caption to match the user selection.
  switch (m_stdButtonType)
  {
  case 0:
    m_modalResult = mrNone;
    COleControl::SetText("Button");
    break;
  case 1:
    m_modalResult = mrOK;
    COleControl::SetText("OK");
    break;
```

continues

Listing 18.3. **continued**

```
  case 2:
    m_modalResult = mrCancel;
    COleControl::SetText("Cancel");
    break;
  case 3:
    m_modalResult = mrAbort;
    COleControl::SetText("Abort");
    break;
  case 4:
    m_modalResult = mrRetry;
    COleControl::SetText("Retry");
    break;
  case 5:
    m_modalResult = mrIgnore;
    COleControl::SetText("Ignore");
    break;
  case 6:
    m_modalResult = mrYes;
    COleControl::SetText("Yes");
    break;
  case 7:
    m_modalResult = mrNo;
    COleControl::SetText("No");
    break;
  case 8:
    m_modalResult = mrOn;
    COleControl::SetText("On");
    break;
  case 9:
    m_modalResult = mrOff;
    COleControl::SetText("Off");
  }


  //Set the OnOff property to false since the user selected another type.
  m_onOff = FALSE;

  //Set the modified flag.
  SetModifiedFlag();
}
```

Listing 18.4. **OCXEXMPLCtl. H file.**

```
// OCXEXMPLCtl.h : Declaration of the COCXEXMPLCtrl OLE control class.

/////////////////////////////////////////////////////////////////////////////
// COCXEXMPLCtrl : See OCXEXMPLCtl.cpp for implementation.

class COCXEXMPLCtrl : public COleControl
{
  DECLARE_DYNCREATE(COCXEXMPLCtrl)

// Constructor
public:
  COCXEXMPLCtrl();
```

```
// Overrides

  // Drawing function
  virtual void OnDraw(
        CDC* pdc, const CRect& rcBounds, const CRect& rcInvalid);

  // Persistence
  virtual void DoPropExchange(CPropExchange* pPX);

  // Reset control state
  virtual void OnResetState();

  // A new OnClick routine.
  virtual void OnClick(USHORT iButton);

// Implementation
protected:
  ~COCXEXMPLCtrl();

  DECLARE_OLECREATE_EX(COCXEXMPLCtrl)     // Class factory and guid
  DECLARE_OLETYPELIB(COCXEXMPLCtrl)       // GetTypeInfo
  DECLARE_PROPPAGEIDS(COCXEXMPLCtrl)      // Property page IDs
  DECLARE_OLECTLTYPE(COCXEXMPLCtrl)       // Type name and misc status

  // Subclassed control support
  BOOL PreCreateWindow(CREATESTRUCT& cs);
  BOOL IsSubclassedControl();
  LRESULT OnOcmCommand(WPARAM wParam, LPARAM lParam);

// Message maps
  //{{AFX_MSG(COCXEXMPLCtrl)
    // NOTE - ClassWizard will add and remove member functions here.
    //    DO NOT EDIT what you see in these blocks of generated code !
  //}}AFX_MSG
  DECLARE_MESSAGE_MAP()

// Create a new enumerated type for the modal result.
  typedef enum
  {
    mrNone = -1L,
    mrOK = 1L,
    mrCancel = 2L,
    mrAbort = 3L,
        mrRetry = 4L,
        mrIgnore = 5L,
        mrYes = 6L,
        mrNo = 7L,
        mrOn = 8L,
        mrOff = 9L,
  }MODALTYPE;


// Dispatch maps
  //{{AFX_DISPATCH(COCXEXMPLCtrl)
  BOOL m_onOff;
  afx_msg void OnOnOffChanged();
  long m_modalResult;
```

continues

Listing 18.4. **continued**

```
  afx_msg void OnModalResultChanged();
  long m_stdButtonType;
  afx_msg void OnStdButtonTypeChanged();
  //}}AFX_DISPATCH
  DECLARE_DISPATCH_MAP()

  afx_msg void AboutBox();

// Event maps
  //{{AFX_EVENT(COCXEXMPLCtrl)
  //}}AFX_EVENT
  DECLARE_EVENT_MAP()

// Special On/Off state variable.
  BOOL m_SetOn;

// Dispatch and event IDs
public:
  enum {
  //{{AFX_DISP_ID(COCXEXMPLCtrl)
  dispidOnOff = 1L,
  dispidModalResult = 2L,
  dispidStdButtonType = 3L,
  //}}AFX_DISP_ID
  };
};
```

How Does the OCX Work?

Your initial reaction to all this code might be one of sheer terror—it's actually pretty easy to figure it out if you take it one function at a time. In fact, about 20 percent of this code is generated automatically for you as part of the procedure we followed to get to this point. The application framework will save you quite a bit of time.

Let's start taking this code apart. The first function that you'll need to modify is DoPropExchange. This function performs only one service in this example—it allows you to make your custom properties persistent. Remember the "stored" key word in our component example? The PX_ series of function calls does the same thing for Visual C++. There is one function call for each variable type that you define. Each one of them accepts four variables like this: PX_Bool(pPX, "OnOff", m_onOff, FALSE);. The first variable is a pointer to a property exchange structure. Visual C++ defines this structure for you automatically—all you need to do is use it. The second parameter contains the external name of the property, the one that the user will see in the Object Inspector. The third parameter is the internal name for the property. That's the one you'll use throughout the program to define the property. Finally, we have to define a default value for the property (unless you want the user to see a blank field in the Object Inspector).

The next function you have to modify is OnResetState. This function provides some of the aesthetic details that the user will see when he adds the component to a form. In this case I give the component a default caption and resize it to match those provided with Delphi. The default component size used by Microsoft is about twice the size of the one provided by Delphi.

At least two of the three modified functions in the message handle sections of the code. (The ModalResultChanged function doesn't require any modification, so I won't talk about it here.) The OnOnOffChanged function is the first one we'll look at. As you can see, it performs the same task as its counterpart in the Delphi Component example in Chapter 17. What we need to do is set an internal caption flag and the initial caption. Notice that I use the m_onOff internal property variable to track the status of the flag.

The OnClick also looks similar to the one in our component programming example. If this is an OnOff multi-button, then we change the internal state variable and the button caption. The function switches the button state between on and off as needed. Once we get done with the internal processing needed to make the button work, we call the default OnClick processing routine. Like the Delphi component example, failure to call this default routine will cause the OCX to skip any Delphi specific code that you attach to button events.

Now it's time to look at the processing required for the Property Page feature of this OCX. The OnStdButtonTypeChanged function is nothing more than a simple case statement. It changes the button Caption and ModalResult properties as needed to create various default button types. Notice that I also turn off the OnOff multi-button processing if the user selects a default button type.

The header file required only a few changes, but they're pretty important. The first is the addition of a virtual void OnClick(USHORT iButton); declaration to the public section of the component definition. Visual C++ doesn't add this declaration automatically. Since we need it to modify the handling of OnClick events, you'll have to add it manually. This is an important point to remember when writing your own components as well. Assume that nothing is declared public until you actually see it in the code.

The only other addition to the header is an enumerated type definition—MODALTYPE—which allows me to use the same ModalResult settings in the source code that Delphi uses. I found that this was a small, but very important change. Otherwise, the code I wrote could easily get out of sync with that provided by Delphi. It's going to be less of a consideration for you if you plan to write generic OCXs that could work in any environment. You'll want to keep this idea handy though, if the OCXs you create are for use with Delphi applications.

Before you can use this component in Delphi, you'll have to build it within Visual C++. Part of the build process is to register the component for you. I really liked this feature because it saved me some time when working with Delphi. After you build the OCX, you'll need to follow the procedures in Chapter 17 for adding the component to your library.

Testing the OCX

Writing the OCX is only part of the process. Now we have to test it. I created the Delphi form in Figure 18.17. If you read through Chapter 17 this form should look familiar. It uses the same layout as the one in Chapter 17. The only difference is that I'm using an OCX instead of a Delphi component in this case.

Figure 18.17.
Our test form for OCX testing looks just like the one used for component testing—only the components are different.

One of the things that you should notice right away is that our OCX components contain the same context menu that I showed you previously. Open the About Box and you'll see something like Figure 18.18. Open the Properties page and you'll see a working example of the buttons that we created as part of the OCX design process (see Figure 18.19). Try out the various features to see how they work. All you'll need now to make this example function is the code in Listing 18.5.

Figure 18.18.
The About Box for our example is about the same as you'll see in other OCX components.

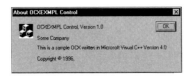

Figure 18.19.
Adding the example OCX to Delphi activates the property page shown here.

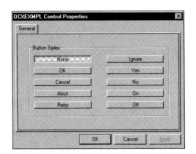

Listing 18.5. **Testing OCXs.**

```
unit OCXComp1;

interface
```

```
uses
  Windows, Messages, SysUtils, Classes, Graphics, Controls, Forms, Dialogs,
  OleCtrls, OCXEXMPL, MultiBtn;

type
  TForm1 = class(TForm)
    OCXMultiButton1: TOCXMultiButton;
    OCXMultiButton2: TOCXMultiButton;
    procedure OCXMultiButton1Click(Sender: TObject);
    procedure OCXMultiButton2Click(Sender: TObject);
  private
    { Private declarations }
  public
    { Public declarations }
  end;

var
  Form1: TForm1;

implementation

{$R *.DFM}

procedure TForm1.OCXMultiButton1Click(Sender: TObject);
begin
  {Check the modal result of our pushbutton press.}
  case OCXMultiButton1.ModalResult of
    mrNone: ShowMessage('Modal Result is None');
    mrOK: ShowMessage('Modal Result is OK');
    mrCancel: ShowMessage('Modal Result is Cancel');
    mrAbort: ShowMessage('Modal Result is Abort');
    mrRetry: ShowMessage('Modal Result is Retry');
    mrIgnore: ShowMessage('Modal Result is Ignore');
    mrYes: ShowMessage('Modal Result is Yes');
    mrNo: ShowMessage('Modal Result is No');
    mrOn: ShowMessage('Button is on.');
    mrOff: ShowMessage('Button is off.');
    end;
end;

procedure TForm1.OCXMultiButton2Click(Sender: TObject);
begin
  {End the application.}
  Application.Terminate;
end;

end.
```

So, how does our example look in operation? Figure 18.20 shows the results. As you can see, we've gotten about the same result from using an OCX that we got from a Delphi component. Obviously, you don't have to stop where I did. The OCX components that we looked at earlier in the chapter certainly provided a lot more. There are two big reasons to use an OCX in place of a Delphi component. The first is portability—I can use the OCX I created with any programming language that accepts them. Second, an OCX can provide an OLE connection—something that you can do with a Delphi component as well, but you'll probably find it more difficult to do.

Figure 18.20.
The final result of using an
OCX for a multi-button
component is similar to that
provided by the Delphi
version.

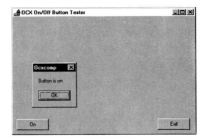

Summary

The best way to look at this chapter is as introducing the three steps needed to fully understand OCXs. The first section contains the theoretical information you'll need to get started. We fully explored what an OCX is in terms of other kinds of Windows executable files that we've looked at in the past and in terms of Delphi components.

The second section shows how to use OCXs. I didn't really do much more than give you a quick overview of the topic. It's important that you take the time to read through the vendor documentation for any OCX that you purchase. I think you're going to find that they're all different. The one drawback to using a commercially available OCX is going to be the Visual BASIC orientation that I told you about.

The third section is where I spent the bulk of my time. This is a simple overview of how to create an OCX of your own. I think that most texts on the subject make the process of creating an OCX a lot more difficult than it needs to be. If you follow the procedure that I showed you here, you'll at least end up with a working OCX that you can enhance as needed. Get the OCX framework in place first, add some basic code to it, then test each function as you embellish the result.

V

Appendixes

A

A Guide to VBXs and OCXs

Delphi surpasses most programming languages in its flexibility. One of the ways it shows this flexibility off is by providing support for more tool types than the competition does. If you're using Delphi 1.0, you can choose between VBXs and Delphi components. If you're using Delphi 2.0, you have a choice between OCXs and Delphi components.

Some people are under the mistaken impression that most components help you manage graphics better, provide file support, or act as some kind of utility. Nothing could be further from the truth. You can buy third-party components as varied as the kinds of applications that you write. In fact, I doubt that I would be too far off in saying that there's a component somewhere out there that's designed to meet your special needs—no matter how esoteric they may be.

This appendix looks at some of the third-party components available on the market. Except for the Delphi component section, you'll probably find most of these products in the Visual Basic section of your favorite computer store or programmer's catalog. I've tried to include a selection of components from a variety of vendors. That way if you don't see what you need, you can always contact one of the vendors listed here to see if they can provide the component you do need.

Note: A lot of the products in this appendix are from other countries. For example, you'll find more than a few marketed by companies in England. There are some cases when developers in the United States may want to try to purchase the products locally instead of relying on an overseas vendor. Pinnacle Publishing, Inc., also markets many of these products. You can contact them at:

P.O. Box 888
Kent, WA 98035-0888
Voice: (800)231-1293
FAX: (206)251-5057

Before I launch into the product descriptions, let's look at some of the criteria you should use when selecting a component. I usually use this list as part of my evaluation before I buy a product. You'll probably want to add some of your own personal criteria to this list as well.

- Royalties—Some companies charge a royalty when you use their product for commercial purposes. If you plan to use their product in your application and then sell your application to other people, you may have to pay the company royalties to maintain the licensing arrangement. I always look for products that don't charge a royalty first. That way I don't have to worry about licensing the product at all. If I don't find one in this category, I start looking for an OEM licensing arrangement. There are some cases when you can get by with an annual fee or other "one-shot" licensing scheme. Obviously, using a product that requires a royalty will also increase the price of your product, so looking around for a royalty free product is always a good idea.

- Source Code—Most of the Delphi components you buy will come with some level of source code support. Some of them will require an additional purchase to get the source. If you're a professional consultant or someone who distributes applications commercially, the cost of buying that source is minimal compared to what you'll gain by having it. Not only will having the source allow you to learn new programming techniques, but you can use it to enhance the component you've purchased. Needless to say, source code is a rarity when buying an OCX or VBX component, but you do see it offered. Normally you'll need to know C to use the VBX or OCX source code.

- Other Programmer Recommendation—I once got bit by a piece of software that was so buggy and ill-conceived that it was unusable. The literature for this particular library offered me the sun, the moon, and the stars; but the product itself didn't offer anything even close. It didn't take me very long to figure out that I should have gotten a few recommendations from other people before I bought the product. You should, too. A lot of times someone has purchased a product that you're thinking about buying. See if you can get a few opinions before you buy.

- Demo or Shareware Versions—There are times when you can't get a recommendation from another programmer. Perhaps no one has really used the product in the same way that you intend to use it. In this case I try to find a demo or shareware version of the product I want to use. Sure, it won't be full-featured and some vendors actually make the shareware or demo version hide flaws in the full-featured product, but it's better than buying the product without even viewing it first. If you do try a shareware or demo version, see if someone else has tried both versions as well. The feedback she provides will help you understand how the shareware or demo version of the product varies from what you'll actually buy. You may want to check out the Delphi 2.0 forum (BDELPHI32) on CompuServe as well. There is a active third-party support section (22) which includes shareware products.

Tip: You'll want to check Borland's other forums as well such as BPASCAL (the Delphi 1.0 forum). There are some great shareware components out there with source code that the authors have yet to convert to 32-bit format. Making a few changes and recompiling the component using Delphi 2.0 may get you a new component that isn't listed elsewhere.

- Money Back Guarantee—Vendors are getting smarter as the software industry matures. I'm often surprised at how many vendors offer a 30- to 60-day money back guarantee with their product these days. What you'll need to find out first though is just what the terms of that money back guarantee are. Make sure you can try the product out on a small project or two, then return it if it doesn't work as advertised. You'll also need to check the return policy of the third-party vendor you buy a product through. There have been a few cases

I've heard of where a vendor wouldn't honor her money back guarantee when a programmer bought a product through a third party. Since the third party didn't have a money back guarantee either, the programmer ended up eating the cost of the purchase.

- Company Stability and Support—Programmers rely on a vendor to provide them with good updates on a fairly regular basis to remain competitive. If the small, one-man shop you buy your component from goes out of business tomorrow, how will you support the product you build with it? The problem just doesn't extend to practical matters like new technology; you'll need that support when a customer calls in with a bug that isn't in your code. You'll find that interactions between your program and a third-party product happen more often than you'd like. If the company you're working with goes out of business or charges by the minute for support, you may be out of luck when it comes time to fix that bug the user reported.

- Cost per Component Versus Quality—There are some vendors in this appendix that offer a grab bag of all kinds of components at a very low cost. The thing you need to realize is that those components may or may not be the best quality. Think about your business. Could you afford to offer a lot of product for a low cost if it took a lot of time to put the application together? I think you'll agree that a vendor who offers a lot of product at a low cost has to have cut corners somewhere. (Of course, some people just charge too much, the opposite side of the coin.) If someone's willing to offer me something for close to nothing, I take a much harder look at it before I buy.

- Flexibility—One of the products in this appendix—Graphics Server—offers no less than six levels of platform support: DLL, VBX, VCL (Delphi component), OCX, FLL, and C++ class. I view this as a real plus because you never know when you'll need to use a component you bought for Delphi on some other platform like Visual Basic. This is especially true for consultants because the job or the client often dictates which language you'll use for a particular project. There are other forms of flexibility as well. What about a communications package that lets you use nine or ten different protocols or a network package that works with NetWare 3.x and 4.x? Products that allow you to do more than the minimum needed are always a better deal than those that don't.

- Efficiency—I've run into a few components that I wouldn't buy for a very good reason—they required too many resources to use. Some vendors try to stick every bit of functionality known to programmers into one component. Sure, it'll allow you to write any kind of program in just ten minutes; but the fact that it requires 16 MB of memory to run should tell you something—no one is going to be able to run the application you build. Obviously I've exaggerated here, but I did so for an important reason. You're going to run into situations when you think you just have to add one more bell or whistle to an application only to find that users complain it's slow or won't run well on their machine. Look for the small and efficient component. Get the job done with the least number of resources possible, and you'll find that the people using your program are a lot happier.

Now that you have a better idea of what to look for, let's start looking at some products. I'm not going to list each and every third-party product available on the market today in this appendix—that would take an entire book by itself. What I am going to do is provide you with some ideas of the type of support that's available out there. I've concentrated on special tools, OLE, popular, and eso-teric components so that you get a good mix of component types. The chapter is separated into four areas: Delphi component, VBX, OCX, and tools so that you can find a particular product with ease.

> **Note:** All prices in this chapter are current as of the time of writing. The prices may change without notice. All prices are list price for the product.

Components—The Third-Party Solution for Delphi

The obvious place to start looking for third-party components as a Delphi programmer is in the Delphi components area. There are more than a few reasons to go the Delphi component route. Just think of all those programmers who made an investment in VBXs, only to find out that they had to buy OCXs to get into the 32-bit world. If those people had bought components, they would have saved some money when making the transition. I also find that VCL components are a lot less work to use in Delphi, if for no other reason than they provide native code support. You can also get full source code support for some components—especially those made by some smaller companies. (Chapter 17, "Building a Delphi VBX," provides a look at how to write your own components; you could use this information to modify any Delphi components that come with full source code support to meet your needs.) Finally, components get compiled into your application; there isn't any need to pro-vide a lot of VBX or OCX files on disk. You also won't need to worry about the user accidentally overwriting your OCX or VBX with a file from someone else's application.

Delphi components aren't as widely used as VBXs and OCXs. However, I recently received a 34- page catalog of Delphi components and was surprised at just how much variety I saw. It's unfor-tunate that I don't have space to list every one of those components here, but space just won't allow for it. What the following paragraphs will provide you with is some ideas of where to start looking for the components you need to get that next big programming job started.

> **Note:** While most Delphi components come with full source code, some, like Graphics Server, don't. I tried to find out which components do and do not come with source code when writing this appendix. The information is current as of the time of writing. You'll definitely want to check with the vendor before you buy if source code support is important to you. Other vendors charge one price for just the component and another for the component

with source code. You'll find two prices for the vendors that do: one for the component alone and another for the component with source. Make sure you find out if all the source code is provided if you plan to use the same component for both 16-bit and 32-bit development since you'll have to recompile it to move from one environment to the other (we covered this procedure in Chapter 17).

WinG SpriteKit
$159.00
DirectDraw SpriteKit
$159.00
Autosizer
$35.00
Mike Scott Software
3 East End
West Calder
West Lothian EH55 8AB
United Kingdom
Tel/fax: +44 1506 871943
E-mail: 100140.2420@compuserve.com

Mike Scott Software actually produces three different products that I'll cover here. By the way, you may have previously known this company under the name Mobius.

The WinG SpriteKit components provide an interface to the Microsoft WinG API extensions for Windows 3.x, Windows 95, and Windows NT. They do the same thing as a lot of Delphi components by encapsulating WinG and making it easier to access. These easy to use components include a full sprite engine. You won't have to add any code for basic sprite movement and animation. This product ships with full source code that is compatible with Delphi 1 and Delphi 2.

The DirectDraw SpriteKit components provide an interface to the DirectDraw objects in the Windows 95 Game SDK. You need Delphi 2.0 to use this product. Mike Scott Software has fully translated the DirectDraw headers, making Delphi 2.0 the tool of choice for Windows 95 game development. The product includes a complete sprite engine built on top of DirectDraw. As with WinG SpriteKit, this product comes with full source code.

You'll find that AutoSizer is an essential tool for graphics programs or if you have to support an application across a wide range of machine types. It provides a set of components that can automatically size components when the user changes the form's size. Sizing options are set per component using a graphical component editor. The best part is that you don't have to add any code to use this product; just drop it on the form and change the appropriate properties. The product includes full source code.

Graphics Server SDK
$245.00
Bits Per Second, Ltd.
14 Regent Hill, Brighton BN1 3ED, UK
Telephone: 01273-727119
Fax: 01273-731925
CompuServe: >MHS:rflowers@bits
Internet: rflowers@bits.mhs.compuserve.com

This is the full-fledged version of the runtime product included with Visual Basic and Delphi. It comes with DLL, VBX, VCL (Delphi component), OCX, FLL, and C++ class support, making it just about the most versatile tool in this appendix. Just like the runtime version, the server runs as an independent application outside of your Delphi or Visual Basic application. However, this product provides a lot more than the runtime does.

Graphics Server is an OLE 2 graphics primitive engine. It supports commands that draw circles or squares. You can use it to perform a variety of complex drawing tasks with products other than Delphi or Visual Basic, even those that don't support OLE directly (CA-Visual Objects is one of them). This feature makes Graphics Server more than just a Delphi tool; it's a tool that you could potentially use with a variety of products in a lot of different environments.

If you don't want to work with graphics primitives and a graph or chart is your goal, then you can use the included ChartBuilder product. This is the full-featured version of the Graph control included with Visual Basic. (The latest version of Graphics Server incorporates all of these capabilities into a single product.) All you need to do is tell ChartBuilder what data points you want to display and what type of graph or chart to display them on. It takes care of all the details.

The features don't end here. You can also use Graphics Server SDK with products like Microsoft Excel and Word for Windows. The new 4.5 version fully supports VBA. It also includes support for pareto charts, floating bar graphs, and error bars on all log graphs. In fact, this product contains so many features that I really can't talk about them all in this appendix. About the only thing that you won't find here is source code. Obviously Bits Per Second wants to protect their investment, so you'll have to be satisfied with the compiled code. (As with all Delphi components, you need a PAS file to use the product, but this file only contains the interface elements, not the graphics server code itself.)

VisualPROS for Delphi
Component: $149.95
Component with Source Code: $289.95
Shoreline Software
35-31 Talcottville Road, Suite 123
Vernon, CT 06066-4030
Voice: (203)870-5707
FAX: (203)870-5727

Users like applications that are easy to use. Delphi certainly helps you to do that by providing a combination of standard Windows components for you to use. However, there are times when the standard components just won't do everything you need, and that's when VisualPROS comes into play.

This product provides a variety of user interface enhancements. For example, you might want to add a tear off menu to your application so that the user can put it where they want instead of at the top of the window. Delphi 2.0 provides help clouds as a standard feature, but you can still use this product to add them to your Delphi 1.0 applications. In fact, a lot of programmers will probably need this feature as they move people from the 16-bit to the 32-bit environment. Wouldn't it be nice if applications on all the machines in an office looked the same—even if one machine still used Windows 3.x while the others used Windows 95 or Windows NT? Other types of components include expanding edit fields, bitmap tile, and gradient controls. You also get multi-language prompt support.

Note: Multi-language prompt support won't change the data you display. If your database contains information in English, using this product won't magically change it into Spanish. The only things that'll change are the prompts used within the application. This is still a major feature since knowing what kind of data you're working with is better than seeing an entire screen in a language you don't speak.

VisualPROS isn't just a user-oriented tool. It also includes both INI and registry file support. This isn't such a big deal with Delphi 2.0 because it provides support for both file types right out of the box. However, you'll probably find that the VisualPROS components are easier to use.

InfoPower
Component: $199.00
Additional for Source: $99.00
Woll2Woll Software
2217 Rhone Dr.
Livermore, CA 94550
Voice: (510)371-1663
FAX: (510)371-1664
CompuServe: 76207,2541

One of the benefits of using Delphi over other products on the market is its strong database support. Programs that manage a lot of data tend to get cluttered rather quickly—anything you can do to reduce that clutter is going to help the user and reduce support costs. That's the whole purpose behind this product.

InfoPower provides data-aware controls like a three-dimensional multi-table grid. This grid reminds me a little of the DBCtrlGrid provided with Delphi 2.0, but with a lot more power. Other components allow you to display pop-up resizable memo field editors and custom dialog boxes. One of the components even allows you to display the active index. A special filtering mechanism allows the user to select a different index from a drop-down list. In addition, InfoPower includes a Query By Example (QBE) component that operates just like its Paradox counterpart. (According to the vendor, there are 15 components in all.)

This is a Delphi-component-only product—meaning you probably won't be able to use it in other environments. It does provide full source code written in pure Delphi (i.e., Object Pascal). Best of all, InfoPower is royalty free—an important feature for a database component where some vendors do charge a royalty.

> Orpheus
> $199.00
> TurboPower Software
> P.O. Box 49009
> Colorado Springs, CO 80949
> Voice: (719)260-9136
> FAX: (719)260-7151

There are a lot of features to like about this particular product. One of the features I really like is that all of the components use the Windows 95 interface. This may not seem like a big deal until you consider that this product comes with full source code. You can use it to make your 16-bit applications look like the ones you write with Delphi 2.0. TurboPower even guarantees that Orpheus will work equally well in both the 16-bit and 32-bit environments (something that a few vendors I talked to were afraid to say).

Some of the features in Orpheus include validated data-aware fields for string, numeric, currency, and date/time variables. It also provides a text editor that can hold a whopping 16 MB of text (not such a big deal in the 32-bit environment, but something worth noting for those occasions when you still have to write a 16-bit application). Other features include a notebook page with top or side tabs and a flexible table that holds edit fields, combo boxes, and bitmaps (among other things). According to the vendor, Orpheus includes 24 components in all. Orpheus also includes a 60-day money back guarantee and a royalty free license.

Power Controls for Delphi
Eschalon Development, Inc.
Component: $99.95
Additional for Source: $49.95
24-2979 Panorama Drive
Coquitlam, BC V3E 2W8 Canada
Voice: (604)945-3198
FAX: (604)945-7602

This package contains a veritable Swiss army knife of gadget type components. You'll find some mundane selections like an About Dialog and Windows 95 borders to add to your 16-bit applications. Some of the more unusual offerings include a "Tip of the Day" dialog like the ones that Microsoft has started including in their products.

Most of the other components are useful additions to your tool kit. For example, there is a slider/volume switch component for those of you who build multimedia applications. The meter bar/LED component would come in handy for communication programs, but you could use it for other purposes as well. One enterprising programmer included such a light to help administrators monitor network activity. The light would get brighter and change colors as certain types of activity increased.

VBtrv Toolbox Controls for Btrieve
$249.95
Classic Software, Inc.
900 Victors Way, Suite 170E
Ann Arbor, MI 48108
Voice: (313)913-8075
FAX: (313)994-7330
Orders: (800)677-2952

If you work with Btrieve, then you may want to take a look at this package. It provides a set of nine components designed to make writing a program quick. The actual components look similar to the ones that you already use with Delphi—their biggest difference is a Btrieve twist. Some of these components include capabilities like automatic data type conversion, field based access, and SQL support.

This product also includes a special utility called DDF Maker. It's a Windows hosted Btrieve DDE File editor. Essentially this tool allows you to visually define your database using a Windows interface. You can also use it to allow access to your Btrieve data by third-party report writers and other tools—even if they don't natively support Btrieve.

The one downside to this product is the lack of full source code support. You'll get a DLL that contains the majority of the code required to make this product work. The vendor doesn't provide any source code support.

VBXs—Available Today

Visual Basic eXtensions (VBXs) changed the way that most programmers worked. In the past, a programmer would write procedural code to accomplish a task. There wasn't any way to see what you were doing until you actually compiled and ran the application. A VBX allows a programmer to see what he's putting together as he writes the application. The result is better applications written in a shorter amount of time. However, VBXs have a few flaws. The first version of the VBX was very flawed, so Microsoft introduced a new type with Visual Basic 2.0. Unfortunately, the two forms of VBX aren't compatible. In addition, a VBX doesn't provide any form of OLE capability, which is becoming a major issue today. As a result, Microsoft dropped the VBX in favor of the OCX when they introduced a 32-bit programming environment.

Note: There's nothing to prevent you from using a 16-bit VBX with your 32-bit application. However, you'd have to write a thunking layer to do it using Microsoft's thunking compiler. The short story on this compiler is that it's so complicated to use that you probably wouldn't want to except in extraordinary circumstances. In essence, Delphi 2.0 doesn't provide VBX support because Microsoft doesn't provide it as part of its 32-bit programming strategy.

The majority of this section is going to appeal to the Delphi 1.0 programmer since Delphi 2.0 doesn't support VBXs. OK, so VBXs are the 16-bit solution of yesterday. Delphi 2.0 doesn't support them, so why should you even bother to look at this section? A lot of these VBX vendors are creating OCX versions of their product—they just weren't available at the time I was writing this appendix. So, whether or not you're a Delphi 2.0 programmer, you'll probably want to at least browse through this section. If you see something interesting, contact the vendor to see if they're going to provide an updated version of their product.

> ImageKnife/VBX
> $199.00
> Media Architects
> 1075 NW Murray Road, Suite 230
> Portland, OR 97229-5501
> Voice: (503)297-5010
> FAX: (503)297-6744

This is a very complex graphics VBX that supports the Microsoft Access Paintbrush Picture OLE Object format. It helps you acquire images using the TWAIN scanner interface. That's the same interface used by products like CorelDRAW!. Once you acquire an image, you can change its appearance and store it in either a file or database. Delphi can interact with Access using ODBC. I showed you how to do just that in Chapter 12, "Database Management Under Delphi." You could use this library to provide an added level of support for graphics databases using the Access database format. Of course, you aren't limited to Access databases; you can also use this product with other DBMSs that support this graphics format.

Don't get the idea that you can't use ImageKnife for some of the more mundane graphics chores in your application. It also supports a variety of other file formats, including: BMP, DIB, JPEG, GIF, PCX, TIFF, and Targa. You can display those files as true color (24-bit), Super VGA (8-bit), VGA (8-bit), or monochrome images. This versatility makes ImageKnife a good graphics library selection for most applications.

Some of the fancier graphic changes this product supports include: rotating, mirroring, negation, sharpening, and matrix filtering. If that isn't enough, the product also allows you to perform image resizing, compositing, and masking for cropping and combining images. Let's just say it can do a lot of stuff and let it go at that.

> App-Link
> $99.95
> Synergy Software Technologies, Inc.
> 159 Pearl Street
> Essex Junction, VT 05452
> Voice: (800)294-8514 or (802)879-8514
> FAX: (802)879-3754

We talked about implementing DDE in Chapter 10, "Using Delphi with OLE." If you'll remember, even the simple example I provided was a fairly complex operation, and I only showed you how to perform DDE tasks on the local machine. Communicating DDE commands over a network may seem like an impossible task, and it is unless you have help. Some products, like LANtastic, provide this support as a built-in option. Other products, like NetWare, don't.

App-Link helps you create DDE links over a network. Using a network DDE link would allow you to create an OLE connection between an application on one workstation and a different application on another workstation. Some magazines call this distributed processing, but that's such a nebulous and ill-used term that we'll avoid using it here. (It really isn't distributed processing that requires the RPC support that Microsoft and other companies are still working on.)

So, how does App-Link get the job done? It uses something called a socket. If your network supports sockets (like both NetWare and Microsoft Network do), then you can use this product. You'll probably want to talk to your network operating system vendor before you buy this product.

One of the nice features of App-Link is that it doesn't force you to use a specific message format. You can create user-defined data formats. This comes in handy for applications like database managers that support DDE, but use a variety of data formats. Since Delphi's DDE implementation is pretty open, you could literally create a network application that could move data in just about every way conceivable.

Visio
$199.00
Shapeware Corporation
520 Pike Street, Suite 1800
Seattle, WA 98101
Voice: (800)446-3335

If your application makes heavy use of flowcharts and network diagrams, then this is probably the product you're looking for. Visio provides a wide variety of presentation quality flowchart symbols. All you need to do is provide a drawing window, and it takes care of the rest.

Visio supports both OLE 2 and VBA. You can use it as either an OLE client or a server. VBA support means you can use it with applications like Microsoft Excel and Word for Windows.

HypertextManager
$89.00
BrainTree, Ltd.
42-42 204th Street
Bayside, NY 11361
Voice: (800)745-4645
FAX: (718)224-4728

You can use this product to create standard hypertext files. In essence, you can create connections between various objects on a user's machine. In addition, those connections can use pictures instead of words as a means of communication. For example, instead of providing a word for the user to click on, you could have her click on an icon or picture instead. You could even show a screenshot of an application and allow the user to click on the part of the screen that she needs help with. All of this is accomplished using OLE as the communication medium.

Note: Don't confuse this product with something that can produce Internet compatible hypertext markup language (HTML) files. It uses hypertext in the same way that most Macintosh users do—as a means of creating connections between two objects on the same machine. HTML had its roots in this idea, but has expanded well beyond what the Macintosh originally provided.

So how would this help you as a programmer? If you use the built-in help provided with Windows, you need to keep a copy of each graphic right with the HLP file. You can't create a link to the file; the file itself must appear within the help file. If you use the same graphic more than one time, it must appear in the file each time you use it. Talk about a nightmare to fix when it comes time to change the graphic! Microsoft also limits you as to what kind of graphic you can use. Using an OLE link means that you can use virtually any kind of graphic image that an OLE server on the local machine can support.

Using OLE to create a link to the graphics in your text file allows you to reduce the size of the file and allows you to change every occurrence of the graphic by changing one file. It also means you don't have to recompile the file every time you make a change since the graphics exist outside the hypertext file.

> ALLText HT/Pro
> $350.00
> Bennet-Tec Information Systems
> 10 Steuben Drive
> Jericho, NY 11753
> Voice: (516) 433-6283
> FAX: (516) 822-2679
> CompuServe: 71201.1075

This product is essentially a word processor with a little extra oomph. It includes: Hypertext support, embedded OLE 1 objects for graphics or other document embedding, RTF input and output, and data aware support. This makes the component a little better than Delphi's TRichEdit component, but not much. However, it does provide this support with little or no programming on your part, which is a plus.

Rich text format (RTF) is the word processing format used by the Windows help compiler. Many word processors use this format as a means for exchanging data with other word processors. The data aware support means that ALLText includes the name of the application that created an object as part of the object. You could theoretically provide a small text processor in your application, and then allow the user to export the file to a full-fledged word processor like Microsoft Word without too many problems.

ALLText HT/Pro supports embedded (not linked) OLE 1 objects like bitmaps and spreadsheets. You can't see the object in its native form; all objects appear as an icon in the word processed document. What you see looks much like the objects created by the Object Packager utility provided with Windows 3.x. Double-clicking on the object will launch the server application. ALLText does not provide OLE server support.

> Crystal Reports Pro
> $345.00
> Crystal Services
> 1050 West Pender Street, Suite 2200
> Vancouver, B.C. Canada V6E-3S7
> Voice: (800)663-1244 or (604)681-3435

This is a full-featured version of the product provided with Visual Basic. In some respects it acts like ReportSmith by providing a word processor-like interface for painting your report. In other respects it allows the ease of integration provided by the Quick Report components in Delphi 2.0.

Crystal Reports Pro provides a 2-pass report generator that allows you to include groups and cross-tabs in your report. It also provides a variety of data sorting methods. Most important of all, any of the fields in your report can contain OLE 1 or 2 objects.

Other product features include a Print Preview window and a runtime engine. You can use the Crystal Reports Formula Editor to add calculated fields to your reports. Unlike ReportSmith, Crystal Reports Pro allows you to interact with the components using Delphi—something that I see as a real plus for the Delphi programmer.

According to the vendor, you get most of this functionality without a single line of code. Crystal Reports Pro converts the report picture that you draw on-screen into a report on paper. In that regard it works exactly the same as ReportSmith.

> Custom Control Factory
> $48.00
> DesaWare
> 5 Town and Country Village #790
> San Jose, CA 95128
> Voice: (408)377-4770
> FAX: (408)371-3530

Ever wonder what you would do if you couldn't find the custom control you needed? You could always create one the hard way like we did in Chapter 17 (and that would be the best way as far as I'm concerned if you plan to keep the component around for any length of time). There's another way to get the job done if you need something fast, but it's not what you would call the ultimate level of help. You'll still end up adding VBX components to Delphi and writing some amount of code to get the job done. Using the Custom Control Factory is faster than starting from scratch, but it's not automatic.

Custom Control Factory will help you with a wide range of custom controls that don't quite fit a specific category (it's like attending a potluck supper—you never know what you're getting into until the dinner has started). This includes the ability to create animated and multi-state buttons, toolbars, and both standard and animated cursors. You can even create cursors from standard icons.

One of the best features of this product is its DDE support. You can use it to communicate better with another application without writing a lot of code or getting involved with Delphi's DDE components. Overall, this product is a lot easier to use than Delphi's native capabilities in some regards, but you pay the price by having to drag some VBXs around with you.

Other product features include 256- and 24-bit color support for graphics and automatic 3D backgrounds. You'll also find image compression and some other graphics related stuff thrown in for good measure. The package includes over 50 custom controls of various types and sizes.

Rocket
$249.00
SuccessWare 90, Inc.
27349 Jefferson Avenue
Temecula, CA 92590
Voice: (800)683-1657 or (909)699-9657
FAX: (909)695-5679
CompuServe: Go SWARE

You'd think with all of the database capability that Delphi has built into it that the last thing you would need is database components. I think you'll find that this product is special because it adds a superior level of Xbase database capability to your application. In fact, it actually enhances native Xbase capabilities, something that Delphi won't do for you. Rocket supports FoxPro, Clipper, and HiPer-Six index formats. Unlike a standard Xbase DBF file though, you get both variable length fields (VariField) and BLOBs (supported through memo fields).

Speed is no problem with this product since it uses the Mach Six query optimizer. A query optimizer takes your request as input and comes up with the most efficient way possible to satisfy it. Add to this the ability to create sub-indexes, and you have a real performance enhancement for those older technology Xbase files.

Rocket also comes with two utility programs: Visual Navigator (database maintenance) and Filter-Builder (query maintenance). You'll also find that it includes an encryption engine so that you can protect your sensitive data from prying eyes. Normal DBF files are wide open; anyone with a little spare time and a standard viewer can figure out exactly what your company is doing. Fortunately, you get all of this support royalty free.

NetPak Professional
$179.00
Cresent
11 Bailey Avenue
Ridgefield, CT 06877-4505
Voice: (800)352-2742 or (203)438-5300
FAX: (203)431-4626

Remember in Chapter 13, "Delphi on a LAN," when we looked at using Delphi on a LAN? I mentioned that there were some products out on the market that would make life a lot easier for you. NetPak Professional is one of those products.

NetPak includes: NetWare 386 F2, bindery, communications, connection, directory, message, print, TTS, and workstation functions. (There are other functions too numerous to mention here—according to the vendor there are over 100 network functions in all.) In other words, if there is a

NetWare feature that you need to change, you can do it with this package. Best of all, this set of components encapsulates many of the Windows API network functions for you.

One of the things I found interesting about this product is that it comes with an NLM. You load the NLM on the file server. Once loaded, it can receive IPX packets from any workstation on the network. An administrator could monitor several kinds of information using this technique—up to and including the user's workstation configuration. What you'd need to provide on each workstation is an agent to gather and send the required information to the server. (The administrator requests information using a combination of a socket number and password.)

The bottom line is that you would use NetPak to do things like implement security and monitor transactions. You could also use it in a variety of other ways. For example, you could use it to monitor who is and isn't logged into the network. This might have advantages other than acting as "big brother." You could use it as part of a strategy for sharing data on the network using one of the other products in this appendix like App-Link.

> JustButtons
> Standard Edition: $99.00
> Developers Edition: $199.00
> Professional Edition: $299.00
> Chrisalan Designs, Inc.
> P.O. Box 775
> 815 Lambert Street
> Wenatchee, WA 98807-0775
> Voice: (509)663-7770
> FAX: (509)662-5948

I never realized just how time-consuming it could be to create anything more than standard buttons. Just look at the code required to create a multi-state button in Chapter 17. Every dialog you'll ever see contains at least one button, OK. You could probably say the same thing about windows: They contain buttons. Using buttons helps make Windows a lot easier to use. Suffice it to say that the developer pays for that ease of use in programming time.

You can use JustButtons to reduce the amount of time it takes to create buttons. The types of buttons in this package include: Command Line, Memo, Control Panel Applet, WinFile, Talking Time, and many more. Each of these button types is an enhanced version of the basic button that we take for granted. The best part is that you get this enhanced capability without any programming.

Unlike a standard Delphi button, all of these buttons are OLE 2 compliant. You can even use drag and drop with your new buttons. A button scheduler allows you to attach timed events to a button or even wake the button up at a specific time.

Sax Basic Engine
Standard Edition: $149.00
Professional Edition: $495.00
Sax Software
950 Patterson Street
Eugene, OR 97401
Voice: (503)344-2235
FAX: (503)344-2459
Orders: (800)645-3729

There are a lot of situations when it would be nice to add a macro language to your application. However, if you've ever tried to write such a language, you know why compilers are so expensive. Writing a good macro language is akin to writing a good compiler. If you're writing an application for commercial distribution, it might be worth the effort. Otherwise, it's a need that often gets overlooked.

The Sax Basic Engine is a macro language in a component. All you need to do is drop the component on your application and do a little additional programming. Voila, for just a little effort you've added a macro language that supports VBA to your application. You can also enhance the capabilities of this product by adding OLE automation support to your application.

If you get the professional edition, Sax Software will include an IDE and complete macro editor in the picture. This allows you to redefine and enhance particular areas of the macro language provided with the product. The professional edition also includes a debugger, something that the standard edition lacks (since you can't modify the language, the lack of a debugger isn't too big a deal).

Scientific Imaging
$495.00
Evergreen Technologies
Main Street, P.O. Box 795
Castline, Maine 04421
Voice: (207)325-8300
FAX: (207)326-8333

Have you ever thought about adding engineering or scientific graphics capabilities to your application? Unless you have a lot of time to write the application, you're in for a lot of long nights. Scientific and engineering drawings are some of the most complex anywhere. Just think about the detail required to display an adequate picture of the human brain or the inside of a computer chip.

Scientific Imaging uses a combination of VBXs and DLLs to allow you to display and manipulate complex scientific and engineering diagrams with very little programming. The use of DLLs enhances the component's speed and allows you to display the information in a reasonable amount of time. The components support 1-bit, 4-bit, 8-bit, 16-bit (signed and unsigned), 32-bit, floating point, and 24-bit color raw data. You'll also find that it provides overlay support in the form of lines, arrows, rectangles, ovals, and polygons. Magnification, scrolling, and full color palette control allow the user to manipulate the image as needed.

Displaying the image is one thing; storing it is another. Scientific imaging provides some good support in this area as well. You'll find that it can handle the BMP, GIF, PCX, TIFF, generic raw, TWAIN, and MedVision file formats. It also provides the hooks required to add other file formats to its list of capabilities.

About the only drawback with this product is that Evergreen Technologies has a one user, one machine licensing policy. Fortunately they also allow you to purchase a site license, reducing the cost of buying a lot of copies of the product.

> VB-EZ
> $195.00
> Data Translation
> 100 Locke Drive
> Marlboro, MA 01752-1192
> Voice: (800)525-8528
> FAX: (508)481-8620

Real time data acquisition is an important part of many scientific applications. It's also an important part of other applications like inventory and process control. This package provides a set of general components designed to help you gather and analyze data in real time.

Data analysis in real time usually means adding hardware to your system in the form of A/D (analog to digital) and D/A converters. I was surprised to find that Data Translation also provides this kind of hardware for the scientific community. The components in this package are designed to monitor the boards to collect the data you need. The component included in the package also allows you to monitor digital I/O and counter/timer boards. You can display the data on-screen or stream it to disk for analysis later.

Most of the analog analysis features of this product seem to revolve around FFT (Fast Fourier Transform) analysis. You can also plot the raw input data directly on-screen. There are a variety of pseudo-screen types including an oscilloscope, waveform analyzer, and a spectrum analyzer. Analog output functions include the ability to send a variety of waveform types including sine, square, or triangular wave. Besides the analog features, you can also perform a variety of digital sampling and output functions.

OCXs—The Wave of the Future

If you're a Delphi 2.0 programmer, you'll want to pay close attention to this section of the chapter. I've included a list of some of the better OCXs out there today. Obviously, as with every other part of the chapter, this isn't meant as an all inclusive list.

Some of the components in this section provide more than one type of support. You'll find that some of them provide both OCXs and VBXs. I even found a few that provide DLL versions of their product. One of the requirements for using most of these packages is the inclusion of OLE container support with your application. We looked at that requirement in Chapter 10. Essentially you'll start with a TOleContainer component as a starting point for your application development. Needless to say, you'll want to weigh the various options carefully.

Make sure you review the previous section of the appendix as well. A number of the vendors I talked to wouldn't commit at the time of this writing to produce an OCX version of their VBX product; yet it's pretty apparent that they will if they intend to stay in business. If you see a VBX that appeals to you, take the time to call the vendor to see if an OCX version release is imminent.

Peter's Principle: OCXs Are Not Created Equal—Read the Label Before Buying

By now you know that for the most part, VBXs are a 16-bit tool and OCXs are a 32-bit tool. In both cases you're looking at a tool originally designed to expand Visual Basic's functionality. The differences go a lot further than that, though.

Normally you can use a VBX with any programming language that supports it. The only exceptions to this rule are when the VBX vendor failed to completely follow the Microsoft guidelines in creating the VBX or if your programming language will use Visual Basic 1.0 controls and the one you want to use is designed for Visual Basic 2.0. OCXs aren't quite as easy to figure out until you learn one rule. Visual Basic supports OCX controls in either bound or unbound mode. A bound control resides in the application. An unbound control resides outside the application.

Access and other programming languages don't support bound controls. Unfortunately, there isn't any way to know this immediately unless you're very careful in looking at the package before you buy. In addition, you probably won't get the same level of support from Access for an OCX that you would from Visual Basic. For example, the OCX won't provide all of the interface functionality that it's designed to provide. The reason is simple: Visual Basic is a better container than Access is when it comes to OCXs.

Delphi, like Access, has problems with bound controls. It does provide full support for the OCX interface. Unlike Access, Delphi lets you know immediately when it won't support an OCX. We looked at the process for registering an OCX with Delphi in Chapter 17. During the registration process Delphi actually tries to open the OCX. If it can't open the OCX, it won't register it. You'll know immediately if Delphi supports a component or not.

> The bottom line is that you need to avoid bound controls in most cases if there is an unbound alternative. Always check the vendor's return policy to see if you can return a control if Delphi won't register it. When buying OCXs it always pays to read the label before you make the investment.

There are a few future OCX developments that you'll probably want to know about. One of them involves the engine for CompuServe Information Manager (CIM). Soon you'll be able to get an SDK that allows any programmer to embed CompuServe Information Service (CIS) connectivity into an application. This means that you'll be able to add a button to your program that allows the user to access her mail or a specific forum. This may seem a bit far-fetched until you consider that the Navy and other government agencies use CIS as one source for price quotes from a variety of companies. (There are hidden forums all over the place on CIS that allow companies to conduct business.) Of course, the OCX will help developers create mainstream applications as well. As of this writing there wasn't any release date or pricing information for this particular OCX.

Another set of OCXs will help the developers add Internet access to their application. Not only is the Internet a good place to go for research, but the trade press is filled with stories of companies who are using it to allow employees to interact with the company in real time, even if they have to work off-site. As of this writing, there are at least three different companies (and probably more) planning to introduce OCXs for the Internet including: Sax (503)344-2235, Cresent (800)352-2742, and NetManage (408)973-7171. You can even download a beta copy of the NetManage product from the Internet at Web site `http://www.netmanage.com/netmanage/dev_info.html`.

So what will you get with the NetManage Chameleon Internet SDK? It includes a WinSock OCX for communication purposes. Anyone accessing your Web server will get authenticated by the Secured Sockets OCX. The package will also include a variety of other OCXs for creating and reading HTML pages, an FTP-client OCX, an OCX for building news group readers, and an OCX mail client. Pricing for the package wasn't available at the time of this writing.

The Cresent Internet ToolPak is similar in functionality to Chameleon. One feature sets it apart. This product includes a wizard code generator to make the task of writing an application easier. The mail OCX also includes support for multiple servers. Pricing for this package is $199.00.

The Sax Webster OCX provides a different kind of functionality from the other two. It's designed to work at the user interface end. This OCX will allow a developer to set up a browse for a specific Web site. Anyone who has spent time on the Internet realizes just how important this functionality is. Another OCX will act as a filter by scanning the contents of the Web page before loading it on-screen. A company could use this capability to control what level of access a user receives to specific Web sites. The price for this package is $149.00.

Communications Library 3
$149.00
Fax Plus
$249.00
MicroHelp
4359 Shallowford Ind. Parkway
Marietta, GA 30066
Voice: (800)922-3383 or (404)516-0899
FAX: (404)516-1099

Communications Library 3 is a general communications library, which means that it provides a lot of generic capabilities that will allow you to build a specific type of communication program. It supports five terminal emulations including: ANSI, TTY, VT52, VT100, and VT220. In addition, it provides support for eight file transfer protocols, including: Kermit, CompuServe B+, X, Y, and Z Modem. Unlike some packages, the Z Modem support in this package also provides auto recovery support. You can use Communications Library 3 up to speeds of 25.6 Kbps.

Trying to support the wide variety of modems out there is one of the big problems in writing a communications program. Communications Library 3 comes with over 150 initialization strings to support the most common modems. You'll also find a selection of Pascal subprograms and forms. The forms include those required for serial port and parameter selection, dialing the phone, and many other functions.

MicroHelp includes VBXs, DLLs, and 16/32-bit OCXs with Communications Library 3. It provides OLE 2 support for all of your file transfer needs. The library will support multiple communication ports (eight is the practical limit).

Fax Plus is another communications product from MicroHelp. You can use it with any Class 1 or 2 fax modem. Fortunately, the product also includes some components you can use to detect the type of modem—a requirement if you plan to distribute your application commercially.

One of the more interesting features of Fax Plus is that it supports faxes through printed output. In other words, you can build an application in such a way that it can take the printed output from another application and send it as a fax. You can also import BMP, PCX, DCX, or TIFF files to send as faxes. The standard fax format is ASCII text.

Unlike Communications Library 3, Fax Plus automatically handles the fax modem initialization for you. Obviously this is limited to the set of modems it supports. You'll need to check whether the fax modem you want to use with Fax Plus is supported before you try to use it. The package also contains a variety of sample programs and other documentation to show you how to use the product. Both Fax Plus and Communications Library 3 are royalty free.

FaxMan
Data Techniques, Inc.
340 Bowditch Street, Suite 6
Burnsville, NC 28714
Voice: (800)955-8015 or (714)682-4111
FAX: (714)682-0025

As its name implies, FaxMan will help you add fax capability to your application. It supports Class 1 and Class 2 fax modems. One of the nicer features of this program is that you can chain several faxes together into one job. That means you could get all your faxes ready in the morning and send them that night when the rates are low. Products like Fax Plus from MicroHelp don't provide this type of support (in Fax Plus's favor, FaxMan doesn't provide automatic fax initialization).

Unlike most of the products in this appendix, FaxMan comes as a DLL, VBX, or OCX. That means you should be able to use it with just about any development environment in Windows, not just programming languages that support VBXs. It also means that you can use FaxMan with both the 16-bit and 32-bit versions of Delphi or even build your own components around it using the techniques I showed you in Chapter 17.

Other product features include a printer type interface from the user's perspective and a user definable log. The printer interface is similar to the one provided by MicroHelp's Fax Plus—it allows you to grab the printed output from an application and send it as a fax. The user log allows you to track specific events. This makes it possible to use FaxMan at night and check the next morning for any errors in faxing. FaxMan also supports multiple fax modems on a single machine. One of the things I like about this company is the level of commitment to their product. You can try FaxMan out for a whopping 90 days and still return it for a full refund.

Sax Comm Objects
Standard Edition: $149.00
Professional Edition: $495.00
Sax Software
950 Patterson Street
Eugene, OR 97401
Voice: (503)344-2235
FAX: (503)344-2459
Orders: (800)645-3729

Communication is becoming a major issue in today's computing environment. Just look at the proliferation of services like CompuServe and The Microsoft Network. Add the Internet into the mix, and you'll find that there aren't too many things you can do without talking with someone electronically these days. Applications will need to add communication support or at least know how to use an operating system's built-in support to survive.

Sax Comm Objects provides one thing that most communication packages don't right now—100 percent compatibility with the Windows COMM driver. I see this as a major issue with the release of Windows 95 since more and more of your computer's communication needs will go through the operating system. Needless to say, COMM driver compatibility is going to be a big first step in making this happen.

You'll also find that this product provides a wealth of features. For one thing it supports quite a few protocols, including: X, Y, and Z Modem, Kermit, and CompuServe B+. The Sax Comm Objects package provides both VBX and OCX support, so you can use it with both versions of Delphi.

Getting the professional edition will add a couple of utility programs to the package. The CommSpy utility will allow you to fully monitor what's going on with the serial port as you debug your application. You'll also get a debugger called BugTrap with the professional edition.

Tools That You Can Use Today

There just aren't all that many tools that Delphi needs—it's a pretty complete product. However, there are some areas where it can still use a hand in dealing with the complexities of today's programming environment. The following sections will look at a few of those tools. I think you'll find this section is a lot more complete than the others simply because there aren't that many tools available.

> The Conversion Assistant
> $79.00
> EarthTrek
> 79 Montvale Avenue, Suite 5
> Woburn, MA 01801
> Voice: (617)273-0308
> FAX: (617)270-4437

If you were a Visual Basic programmer before coming to Delphi, you may want to take a look at this tool. It allows you to move your Visual Basic code to Delphi intact—well, at least for the most part. Even the vendor admits that this tool doesn't work 100 percent of the time, but it does provide about an 80 percent conversion rate. I consider that pretty good when you consider some of the basic differences between Delphi and Visual Basic.

The version of The Conversion Assistant I looked at was Delphi 1.0–specific. Hopefully EarthTrek will come out with a version for Delphi 2.0 soon after you read this. The current product will provide event code translation and VBX mapping for common controls. The next version will probably replace VBX mapping with OCX mapping. I was also surprised to find that it included VB control array translation and DLL support. This support makes it possible to move your Visual Basic application even if it requires a DLL or two to work.

Setup Pro
Eschalon Development, Inc.
$199.95
24-2979 Panorama Drive
Coquitlam, BC V3E 2W8 Canada
Voice: (604)945-3198
FAX: (604)945-7602

Anyone who has tried to write a setup program for her application soon realizes that the task isn't nearly as easy as it should be. The problems you'll run into include getting large files compressed onto small floppies, a monumental task in some cases. You also have to play around with making the various setup options work. Suffice it to say, you can spend a lot of time getting things to work.

While I applaud Borland's addition of InstallShield Express Lite with Delphi 2.0, it really isn't a full-fledged utility. For example, you'll can't really provide any kind of setup other than a full setup with your application. While that'll work in some cases, it won't in others. Fortunately, you can upgrade the InstallShield product to the full-fledged version, but you may want to give Setup Pro a look as well.

PinPoint VB
$199.00
Avanti Software, Inc.
385 Sherman Avenue, Unit 6
Palo Alto, CA 94306
Voice: (800)758-7011
International: +1-415-329-8999
FAX: (415)329-8722
CompuServe: 76260,266

PinPoint uses logs to help you trace the activities of your Delphi programs. This means that you can find out what happened, even if a system crash prevents you from using a normal debugger. The traces cover both client and server activities, making it perfect for debugging both OLE and DDE projects.

Other product features include the ability to profile your programs. Since Delphi 2.0 doesn't provide a profiler, this alone could make PinPoint worth the purchase price. A profiler tells you how much time the program spends in each module. Knowing this information allows you to optimize the program for best performance. PinPoint even provides aesthetically pleasing output by providing both 2D and 3D bar and pie charts.

SpyWorks
Standard: $129.00

Professional: $249.00
Version Stamper
$129.00
DesaWare
1100 East Hamilton Avenue
Suite 4
Campbell, CA 95008
Voice: (408)377-4770
FAX: (408)371-3530
CompuServe: 74431,3534

There are two very useful tools from DesaWare that can make your life as a programmer considerably easier. The first one is Version Stamper. How often has a user called to say that her application no longer works and after a few hours of troubleshooting you've found that it's because they overwrote a DLL, OCX, or VBX with an older version while installing another application? It's happened to me a few times as well (although not as much when using Delphi since it supports native code compilation).

Version Stamper can help you out of this situation by stamping DLLs, OCXs, and VBXs. All you need to do when starting your application is check the stamp to see if the files in the SYSTEM folder are current. If not, you simply display a message telling the user exactly which file got corrupted or overwritten. Fortunately, Version Stamper comes with both an OCX and VBX component. The only other requirement is that your application provide OLE container support—which means that you'll need to add a TOleContainer component to your Delphi application.

SpyWorks is another OLE container product. It allows you to create journaling hooks and perform other low-level tasks without resorting to the programming techniques that I've shown you in this book. For example, you can create a playback journal hook without writing your own DLL when using this product. As with Version Stamper, you'll find both 16-bit and 32-bit versions of SpyWorks included with the package. There are four OCXs provided in the package that help you get the job done: Windows message stream subclassing, hook control, window callback, and common subclassing. The common subclassing control allows you to create objects like virtual forms, MouseEnter/MouseExit detection (for OLE in-place activation tasks), menu selection events, roll-up windows, and caption buttons. You'll also find a DLL that contains an array of library functions designed to make using the Windows API and SpyWorks itself easier to use.

The professional version of the product doesn't include much more in the way of features. It does include quarterly updates to the entire package and some additional aids designed to help you learn to use the package quickly. You'll also receive a copy of the SpyWorks 2.1 package (which contains additional components) and the Common Dialog Toolkit.

B

Glossary

American Standard Code for Information Interchange   See ASCII.

ANSI   American National Standards Institute

API (Application Programming Interface)   A method of defining a standard set of function calls and other interface elements. It usually defines the interface between a high-level language and the lower-level elements used by a device driver or operating system. The ultimate goal is to provide some type of service to an application that requires access to the operating system or device feature set.

Applet   Normally a control panel application in Windows. Most applets allow you to perform some type of system configuration or monitoring. For example, the ODBC applet allows you to define sources of data. Specific applications like Microsoft Mail also place applets in the control panel for configuration purposes.

Application Independence   A method of writing applications so that they don't depend on the specific features of an operating system or hardware interface. It normally requires the use of a high-level language and an API. The programmer also needs to write the application in such a way as to avoid specific hardware or operating system references. All user and device interface elements must use the generic functions provided by the API.

Application Programming Interface   See API.

ASCII (American Standard Code for Information Interchange)   A standard method of equating the numeric representations available in a computer to human-readable form. For example, the number 32 represents a space. There are 128 characters (7 bits) in the standard ASCII code. The extended ASCII code uses 8 bits for 256 characters. Display adapters from the same machine type usually use the same upper 128 characters. Printers, however, might reserve these upper 128 characters for nonstandard characters. For example, many Epson printers use them for the italic representations of the lower 128 characters.

AVI (Audio/Video Interface)   The standard file format used for Windows video clips.

B-Step Processor   An older 80386 processor type that incorporated elements that are incompatible with Windows 95. The normal reason for using this processor type was to provide additional system functionality or improved speed characteristics.

BDE   Borland Database Engine

Bidirectional Support   Defines a printer's ability to transfer information both ways on a printer cable. Input usually contains data or printer control codes. Output usually contains printer status information or error codes.

Binary Large Objects   See BLOB.

Binary Value   Refers to a base 2 data representation (base 2 means that there are only two values: 1 and 0) in the Windows registry. Normally used to hold status flags or other information that lends itself to a binary format.

BIOS (Basic Input/Output System)   A set of low-level computer interface functions stored in a chip on a computer's motherboard. The BIOS performs basic tasks like booting the computer during startup and performing the power-on startup tests (POST). DOS relied heavily on the BIOS to perform all types of low-level device interface tasks. In most cases, Windows 95 relies on the BIOS a lot less and Windows NT not at all (except for the act of booting the computer system initially).

Bitmap   A file or OLE object containing the binary representation of a graphic image in raster format. Each pixel on the display is represented as one entry in the file. The size of the entry depends on the number of colors the image supports. Common sizes include monochrome (1-bit), VGA (4-bits), SVGA (8-bits), and true color (24-bits).

BLOB (Binary Large Object)   A special field in a database table that accepts objects such as bitmaps, sounds, or text as input. This field type is normally associated with the OLE capabilities of a DBMS, but some third party products make it possible to add BLOB support to older database file formats such as the Xbase DBF file format. BLOB fields always imply OLE client support by the DBMS.

.BMP Files   Windows standard bitmap graphics data format. This is a raster graphic data format that doesn't include any form of compression. OS/2 can also use this data format to hold graphics of various types.

Browse   A special application interface element designed to show the user an overview of a database or other storage media (like the thumbnail sketches presented by some graphics applications). Think of a browse as the table of contents to the rest of the storage area. A browse normally contains partial views of several data storage elements (records or picture thumbnails in most cases) that a user can then zoom to see in their entirety. A browse form normally contains scroll bars or other high speed interface elements to make it easier for the user to move from one section of the overall storage media to the next.

CAD (Computer Aided Design)   A special type of graphics program used for creating, printing, storing, and editing architectural, electrical, mechanical, or other forms of engineering drawings. CAD programs normally provide precise measuring capabilities and libraries of predefined objects such as sinks, desks, resistors, and gears.

CCITT   Consultative Committee for International Telegraphy and Telephony

CDFS (Compact Disc File System)   The portion of the file subsystem specifically designed to interact with compact disc drives. It also provides the user interface elements required to tune this part of the subsystem. The CDFS takes the place of an FSD for CD-ROM drives.

CD-ROM (Compact Disc Read-Only Memory)   A device used to store up to 650Mb of permanent data. In most cases you can't use a CD-ROM the same as a hard or floppy disk drive because you can't write to it. A CD-ROM recorder allows you to record CDs on a PC, but this is a one-time process. The disks look much like audio CDs, but require a special drive to interface them with a computer.

CGA   Color Graphics Adapter

Class ID   See CLSID.

Client   The recipient of data, services, or resources from a file or other server. This term can refer to a workstation or an application. The server can be another PC or an application.

CLSID (Class ID)   A method of assigning a unique identifier to each object in the registry. Also refers to various high-level language constructs.

CMOS (Complimentary Metal Oxide Semiconductor)   Normally refers to a construction method for low-power, battery-backed memory. When used in the context of a PC, this term usually refers to the memory used to store system configuration information and the real-time clock status. The configuration information normally includes the amount of system memory, the type and size of floppy drives, the hard drive parameters, and the video display type. Some vendors include other configuration information as part of this chip as well.

Computer Aided Design   See CAD.

Compact Disc File System   See CDFS.

Complimentary Metal Oxide Semiconductor   See CMOS.

Container   Part of the object-oriented terminology that has become part of OLE. A container is a drive, file, or other resource used to hold objects. The container is normally referenced as an object itself.

DAT (Digital Audio Tape) Drive   A tape drive that uses a cassette to store data. The cassette and the drive use the same technology as the audio version of the DAT drive. However, the internal circuitry of the drive formats the tape for use with a computer system. The vendor must also design the interface circuitry with computer needs in mind. DAT tapes allow you to store large amounts of information in a relatively small amount of space. Typical drive capacities range from 1.2 GB to 8 GB.

Database Management System   See DBMS.

Datacentric   The method used by modern operating systems to view the user interface from a data perspective rather than from the perspective of the applications used to create the data. Using this view allows users to worry more about manipulating the data on their machines than the applications required to perform a specific task.

DBF (Database File)   An older technology single table database format used by all Xbase DBMS. The DBF format is used by products like FoxPro and dBASE for Windows. Products like Delphi view the folder (directory) holding the DBF files as the database and the individual DBF files as tables.

DBMS (Database Management System) A collection of tables, forms, queries, reports, and other data elements. It acts as a central processing point for data accessed by one or more users. Most DBMSs (except free-form or text-based) rely on a system of tables for storing information. Each table contains records (rows) consisting of separate data fields (columns). Common DBMSs include Access, Paradox, dBASE, and FileMaker Pro.

DCB (Device Control Block) A Windows structure used to create an interface between an application and a device. In most cases the DCB contains pointers to configuration information in the application's data area. DCBs allow the programmer to request information about the device or to change its current status. Some devices also provide a method for retrieving data using a DCB.

DDE (Dynamic Data Exchange) The ability to cut data from one application and paste it into another application. For example, you could cut a graphic image created with a paint program and paste it into a word processing document. Once pasted, the data doesn't reflect changes made to it by the originating application. DDE also provides a method for communicating with an application that supports it and requesting data. For example, you could use an Excel macro to call Microsoft Word and request the contents of a document file. Some applications also use DDE to implement file association strategies. For example, Microsoft Word uses DDE in place of command line switches to gain added flexibility when a user needs to open or print a file.

Device-Independent Bitmap See DIB.

Device Control Block See DCB.

DHCP (Dynamic Host Configuration Protocol) Manager A special Windows NT utility designed to change its TCP/IP configuration. The DHCP Manager creates IP addresses for client workstations dynamically from a pool of addresses. Normally you would assign a user a static IP address, which could lead to conflicts somewhere along the way.

DIB (Device-Independent Bitmap) A method of representing graphic information that doesn't reflect a particular device's requirements. This has the advantage of allowing the same graphic to appear on any device in precisely the same way, despite differences in resolution or other factors that normally change the graphic's appearance.

Digital Audio Tape Drive See DAT Drive.

Direct Memory Access See DMA.

Disk Defragmenter An application used to reorder the data on a long-term storage device such as a hard or floppy disk drive. Reordering the data so that it appears in sequential order (file by file) reduces the time required to access and read it. The sequential order allows you to read an entire file without moving the disk head at all in some cases and only a little in others. This reduction in access time normally improves overall system throughput and therefore enhances system efficiency.

DLL (Dynamic Link Library)   A special form of application code loaded into memory by request. It is not executable by itself. A DLL does contain one or more discrete routines that an application may use to provide specific features. For example, a DLL could provide a common set of file dialogs used to access information on the hard drive. More than one application may use the functions provided by a DLL, reducing overall memory requirements when more than one application is running.

DMA (Direct Memory Access)   A memory addressing technique in which the processor doesn't perform the actual data transfer. This method of memory access is faster than any other technique.

DOS Protected-Mode Interface   See DPMI.

DPMI (DOS Protected-Mode Interface)   A method of accessing extended memory from a DOS application using the Windows extended memory manager.

Drag and Drop   A technique used in object-oriented operating systems to access data without actually opening the file using conventional methods. For example, this system allows the user to pick up a document file, drag it to the printer, and drop it. The printer will print the document using its default settings.

Dual-Ported Video RAM   See VRAM.

Dvorak Layout   An alternative method of laying out the keyboard so that stress is reduced and typing speed is increased. It's different from the more familiar "QWERTY" layout used by most keyboards and typewriters.

Dynamic Data Exchange   See DDE.

Dynamic Host Configuration Protocol Manager   See DHCP Manager.

Dynamic Link Library   See DLL.

EGA   Enhanced Graphics Adapter

EIA   Electronic Industries Association

Embedded Systems   A combination of processor, operating system, and device-specific applications used in concert with a special-purpose device. For example, the control used to set the time and temperature on a microwave is an embedded system. Another form of embedded system is the computer that controls engine efficiency in a car.

EMF (Enhanced Metafile)   Used as an alternative storage format by some graphics applications. This is a vector graphic format, so it provides a certain level of device independence and other features that a vector graphic normally provides.

EMM (Expanded Memory Manager)   A device driver like EMM386.EXE that provides expanded memory services on 80386 and above machines. (Special drivers work with 80286 and a few 8088/8086 machines.) An application accesses expanded memory using a page frame or other memory-mapping techniques from within the conventional or upper memory area (0 to 124 KB).

The EMM usually emulates expanded memory using extended memory managed by an extended memory manager (XMM) like HIMEM.SYS. An application must change the processor's mode to protected mode in order to use XMS. Some products, such as 386MAX.SYS and QEMM.SYS, provide both EMM and XMM services in one driver.

EMS (Expanded Memory Specification)   Several versions of this specification are in current use. The most popular version is 3.2, even though a newer 4.0 specification is available. This specification defines one method of extending the amount of memory that a processor can address from the conventional memory area. It uses an area outside of system memory to store information. An EMM provides a window view into this larger data area. The old 3.2 specification requires a 64 KB window in the UMB. The newer 4.0 specification can create this window anywhere in conventional or UMB memory.

Enhanced Metafile   See EMF.

ER (Entity Relationship) Diagram   A special type of graphical notation used by DBMS programmers to show the relationship between various database elements. For example, such a diagram would show data sources and the types of data they would contain. ER diagrams are useful in analyzing data flow problems in a DBMS. A programmer would use them much like a flow chart for standard programming code.

Expanded Memory Manager   See EMM.

Expanded Memory Specification   See EMS.

FAT (File Allocation Table)   The method of formatting a hard disk drive used by DOS and other operating systems. This technique is one of the oldest formatting methods available.

File Allocation Table Disk Format   See FAT.

File System Driver   See FSD.

FK (Foreign Key)   A database table column that references the PK (Primary Key) value in another (or even the same) table. FKs are normally used to link a child table to its parent. For example, a table containing invoices would most likely contain an FK pointing to the PK in a customer name and address table. An FK could also provide the means for sorting the table's data.

Foreign Key   See FK.

Frame Buffer   A special area of video memory set aside to allow smooth animation display or video capture. There are two types of common frame buffer. The hardware version is usually part of a display adapter or resides on a specially equipped dual-processor motherboard. It normally creates the frame buffer using high speed VRAM. The software version emulates the capabilities of the hardware version using DRAM.

FSD (File System Driver)   A file subsystem component responsible for defining the interface between Windows and long-term storage. The FSD also defines features such as long filenames and what types of interaction the device supports. For example, the CD-ROM FSD wouldn't support file writes unless you provided a device that could perform that sort of task.

Gallery   A special area of the Delphi speed bar that is set aside to display VCL (visual component library) icons. Clicking on a VCL icon and then on a form creates a copy of the component. Delphi 2 links the gallery to the object repository—the mechanism used to store a variety of objects including components and templates.

GDI (Graphics Device Interface)   One of the main Windows root components. It controls the way that graphic elements are presented on-screen. Every application must use the API provided by this component to draw or perform other graphics-related tasks.

GDT (Global Descriptor Table)   A memory construct that contains the information required to control all the extended memory in 80386 or above processors. The GDT normally passes control of smaller memory segments to the LDTs used by an individual application.

General Protection Fault   See GPF.

Global Descriptor Table   See GDT.

GPF (General Protection Fault)   A processor or memory error that occurs when an application makes a request that the system can't honor. This type of error results in some type of severe action on the part of the operating system. Normally, the operating system terminates the offending application.

Graphical User Interface   See GUI.

Graphics Device Interface   See GDI.

Graphics Primitives   A set of basic drawing elements used to create more complex drawings. Graphics primitives normally include rectangles, circles, ellipses, and polygons. Programmers normally include the various commands used to enhance a graphics primitive in this area. These include color, brushes, and various fills like hatching.

GUI (Graphical User Interface)   A system of icons and graphic images that replaces the character-mode menu system used by many machines. The GUI can ride on top of another operating system (such as DOS or UNIX) or reside as part of the operating system itself (such as Windows or OS/2). Advantages of a GUI are ease of use and high-resolution graphics. Disadvantages are higher workstation hardware requirements and lower performance over a similar system using a character-mode interface.

HAL (Hardware Abstraction Layer)   A conceptual element of the Windows NT architecture. Microsoft wrote the drivers and other software elements in such a way that they could easily move Windows NT to other platforms. That's how they moved Windows NT to the MIPS and Alpha machines. The basic architecture of Windows NT is the same, but the low-level drivers—the ones that directly interface with the hardware—are different. The important thing to remember is that as far as your application is concerned, it's still running on an Intel machine. The only time you'll run into trouble is if your application bypasses the Windows API and goes directly to the hardware.

Hardware Abstraction Layer   See HAL.

High Memory Area   See HMA.

High-Performance File System   See HPFS.

HMA (High Memory Area)   The 64 KB area of memory beyond the 1 MB boundary that the processor can access in real mode on 80286 or above processors.

HPFS (High-Performance File System)   The method of formatting a hard disk drive used by OS/2. Formatting in this case includes the addressing scheme and security features used by HPFS. This formatting method also provides added reliability in the form of a hot fix capability where bad disk sectors are replaced dynamically. Although it provides significant speed advantages over other formatting techniques, only the OS/2 operating system and applications designed to work with that operating system can access a drive formatted using this technique. (Windows NT also provides HPFS capability, although that capability won't be present in versions 4.0 and above. NTFS is the preferred disk format under Windows NT.)

ICM (Image Color Matcher)   A special component of the graphics subsystem that allows Windows to match the colors produced by one device with those available on another device. The result is that the output of both devices doesn't show the normal variations in color that Windows applications currently produce.

Icon   A symbol used to graphically represent the purpose or function of an application or file. For example, a text file might appear as a sheet of paper with the filename below the icon. Applications designed for the environment or operating system usually appear with a special icon depicting the vendor's or product's logo. Icons normally are part of a GUI environment or operating system such as Windows or OS/2.

IDAPI   Independent Database Application Programming Interface

IDE (Integrated Development Environment)   A programming language front end that provides all the tools you need to write an application through a single editor. Older DOS programming language products provided several utilities—one for each of the main programming tasks. Most (if not all) Windows programming languages provide some kind of IDE support.

IDE (Integrated Device Electronics)   A form of disk drive that places the electronics required to control drive functions on the drive itself. The drive communicates with the PC through a host adapter—a generalized set of electronics designed for communication only. Early IDE devices included hard drives only. Newer IDE devices include tape and CD-ROM drives as well.

IDX (Index)   A type of index file used by Xbase DBMS. An index file allows the DBMS to sort the information in a table without actually changing the table's data. The index file performs the same function as an index in a book—it allows the DBMS to look up table records in a specific order.

IFS (Installable File System) Manager   The API component of the file subsystem. It provides a consistent interface that applications can use to access a variety of devices, local and remote. This component also provides a standard interface that device drivers can use to provide services such as file opening and drive status.

Image Color Matcher   See ICM.

.INF File   A special form of device or application configuration file. It contains all the parameters that Windows requires to install or configure the device or application. For example, an application .INF file might contain the location of data files and the interdependencies of DLLs. Both application and device .INF files contain the registry and .INI file entries required to make Windows recognize the application or device.

Integrated Development Environment   See IDE.

Integrated Device Electronics   See IDE.

Installable File System Helper   A special real-mode component of the IFS manager used to allow access of Windows drive functions by DOS applications. It uses the same DOS interface as before, but all processing is performed by the protected-mode manager.

Installable File System Manager   See IFS Manager.

Interrupt Request   See IRQ.

IRQ (Interrupt Request)   The set of special address lines that connect a peripheral to the processor. Think of an IRQ as an office telephone with multiple incoming lines. Every time a device calls, its entry lights up on the front of the telephone. The processor selects the desired line and picks up the receiver to find out what the device wants. Everything works fine as long as there is one line for each device that needs to call the processor. If more than one device were to try to call in on the same line, then the processor wouldn't know who was at the other end. This is the source of IRQ conflicts that you hear about from various sources. Older PC class machines provided 8 interrupt lines. The newer AT class machines provide 16. However, only 15 of those lines are usable since one of them is used for internal purposes.

Kernel   The set of drivers, low-level functions, executables, and other constructs required to create the core of an operating system. The kernel is responsible for honoring application requests for device and data access. It also provides security and system level functionality.

LAN (Local Area Network) A combination of hardware and software used to connect a group of PCs to each other or a mini or mainframe computer. There are two main networking models in use: peer-to-peer and client/server. The peer-to-peer model doesn't require a dedicated server. In addition, all the workstations in the group can share resources. The client/server model uses a central server for resource sharing, but some special methods are provided for using local resources in a limited fashion.

LDT (Local Descriptor Table) A memory construct that controls access to the memory used by a single application or a group of applications that share the same memory. The LDT is subservient to the GDT that manages system memory overall.

Light Remote Procedure Call See LRPC.

Listbox A windowing construct that contains a list of items. Normally the user selects one or more of these items in order to respond to an application or operating system query.

Local Area Network See LAN.

Local Descriptor Table See LDT.

Locally Unique Identifier See LUID.

LRPC (Light Remote Procedure Call) Essentially a method for calling a procedure not associated with the current application or local machine. OLE 2 allows you to create links to other documents, even if they aren't physically located on the local drive. It implements this using an LRPC mechanism. Unfortunately, this linking mechanism has limitations. For example, you'll find that it works fine with some peer-to-peer networks, but it works only marginally with other network types.

LUID (Locally Unique Identifier) Essentially a pointer to an object, the LUID identifies each process and resource for security purposes. In other words, even if a user has two copies of precisely the same resource option (like a document), both copies would have a unique LUID. This method of identification prevents some types of security access violations under Windows NT.

Macro A form of programming that records keystrokes and other programming-related tasks to a file on disk or within the current document. Most applications provide a macro recorder that records the keystrokes and mouse clicks you make. This means you don't even have to write them in most cases. Macros are especially popular in spreadsheets. Most macros use some form of DDE to complete OLE-related tasks.

MAPI (Messaging API) The set of functions and other resources that Windows provides to communication programs. It allows the application to access a variety of communication channels using a single set of calls and without regard to media. This is the component of Windows 95 that allows Exchange to process information from e-mail and online services using the same interface.

MCA (Microchannel Architecture)   A specialized bus introduced by IBM. It's faster than the old ISA bus and gives the operating system information about the peripheral devices connected to the bus. It also provides the means for devices to become self-configuring.

MCI (Media Control Interface)   The set of low-level commands provided by Windows to access media devices like CD-ROM drives and soundboards. Each media driver adds its set of commands to the interface. Since each driver uses a similar command set, the programmer can access any device with a minimal amount of code changes.

MDI (Multiple Document Interface)   A method for displaying more than one document at a time within a parent window. The Program Manager interface is an example of MDI. You see multiple groups within the Program Manager window.

MDX (Multiple Index)   A type of index file used by Xbase DBMSs. An index file allows the DBMS to sort the information in a table without actually changing the table's data. The index file performs the same function as an index in a book—it allows the DBMS to look up table records in a specific order. The advantage to this file format is that it can store more than one index in each file. Older index file formats store a single index in each file.

Messaging API   See MAPI.

Microchannel Architecture   See MCA.

MIDI (Musical Instrument Digital Interface)   There are two components to MIDI. The hardware component provides a physical connection between a computer and a musical instrument. The software component provides the means to represent music in digital format. This includes storage of the information in either an RMI or MID file.

Miniport Driver   A specialized Windows component that provides access to a resource, normally a peripheral device of some type. It's also used to access pseudo-devices and network resources.

Motion Picture Experts Group   See MPEG.

MPEG (Motion Picture Experts Group)   A standards group that provides file formats and other specifications in regard to full-motion video and other types of graphic displays.

MSSHURI (Microsoft Share User Interface)   This module responds to external requests from the user for network resource configuration. Every time you right-click on a resource and tell Windows 95 that you want to share it, this module fields that request. It works with the access control module to set password protection. An interface to the MPR and ADVAPI32.DLL allows the MSSHRUI to set the proper entries in the registry. You'll find it in the MSSHRUI.DLL file in your \SYSTEM folder. Windows NT has a similar version of this file called NTSHRUI.DLL. It provides many of the same capabilities with a heavier emphasis on security. You'll find NTSHRUI.DLL in the \SYSTEM32 folder.

Multiple-Boot Configuration A method of creating a configurable environment that was first introduced with DOS 5.0. The user simply selects the operating environment from a list of environments presented prior to the boot sequence. This technique provides an additional layer of flexibility and allows the user to optimize the operating environment to perform specific tasks.

Multiple Document Interface See MDI.

Multitasking The ability of some processor and environment/system combinations to perform more than one task at a time. The applications appear to run simultaneously. For example, you can download messages from an online service, print from a word processor, and recalculate a spreadsheet all at the same time. Each application receives a slice of time before the processor moves to the next application. Because the time slices are fairly small, it appears to the user that these actions are occurring simultaneously.

Musical Instrument Digital Interface See MIDI.

National Language Support See NLS.

NDS (NetWare Directory Service) An object-oriented approach to managing network resources. It includes a set of graphical utilities that allow the network administrator to view the entire network at once, even if it includes more than one server or more than one location. There are a variety of object types including servers, printers, users, and files. NDS not only allows the administrator to manage the resource, but it provides security as well. As with any object-oriented management approach, NDS gives each object a unique set of properties that the administrator can change as needed.

NDX (Index) The original index file format used by Xbase DBMSs. An index file allows the DBMS to sort the information in a table without actually changing the table's data. The index file performs the same function as an index in a book—it allows the DBMS to look up table records in a specific order.

Nested Objects Two or more objects that are coupled in some fashion. The objects normally appear within the confines of a container object. Object nesting allows multiple objects to define the properties of a higher-level object. It also allows the user to associate different types of objects with each other.

NetWare Directory Services See NDS.

NetWare Loadable Module See NLM.

Network Interface Card See NIC.

Network Operating System See NOS.

NIC (Network Interface Card) The device responsible for allowing a workstation to communicate with the file server and other workstations. It provides the physical means of creating the connection. The card plugs into an expansion slot in the computer. A cable that attaches to the back of the card completes the communication path.

NLM (NetWare Loadable Module)   An executable file that loads on a NetWare 3.x/4.x file server. An NLM usually adds some capability that the entire network shares. Examples of NLMs include tape backup software, virus protection, UPS detection/management, and database servers. The NLM replaces the VAP provided in NetWare 2.x. Unlike a VAP, you can load and unload an NLM while the file server is active.

NLS (National Language Support)   A method of reconfiguring the keyboard and other system components to support more than one language through the use of code pages. Each code page defines a different language configuration. Unfortunately, this technique doesn't change the language used for display purposes. In other words, NLS won't cause your English-language version of Windows to suddenly display prompts and other text in German.

NOS (Network Operating System)   The operating system that runs on the file server or other centralized file/print sharing devices. This operating system normally provides multi-user access capability and user accounting software in addition to other network-specific utilities.

NTFS (Windows NT File System)   The method of formatting a hard disk drive used by Windows NT. Although it provides significant speed advantages over other formatting techniques, only the Windows NT operating system and applications designed to work with that operating system can access a drive formatted using this technique.

NTX (Index)   A type of Xbase index file introduced by Nantucket Corporation for use with Clipper. An index file allows the DBMS to sort the information in a table without actually changing the table's data. The index file performs the same function as an index in a book—it allows the DBMS to look up table records in a specific order. The advantage to this particular index file is that it uses less disk space and provides faster data access. It doesn't provide multiple index storage capabilities.

Object Conversion   A method of changing the format and properties of an object created by one application to the format and properties used by another. Conversion moves the data from one application to another, usually without a loss in formatting, but always without a loss of content.

Object Linking and Embedding   See OLE.

Object-Oriented Programming   See OOP.

Object Repository   See Gallery.

ODBC (Open Database Connectivity)   One of several methods of exchanging data between DBMSs. ODBC normally relies on SQL to translate DBMS-specific commands from the client into a generic language. The ODBC agents on the server translate these SQL requests into server-specific commands.

OBJ (Object)   An intermediate file format used to store compiled code. OBJ files are not linked and therefore not executable. DOS applications store them in LIB files. You can also use OBJ files in certain Windows environments, including some C compilers and Delphi.

OCX (OLE Custom eXtension)   A special form of VBX designed to make adding OLE capabilities to an application easier for the programmer. Essentially, an OCX is a DLL with an added programmer and OLE interface.

OLE (Object Linking and Embedding)   The process of packaging a filename and any required parameters into an object and then pasting this object into the file created by another application. For example, you could place a graphic object within a word processing document or spreadsheet. When you look at the object, it appears as if you simply pasted the data from the originating application into the current application (similar to DDE). When linked, the data provided by the object automatically changes as you change the data in the original object. When embedded, the data doesn't change unless you specifically edit it, but the data still retains its original format and you still use the original application to edit the data. Often you can start the originating application and automatically load the required data by double-clicking on the object. The newer OLE 2 specification allows for in-place data editing as well as editing in a separate application window.

OLE Custom eXtension   See OCX.

OOP (Object-Oriented Programming)   A method of programming that relies on objects. An object is one fully described section of code that includes properties and methods. Unlike procedural code, everything needed to describe a particular task is included in one object. OOP encourages code reuse and reduces interaction-type programming errors since each object is self-contained.

Open Database Connectivity   See ODBC.

Password Caching   A method of saving the passwords for resources that a user might need to access. The user still needs to enter the main password required to access Windows, but Windows remembers the passwords required to access other resources like a network or an online service that directly supports Windows password caching capability.

PCX File   A raster graphic data format originally used by ZSoft Paintbrush. This format has gone through many nonstandard transitions and occasionally presents problems when accessed by applications other than the original. It provides for various levels of color and includes data compression.

PD (Port Driver)   Performs the task of communicating with the device through an adapter. It's the last stage before a message leaves Windows and the first stage when a message arrives from the device. The PD is usually adapter-specific. For example, you would have one VxD for each hard drive and one PD for each hard drive adapter.

PIF (Program Information File)   A special configuration file that Windows and OS/2 use to define the environment for a DOS application. The PIF usually includes various memory settings along with the application's command path and working directory.

PK (Primary Key)   A set of database table columns that describes a unique row within the table. For example, a PK for a name and address table would probably include the person's name plus some unique identifier like his or her ZIP code. The PK is normally used as the main method for ordering the table. It defines each row as a unique entity and is therefore used as the primary search key as well.

Plug and Play   See PNP.

PNP (Plug and Play)   The combination of BIOS, operating system, and peripheral device components that provides a self-configuring environment. This self-configuring feature allows the operating system to avoid potential hardware conflicts by polling the peripheral devices, assessing their requirements, and determining and implementing optimal settings for each device.

Port Driver   See PD.

POST (Power-On Self Test)   The set of diagnostic and configuration routines that the BIOS runs during system initialization. For example, the memory counter you see during the boot sequence is part of this process.

Power-On Self Test   See POST.

Primary Key   See PK.

Program Information File   See PIF.

Protected Mode   The processor mode in which the processor can access all of extended memory. This mode also provides a better level of application error detection as part of the processing cycle.

Protected-Mode Mapper   A special application that converts real-mode device driver calls into those used by a protected-mode counterpart. It enables you to use your DOS drivers under Windows. Without the support of this VxD, Windows couldn't support legacy devices that lack Windows-specific drivers.

RAD (Rapid Application Development)   A tool that lets you design your program's user interface and then write the commands to make that user interface do something useful. Visual Basic and Delphi are both examples of RAD programs.

Rapid Application Development   See RAD.

Real Mode   A Windows operating mode that supports the capabilities of the 8088/8086 processor. This essentially limits you to loading one application within the confines of conventional memory. Windows versions after 3.0 don't support this mode. You must use these versions with workstations containing 80286 or higher processors.

Referential Integrity   See RI.

REG File   A special file used by the registry to hold a text version of the keys and values it contains. Some applications provide REG files that you can use to incorporate their file associations and OLE capabilities into Windows.

Registry Key   This is a registry heading. It provides the structure required to hold configuration values and other information required by both Windows and the applications it runs.

Registry Value   Each value provides some type of Windows configuration information. There are three types of registry values: string, DWORD, and binary. Of the three, the only human-readable form is string.

Remote Access   The ability to use a remote resource as you would a local resource. In some cases, this also means downloading the remote resource to use as a local resource.

Remote Procedure Call   See RPC.

RI (Referential Integrity)   This is a special rule of database management that says that every FK (Foreign Key) must match some existing PK (Primary Key) value. What this means is that you can't have an entry in a child table without some matching entry in the parent. For example, you can't have an invoice for a non-existent company. The parent table must contain a company name for every invoice in the invoice table.

Rich Text Format   See RTF.

RPC (Remote Procedure Call)   The ability to use code or data on a remote machine as if it were local. This is an advanced capability that will eventually pave the way for decentralized applications.

RTF (Rich Text Format)   A file format originally introduced by Microsoft that allows an application to store formatting information in plain ASCII text. All commands begin with a backslash. For example, the \cf command tells an RTF capable editor which color to use from the color table when displaying a particular section of text.

SCSI Manager   Windows NT introduced something called the miniport driver. With Windows 95, you can use the Windows NT miniport binaries. However, before you can actually do this, Windows 95 must translate its commands to a format that the miniport driver will understand. The SCSI manager performs this service.

SCSIZER   This is a file subsystem component that deals with the SCSI command language. Think of the command language as the method that the computer uses to tell a SCSI device to perform a task. The command language isn't the data the SCSI device handles; rather, it's the act the SCSI device will perform. There's one SCSIZER for each SCSI device.

SDI (Single Document Interface)   A method of displaying information where each window is independent of the other—there is no main window. This is the direction that Microsoft is taking with Windows. It's the interface used by Explorer and the Windows Desktop.

Security Identifier   See SID.

Server   An application or workstation that provides services, resources, or data to a client application or workstation. The client usually makes requests in the form of OLE, DDE, or other command formats.

Shell Extension   A special application that gives some type of added value to the operating system interface. In most cases, the application must register itself with the registry before the operating system will recognize it.

SID (Security Identifier)   The part of a user's access token that identifies the user throughout the network—it's like having an account number. The user token that the SID identifies tells what groups the user belongs to and what privileges the user has. Each group also has a SID so the user's SID contains references to the various group SIDs that he belongs to, not a complete set of group access rights. You would normally use the User Manager utility under Windows NT to change the contents of this access token.

Single Document Interface   See SDI.

SQL (Structured Query Language)   Most DBMSs use this language to exchange information. Some also use it as their native language. SQL provides a method for requesting information from the DBMS. It defines which table or tables to use, what information to get from the table, and how to sort that information.

String Value   A plain text entry in the Windows registry that provides a lot of information about the application and how it's configured. Hardware usually uses string values as well for interrupt and port information. String values are the one type of registry entry that you can read without interpretation. Other registry entry values include binary and DWORD.

Structured Query Language   See SQL.

SVGA   Super Video Graphics Array

System Resource   Data, peripheral devices, or other system components used to create, delete, or manipulate documents and produce output.

System VM (Virtual Machine)   The component of the Windows operating system tasked to create virtual machines and manage DOS applications.

TAPI (Telephony API)   An interface used by applications to interface with various types of communication equipment. This currently includes both modems and fax devices.

Task Switching   The ability of an operating system to support more than one application or thread of execution at a time. The foreground application or task is the only one that executes. All other threads of execution are suspended in the background. Contrast this with multitasking where all threads—background and foreground—execute.

TCP/IP (Transmission Control Protocol/Internet Protocol)   A standard communication line protocol developed by the United States Department of Defense. The protocol defines how two devices talk to each other. Think of the protocol as a type of language used by the two devices.

Telephony API   See TAPI.

Terminate and Stay Resident Program   See TSR.

Thunk   The programming interface that translates 32-bit data and system calls to their 16-bit counterpart. The opposite translation takes place going from a 16-bit application to its 32-bit counterpart.

Transmission Control Protocol/Internet Protocol   See TCP/IP.

TrueType   A special form of vector font originally provided with Windows but used with other operating systems as well. This vector font provides hinting and other features that give it a smoother appearance on-screen.

TSD (Type-Specific Driver)   Part of the file subsystem, this layer deals with logical device types rather than specific devices. For example, one TSD handles all the hard drives on your system, and another TSD handles all the floppy drives. A third TSD would handle all network drives.

TSR (Terminate and Stay Resident)   An application that loads itself into memory and stays there after you execute it. The program usually returns you directly to the DOS prompt after loading. Pressing a hot key combination activates the application, allowing you to use the application. In most cases, TSRs provide some type of utility, print spooling, or other short-term function.

Type-Specific Driver   See TSD.

UAE (Unrecoverable Application Error)   A processor or memory error that occurs when an application makes a request that the system can't honor. The operating system normally doesn't detect an error of this type. The result is that the system freezes or becomes unstable to the point of being unusable. Also see GPF.

UMB (Upper Memory Block)   The area of memory between 640 KB and the 1 MB boundary. IBM originally set aside this area of memory for device ROMs and special device memory areas. Use of various memory managers allows you to load applications and device drivers in this area.

UNC (Universal Naming Convention)   A method for identifying network resources without using specific locations. In most cases this convention is used with drives and printers, but it can also be used with other types of resources. A UNC normally uses a device name in place of an identifier. For example, a disk drive on a remote machine might be referred to as "\\AUX\DRIVE-C." The advantage of using UNC is that the resource name won't change, even if the user's drive mappings do.

Universal Naming Convention   See UNC.

Unrecoverable Application Error   See UAE.

Upper Memory Block   See UMB.

VBX (Visual BASIC eXtension)   A special form of DLL that contains functions as well as a programmer interface. The DLL part of the VBX accepts requests from an application for specific services such as opening a file. The programmer interface portion appears on the toolbar of a program, such as Visual Basic, as a button. Clicking the button creates one instance of that particular type of control.

VCL (Visual Component Library)   A stored set of reusable Delphi objects similar in function to a VBX.

VCPI (Virtual Control Program Interface)   A method of accessing extended memory from a DOS application using a third-party XMM. Also see DPMI.

VDD (Virtual Display Driver)   Windows 3.x used this module as its sole source of communication with the display adapter. Windows 95 provides it for compatibility purposes and for DOS applications. It translates application requests into graphics commands and draws the result in video memory.

VDM (Virtual DOS Machine)   Essentially a single copy of a DOS machine created in memory. This machine provides all the access features of the real thing, but it doesn't physically exist. Windows NT places each DOS application in its own VDM. The reason is simple. To provide the higher level of system reliability that Windows NT users demand, Microsoft had to make sure that each application had its own environment, an environment that is completely separate from that used by every other application. It's also important to remember that 16-bit Windows applications share one VDM. You need to remember that Windows NT always starts a VDM, and then runs a copy of 16-bit Windows in it to service the needs of 16-bit Windows applications. This effectively adds two layers to every interaction—one for the VDM and another for the WIN32 Subsystem. As with everything else, this additional layering is transparent to the programmer. You still use the same interfaces as before.

Vector Font   A type of font that uses mathematical expressions instead of a bitmap to define its characteristics.

Vector Table   The place in lower memory where ROM and DOS store pointers to operating system-specific routines. Most of these routines allow an application to access a device or perform some specific task, such as opening a file.

VESA (Video Electronics Standards Association)   A standards group responsible for creating display adapter and monitor specifications. This group has also worked on other standards, such as the VL bus used in some PCs.

VFAT (Virtual File Allocation Table)   An enhanced method of disk formatting based on the FAT system. It allows for additional functionality such as long filenames.

VGA   Video Graphics Array

Video Electronics Standards Association   See VESA.

Virtual Anything Driver   See VxD.

Virtual Control Program Interface   See VCPI.

Virtual Display Driver   See VDD.

Virtual DOS Machine   See VDM.

Virtual File Allocation Table   See VFAT.

Visual BASIC eXtension   See VBX.

Visual Component Library   See VCL.

Volume Tracking Driver   See VTD.

VRAM (Dual-Ported Video RAM)   A special form of memory that allows simultaneous reads and writes. It provides a serial-read interface and a parallel-write interface. The advantage of using VRAM is that it's much faster and doesn't require as much detection code on the part of the application or device driver.

VTD (Volume Tracking Driver)   This file subsystem component handles any removable devices attached to your system.

VxD (Virtual Anything Driver)   A special form of DLL that provides low-level system support.

WAN (Wide Area Network)   A grouping of two or more LANs in more than one physical location.

WEP (Windows Entry Point)   The initial starting point of most Windows applications including DLLs. Older 16-bit applications actually have a WEP function. Newer 32-bit applications provide the equivalent of a WEP function, but it doesn't necessarily have that name. The WEP function initializes the application before Windows allows it to start processing data or perform other tasks.

Wide Area Network   See WAN.

Windows Entry Point   See WEP.

Windows Internet Name Service Manager   See WINS.

Windows NT File System   See NTFS.

WINS (Windows Internet Name Service) Manager   A Windows NT utility designed to work with TCP/IP networks. The WINS Manager makes it easier for a user to use the network by assigning names to IP addresses. Instead of looking at a bunch of numbers and trying to figure out whom they belong to, the WINS Manager would assign the client a name like Joe's Computer.

Wizard   A specialized application that reduces the complexity of using or configuring your system. For example, the Printer Wizard makes it easier to install a new printer.

WMF (Windows MetaFile)   A special form of the EMF file format, the WMF is used as an alternative storage format by some graphics applications. It is also used by a fairly broad range of application programming languages. This is a vector graphic format, so it provides a certain level of device independence and other features that a vector graphic normally provides.

WYSIWYG   What You See Is What You Get

XGA   eXtended Graphics Array

Index

Add to Your Sams Library Today with the Best Books for Programming, Operating Systems, and New Technologies

The easiest way to order is to pick up the phone and call

1-800-428-5331

between 9:00 a.m. and 5:00 p.m. EST.
For faster service please have your credit card available.

ISBN	Quantity	Description of Item	Unit Cost	Total Cost
0-672-30863-0		Teach Yourself Delphi 2 in 21 Days	$35.00	
0-672-30871-1		Borland's Official No-Nonsense Guide to Delphi 2	$25.00	
0-672-30858-4		Delphi 2 Unleashed, Second Edition (book/CD)	$55.00	
0-672-30704-9		Delphi Developer's Guide (book/CD)	$49.99	
0-672-30862-2		Database Developer's Guide with Delphi 2 (book/CD)	$55.00	
0-672-30913-0		Database Developer's Guide with Visual C++ 4, Second Edition (book/CD)	$59.99	
0-672-30474-0		Windows 95 Unleashed (book/CD)	$39.99	
0-672-30602-6		Programming Windows 95 Unleashed (book/CD)	$49.99	
0-672-30745-6		HTML & CGI Unleashed (book/CD)	$49.99	
0-672-30837-1		Visual Basic 4 Unleashed (book/CD)	$45.00	
0-672-30568-2		Teach Yourself OLE Programming in 21 Days (book/CD)	$39.99	
0-672-30620-4		Teach Yourself Visual Basic 4 in 21 Days, Third Edition	$35.00	
0-672-30736-7		Teach Yourself C in 21 Days, Premier Edition	$35.00	
❏ 3 ½" Disk		Shipping and Handling: See information below.		
❏ 5 ¼" Disk		TOTAL		

Shipping and Handling: $4.00 for the first book, and $1.75 for each additional book. Floppy disk: add $1.75 for shipping and handling. If you need to have it NOW, we can ship product to you in 24 hours for an additional charge of approximately $18.00, and you will receive your item overnight or in two days. Overseas shipping and handling adds $2.00 per book and $8.00 for up to three disks. Prices subject to change. Call for availability and pricing information on latest editions.

201 W. 103rd Street, Indianapolis, Indiana 46290

1-800-428-5331 — Orders   1-800-835-3202 — FAX   1-800-858-7674 — Customer Service

Book ISBN 0-672-30898-3